A FIRST COURSE ON CLOUD-BASED MICROSERVICES

A COMPETENCY-BASED TEXTBOOK FOR UNIVERSITIES

ARSHDEEP BAHGA | VIJAY MADISETTI

A First Course on Cloud-Based Microservices:
A Competency-based Textbook for Universities

Published by Arshdeep Bahga & Vijay Madisetti

ISBN: 978-1-949978-03-2

Book Website: https://hands-on-books-series.com

The contents of this book have been timestamped on the Ethereum blockchain as a permanent proof of existence. Scan the QR code or visit the URL given on the back cover to verify the blockchain certification for this book.

TABLE OF CONTENTS

PREFACE

ABOUT THE BOOK

Companies today are undergoing digital transformation to build agile IT infrastructures that not only provide traditional IT support functions, but also enable innovation in business operations and planning. Rather than custom solutions that lock them into legacy systems, companies want flexible and cost-effective solutions that leverage the cloud's potential. Migrating to the cloud opens exciting new opportunities.

Microservices architecture offers a way to realize complex, cloud-native systems by decomposing functionality into numerous independent services that work together. This reduces overall complexity, allows quicker changes to meet shifting business needs, and enables efficient scaling for performance and reliability. Microservices are especially well-suited for cloud platforms and facilitate reorganization of development and operations (DevOps) methods to suit faster delivery schedules.

However, a gap exists between academic coverage of microservices patterns and actual deployment of microservices-based solutions on real cloud platforms. Many excellent resources focus on architectural principles but do not provide clear guidance on implementation. Conversely, books on specific cloud providers emphasize hands-on skills but fail to provide foundational knowledge to evaluate solutions properly or transfer learning across platforms.

This textbook bridges the gap by enabling readers to rapidly grasp microservices concepts and then deploy practical microservices applications on real cloud platforms. We provide the requisite technical grounding to assess and utilize various cloud services while explaining why particular implementation choices are made. With hundreds of figures and tested code samples, we offer a rigorous, hype-free guide to developing robust cloud-native apps.

The book meets the need for educational programs at colleges and universities to train the next generation of cloud solutions architects and DevOps engineers. It accompanies cloud computing curricula and certification programs where students seek valuable hands-on experience on commercial cloud platforms to complement conceptual knowledge.

The typical reader is a senior undergraduate or beginning graduate student in science, technology, engineering, or mathematics (STEM) fields who has completed introductory programming courses. The book provides the necessary guidance and knowledge for readers to develop working code for cloud-based microservices applications. We believe augmenting traditional classroom learning with practical coding exercises significantly enhances the learning process. Additional student support resources are available on the book's companion website.

The textbook comprises twelve chapters delivering in-depth coverage of key concepts, technologies, and architectural patterns for cloud-based microservices. Our competency development approach aims to equip readers with practical skills rather than dwell on theory covered adequately elsewhere. While we refer frequently to commercial cloud providers' offerings, this textbook does not constitute an endorsement of any vendor, product, or service. All trademarks belong to their respective owners. The perspectives presented reflect the authors' opinions solely.

We offer a book that allows readers to quickly understand what microservices are and then deploy them on real cloud platforms, while providing the necessary technical background to guide them to improve their understanding and competency in evaluating and using cloud-based platforms. We have organized it so that it can be taught within a semester. We have provided running examples that explain the foundations of how and why the applications are implemented in a particular way, be they in a 'serverless manner' or a 'container-based approach'. Such a course can then be followed by a course that applies and extends these principles to establish a DevSecOps framework for efficient and powerful cloud application development and deployment.

Please also refer to our books "Cloud Computing: A Hands-On Approach", "Internet of Things: A Hands-On Approach", "Big Data Science & Analytics: A Hands-On Approach", "Blockchain Applications: A Hands-On Approach", and "Cloud Computing Solutions Architect: A Hands-On Approach" that provide additional and complementary information on these topics. We are grateful to the Association of Computing Surveys (ACM) for recognizing our book on cloud computing as a "Notable Book of 2014" as part of their annual literature survey. We are also grateful to the universities worldwide that have adopted these textbooks as part of their program offerings for providing us feedback that has helped us in improving our offerings

▓ BOOK WEBSITE

For more information on the book, the copyrighted source code of all examples in the book, lab exercises, and instructor material visit the book website: www.hands-on-books-series.com

ACKNOWLEDGMENTS

From Arshdeep Bahga

I would like to thank my father, Sarbjit Bahga, for inspiring me to write books and sharing his valuable insights and experiences on authoring books. This book could not have been completed without the support of my mother Gurdeep Kaur, wife Navsangeet Kaur, sons Navroz and Nivaaz, who have always motivated me and encouraged me to explore my interests.

From Vijay Madisetti

I thank my family, especially Anitha and Jerry (Raj), and my parents (Prof. M. A. Ramlu and Mrs. Madhavi Saroja Ramlu) for their support.

From the Authors

We would like to acknowledge the instructors who have adopted our earlier books in the "A Hands-On Approach"™ series, for their constructive feedback.

ABOUT THE AUTHORS

■ ARSHDEEP BAHGA

Arshdeep Bahga is a computer science researcher noted for his research work and textbooks in the areas of Blockchain, Internet of Things, Cloud Computing and Big Data. Arshdeep completed Masters degree in Electrical & Computer Engineering from Georgia Institute of Technology in 2010. He worked as Research Scientist with Georgia Tech from 2010-2016. Arshdeep has to his credit several scientific publications in peer-reviewed journals and technology patents. Arshdeep received the 2014 Roger P. Webb - Research Spotlight Award from the School of Electrical and Computer Engineering, Georgia Tech.

■ VIJAY MADISETTI

Vijay Madisetti is a Professor in the School of Cybersecurity and Privacy (SCP) in the College of Computing at Georgia Institute of Technology. Vijay is a Fellow of the IEEE, and received the 2006 Terman Medal from the American Society of Engineering Education and HP Corporation.

COMPANION BOOKS FROM THE AUTHORS

■ CLOUD COMPUTING: A HANDS-ON APPROACH

Recent industry surveys expect the cloud computing services market to be in excess of $20 billion and cloud computing jobs to be in excess of 10 million worldwide in 2014 alone. In addition, since a majority of existing information technology (IT) jobs are focused on maintaining legacy in-house systems, the demand for these kinds of jobs is likely to drop rapidly if cloud computing continues to take hold of the industry. However, there are very few educational options available in the area of cloud computing beyond vendor-specific training by cloud providers themselves. Cloud computing courses have not found their way (yet) into mainstream college curricula. This book is written as a textbook on cloud computing for educational programs at colleges. It can also be used by cloud service providers who may be interested in offering a broader perspective of cloud computing to accompany their customer and employee training programs.

■ INTERNET OF THINGS: A HANDS-ON APPROACH

Internet of Things (IoT) refers to physical and virtual objects that have unique identities and are connected to the Internet to facilitate intelligent applications that make energy, logistics, industrial control, retail, agriculture, and many other domains "smarter". Internet of Things is a new revolution of the Internet that is rapidly gathering momentum driven by the advancements in sensor networks, mobile devices, wireless communications, networking, and cloud technologies. Experts forecast that by the year 2020 there will be a total of 50 billion devices/things connected to the Internet. This book is written as a textbook on the Internet of Things for educational programs at colleges and universities, and also for IoT vendors and service providers who may be interested in offering a broader perspective of Internet of Things to accompany their customer and developer training programs.

■ BIG DATA SCIENCE & ANALYTICS: A HANDS-ON APPROACH

Big data is defined as collections of datasets whose volume, velocity, or variety is so large that it is difficult to store, manage, process, and analyze the data using traditional databases and data processing tools. Big data science and analytics deal with the collection, storage, processing, and analysis of massive-scale data. We have written this textbook for educational programs at colleges and universities, and also for big data service providers who may be interested in offering a broader perspective of this emerging field to accompany their customer and developer training programs. The book is organized into three main parts, comprising a total of twelve chapters. Part I provides an introduction to big data, applications of big data, and big data science and analytics patterns and architectures. Part II introduces the reader to various tools and frameworks for big data analytics, and the architectural and programming aspects of these frameworks, with examples in Python. Part III introduces the reader to various machine learning algorithms.

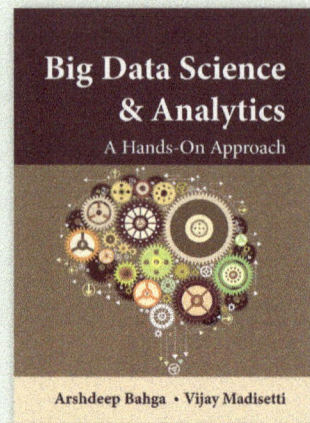

■ BLOCKCHAIN APPLICATIONS: A HANDS-ON APPROACH

Blockchain is a distributed and public ledger that maintains records of all the transactions on a blockchain network comprising suppliers of products and services and consumers. With the blockchain's ability to establish trust in a peer-to-peer network through a distributed consensus mechanism rather than relying on a powerful centralized authority, the technology is being seen by the industry experts as one of the greatest innovations since the invention of the Internet. The book is organized into three main parts, comprising a total of ten chapters. Part I provides an introduction to blockchain concepts, design patterns, and architectures for blockchain applications. A blockchain stack comprising a decentralized computation platform, a decentralized messaging platform, and a decentralized storage platform is described. Part II introduces the readers to tools and platforms for blockchain. Implementation examples of various smart contracts and decentralized applications (Dapps) are provided. The reader is introduced to the Whisper decentralized messaging platform and Swarm decentralized storage platform. Part III focuses on advanced topics such as the security and scalability related challenges for the blockchain platforms.

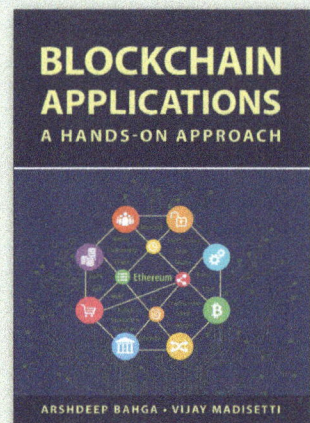

CLOUD COMPUTING SOLUTIONS ARCHITECT: A HANDS-ON APPROACH

Cloud computing is a transformative paradigm that enables scalable, convenient, on-demand access to a shared pool of configurable computing and networking resources, for efficiently delivering applications and services over the Internet. Amazon Web Services (AWS), a leading provider of cloud platforms and services, defines a cloud solutions architect as one who can provide solution plans for the best architectural practices for cloud applications, can design and deploy highly scalable and fault-tolerant services, can assist in lifting legacy applications and shifting them to the cloud, and can identify and plan for data entry and exit from the cloud platform, choose suitable cloud services based on data, compute, and security requirements. Further, the cloud solutions architect also ensures that enterprise offerings conform to sound principles, such as AWS Well-Architected Framework (WAF) for cloud applications and services. This book is written as a textbook for training the next generation of cloud solutions architects for educational programs at colleges and universities, and also accompanying cloud certification programs where students would be interested in obtaining valuable hands-on skills on actual cloud platforms to further develop their knowledge and competency base. The book is organized into twenty chapters that provide in-depth coverage of concepts, technologies, and architectures related to cloud computing environments and cloud applications. The reader is also introduced to specialized aspects of cloud computing, including serverless computing, cloud security, and big data analytics.

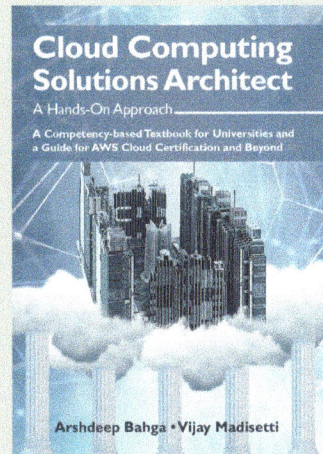

PART I

CONCEPTS & TECHNOLOGIES

INTRODUCTION TO CLOUD COMPUTING

THIS CHAPTER COVERS

- Introduction to Cloud Computing
- Characteristics of Cloud Computing
- Cloud Service and Deployment Models
- Cloud Computing Concepts & Technologies
- Cloud Computing Reference Model
- Open Source Private Cloud Software
- Design Considerations for Cloud Applications
- Reference Architectures for Cloud Applications

1.1   Introduction

Cloud computing is a new computing paradigm that involves delivering applications and services over the Internet. Though cloud computing is being seen as the next big thing for information technology (IT), the underlying technologies that are the foundation of cloud computing have existed for quite some time. The cloud computing model came into existence with the evolution of a variety of technologies such as virtualization and distributed computing. Improved Internet speeds, greater Internet penetration, wired and wireless broadband technologies, the proliferation of Internet access devices such as smartphones and tablets, and increased demands for the outsourcing of IT infrastructures have accelerated the growth and adoption of cloud computing.

The computing paradigm of the cloud provides an abstraction of physical systems delivering hosted services from the user. For the user, the computing resources provided by the cloud are virtual and limitless. Cloud computing, which is also commonly referred to as 'the cloud', brings the concept of utility computing that involves provisioning of computing and storage resources on demand, and providing these resources as metered services to the users. Cloud computing comprises both hardware and software. Virtual and on-demand computing, pay-as-you-go, rapid elasticity, flexibility, ease of implementation, pooling of resources, multi-tenancy, and reduced IT costs are the key driving factors for the adoption of cloud computing. In this chapter, we describe various deployment models, service models, characteristics, driving factors, and challenges of cloud computing.

1.1.1   Definition of Cloud Computing

The U.S. National Institute of Standards and Technology (NIST) defines cloud computing as [1]:

> **Definition:** Cloud computing is a model for enabling ubiquitous, convenient, on-demand network access to a shared pool of configurable computing resources (e.g., networks, servers, storage, applications, and services) that can be rapidly provisioned and released with minimal management effort or service provider interaction.

Let us deep dive into the key terms of the cloud computing definition:
- **Ubiquitous:** Cloud computing allows ubiquitous access to computing and storage resources over the Internet. Any device connected to the Internet, be it a personal computer, laptop, smartphone, or tablet can be used to access cloud services.
- **Convenient:** The utility computing model of the cloud makes it convenient for individual users, small and medium enterprises, large organizations, and governments to provision computing and storage resources required for their IT operations without any upfront capital expenditure in the IT infrastructure.
- **On-Demand:** Cloud computing model allows provisioning computing and storage resources on-demand, i.e., as and when required. This saves the upfront investments in IT infrastructure, and brings cost benefits for IT operations as only as many resources as required can be provisioned.
- **Shared pool:** Cloud computing involves the pooling of computing and storage resources to serve multiple users using the multi-tenant model. Multi-tenancy is enabled by virtualization technologies that allow multiple virtual resources to run on

the same physical resources. The virtual resources are dynamically provisioned and de-provisioned based on user demand.

- **Rapidly Provisioned:** The virtual resources provided by cloud computing can be rapidly and automatically provisioned without requiring human interaction with the service provider.
- **Minimal Management:** Cloud computing model requires minimal management efforts for provisioning and de-provisioning of computing and storage resources.

1.2 Characteristics of Cloud Computing

Cloud computing has five essential characteristics according to the NIST definition of the cloud [1] described as follows:

On-demand self service

Cloud computing resources can be provisioned on-demand by the users, without requiring interactions with the cloud service provider. The process of provisioning resources is automated.

Broad network access

Cloud computing resources can be accessed over the network with standard access mechanisms that provide platform-independent access through the use of heterogeneous thin and thick client platforms such as workstations, laptops, tablets and smartphones.

Resource pooling

The computing and storage resources provided by cloud service providers are pooled to serve multiple users using multi-tenancy. Multi-tenant aspects of the cloud allow multiple users to be served by the same physical hardware. Users are assigned virtual resources that run on top of the physical resources.

Rapid elasticity

Cloud computing resources can be provisioned rapidly and elastically. Cloud resources can be rapidly scaled up or down based on demand. Two types of scaling options exist:

- **Horizontal Scaling (scaling out):** Horizontal scaling or scaling-out involves launching and provisioning additional server resources.
- **Vertical Scaling (scaling up):** Vertical scaling or scaling-up involves changing the computing capacity assigned to the server resources while keeping the number of server resources constant.

Measured service

Cloud computing resources are provided to users on a pay-per-use model. The usage of the cloud resources is measured, and the user is charged based on some specific metrics. Metrics such as the amount of CPU cycles used, amount of storage space used, and number of network I/O requests are used to calculate the usage charges for cloud resources.

In addition to the five essential characteristics of cloud computing, other characteristics include:

Performance

Cloud computing provides improved performance for applications since the resources provisioned for the applications can be scaled up or down based on the application workloads. Using horizontal or vertical scaling options, the performance requirements of the applications can be met.

Reduced costs

Cloud computing provides cost benefits for applications as only as much computing and storage resources as required can be provisioned. Applications can experience large variations in the workloads, which can be due to seasonal or other factors. For example, E-Commerce applications typically experience higher workloads in festive seasons. To ensure market readiness of such applications, adequate resources need to be provisioned so that the applications can meet the demands of specified workload levels, and at the same time ensure that service level agreements are met. Over-provisioning in advance for such systems is not economically feasible. Cloud computing provides a promising approach of dynamically scaling up or scaling down the capacity based on the application workload.

Outsourced Management

Cloud computing allows the users (individuals, large organizations, small and medium enterprises, and governments) to outsource the IT infrastructure requirements to external cloud providers. Thus, the users can save large upfront capital expenditures in setting up the IT infrastructure and pay only for the operational expenses for the cloud resources used. The outsourced nature of cloud services provides a reduction in IT infrastructure management costs.

Reliability

Applications deployed in cloud computing environments have higher reliability as the underlying IT infrastructure is managed by the cloud service and kept up to date with the most recent software updates and patches. Cloud service providers specify the reliability and availability levels for their cloud resources in the form of service level agreements (SLA). Most cloud providers promise 99.99% uptime guarantee for the cloud resources, which is difficult and expensive to achieve with in-house IT infrastructure.

Multi-tenancy

The multi-tenanted approach of the cloud allows multiple users to make use of the same shared resources. Modern applications such as E-Commerce, Business-to-Business, Banking and Financial, Retail, and Social Networking applications that are deployed in cloud computing environments are multi-tenant applications. Multi-tenancy can be of different forms:
- **Virtual multi-tenancy:** In virtual multi-tenancy, computing and storage resources are shared among multiple users. Multiple tenants are served from virtual machines (VMs) that operate concurrently on top of the same computing and storage resources.
- **Organic multi-tenancy:** In organic multi-tenancy, every component in the system architecture is shared among multiple tenants, including hardware, OS, database

servers, application servers, and load balancers. Organic multi-tenancy exists when explicit multi-tenant design patterns are coded into the application.

1.3 Cloud Models

1.3.1 Service Models

Cloud computing services are offered to users in different forms. NIST defines three cloud service models as follows:

Infrastructure-as-a-Service (IaaS)

IaaS provides users with the ability to provision computing and storage resources. These resources are provided to the users as virtual machine instances and virtual storage. Users can start, stop, configure, and manage virtual machine instances and virtual storage. Users can deploy operating systems and applications of their choice on the virtual resources provisioned in the cloud. The cloud service provider manages the underlying infrastructure. Virtual resources provisioned by the users are billed based on a pay-per-use paradigm. Common metering metrics used are the number of virtual machine hours used or the amount of storage space provisioned.

Platform-as-a-Service (PaaS)

PaaS provides users with the ability to develop and deploy applications in the cloud using the development tools, application programming interfaces (APIs), software libraries, and services provided by the cloud service provider. The cloud service provider manages the underlying cloud infrastructure, including servers, network, operating systems, and storage. The users are responsible for developing, deploying, configuring, and managing applications in the cloud.

Software-as-a-Service (SaaS)

SaaS provides users with a complete application environment, including software and hardware infrastructure. The cloud service provider manages the underlying cloud infrastructure, including servers, network, operating systems, storage, and application software. Applications are provided to the user through a thin client interface (e.g., a browser). SaaS applications are platform-independent and can be accessed from various client devices such as workstations, laptops, tablets, and smartphones, running different operating systems. Since the cloud service provider manages both the application and data, the users are free to access the applications from anywhere.

Figure 1.1 shows the cloud computing service models and Figure 1.2 lists the benefits, characteristics, and adoption of IaaS, PaaS, and SaaS.

1.3.2 Deployment Models

NIST defines four cloud deployment models as follows:

Public cloud

In the public cloud deployment model, cloud services are available to the general public or a large group of companies. The cloud resources are shared among different users (individuals, large organizations, small and medium enterprises, and governments). The cloud services are

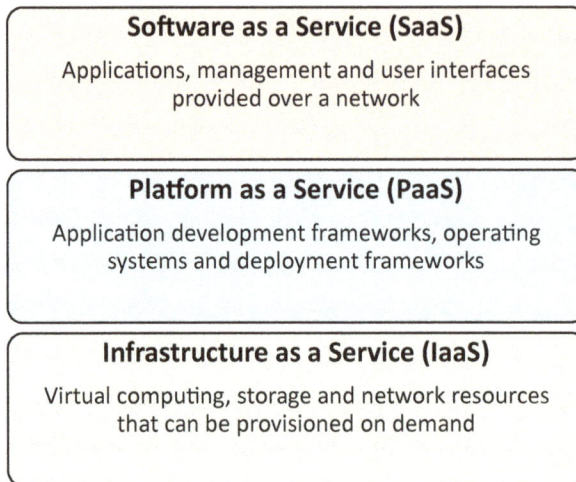

Figure 1.1: Cloud computing service models

provided by a third-party cloud provider. Public clouds are best suited for users who want to use cloud infrastructure for the development and testing of applications and host applications in the cloud to serve large workloads, without upfront investments in IT infrastructure.

Private cloud

In the private cloud deployment model, cloud infrastructure is operated for the exclusive use of a single organization. Private cloud services are dedicated to a single organization. Cloud infrastructure can be set up on-premises or off-premises, and may be managed internally or by a third-party. Private clouds are best suited for applications where security is important, and organizations that want to have control over their data.

Hybrid cloud

The hybrid cloud deployment model combines the services of multiple clouds (private or public). The individual clouds retain their unique identities but are bound by standardized or proprietary technology that enables data and application portability. Hybrid clouds are best suited for organizations that want to take advantage of secured application and data hosting on a private cloud, and at the same time benefit from cost savings by hosting shared applications and data in public clouds.

Community cloud

In the community cloud deployment model, the cloud services are shared by several organizations that have the same policy and compliance considerations. Community clouds are best suited for organizations that want access to the same applications and data, and want the cloud costs to be shared with the larger group.

Figures 1.3 and 1.4 show the cloud deployment models.

IaaS		
Benefits	**Characteristics**	**Examples**
- Shift focus from IT management to core activities - No IT infrastructure management costs - Pay-per-use/pay-per-go pricing - Guaranteed performance - Dynamic scaling - Secure access - Enterprise grade infrastructure - Green IT adoption	- Multi-tenancy - Virtualized hardware - Management & monitoring tools - Disaster recovery **Adoption** - Individual users: Low - Small & medium enterprises: Medium - Large organizations: High - Government: High	1. Amazon Web Services (AWS) EC2 2. Microsoft Azure Virtual Machines 3. Google Compute Engine 4. DigitalOcean Droplets 5. Linode 6. IBM Cloud Virtual Servers 7. Oracle Cloud Infrastructure 8. Rackspace Cloud 9. Vultr 10. Liquid Web

PaaS		
Benefits	**Characteristics**	**Examples**
- Lower upfront & operations costs - No IT infrastructure management costs - Improved scalability - Higher performance - Secured access - Quick & easy development - Seamless integration	- Multi-tenancy - Open integration protocols - App development tools & SDKs - Analytics **Adoption** - Individual users: Low - Small & medium enterprises: Medium - Large organizations: High - Government: Medium	1. AWS Elastic Beanstalk 2. AWS Lambda 3. AWS EMR 4. Google App Engine 5. Heroku 6. Microsoft Azure App Service 7. IBM Cloud Foundry 8. Red Hat OpenShift 9. Apprenda 10. Engine Yard

SaaS		
Benefits	**Characteristics**	**Examples**
- Lower costs - No infrastructure required - Seamless upgrades - Guaranteed performance - Automated backups - Easy data recovery - Secure - High adoption - On-the move access	- Multi-tenancy - On-demand software - Open integration protocols - Social network integration **Adoption** - Individual users: High - Small & medium enterprises: High - Large organizations: High - Government: Medium	1. Google Workspace 2. Microsoft Office 365 3. Salesforce 4. Dropbox 5. Zoom 6. ServiceNow 7. Zendesk 8. Workday 9. Slack 10. Atlassian Jira

Figure 1.2: Benefits, characteristics and adoption of IaaS, PaaS and SaaS

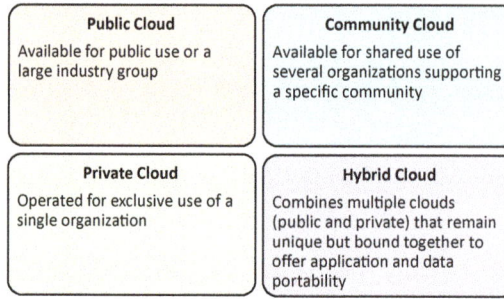

Figure 1.3: Cloud deployment models

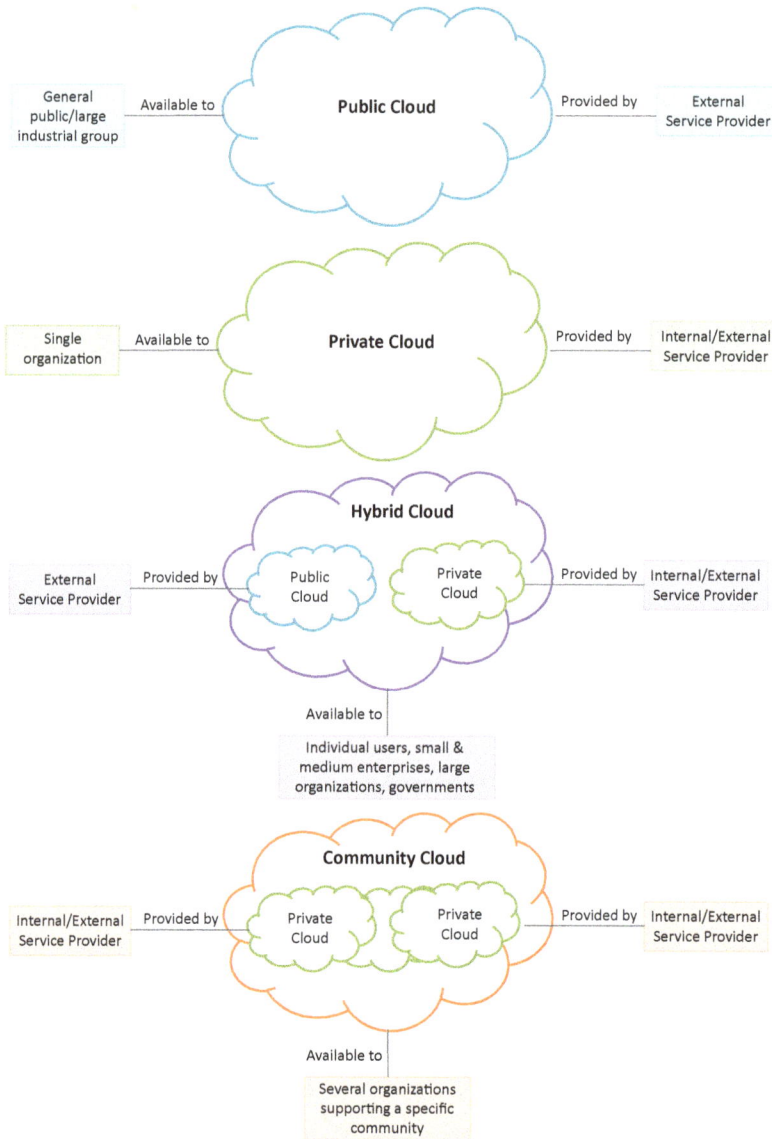

Figure 1.4: Cloud deployment models

1.4 Cloud Computing Concepts & Technologies

In this section, we describe the key concepts and enabling technologies of cloud computing. While cloud computing is a relatively new computing paradigm, the underlying technologies that enable cloud computing have existed for quite some time. Cloud computing is an emerging computing paradigm that builds upon concepts and technologies such as virtualization, load balancing, and on-demand provisioning.

1.4.1 Virtualization

Virtualization refers to the partitioning the resources of a physical system (such as computing, storage, network, and memory) into multiple virtual resources. Virtualization is the key enabling technology of cloud computing and allows the pooling of resources. In cloud computing, resources are pooled to serve multiple users using multi-tenancy. Multi-tenant aspects of the cloud allow multiple users to be served by the same physical hardware. Users are assigned virtual resources that run on top of the physical resources. Figure 1.5 shows the architecture of virtualization technology in cloud computing. The physical resources such as computing, storage memory, and network resources are virtualized. The virtualization layer partitions the physical resources into multiple virtual machines. The virtualization layer allows multiple operating system instances to run as virtual machines on the same underlying physical resources. Virtual machines abstract the operating system and applications from the hardware and enable resource pooling. Virtual machines provide several benefits such as efficient utilization of resources, rapid deployment, isolation, and encapsulation. Virtual machines are portable and allow applications to be migrated from one machine to another. Cloud computing resources can be provisioned in the form of virtual machine instances on demand. Multiple virtual machines running on the same physical resources enable multi-tenancy. The multi-tenanted approach of the cloud allows multiple users to make use of the same shared resources.

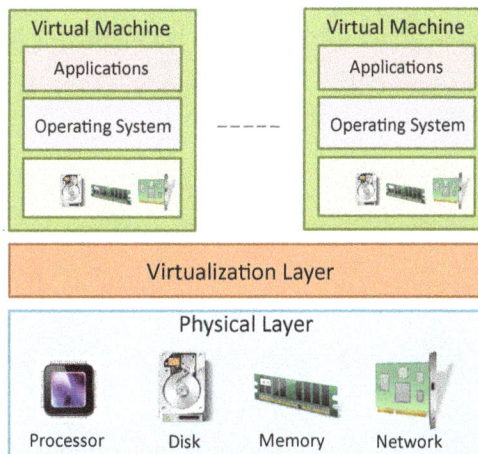

Figure 1.5: Virtualization architecture

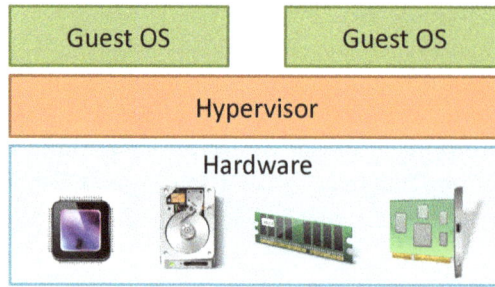

Figure 1.6: Hypervisor design: Type-1

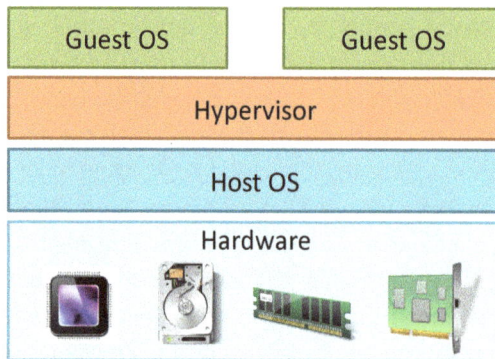

Figure 1.7: Hypervisor design: Type-2

Hypervisor

The virtualization layer consists of a hypervisor or virtual machine monitor (VMM). The hypervisor presents a virtual operating platform to the guest operating system. There are two types of hypervisors as shown in Figures 1.6 and 1.7 . Type-1 hypervisors or the native hypervisors run directly on the host hardware, control the hardware, and monitor the guest operating systems. Type 2 hypervisors or hosted hypervisors run on top of a conventional operating system and host guest operating systems.

Guest OS

A guest OS is an operating system that is installed in a virtual machine in addition to the host or main OS. In virtualization, the guest OS can be different from the host OS.

Various forms of virtualization approaches exist:

Full Virtualization

In full virtualization, the virtualization layer completely decouples the guest OS from the underlying hardware. The guest OS requires no modification and is not aware that it is being virtualized. Full virtualization is enabled by direct execution of user requests and binary translation of OS requests. Figure 1.8 shows the full virtualization approach.

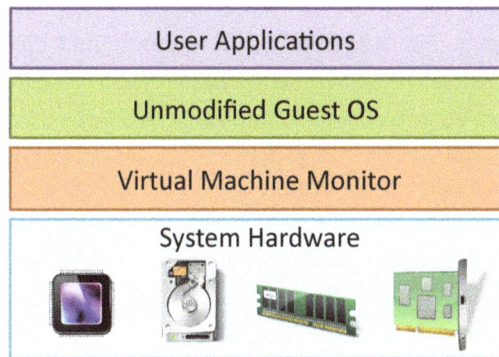

Figure 1.8: Full virtualization

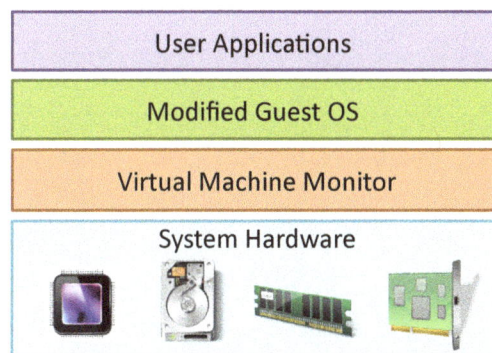

Figure 1.9: Para-virtualization

Para-Virtualization

In para-virtualization, the guest OS is modified to enable communication with the hypervisor to improve performance and efficiency. The guest OS kernel is modified to replace non-virtualizable instructions with hypercalls that communicate directly with the virtualization layer hypervisor. Figure 1.9 shows the para-virtualization approach.

Hardware Virtualization

Hardware-assisted virtualization is enabled by hardware features such as Intel's Virtualization Technology (VT-x) and AMD's AMD-V. In hardware-assisted virtualization, privileged, and sensitive calls are set to trap to the hypervisor automatically. Thus, there is no need for either binary translation or para-virtualization.

1.4.2 Containerization

Containers are a lightweight alternative to full virtual machines that allow applications to be packaged with all their dependencies into standardized units for software development and deployment. Rather than virtualizing the entire machine as VMs do, containers virtualize at the operating system level. This enables containers to share the host machine's operating system kernel while isolating the application's code, libraries, and dependencies. Containers offer greater efficiency and portability compared to traditional VMs since they avoid the overhead of full operating system virtualization. This emerging technology is rapidly gaining adoption due to advantages like consistent environments across development and production, optimized utilization of system resources, and simplified DevOps workflows. Containers are particularly well-suited for building and deploying microservices architectures, as each microservice can be isolated into its own container for independent scaling, updates, and resource allocation. The lightweight and portable nature of containers facilitates a seamless transition from developing microservices locally to deploying them across distributed clusters in the cloud. Later chapters will cover how to build, deploy, and orchestrate containers for microservices applications using industry-standard tools and platforms. Figure 1.10 shows a comparison of virtualization and containerization.

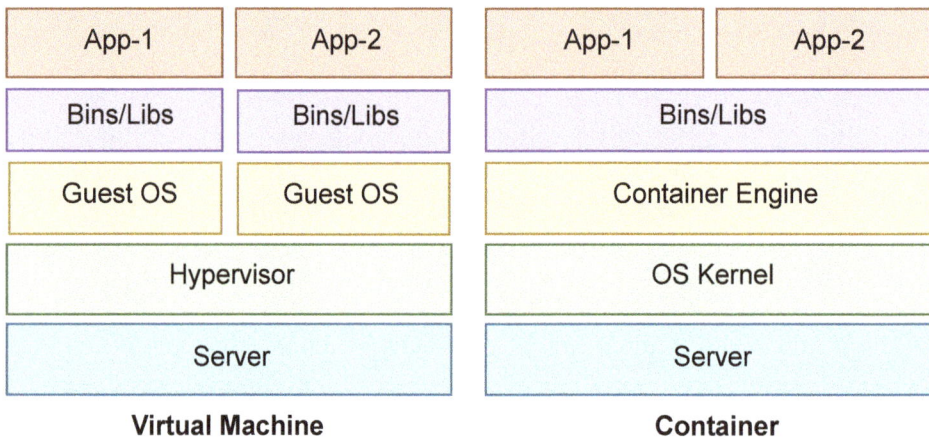

Figure 1.10: Virtualization versus Containerization

1.4.3 Load Balancing

One of the key characteristics of cloud computing is scalability. Cloud computing resources can be scaled up on demand to meet the performance requirements of applications. Load balancing is a key enabling technology that provides scalability for cloud environments. When the workload on servers increases, the response times of applications increase, and their throughput decreases. To meet the higher workloads, either the servers can be upgraded to higher computing capacity, or additional servers of the same capacity can be launched. The latter scenario is more scalable and easy to accomplish. Load balancing distributes workloads across multiple servers to meet the application workloads. Load balancing can be for different types of resources such as computing, storage, or network. The goals of load balancing techniques are to achieve maximum utilization of resources, minimizing the response times, and maximizing throughput. Load balancing distributes the incoming user requests across multiple resources. With load balancing, cloud-based applications can achieve high availability and reliability. Since multiple resources under a load balancer are used to serve the user requests, in the event of failure of one or more of the resources, the load balancer can automatically reroute the user traffic to the healthy resources.

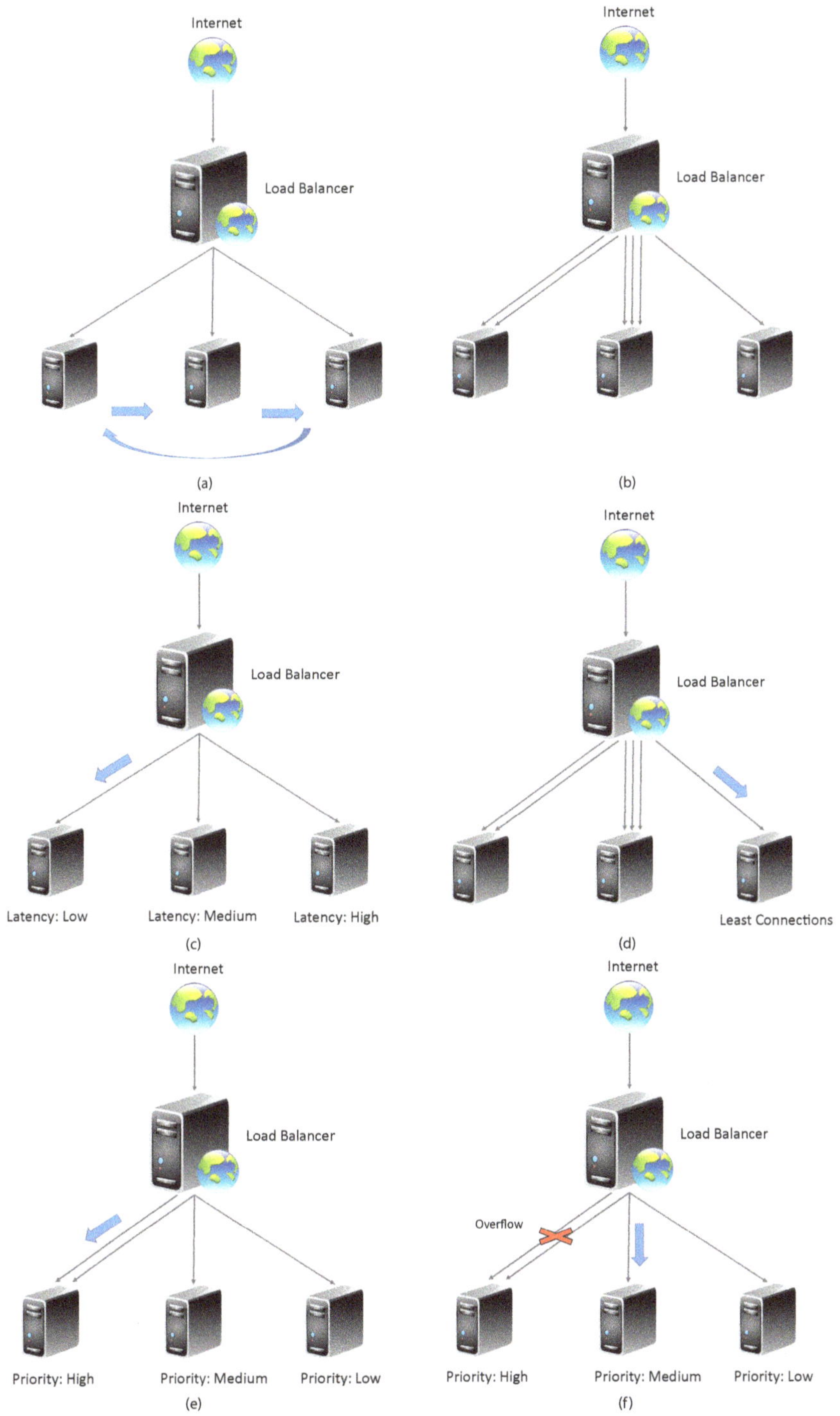

Figure 1.11: (a) Round-robin load balancing, (b) Weighted round-robin load balancing, (c) Low latency load balancing, (d) Least connections load balancing, (e) Priority load balancing, (f) Overload load balancing

To the end user accessing a cloud-based application, a load balancer makes the pool of servers under the load balancer appear as a single server with high computing capacity. The routing of incoming requests is transparent to the users and is determined based on a load balancing algorithm. Commonly used load balancing algorithms include:

Round-Robin

In round-robin load balancing, the servers are selected one by one to serve the incoming requests in a non-hierarchical circular fashion with no priority assigned to a specific server.

Weighted Round-Robin

In weighted round robin load balancing, servers are assigned some weights. The incoming requests are proportionally routed in the specified ratio.

Low Latency

In low latency load balancing, the load balancer monitors the latency of each server. Each incoming request is routed to the server, which has the lowest latency.

Least Connections

In the least connections load balancing, the incoming requests are routed to the server with the least number of connections.

Priority

In priority load balancing, each server is assigned a priority. The incoming traffic is routed to the highest priority server as long as the server is available. When the highest priority server fails, the incoming traffic is routed to a server with a lower priority.

Overflow

Overflow load balancing is similar to priority load balancing. When the incoming requests to the highest priority server overflow, the requests are routed to a lower priority server.

Figure 1.11 shows the various load balancing approaches. For session-based applications, an important issue to handle with load balancing is the persistence of multiple requests from a user session. Since load balancing can route successive requests from a user session to different servers, maintaining the state or the information of the session is essential. The commonly used persistence approaches are described below:

Sticky sessions

In this approach, all the requests belonging to a user session are routed to the same server. Thus, the sessions are called sticky sessions. The benefit of this approach is that it makes session management simple. However, a drawback of this approach is that if a server fails all the sessions belonging to that server are lost since there is no automatic failover possible.

Session Database

In this approach, all the session information is stored externally in a separate session database, which is often replicated to avoid a single point of failure. Though, this approach involves the additional overhead of storing the session information; however, unlike the sticky session approach, this approach allows automatic failover.

Browser cookies

In this approach, the session information is stored on the client side in the form of browser cookies. The benefit of this approach is that it makes the session management easy and has the least amount of overhead for the load balancer.

URL re-writing

In this approach, a URL re-write engine stores the session information by modifying the URLs on the client side. Though this approach avoids overhead on the load balancer, a drawback is that the amount of session information that can be stored is limited. For applications that require larger amounts of session information, this approach does not work.

Load balancing can be implemented in software or hardware. Software-based load balancers run on standard operating systems, and like other cloud resources, load balancers are also virtualized. Hardware-based load balancers implement load balancing algorithms in Application Specific Integrated Circuits (ASICs). In a hardware load balancer, the incoming user requests are routed to the underlying servers based on some pre-configured load-balancing strategy and the response from the servers is sent back either directly to the user (at layer-4) or back to the load balancer (at layer-7) where it is manipulated before being sent back to the user. Table 1.1 lists some examples of load balancers.

Load Balancer	Type
Nginx	Software
HAProxy	Software
Pound	Software
Varish	Software
Cisco Systems Catalyst 6500	Hardware
Coyote Point Equalizer	Hardware
F5 Networks BIG-IP LTM	Hardware
Barracuda Load Balancer	Hardware

Table 1.1: Examples of popular load balancers

1.4.4 Scalability & Elasticity

Multi-tier applications (such as E-Commerce, banking, social networking, and business-to-business) can experience rapid changes in their traffic. Each web application has a different traffic pattern which is determined by several factors, and is hard to predict. Modern web applications have multiple tiers of deployment with a different number of servers in each tier. Capacity planning is an essential task for such applications. Capacity planning involves determining the right sizing of each tier of the deployment of an application in terms of the number of resources and the capacity of each resource. Capacity planning may be for computing, storage, memory, or network resources. Figure 1.12 shows the cost versus capacity curves for traditional and cloud approaches.

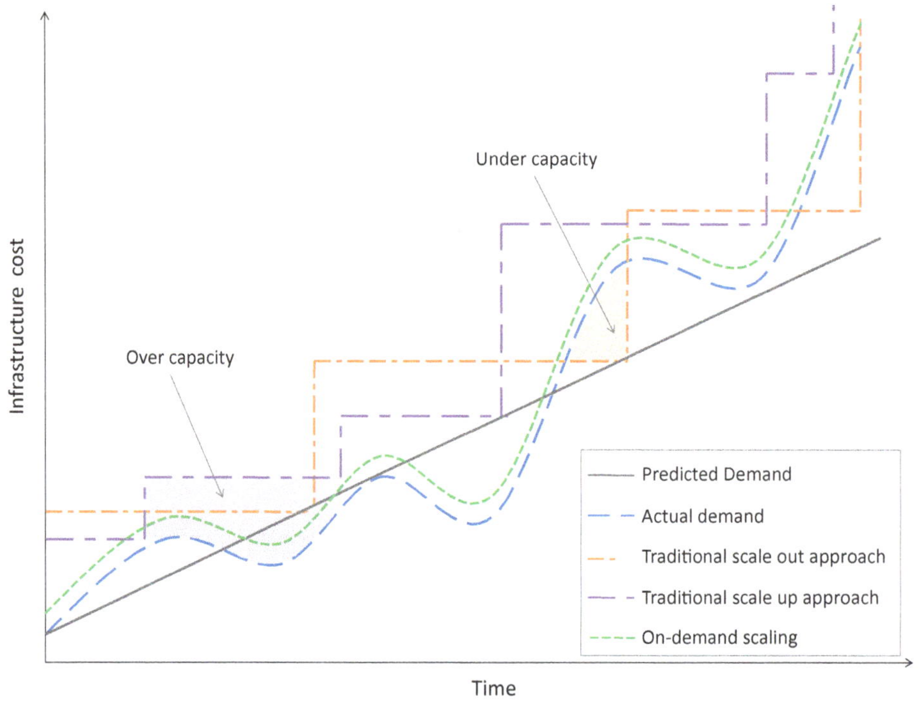

Figure 1.12: Cost versus capacity curves

Traditional approaches for capacity planning are based on predicted demands for applications and account for peak loads of applications. When the workloads of applications increase, the traditional approaches have been either to scale-up or scale-out. Scaling-up involves upgrading the hardware resources (adding additional computing, memory, storage, or network resources). Scaling-out involves the addition of more resources of the same type. Traditional scaling-up and scaling-out approaches are based on demand forecasts at regular intervals of time. When variations in workloads are rapid, traditional approaches are unable to keep track of the demand and lead to either over-provisioning or under-provisioning of resources. Over-provisioning of resources leads to higher capital expenditures than required. On the other hand, under-provisioning of resources leads to traffic overloads, slow response times, low throughputs, and hence, loss of opportunity to serve the customers. Traditional capacity planning approaches that are designed to meet the peak loads result in excess capacity and under-utilization of resources. Moreover, the infrastructure resources for traditional applications are fixed, rigid, and provisioned in advance. This involves up-front capital expenditures for setting up the infrastructure.

Cloud computing provides rapid elasticity and on-demand scaling of resources to meet the application workloads. Therefore, there is no over or under-provisioning of resources. On-demand scaling of cloud computing reduces the need for demand forecasting. On-demand scaling improves resource utilization and allows organizations to meet the peak workloads for their applications without overspending on infrastructure. Cloud computing allows organizations to save on the upfront capital expenditures for setting up the infrastructure for their applications. Cloud computing resources can be provisioned on pay-per-use/pay-as-you-go pricing models without the need for making upfront investments in infrastructure. Thus, cloud computing reduces the time to market for organizations by shifting their focus from capital expenditures (CapEx) to operating expenditures (OpEx). To leverage on-demand scaling and rapid elasticity, the deployment and configuration processes of cloud-based applications are automated. The utilization of resources of cloud applications is continuously monitored. On-demand scaling is enabled by triggers or events that signal the need for scaling up or down.

1.4.5 Deployment

Figure 1.13 shows the cloud application deployment lifecycle. Deployment prototyping can help in making deployment architecture design choices. By comparing the performance of alternative deployment architectures, deployment prototyping can help in choosing the most cost-effective deployment architecture that can meet the application performance requirements.

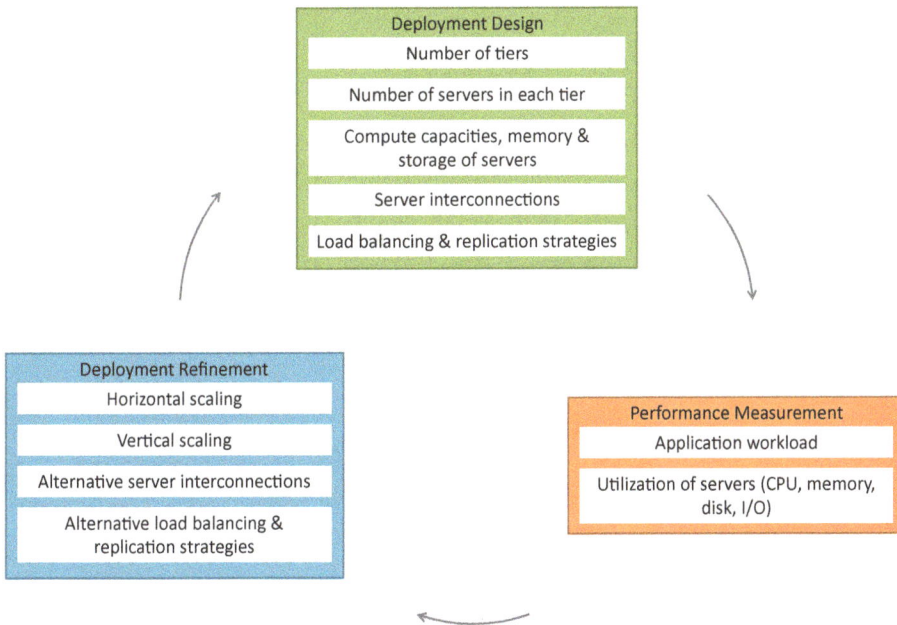

Figure 1.13: Cloud application deployment lifecycle

Deployment lifecycle includes the following steps:

Deployment Design

In this step, the application deployment is created with various tiers as specified in the deployment configuration. The variables in this step include the number of servers in each tier, computing, memory, and storage capacities of servers, server interconnection, load balancing, and replication strategies. Deployment is created by provisioning the cloud resources as specified in the deployment configuration. The process of resource provisioning and deployment creation is often automated and involves several steps such as the launching of server instances, configuration of servers, and deployment of various tiers of the application on the servers.

Performance Evaluation

Once the application is deployed in the cloud, the next step in the deployment lifecycle is to verify whether the application meets the performance requirements with the deployment. This step involves monitoring the workload on the application and measuring various workload parameters such as response time and throughput. In addition to this, the utilization of servers (CPU, memory, disk, and I/O) in each tier is also monitored.

Deployment Refinement

After evaluating the performance of the application, the deployment is refined so that the application can meet the performance requirements. Various alternatives can exist in this step, such as vertical scaling (or scaling-up), horizontal scaling (or scaling-out), alternative server interconnections, alternative load balancing, and replication strategies.

1.4.6   Replication

Replication is used to create and maintain multiple copies of the data in the cloud. Replication of data is essential for business continuity and disaster recovery. In the event of data loss at the primary location, organizations can continue to operate their applications from secondary data sources. With real-time replication of data, organizations can achieve faster recovery from failures. Traditional business continuity and disaster recovery approaches don't provide efficient, cost-effective, and automated recovery of data. Cloud-based data replication approaches provide replication of data in multiple locations, automated recovery, low recovery point objective (RPO), and low recovery time objective (RTO). Cloud enables the rapid implementation of replication solutions for disaster recovery for small and medium enterprises and large organizations. With cloud-based data replication, organizations can plan for disaster recovery without making any capital expenditures on purchasing, configuring, and managing secondary site locations. Cloud platforms provides affordable replication solutions with pay-per-use/pay-as-you-go pricing models. There are three types of replication approaches, as shown in Figure 1.14 and described as follows:

Array-based Replication

Array-based replication uses compatible storage arrays to automatically copy data from a local storage array to a remote storage array. Arrays replicate data at the disk sub-system level; therefore, the type of hosts accessing the data and the type of data is not important. Thus, array-based replication can work in heterogeneous environments with different operating systems. Array-based replication uses Network Attached Storage (NAS) or Storage Area Network (SAN), to replicate. A drawback of array-based replication is that it requires similar arrays at local and remote locations. Thus, the costs for setting up array-based replication are higher than the other approaches.

Network-based Replication

Network-based replication uses an appliance that sits on the network and intercepts packets that are sent from hosts and storage arrays. The intercepted packets are replicated to

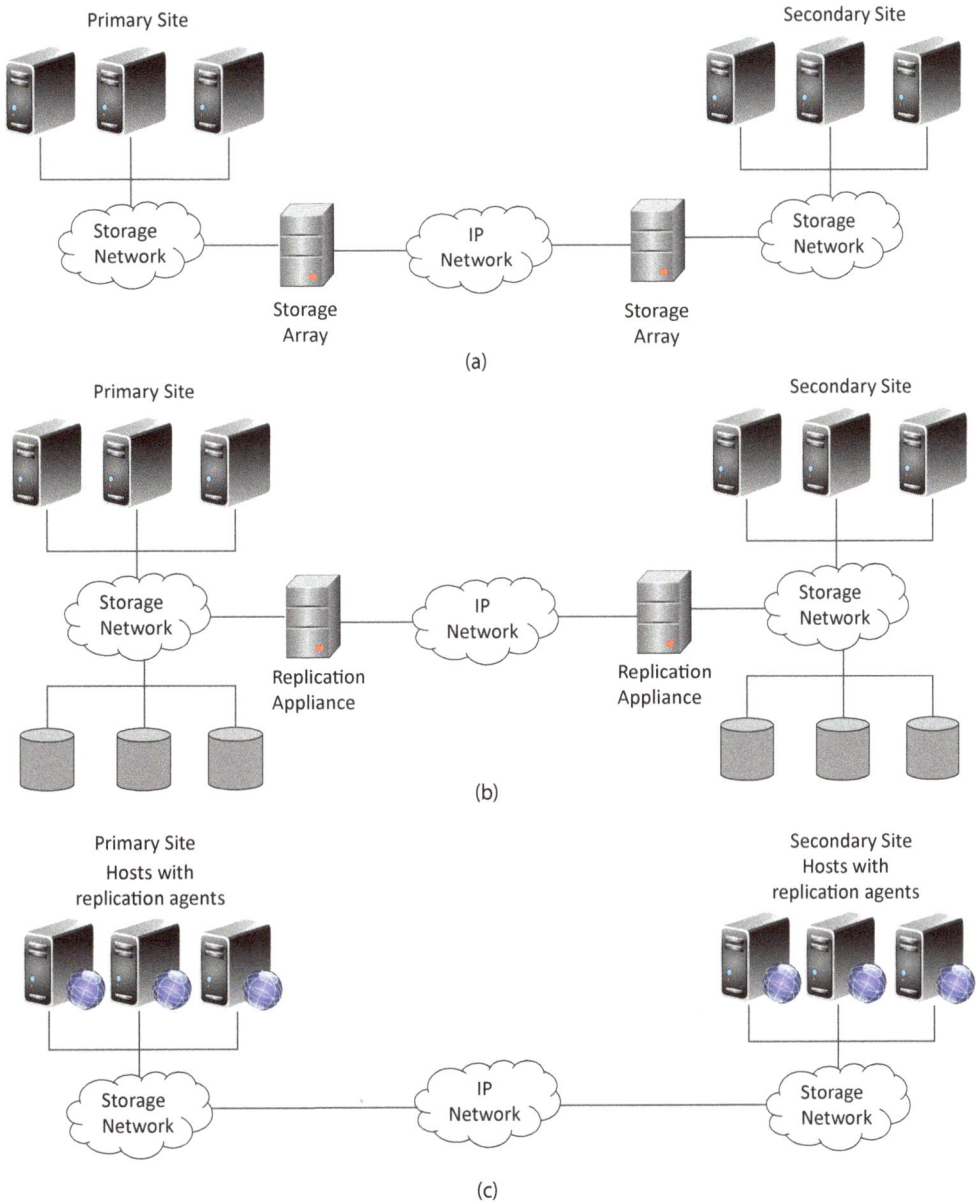

Figure 1.14: Replication approaches: (a) Array-based replication, (b) Network-based replication, (c) Host-based replication

a secondary location. The benefits of this approach are that it supports heterogeneous environments and requires a single point of management. However, this approach involves higher initial costs due to the replication of hardware and software.

Host-based Replication

Host-based replication runs on standard servers and uses software to transfer data from a local to a remote location. The host acts as the replication control mechanism. An agent is installed on the hosts that communicate with the agents on the other hosts. Host-based replication can either be block-based or file-based. Block-based replication typically requires dedicated volumes of the same size on both the local and remote servers. File-based replication requires less storage as compared to block-based storage. File-based replication allows the administrators to choose the files or folders to be replicated. Host-based replication with cloud infrastructure provides affordable replication solutions. With host-based replication, entire virtual machines can be replicated in real-time.

1.4.7 Monitoring

Cloud resources can be monitored by monitoring services provided by cloud service providers. Monitoring services allow cloud users to collect and analyze the data on various monitoring metrics. Figure 1.15 shows a generic architecture for a cloud monitoring service. A monitoring service collects data on various system and application metrics from the cloud computing instances. Monitoring services provide various pre-defined metrics. Users can also define their custom metrics for monitoring cloud resources. Users can define various actions based on the monitoring data, for example, auto-scaling a cloud deployment when the CPU usage of monitored resources becomes high. Monitoring services also provide various statistics based on the monitoring data collected. Table 1.2 lists the commonly used monitoring metrics for cloud computing resources. Monitoring of cloud resources is necessary because it allows the users to keep track of the health of applications and services deployed in the cloud. With the monitoring data, users can make operational decisions such as scaling-up or scaling-down cloud resources.

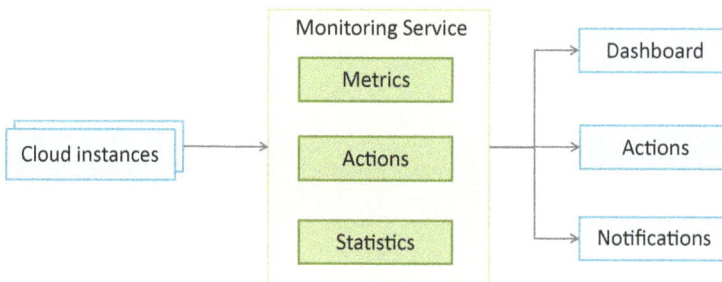

Figure 1.15: Typical cloud monitoring service architecture

Type	Metrics
CPU	CPU-Usage, CPU-Idle
Disk	Disk-Usage, Bytes/sec (read/write), Operations/sec
Memory	Memory-Used, Memory-Free, Page-Cache
Interface	Packets/sec(incoming/outgoing), Octets/sec(incoming/outgoing)

Table 1.2: Typical monitoring metrics

1.4.8 Software Defined Networking

Software-Defined Networking (SDN) is a networking architecture that separates the control plane from the data plane and centralizes the network controller. Figure 1.16 shows the conventional network architecture built with specialized hardware (switches and routers). Network devices in conventional network architectures are getting increasingly complex with the growing number of distributed protocols being implemented and the use of proprietary hardware and interfaces. In the conventional network architecture, the control plane and data plane are tightly coupled. Control plane is the part of the network that carries the signaling traffic, and the data plane is the part of the network that bears the traffic.

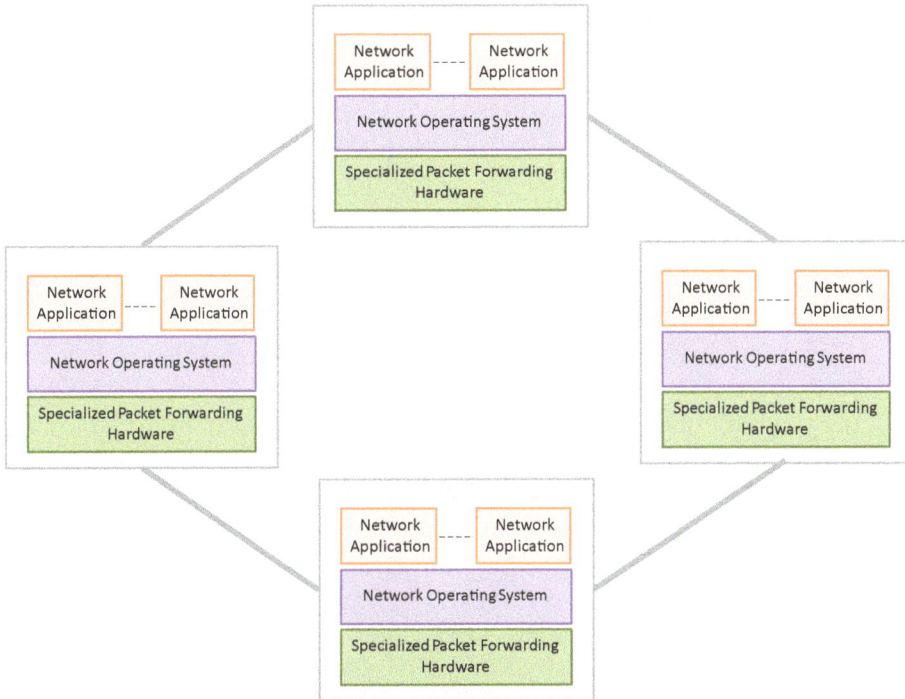

Figure 1.16: Conventional network architecture

The limitations of the conventional network architectures are as follows:

- **Complex Network Devices**: Conventional networks are getting increasingly complex with more and more protocols being implemented to improve link speeds and reliability. Interoperability is limited due to the lack of standard and open interfaces. Network devices use proprietary hardware and software and have slow product lifecycles limiting innovation. The conventional networks were well-suited for static traffic patterns and had a large number of protocols designed for specific applications. With the emergence of cloud computing and the proliferation of Internet access devices, traffic patterns are becoming more and more dynamic. Due to the complexity of conventional network devices, making changes in the networks to meet the dynamic traffic patterns has become increasingly difficult.

- **Mangement Overhead**: Conventional networks involve significant management overhead. Network managers find it increasingly difficult to manage multiple network

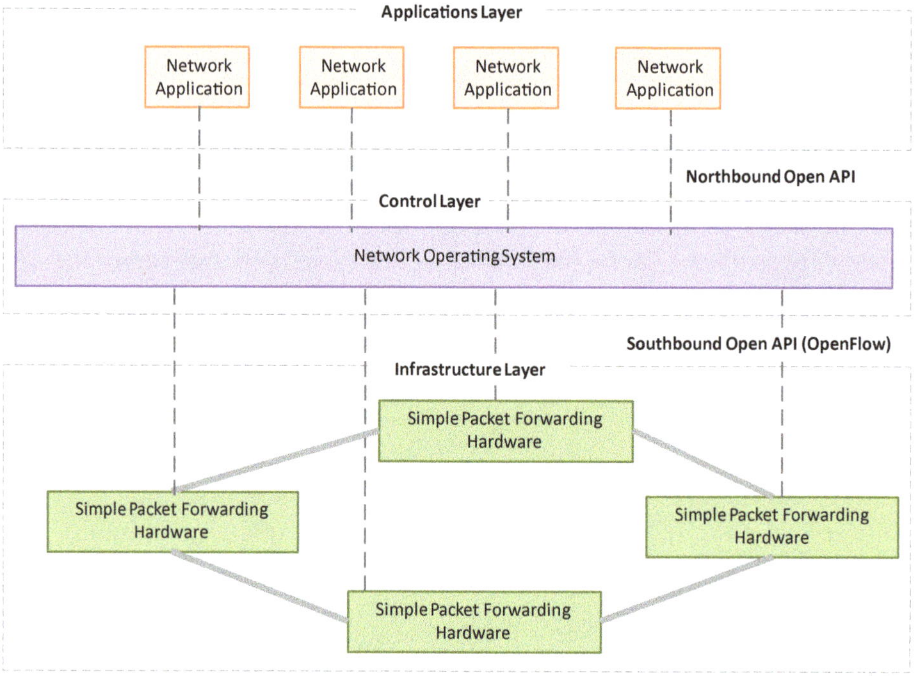

Figure 1.17: SDN architecture

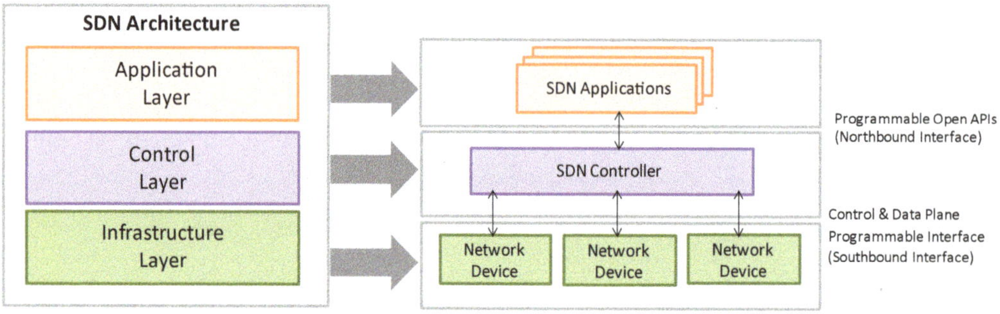

Figure 1.18: SDN layers

devices and interfaces from multiple vendors. Upgradation of a network requires configuration changes in multiple devices (switches, routers, and firewalls).

- **Limited Scalability**: The virtualization technologies used in cloud computing environments have increased the number of virtual hosts requiring network access. Multi-tenanted applications hosted in the cloud are distributed across multiple virtual machines that require the exchange of traffic. Big data applications run distributed algorithms on a large number of virtual machines that require vast amounts of data exchange between virtual machines. Such computing environments require highly scalable and easy to manage network architectures with minimal manual configurations, which is becoming increasingly difficult with conventional networks.

SDN aims to make the network architectures simpler, scalable, agile, and easy to manage. Figures 1.17 and 1.18 show the SDN architecture and the SDN layers in which the control and data planes are decoupled, and the network controller is centralized. Software-based SDN controllers maintain a unified view of the network and make configuration, management, and provisioning simpler. The underlying infrastructure in SDN uses simple packet forwarding hardware as opposed to specialized hardware in conventional networks. The underlying network infrastructure is abstracted from the applications. Network devices become simple with SDN as they do not require implementations of a large number of protocols. Network devices receive instructions from the SDN controller on how to forward the packets.

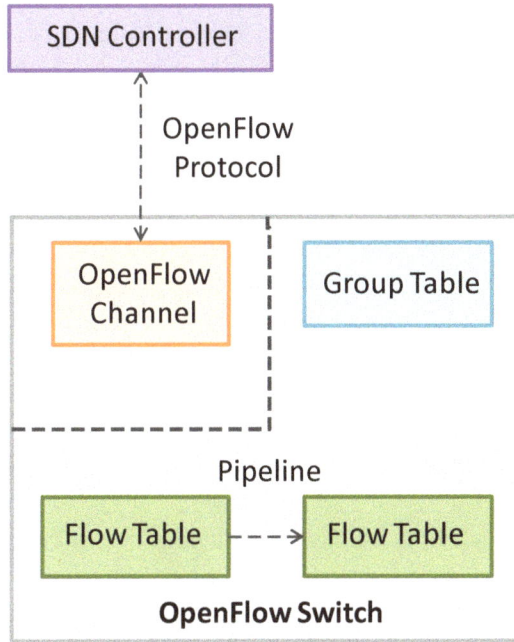

Figure 1.19: OpenFlow switch

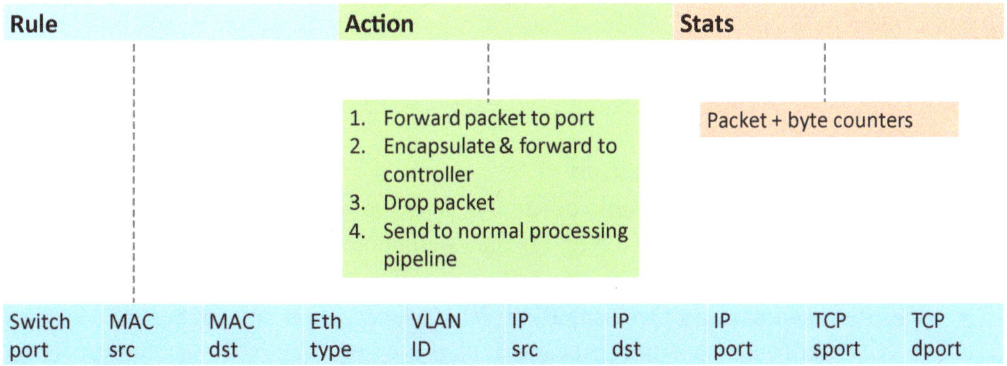

Figure 1.20: OpenFlow flow table

The key elements of SDN are as follows:

- **Centralized Network Controller**: With decoupled control and data planes, and a centralized network controller, the network administrators can rapidly configure the network. SDN applications can be deployed through programmable open APIs. This speeds up innovation as the network administrators no longer need to wait for the device vendors to embed new features in their proprietary hardware.
- **Programmable Open APIs**: SDN architecture supports programmable open APIs for the interface between the SDN application and control layers (Northbound interface). These open APIs allow implementing various network services such as routing, quality of service (QoS), and access control.
- **Standard Communication Interface (OpenFlow)**: SDN architecture uses a standard communication interface between the control and infrastructure layers (Southbound interface). OpenFlow, which is defined by the Open Networking Foundation (ONF) is the broadly accepted SDN protocol for the Southbound interface. With OpenFlow, the forwarding plane of the network devices can be directly accessed and manipulated. OpenFlow uses the concept of flows to identify network traffic based on pre-defined match rules. Flows can be programmed statically or dynamically by the SDN control software. Figure 1.19 shows the components of an OpenFlow switch comprising one or more flow tables and a group table, which perform packet lookups and forwarding, and OpenFlow channel to an external controller. OpenFlow protocol is implemented on both sides of the interface between the controller and the network devices. The controller manages the switch via the OpenFlow switch protocol. The controller can add, update, and delete flow entries in flow tables. Figure 1.20 shows an example of an OpenFlow flow table. Each flow table contains a set of flow entries. Each flow entry consists of match fields, counters, and a set of instructions to apply to matching packets. Matching starts at the first flow table and may continue to additional flow tables of the pipeline [5].

1.4.9   Network Function Virtualization

Network Function Virtualization (NFV) is a technology that leverages virtualization to consolidate the heterogeneous network devices onto industry standard high-volume servers, switches, and storage. NFV is complementary to SDN as NFV can provide the infrastructure on which SDN can run. NFV and SDN are mutually beneficial to each other but not dependent. Network functions can be virtualized without SDN; similarly, SDN can run without NFV.

Figure 1.21 shows the NFV architecture, as being standardized by the European Telecommunications Standards Institute (ETSI) [4]. Key elements of the NFV architecture are as follows:

- **Virtualized Network Function (VNF)**: VNF is a software implementation of a network function that is capable of running over the NFV Infrastructure (NFVI).
- **NFV Infrastructure (NFVI)**: NFVI includes compute, network, and storage resources that are virtualized.
- **NFV Management and Orchestration**: NFV Management and Orchestration focuses on all virtualization-specific management tasks and covers the orchestration and lifecycle management of physical or software resources that support the infrastructure virtualization and the lifecycle management of VNFs.

Figure 1.21: NFV architecture

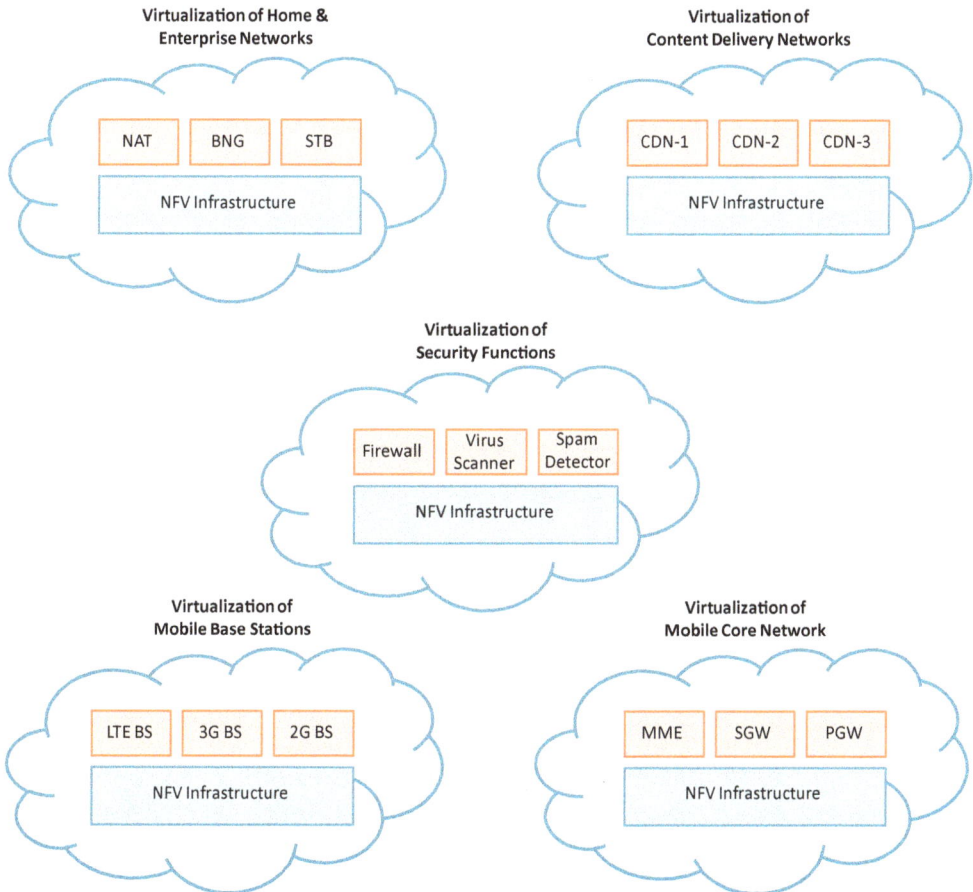

Figure 1.22: NFV use cases

NFV comprises network functions implemented in software that run on virtualized resources in the cloud. NFV enables a separation of the network functions which are implemented in software, from the underlying hardware. Thus, network functions can be easily tested and upgraded by installing new software, while the hardware remains the same. Virtualizing network functions reduces equipment costs and also reduces power consumption. The multi-tenanted nature of the cloud allows virtualized network functions to be shared for multiple network services. NFV applies only to the data plane and control plane functions in fixed and mobile networks. Figure 1.22 shows the use cases of NFV for home and enterprise networks, content delivery networks, mobile base stations, mobile core network, and security functions.

1.4.10   Identity and Access Management

Identity and Access Management (IAM) for cloud describes the authentication and authorization of users to provide secure access to cloud resources. Organizations with multiple users can use IAM services provided by the cloud service provider for the management of user identifiers and user permissions. IAM services allow organizations to centrally manage users, access permissions, security credentials, and access keys. Organizations can enable role-based access control to cloud resources and applications using IAM services. IAM services allow the creation of user groups where all the users in a group have the same access permissions. Identity and Access Management is enabled by several technologies such as OAuth, Role-based Access Control (RBAC), Digital Identities, Security Tokens, and Identity Providers.

OAuth is an open standard for authorization that allows resource owners to share their private resources stored on one site with another site without sharing the credentials. Figure 1.23 shows an example of OAuth. In the OAuth model, an application (which is not the resource owner) requests access to resources controlled by the resource owner (but hosted by the server). The resource owner grants permission to access the resources in the form of a token and a matching shared-secret. Tokens make it unnecessary for the resource owner to share its credentials with the application. Tokens can be issued with a restricted scope and limited lifetime, and can be revoked independently.

RBAC is an approach for restricting access to authorized users. Figure 1.24 shows an example of a typical RBAC framework. Users who wants to access the cloud resources are required to send their data to the system administrator who assigns permissions and access control policies which are stored in the User Roles and Data Access Policies databases respectively. RBAC is an important concept for managing permissions in cloud environments. With RBAC, permissions are assigned to roles rather than individual users. Users are then assigned to appropriate roles based on their responsibilities and job functions. This provides a simple yet powerful mechanism for managing access to cloud resources. Effective implementation of RBAC requires carefully planning roles, mapping job functions to roles, assigning users to roles and auditing role use over time. Roles should be limited in number and reflect broad responsibilities. With cloud environments becoming ubiquitous, RBAC provides an indispensable mechanism for managing permissions to cloud resources. The ability to assign access based on roles rather than individual user accounts saves time, reduces risk, improves security and enables organizations to manage access at cloud scale.

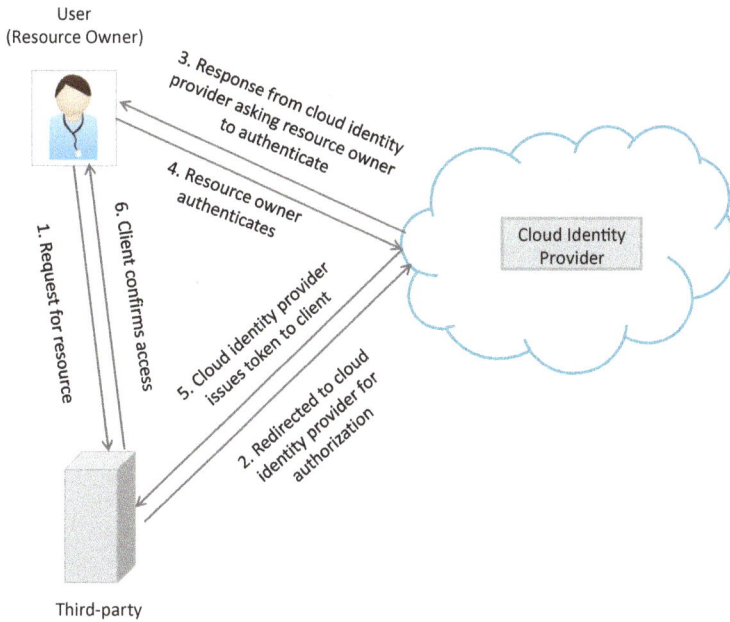

Figure 1.23: OAuth example

Figure 1.24: Role-based Access Control example

1.4.11   Service Level Agreements

A Service Level Agreement (SLA) for cloud specifies the level of service that is formally
defined as a part of the service contract with the cloud service provider. SLAs provide
a level of service for each service, which is specified in the form of a minimum level of
service guaranteed and a target level. SLAs contain several performance metrics and the
corresponding service level objectives. Table 1.3 lists the common criteria of cloud SLAs.

Criteria	Details
Availability	Percentage of time the service is guaranteed to be available
Performance	Response time, Throughput
Disaster Recovery	Mean time to recover
Problem resolution	Process to identify problems, support options, resolution expectations
Security and privacy of data	Mechanisms for security of data in storage and transmission

Table 1.3: List of criteria for cloud SLAs

1.4.12   Billing

Cloud service providers offer several billing models described as follows:

Elastic Pricing

In the elastic pricing or pay-as-you-use pricing model, the customers are charged based on
the usage of cloud resources. Cloud computing provides the benefit of provisioning resources
on-demand. On-demand provisioning and elastic pricing models bring cost savings for
customers. The elastic pricing model is suited for customers who consume cloud resources
for short durations, and cannot predict the usage.

Fixed Pricing

In fixed pricing models, customers are charged a fixed amount per month for cloud resources.
For example, a fixed amount can be charged per month for running a virtual machine instance,
irrespective of the actual usage. The fixed pricing model is suited for customers who want to
use cloud resources for longer durations, and want more control over the cloud expenses.

Spot Pricing

Spot pricing models offer variable pricing for cloud resources, which is driven by market
demand. When the demand for cloud resources is high, the prices increase, and when the
demand is lower, the prices decrease.

Table 1.4 lists the billable resources for cloud, including virtual machines, network,
storage, data services, security services, support, application services, deployment, and
management services.

Resource	Details
Virtual machines	CPU, memory, storage, disk I/O, network I/O
Network	Network I/O, load balancers, DNS, firewall, VPN
Storage	Cloud storage, storage volumes, storage gateway
Data services	Data import/export services, data encryption, data compression, data backup, data redundancy, content delivery
Security services	Identity and access management, isolation, compliance
Support	Level of support, SLA, fault tolerance
Application services	Queuing service, notification service, workflow service, payment service
Deployment and management services	Monitoring service, deployment service

Table 1.4: List of billable resources for cloud

1.5 Cloud Computing Reference Model

Figure 1.25 (a) shows the cloud computing reference model, along with the various cloud service models (IaaS, PaaS, and SaaS). Infrastructure-as-a-Service (IaaS) provides virtualized and dynamically scalable resources using a virtualized infrastructure. Platform-as-a-Service (PaaS) simplifies application development by providing development tools, application programming interfaces (APIs), and software libraries that can be used for a wide range of applications. Software-as-a-Service (SaaS) provides multi-tenant applications hosted in the cloud. The bottommost layer in the cloud reference model is the infrastructure and facilities layer that includes the physical infrastructure such as data center facilities, electrical and mechanical equipment. On top of the infrastructure, layer is the hardware layer that includes physical compute, network, and storage hardware. On top of the hardware layer, the virtualization layer partitions the physical hardware resources into multiple virtual resources that enable the pooling of resources. The platform and middleware layer builds upon the IaaS layers below and provides standardized stacks of services such as database service, queuing service, application frameworks, run-time environments, messaging services, monitoring services, and analytics services. The service management layer provides APIs for requesting, managing, and monitoring cloud resources. The topmost layer is the applications layer that includes SaaS applications.

Figure 1.25 (b) shows various types of cloud services. Some key categories of cloud services include deployment and management services which help deploy and manage infrastructure and applications in the cloud. Analytics services provide tools for analyzing and visualizing data. Application services allow organizations to develop, deploy and manage applications. Network services provide connectivity between cloud resources and on-premise infrastructure. Compute services provide access to scalable computing resources like virtual machines and containers. Identity and access management services handle user authentication and access controls. Storage services offer file, block or object storage capabilities.

(a) Cloud reference model

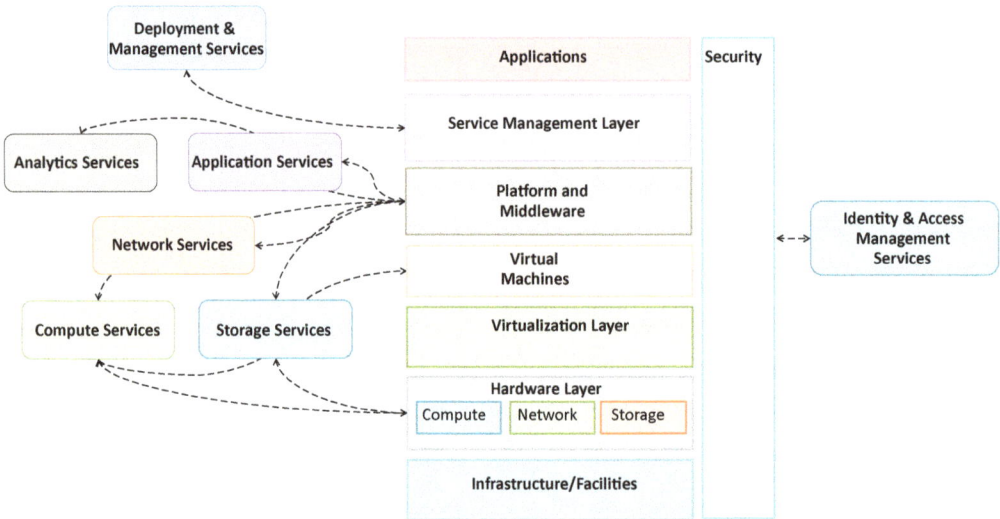

(b) Cloud services

Figure 1.25: Cloud Computing reference model & services

1.6 Open Source Private Cloud Software

In this section, we describe popular open-source cloud software that can be used to build private clouds.

1.6.1 CloudStack

Apache CloudStack is an open-source cloud software that can be used for creating private cloud offerings [6]. CloudStack manages the network, storage, and compute nodes that make up a cloud infrastructure. A CloudStack installation consists of a Management Server and the cloud infrastructure that it manages. The cloud infrastructure can be as simple as one host running the hypervisor or a large cluster of hundreds of hosts. The Management Server allows you to configure and manage the cloud resources. Figure 1.26 shows the architecture of CloudStack, which is the Management Server. The Management Server manages one or more zones where each zone is typically a single data center. Each zone has one or more pods. A pod is a rack of hardware comprising a switch and one or more clusters. A cluster consists of one or more hosts and primary storage. A host is a compute node that runs guest virtual machines. The primary storage of the cluster stores the disk volumes for all the virtual machines running on the hosts in that cluster. Each zone has a secondary storage that stores templates, ISO images, and disk volume snapshots.

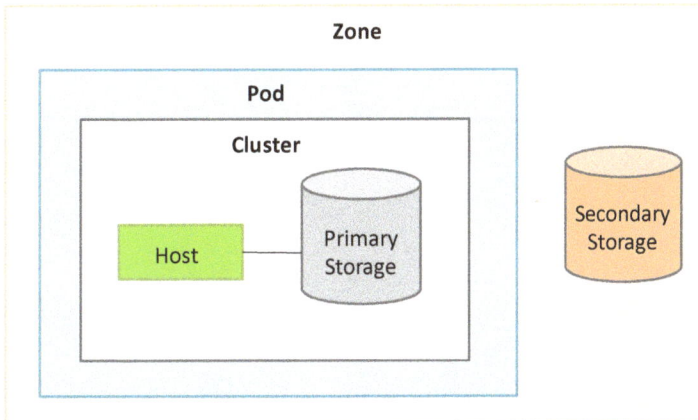

Figure 1.26: CloudStack architecture

1.6.2 Eucalyptus

Eucalyptus is an open-source private cloud software for building private and hybrid clouds that are compatible with Amazon Web Services (AWS) APIs [7]. Figure 1.27 shows the architecture of Eucalyptus. The Node Controller (NC) hosts virtual machine instances and manages the virtual network endpoints. The cluster-level (availability-zone) consists of three components - Cluster Controller (CC), Storage Controller (SC), and VMware Broker. The CC manages the virtual machines and is the front-end for a cluster. The SC manages the Eucalyptus block volumes and snapshots to the instances within its specific cluster. SC is equivalent to AWS Elastic Block Store (EBS). The VMware Broker is an optional component that provides an AWS-compatible interface for VMware environments. At the cloud-level, there are two components - Cloud Controller (CLC) and Walrus. CLC provides an administrative interface for cloud management and performs high-level resource scheduling, system accounting, authentication, and quota management.

Walrus is equivalent to Amazon S3 and serves as persistent storage to all of the virtual machines in the Eucalyptus cloud. Walrus can be used as a simple Storage-as-a-Service solution.

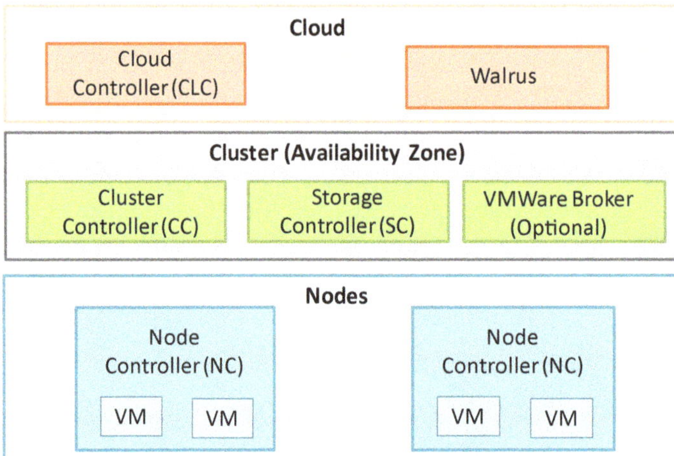

Figure 1.27: Eucalyptus architecture

1.6.3 OpenStack

OpenStack is a cloud operating system comprising a collection of interacting services that control computing, storage, and networking resources [8]. Figure 1.28 shows the architecture of OpenStack. The OpenStack compute service (called nova-compute) manages networks of virtual machines running on nodes, providing virtual servers on demand. The network service (called nova-networking) provides connectivity between the interfaces of other OpenStack services. The volume service (cinder) manages storage volumes for virtual machines. The object storage service (swift) allows users to store and retrieve files. The identity service (keystone) provides authentication and authorization for other services. The image registry (glance) acts as a catalog and repository for virtual machine images. The OpenStack scheduler (nova-scheduler) maps the nova-API calls to the appropriate OpenStack components. The scheduler takes the virtual machine requests from the queue and determines where they should run. The messaging service (rabbit-mq) acts as a central node for message passing between daemons. Orchestration activities such as running an instance are performed by the nova-api, which accepts and responds to end-user compute API calls. The OpenStack dashboard (called horizon) provides a web-based interface for managing OpenStack services.

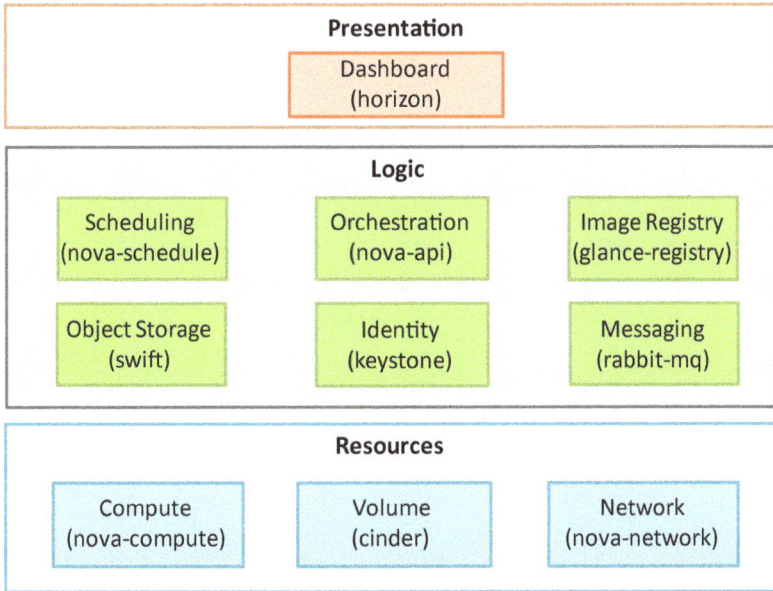

Figure 1.28: OpenStack architecture

1.7 Design Considerations for Cloud Applications

Modern web applications are dynamic in nature allowing users to interact and collaborate, include user generated content such as comments and discussions, integrate social networks and multimodal content such as text, images, audio, video, and presentations, in various formats. Due to this dynamic nature of modern web applications, the traffic patterns for such applications are becoming more and more unpredictable. Some applications experience seasonal variations in their workloads. The 'one size fits all' paradigm no longer works for modern applications. In this section, we describe the design considerations for cloud applications, and the reference architectures for various types of applications.

1.7.1 Scalability

Scalability is an important factor that drives the application designers to move to cloud computing environments. Building applications that can serve millions of users without taking a hit on their performance has always been challenging. With the developments in cloud computing technologies, application designers can provision adequate resources to meet their workload levels. However, simply provisioning more and more resources may not bring performance gains if the applications are not designed to scale well. There are several design considerations that the developers need to keep in mind. Traditional approaches were based on either over-provisioning of resources to handle the peak workload levels expected or provisioning based on average workload levels. Both approaches have their disadvantages. While the over-provisioning approach leads to underutilization of resources and increased costs, the approach based on average workload levels can lead to traffic overloads, slow response times, low throughputs and hence loss of opportunity to serve the customers. To leverage the benefits of cloud computing, such as dynamic scaling, the following design considerations must be kept in mind:

- **Loose coupling of components:** Traditional application design methodologies with tightly coupled application components limit the scalability. Tightly coupled components use procedure-based tight coupling and hard-wired links, which make it difficult to scale application components independently. By designing loosely coupled components, it is possible to scale each component independently.

- **Asynchronous communication:** Synchronous communication limits the scalability of the application. By allowing asynchronous communication between components, it is possible to add capacity by adding additional servers when the application load increases.

- **Stateless design:** Stateless designs that store the state information outside of the components in a separate database or cloud storage, allow scaling the application components independently.

- **Database choice and design:** The choice of the database and the design of data storage schemes affect the application scalability. Decisions such as whether to choose a traditional relational database (SQL approach) with strict schemas or a schema-less database (NoSQL approach) should be made after careful analysis of the application's data storage and analysis requirements.

1.7.2 Reliability & Availability

Reliability of a system is defined as the probability that a system performs the intended functions under stated conditions for a specified amount of time. Availability is the probability that a system performs a specified function under given conditions at a prescribed time. The important considerations to be kept in mind while developing highly reliable and available applications are:

- **No single point of failure:** Traditional application design approaches that have single points of failure, such as a single database server or a single application server, have the risk of complete breakdowns in case the of failure of the critical resource. To achieve high reliability and availability, having a redundant resource or an automated fallback resource is important.

- **Trigger automated actions on failures:** Traditional application design approaches handled failures by giving exceptions. By using failures and triggers for automated actions, it is possible to improve the application reliability and availability. For example, if an application server experiences high CPU usage and is unable to serve new requests, a new application server is automatically launched.

- **Graceful degradation:** Applications should be designed to gracefully degrade in the event of outages of some parts or components of the application. Graceful degradation means that if some component of the application becomes unavailable, the application as a whole would still be available and continue to serve the users, though, with limited functionality. For example, in an E-Commerce application, if a component that manages a certain category of products becomes unavailable, the users should still be able to view products from other categories.

- **Logging:** Logging all events in all the application components can help in detecting bottlenecks and failures so that necessary design/deployment changes can be made to improve application reliability and availability.

- **Replication:** All application data should be replicated. Replication is used to create and maintain multiple copies of the data in the cloud. In the event of data loss at the primary location, organizations can continue to operate their applications from secondary data sources.

1.7.3 Security

Security is an important design consideration for cloud applications given the outsourced nature of cloud computing environments. Key security considerations for cloud computing environments include:

- **Securing data at rest**: Data at rest should be encrypted to prevent unauthorized access if storage is compromised. Access controls should also limit who can access stored data.
- **Securing data in motion**: Data should be encrypted in transit over networks and between cloud services to prevent eavesdropping or tampering during transmission.
- **Authentication**: Multi-factor authentication and strong passwords should be used to verify users are who they claim to be when accessing cloud services.
- **Authorization**: Role-based access controls should be implemented to restrict user actions to only what is needed for their role.
- **Identity and access management**: Cloud providers and organizations should have systems to provision, manage, and revoke access to cloud resources.
- **Key management**: Keys used for encryption should be securely generated, stored, rotated, and access should be tightly controlled.
- **Data integrity**: Cryptographic checksums or signatures should be used to detect unauthorized changes to data in the cloud.
- **Auditing**: Cloud activity should be logged to provide visibility into user actions for auditing and forensic purposes.

1.7.4 Maintenance & Upgradation

To achieve a rapid time-to-market, businesses typically launch their applications with a core set of features ready and then incrementally add new features as and when they are complete. Businesses may need to adapt their applications based on the feedback from the users. In such scenarios, it is important to design applications with low maintenance and upgradation costs. Design decisions such as loosely coupled components and microservices help in reducing the application maintenance and upgradation time. In applications with loosely coupled components, changes can be made to a component without affecting other components. Moreover, components can be tested individually. Other decisions such as logging and triggering automated actions also help in lowering maintenance costs.

1.7.5 Performance

Applications should be designed while keeping the performance requirements in mind. Performance requirements depend on the type of application. For example, applications that experience database read-intensive workloads, can benefit from read-replication or caching approaches. Various metrics are used to evaluate application performance, such as latency, traffic, errors, and saturation, which are also called the golden signals. Latency measures the time it takes to service a request. Traffic monitors the rate of requests. Errors track failed requests and exceptions. Saturation indicates how 'full' resources are, like CPU, memory, or disk. Tracking these four signals provides a comprehensive view into overall system health, helps identify bottlenecks and issues, and enables proactive capacity planning. The golden signals allow cloud teams to monitor service-level objectives and quickly diagnose problems to maintain high availability and performance.

1.8   Reference Architectures for Cloud Applications

Multi-tier cloud applications can have various deployment architecture alternatives. Choosing the right deployment architecture is important to ensure that the application meets the specified performance requirements. In this section, we describe the reference architectures for different classes of multi-tier cloud applications.

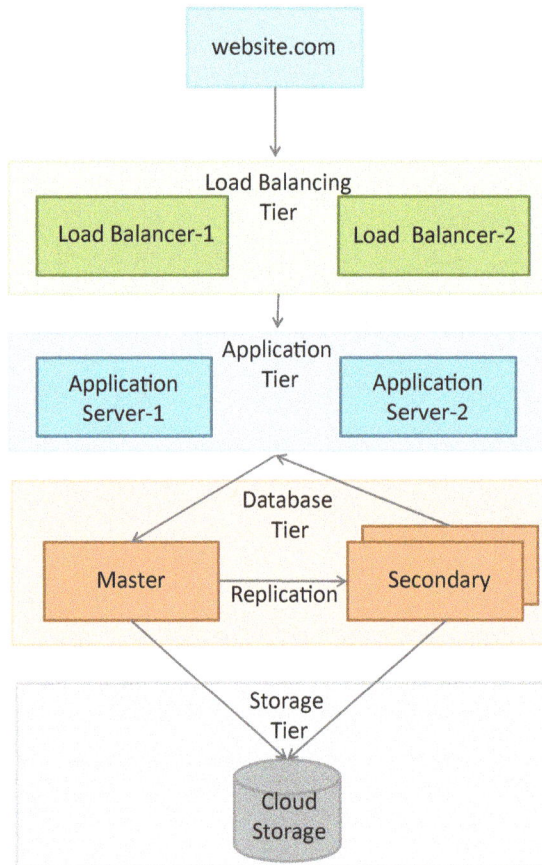

Figure 1.29: Typical deployment architecture for E-Commerce, Business-to-Business, Banking and Financial applications.

Figure 1.29 shows a typical deployment architecture for E-Commerce, Business-to-Business, Banking, and Financial applications. The various tiers in this deployment include:

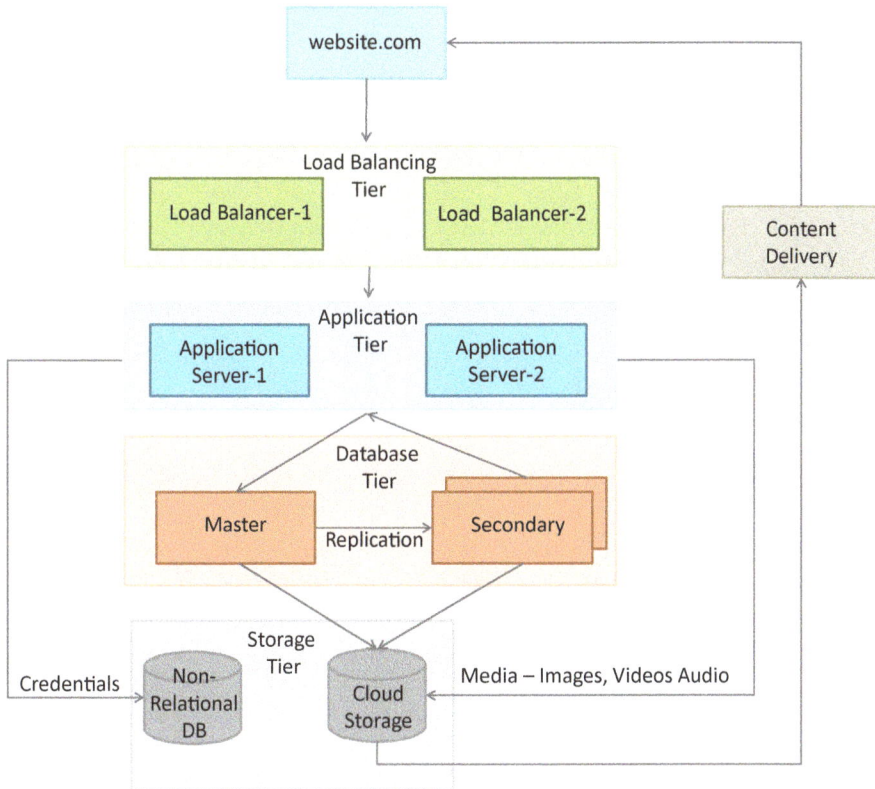

Figure 1.30: Typical deployment architecture for content delivery applications such as online photo albums, video webcasting, etc.

- **Load Balancing Tier:** The first tier is the load balancing tier. The load balancing tier consists of one or more load balancers. It is recommended to have at least two load balancer instances to avoid the single point of failure. Whenever possible, it is also recommended to provision the load balancer instances in separate availability zones of the cloud service provider to improve reliability and availability.

- **Application Tier:** The second tier is the application tier that consists of one or more application servers. For this tier, it is recommended to configure auto-scaling. Auto-scaling can be triggered when the recorded values for any of the specified metrics such as CPU or memory usage go above defined thresholds. The minimum and maximum size of the application server auto-scaling groups can be configured. It is recommended to have at least two application servers running at all times to avoid a single point of failure. When an auto-scaling event occurs, a new instance is launched. It may take a few minutes for the instance to get fully operational. Within this period, if the workload increases rapidly, the existing application server instances may fail to serve all requests. Therefore, it is recommended to set the threshold values for the auto scaling metrics conservatively to take care of the time lag involved in the new instances becoming operational. In the auto-scaling options, the threshold for scaling down is also specified.

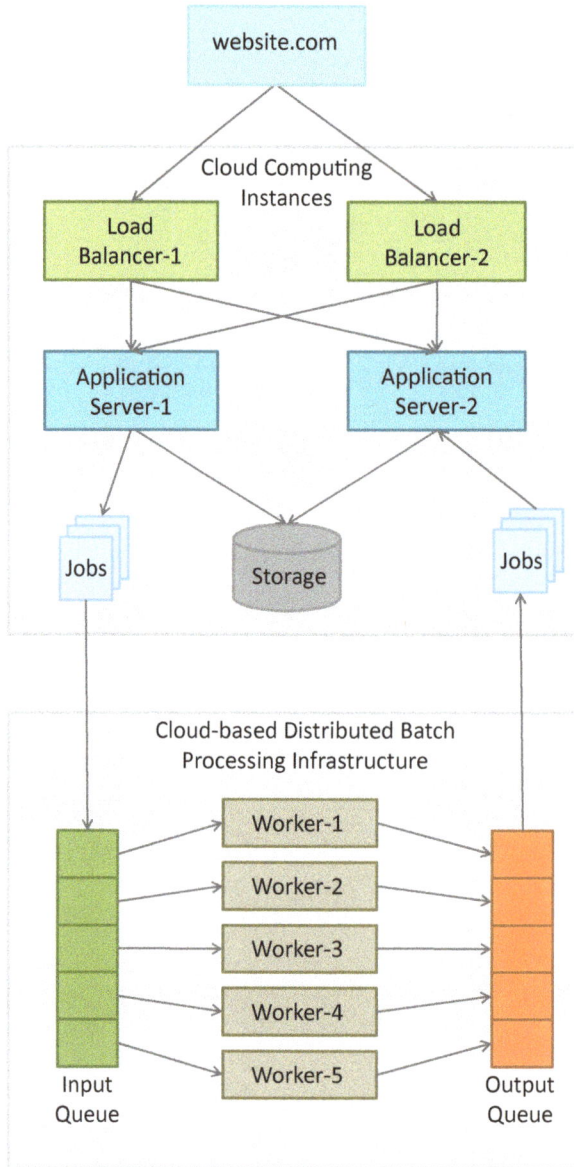

Figure 1.31: Typical deployment architecture for compute-intensive applications such as Data Analytics, Media Transcoding, etc.

- **Database Tier:** The third tier is the database tier, which includes a master database instance and multiple secondary instances. The master node serves all the write requests, and the read requests are served from the secondary nodes. This improves the throughput for the database tier since most applications have a higher number of read requests than write requests. Multiple secondary nodes also serve as a backup for the master node. In the event of failure of the master node, one of the secondary/standby nodes can be automatically configured to become the master. For both master and secondary nodes, it is highly recommended to use a disk subsystem for storage and not the instance-attached store. This is essential to ensure reliability and availability because in the event of failures if the instance-attached storage is used for the database, all data will be lost. Whereas, in the case of separate disk volumes, it is possible to restore the database. Regular snapshots of the database are recommended. The frequency of snapshots may be configured to be daily or hourly. It is recommended to store snapshots in distributed persistent cloud storage solutions (such as Amazon S3).

Figure 1.30 shows a typical deployment architecture for content delivery applications such as online photo albums and video webcasting. Both relational and non-relational data stores are shown in this deployment. A content delivery network (CDN) is used for media delivery. CDN comprises a global network of edge locations that help in speeding up the delivery of static content such as images and videos.

Figure 1.31 shows a typical deployment architecture for compute-intensive applications such as Data Analytics and Media Transcoding. The figure shows the web, application, storage, computing/analytics, and database tiers. The analytics tier consists of cloud-based distributed batch processing frameworks such as Hadoop, which are suitable for analyzing big data. Data analysis jobs (such as MapReduce) jobs are submitted to the analytics tier from the application servers. The jobs are queued for execution, and upon completion, the analyzed data is presented from the application servers.

Summary

In this chapter, we described the definition and key characteristics of cloud computing. Cloud computing offers Internet-based access to low-cost computing resources and applications provided using virtualized resources. The key characteristics of cloud computing that we explained include on-demand self-service, broad network access, resource pooling, rapid elasticity, and measured service. We covered the three main cloud service models - Infrastructure-as-a-Service (IaaS), Platform-as-a-Service (PaaS), and Software-as-a-Service (SaaS). IaaS allows users to provision computing and storage resources on-demand. PaaS allows users to develop and deploy applications using tools, APIs, and services provided by the cloud platform. SaaS provides complete applications hosted in the cloud and accessed through thin client interfaces. We also presented the four main cloud deployment models - public, private, hybrid, and community cloud. Public cloud services are available to the general public or large industry groups. Private cloud infrastructure is used exclusively by a single organization. Hybrid cloud combines private and public cloud services. Community cloud is shared by organizations with similar requirements. Key cloud computing concepts and enabling technologies were explained including virtualization, load balancing, scalability, elasticity, deployment, replication, monitoring, software defined networking, network function virtualization, identity and access management, service level agreements and billing models. The cloud computing reference model was described which includes layers for facilities, hardware, virtualization, platform and middleware, service management, applications and security. Different types of cloud services were also covered such as compute, storage, database, application, analytics, deployment, management, identity and access. Design considerations for building cloud-native applications were presented including scalability, reliability, availability, security, maintenance, upgradability and performance. Finally, we explained reference architectures for various classes of multi-tier cloud applications, content delivery, and compute-intensive big data applications. This chapter provided a comprehensive overview of cloud computing concepts, technologies, services, deployment models, design considerations, and reference architectures for building robust and scalable cloud-based applications.

2 FUNDAMENTALS OF MICROSERVICES

THIS CHAPTER COVERS

- Definition of a Microservice
- Characteristics of a Microservice
- Microservices Architecture
- Monolithic versus Microservice Architecture
- Benefits & Challenges of Microservices
- Decomposing a Monolith into Microservices
- Decomposition Strategies and Steps
- Case Study on Transitioning a Monolithic Application to Microservices

2.1   Definition of a Microservice

Microservices are **independent and self-contained** software services **aligned to business capabilities**. They are **loosely coupled**, **own their own data** and persistence, and can be developed, deployed, scaled, and managed independently. **Independent and automated deployments** enable continuous delivery of microservices. The **modular and replaceable design** provides flexibility to adopt new technologies or migrate functionality as needs evolve.

2.2   Characteristics of a Microservice

Microservices have emerged as an important architectural approach for building modular and scalable applications. As an architectural style, microservices possess some key characteristics that distinguish them from traditional monolithic applications. In this section, we will describe the characteristics of microservices which are highlighted in the definition above. Figure 2.1 shows the characteristics of a microservice.

Independent and Self Contained

A defining characteristic of microservices is their independence from other microservices. Each microservice is modular, fully self-contained, and implements a focused set of capabilities aligned with a business domain or subsystem. The source code, persistent storage, messaging endpoints, APIs, deployment mechanisms, and all components for a microservice are packaged independently.

This independence has several advantages. It allows separate development of the services. Teams can build, test, deploy, and scale their services without coordination with developers working on other microservices. It also enables polyglot programming approaches, where the services can leverage different languages, databases, and other technologies appropriately for their context rather than having to conform to broader application-wide technology choices.

The independence extends to deployment as well, which increases architectural flexibility. Services can be deployed separately across clouds, containers, servers, and availability zones to improve resilience. The production environments can also diverge between teams, allowing gradual updates rather than big bang releases.

Aligned to Business Capabilities

A key driver for microservices architectures is to shift organization around business capabilities rather than technologies. So the microservices created should align to capabilities delivered to the customer. This represents a shift from traditional applications that structure teams across technical components such as database, backend, frontend, and testing. Aligning to business capabilities enhances the focus for developers and improves efficiency in delivering business functionality.

The size of a microservice is determined by the scope of a single capability or subdomain. Capability scope also determines the size, structure, and focus area for the development team maintaining that microservice. So an architecture that is aligned to business capability promotes better modularization for both system design and team organization.

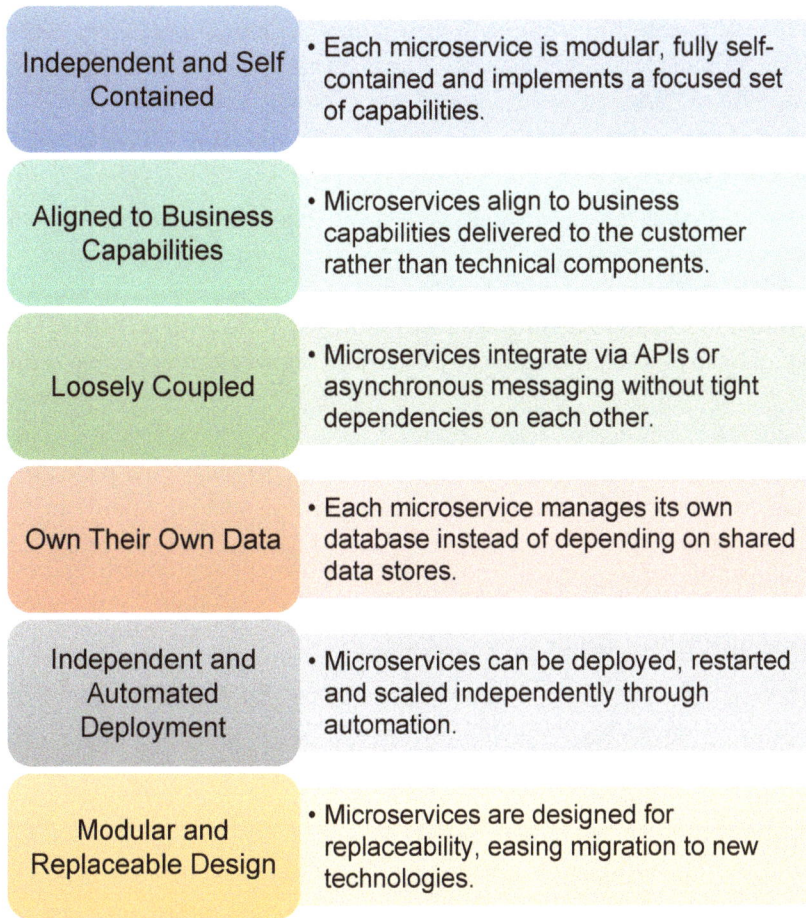

Independent and Self Contained	• Each microservice is modular, fully self-contained and implements a focused set of capabilities.
Aligned to Business Capabilities	• Microservices align to business capabilities delivered to the customer rather than technical components.
Loosely Coupled	• Microservices integrate via APIs or asynchronous messaging without tight dependencies on each other.
Own Their Own Data	• Each microservice manages its own database instead of depending on shared data stores.
Independent and Automated Deployment	• Microservices can be deployed, restarted and scaled independently through automation.
Modular and Replaceable Design	• Microservices are designed for replaceability, easing migration to new technologies.

Figure 2.1: Characteristics of a Microservice

Loosely Coupled

Microservices are loosely coupled and independent from the implementation of other services. Although a microservices-based application comprises multiple different services, these services need to integrate together somehow for the system to function as a whole. Microservices promote loose coupling between services to preserve their independence while still enabling seamless integration.

There are two common patterns used for loose coupling - API endpoints and asynchronous event messaging. In the endpoint approach, microservices expose REST APIs that other services invoke as needed through simple HTTP requests. The APIs carry out some business operation of that service while enclosing implementation details behind the endpoint interface.

For integration using asynchronous event messaging, the microservices communicate by publishing event messages to a streaming event bus or message broker, without directly integrating with each other. Other services subscribe to event streams relevant to them and design their logic around responding to published events.

In both cases, the microservices integrate without tight dependencies on each other's code, libraries, protocols, or runtime environments. This prevents changes in one service from cascading across the application. It also promotes their independent evolution. The implementation of a service can be refactored or even rewritten without requiring change by consumers as long as the APIs or message contracts remain consistent.

Own Their Own Data

Each microservice manages its own database and data persistence. Data persistence is a key architectural consideration for microservices, especially given their independence from each other. The easiest approach conceptually is to create a single logical database for the overall application with all services accessing necessary tables or documents as needed. However, in practice, that creates tight coupling between services and constraints on their independent evolution.

Instead, microservices embrace data decentralization with each microservice managing its own database rather than depending on shared data stores. The database platforms, schemas, and size can be optimized for the specific workload and access patterns of that service domain. The development team can evolve the data layer to meet emerging functionality needs without external dependencies.

Independent and Automated Deployment

Microservices can be deployed, restarted, and scaled without affecting other services. Microservice architectures require higher degrees of automation to manage many moving parts including separate services and infrastructure components such as databases, message streams, and API gateways.

When a development team completes an update to their microservice code, with all testing and review completed, deployment processes execute any steps needed to release and launch that service. This includes steps such as packaging of binaries/containers, application of configuration changes, publishing to environments, dynamic scaling, and monitoring. This deployment occurs independently without manual intervention and without impacting other microservices.

Independent deployment promotes faster innovation by removing delays and bottlenecks around centralized releases. It also reduces risk from changes, for example, an issue with one service can be rolled back without reverting functionality of other services. Automation frees up developer teams to focus on innovation rather than bureaucratic processes.

Microservices leverage automation and infrastructure-as-code for deployment and scaling. The independent nature of microservices enables continuous delivery of updates through automation tooling for builds, testing, and deployment. Manual processes create bottlenecks given the volume of services and frequency of changes. So microservices architectures invest heavily in infrastructure automation and scripting capabilities.

For most applications, the deployment pipeline flows through build automation to compile updated service code and dependencies. Automated testing frameworks then execute integrated tests, performance benchmarking, and other validation against the recent changes. Containerization or virtualization tools package the service for portability across environments. Finally, release automation handles dynamic configuration updates, publishing the service onto runtime platforms, routing integration traffic to new versions, and appropriate scaling of resources.

Test automation, in particular, increases confidence for development teams to release changes frequently and independently without quality risk. Automation provides a consistent safety net allowing developers to focus on innovation and solving the business problems.

Modular and Replaceable Design

Microservices are designed for replaceability, easing migrations to new technology. Given their independence, microservices are intended to minimize long-term commitment to a single implementation. As business or technical needs evolve, teams need the flexibility to reassess previous decisions around code, technologies, or architectural approaches used. Microservices better support service replacement or migration through clear encapsulation and stable service contracts.

A common scenario is the need to migrate an outdated service leveraging legacy systems to new platforms such as cloud, containers, or serverless environments. Without microservices, entire systems may need to be rewritten together at considerable cost and risk. With microservices, teams can pilot migrations focused on specific services first before incrementally expanding across other areas. No changes are needed by consumers if APIs remain consistent. Data migration tools can synchronize information across old and new systems running in parallel during transition periods.

The flexibility to replace services without high risk, as needs change, enables architects and developers to more confidently build systems with the latest technologies aligned to business problems at hand. It avoids the need to compromise innovation due to legacy constraints.

2.3 Microservices Architecture

Microservices architecture (MSA) refers to an approach to build an application as a collection of small, modular, independently deployable services rather than as a single, monolithic application. Each microservice focuses on completing one capability or business function, utilizes its own data storage, and exposes APIs for integration with other services through lightweight protocols like HTTP.

The isolation and decentralization of microservices bring significant benefits around agility, scalability, reliability, and organizational alignment. The small independent units with isolated responsibilities reduce complexity, allowing developers to innovate faster. The modular deployment model allows incremental updates, easing continuous delivery. Different services can scale resources appropriately to their individual workloads. Failure isolation limits the blast radius when instances fail. Teams organize centrally around business capabilities rather than technologies.

However, the distributed nature of microservices also introduces complexities and trade-offs. When planned effectively, microservices appropriately balance the increased engineering complexities with the benefits around organizational agility, accelerated feature delivery, incremental modernization, and other architectural advantages that enable success in competitive digital markets.

Services	• Independent, focused capabilities modeled around business domains
Service Code	• Business logic and functionality implementing the microservice
Service APIs	• Interfaces enabling integration of the microservice
Message Endpoints	• Components producing/consuming async event streams
API Gateway	• Centralized control point managing APIs
Service Discovery	• Lookup service providing network locations of services
Persistent Storage	• Private data store optimized for the microservice
Event Streaming	• Asynchronous event-driven integration using message brokers
Deployment Infrastructure	• Automation of provisioning, deployment, scaling using containers/orchestrators
Monitoring & Telemetry	• Logging, metrics and tracing for observability

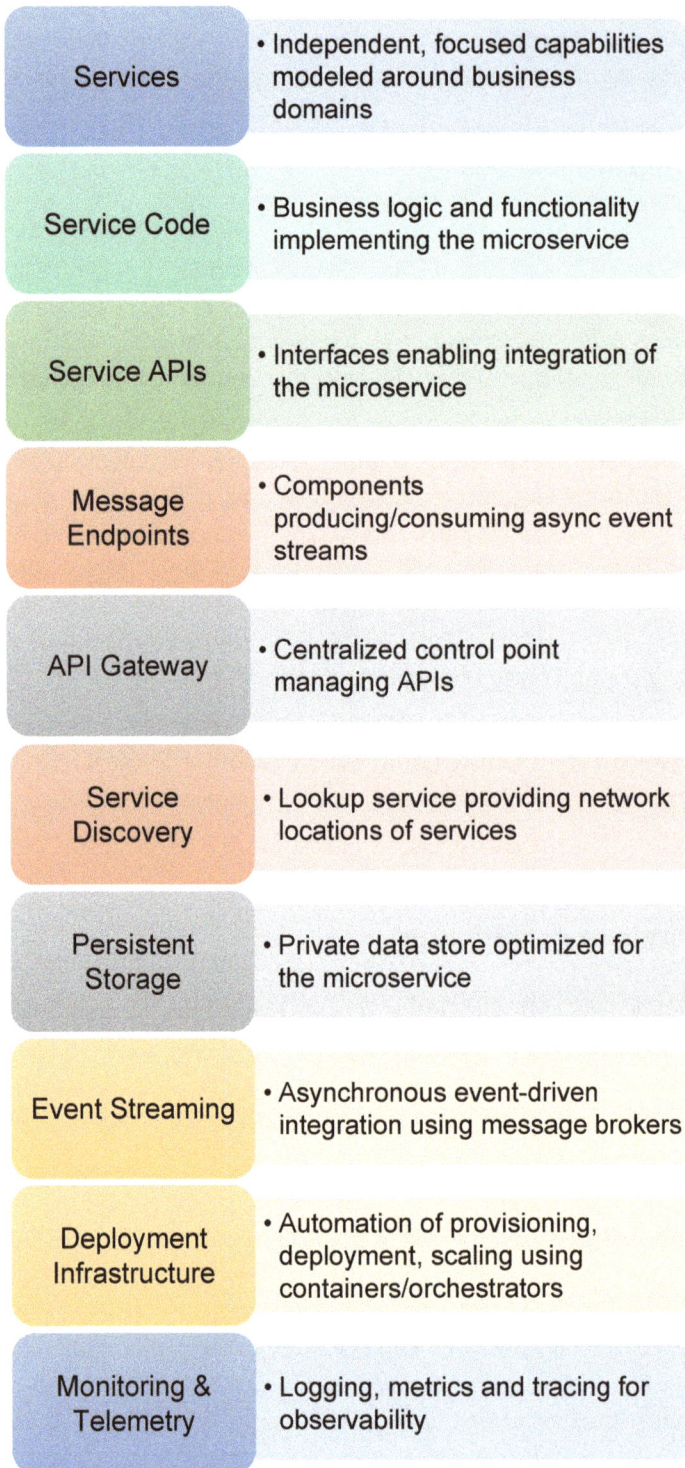

Figure 2.2: Components of Microservices Architectures

2.3.1 Components of Microservices Architectures

Services

The microservices themselves act as the fundamental building blocks in this microservices architecture approach. Microservices are typically aligned with specific business capabilities or modeled as domain concepts. Their sizes generally allow a small team to develop and maintain each microservice. Microservices are designed and focused around specific capabilities. There is loose coupling between services which communicate through well-defined interfaces. This enables independent development, testing, and deployment of each service. Figure 2.2 shows the components of microservices architectures.

Service Code

The core of a microservice is the service code containing the business logic and functionality aligned to its focused capability and subdomain. The code defines request handling workflows, business operations, domain entity constructs, processing rules, and behaviors. The service implementation leverages modularity through class decomposition and low coupling to keep the service cohesive. Code bases are kept lean through emphasis on core capability versus generic infrastructure.

Service APIs

Well-designed interfaces enabling integration are essential for microservices. REST APIs are most common, providing a lightweight approach to integrate over HTTP. gRPC is another option for more efficient binary serialization. APIs expose operations allowing create, read, update, delete (CRUD) against resources of that service. API gateways acts as a single entry point for client applications to access backend services, handling tasks like request routing, authentication, rate limiting, monitoring, and security to abstract backend complexity. Load balancers route requests across service instances. A good API design applies standards around resources, CRUD verbs, versioning, and status codes.

Message Endpoints

Microservices using asynchronous messaging require implementation of the endpoints which produce and consume event streams. This is handled either through a centralized message broker or lightweight event bus. Domain-driven design identifies key domain events that services react to, such as *Payment-Accepted*, *Shipping-Address-Updated*, for instance. Service endpoints apply business logic triggered by messages containing these events.

API Gateway

Public endpoints exposed for client consumption often route through an intermediary API Gateway rather than directly to backend service instances. API gateways encapsulate the common capabilities from service implementations. They provide centralized control points to manage API behavior. API Gateways provide the following functionalities:
- Authentication: Verify identity and access control
- Transport security: Encryption, certificates, secure channels
- Protocol translation: Support multiple protocols like HTTP, gRPC
- Rate limiting: Throttle requests to protect services
- Load balancing: Distribute requests across instances

- Observability: Logging, metrics, and tracing
- Request aggregation: Optimize data fetches across services

Service Discovery

Service discovery components provide runtime mappings of service instances to network locations and ports. This mapping enables dynamic request routing across infrastructure. Service discovery acts as a phone book that clients can look up to find the network locations of desired services. The lookups provide load-balanced endpoints to distribute requests across service replicas. Service discovery tracks configuration changes triggered automatically through orchestrators when services scale out/in or get redeployed.

Some common service discovery patterns include:
- DNS: Service locations are stored in DNS records with automated updates
- Load balancers: Maintain dynamic configuration of service backends
- Service registries: Key-value stores that services register with

Persistent Storage

Managing data persistence is a key responsibility in microservices architecture. Microservices adopt encapsulation and information hiding techniques, as a result, the storage implementation details are abstracted behind interfaces like repositories and entity classes. Microservices typically leverage their own private database or datastore. This allows optimizing the data model around the specific domain entities and logic of that microservice.

Event Streaming

To enable high performance and reliable integration between services, many architectures adopt asynchronous event streaming. This event-driven approach provides loose coupling. Rather than direct API requests, services publish event messages to a centralized message broker or event bus to propagate state changes. The broker ensures reliable delivery across publishers and subscribers. Other services subscribe to specific event streams and apply corresponding logic when domain events occur, such as *Payment-Accepted* or *Shipping-Address-Updated*, for instance. The publisher does not need to block, waiting on subscriber processing.

Deployment Infrastructure

Fully automating the deployment of a microservice requires codifying everything the service needs to successfully run. This includes the base OS, binaries, third-party libraries, configuration, networking rules, resource allocation, and scaling rules.

Containers (such as Docker) allow packaging services consistently as container images for portability across environments. Container images include the service binary, dependencies, libraries, configuration, and startup scripts. This provides a standard unit of deployment for microservices. Containers isolate services from each other and the underlying infrastructure.

Container orchestrators (such as Kubernetes) automate the deployment, scaling, networking, upgrades, and healing of container fleets across clusters. Orchestrators like Kubernetes provide abstractions that enable declaring desired state through YAML config files. The orchestrator then continuously works to match the actual state against the desired state for container lifecycle management. Orchestrators also handle service discovery, load balancing, storage, secrets management, and other operations.

Infrastructure-as-Code (IaC) and Configuration Management tools such as Terraform, Ansible, and Chef enable the definition of declarative specifications, versioning, and repeatability of deployment across environments. These tools manage the provisioning and configuration of infrastructure and platforms across the full application stack including network, storage, compute, and databases. These tools treat infrastructure like code, enabling instrumentation and frequent iteration similar to application code.

Cloud platforms provide the scalable underlying infrastructure for deploying microservices. Public cloud platforms such as AWS, Azure, and GCP provide APIs to programmatically manage the infrastructure. Cloud auto-scaling handles spikes in traffic by automatically adding or removing capacity.

Monitoring & Telemetry

Given the complexities of distributed systems, microservices require robust observability mechanisms for monitoring, logging, and tracing. Instrumentation is added both on individual services and end-to-end transaction flows across services.

Teams incorporate logging frameworks and agents for collecting metrics and traces emitted from application code and infrastructure. Monitoring systems aggregate this telemetry data into dashboards for real-time awareness while providing alert automation.

Many vendors provide specialized observability and monitoring solutions for microservices architectures. These solutions provide out-of-the-box visibility for common technologies such as Docker, Kubernetes, service meshes, and message brokers.

2.4 Monolithic versus Microservice Architecture

2.4.1 Monolithic Application Architecture

A monolithic application refers to a software application architecture style where components of the application are tightly coupled and bundled together into a single, unified application. Typically, a monolithic application combines the user interface layer, business logic layer, and data access layer, all into a single executable. Figure 2.3 shows the characteristics of monolithic architecture, including:

Tightly Coupled Components

In a monolithic application, the different components making up the application logic tend to be heavily interdependent and interconnected. There are direct references between different components rather than clearly defined interfaces. This tight coupling ties the components together such that it is difficult to isolate services or pull components out of the application.

Single Package Deployment

The components of a monolithic application are packaged together and deployed as a single unit. The entire application is compiled into a single binary executable which runs as a stand-alone piece. As a result, the whole application needs to be repackaged, recompiled, and redeployed even if only one minor change was made to any individual component.

Scaling Entire Application

In monolithic applications, scaling has to happen at the level of the entire application. It is not possible to scale individual application components independently. If one particular

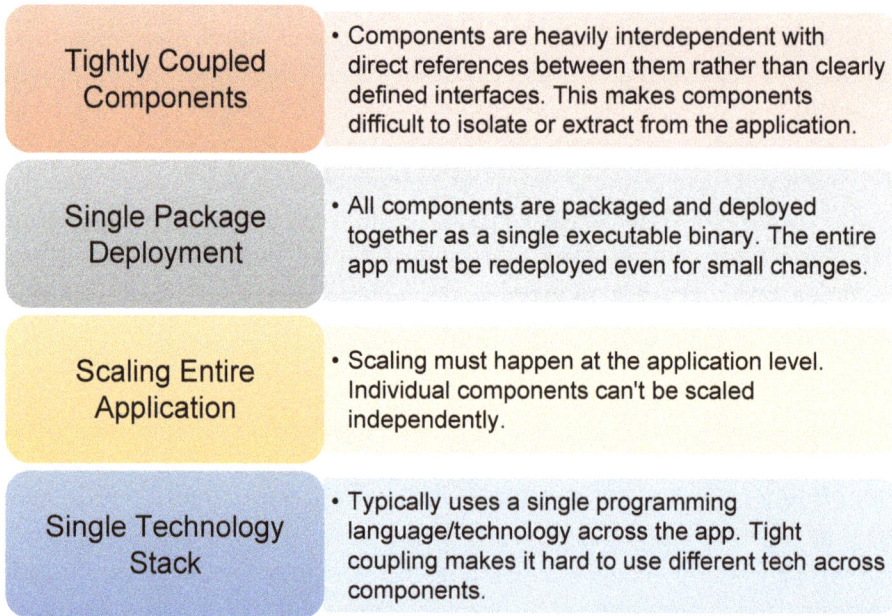

Figure 2.3: Characteristics of monolithic architecture

service or component reaches its resource limits, the only option is to scale-out the entire application tier which often requires a proportional increase in hardware capacity.

Single Technology Stack

Monolithic applications are typically built using a single programming language and technology stack. For example, a Java application would be built using Java, a Java web framework like Spring, and a MySQL database. The tight coupling between components makes it impractical to use different technologies across the application.

2.4.2   Drawbacks of Monolithic Applications

While monolithic applications represent a simple architectural approach in principle, as the scale and complexity of applications grow, monolithic architectures start demonstrating major inefficiencies which impact agility, reliability, and scalability.

Complex and Rigid Codebase

As more and more features and components are added to a monolithic application over time, it results in a large and complex codebase spanning hundreds of classes, services, and interfaces. Understandability, maintainability, and testability of the application suffer. Adding new developers to work on the monolith requires significant ramp-up time to grasp the application. Dependencies between components also keep accumulating, making the codebase rigid and fragile to change.

Deployment Inefficiencies

In monolithic applications, even small one-line changes require recompiling and redeploying the entire application binary. As the codebase grows to hundreds of thousands of lines of code, build and deployment cycles become longer. For large applications with many teams of developers, coordination is required around deployments. Continuous software delivery gets hindered.

Absence of Fault Isolation

In monolithic applications, a runtime error or bug in any one component can potentially bring down or corrupt the whole application. For example, a memory leak generated in one component could cause the application server to crash, impacting availability across the application. Fault isolation is difficult as faults can propagate across component boundaries.

Lack of Independent Scalability

Monolithic applications have to be scaled in their entirety rather than individual components. Attempting to scale-out certain application servers or services more than others creates resource and capacity imbalances. Additional computing capacity has to be uniformly added to scale-out the application tier as a whole. This wastes resources as components with lower resource needs also get overprovisioned.

Technology Lock-in

Rewriting or migrating monolithic applications to newer languages or technologies is an arduous task due to the significant upfront rewrite effort and risk involved. Monolithic architectures severely limit the ability to iteratively improve parts of the application through technology modernization. New libraries and frameworks also cannot be selectively adopted for individual components.

Negative Impact on Innovation Velocity

Innovating on large monolithic applications requires coordination between a large set of developers and testers, creating a bottleneck around release cycles. Adding new features requires changing code in multiple places, making the codebase rigid. Integration risks amplify due to two-way dependencies between components. Continuous experimentation and testing of new ideas gets delayed.

2.4.3 Benefits of Microservices

Microservices offer several key benefits that make them an attractive architectural approach compared to traditional monolithic applications, as shown in Figure 2.4. These include:

Strong Modularization

One of the core advantages of microservices is the clear module boundaries that get established between the different services. In a monolithic application, it is easy for unwanted dependencies and coupling to accumulate between components over time, resulting in code that is hard to maintain. Microservices provide much stronger encapsulation, with the services explicitly defining their APIs and data models, which forms a contract for how the services can be accessed.

This strict separation makes it far less likely for unintentional dependencies to creep up inside the codebase. For example, in a monolithic application, a developer may start using

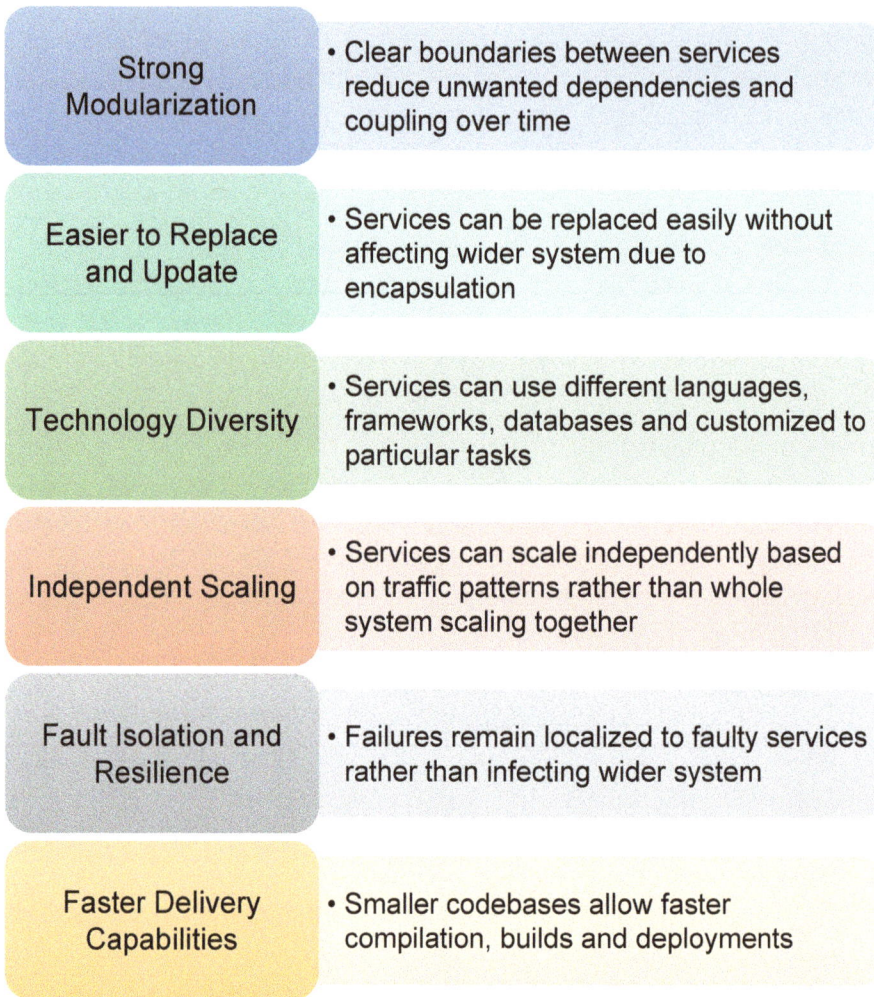

Figure 2.4: Benefits of microservices

functionality from another module just because it seems convenient, slowly creating tighter coupling where it was not intended in the architecture. With microservices, calling another service requires much more deliberate coding against the public interfaces. This ensures the microservices remain decoupled unless integration is consciously set up.

The strong module boundaries promote better architectural integrity over the lifetime of the application. The risk of erosion, where the implementation drifts away from the planned architecture, is greatly reduced. This also eases long-term maintenance, as unwanted dependencies do not accumulate inside the services over many years.

Easier to Replace and Update

Due to the clear isolation of microservices into independent deployment components, they can be replaced and updated extremely easily without affecting the wider application. This enables aging services suffering from quality issues to be incrementally reworked over time, restoring the maintainability and extensibility of the system.

Monoliths typically require full rewrites when they degrade, as it is hard to disentangle the parts needing improvement from the rest of the complex application logic. With microservices, only that small service needs to be thrown away and replaced. This surgical updating prevents the need for risky changes which can result in catastrophic failures. The interfaces and data models act as a buffer from change impacting the whole system. As long as the new service preserves the same API, other services don't even need to know it was swapped out.

The ability to plug in new implementations means developers are not constrained by old technology choices. New languages, frameworks, and infrastructure can be introduced to particular services without requiring overall coordination. Microservices maximize developer freedom and minimize friction to improve parts of the system independently.

Technology Diversity

Microservices encourage greater diversity in technologies across an application architecture. Because services only interact through relatively limited APIs and messaging, the internal implementations of the services can vary widely. Different services in an application can use different programming languages, frameworks, and database models.

The developers can choose what they feel is most appropriate for the task at hand rather than having to abide by "one size fits all" technology decisions. Specialized or unconventional programming languages can be tested and confined to specific services. The loose coupling means most new technologies can be tried and tested with little risk of impacting the whole system.

The technology options even extend to hardware and infrastructure choices. Services requiring high computation or memory for intensive tasks (like machine learning) could use GPU-optimized instances, while simpler services operate on cheaper hardware. Some services might incorporate third-party managed services (for example, messaging and notifications) or proprietary appliances. Microservice architectures are easily customizable within the constraints of API compatibility.

Independent Scaling

Because microservices can deploy onto infrastructure independently, auto-scaling policies can also be defined at the granular level of individual services. If a particular service experiences fluctuating traffic and demand patterns, more computing resources can be spun up or down for that service alone without requiring proportional scaling across the rest of the application.

This is far more efficient than monolithic applications that scale in a fixed ratio across the whole system, resulting in over-provisioning for steady-state services. The loose coupling between microservices allows the architecture to right-size for variable workloads in different parts of the application.

Independent scaling allows cheaper incremental growth in underlying infrastructure to meet increasing application demand over time. The system can scale out just the most constrained bottlenecks rather than forcing everything to scale together. Microservice architectures maximize utilization of available cloud and hardware capacity by scaling more intelligently along service boundaries.

Fault Isolation and Resilience

Because microservices deliberately separate components across the process and network boundaries, failures remain localized to the service where problems occur. A single service crashing or behaving abnormally does not directly take down other services still running correctly. The system as a whole gains fault tolerance from this isolation into independent units of failure.

Monolithic applications offer no such protection, as a result, buggy code or exceptions anywhere in application logic can bring the entire system down. The lack of isolation leads to domino effects spreading across components. With microservices, failures are contained within that domain's service. No matter how unstable, its problems cannot directly infect its peers. This resilience and fault isolation foster more reliable systems overall.

Microservice architectures are also designed to gracefully handle degraded service capabilities when failures do happen. Services use patterns like timeout calls, default return values, and circuit breaker self-monitoring to integrate seamlessly across unreliable networks. If one service call fails or times out, the rest of the system marches on unaffected by having contingency planning built-in at the architecture level. Sophisticated microservice platforms provide libraries and tools to harden fault tolerance mechanisms consistently across services.

Faster Delivery Capabilities

The smaller and more focused codebases of individual microservices allow for much faster compile and build speeds compared to large, complex monolithic applications. Because microservices have fewer code dependencies in general, changes made to one service also require recompilation of less additional code. These lightweight services can build, package, and deploy quickly.

This agility combines powerfully with continuous delivery practices. New changes can progress from developer systems to production environments quickly because microservices reduce friction throughout the deployment pipeline. Easy rollbacks are also supported using advanced platform capabilities like blue/green deployments.

Microservices are designed to facilitate continuous deployment because of their decomposability into small and independent units. The granularity of change is much finer, allowing small incremental improvements to be tested and delivered often into production. Teams can focus on enhancing or bug fixing their microservice without touching the rest of the application.

2.4.4   Challenges of Microservices

While microservices provide significant benefits, there are also inherent complexities and challenges as shown in Figure 2.5. These include:

Distributed Complexity

One of the biggest trade-offs with microservices is the added complexity that comes from distributing components across processes and machines. Local function calls get replaced with API requests that carry extra overhead. Instead of performing operations directly inside application memory, execution happens across a network. All the inter-service communication introduces latency, reliability issues, and hardware dependencies absent in monoliths.

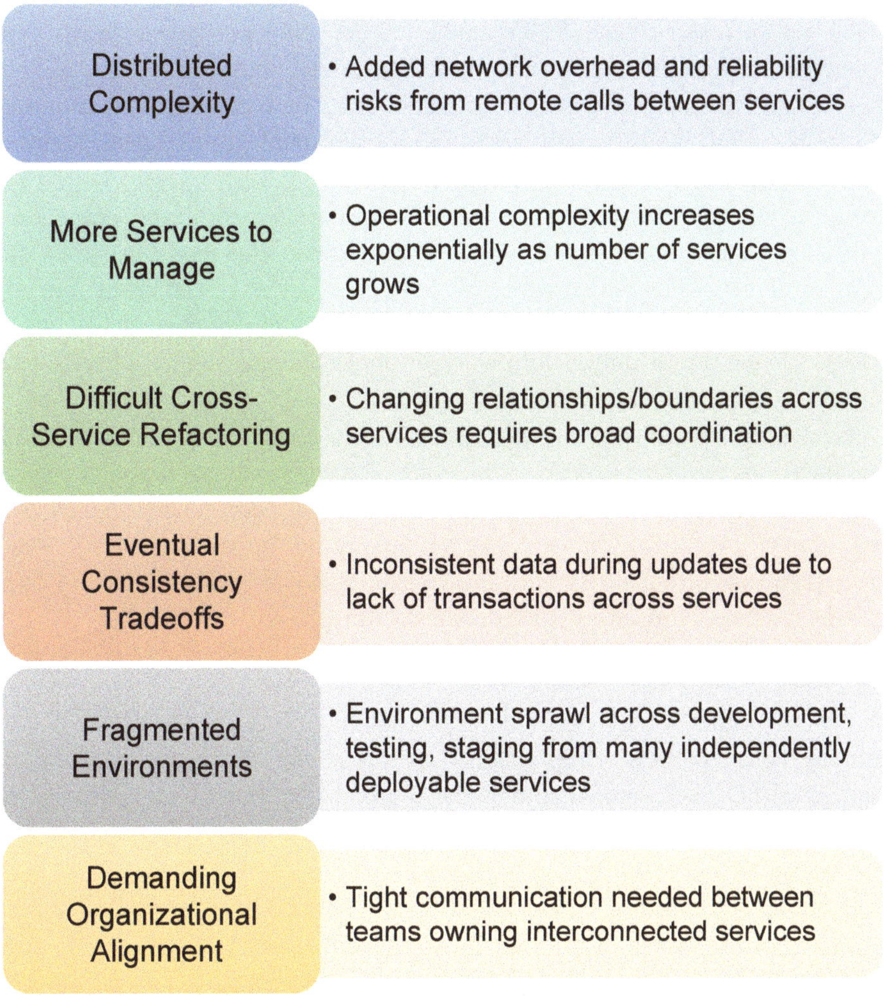

Distributed Complexity	• Added network overhead and reliability risks from remote calls between services
More Services to Manage	• Operational complexity increases exponentially as number of services grows
Difficult Cross-Service Refactoring	• Changing relationships/boundaries across services requires broad coordination
Eventual Consistency Tradeoffs	• Inconsistent data during updates due to lack of transactions across services
Fragmented Environments	• Environment sprawl across development, testing, staging from many independently deployable services
Demanding Organizational Alignment	• Tight communication needed between teams owning interconnected services

Figure 2.5: Challenges of microservices

This distributed computing approach is fundamentally slower and less efficient at pure computation compared to local calls within a single program. This overhead can significantly increase the response times if the services run on separate machines. Even within the same physical server, the network stack and serialization burdens add to the latency. Load balancing across instances of the same microservice also increases variability in response times.

The multitude of network hops can result in failures that are external to the application code itself. Unreliable networks can lose packets or hang connections at inopportune times. Even with circuit breakers and timeout calls, real-world environments risk hampering uptime. Operations teams need to monitor and manage the intricate web of microservices dependencies to ensure acceptable performance. Site Reliability Engineering (SRE) and Observability have grown as major disciplines to combat the distributed complexities of microservices.

More Services to Manage

By definition, a microservice architecture multiplies the number of independently deployable components in an application. What was once a single monolithic system becomes multiple distinct microservices depending on the functional scope involved. This increase in the number of services immediately compounds operational complexity across the entire software delivery lifecycle.

Instead of worrying about one application, the infrastructure and operations teams need to wrangle many more moving parts. Each microservice likely demands dedicated computing resources, whether via virtual machines, containers, or serverless functions. The infrastructure requirements around managing and orchestrating these environments multiply. Automation around provisioning, configuration management, and coordination becomes mandatory.

The burden further cascades across release management. Each microservice needs its own continuous integration and delivery pipeline with environments for testing and staging. Updates must be planned and deployed in coordination with dependent services. Rollbacks also require intricate choreography. Logging, monitoring, metrics gathering, and tracing need to aggregate data from all services into holistic dashboards. The number of operational tools grows significantly in such distributed environments.

Difficult Cross-Service Refactoring

A clear benefit inside microservices comes from the ability to overhaul aging services by replacing them with newer implementations. However, changing and refactoring the relationships across microservices proves far more challenging by comparison. Altering, moving, or consolidating functionality that spans different services requires significant coordination and coding changes.

For example, decomposing a monolith into microservices requires care around defining initial service boundaries and picking an initial domain-based partitioning approach. Early design decisions get baked into the interfaces, formats, and communication channels between microservices once integration develops. Over time as learning increases, teams often wish to rebalance responsibilities or rearrange models for better coherence. However, this requires almost rewiring services from scratch.

While the functions and classes inside a monolith can be shuffled around to refactor functionality, extracting and merging units of logic across microservices demands heavyweight changes across all participating services, databases, tools, and deployment pipelines impacted. The effort level rises exponentially once initial service boundaries have been defined and integration is completed. Refactoring can risk destabilizing the broader application functionality until all constituent services get transitioned.

Eventual Consistency Tradeoffs

Distributed data presents another core challenge with microservices, as the traditional ACID (atomicity, consistency, isolation, durability) transaction capabilities of relational databases are avoided in favor of faster access. Keeping strongly consistent data models proves extremely difficult across independent services because of the two-phase commit coordination required. Instead, microservices typically adopt BASE (basically available, soft state, and eventual consistency) semantics offered by non-relational databases.

This means developers must anticipate and accommodate periods of time when related data across services can drift out of sync during updates. The system trades off immediate accuracy for better availability and partition tolerance across services. Developers have to think through the edge cases and program mitigating solutions to reconcile the data. Various caching strategies also emerge to minimize the window for inconsistencies cropping up during execution.

Eventual consistency works well for situations that tolerate minor delays or fixes before all users access the same updated state. But some architectures require fully atomic distributed transactions to avoid corrupting processes or calculations. The looser coupling of microservices makes credible distributed transactions nearly impossible. Teams have to assess if their problem space allows the complexities of eventual consistency by design.

Fragmented Environments

The prevalence of microservices tends to propagate environment sprawl across development, testing, staging, and production landscapes. Because each microservice operates independently, the degree of dependency between environments goes up exponentially as more services get introduced. Each service team needs their own environments. Managing the matrices of configuration, automation, tools, and inter-environmental connectivity becomes challenging.

Drifts can emerge in service software or schema versions between environments that corrupt attempts at integration testing. Test automation can break due to outdated stubs, deprecated endpoints, or protocols. Without extensive DevOps practices around environment management, microservices risk environmental fragility and fragmentation.

Demanding Organizational Alignment

Microservice architectures impose additional burdens on organizational communication and alignment. Since service boundaries typically follow domain boundaries that get staffed by separate teams, the approach demands some decentralized decision-making and accountability. However, teams still need to collaborate tightly around contracts, standards, interfaces, guidelines, shared technologies, release planning, infrastructure, security policies, and data flows.

With a dozen microservices, hundreds of environment permutations, many languages and frameworks in play all changing frequently, the coherence depends heavily on organizational maturity. Loosely coupled architectures still require tightly managed organizational partnerships between teams owning interconnected services. Communications demands intensify despite the technical decoupling. Microservices shift complexity from code to teams.

Figure 2.6 shows a comparison of Monolithic and Microservices architectures.

2.5 Decomposing a Monolith into Microservices

2.5.1 Decomposition Strategies

Transitioning enterprise-scale monolithic applications into collections of collaborating microservices involves systematically identifying domain boundaries and scoping services appropriately. Teams can employ a combination of strategies for decomposing monolithic applications into microservices as shown in Figure 2.7. These include:

Architecture	Monolithic	Microservices
Components	Bundled into single application	Decomposed into discrete services
Coupling	Tight coupling between components	Services are loosely coupled
Scalability	Scales by increasing resource capacity of entire system	Independently scalable at service level
Codebase	Single codebase with one tech stack	Technology heterogeneity - different languages per service
Deployment	Code compiled and deployed as single unit	Services are independently deployable
Releases	Changes impact entire application	Services can be updated and released independently
Resilience	Fault in one module can bring entire system down	Isolated functionality and data per service
Debugging	Hard to isolate issues due to tight coupling	Services can be debugged and fixed independently
Innovation	Technology lock-in hinders incremental innovation	Supports continuous experimentation and innovation
Velocity	Requires coordination between a large set of developers and testers, hindering velocity	Smaller teams working independently on different services increases velocity

Figure 2.6: Comparison of Monolithic and Microservices architectures

Business Capabilities-Based Decomposition

This approach involves identifying key business functions that the monolithic application implements and using those to carve out microservices. The steps involved in business capabilities-based decomposition are as follows:

- Catalog the end-to-end business processes facilitated by the system
- Deconstruct processes into discrete steps such as data input, validation, transaction, and record
- Group functions into those managing related data entities or executing similar tasks
- Encapsulate business functions requiring extreme scale or throughput into services

For example, an E-Commerce application may decompose into an accounts service, product catalog service, and separate checkout and fulfillment services. Enterprise integration apps could have distinct services for message processing, data mapping, protocol mediation, and routing.

Each service maps to an organizational team managing a business domain. Loose coupling between services prevents changes from rippling across domains. This decomposition allows scaling-out at the individual service-level rather than uniformly.

Subdomain-Oriented Decomposition

In this approach, different subdomains or subject areas within the application act as boundaries for extracting microservices.

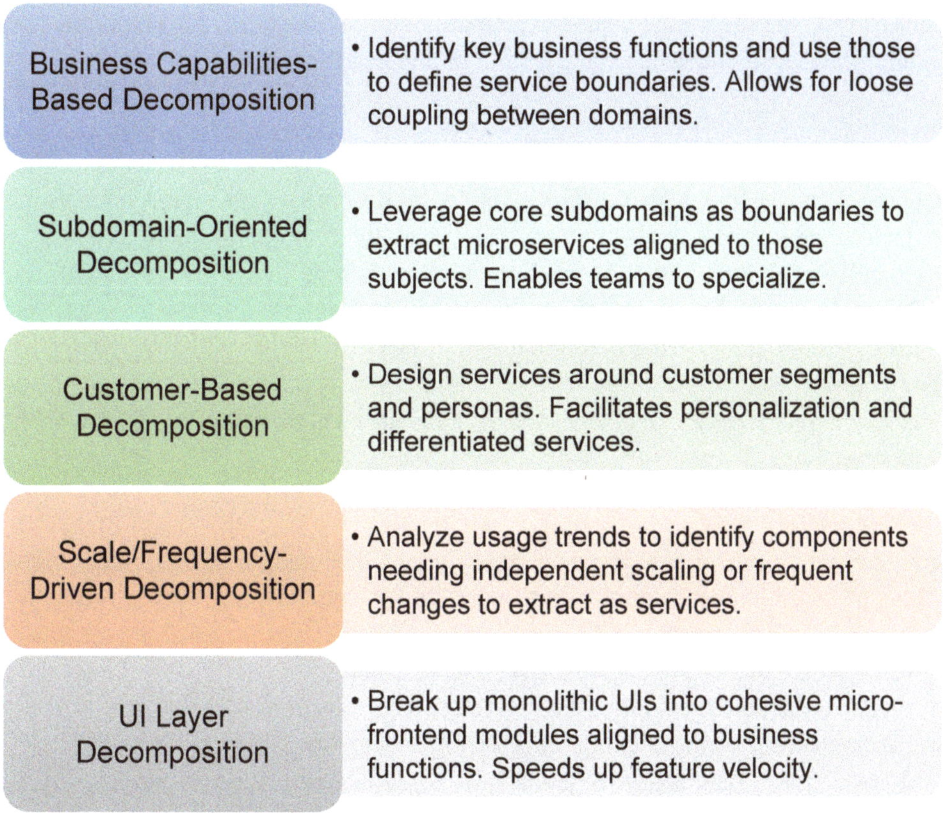

Figure 2.7: Strategies for decomposing a monolith into microservices

The steps involved in subdomain-oriented decomposition are as follows:
- Identify core subdomains such as sales, inventory, accounting, and analytics
- Explore contextual domain boundaries via bounded context modeling
- Discover subdomain relationships
- Strategically identify services aligned to subdomains

For example, an ordering system could have services for order submission, order processing, warehousing/inventory, and order history/analytics. Media services can be decomposed into content ingestion, metadata management, storage, and delivery services. Alignment to subdomains allows teams to specialize and accelerate feature velocity within that problem space.

Customer-Based Decomposition

For consumer-facing applications, microservices could be designed around customer personas and segments. The steps involved in customer-based decomposition are as follows:
- Understand categories such as retail buyers and enterprise customers, for instance.
- Analyze journeys across user types and their variants
- Identify functionality only applicable to certain customers
- Strategically scope microservices around user base differences

For example, in a banking and financial application, the application functionality can be segmented between high-value and standard customer service tiers. This facilitates greater personalization, differentiated service levels, and targeted scaling.

Scale/Frequency-Driven Decomposition

In this approach, the usage trends of an application are analyzed to strategically decompose the monolithic application. The steps involved in this decomposition approach are as follows:
- Determine workflow peaks and troughs via analytics
- Identify modules undergoing frequent modification
- Breakdown components needing independent scaling
- Shift volatile but isolated functionality into services

For example, retail applications may extract the catalog, promotions, or cart components into dedicated microservices to independently scale during high-traffic campaigns and festive seasons.

UI Layer Decomposition

Beyond service decomposition, monolithic UIs could also modularize into micro-frontends. The steps involved in this decomposition approach are as follows:
- Identify logical groups of UI screens and workflows
- Encapsulate related screens into cohesive modules
- Establish module boundaries aligned to business functions
- Enable teams to independently develop UI components

This breaks up integrated frontends into self-contained micro-frontends aligned to domains that can render independently. Micro-frontends help to speed up UI feature development, facilitate tech diversity, and prevent contention across teams.

2.5.2   Steps for Decomposing a Monolithic Application into Microservices

Transitioning a monolithic application to a microservices architecture is a major task that requires carefully analyzing dependencies, planning appropriate service boundaries, and rearchitecting the supporting infrastructure. Transitioning to microservices can result in substantial gains in software agility, resiliency, and innovation velocity. Figure 2.8 shows the steps for decomposing a monolith into microservices. These include:

Understand and Map Existing Architecture

As a starting point, diagram the architecture of the existing monolithic application to visualize its key components, relationships, and dependencies. The following tasks are performed at this step:
- Capture modular structure and layering
- Document major classes/packages
- Identify shared libraries and frameworks
- Identify shared persistent data stores
- Identify services communicating via APIs
- Capture synchronous versus asynchronous communication

This exercise reveals duplication, bottlenecks, and cross-cutting concerns and highlights modular structures usable in the microservices architecture. Analyzing layering and packaging

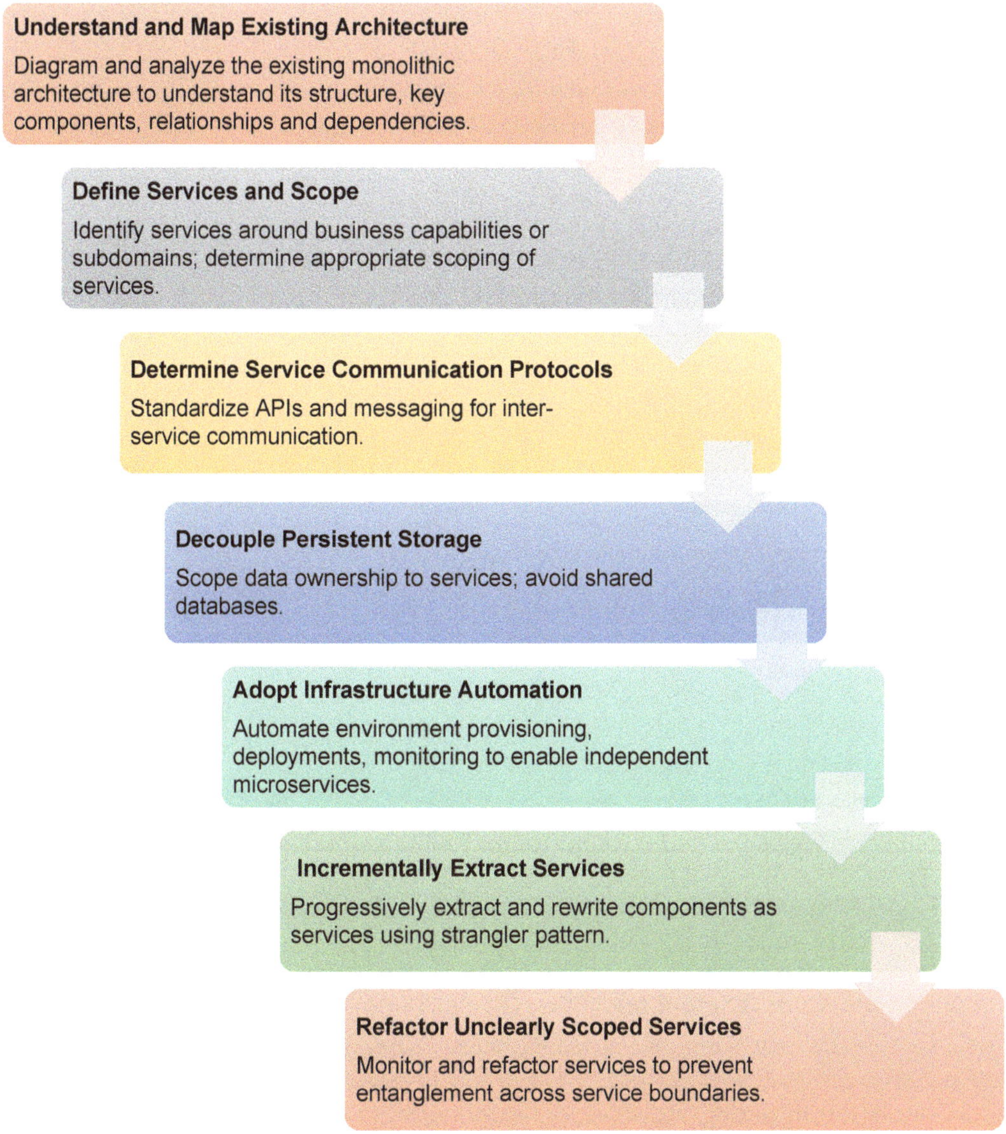

Understand and Map Existing Architecture

Diagram and analyze the existing monolithic architecture to understand its structure, key components, relationships and dependencies.

Define Services and Scope

Identify services around business capabilities or subdomains; determine appropriate scoping of services.

Determine Service Communication Protocols

Standardize APIs and messaging for inter-service communication.

Decouple Persistent Storage

Scope data ownership to services; avoid shared databases.

Adopt Infrastructure Automation

Automate environment provisioning, deployments, monitoring to enable independent microservices.

Incrementally Extract Services

Progressively extract and rewrite components as services using strangler pattern.

Refactor Unclearly Scoped Services

Monitor and refactor services to prevent entanglement across service boundaries.

Figure 2.8: Steps for decomposing a monolith into microservices

conventions also signals potential fault line boundaries along which the application can be decomposed.

Define Services and Scope

Leveraging the architectural visualization and dependency analysis in the previous step, define the strategy to carve out services from the monolith. The following tasks are performed at this step:

- Split by business capability or subdomain
- Identify shared capabilities needing scale
- Separate customer-facing functions

- Distill reusable utilities as services
- Capture volatile components likely to change

Services should support related capabilities that serve a specific sub-domain or business function. This ensures that future changes are largely isolated within service boundaries. Appropriately scoped services also enable independent lifecycle management of specific functions.

Determine Service Communication Protocols

With services and capabilities defined, standardize protocols for inter-service communication. The following tasks are performed at this step:

- Adopt REST APIs for synchronous request/response
- Leverage asynchronous events for push notification
- Design APIs and events around domains or technology
- Reuse APIs where external consumers are involved

Well-defined APIs and messaging allow loose coupling between services. This facilitates changes to service implementations without impacting consumers.

Decouple Persistent Storage

To eliminate state-based dependencies, decouple database access by scoping data ownership to services. The following tasks are performed at this step:

- Reorganize logical schema around business domains
- Distribute tables to relevant microservices
- Denormalize schemas as needed for efficiency
- Employ database access layer per service
- Connect services to their own data store

Directly sharing databases between microservices can risk tight coupling. Cross-over data access can be provided via APIs where needed.

Adopt Infrastructure Automation

The infrastructure underpinning monoliths won't sustain hundreds of smaller services. Infrastructure automation must be adopted for microservices to independently release and iterate on services. The following tasks are performed at this step:

- Automate environment provisioning
- Create pipelines for building services
- Standardize application configuration
- Automate application deployments
- Instrument logging and monitoring
- Use containerization and orchestration

Infrastructure automation, containers, and orchestrators help in rapid provisioning, deployment, and management of services across environments.

Incrementally Extract Services

With the transformed architecture defined, start extracting services from the monolith. The following tasks are performed at this step:

- Prioritize fault-prone components first
- Rewrite components via strangler pattern

- Build adapters to call existing code
- Phase out replaced modules over time
- Retain legacy application as residual services

Strangler pattern incrementally redirects functionality to new services while keeping the legacy application intact. This reduces risk, allowing old and new implementations to coexist while directing traffic progressively to the new.

Refactor Unclearly Scoped Services

Monitor the emerging architecture for violations of interface segregation and service aggregation principles. Watch for:

- Microservices with too many responsibilities, indicated by high code churn
- Microservice interfaces growing too large
- Microservices calling too many other services
- Microservices sharing infrastructure with other services

Refactoring by extracting new microservices can help enforce service boundaries and prevent entanglement across services. New microservices should aim for high cohesion by focusing on a single business capability. Loose coupling is achieved by minimizing dependencies on other services through narrow interfaces.

The decomposition process described above requires careful planning, executing, and governing service boundaries. If the above steps are done methodically, enterprises can unlock software modernization benefits while minimizing risk through incremental transition. The decomposition and transition process also helps in documentation and understanding of the inherited architecture. With clear ownership, services can subsequently be optimized leveraging appropriate languages and technologies.

2.6 Case Study: Transitioning a Monolithic App to Microservices

In this section, we describe a case study of transitioning a monolithic E-Commerce application to microservices architecture. E-commerce applications have complex and evolving demands around agility, scalability, and resilience. Figure 2.9 shows the architecture of an E-Commerce application that has been built as a monolith. The presentation layer components are tightly coupled to business functions like account management, checkout, and inventory lookup. The business components, in turn, either directly access the database or call common data access components that query the single logical database.

The drawbacks of the monolithic E-Commerce application architecture are as follows:

- **Agility Limitations**: A monolithic architecture requires redeploying the entire application for any change, no matter how small. This makes it difficult to scale delivery teams since parallel work requires substantial coordination. Any rollout or rollback often impacts unrelated features as everything is tightly coupled. Overall, this limits the agility of developers and the business.
- **Poor Reliability**: The monolithic design represents a single point of failure. If the application goes down, the entire business goes down. Furthermore, any changes have the risk of impact across the entire application, slowing fault isolation and tying up precious developer resources. There is often no redundancy for core functions either.
- **Cost and Scale Inefficiencies**: A monolithic application relies on uniform vertical scaling, which leads to underutilized resources when scaling-out. Teams usually have

UI Layer

- Contains storefront UI and shopping flows across buyer scenarios
- Renders catalog, recommendations, cart, and order history
- Implements account management capabilities

Business Logic Layer

- Comprises business rules and processes like pricing, promotions, fulfillment
- Executes order orchestration, payment processing, and inventory management
- Tracks and calculates analytics like sales, trends, and KPI reporting

Data Layer

- Persists customer data, order history, product catalog, promotions and pricing
- Stores user sessions and shopping cart data
- Logically organized across entities but stored together physically

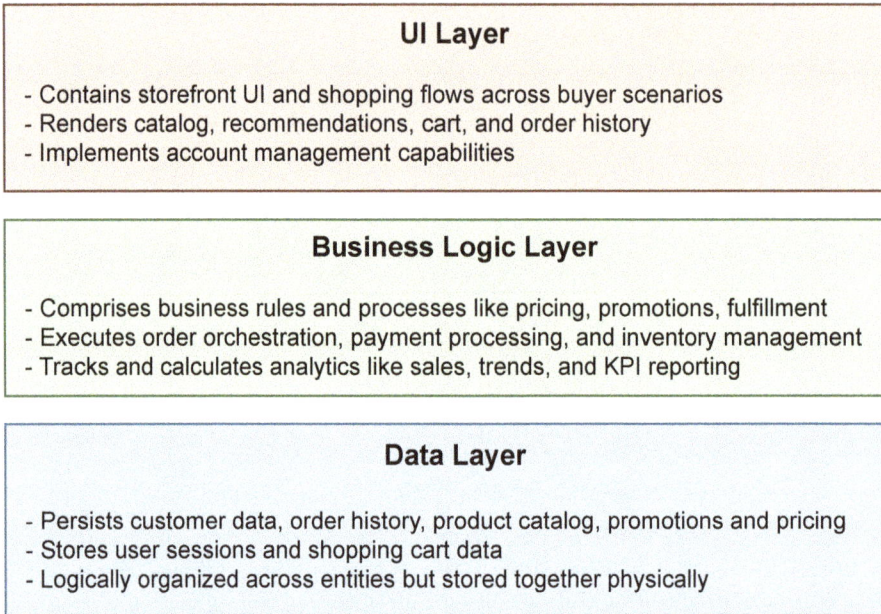

Figure 2.9: Monolithic architecture for an E-Commerce application

to overprovision across less busy tiers just to accommodate peak capacity. All of this contributes to infrastructure cost and scale inefficiencies.

- **Technology Lock-in**: Monolithic architectures make it extremely difficult to modernize technology over time. Typically, an entire application rewrite is required to switch frameworks or languages. What results is a disjointed mix of legacy and modern technologies. This also severely limits the ability to take advantage of the latest cloud innovations.

Monolithic architectures prove inefficient in meeting these demands over time. By decomposing the monolith architecture into microservices, E-Commerce applications can accelerate development and innovation velocity, scale cost-effectively, and isolate faults due to well-defined service boundaries.

To overcome these limitations, the monolith can be iteratively decomposed into specialized microservices as shown in Figure 2.10. The microservices in the E-Commerce application are as follows:

- **Customer Service**: The Customer Service microservice encapsulates account management, profiles, loyalty programs, and engagement capabilities. It owns customer-related data and makes it available to other services via APIs. It accelerates customer feature velocity, scales easily for traffic surges, and provides fault containment away from orders.
- **Catalog Service** The Catalog Service owns the product catalog, categories, inventory statuses, pricing, and merchandising capabilities. Other services consume product data via the provided APIs. It enables rapid iteration of catalog features, cost-efficient scaling for traffic bursts, and increased product team agility from being decoupled.

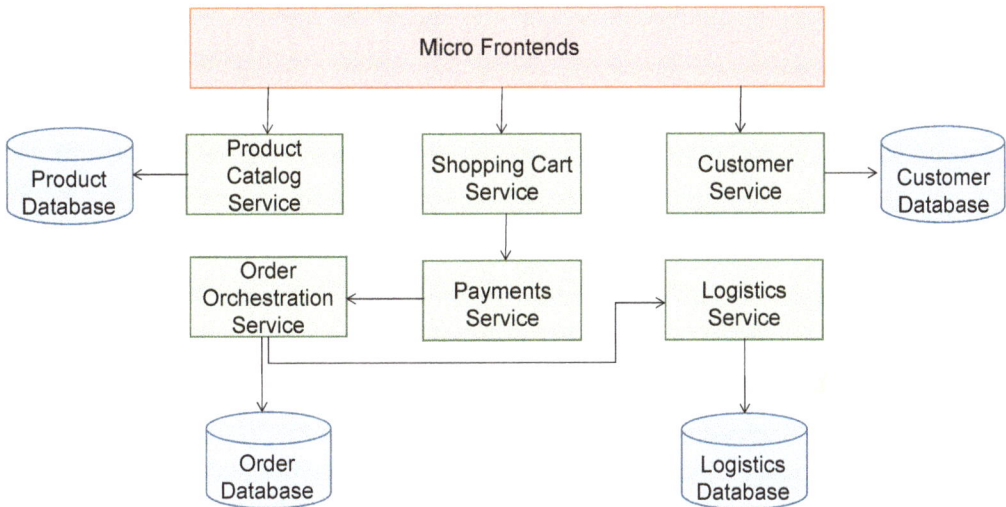

Figure 2.10: Microservices architecture for an E-Commerce application

- **Shopping Cart Service** The Shopping Cart Service handles shopping cart actions, validations, update events, and cart data. It is used by the UI layer during buyer flows. It helps in improving resilience against surges, increased shopping domain team ownership, and flexible promotions.
- **Order Orchestration Service** The Order Orchestration Service orchestrates order fulfillment across pricing, payment, and inventory services. It owns order data, including history. Other services integrate via events and APIs. This provides business agility over order rules, scalability for sales spikes, and increased reliability against dependent service failures.
- **Payments Service** The Payments Service encapsulates payment integrations, fraud analysis, and payment events/statuses/logs. It is used internally by the order service. This helps in fault isolation from payment failures, ownership by the payments team, and enabling cost-efficient independent scaling.
- **Logistics Service** The Logistics Service owns delivery management, shipment events, carrier integrations, and tracker APIs. It is used by the Order Orchestration service. This helps to increase agility over supply chain integration, ability to scale to address volatility, and ownership by the logistics team.
- **Micro Frontends** Besides backend services, the UI layer can also be broken down into independently deliverable components owned by domain teams such as Account Management UI, Catalog Browsing UI, Cart and Checkout UI, Order Tracking UI, for instance. This divides UI by user journeys while accelerating component capability, feature velocity, and resiliency.

The microservices architecture overcomes the limitations of monolithic architecture such as agility, reliability, cost efficiency, and technology lock-in as described previously. Let us review how each drawback of the monolithic architecture is addressed by the microservices architecture:

- **Addressing agility limitations**: Microservices are independently deployable, allowing changes to be made to individual services without impacting unrelated services. This enables parallel work and faster delivery of features. Services have well-defined boundaries, reducing coordination needs across teams. Rollouts/rollbacks impact isolated services only.

- **Addressing reliability issues**: Microservices establish fault isolation boundaries, limiting failures to individual services. There is redundancy for core functions via multiple service instances. Changes carry lower risk as the impact is contained within a service. This improves overall reliability.
- **Addressing cost and scale inefficiencies**: Microservices can scale independently based on resource needs, eliminating overprovisioning. Services can scale horizontally without being limited by load balancers. This enables cost-efficient scaling aligned to traffic patterns.
- **Addressing the technology lock-in problem**: Microservices encapsulate technology choices, enabling different technology stacks per service. Individual services can be modernized via rewrite/replatforming without impacting other services. This reduces legacy drag and allows faster adoption of the latest technologies.

Summary

In this chapter, we provided an overview of microservices, which are small, independent, self-contained software services, each aligned to a distinct business capability. Microservices own their own data persistence layer and expose well-defined interfaces for integration. Key characteristics include strong modularity and encapsulation into cohesive services, loose coupling between services to prevent cascading changes, and alignment to business functions rather than technologies. Microservices provide several benefits over traditional monolithic applications, such as easier updating and scaling of individual services, enabling greater technology diversity across services, and accelerating feature delivery by allowing independent deployment of each service without coordination. However, microservices also introduce complexities of distributed execution across process and network boundaries which demands more operational coordination. Tradeoffs emerge around eventual data consistency across services and difficulty of cross-service refactoring. We described various strategies for systematically decomposing monolithic applications into microservices based on business capabilities, subdomains, customer needs, scale requirements, and volatility. The process involves defining service scopes and interfaces upfront, decentralizing persistent storage, and adopting infrastructure automation to facilitate independent deployment. Functionality can then be incrementally ported from monoliths to microservices while retaining legacy systems, reducing risk. A case study demonstrating the decomposition of an E-Commerce monolith into specialized microservices was described. The microservices architecture addressed limitations of the monolith around agility, reliability, cost efficiency, and technology lock-in.

3

MICROSERVICE ARCHITECTURE PATTERNS

THIS CHAPTER COVERS

- Decomposition Patterns
- Composition & Integration Patterns
- Database Patterns
- Observability Patterns
- Deployment & Operational Patterns
- Communication Patterns

3.1   Introduction

Microservices architecture has rapidly emerged as a popular approach for building large scale enterprise applications. It breaks down an application into hundreds of independent, loosely coupled services representing different business capabilities. Each microservice can be developed, tested, deployed and scaled independently.

While this distributed and independent services-based approach enables better agility, scalability, and resilience, microservices also introduce major complexities around distributed state, dynamic scale, fault isolation, fragmented visibility, and greater management overhead. Addressing these intrinsic complexities requires a whole new set of architectural patterns compared to traditional monolithic systems. Over the last decade, many such microservices patterns have emerged from both academic research and real-world enterprise application development experiences. Just like design patterns provide proven solutions to common object-oriented programming scenarios, microservices patterns codify recommended practices to solve recurring distributed architecture challenges.

In this chapter, we present a comprehensive catalog of microservices patterns. We have categorized the patterns into the following - Decomposition Patterns, Composition & Integration Patterns, Database Patterns, Observability Patterns, Deployment & Operational Patterns, and Communication Patterns. The patterns enable simplifying inherent complexities in designing, building, and operating microservices-based applications.

3.2   Decomposition Patterns

Microservices architectures are used to build large applications from small, independent, and loosely coupled services. Decomposing monolithic applications into microservices is a major challenge. Breaking down monolithic systems into well-bounded microservices is more of an art than science. Decomposition patterns provide proven strategies to systematically extract microservices from existing monoliths or design them for new applications.

Effective decomposition is crucial for realizing microservices benefits like independent deployability, fault isolation, and scalability. Poor decomposition can lead to tightly coupled microservices, defeating the architecture's purpose. Decomposition patterns leverage principles like domain-driven design, organizational alignment, transactions, and fault isolation to divide functionality.

3.2.1   Decompose by Business Capability

As monolithic applications grow massive, modifying them becomes extremely hard, slowing innovation. This pattern breaks down monoliths into lightweight, independent services aligned to business capabilities. The key design considerations for decomposition by business capability are described as follows:

Defining Business Capabilities

A business capability represents an ability that an organization needs to achieve its goals, such as marketing, selling, distributing products, etc. Capabilities map clearly to business functions, unlike technical functions such as communication, messaging, data access, and monitoring, for instance. For example, the business capabilities of an online store include - product catalog management, inventory management, order management, delivery management, and customer management. Each capability offers stand-alone business value.

Granularity of Capabilities

Capabilities can decompose into finer-grained units called sub-capabilities if needed. For example, inventory management can be further divided into sub-capabilities such as inventory tracking, inventory optimization, warehouse management, inventory forecasting, and inventory visibility. Similarly, customer management can be further divided into sub-capabilities such as profile management, order history, rewards programs, customer service, and customer analytics. However, excessive granularity leads to too many services, increasing overhead. So it is recommended to keep services representing higher-level capabilities, except where lower-level subdivision significantly aids organizational agility.

Aligning to Business Capabilities

This decomposition technique aligns services to business functions rather than technology concerns. It creates services matching how the business operates to serve customers. For instance, the customer onboarding capability can facilitate opening accounts through online applications, in-person verification, call center-based enrollment, etc. The business process variations do not warrant separate services.

Evolution of Business Capabilities

Business capabilities are relatively stable compared to rapidly changing solution implementations involving newer technologies, tools, and frameworks. Aligning service boundaries to capabilities insulates services from such solution-level volatility. For example, delivery management might expand to include additional functionality such as delivery route optimization, carrier integration, real-time tracking, and delivery performance monitoring. Over time, however, the customer management service boundary remains unchanged.

Organizational Alignment

Aligning teams to services that represent capabilities also improves organizational alignment between business and IT groups for faster delivery. Teams can become full-stack owners of services supporting related capabilities. Focused service teams enhance productivity, accountability, and agility. However, some duplication of effort can occur due to redundant implementations across teams.

Example of Decomposing an E-Commerce Application by Business Capability

The core business capabilities of an E-Commerce business include Product catalog management, Inventory management, Order management, Delivery management, and Customer Management. By leveraging the decomposition by business capability pattern, a monolithic E-Commerce application can be broken down into the following microservices:
- Product Catalog Management
  - Product Catalog Service: manages product catalog data, classifications, pricing, inventory status, etc.
  - Content Management Service: manages product images, videos, rich descriptions
- Inventory Management
  - Warehouse Management Service: tracks inventory across multiple warehouses, inventory movement, and availability

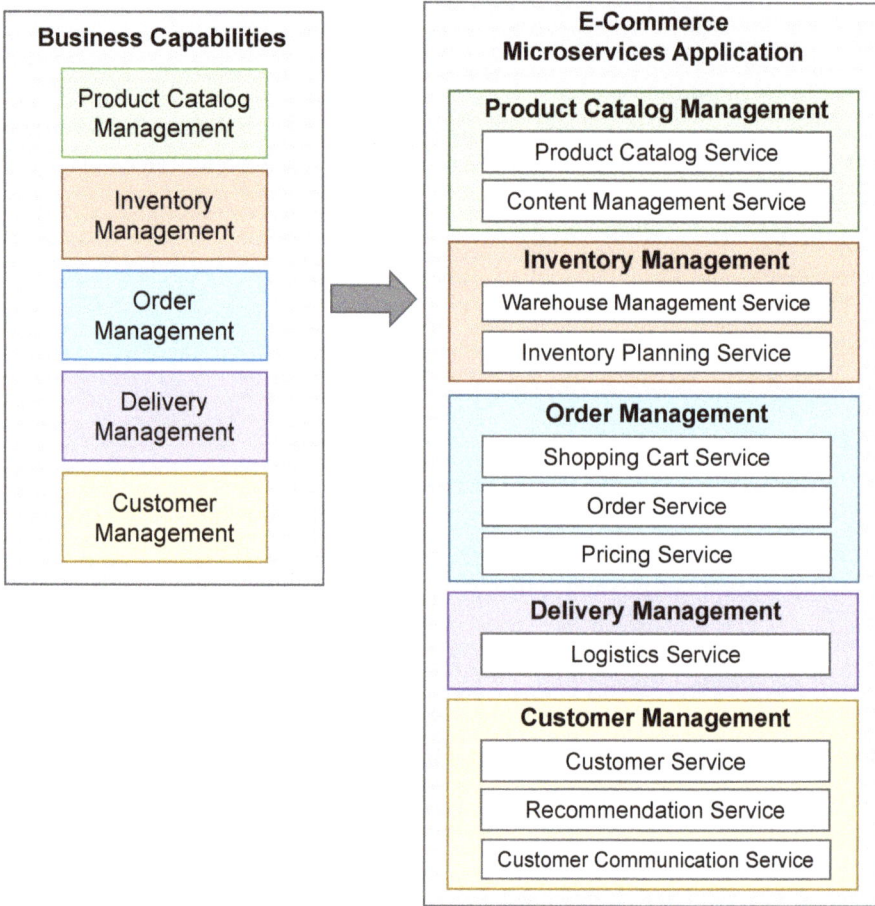

Figure 3.1: Decomposing an E-Commerce application by business capability

- Inventory Planning Service: forecasts demand and optimizes inventory levels across the network
- Order Management
  - Shopping Cart Service: encapsulates shopping cart actions and order creation
  - Order Service: handles order fulfillment workflow orchestration
  - Pricing Service: applies pricing rules, promotions, and calculates order totals
- Delivery Management
  - Logistics Service: optimizes delivery routing, tracks shipments, carrier integrations
- Customer Management
  - Customer Service: manages user accounts, profiles, self-service, loyalty programs
  - Recommendation Service: personalized product recommendations engine
  - Customer Communication Service: manages customer communication across channels

Figure 3.1 shows an example of decomposing an E-Commerce application by business capability.

3.2.2 Decompose by Subdomain

Breaking monolithic applications down into flexible microservices speeds up feature delivery through independent development and deployment. The decomposing by subdomain pattern leverages domain-driven design (DDD) concepts to systematically extract microservices. The key design considerations for decomposition by subdomain are described as follows:

Understanding Subdomains

A domain refers to an organization's complete business functionality. Within a domain, subdomains represent specific business areas such as inventory, logistics, and accounting, for instance. Subdomains have clear boundaries and can function semi-independently. For example, an E-Commerce business domain consists of subdomains such as product catalog, order processing, customer management, and fulfillment. Each subdomain implements a cohesive functionality.

Bounded Contexts

In domain-driven design, bounded contexts delineate the applicability of a domain model for particular subdomains. They clarify what specific terms and rules mean within that context. Microservices then encapsulate the domain logic for corresponding bounded contexts. For example, the concept of an 'account' is different in E-Commerce, Banking, and Telecom systems. The account management microservice only focuses on accounts as applicable to that industry domain.

Structuring Subdomains

Some subdomains are core to the business, such as product sales and delivery for an E-Commerce business. Some subdomains provide supporting capabilities such as customer relationship management. Some subdomains are generic, such as logging, security, and messaging, which span different domains. The nature and relationships between subdomains guide microservices decomposition priorities. Core and complex subdomains often deserve finer-grained microservices earlier. More generic or peripheral subdomains can be consolidated into shared services later.

Analyzing Domain and Context

Domain analysis to identify optimal subdomains requires thoroughly understanding existing systems. Context mapping helps position subdomains concerning external parties like customers and vendors. This analysis models realistic rather than ideal domain boundaries.

Evolutionary Decomposition

The decomposed microservices should be minimally sized to migrate out of any legacy entanglements. This keeps the initial scope small while validating chosen subdomain boundaries through real-world usage and feedback. Any suboptimal subtype microservices can later merge or split as business needs evolve if initial service interfaces encapsulate related logic well. Teams should expect occasional refactoring as domain knowledge improves over time.

Figure 3.2 shows an example of decomposing an E-Commerce application by business subdomain.

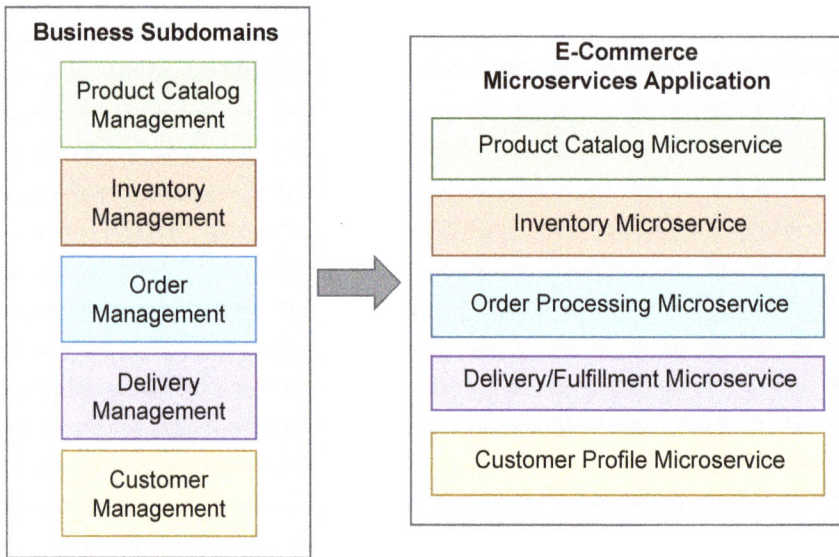

Figure 3.2: Decomposing an E-Commerce application by business subdomain

Example of Decomposing an E-Commerce Application by Subdomain

An E-Commerce business has the following subdomains:

- Product Catalog Management: manages the catalog of products, product information, and categories.
- Inventory Management: manages inventory levels, availability, and restocking for products.
- Order Management: manages orders placed by customers, order status, and billing.
- Delivery Management: manages delivery/fulfillment of orders to customers.
- Customer Management: manages customer accounts, profiles, and order history.

The subdomains are broken down into separate bounded contexts and encapsulated in microservices. By leveraging the decomposition by subdomain pattern, a monolithic E-Commerce application can be broken down into the following microservices:

- Product Catalog Microservice: provides APIs for accessing and managing the product catalog.
- Inventory Microservice: provides inventory availability and management capabilities.
- Order Processing Microservice: provides capabilities for placing orders, tracking status, and billing.
- Delivery/Fulfillment Microservice: handles delivery scheduling, status, and reverse logistics.
- Customer Profile Microservice: provides customer account and profile management.

This allows the different capabilities to be developed, deployed, and scaled independently. Optimal service boundaries can be refined over time as business needs evolve. Supporting subdomains like logging can be consolidated into shared services later.

3.2.3 Decompose by Transaction

This pattern groups functionally related operations into microservices based on transaction boundaries. All operations of a transaction execute within one service. This optimizes performance, availability, and data consistency. As monolithic applications accumulate vast complexity, modifying them becomes extremely hard, slowing feature delivery. Breaking them down into flexible microservices promises accelerated deployment. The 'decompose by transaction' pattern takes a unique approach based on transaction boundaries.

The key design considerations for decomposition by transaction are described as follows:

Understanding Transactions

Transactions represent units of business activity involving multiple steps that must fully complete or fail altogether to maintain data integrity. For example, an online purchase in an E-Commerce application translates into a transaction spanning multiple services such as payment service, inventory management service, and order management service.

Transactions Demarcate Activities

Transaction boundaries demarcate the start, execution scope, and end of complete workflow activities. They have clearly identified inputs, processing workflow, and outputs or events upon completion. For example, a checkout transaction encompasses multiple steps like payment deduction, order creation, and shipment scheduling.

Transaction-aligned Microservices

This decomposition style groups together all transaction participant components into standalone microservices by transaction type. This differs from decomposition by business capability or subdomain approaches. For example, an E-Commerce platform could offer separate microservices for managing shopping cart transactions, order placement transactions, payment transactions, and delivery transactions independently.

Improved Consistency and Performance

The key benefit here is data consistency within the microservice's scope. Since all transaction logic for a workflow resides in one service, data modifications either fully complete or rollback together there itself using ACID properties. Calls to external services are minimized. This also improves performance and availability. Grouping related operations avoids higher network latency with no intermediate service calls. Entire business functions remain available independently despite dependent service failures. For example, by keeping the order placement operations within one service, data consistency issues are avoided, and performance improves from less network chatter.

System-wide Transactions Still Complex

Composite system-wide business transactions being fulfilled via multiple microservices collaborating are not fully optimized. For example, the checkout transaction spans inventory update, payment deduction, and order persistence across services having their own data stores. Teams sometimes selectively compromise on consistency to favor availability and performance.

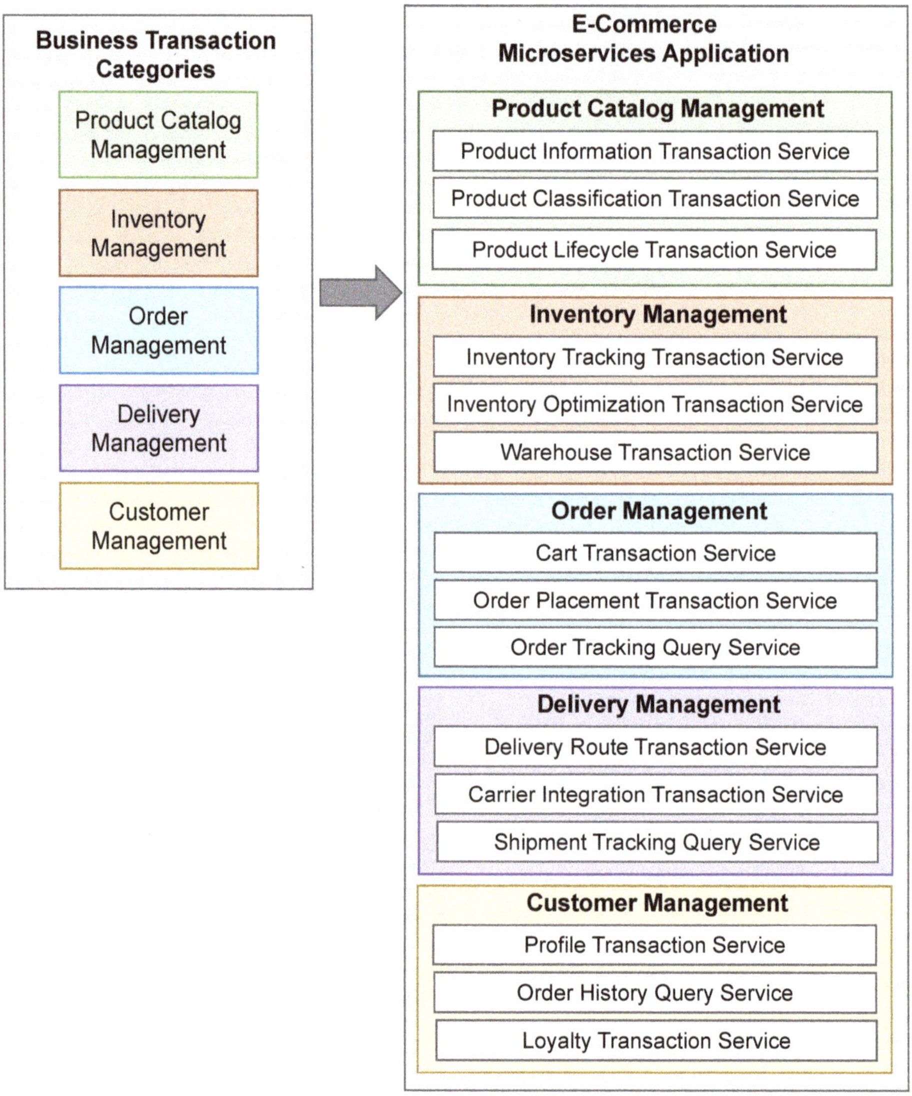

Figure 3.3: Decomposing an E-Commerce application by transactions

Legacy Migration Suitability

This decomposition style suits newer systems better as compared to legacy systems where carving out transactional boundaries across pre-existing tightly coupled modules proves complicated and time-consuming. Other incremental migration patterns often work better for transitioning monolithic capabilities.

The decompose by transaction pattern accelerates delivery of independent business transaction workflows crucial for an organization. It brings consistency, performance, and robustness benefits through appropriate grouping of operations for such scenarios. However, these microservices risk becoming very complex monoliths themselves over time. Maintaining cohesion during additional capability inclusion poses challenges. There are also deployment challenges around running multiple versions of transactional services.

Example of Decomposing an E-Commerce Application by Transactions

Let us look at an example of decomposition of an E-Commerce application's capabilities into microservices based on transaction boundaries as shown in Figure 3.3. For better organization and presentation, we have grouped the transaction-related services based on the function. The related operations within the same transaction boundary are kept in a microservice.

- Product Catalog Management:
  - Product Information Transaction Service: Add, update, delete product details
  - Product Classification Transaction Service: Classify products into categories
  - Product Lifecycle Transaction Service: Manage product lifecycle stages
- Inventory Management:
  - Inventory Tracking Transaction Service: Record inventory counts
  - Inventory Optimization Transaction Service: Replenish and redistribute inventory
  - Warehouse Transaction Service: Manage warehouse storage and retrieval operations
- Order Management:
  - Cart Transaction Service: Allow customers to add/remove items to cart
  - Order Placement Transaction Service: Place orders and process payments
  - Order Tracking Query Service: View real-time order status
- Delivery Management:
  - Delivery Route Transaction Service: Optimize delivery routes
  - Carrier Integration Transaction Service: Integrate with shipping carriers
  - Shipment Tracking Query Service: Track real-time shipment location
- Customer Management:
  - Profile Transaction Service: Update customer account details
  - Order History Query Service: View past order details
  - Loyalty Transaction Service: Manage loyalty program signups and points crediting

3.2.4 Strangler Pattern

The Strangler pattern is an incremental approach to modernizing monolithic legacy applications. It works by gradually migrating functionality over time into new microservices, while keeping the legacy application running to serve remaining features. This reduces risk compared to big-bang rewrites attempted in one shot. The incremental strangler migration pattern offers an effective and pragmatic approach for migrating monolithic applications to microservices on modern stacks, while operating existing systems in parallel.

Strangler Facade or Router

The first step is to ring-fence the monolith by exposing its capabilities through APIs built as a facade or router layer. The strangler facade or router sits in front of the legacy app to abstract it behind a well-defined API interface. This layer routes requests either to the monolith or the new microservices transparently. The facade ensures external consumers remain unaffected by internal changes. Over time, microservices take over functionality completely from inside this facade as the monolith gets 'strangled'.

Analyze Before Extracting

The next step analyzes monolith flows, data structures, and code dependencies to identify slices of logic to extract. Business capabilities like accounts, payments, or subdomains are

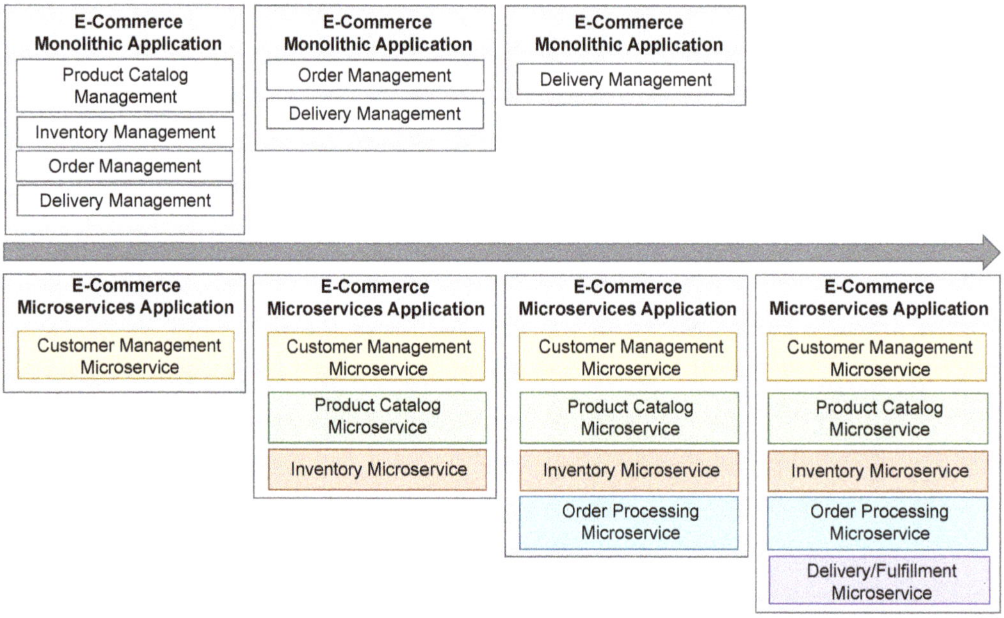

Figure 3.4: Decomposing an E-Commerce application using strangler pattern

common extraction criteria. Legacy refactoring techniques help here too. Teams model target
state microservices and underlying domain models to guide appropriate slicing. This guides
extraction of cohesive microservices with clear boundaries.

Building Initial Microservices

The next step is to build simple thin microservices reproducing existing monolith logic. The
initial microservices focus on testing integration and end-to-end functionality with minimal
logic. As capabilities shift across, common libraries get refactored out for reuse to prevent
duplication.

Migrating Users

After successful internal testing, the strangler facade or router starts redirecting a subset of
user traffic to the new microservices. This allows testing real-world usage at a smaller scale
while debugging. Traffic migration accelerates as confidence builds.

Legacy Retirement

Eventually, as features fully migrate, components of legacy apps are permanently retired
after thorough testing. Any remaining traffic is redirected to microservices and that portion
of the monolith is decommissioned.

Multi-phase Migrations

For large monoliths, migration occurs incrementally across multiple product release cycles
rather than in one shot. Targeted critical capabilities are migrated first. Then auxiliary
functions are migrated in subsequent product release cycles. Careful facade design is vital so
that such phased migration remains transparent to end-users throughout multiple coexistence
periods.

Example of Decomposing an E-Commerce Application by Strangler Pattern

Let us look at an example of applying the Strangler pattern to migrate an E-Commerce application from a monolith to microservices as shown in Figure 3.4. The strangler pattern is applied in the following phases:

- Phase 1:
  - Build a strangler facade or router to abstract the legacy system and adapt interfaces while new microservices are built behind it. The facade keeps end users unaffected by behind-the-scenes incremental changes from monolith to microservices.
  - Build new microservices for the customer management capabilities as this can likely be built independently without much dependence on other systems. This would handle functionality like user profiles, authentication, preferences, etc.
  - Build a simple customer UI that consumes the new customer microservice API as well as legacy APIs. Redirect a segment of users to this UI for testing.
- Phase 2:
  - Build product catalog management and inventory management as separate microservices.
  - The strangler facade continues routing non-customer and non-order requests to legacy systems while directing segmented user traffic to new UIs hitting microservices.
- Phase 3:
  - Build order management as a separate microservice.
  - Build a separate order processing UI application for staff that uses the new order microservice. This allows testing order-related microservices at a smaller scale.
- Phase 4:
  - Build delivery management as a microservice. Integrate fully with the existing microservices.
  - Migrate remaining legacy capabilities bit by bit with careful testing.
  - As new microservices take over capabilities fully, roll out to larger user segments, and eventually full production traffic.

3.3 Composition & Integration Patterns

As monolithic applications are decomposed into microservices, the services need to integrate and compose together to provide complete business functionality. Composition and integration patterns help connect the distributed services and data to enable applications built with microservices architecture.

The composition and integration patterns provide loose coupling, flexibility to change the implementation of services, consolidated APIs tailored for different client needs, reduced complexity for clients, and optimized request routing and data flows. They are essential for connecting the distributed capabilities delivered via microservices into full-featured, integrated applications.

3.3.1 Aggregator Pattern

The Aggregator pattern collects responses from multiple microservices and combines them into an integrated API response for clients. This consolidates data lookup logic behind the scenes so clients make fewer requests. The Aggregator may apply additional business logic as well while aggregating data.

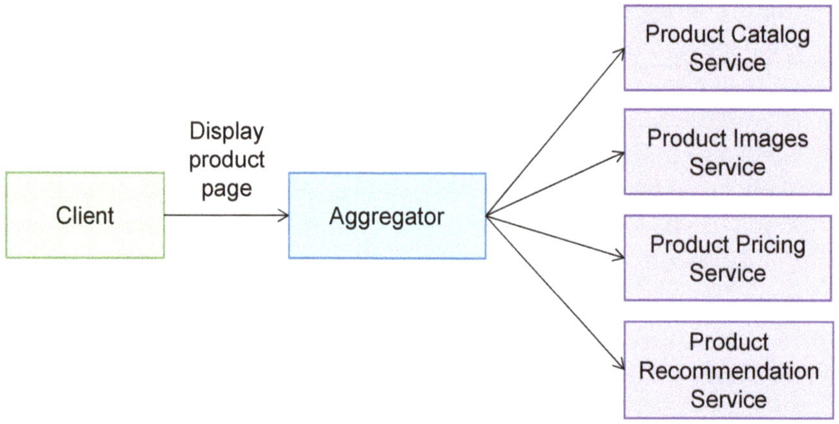

Figure 3.5: Using Aggregator pattern for an E-Commerce application

In a microservices architecture, related data is distributed across services. For example, an E-Commerce application may have separate services for product catalog, product images, product pricing, and product recommendations. Displaying a product page would require aggregation of data from several of those services. A product aggregator can provide the complete product information by calling the product catalog, product images, product pricing, and product recommendation services and then combining those into the integrated product data response, as shown in Figure 3.5.

Without an aggregator, the client application would need to call multiple services directly. This exposes the microservices landscape to the client with all its complexities. It also requires multiple round trips impacting performance. An Aggregator pattern can simplify things for the client application. The Aggregator sits in front of the other microservices, handling cross-service data aggregation on behalf of clients. The client only needs to call the Aggregator.

Aggregators typically use asynchronous, non-blocking calls (like REST API calls) to retrieve data from services. This avoids long delays if any particular service call is slow. The Aggregator assembles responses asynchronously as they return. Some Aggregators may cache common requests so similar future calls return even faster without having to re-retrieve the same data. Aggregators can reduce overall coupling in the system by hiding the actual services from clients. This abstracts the implementation allowing services to change without impacting clients.

Aggregators can also apply additional cross-cutting business logic while aggregating responses. For example, applying rules to calculate product discounts based on customer tier and product type. However, adding too much logic can increase complexity and reduce their reusability.

3.3.2   API Gateway Pattern

As an application is decomposed into microservices, direct integration between client apps and all the services becomes increasingly complex. Clients may need to call multiple services to satisfy a single user request. Different clients also have diverse integration needs - mobile apps require API optimization while analytics systems need data ingestion from services.

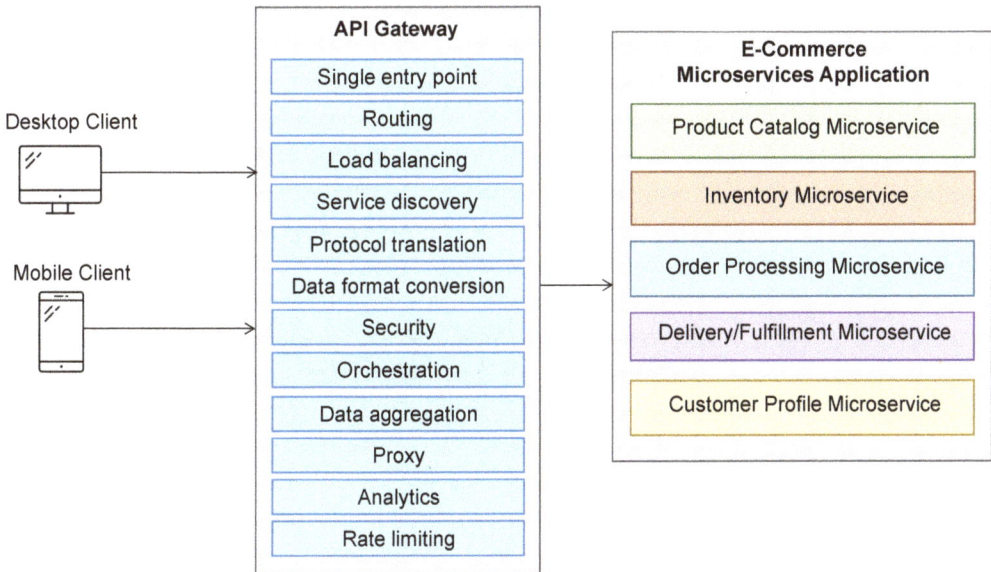

Figure 3.6: Using API Gateway pattern for an E-Commerce application

The API Gateway pattern provides a single entry point or facade to handle all client interactions with the microservices ecosystem. The gateway abstracts the actual services implementation from consumers. This keeps service evolution isolated from client impact.

The API Gateway can route requests to appropriate service APIs while aggregating data across multiple services for the client response. Cross-cutting concerns like authentication, security, monitoring, and rate limits can be handled in one place instead of duplicating them across services. Requests can be fanned out to multiple services in parallel to improve responsiveness. Figure 3.6 shows an example of using API Gateway pattern for an E-Commerce application.

For mobile devices using REST APIs, the API Gateway enables a different optimized REST API channel as compared to XML SOAP API optimized for certain enterprise on-prem systems. Common protocols like HTTP and WebSocket can proxy to efficient binary protocols like gRPC or Thrift being used internally between services.

API Gateways provide the following major benefits:
- Single entry point: Centralized external entry point into a microservices architecture.
- Routing: Route requests to appropriate services based on rules.
- Load balancing: Distribute requests across instances of services.
- Service discovery: Abstract actual locations of services.
- Protocol translation: Convert between protocols such as HTTP and gRPC.
- Data format conversion: Transform between data formats like JSON and XML.

- Security implementation: Externalize authentication, authorization, TLS termination.
- Orchestration: Sequence calls between multiple services.
- Data aggregation: Gather data from multiple services into a single response.
- Proxy: Act as a reverse proxy to services.
- Analytics: Collect metrics, logs, and traces on API activity.
- Rate limiting: Throttle requests to prevent overloading of services.

In effect, the API Gateway encapsulates the complex mesh of services behind a facade, reducing the integration complexity.

3.3.3 Proxy Pattern

Proxy is an integration pattern that uses a proxy service in front of actual microservice APIs to control and manage access. The proxy enables additional processing on requests and responses without code changes to the microservices. This is another abstraction mechanism that reduces coupling between clients and microservices.

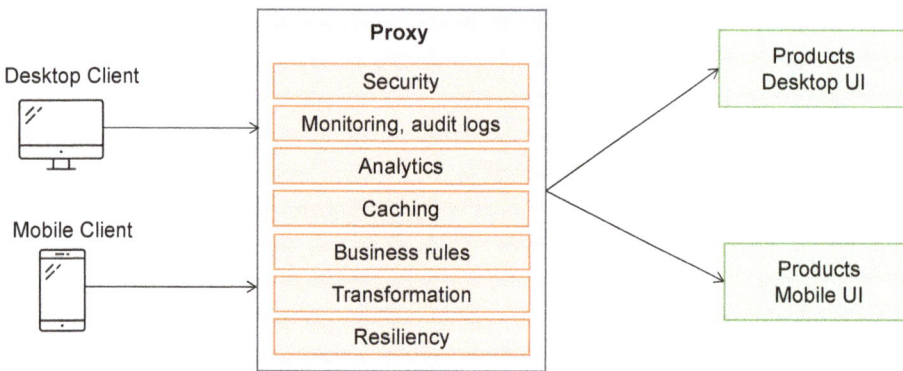

Figure 3.7: Using Proxy pattern for an E-Commerce application

Figure 3.7 shows an example of using the Proxy pattern for an E-Commerce application. The proxy hides direct access to microservices so that clients don't rely on tight integration with the actual API structures. Clients communicate through the proxy, which handles requests by invoking services.

The proxy abstracts access to microservices so clients don't directly integrate with service APIs. This reduces coupling for easier refactoring of services without needing to upgrade all clients. The proxy handles data, protocol, and interface transformations on behalf of services.

The common use cases of a proxy are as follows:

- Security: Applying authentication and rate limits before routing service requests
- Monitoring, audit logs and analytics
- Caching: Serving responses first from a cache for reduced requests
- Business rules: Applying rules like service request orchestration logic
- Transformation: Converting between data formats, protocols, and interfaces
- Resiliency: Retry policies and circuit breakers if services are unavailable

In essence, proxies act as intermediaries that augment and control access to microservices. The proxy pattern is useful for abstraction, cross-cutting features, and access control in microservices architectures.

3.3.4   Client-Side UI Composition

In the Client-Side UI Composition pattern, the UI is structured as a layout skeleton that loads different regions or components independently. This enables different teams to develop UI components tying into their own microservices. The components integrate together at runtime to create the full cohesive page.

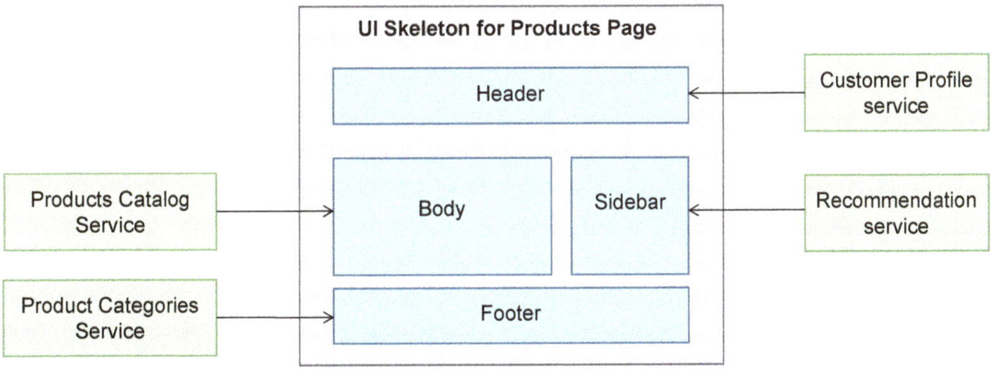

Figure 3.8: Using Client-Side UI Composition pattern for an E-Commerce application

Microservices architectures distribute capabilities across bounded contexts. A client page may need to integrate data, logic, and UI from multiple different services representing different business areas. Building a monolithic page becomes challenging both technically and organizationally across teams.

Figure 3.8 shows an example of using the Client-Side UI Composition pattern for an E-Commerce application. With client-side UI composition, the page layout provides regions, slots, or placeholders for UI components to load into. For example, a Page Header, Sidebar, Body Content, and Footer. The header may load customer profile data from the Customer service. The sidebar may display product recommendations calling the Recommendation service.

This provides a separation of concerns allowing teams to focus on their components. The components call their own microservices for data, isolate related business logic, and manage their own state and dependencies. At runtime, the lightweight page skeleton, router, and component model handle seamlessly loading the distributed components into an integrated page. Developing components as isolated building blocks also maximizes their reusability across the application.

The Client-Side UI Composition pattern has the following benefits:

- Separates UI concerns across components and teams
- Pages load dynamically in a responsive, asynchronous way
- Maximizes reuse of components across the application
- Components manage integration only with their microservices
- Enables independent development with less coordination

This pattern is commonly realized using modern Single Page Application frameworks with reusable UI component models. Commonly used UI component frameworks enabling these capabilities include React, Angular, and Vue.

3.3.5 Chained Microservices

The chained microservice design pattern links together a sequence of microservices, each performing a specific task, to collectively handle a client request. In this pattern, the output of one microservice becomes the input to the next one in the chain. The pattern allows building complex services from smaller, focused services that work together.

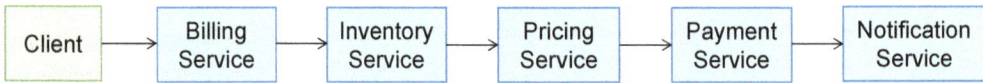

Figure 3.9: Using chained microservice pattern for an E-Commerce application

Figure 3.9 shows an example of using the chained microservice pattern for an E-Commerce application. In an E-Commerce application, several steps need to be performed to handle orders placed by customers, such as validating billing information, checking inventory availability, calculating taxes and shipping, submitting payment, and sending order confirmation. Rather than build one monolithic application to handle every aspect of placing an order, the chained pattern can be leveraged to break this into smaller microservices as follows:
- Billing Service: Validates credit card details, billing address, etc.
- Inventory Service: Checks if items ordered are in stock and reserves them
- Pricing Service: Calculates cost of items, promotions, shipping, and taxes
- Payment Service: Submits payment details and processes transaction
- Notification Service: Sends order confirmation and tracking info to customer

In this example, when an order is placed, the Order Service would invoke each downstream service in sequence, passing key information and outcomes to the next service. Once the payment is processed, the order confirmation can be sent to the customer. If any service fails, the sequence would be broken, and the order is not finalized. This chained approach allows each service to focus on one capability, scale independently, and be developed by separate teams if needed. New services like a Recommendation Service could also be added to the sequence to provide upsell suggestions.

The chained microservice design pattern has the following benefits:
- Modularity: Each microservice focuses on a specific task and can be developed, updated, and scaled independently.
- Resilience: If one service in the chain fails, only that part breaks instead of the entire application.
- Reusability: The individual microservices can be reused for other applications.
- Scalability: Services can scale independently based on demand.
- Performance: Calls between internal services are faster than external requests.

The trade-off of this pattern is added latency, testing, and monitoring needs. The chained microservices can result in cascading failures when an issue with one service impacts the entire chain's ability to function properly. The testing and monitoring complexity increases as the interdependencies between services make the system as more complex. For many applications such as E-Commerce, however, the benefits outweigh the downsides.

3.3.6 Branched Microservices

The branched microservice design pattern is an architectural pattern used to model interactions between services in complex distributed systems. It extends common microservice patterns like the aggregator and chained service patterns to allow services to invoke multiple chains of other services simultaneously.

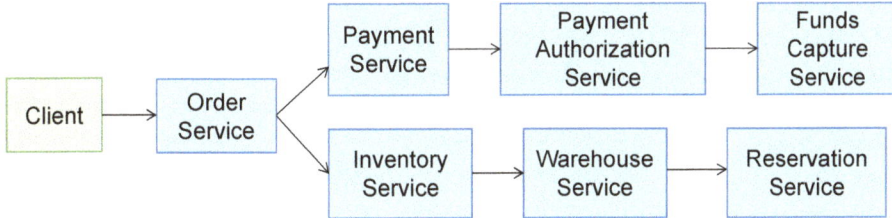

Figure 3.10: Using branched microservice pattern for an E-Commerce application

The branched microservice design pattern allows complex orchestration of multiple chains of microservices to achieve parallel processing. It encapsulates implementation details behind root services while also keeping services decoupled. A root parent service brokers requests from consumers to one or multiple chains of child services. Each chain executes its own workflow and returns output to the parent service. The parent service aggregates responses from the different branches and forms a consolidated response back to the calling consumer.

The branched microservice design pattern has the following benefits:

- Parallel Processing: By splitting flows into multiple chains that can execute in parallel, the overall request processing time can be reduced compared to sequential chains.
- Simplified Services: Each branch can be developed and maintained independently as a simple sequence of services focused on specific goals.
- Isolation of Concerns: Branches usually group related functionality, isolating those functions from other branches.
- Improved Resiliency: If one branch fails, other branches may still succeed. The aggregating service can apply compensating logic on failures and partial successes.
- Flexible Consumption: Consumers can call the root service without knowing complex branching logic, reducing coupling to internal implementation details.

Figure 3.10 shows an example of using the branched microservice pattern for an E-Commerce application. When a customer places an order, multiple services need to be invoked to complete the order. Using the branch pattern, the order service can invoke the payment service and the inventory service simultaneously. The order service receives the order details from the client. It then calls the payment service to authorize and capture payment. At the same time, it also calls the inventory service to reserve the items in the customer's cart and ensure they are in stock. The payment service has its own chain that authorizes the payment method, captures funds, and confirms payment. The inventory service has a chain that checks inventory levels at different warehouses, reserves items at specific locations, and commits the reservation. Once the order service receives responses from both the payment and inventory chains, it aggregates the results.

3.4 Database Patterns

Microservices promote building applications with small, independent, and loosely coupled services. This presents both challenges and opportunities in managing and persisting data within such systems. Monolithic applications can rely on a large central database underpinning the entire application. But decentralized microservices require rethinking traditional approaches.

The database patterns embody strategies for distributing and sharing data across boundaries between self-contained services. Key patterns that have emerged include decentralizing data ownership down to the level of individual services, separating specialized read and write data pipelines, coordinating business transactions across microservice boundaries, and legacy integration tactics.

3.4.1 Database per Service

The database per service pattern prescribes that each microservice in an application architecture should have its own private database instance. The goal is to achieve loose coupling between services and avoid situations where services are dependent on shared databases. In this pattern, the database access is strictly controlled through the APIs provided by the microservice that owns the database. No other services have direct access to the database. Figure 3.11 shows an example of using the database per service pattern for an E-Commerce application.

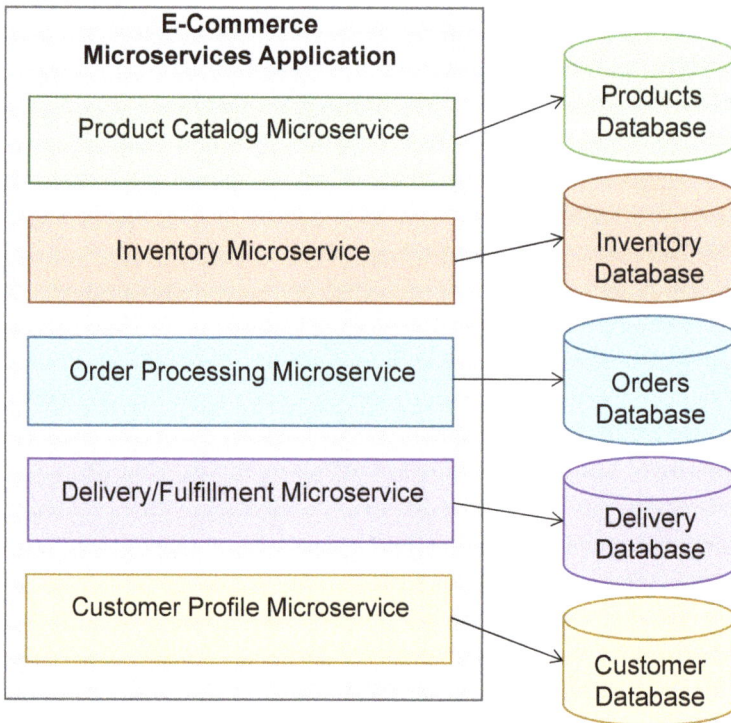

Figure 3.11: Using database per service pattern for an E-Commerce application

The database per service pattern has the following benefits:
- Independence and Isolation: With a database per service, each microservice team can manage their own database schema and make changes without coordination with other teams. There is no risk of schema changes breaking other services. Upgrades or migrations can be performed independently as well. Additionally, if there are issues with one database, the outage is isolated to only that service. The blast radius is limited compared to situations where many services rely on the same database server.
- Flexibility: Microservices typically handle different kinds of data and workflows. The database per service approach allows each service to select the database type that fits its needs, whether relational, document, graph, time-series, or other NoSQL varieties. Teams can choose their ideal database technology rather than being constrained to the limitations of a monolithic database.
- Scalability: Demand and load patterns tend to differ between microservices. By separating databases, the data storage for each service can be scaled up or out appropriately to handle just the load for that service. With a shared database server, it becomes quite difficult to scale resources in a tailored way.
- Security: Access control and permissions can be managed at the service level more easily when databases are fully separated. Rather than managing access control centrally across all applications and users, each microservices team only needs to secure access within the scope of their own service database. This makes security management decentralized similar to the services themselves.

There are a few variants when adopting the database per service approach such as using private-tables-per-service, database schema-per-service, or database-server-per-service. The choice depends on resource constraints and the need for full isolation. As microservices expand, starting with shared database servers and evolving towards dedicated servers is a pragmatic approach.

3.4.2   Shared Database per Service

In the shared database per service pattern, multiple microservices share access to the same database instance or database schema. While this pattern may seem to contradict the decentralized nature of microservices, however, there are some scenarios where sharing a database can simplify the initial decomposition of a monolithic application.

For instance, large legacy applications often have a single monolithic database powering the entire application. Migrating all at once to a fully isolated database per service architecture requires significant upfront effort. An incremental approach is easier for large systems with hundreds of tables and complex schema dependencies. In this approach, the application logic and messaging are first separated by refactoring into microservices. But the database layer itself is left untouched initially. All services continue accessing the original central database.

The database per service pattern has the following benefits:
- Simplifies Initial Migration: Teams can focus on decomposing the application into services first without taking on complex database migration in parallel. The services access the existing database using well-defined APIs only rather than direct database access.
- Atmosphere of a Shared Database: Many legacy systems rely on stored procedures, triggers, foreign key constraints, and transactions spanning multiple entities.

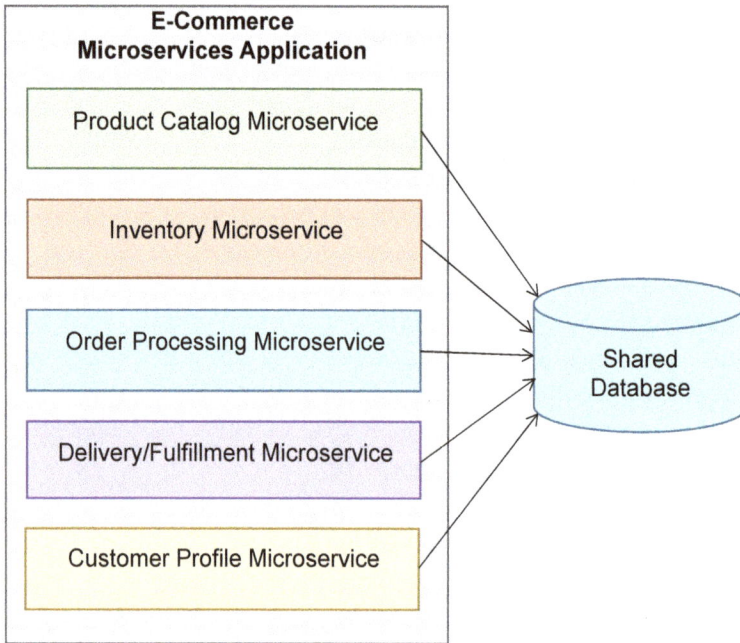

Figure 3.12: Using Shared Database per Service pattern for an E-Commerce application

These constructs stop working properly when decentralized into microservices unless redesigned. Keeping the central database preserves this functionality temporarily while services are extracted.

- Application-Level Isolation: Even with a shared database, the microservices themselves interact via APIs, not direct database calls. This enforces some isolation of responsibilities at the application level. As far as services are concerned, they are only accessing their own data store via their own APIs.
- Gradual Decentralization: After an initial migration to services sharing a database, the database can then be gradually broken apart into decentralized schemas owned by each service team. This incremental approach gets value from microservices faster without a complex initial data migration.

Figure 3.12 shows an example of using the shared database per service pattern for an E-Commerce application. This pattern is useful as an interim step when decomposing monolithic systems.

A shared database between microservices can undermine some of the benefits of a microservices architecture like loose coupling, independent scalability, and clear ownership boundaries. It introduces contention risks and tightly couples service teams through the database schema. In the long term, the database per service pattern is preferred from the perspective of loose coupling, isolation, and independent scaling.

3.4.3 Command Query Responsibility Segregation (CQRS)

The Command Query Responsibility Segregation (CQRS) pattern is an architectural pattern that separates read and update operations into two separate application stacks. The goal is to scale and optimize each stack specifically for the very different usage patterns of reads as compared to writes.

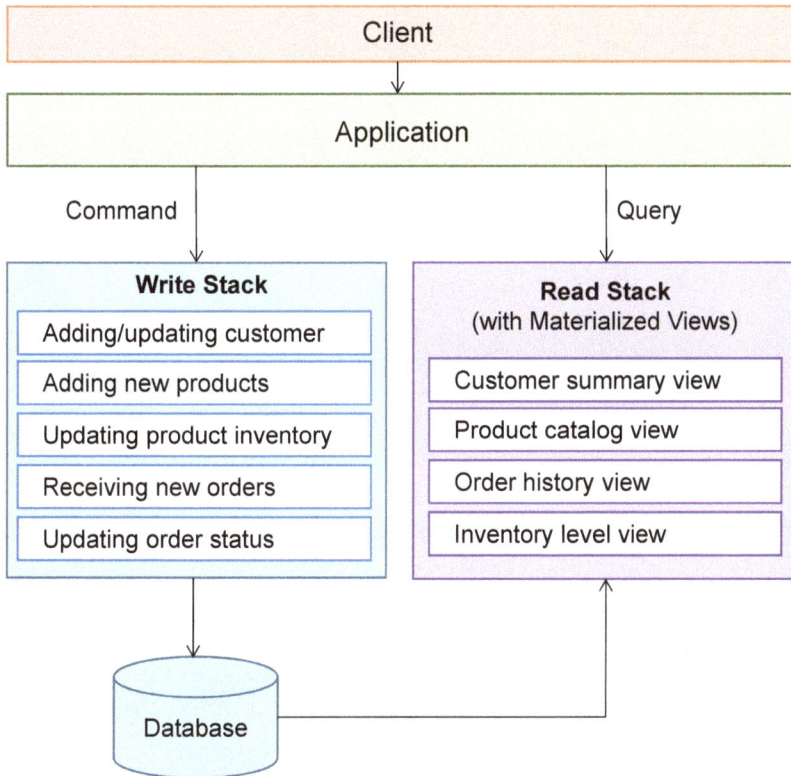

Figure 3.13: Using CQRS pattern for an E-Commerce application

In a traditional monolithic application, the same application layer handles UI displays, user inputs for updates, business logic, and database operations. In complex applications with many concurrent users, the database tier often suffers from contention issues around mixed read/write workloads.

By adopting the CQRS approach, the application routes all write operations through one stack focused purely on accepting and processing updates efficiently. Reads route through an entirely separate stack optimized for fast reads.

The write stack focuses purely on handling user input and making rapid updates or inserts to the data store. The write stack uses common optimizations such as using a queuing infrastructure ahead of the database to smooth spikes in traffic and aggregating/batching updates when possible. The event sourcing pattern can be used to log all state changes as immutable events.

The ready stack aims solely at querying and displaying data for users. The read replicas provide insulation from lock contention with writes. To avoid hotspots going directly to the database, cached views are used. The read stack uses indexes and materialized views that are optimized for common queries. The read side maintains up-to-date views of the data by subscribing to events streamed out of the write side and applying any business logic or projection logic to form the read model.

The CQRS pattern has the following benefits:
- Allows scaling resources on each side independently
- Allows using different storage types tailored to workflows
- Avoids read contention during write-heavy workloads
- Provides more flexibility around consistency and isolation levels

Figure 3.13 shows an example of using the CQRS pattern for an E-Commerce application. The CQRS pattern is used to separate read and update operations into two separate application stacks. The write stack handles tasks such as:
- Adding/updating customer details
- Adding new products
- Updating product inventory
- Receiving new orders
- Updating order status as it ships

These write operations funnel through a message queue to smooth spikes in traffic. An event store database logs these events immutably. Additional services in the write stack handle business logic processing on the events, apply validation rules, handle payments, update legacy systems, etc.

The read stack maintains materialized views of the data optimized for different display contexts such as:
- A customer summary view for the customer profile page
- A product catalog view for browsing inventory
- An order history view for a customer's previous orders
- Inventory level views for reordering products

As write operations occur, events publish to message streams. The read stack services subscribe to relevant streams and update their view models.

The CQRS pattern essentially scales an application on two axes. The writes are scaled up vertically via the write stack, and the reads are scaled out horizontally via the read stack.

3.4.4 Event Sourcing Pattern

Event sourcing is an architectural pattern for microservices which is centered around persistence of all changes to the application state as an immutable sequence or log of events. The core idea is that the application state is not stored in database rows or objects as the 'current' state. Instead, every change to the state generates an event object capturing the intent and relevant details about the state change.

The event sourcing pattern has the following benefits:
- Audit History: The sequenced event log provides a full history to reconstruct past states from any point in time.
- Debugging: Bugs can be debugged by replaying events leading up to failure scenarios, revealing what happened.
- Rollbacks: Reversing state changes is simple using compensation events that undo previous application events.

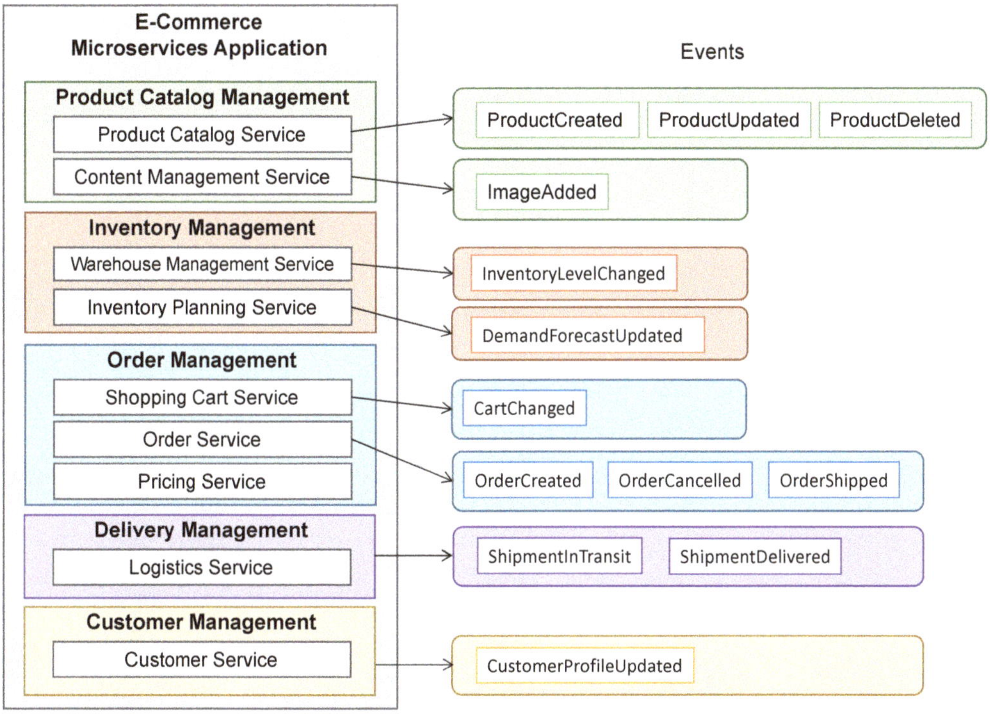

Figure 3.14: Using Event Sourcing pattern for an E-Commerce application

- Handling Concurrency: If two users update the same entity concurrently, events end up sequenced, and replaying events handles the concurrency.

The events are appended to an event log or stream in sequence. The events are usually immutable once recorded and include details such as timestamp and intent. To construct the current state, the system replays events from the beginning to essentially rebuild the state by applying events. Event sourcing provides rich history and flexibility around state changes. The challenges of event sourcing include increased storage for large histories and rebuilding state by replaying events which has latency costs.

Let us look at an example of using the event sourcing pattern for an E-Commerce application as shown in Figure 3.14. Event sourcing enables decoupled architecture across E-commerce microservices. Rather than directly updating state, services emit immutable event objects as follows:

- Product Catalog Management:
  - Product Catalog Service emits events like *ProductCreated*, *ProductUpdated*, and *ProductDeleted*
  - Content Management Service emits events for content changes like *ImageAdded*
- Inventory Management:
  - Warehouse Management Service emits *InventoryLevelChanged* events when stock changes
  - Inventory Planning Service emits events like *DemandForecastUpdated*

- Order Management:
  - Shopping Cart Service emits *CartChanged* events for additions or removals
  - Order Service emits *OrderCreated*, *OrderCancelled*, and *OrderShipped* events
  - Pricing Service listens for *OrderCreated* and applies pricing rules
- Delivery Management:
  - Logistics Service listens to *OrderShipped* events and plans delivery
  - Emits shipping events like *ShipmentInTransit* and *ShipmentDelivered*
- Customer Management:
  - Customer Service emits *CustomerProfileUpdated* when profiles change

3.4.5 Saga Pattern

The Saga pattern is a way to maintain data consistency across multiple services in a microservice architecture without using distributed transactions. A saga is a sequence of distributed transactions where each transaction updates data within a single service's database. It breaks a long business transaction into a sequence of localized transactions.

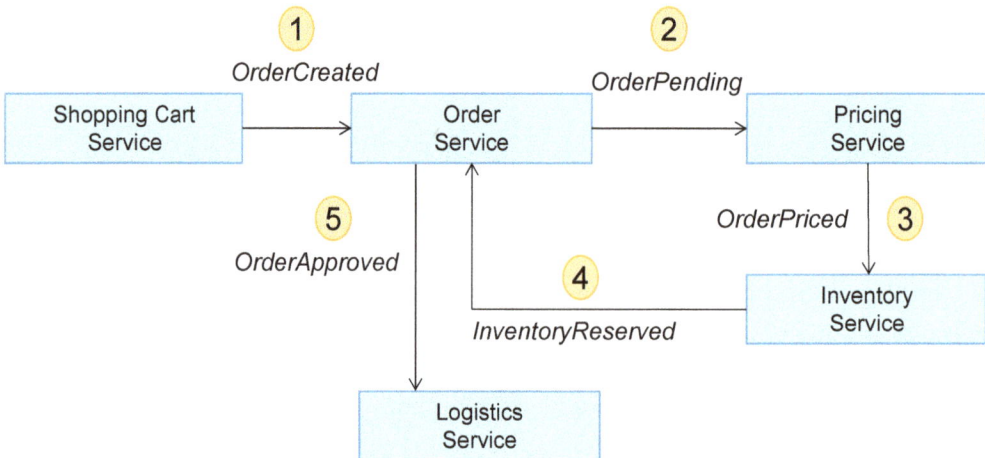

Figure 3.15: Saga for order placement in an E-Commerce application

After each localized transaction, the service publishes an event to trigger the next transaction in the sequence. If any transaction fails due to a business rule violation, the saga executes compensating transactions to rollback the impact of previous transactions.

This enables eventual consistency between services without the overhead of distributed transactions or isolation of localized transactions. Services communicate progress via events.

The Saga pattern has the following benefits:

- Enables consistency: Saga pattern enables consistency across services without distributed transactions and avoids performance overhead of coordinating distributed transactions.
- Loose coupling: Saga pattern maintains loose coupling between services which communicate via events rather than direct calls.
- Asynchronous and non-blocking: Transactions execute independently without services blocking each other, which improves responsiveness and scalability.

- Fault tolerance: Saga pattern improves fault tolerance as compensating transactions provide rollback and recovery.
- Decentralized data ownership: Saga pattern improves autonomy of services as each service manages its own database transactions.
- Incrementally adoptable: Saga pattern can be adopted in an incremental manner for specific business transactions.

Some drawbacks of Saga pattern include programming complexity to handle rollbacks, and the need for services to atomically update the database and publish events. Additional mechanisms are required for clients to determine async saga outcomes.

Let us look at an example of using the Saga pattern for an E-Commerce application as shown in Figure 3.15. The Saga pattern can be used to coordinate transactions across services in this E-commerce application. A saga for order placement can be defined as follows:

- Shopping Cart Service: Creates order and emits *OrderCreated* event
- Order Service: Receives *OrderCreated* event, creates pending order, and emits *OrderPending* event.
- Pricing Service: Receives *OrderPending* event, calculates prices, and emits *OrderPriced* event.
- Inventory Service: Receives *OrderPriced* event, reserves inventory, and emits *InventoryReserved* event.
- Order Service: Receives *InventoryReserved* event, approves order, and emits *OrderApproved* event.
- Logistics Service: Receives *OrderApproved* event and schedules delivery.

Similarly, other sagas can be defined for workflows like order cancellation, payment capture, and refunds.

3.5 Observability Patterns

Microservices architecture has become mainstream for building large-scale, business-critical cloud-native applications. Microservices break down software into hundreds of independent, scalable components interacting to drive complex workflows. While this distributed approach has clear advantages like accelerated feature development and resilience, microservices also introduce complexities related to distributed services, dynamic scaling, and fragmented visibility. These factors impair the ability of developers and operators to understand and manage system behavior. Without system comprehension, developers cannot effectively build new features or troubleshoot issues in production. For operators, it becomes challenging to track Service Level Objectives (SLOs), optimize infrastructure spending, and prevent outages.

Observability Patterns address these challenges around microservices visibility and comprehension. Observability refers to techniques enabling teams to measure, understand, and improve system behavior. As opposed to mere monitoring, observability facilitates interpreting monitoring signals in the context of business and customer objectives.

Such observability into overall system behavior is invaluable for developers building new capabilities and operators running mission-critical software reliably, efficiently, and cost-effectively. Other benefits include faster root cause analysis of issues, proactive capacity planning based on usage trends, preventing outages, and optimizing infrastructure spends.

3.5.1 Log Aggregation Pattern

The log aggregation pattern is critical for observability in microservices architectures. Since a microservices application comprises many small services, logs get scattered across servers running different services. This makes debugging difficult.

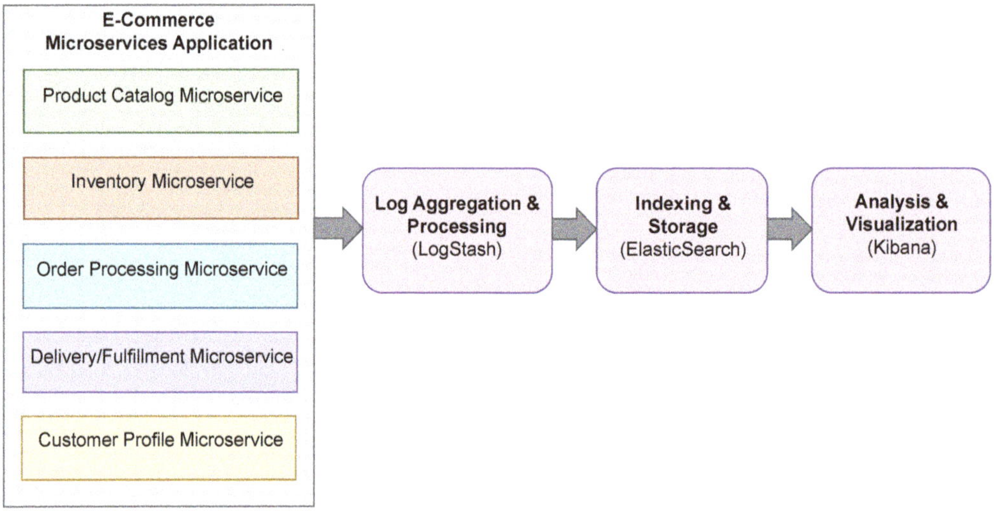

Figure 3.16: Using Log Aggregation pattern for an E-Commerce application

The log aggregation pattern collects logs from all microservice instances and aggregates them in a centralized log store. Log aggregators have three main components as follows:
- Data Collection: Lightweight agents are installed on all microservice hosts to collect application and system logs.
- Central Data Store: Collected log data is stored centrally in a searchable data store. Data is indexed for fields to enable filtering logs by attributes such as timestamps, log levels, and hosts, for instance.
- Data Analysis: Aggregated logs are analyzed using a powerful search and visualization engine. Users can search logs, create custom charts, set alerts for log patterns indicating errors, and find trends. Machine learning can also be applied to detect anomalies.

The log aggregation pattern has the following benefits:
- Enables centralized logging and monitoring instead of logging individual services
- Correlates logs spanning multiple services to simplify troubleshooting
- Helps identify issues like exceptions and performance bottlenecks
- Provides historical log data for auditing and compliance
- Real-time dashboards give operational visibility
- Alerts notify teams of application or infrastructure issues
- Aids optimization and capacity planning using log analytics

Let us look at an example of using the log aggregation pattern for an E-Commerce application as shown in Figure 3.16. The pattern is implemented as follows:
- All the microservices in the E-Commerce application (like Product Catalog Service, Order Management Service, Inventory Management, Customer Management, and

Delivery Management) stream logs to a centralized log aggregation system like ELK stack (that includes Elasticsearch, Logstash, and Kibana).

- The log aggregation system ingests logs from the disparate services and store them in a database like Elasticsearch. This provides a single place to access and analyze logs spanning services.
- Kibana dashboards on top of Elasticsearch provide real-time operational visibility. For example, dashboards can track order throughput, inventory levels, and shipping performance across the logistics network.
- Alerts can be set up to notify teams about issues. For instance, alerts for spikes in checkout errors, inventory stock-outs, delivery delays, etc. This enables rapid incident response.
- Log correlation across services aids debugging. For example, tracing a failed order end-to-end through the workflow spanning Order Service, Pricing Service, Inventory Service, etc.
- Log analytics provides insights into customer behavior from data across Customer Service, Recommendation Service, Order Service, etc. This helps in planning personalized promotions.

3.5.2   Distributed Tracing Pattern

Distributed tracing tracks the flow of requests across microservices in complex, distributed environments. It traces every step of a transaction, making reference data available during monitoring, debugging, and auditing.

The key concepts in distributed tracing are as follows:
- Trace: The overall distributed transaction that propagates across systems and processes.
- Span: A logical unit of work within a trace that has an operation name, start time, duration, and metadata.
- Tag: Key-value metadata that provides contextual information about a span.
- Log: Additional timestamped messages associated with a span providing debug or insight data.
- Span Context: The tracing state that propagates from parent to child spans and across process boundaries.
- Parent Span: The span that invokes an operation resulting in a child span being created.
- Child Span: The span created as a result of an operation invoked by a parent span.

Each external request gets assigned a unique trace ID which passes through all microservices touched by that request. All logs emitted by each microservice contain this trace ID, linking them to the specific end-to-end transaction.

The key steps are involved in distributed tracing are as follows:
- Generate a trace ID for every incoming external request.
- Propagate the ID across all microservices handling this request, generally by putting it in the request headers.
- All application logs should output the trace ID if enabled.
- Agents installed on microservice hosts collect and export tracing data in formats like OpenTracing.
- Tracing analysis tools aggregate, visualize, and monitor tracing data to provide distributed tracing views.

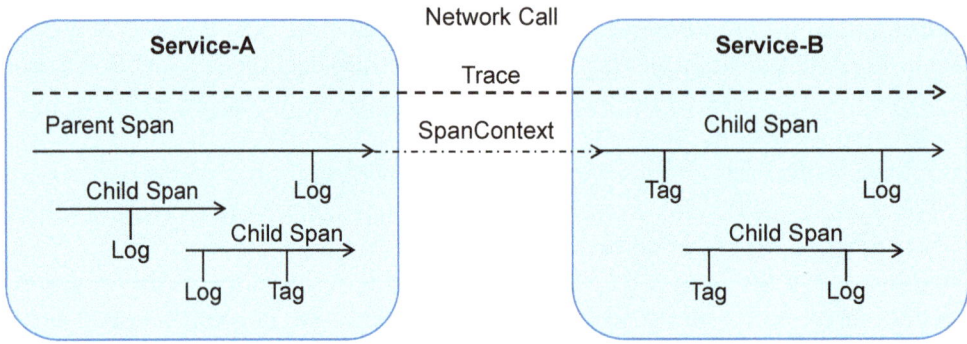

Figure 3.17: Distributed Tracing pattern

With hundreds of microservices, developers can't keep track of all dependencies. Tracing tools automatically construct visual transaction flows, depicting how requests get routed across services. Developers see which services called which other services, latency at each hop, and total transaction time.

The distributed tracing pattern has the following benefits:

- Visualize end-to-end transaction flows across all microservices, understanding how requests get routed
- Identify service dependencies automatically
- Pinpoint high-latency services or failures causing cascading downstream failures
- Gain code-level visibility into traces to debug issues faster
- Understand overall transaction performance and SLAs
- Enable filtering and segmentation of tracing data
- Correlate logs with traces to access logs for requests
- Integrate with monitoring tools like Grafana for alerts and metrics
- Faster resolution for microservices issues

Let us look at an example using the distributed tracing pattern for an E-Commerce application as shown in Figure 3.17. The pattern is implemented as follows:

- Every incoming customer request is assigned a unique trace ID that is propagated across all services that handle that request.
- The trace ID is inserted into all request headers and logged with all logs emitted by each service.
- A customer placing an order, for example, would trigger the Shopping Cart Service to create an order. This generates a trace ID that is sent to the Order Service when it is called.
- The Order Service forwards this trace ID to the Pricing Service when asking for order total calculation and also to the Inventory Management services to validate and commit inventory.
- Similarly, trace ID propagates downstream to Delivery Management and Customer Management systems.
- All logs across Order, Pricing, Inventory, Delivery, and Customer services are correlated by trace ID.

- If there is an issue with the order, the trace ID can be used to pull relevant logs across all services.
- Trace analysis tools create a visual end-to-end transaction flow for the order placement, showing how the request moved across all services.
- Linking distributed traces with a visualization tool like Grafana can provide visibility into order placement SLAs, metrics on trace durations, and alerts around traces exceeding SLAs.

3.5.3 Performance Metrics Pattern

The performance metrics pattern collects monitoring statistics from each microservice instance to provide centralized visibility into the entire software system. In monolithic applications, performance monitoring is straightforward as everything runs as a single process. In contrast, microservices applications comprise hundreds of services running across an elastic infrastructure. No single team has end-to-end visibility. The performance metrics pattern addresses this fragmented view via centralized collection and aggregation of metrics.

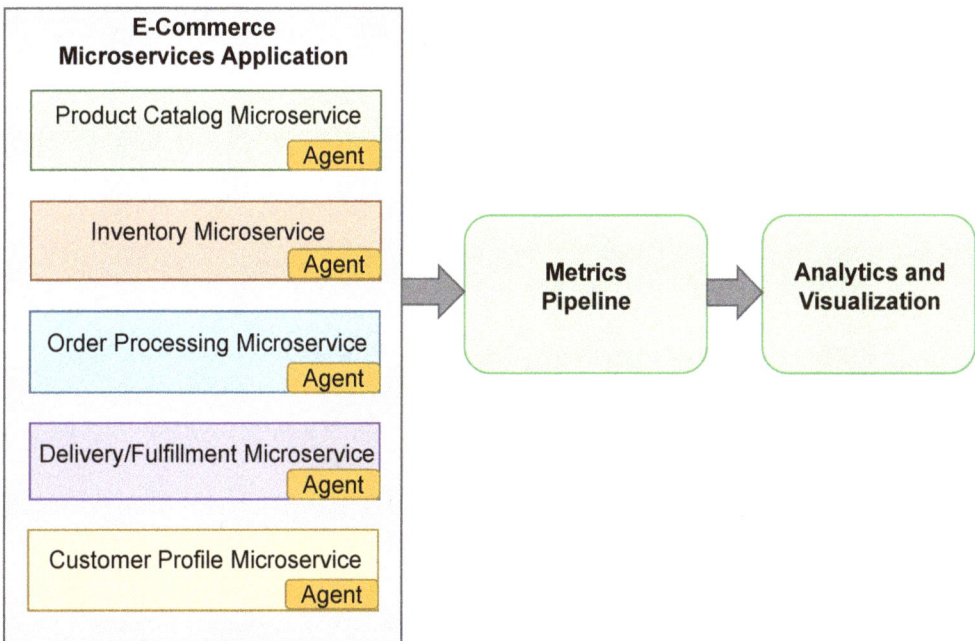

Figure 3.18: Using Performance Metrics pattern for an E-Commerce application

Every service instance in the application needs to be instrumented to export metrics like hardware (such as CPU, memory, I/O), software (such as request rates, response times, uptime, traffic), and business metrics (such as checkout conversions, orders per minute).

The performance metrics pattern has the following benefits:

- Provides centralized visibility into the performance of the entire microservices application, overcoming the fragmented view that results from hundreds of services

running across an elastic infrastructure.
- Enables easy debugging of performance issues across microservices without needing access to hosts.
- Facilitates performance testing to validate fixes to issues.
- Allows detection of trends to help teams scale infrastructure proactively to meet demand, keeping costs low.
- Supports creation of sophisticated dashboards and charts to slice and dice performance data, revealing insights into the application behavior.
- Alerts teams when performance thresholds are breached to avoid outages.
- Fundamental not just for monitoring reliability, but also for cost-effective operations of microservices.

Let us look at an example of using the performance metrics pattern for an E-Commerce application as shown in Figure 3.18. The pattern is implemented as follows:
- Agents and Instrumentation:
  - Deploy monitoring agents on all hosts running the microservices.
  - Instrument all services to export metrics such as HTTP request metrics, hardware metrics, custom business metrics, etc.
- Metrics Pipeline:
  - Agents aggregate and push all monitoring data to a central metrics database.
  - The metrics database handles ingestion from multiple hosts and relates metrics using attributes like service name and environment.
  - Mathematical aggregations (such as averages, percentiles, min, max) are applied.
- Analytics and Visualization:
  - Sophisticated dashboards, charts, and alerts are layered on top, providing insights into the application performance.
  - Grafana is popular for rich metrics visualization enabling teams to slice and dice data.
  - Create a dashboard for each business workflow such as order placement performance and catalog update performance, for instance.
  - Visualize request latency SLA compliance for key services like Order and Cart.
- Business Insights:
  - Show average checkout conversion rates across environments to analyze customer experience.
  - Track inventory utilization by warehouse to optimize inventory planning.
- Debugging:
  - Pinpoint the root cause services contributing to order placement performance issues.
  - Check if pricing rule updates affect order pricing performance.
  - Identify if inventory sync delays affect order fulfillment SLAs.

The performance metrics pattern does add complexity to the deployment and management of monitoring agents across the infrastructure. The volume of instrumentation data also grows exponentially with scale. Thus, the metrics pipeline needs to handle ingestion from thousands of hosts while making metrics searchable and consumable across teams. However, despite the overheads, the performance metrics pattern is hugely beneficial for managing a distributed microservices application cost-effectively.

3.5.4   Health Check Pattern

This pattern enables checking the health and availability of microservice instances before sending requests. Given the ephemeral nature of microservices, their availability keeps fluctuating. The health check pattern prevents directing traffic to unhealthy or overloaded instances which would fail or perform slowly.

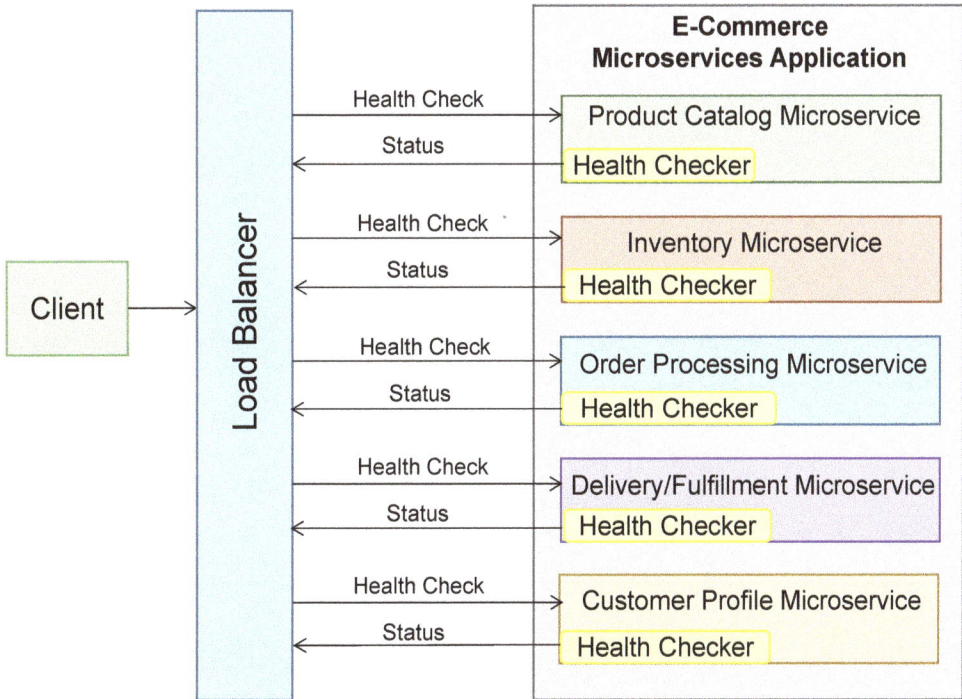

Figure 3.19: Using Health Check pattern for an E-Commerce application

Each service instance exposes a health check API endpoint. The endpoint runs self-diagnostics to assess if the instance can successfully serve requests currently. Simple checks verify if the process is running. Sophisticated checks may run integration tests against backend services to test connectivity.

A load balancer continually polls each instance on the health endpoint. Based on the response code, it determines whether to keep the instance in or remove it from the load balancer pool. For example, a 200 status code may signify the instance is healthy. Similarly, an API Gateway polls the health check endpoints periodically to check health status codes before routing traffic to service instances. Unhealthy instances are removed from the backend pool, preventing outages.

The health check pattern has the following benefits:
- Prevent outages by shifting traffic away from instances projected to fail soon
- Help scale instances based on health to maintain performance
- Pinpoint failures via status code patterns from health checks
- Implement gradual rollout/phased deployment of new versions

Let us look at an example of using the health check pattern for an E-Commerce application as shown in Figure 3.19. The pattern is implemented as follows:

- Each microservice exposes a health check endpoint that performs self-diagnostics.
- Product Catalog Service health check connects to the database and verifies that it can execute a simple query to validate database connectivity.
- Content Management Service health check checks if it can access the storage bucket for images/videos successfully.
- Warehouse Management Service health check runs a test query against the warehouse database and checks recent inventory updates to validate connectivity.
- Shopping Cart Service health check tests CRUD operations against a test cart in the database.
- Order Service health check validates workflows by executing a sample order.
- Pricing Service health check tests pricing rules against a predefined basket.
- Logistics Service health check makes test API calls to carrier systems to check connectivity.
- Customer Service health check connects to the database and verifies sample reads/writes.
- Recommendation Service health check runs sample recommendation engine logic.
- Customer Communication Service health check attempts to send test emails/SMS/push notifications.

Health checks, though simple, bring sanity to the volatile world of microservices. The pattern is invaluable for applications demanding high availability and also enables progressive delivery processes.

3.6   Deployment & Operational Patterns

Deploying software applications and keeping them running smoothly is critical yet challenging, especially for large, complex systems built on microservices architectures. Deployment and operational patterns provide proven solutions to tackle such challenges across the application lifecycle. These patterns allow software teams to release faster, reduce risks in rollouts, efficiently administer dynamic microservices architectures at scale, and build extremely resilient systems. Leveraging such patterns is key for successfully running modern applications with minimal downtime as teams embrace continuous delivery processes.

3.6.1   Blue-Green Deployment Pattern

The Blue-Green deployment pattern reduces risk and downtime when deploying new versions of applications and services by running two production environments. One stays active while the other remains inactive as the updated version gets deployed. This avoids impacting end users and allows safer testing before switching live traffic.

In traditional deployment models, updating applications requires bringing down the current production instance, deploying the update, restarting, and testing before finally opening up again to users. For complex microservices-based applications with many services, this approach leads to long downtimes and outage windows affecting users. Rollbacks in case of failures further compound headaches.

The Blue-Green pattern mitigates this by maintaining two identical production environments for the application that are as similar as possible.

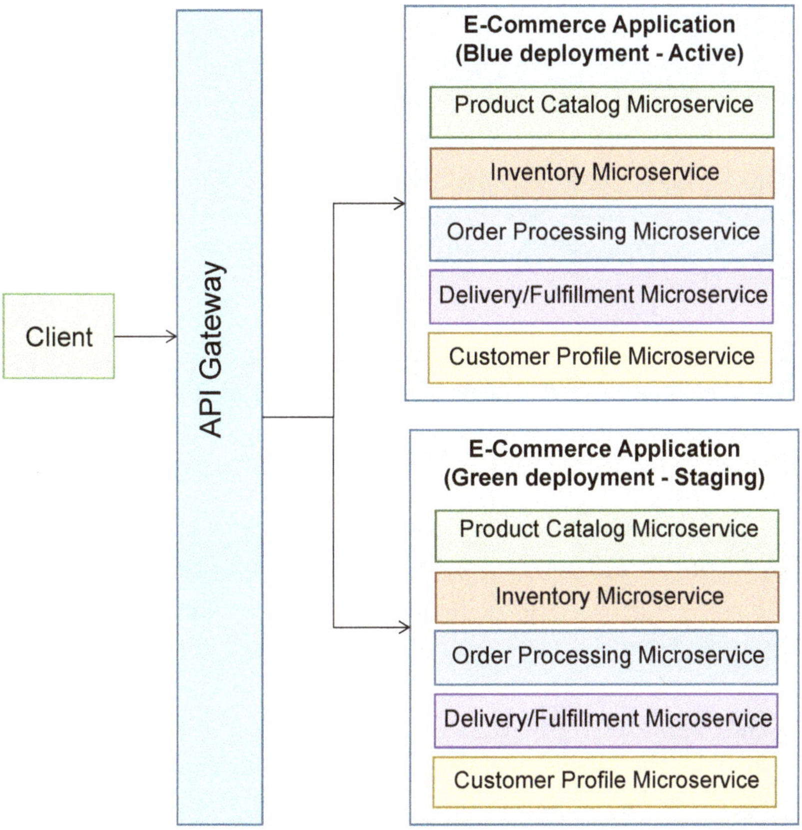

Figure 3.20: Using Blue-Green Deployment pattern for an E-Commerce application

The two production environments are as follows:
- Blue: Active and live environment handling all production traffic initially
- Green: Stands ready to take over when new versions are deployed

At any point, only one environment handles live user traffic while the other remains inactive. The Blue and Green must be replicas with the same software versions and configurations.

The Blue-Green deployment pattern has the following benefits:
- Zero downtime: There is zero downtime during releases as no user traffic is dropped.
- Lower risk rollbacks: Allows instantly switching back to the old environment if issues emerge.
- Faster and continuous testing: New environments enable extensive QA automation.
- Progressive traffic shifting: Route partial traffic first to reduce risk.
- Shorter release cycles: Small incremental updates can be launched more often.
- User experience: Seamless user experience even during frequent updates.
- Facilitates Continuous Delivery: Frequent updates without impacting users.

Let us look at an example of using the Blue-Green deployment pattern for an E-Commerce application as shown in Figure 3.20. Since the application has multiple critical microservices, using the Blue-Green pattern allows us to update them incrementally with no downtime.

For each service:
- Maintain two identical 'Blue' and 'Green' environments for the service.
- Develop and test updates to the service on local development environments.
- Deploy the v2 of the updated service into the idle Green environment.
- Perform QA automation, security, and performance testing on Green.
- Route a small percentage of live traffic to Green v2 from Blue v1.
- If testing passes, shift all traffic from old Blue v1 to new Green v2.
- The idle old environment Blue v1 remains intact as the new inactive environment for the next update.
- When v3 releases for the service, deploy it on old Blue v1, which now becomes Green.
- Repeat the process after full testing.

This approach lets us build, test, and roll out updates for each microservice independently without affecting others. Such automated incremental updates across services using the Blue-Green pattern allows continuous delivery of new features, fixing bugs faster, trying out changes with subsets of users, and preventing downtime.

The overhead of maintaining dual environments is offset by business gains from releases with shorter cycles, higher safety, and zero user impact. For most modern web and mobile applications built on microservices or cloud platforms, the Blue-Green pattern serves as a robust deployment strategy.

3.6.2 Service Registry Pattern

The Service Registry pattern enables service discovery by acting as a directory of available service instances. It provides a decoupling between service providers and consumers, allowing services to be dynamically discovered by name rather than hardcoding endpoints.

In a complex microservices architecture, services and their instances constantly get updated, moved, added, and removed. Hardcoding the endpoints of dependent services in consumer applications can lead to tight coupling, making changes painful.

The Service Registry provides a lookup service where each service instance registers its availability as it starts up. The registry maintains the state and location information for all registered services. When a consumer needs to access a service, it simply requests the service name from the registry, which returns the appropriate location and endpoints to access it. Consumers can then directly invoke this service dynamically based on the registry's response. This decoupling avoids the need to actively update the consumer applications.

Two common approaches for service discovery are:
- Client-side Discovery: With Client-side Discovery, the consumer handles all communication with the registry and instances. When first invoking a service, it queries the registry, caches the results, and balances loads across the instances. Caching avoids having to repeatedly access the registry. If new instances appear, the cache can be refreshed efficiently. Client-side discovery easily supports rich load balancing strategies across available instances.
- Server-side Discovery: With Server-side Discovery, the API Gateway handles service discovery on behalf of consumers. This saves duplicate effort across consumers and moves complexity to the Gateway tier. But the Gateway can become a performance bottleneck if all traffic routes via it, so appropriate scaling is vital.

Client-side discovery

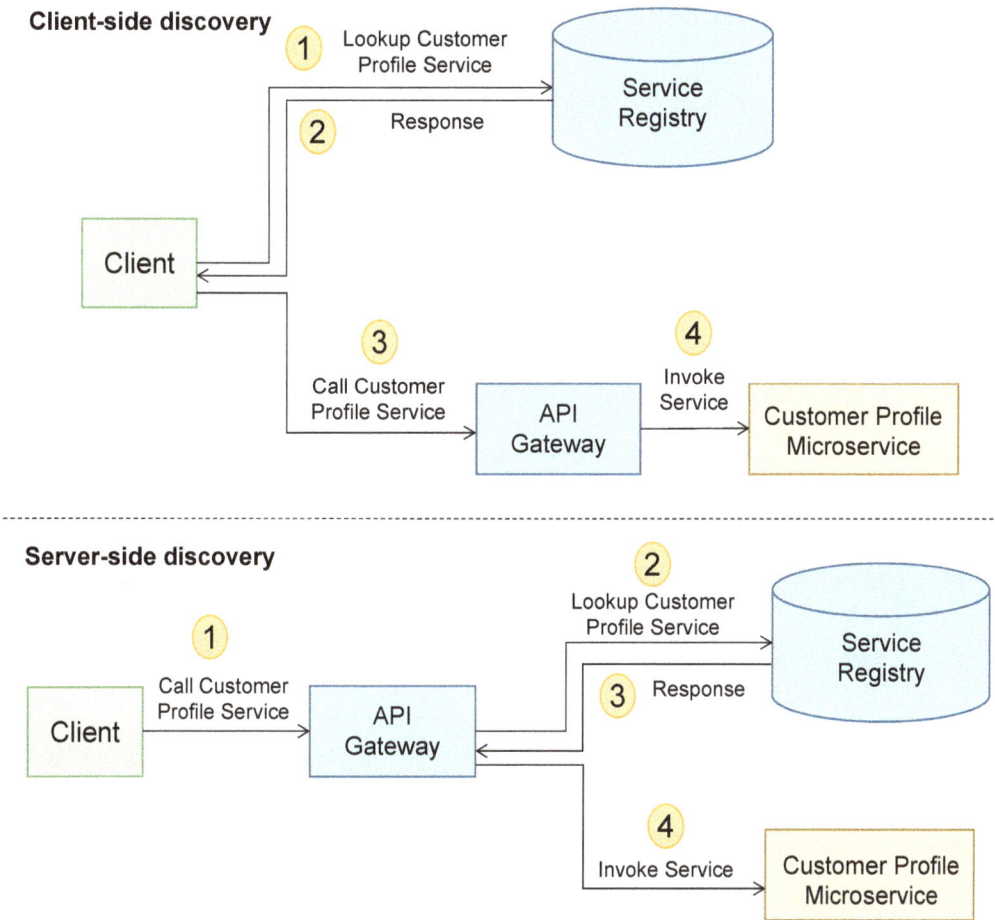

Server-side discovery

Figure 3.21: Using Service Registry pattern for an E-Commerce application

In either case, services have to register themselves with the registry when starting up. They also need to send heartbeat pings to indicate their health so that unhealthy instances can be removed. The service registry pattern has the following benefits:

- Decouples service providers from consumers, enabling independent management and evolution.
- Allows services to be dynamically discovered by name rather than hardcoding endpoints.
- Enables consumer applications to dynamically look up and invoke available service instances.
- Avoids the need to actively update consumer applications when service instances change.
- Supports various load balancing strategies across service instances.
- Reduces dependency management between providers and consumers.
- Loosely couples providers and consumers through an abstraction layer.
- Can enable both client-side and server-side discovery approaches.
- Facilitates scaling and resilience of services and consumer applications.

Let us look at an example of using the service registry pattern for an E-Commerce application as shown in Figure 3.21. The E-Commerce application has services like product catalog service, order management service, customer management, and delivery management service. A Service Registry would be deployed independently to act as a lookup directory for services. Each service would register with the registry on startup, providing a unique name, URL, and any metadata like supported protocols. Consumer-facing applications (like the shopping cart service or pricing service) would look up dependent services via the service registry instead of hardcoded endpoints. For example, when calculating pricing, the pricing service would ask the service registry for the URL of the product catalog service. The service registry returns the currently available URLs for the requested service. The consumer application can then load balance requests across the service instances.

3.6.3 External Configuration Store Pattern

The External Configuration Store pattern decouples an application's configuration from its code by extracting all configurable parameters into an external centralized configuration store. This avoids the need to rebuild and redeploy applications whenever configurations need to change.

In a typical application, configurations such as database URLs, credentials, feature flags, service endpoints, and other environment-specific parameters are hardcoded into configuration files that are packaged with the application code. This tight coupling makes changing configurations difficult as it requires rebuilding and redeploying the application whenever any parameters need to be updated.

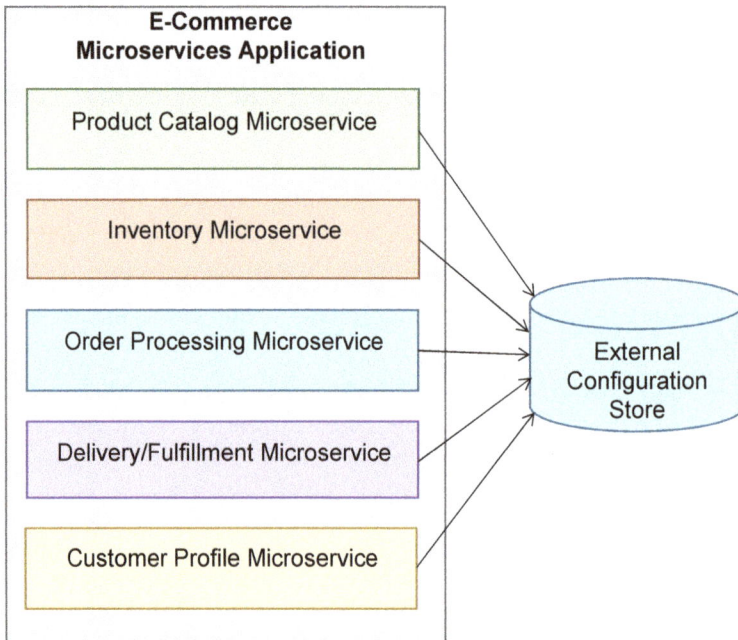

Figure 3.22: Using External Configuration Store pattern for an E-Commerce application

With the external configuration store pattern, all configurable parameters are centralized into an external store that is independent of the application code. The store acts as the single source of truth for configurations across all environments. Applications access this store at runtime to load the necessary config values.

When starting up, the application contacts the configuration store to load the initial config values. It also implements a polling mechanism to periodically check for changes, refreshing any updated parameters automatically without needing restarts or rebuilds.

The external configuration store pattern has the following benefits:

- Decouples configuration from code: Enables changing configuration without rebuilding or redeploying code.
- Faster configuration changes: Updates to external store immediately propagate without needing application restarts.
- Enables environment independence: Same code can run across environments by changing the external configuration.
- Centralizes configuration: Single source of truth for configuration instead of being scattered.
- Enhances security: Sensitive configurations such as credentials are stored securely, external to code.
- Supports continuous deployment: System behavior can be modified via configuration changes without touching code.
- Easier configuration management: External store provides a single interface to manage configurations.
- Aids local development: Override configuration easily for local testing.
- Facilitates adjusting parameters: Performance configurations can be tuned without changing code.
- Simplifies feature releases: Feature flags can be used to control rollout via configuration.

Let us look at an example of using the external configuration store pattern for an E-Commerce application as shown in Figure 3.22. A centralized configuration database can act as the store for all configurable parameters required by the various microservices of the E-Commerce application. For example:

- Product Catalog Service can store product classifications, pricing tiers, and inventory refresh intervals.
- Warehouse Management Service can store configurations related to warehouse locations, capacities, and SLA parameters.
- Order Service can store order expiration times, retry policies, and payment provider credentials.
- Logistics Service can store delivery radius thresholds, and carrier integration details.
- Pricing Service can store pricing rules, promotions, discounts, and tax configurations.
- Customer Service can store encryption keys, and password policy rules.

All services initialize by connecting to the configuration database to load the required parameters on startup. The services also implement a polling mechanism to automatically pick up any config changes from the store at runtime. This avoids embedding any environment-specific or variable configurations in the service code or containers. The same packaged services can thus work correctly when deployed across multiple environments by simply pointing them to the appropriate configuration database for that target environment.

3.6.4   Circuit Breaker Pattern

In complex distributed systems built on microservices, failures are inevitable. Services can fail due to high load, timeouts, faults, unhandled exceptions, and other reasons. In tightly coupled systems, one failing service can start a cascading failure chain reaction that ultimately leads to entire systems failing.

The Circuit Breaker pattern aims to prevent this by giving services the ability to detect failures, stop sending requests to unstable services, wait untill services recover, and then transparently resume operations. This ability to 'fail fast' and resume reliably helps build resilient systems.

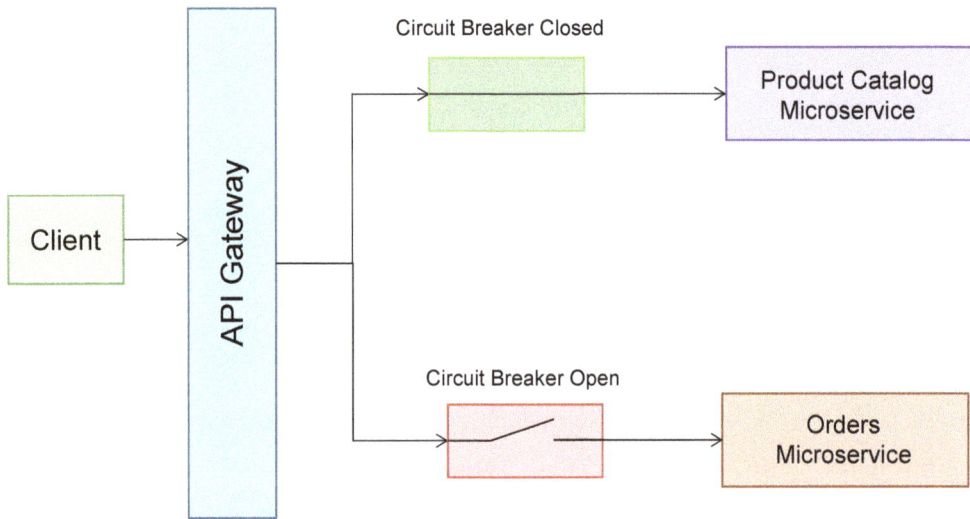

Figure 3.23: Using Circuit Breaker pattern for an E-Commerce application

The analogy to an electric circuit breaker holds well here. Just as electric circuit breakers trip switches when current crosses safe thresholds to prevent overload, similarly application circuit breakers monitor failing calls to downstream services. Once failures cross predefined thresholds, the breakers 'trip' and stop sending requests. This gives the opportunity for services to recover rather than being overwhelmed by a cascading failure effect.

After the breaker trips due to failures, all calls to that service immediately fail without waiting for timeouts or trying to process requests. Optionally, a fallback logic can be executed, such as loading data from a cache or returning a default value. The consumers here are isolated from the failing dependency.

After a suitable 'timeout' period set based on business requirements, the circuit breaker allows some requests to pass through to 'trial probe' the health of the service. If these requests are successful, it assumes service recovery and closes to resume all requests. If errors still occur in the trial, the timeout starts again.

The circuit breaker pattern has the following benefits:

- Prevents cascading failures in complex, distributed systems by failing fast when downstream services become unstable.

- Automates health checks and retries to give failing services the chance to recover independently.
- Improves system resiliency by isolating failures to individual services.
- Provides fallback logic to improve user experience when failures eventually impact end users.
- Reduces human intervention needed to monitor and manage failures through automated circuit state transitions.
- Enables reporting on metrics related to circuit state changes and failure rates.
- Allows 'trial probes' to check service health before resuming processing after failures.
- Containment of failures avoids entire systems going down due to one unstable service.

Let us look at an example of using the circuit breaker pattern for an E-Commerce application as shown in Figure 3.23. The pattern is implemented as follows:

- Calls to downstream services (like Product Catalog, Inventory Management, Pricing, and Logistics) are wrapped in a circuit breaker component.
- Failure thresholds (such as failure rate and latency) are configured for each circuit separately based on the priority and expected load.
- The Shopping Cart and Order services are good candidates for circuit isolation as failures in downstream catalog/inventory/pricing services should not take down order processing.
- If the Product Catalog service circuit trips open, the Shopping Cart service can show a fallback cached catalog or display a banner that catalog browsing is currently unavailable.
- Similarly, if the Inventory service circuit opens, the Order service can estimate delivery dates based on average statistics rather than actual stock checks.
- The Logistics circuit can have a higher failure threshold, and an open circuit would trigger default shipping rules rather than failing orders completely.
- Dashboards to monitor key circuit state metrics can help manually roll back bad service releases. Automated alerting integrated with the circuit breaker metrics can notify development teams if critical services become unstable.

Automated isolation of failure boundaries via circuit breakers, along with graceful fallback handling, prevents localized service issues from snowballing into system-wide outages.

3.7 Communication Patterns

Microservices have unique communication requirements compared to monolithic applications. Since services are independently developed and deployed, the interface contracts between services need to be well-defined. The network interactions also tend to be more chatty and complex with multiple services involved in business transactions. In addition, microservices should communicate asynchronously as much as possible to avoid cascading failures when one service is slow or fails.

There are several common communication patterns used in microservices to address these requirements such as Request-Response, Publish-Subscribe, Exclusive Pair, Remote Procedure Call, and Push-Pull. The communication requirements between any two services depend on factors like latency needs, traffic patterns, and coupling.

Microservices architects must match communication patterns to requirements rather than follow a one-size-fits-all approach. For example, synchronous request-response may make sense for a high-volume web API while asynchronous publish-subscribe is preferred for background notification services.

In this section, we provide an overview of common communication patterns for microservices, and when to use each approach. We discuss the benefits and drawbacks of each pattern and make recommendations on best practices.

3.7.1 Request-Response

Request-Response is the most ubiquitous communication pattern used in microservices architectures. It is typically implemented using REST APIs over HTTP. In this pattern, a service makes a request to another service via its HTTP API and waits for the response before continuing processing. The request usually contains some payload like JSON data.

REST leverages standard HTTP methods like GET, POST, PUT, DELETE to implement CRUD (create, retrieve, update, delete) operations. Since HTTP is ubiquitous, REST APIs provide an easy way for services to expose their capabilities and integrate with each other. There is a large ecosystem of tools and middleware for building, documenting, testing, and consuming REST APIs. Figure 3.24 shows the request-response communication pattern.

Unlike asynchronous messaging, request-response minimizes latency since the caller waits for the result. This makes it suitable for user-facing services that require low latency like web servers and API gateways. The request-response pattern also allows easier tracing of business transactions that span multiple services. Since each service handles one request at a time, it simplifies reasoning about workflows.

However, there are some downsides of the request-response pattern. Firstly, it can lead to very chatty communication between services since fulfilling one user request might require multiple backend requests. This can result in increased network traffic and higher latencies. Secondly, it introduces tight temporal coupling between services. If a backend service is slow or unavailable, it cascades failures to all the dependent services.

Some best practices around using the request-response pattern effectively are:
- Define API contracts upfront using OpenAPI or similar formats
- Make APIs coarser-grained to minimize chatty communication
- Use API Gateways to aggregate requests and cache responses
- Implement client-side load balancing and retries
- Set timeouts on outbound requests to prevent catastrophic backlogs
- Design APIs for backward and forward compatibility

The request-response pattern is well-suited for user-facing services, but teams should be cautious about overusing it for service-to-service communication. Combining REST APIs with asynchronous event-based communication can balance these trade-offs.

3.7.2 Publish-Subscribe

Publish-subscribe (pub-sub) is an asynchronous messaging pattern where sender services publish event messages, and receiver services subscribe to events they are interested in processing. This decouples the interacting services by providing temporal and referential decoupling. The sender does not need to know the receivers upfront, and the exchange is not temporally coupled.

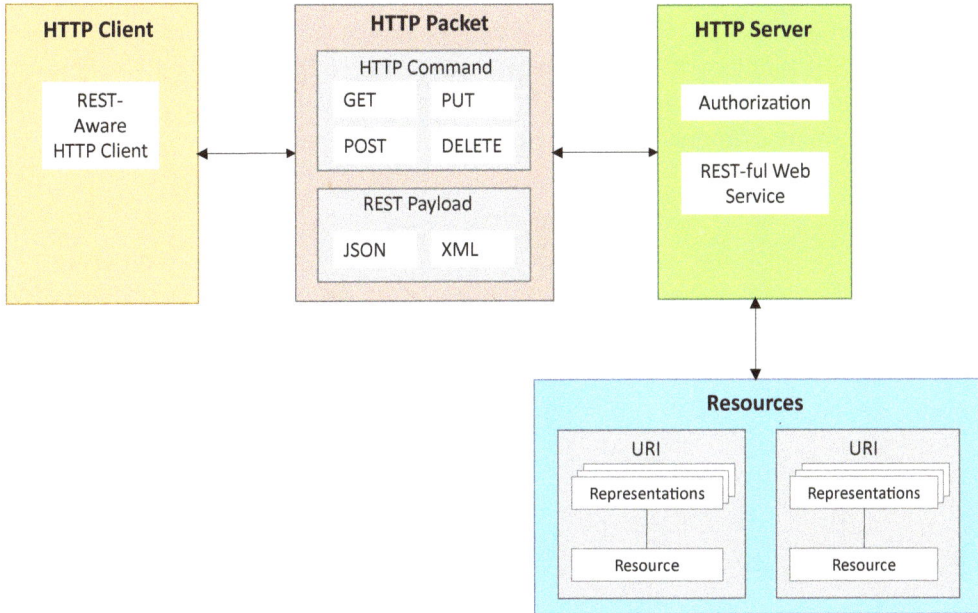

Figure 3.24: Request-Response communication pattern

Publish-subscribe requires an intermediate message broker that buffers and routes event messages. Services do not communicate directly. Popular choices for brokers include MQTT, RabbitMQ, and Kafka. The broker also allows fan-out of messages to multiple subscribers efficiently.

The publish-subscribe pattern provides several benefits for microservices architectures, including enabling push-based updates from publishing services to interested subscribers, decoupling services across time, space, and synchronization needs, and allowing fan-out to multiple subscribed services. Subscribers can also selectively subscribe only to events they care about. Publish-subscribe messaging adds reliability and loose coupling between event producers and consumers. For example, an E-Commerce Order service can publish an *OrderCreated* event that other services like shipping and notification can subscribe to asynchronously. This prevents tight temporal coupling and downstream failures.

However, there are some drawbacks to consider as well. The publish-subscribe pattern adds complexity in operating and scaling centralized message brokers. There are also no guarantees that events will be processed or received in order if subscriber services crash. Subscribers may receive duplicate or redundant messages, and the pattern requires defining standardized event schemas and versioning.

Some best practices for using the publish-subscribe pattern effectively are:
- Define schemas for events using JSON Schema or Protobuf
- Make events self-contained with all necessary data
- Add metadata like IDs, timestamps, and version numbers
- Allow clients to specify delivery guarantees like at-least-once
- Set TTL on events to prevent unbounded accumulation
- Plan for duplicates and inconsistent event ordering

Figure 3.25 shows the publish-subscribe communication pattern. Publish-subscribe messaging is an essential pattern for asynchronous communication and integration between microservices. It complements request-based interactions by providing push notifications and event streaming. Combining REST APIs with asynchronous publish-subscribe provides scalable and resilient communication architectures for microservices.

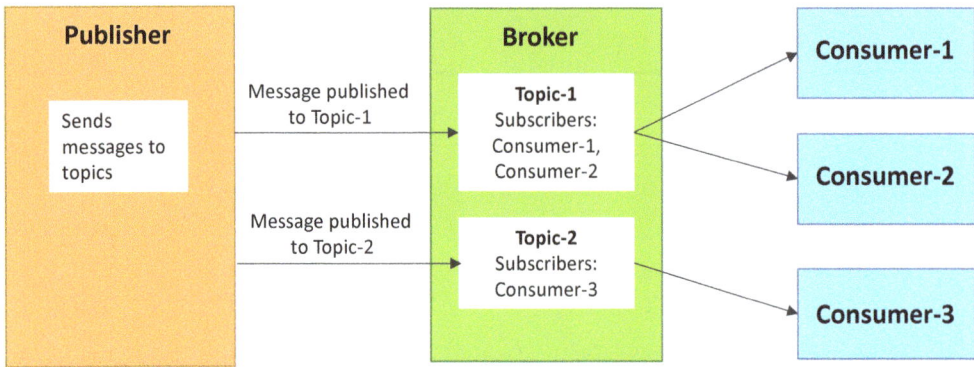

Figure 3.25: Publish-Subscribe communication pattern

3.7.3 Exclusive Pair

The exclusive pair pattern represents a long-lived, low-latency bidirectional communication channel between two services. This is enabled by protocols like WebSocket or Socket.io, which allow a persistent connection between a client and server, unlike transient HTTP requests.

The exclusive-pair pattern establishes a persistent, low-latency, full-duplex, and bidirectional communication channel between two microservices. It is useful for building real-time applications like chat, multiplayer games, live data streaming, and collaborative editing where millisecond latency and instant data syncing are required. The main advantage over request-response is minimized latency since messages can be sent instantly when data changes rather than polling. It also avoids message broker overhead.

However, exclusive-pair has limitations in scalability due to the direct peer-to-peer connection, which does not fan out, along with the potential waste of idle resources. Teams should use exclusive-pair judiciously for latency-sensitive data while leveraging asynchronous patterns like publish-subscribe and message queues more broadly. Careful API design and system constraints are needed to avoid misuse for high data volumes.

Some best practices for using the exclusive pair pattern effectively are:
- Establish the connection using secure web protocols like HTTPS/WSS
- Implement reconnect logic to resume after disruptions
- Send keep-alive pings to detect dead connections
- Batch messages to reduce TCP packet overhead
- Avoid transferring large messages or files over the socket
- Employ a sub-protocol for application-level messages
- Set resource limits for the number of connections per service

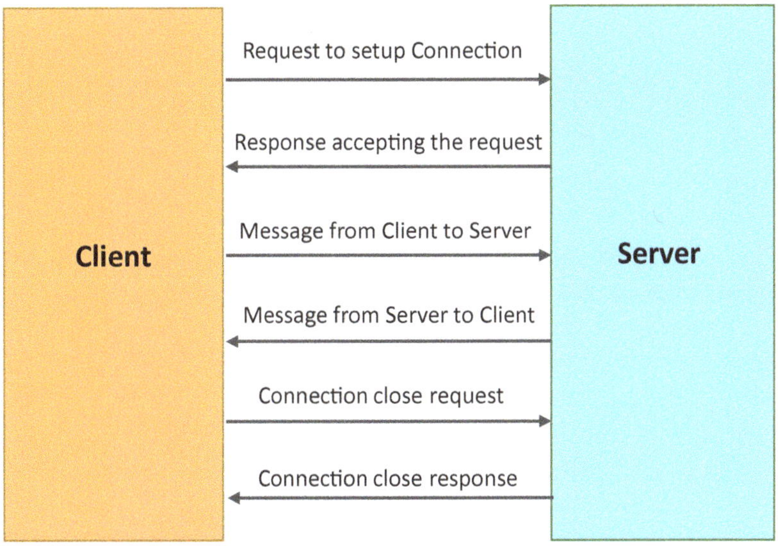

Figure 3.26: Exclusive-pair communication pattern

Figure 3.26 shows the exclusive-pair communication pattern. The exclusive pair pattern allows building real-time services with millisecond latency. It complements asynchronous patterns like publish-subscribe or message queues which have higher overhead.

3.7.4 Remote Procedure Call

Remote Procedure Call (RPC) is a communication pattern that allows a program to call a function or procedure on another system or service. It provides the abstraction of a local function call but executes the function remotely. The RPC pattern has become popular for microservices with frameworks like gRPC.

gRPC is a modern open-source high-performance RPC framework that is useful for communication between microservices. It uses protocol buffers (protobuf) over HTTP/2 for service definition and messaging. gRPC enables services to define request and response schemas using protocol buffers, which generate code for serialization. The gRPC framework then handles the client-server communication using HTTP/2 as the transport layer.

Some of the key benefits of using gRPC over REST APIs are its contract-first approach enabled by protocol buffers, which define the service contract explicitly upfront. This provides better documentation and compliance. gRPC also uses efficient binary serialization rather than JSON or XML, which reduces payload size. Support for bidirectional streaming allows long running stateful calls between services, which is difficult with REST. gRPC has built-in service discovery and load balancing features that simplify client-side load distribution. gRPC tooling exists for many programming languages, enabling easier polyglot microservices.

However, gRPC has some limitations compared to REST APIs. gRPC does not leverage existing HTTP servers and proxies, so additional gateways are required to expose gRPC APIs externally. Browser support for gRPC is still emerging, so REST is better for user-facing applications. The protocol buffer payloads are also not human-readable, which makes debugging harder than REST APIs. Code generation is required on the client and server for serialization, which adds complexity to the build process.

Some best practices for using gRPC effectively are:
- Use protocol buffers for internal APIs, and REST for external
- Implement client-side load balancing and retry logic
- Set timeouts on gRPC calls to prevent hanging requests
- Use TLS and authentication for secure service-to-service communication
- Log and monitor gRPC calls to troubleshoot latency issues

Figure 3.27 shows how to use gRPC for an E-Commerce application. gRPC provides better performance and developer productivity over REST when defining internal service-to-service APIs by leveraging code generation, binary serialization, and bidirectional streaming. For user-facing APIs, REST is likely more appropriate due to wider language and browser support. Using gRPC internally and REST externally combines the benefits of both approaches.

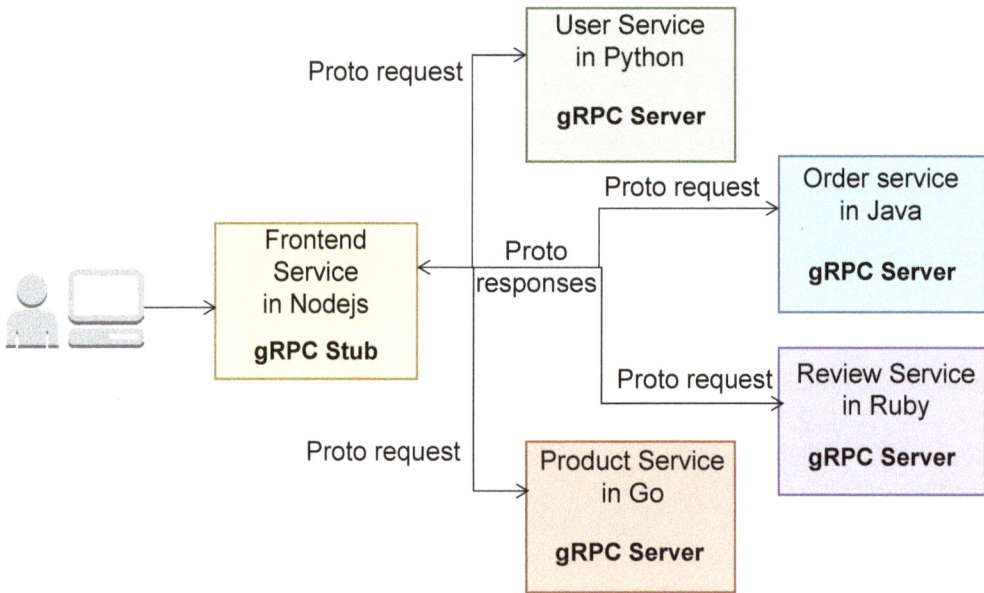

Figure 3.27: Remote Procedure Call communication pattern

3.7.5 Push-Pull

The push-pull pattern involves asynchronously sending messages from producers to consumers via an intermediary message queue or broker. Producers can reliably buffer messages in the queue even when consumers are busy or slow. Consumers can pull messages from the queue at their own pace.

This pattern decouples the production and consumption of messages across time, space, and synchronization boundaries. Popular implementations include Kafka, RabbitMQ, Amazon SQS, etc. The push-pull communication pattern provides several benefits through the use of message queues, including decoupling producers from consumers, smoothing traffic spikes, persisting messages for reliability, and allowing messages to be consumed in a different order than produced. Additionally, queues enable fan-out to multiple consumers and rate limiting on the consumer side.

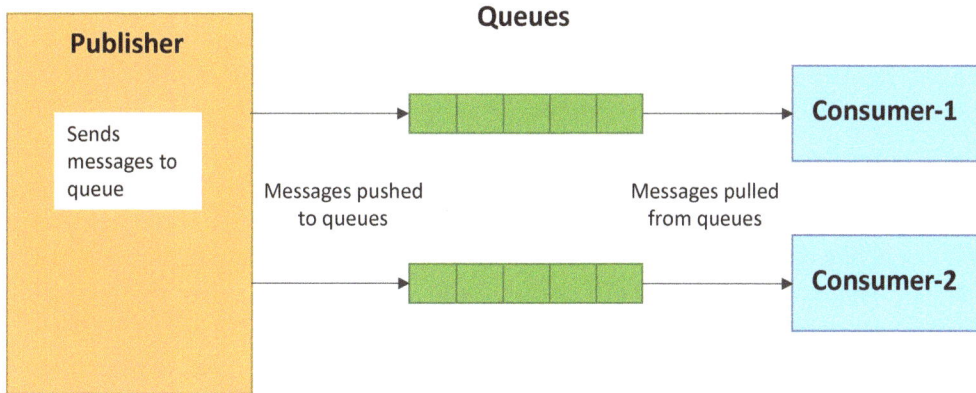

Figure 3.28: Push-Pull communication pattern

However, there are also some drawbacks to consider. Using queues adds complexity and delivery latency, requires monitoring queue sizes, and may result in out-of-order or duplicated messages that need duplicate detection. Queues provide useful capabilities but also incur operational overheads that should be evaluated when considering a push-pull architecture.

Some best practices when using the push-pull communication pattern are:
• Make each message self-contained with all necessary context
• Prefer smaller messages for efficiency
• Support multiple delivery policies like at least once or exactly once
• Do not use queues as a database for large volumes of data
• Monitor queue size as a metric for system health
• Implement retries with exponential backoff for consumers
• Use separate queues per message type or workload

Figure 3.28 shows the push-pull communication pattern. Message queues and brokers enable asynchronous messaging flows in microservices. They add reliability through persistence and decoupling. When used judiciously, push-pull messaging helps build scalable and resilient systems.

Summary

In this chapter, we provided a comprehensive guide to architectural patterns for building and operating microservices-based systems. As microservice architectures gains rapid mainstream adoption, recurring challenges keep emerging around distributed state, dynamic scaling, fault isolation, and end-to-end visibility. We presented a catalog of microservices design patterns that encode proven solutions to these distributed computing concerns based on real-world industry experience and academic research. We covered decomposition patterns that offer systemic ways to break down monolithic applications into well-encapsulated microservices guided by principles like domain-driven design and business capabilities microservices guided by principles like domain-driven design and business capabilities alignment. These patterns include decomposition by business capability, decomposition by subdomain, decomposition by transaction, and strangler pattern. Next, we presented composition patterns which are essential for integrating distributed microservices capabilities into unified application experiences. These patterns include Aggregator, API Gateway, Proxy, Client-Side Composition, Chained Microservices, and Branched Microservices. Next, we described database architecture patterns tailored for decentralized data persistence across services including Database per Service, Shared Database per Service, CQRS, Event Sourcing, and Saga pattern. Next, we covered observability patterns like Log Aggregation, Distributed Tracing, Performance Metrics, and Health Check pattern, that help developers trace requests and diagnose issues across cloud-native environments. Next, we described deployment and operational patterns including Blue-Green Deployment, Service Registry, External Configuration Store, and Circuit Breaker pattern. Finally, we described the common microservices communication patterns such as Request-Response, Publish-Subscribe, Exclusive Pair, Remote Procedure Call, and Push-Pull. The microservices patterns presented in this chapter can serve as an essential reference manual for enterprise architects and developers adopting microservice architectures.

4
DESIGN METHODOLOGIES FOR MICROSERVICES APPLICATIONS

THIS CHAPTER COVERS

- REST Web Services
- Cloud Component Model (CCM)
- Serverless Architecture
- Event-Driven Architecture
- Model View Controller (MVC)

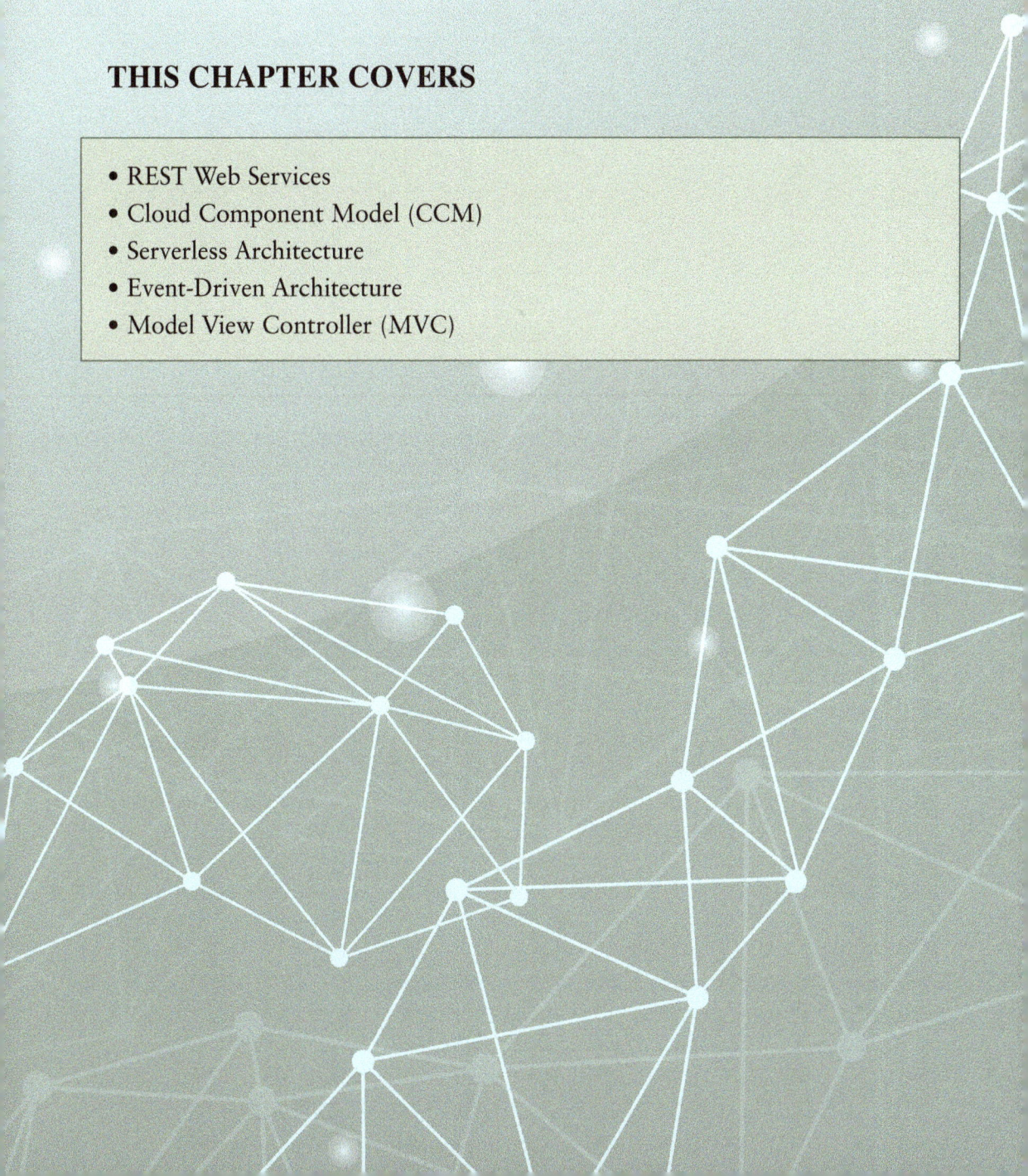

4.1 Introduction

Microservices architecture has rapidly grown in popularity for building scalable, resilient, and maintainable enterprise applications. It involves architecting an application as a collection of small, independent services where each service implements specific business capabilities. These services communicate via well-defined APIs (typically REST APIs over HTTP). Each service can be developed, upgraded, tested, and deployed independently by small, decentralized teams.

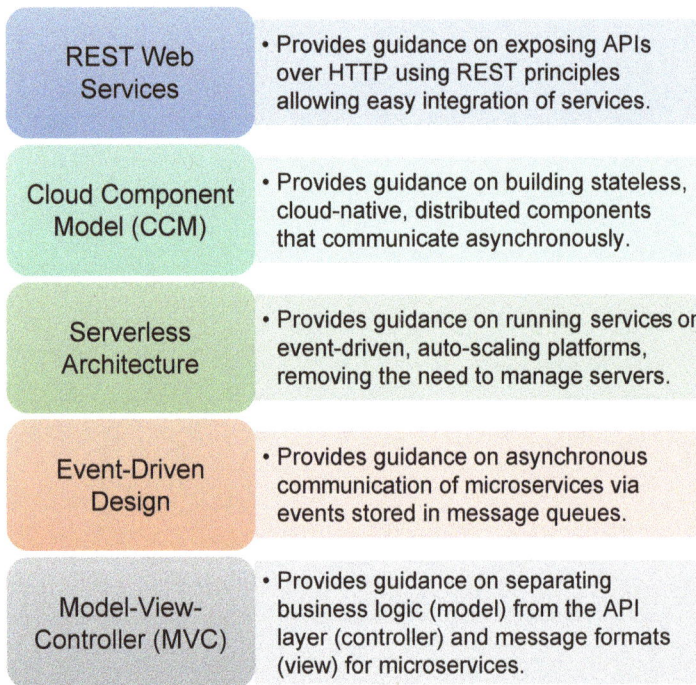

Figure 4.1: Design methodologies for microservices applications

While microservices offer numerous benefits like accelerating feature delivery, enabling technology diversity across stacks, and increasing organizational agility, they also introduce several complexity challenges such as distributed state management across services, handling of complex distributed transactions, data consistency, service decomposition, standardizing service contracts, service communication, managing deployments, and monitoring.

Additionally, teams new to microservices often struggle to identify service boundaries, implement resilient communication protocols between services, address cross-cutting concerns like security, events, and transactions, and set up effective DevOps tooling. These microservices design and development complexities can overwhelm teams, leading to tightly coupled services, inconsistent interfaces, difficulty troubleshooting failures, and eventually impact the productivity that microservices aim to offer.

This highlights the critical need for comprehensive design methodologies aligned specifically to microservices architectures that provide prescriptive guidance across domains like:

- Decomposing monoliths into independent microservices

- Standardizing service contracts and communication mechanisms
- Implementing reliable inter-service communication with loose coupling
- State management, transactions, and data consistency across services
- Optimized deployment topologies across dynamic infrastructure
- Monitoring, logging, and troubleshooting distributed services

In this chapter, we present design methodologies for microservices applications such as REST Web Services, Cloud Component Model, Serverless Architecture, Event-driven Design, and Model-View-Controller. Figure 4.1 summarizes the design methodologies. These design methodologies consist of proven architectural patterns, design guidelines, communication contracts, and infrastructure mapping strategies.

Adopting these methodologies enables architects and developers to avoid common pitfalls when designing microservices. These guiding methodologies allow teams to build systems focused on loose coupling, resilient inter-service communication, decentralized data management, and standardized interfaces required for reliability at scale.

Using guiding methodologies allows teams to get microservices architecture right from the start and reap benefits like accelerated delivery, reliability at scale, and continuous innovation across large engineering groups rather than ending up with a complex web of interconnected services.

4.2 REST Web Services

Representational State Transfer (REST) [15] is a set of architectural principles by which you can design web services and web APIs that focus on a system's resources and how resource states are addressed and transferred.

Microservices architecture has become popular for building scalable and maintainable software systems. The key idea is to architect an application as a collection of loosely coupled services that can evolve independently. Effective communication between these services is vital for realizing the benefits of microservices. This is where RESTful APIs prove invaluable, serving as the glue that connects microservices.

A RESTful web service exposes API endpoints that enable client applications to access and manipulate textual representations of web resources using a uniform and predefined set of stateless operations.

The REST architectural constraints apply to the components, connectors, and data elements within a distributed hypermedia system. The REST architectural constraints are as follows:

- **Client-Server**: The principle behind the client-server constraint is the separation of concerns. For example, clients should not be concerned with the storage of data, which is a concern of the server. Similarly, the server should not be concerned about the user interface, which is a concern of the client. The separation allows the client and server to be independently developed and updated.
- **Stateless**: Each request from the client to server must contain all of the information necessary to understand the request and cannot take advantage of any stored context on the server. The session state is kept entirely on the client.
- **Cacheable**: Cache constraint requires that the data within a response to a request be implicitly or explicitly labeled as cacheable or non-cacheable. If a response is

cacheable, then a client cache is given the right to reuse that response data for later, similar requests. Caching can partially or completely eliminate some interactions and improve efficiency and scalability.

- **Layered System**: Layered system constraint constrains the behavior of components such that each component cannot see beyond the immediate layer with which they are interacting. For example, a client cannot tell whether it is connected directly to the end server or an intermediary along the way. System scalability can be improved by allowing intermediaries to respond to requests instead of the end server, without the client having to do anything different.
- **Uniform Interface**: Uniform Interface constraint requires that the method of communication between a client and a server must be uniform. Resources are identified in the requests (by URIs in web-based systems) and are themselves separate from the representations of the resources that are returned to the client. When a client holds a representation of a resource, it has all the information required to update or delete the resource (provided the client has the required permissions). Each message includes enough information to describe how to process the message.
- **Code on demand**: Servers can provide executable code or scripts for clients to execute in their context. This constraint is the only one that is optional.

A RESTful web service is a web API implemented using HTTP and REST principles. RESTful web service is a collection of resources that are represented by URIs. A RESTful web API has a base URI (e.g., http://example.com/api/tasks/). The clients send requests to these URIs using the methods defined by the HTTP protocol (e.g., GET, PUT, POST, or DELETE). A RESTful web service can support various Internet media types (JSON being the most popular media type for RESTful web services). Figure 4.2 lists the HTTP request methods and actions.

4.2.1   Using REST Principles for Microservices

Microservices aim to decompose monoliths into independent, collaborating services. But distributing business capabilities across multiple services requires an interoperable mechanism for them to communicate effectively. This is where REST principles help. Some key reasons why REST is an ideal approach for microservices are:

- **Separate client-server concern**: Clear separation of client and server keeps services focused.
- **Statelessness**: Services do not have to maintain conversational state.
- **Decoupling**: Well-defined interfaces decouple services from each other.
- **Lightweight**: REST avoids overhead with simple standards like HTTP.
- **Scalability**: Stateless services can be called independently, improving scalability.
- **Reliability**: REST reliably separates failure domains, limiting cascading failures.
- **Reusability**: Clear API contracts allow reusable implementation of services.

Every microservice exposes a REST interface to communicate. Other services and applications interact solely through that interface using simple HTTP requests for full decoupling. The stateless constraints facilitate horizontal scaling while standardized interfaces ease maintainability and evolution.

HTTP Method	Resource Type	Action	Example
GET	Collection URI	List all the resources in a collection	http://example.com/api/tasks/ (list all tasks)
GET	Element URI	Get information about a resource	http://example.com/api/tasks/1/ (get information on task-1)
POST	Collection URI	Create a new resource	http://example.com/api/tasks/ (create a new task from data provided in the request)
POST	Element URI	Generally not used	
PUT	Collection URI	Replace the entire collection with another collection	http://example.com/api/tasks/ (replace entire collection with data provided in the request)
PUT	Element URI	Update a resource	http://example.com/api/tasks/1/ (update task-1 with data provided in the request)
DELETE	Collection URI	Delete the entire collection	http://example.com/api/tasks/ (delete all tasks)
DELETE	Element URI	Delete a resource	http://example.com/api/tasks/1/ (delete task-1)

Figure 4.2: HTTP request methods and actions

4.2.2 Building RESTful Web Services

Constructing robust RESTful web services suited for microservices involves adhering to core design principles across resources, HTTP verbs, URIs, and responses. Let us look at the steps involved in building RESTful web services:

1. Identify Resources

The first step is to identify key business entities that the web services aim to provide, such as users, accounts, and products, for instance. These form the resources that clients can access and manipulate. Define each resource with a unique URI.

2. Support HTTP Methods

Expose standard CRUD (Create, Read, Update, Delete) operations on resources using HTTP methods such as GET (retrieve resource), POST (create new resource), PUT (update existing resource), and DELETE (delete resource).

3. Structure URIs

URIs should follow a consistent, hierarchical scheme to form a clear URL structure for resources. For example, for a user service, some patterns include:
- /users
- /users/{userID}
- /users/{userID}/orders

4. Define Responses

Use consistent naming and structures for response payloads in JSON/XML for clarity. Include relevant metadata such as timestamps and status codes.

5. Implement Hypermedia Controls

Hypermedia links guide state transitions. Responses can include links to details or related actions. For example, the response to an API to retrieve product details in an E-Commerce application may contain links to other related products.

6. Add Security

Enforce authentication, access control, and HTTPS for security. OAuth can be used for managing authorization for secure access.

7. Handle Errors

Use appropriate HTTP status codes to classify response errors for robust error handling.

8. Document Everything

Maintain detailed documentation of resources, URIs, and request/response structure.

4.2.3 Benefits of RESTful Web Services for Microservices

Adhering to REST architectural constraints and API best practices provides several advantages for building reliable, scalable microservices:

- **Loose Coupling**: Well-defined interfaces using resources/HTTP verbs decouple services.
- **Increased Cohesion**: Services can focus on their core capability.
- **Improved Maintainability**: Standards facilitate systematic changes.
- **Enhanced Scalability**: Stateless communication allows easy replication of services.
- **Reliability**: Isolation of failure domains prevents cascading failures.
- **Ease of Evolution**: New API versions can be added without disruption.
- **Developer Friendliness**: Uniform interfaces encourage adoption and testing.

REST defines a mature set of design principles for crafting web services tailored to enable distributed microservices architectures. REST guides the architectural decisions towards building resilient, reliable, and evolvable systems.

4.3 Cloud Component Model (CCM)

The Cloud Component Model (CCM) [17] provides a comprehensive approach for modeling, implementing, and deploying microservices-based cloud applications. It utilizes a component-based design, standardized interfaces between components, asynchronous communication, and external state storage to enable building distributed, event-driven systems.

CCM provides a component-based approach for rapidly building cloud-based applications using reusable and loosely coupled components. It aligns well with microservices principles and can simplify the process of developing microservices.

CCM is an architectural approach for microservices-based cloud applications that are not tied to any specific programming language or cloud platform. Applications designed with the CCM approach can have innovative hybrid deployments in which different components

of an application can be deployed on cloud infrastructure and platforms of different cloud
vendors. CCM allows better portability, interoperability, and scalability by decoupling
application components and providing asynchronous communication mechanisms. CCM
makes maintainability of cloud applications easier as the functionality of individual components
of the application can be improved or upgraded independently of other components. CCM
approach provides cost benefits for cloud applications as components can be carefully mapped
to cloud resources. Cost benefits come by scaling cloud resources up, or scaling out, only for
those components which require additional computing capacity.

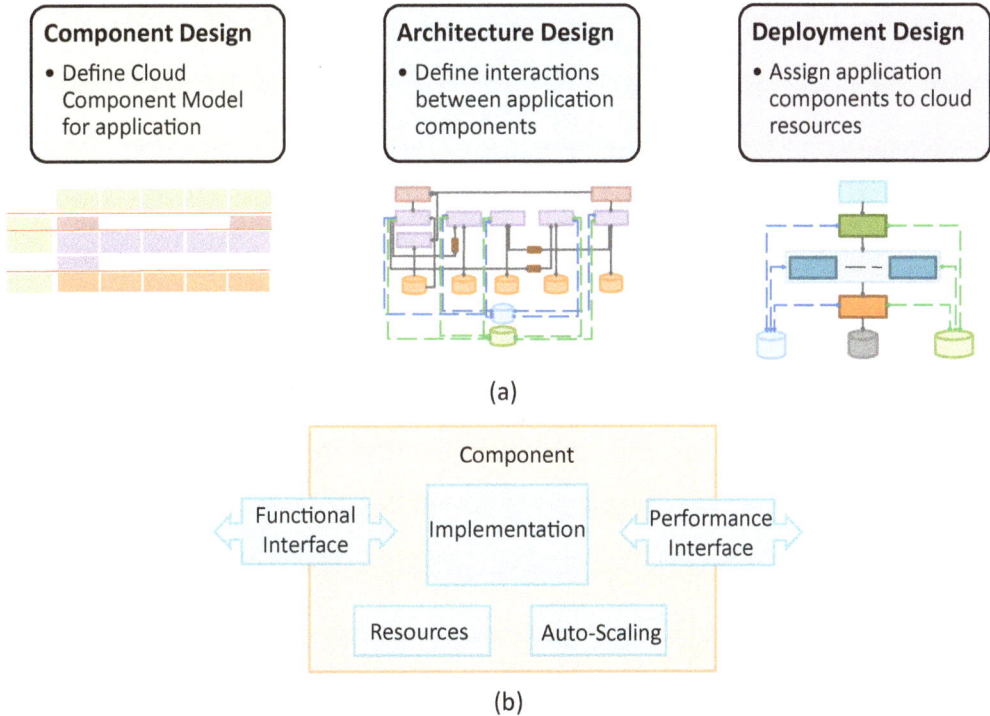

(a)

(b)

Figure 4.3: (a) Steps involved in application design using Cloud component model
methodology, (b) Architecture of a CCM component.

Key aspects of CCM include:
- Components: Self-contained units of functionality that communicate via well-defined
  interfaces. Similar to microservices.
- Loose coupling: Components have little to no knowledge about each other and
  communicate asynchronously. This enables independent scaling.
- Statelessness: Application state is managed externally in a database rather than within
  components. Allows flexibility in scaling components.
- Standard interfaces: Components interact via standard protocols like HTTP and
  RESTful APIs for easy integration.

4.3.1   Using CCM Principles for Microservices

CCM breaks down application design into three phases - component design, architecture design, and deployment design as shown in Figure 4.3(a). It focuses on decomposing application functionality into shared and reusable components that can be combined and deployed in multiple ways.

Component Design

In the first step, a Cloud Component Model is created for the application based on a comprehensive analysis of the application's functions and building blocks. Cloud Component Model allows identifying the building blocks of a cloud application which are classified based on the functions performed and type of cloud resources required. Each building block performs a set of actions to produce the desired outputs for other components. Figure 4.3(b) shows the architecture of a CCM component. Each component takes specific inputs, performs a pre-defined set of actions, and produces the desired outputs. Components offer their functions as services through a functional interface that can be used by other components. Components report their performance to a performance database through a performance interface. Components have several resources, such as web pages, images, documents, and database tables. Auto-scaling performance constraints and conditions can be specified for each component. The component-based approach applies to both web-based applications and mobile applications. Figure 4.4 shows a CCM component map for an E-Commerce application.

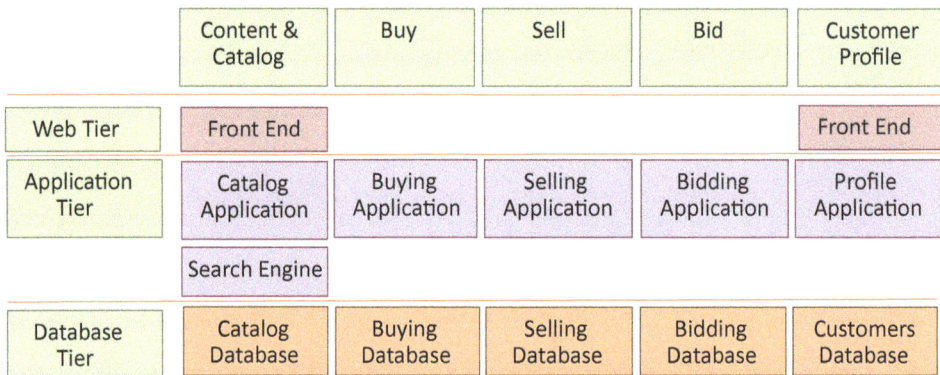

	Content & Catalog	Buy	Sell	Bid	Customer Profile
Web Tier	Front End				Front End
Application Tier	Catalog Application	Buying Application	Selling Application	Bidding Application	Profile Application
	Search Engine				
Database Tier	Catalog Database	Buying Database	Selling Database	Bidding Database	Customers Database

Figure 4.4: Component design step - CCM map for an E-Commerce application

Architecture Design

The second step in the CCM design methodology is architecture design. In this step, interactions between the application components are defined as shown in Figure 4.5.

CCM components have the following characteristics:

- **Loose Coupling:** Components in the Cloud Component Model are loosely coupled. Instead of hard-wiring the links, the components interface through clearly defined functional and service boundaries. Links between the components are established and broken as they respond to service requests. Loose coupling of components relies on

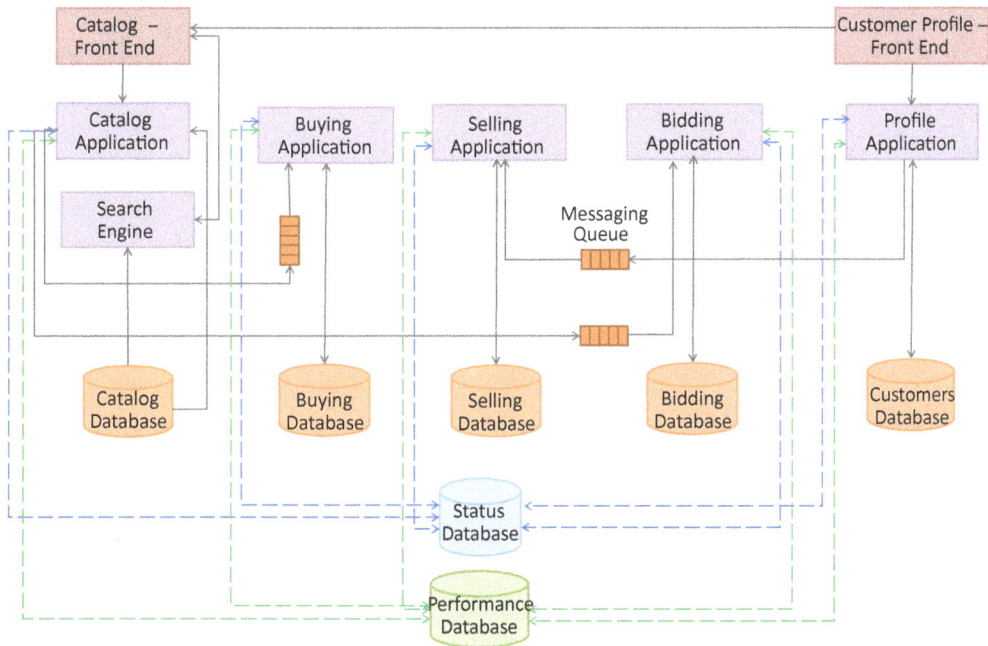

Figure 4.5: Architecture design step - Web interaction diagram for an E-Commerce application

the use of the REST communication protocol that allows components developed in different programming languages to communicate with each other.

- **Asynchronous Communication:** Tightly coupled components use procedure-based tight coupling. Whereas, loosely coupled components communicate asynchronously through message-based communication. Loose coupling isolates various components of the application so that each component interacts asynchronously with the others, treating other components as black boxes. In traditional application designs, it is a common practice to process a request and return immediately. This limits the scalability of the application. By allowing asynchronous communication between components, it is possible to add capacity by adding additional servers when the application load increases. Asynchronous communication is made possible by using messaging queues. The benefit of messaging queues is that the overall application can continue to perform even though individual components may go offline temporarily. If a component becomes temporarily unavailable, the messages are buffered and processed when the component becomes available again.

- **Stateless Design:** Components in the Cloud Component Model are stateless. By storing session state outside of the component (e.g., in a database), the stateless component design enables distribution and horizontal scaling. In distributed computing (with horizontal scaling of components), successive requests to a component may be serviced by different servers. Therefore, the state is maintained outside the components in a database.

Deployment Design

The third step in CCM design methodology is deployment design. In this step, application components are mapped to specific cloud resources such as web servers, application servers, and database servers.

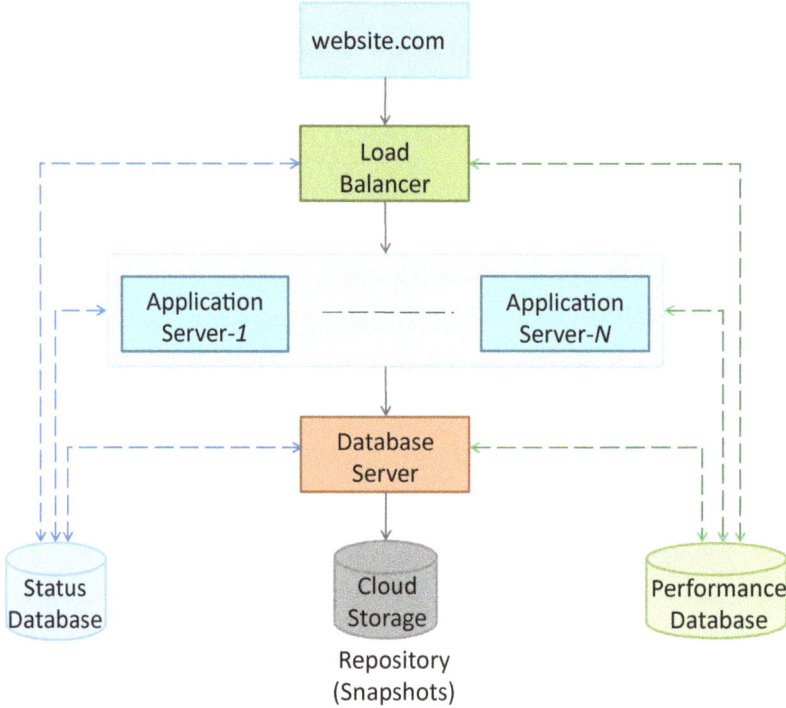

Figure 4.6: Deployment design step - Multi-tier cloud deployment for an E-Commerce application

Since the application components are designed to be loosely coupled and stateless with asynchronous communication, components can be deployed independently of each other. Moreover, multiple cloud platforms can be used for application deployment. This approach makes it easy to migrate application components from one cloud to the other. With this flexibility in application design and deployment, the application developers can ensure that the applications meet the performance and cost requirements with changing contexts. Figure 4.6 shows the deployment design for an E-Commerce application.

4.3.2 Building Microservices with CCM

Let's go through a sample workflow of developing microservices for an E-Commerce application using the CCM methodology:

1. Identify functional areas

Decompose the E-Commerce application functionality into logical areas like product catalog, user authentication, payment processing, order management, etc.

2. Assign microservices

Map identified functional areas to independently deployable and scalable microservices. For example, product catalog can be a microservice while payment processing can be another one.

3. Design APIs

Define APIs through which microservices will interact with each other. For example, Order service calls Payment service to authorize credit card payments.

4. Setup communication

Implement asynchronous event-driven interaction between microservices using message queues or event buses.

5. Externalize state

Store user sessions, shopping carts, and order statuses in databases rather than within microservices to keep them stateless.

6. Multi-cloud deployment

Leverage CCM principles like loose coupling and asynchronous communication to flexibly distribute microservices across multiple clouds, auto-scale them independently, and prevent vendor lock-in.

7. Monitor and refine

Continuously monitor performance to identify bottlenecks, then refine architecture by scaling components or deploying with different cloud configurations for efficiency.

4.3.3   Benefits of using CCM for Microservices

The benefits of the CCM approach are as follows:
- **Improved Performance**: The CCM approach allows applications to be designed using loosely coupled, independently scalable components. This enables selective allocation of additional cloud infrastructure resources only to poorly performing components that are creating bottlenecks. Independent auto-scaling of individual components also improves overall application performance.
- **Better Efficiency**: The use of standardized, reusable software components significantly reduces design, testing, and maintenance time in CCM applications. The ability to decouple components also simplifies the overall application architecture by removing complex interdependencies seen in monolithic applications. This reduces deployment complexity and makes applications easier to manage. CCM also enables granular and highly dynamic cloud resource allocation, allowing infrastructure to be provisioned for specific components based on their runtime performance requirements.
- **Reduced Costs**: As CCM decouples infrastructure scaling from application scaling, resources can be allocated selectively only to poorly performing components instead of uniformly across all modules. This optimized use of cloud infrastructure significantly reduces overall costs. CCM also allows simplification of deployment architectures when feasible through vertical scaling rather than horizontal scaling. Using fewer but more powerful cloud servers improves cost-efficiency.

- **Seamless Scalability**: The loose coupling and stateless nature of components in CCM applications allows them to be scaled seamlessly without impacting other modules. This seamless auto-scaling on demand provides much-needed flexibility and agility to applications. Scaling can be both vertical (using larger servers) or horizontal (adding more instances) based on requirements. Targeted scaling eliminates resource wastage and is more cost-effective than uniformly scaling all application components.
- **Reduced Complexity**: CCM components encapsulate implementation complexity internally and expose only necessary APIs to other services. This abstraction and loose coupling eliminate complex inter-service dependencies seen in monolithic applications. Self-contained components only rely on interfaces and shared data stores to integrate with platforms, which reduces architecture complexity substantially.
- **Improved Maintainability**: The use of standardized interfaces enables the components to act as pluggable, substitutable units. They can be independently upgraded or replaced as needed without necessitating changes in other components. Maintenance overhead is thus greatly reduced. Components can also be extended and improved incrementally to continuously meet evolving business needs.
- **Increased Resilience**: Loose coupling isolates and insulates component failures through well-defined interfaces, preventing them from cascading and bringing down other components or the entire application. Components operate independently, allowing for higher fault tolerance.
- **Multi-Cloud Leverage**: A major advantage of CCM's portable and loosely coupled components is their ability to be deployed across multiple clouds and technology platforms rather than being limited to specific environments. This interoperability allows architects immense flexibility to choose optimal cloud platforms and dynamically distribute components for maximizing efficiency. Multi-cloud deployments also prevent vendor lock-in situations and provide redundancy for continuity.

The Cloud Component Model represents an excellent blueprint for architecting complex yet flexible microservices applications optimally designed for cloud environments. Adopting the CCM principles and design process enables building robust, resilient, and efficient microservice systems.

4.4 Serverless Architecture

Serverless architecture is a cloud computing execution model where the cloud provider dynamically provisions the computing resources required to run application code on demand. Serverless architecture enables building and running applications without having to manage the underlying servers and infrastructure.

In serverless architecture, the application code is broken down into individual functions that run in stateless containers provided by the cloud platform. The functions are event-driven and execute only when triggered by an event such as an HTTP request, adding a message to a queue, updating a database record, or on a schedule.

While in serverless computing, servers (such as physical servers, virtual machines, or containers) are still required for the execution of code, the difference from server-based computing is that in serverless a layer of abstraction is added on top of cloud infrastructure such that the application developers do not need to provision and manage the underlying infrastructure required for the execution of code. Unlike in server-based computing, where servers have to be provisioned and run continuously to run the applications, in serverless computing, there is no need to provision the resources. The cloud provider manages the provisioning and scaling of the infrastructure required to run the functions. Cloud providers charge for the amount of resources used to run the code, which makes serverless computing much more cost-effective than server-based computing where servers have to run continuously.

Serverless architecture is highly scalable and cost-efficient as you only pay for the compute resources when your functions execute rather than paying for servers that are continuously running. It enables focusing on the application code rather than infrastructure management.

Serverless is also referred to as *Functions-as-a-Service (FaaS)*. AWS Lambda is a popular FaaS offering from Amazon Web Services. In the serverless computing model, the code is structured into functions. The functions are triggered by events such as an HTTP request to an API gateway, a record written to a database, a new file uploaded to cloud storage, a new message inserted into a messaging queue, a monitoring alert, a scheduled event, etc. When a function is triggered by an event, the cloud provider launches a container and executes the function within the container. The cloud provider may either use the same container for subsequent executions or terminate the container if the function is not invoked again within a certain period and then launch a new container for subsequent execution of the function. The developers must design the functions to be stateless and assume that the function is executed in a new container every time. If any state information has to be maintained for subsequent executions, it must be saved to a database or cloud storage.

4.4.1   Using Serverless Principles for Microservices

Microservices architecture structures an application as a collection of loosely coupled services where each service implements specific business capabilities. The microservices interact using well-defined APIs. Combining serverless and microservices enables building highly scalable, resilient, and cost-efficient applications.

Figure 4.7 shows transitioning an application from a monolithic to microservices and then to a serverless application. In a monolithic application, all the functionality is within a single process. The different components of a monolithic application are tightly coupled to each other. A monolithic application is run on a server, and application scaling is done by replicating the application on multiple servers. In microservices-based applications, a separate microservice is used for each functionality in the application or related set of functionalities. For example, in an E-Commerce application, user authentication functionality can be implemented as one microservice, product listings can be implemented in another microservice, and shopping cart and checkout can be implemented in another microservice. Each microservice runs on a server or a container. The application is scaled by distributing and replicating the microservices across multiple servers or containers. Going from microservices to a serverless application, the microservices are broken down into individual functions where each function is deployed and run separately in a serverless platform or FaaS. Each function performs a specific task such as user signup and user login. The cloud provider manages the underlying infrastructure, including provisioning and scaling the resources.

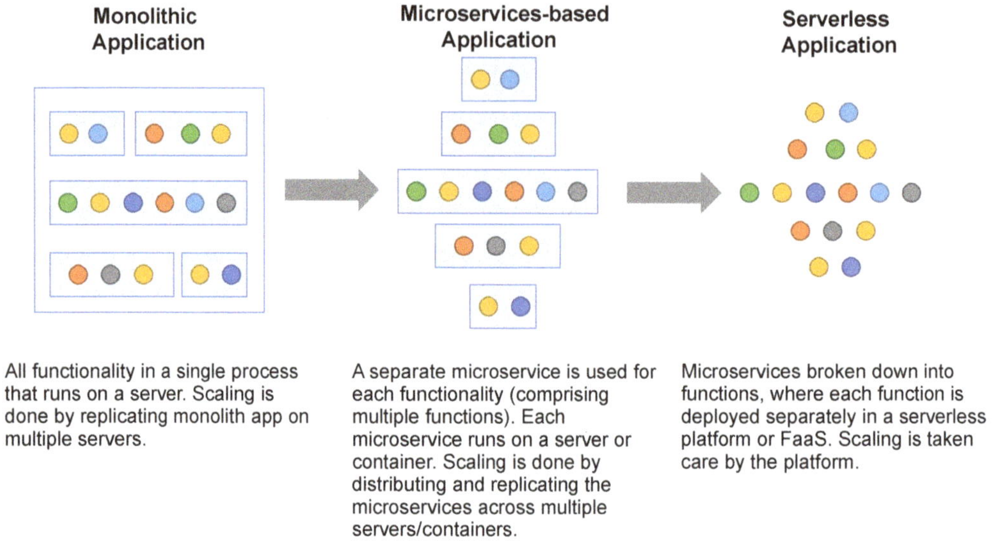

Figure 4.7: Monolith to Microservices to Serverless applications

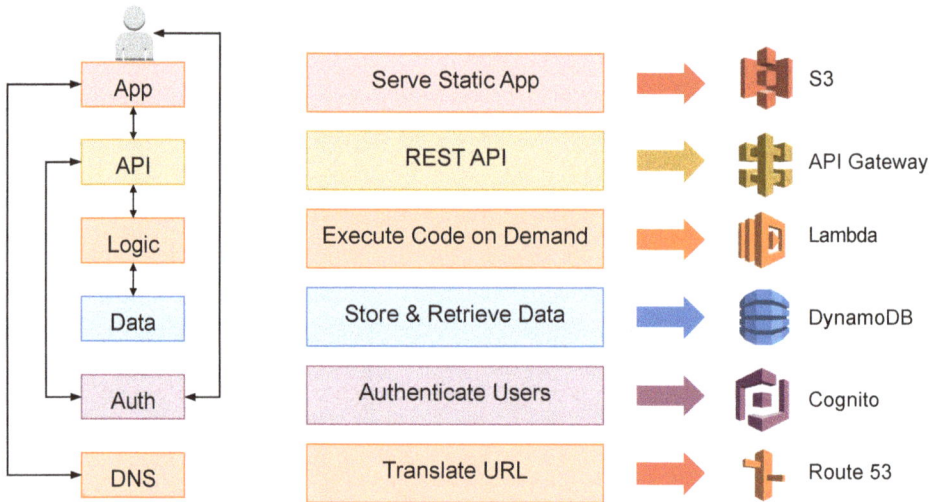

Figure 4.8: Cloud services for implementing serverless applications

Figure 4.8 shows an example of a multi-tier web application implemented with the serverless computing model. The different tiers in the application architecture along with the AWS cloud services which may be used for each tier are shown. The web application comprises a static front-end implemented in HTML, CSS, and JavaScript. The static files for the frontend are deployed on Amazon S3 cloud storage. The application frontend uses a REST API for interacting with the backend. The REST API is implemented using Amazon API Gateway. The application's logic is implemented using Lambda functions. For the database tier, DynamoDB NoSQL database is used. For user authentication, Amazon Cognito service is used. Amazon Route 53 is used as the domain name service (DNS).

4.4.2 Building Serverless Microservices Applications

Let us look at the key steps for building serverless microservices applications on AWS:

1. **Decompose Application into Microservices**: Identify the business capabilities and decompose the application into distinct microservices. For example, an E-Commerce app can have microservices for product catalog, inventory management, order management, customer management, and delivery management.

2. **Design Microservices and Functions**: For each microservice, identify the specific functions to be implemented. Break down the business logic across one or more functions within the microservice.

3. **Develop Functions**: Use a FaaS platform such as AWS Lambda to implement the functions. Wrap units of business logic into separate Lambda functions.

4. **Configure Triggers and Events**: Define triggers for executing the functions such as API Gateway HTTP endpoints, SQS queues, S3 notifications, for instance.

5. **Externalize State**: Store shared, persistent state in data stores such as DynamoDB. Design functions to be stateless.

6. **Set up Monitoring and Logs**: Set up monitoring using a service like Amazon CloudWatch. Configure CloudWatch metrics, alarms, and logs for observability into functions.

7. **Handle Errors and Retries**: Implement error handling using try/catch blocks within the code and set up retry logic using exponential backoff.

8. **Test Functions**: Unit test functions locally (for example, using AWS SAM CLI). Perform integration testing by invoking functions deployed in AWS and validate end-to-end functionality.

9. **Set up CI/CD Pipeline**: Automate builds, tests, and deployments (for example, using AWS CodePipeline) to wrap together build, test, and deploy stages.

10. **Roll out new Versions**: Use versioning to perform rolling deployments of new function versions.

By following these steps, you can build serverless applications using microservices architecture on AWS that are scalable, resilient, cost-efficient, and accelerate time to market. The combination of serverless and microservices enables focusing on delivering business value rather than infrastructure management.

4.4.3 Benefits of using Serverless Architecture for Microservices

The advantages of serverless computing are as follows:

- **Low Operational Cost**: Serverless applications have lower operational costs as there is no need to run servers continuously to serve the applications. The cloud provider provisions the infrastructure required for executing the code only when functions are triggered by events. Cloud providers charge only for the number of invocations of the functions based on a pay-per-invocation billing model. This results in significant cost savings compared to dedicated servers or virtual machines running continuously.

- **Low Maintenance**: The tasks of provisioning, managing infrastructure, OS patching, code monitoring, and logging are handled by the cloud provider in serverless applications. As there are no servers to manage, developers can focus on software design and development rather than infrastructure monitoring and maintenance. Developers are responsible only for their code while other operational tasks are handled by the cloud provider. You only pay for compute resources when functions execute rather than paying for always-on servers.

- **Scalability**: The cloud provider ensures automatic scaling of serverless applications, achieving thousands of executions per second for functions with zero administration. Scaling up and down of infrastructure to execute functions is handled by the cloud provider.
- **Availability & Fault Tolerance**: Cloud providers ensure serverless functions execute in highly available compute environments across multiple availability zones. As cloud providers handle OS patching, there is reduced worry about security vulnerabilities. Serverless platforms run functions on fully managed, highly available infrastructure across zones.
- **Resilience**: Serverless functions execute in stateless containers that are isolated from each other. This isolation ensures that if one function fails or crashes, it does not impact other functions. The functions treat compute infrastructure as a black box without needing awareness of the underlying hosting environment. As the functions are stateless, they can be restarted immediately in case of failures without impacting overall application resilience. This resilience is inherently provided by the serverless platforms without extra effort by the developers.
- **Agility**: Serverless computing enables faster time-to-market for applications as the developers don't need to spend effort on provisioning and managing infrastructure. Developers can focus exclusively on writing application logic and uploading the code, without configuring the infrastructure to run it. This infrastructure agility helps minimize lead time between writing and deploying code into production using simple uploading of function code.
- **Simplified Operations**: In serverless architectures, the cloud provider handles all operational aspects like infrastructure provisioning, deployment, OS patching, capacity planning, monitoring, logging, and more. Developers simply upload code, while the serverless platform handles everything needed to build, run, and scale the code reliably. Operational tasks (such as monitoring thresholds, scaling policies, and patching schedules, for instance) are automatically handled by the platform. This shifts operational responsibilities completely to the platform provider, simplifying the operations from the developer perspective.

4.5   Event-Driven Architecture

Event-Driven architecture (EDA) is becoming increasingly popular for building modern, distributed applications using microservices. Event-driven systems are organized around the production and consumption of events. An event represents a significant change in state, such as a new data entity being created or updated. This enables loose coupling between services, scalability, flexibility, and evolvability of systems.

4.5.1   Using Event-Driven Architecture Principles for Microservices

EDA aligns well with key microservices principles like loose coupling and high cohesion. By adopting an event-driven approach, microservices can interact without tight dependencies, improving flexibility. This results in an asynchronous, decoupled architecture oriented around the flow of events. Let us look at the core principles of event-driven architecture that facilitate building robust microservices:

- **Loose Coupling**: EDA promotes loose coupling by having services interact through events instead of direct call-based dependencies. Services publish events when internal state changes or a notable action occurs. Other interested services subscribe to and consume these events. This asynchronous communication removes the need for producers and consumers to be aware of each other. Services can evolve independently as long as they maintain compatibility with existing event formats.
- **Domain-Driven Boundaries**: Event-driven services have clear boundaries and responsibilities based on domain contexts. Services take on roles of either being producers of certain event types or consumers interested in specific events. This divides up domains cleanly across autonomous, focused services. For example, an Order service in an E-Commerce application produces *OrderCreated* and *OrderCancelled* events, while a Payment service reacts to *OrderCreated* events for collecting payments. This domain-centric alignment of services also prevents cyclic dependencies between domains.
- **Separation of Concerns**: In EDA, different architectural concerns (such as messaging, persistence, transactions, and analytics) are handled by separate components. Domain services focus on core logic while supporting components deal with cross-cutting concerns. This separation of duties results in simpler services that can change independently. For instance, in an E-Commerce system, orders, payments, and fulfillment can change without impacting the messaging infrastructure. This makes the system more adaptable to change.
- **Resilience**: Loose coupling and asynchronous event flow make event-driven microservices more resilient to failures. Component outage impacts a smaller surface area due to isolation. Independent services can retry operations or redirect events to handle errors gracefully. Redundant service instances provide high availability. This reduces system fragility compared to traditional monoliths where a single point of failure can cascade across domains.

4.5.2 Building Microservices with Event-Driven Architecture

Figure 4.9 shows an example of using event-driven architecture for an E-Commerce application. The steps for building a microservices application with EDA are as follows:

1. **Decompose System into Bounded Contexts**: Break down the system into microservices representing different bounded contexts from the domain model. These contexts produce and consume related events.
2. **Identify Events**: Determine the significant events for each bounded context. Useful event types capture state changes like *OrderCreated* or *PaymentProcessed*.
3. **Define Event Schema**: Structure events by defining common and domain-specific attributes such as unique ID, timestamp, and source, for instance.
4. **Model Event Producers and Consumers**: Identify microservices that will publish different event types and those that will subscribe to events. A service may take on both roles.
5. **Implement Message Channels**: Provide an event bus for asynchronous communication between producers and consumers using message brokers (like Kafka or RabbitMQ).

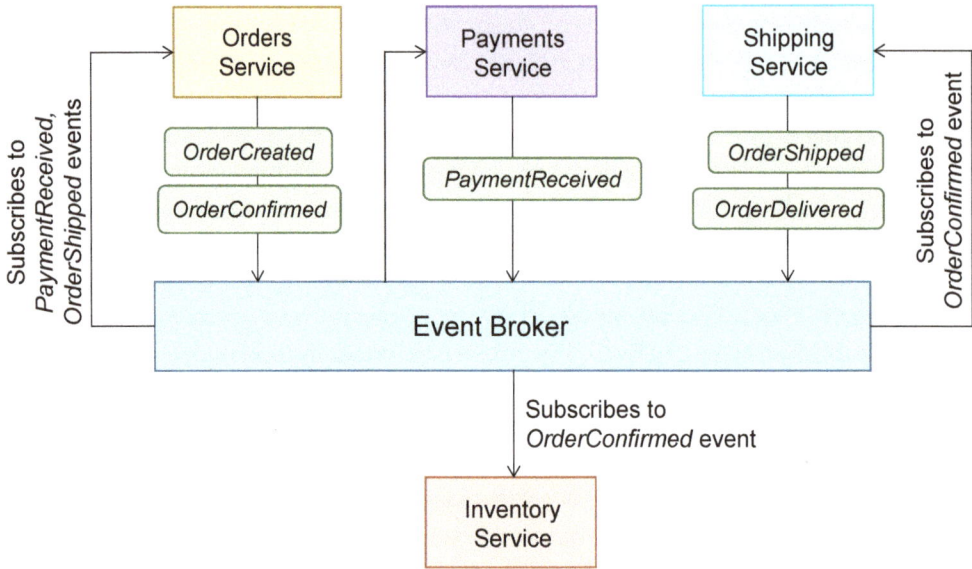

Figure 4.9: Using Event-Driven Architecture for an E-Commerce application

6. **Develop Services**: Build stateless, cohesive microservices that either generate event data or trigger logic on consuming specific event types.
7. **Manage Errors and Retries**: Put retry mechanisms in place. Redirect failed events to a dead letter queue for analysis.

4.5.3   Benefits of using Event-Driven Architecture for Microservices

The benefits of using event-driven architecture for microservices are as follows:

- **Reduced Coupling**: Asynchronous events backed by message brokers eliminate direct point-to-point service dependencies. This reduces coupling, enabling independent service evolvability.
- **Improved Scalability and Availability**: Stateless services can be scaled easily. Message queues are used to absorb traffic spikes. Replication provides high event channel availability, and redundant service instances ensure uptime.
- **Faster Time to Market**: Parallel team development speeds delivery with fewer cross-team dependencies due to decoupling. New features can be added without impacting existing flows.
- **Reliability and Auditability**: Guaranteed event delivery and retry semantics make system interactions reliable. Immutable event logs help in debugging and monitoring.
- **Enables Innovation**: Real-time stream analytics unlocks reactive architectures while event replay enables testing.

The EDA principles align with microservices while bringing key advantages like reduced coupling, easier scaling, improved resilience, and accelerated delivery of business value.

4.6 Model View Controller (MVC)

Model View Controller (MVC) is a popular software design pattern for web applications.

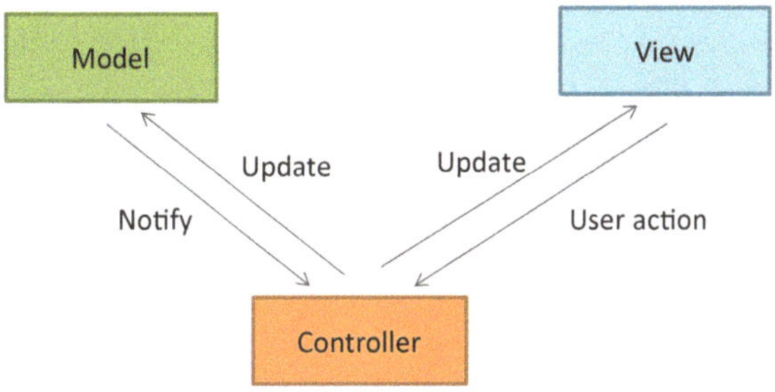

Figure 4.10: Model View Controller

The MVC pattern consists of three parts as shown in Figure 4.10, including:
- **Model**: Model manages the data and the behavior of the applications. Model processes events sent by the controller. Model has no information about the views and controllers. Model responds to the requests for information about its state (from the view) and responds to the instructions to change state (from the controller).
- **View**: View prepares the interface that is shown to the user. Users interact with the application through views. Views present the information that the model or controller tells the view to present to the user and also handle user requests and sends them to the controller.
- **Controller**: Controller glues the model to the view. Controller processes user requests and updates the model when the user manipulates the view. The controller also updates the view when the model changes.

MVC separates the application logic, the data, and the user interface. The benefit of using MVC is that it improves the maintainability of the application and allows reuse of code. The applications built with MVC architecture can be updated easily due to the separation of the model from the view. In MVC, both the view and controller depend on the model; however, the model does not depend on either. This allows the model to be developed and tested independently. Similarly, the separation between the view and the controller is also well-defined for web applications.

In traditional applications, the view is generally tightly coupled with the model. Since views are likely to change more frequently than the model, this tight coupling requires rewiring the links. With MVC, the views can be changed without affecting the model.

4.6.1 Using MVC Principles for Microservices

Microservices can leverage MVC internally to provide separation of concerns within a service. Or more importantly, MVC can be used to design the interaction between multiple microservices themselves. The Model, View, and Controller responsibilities can be implemented in separate microservices as follows:
1. **Model Microservices**: These implement the core business capabilities and database/API access functionality. Model services encapsulate domain logic, data access, validation, and workflows.

2. **View Microservices**: These expose APIs and UIs to access model services. Multiple lightweight view services can reuse capabilities of the model via APIs and display data in different formats.

3. **Controller Microservices**: These handle request flows across services, composition of operations, orchestration, load balancing, messaging, and monitoring. They control coordination between multiple microservices.

In a microservice architecture, capabilities are split into self-contained services with clearly defined responsibilities along MVC paradigms. These services can then scale, evolve, and deploy rapidly to enable greater agility across large applications.

4.6.2   Building Microservices with MVC

Let us look at the steps to build microservices using the MVC pattern:

1. **Domain Analysis**: Break down the system into core domains and sub-domains. Identify services around business capabilities.

2. **Model Services**: Implement key domains as independent model services with data access, processing logic and workflows. Define APIs for access.

3. **View Services**: Create lightweight view services to access model APIs and display data on UI, reports, and other formats.

4. **Controller Services**: Develop controller services that handle cross-cutting needs like request routing, aggregation from multiple models, orchestration, messaging, and monitoring.

5. **Interaction Contracts**: Define loose coupling interaction contracts between services using APIs (REST), events, and message queues.

6. **Independent Delivery**: Model, view, and controller services can be built, upgraded, and scaled independently without impacting others.

7. **Automated Testing**: Implement test automation across service components and contracts early to enable rapid parallel development.

For example, an E-Commerce application built on MVC principles would have separate microservices for managing product catalog data, customer data, inventory data, and orders data, for instance. The view services would expose APIs for web and mobile apps to display pages such as product catalog, customer profile, and order status pages, for instance. Controller services would handle user interactions, route requests, handle orders across model services, and process payments via third-party APIs.

Each component here is delivered independently via automated CI/CD pipelines, even though they work together to provide application capabilities. Changes to the product catalog model would not require changes in payment processing logic. New mobile interfaces can be added without disrupting existing flows. This separation facilitates agility across decentralized teams working on microservices.

4.6.3   Benefits of using MVC for Microservices

The benefits of using MVC principles for microservice architectures are as follows:

- **Loose Coupling**: Clear separation of responsibilities allows services to operate independently without tight coupling.

- **Flexibility**: Services can implement their own data access, logic layers, and expose interfaces without collisions across components, thus enabling parallel development.

- **Reusability**: Common model services with well-defined APIs can be reused across multiple applications.
- **Scalability**: Services can scale vertically and horizontally independently of each other depending on load patterns.
- **Agility**: Faster release cycles due to independent components owned by small teams with localized changes.
- **Resiliency**: Isolated failures due to loosely coupled services.
- **Ease of maintenance**: Much easier to modify, update, rewrite services independently.

The MVC pattern enables the design of complex microservice-driven applications that are resilient, scalable, and easier to maintain in the long run. It brings simplicity in high-scale architectures, teams, and continuous delivery environments.

Summary

In this chapter, we covered popular design methodologies and architectural patterns that provide structured approaches, guidelines, and blueprints tailored towards developing successful microservices applications. We described the need for comprehensive design methodologies aligned specifically for microservices architectures that help address the complexities around distributing business capabilities across independently deployable services. We explained the Cloud Component Model (CCM) methodology, which offers a component-based approach consisting of reusable, loosely coupled components that align well with microservices principles. CCM focuses on stateless components with well-defined communication contracts and separation of cross-cutting capabilities, allowing flexible deployment topologies. We covered the REST architectural style, which establishes constraints and best practices for building scalable and reliable web services suited for inter-service communication in microservices. Guiding principles around resources, uniform interfaces, stateless operations, and hypermedia usage allow the creation of evolvable and maintainable APIs. We covered serverless architectures, which allow splitting microservices into granular serverless functions triggered by events like API requests. This enables scaling and resiliency without infrastructure management overheads. We provided an overview of event-driven architecture where microservices communicate using asynchronous events instead of direct API connections, facilitating loose coupling and independent scalability. Finally, we described using the Model-View-Controller (MVC) pattern for clearly separating microservices into model components focused on business capabilities and state, view components focused on UI and API exposure, and controller components handling service coordination and communication. This separation of concerns facilitates independent evolution of capabilities. This chapter aimed to highlight proven design methodologies consisting of component models, architectural guidelines, and communication approaches for overcoming complexities specific to microservices.

IMPLEMENTATION ON AWS

OVERVIEW OF AMAZON WEB SERVICES

THIS CHAPTER COVERS

- Amazon EC2
- AWS EC2 Auto Scaling
- AWS Elastic Load Balancing (ELB)
- Amazon Simple Storage Service (S3)
- Amazon Elastic File System (EFS)
- Amazon Elastic Block Store (EBS)
- Amazon Relational Data Store (RDS)
- Amazon ElastiCache
- Amazon DynamoDB
- Amazon DocumentDB
- Amazon Neptune
- AWS Lambda
- AWS Identity and Access Management (IAM)
- AWS Key Management Service (KMS)
- Amazon Route 53
- Amazon CloudFront
- Amazon SNS

5.1 Introduction

Amazon Web Services (AWS) is the world's most comprehensive and broadly adopted cloud platform, offering over 200 fully-featured services from data centers globally. Millions of customers, including the fastest-growing startups, largest enterprises, and leading government agencies, trust AWS to power their infrastructure, become more agile, and lower costs. AWS provides a highly reliable, scalable, low-cost infrastructure platform in the cloud. With data center locations in the United States, Canada, Europe, Brazil, Singapore, Japan, India, China, Middle East, South Africa, and Australia, AWS has the ability to enable its customers to run their applications and serve customers from data centers close to their own customers, no matter where they are located. This allows customers to lower latency and improve performance.

In this chapter, we will cover the key services and solutions offered by AWS including:

- **Compute Services**:
  - **Amazon EC2**: Provides secure, resizable compute capacity in the cloud to develop and host applications.
  - **AWS EC2 Auto Scaling**: Automatically adjusts the number of EC2 instances in an Auto Scaling group according to conditions.
  - **AWS Elastic Load Balancing**: Automatically distributes incoming application traffic across multiple targets and EC2 instances.
- **Storage Services**:
  - **Amazon Simple Storage Service (S3)**: Provides scalable object storage that allows storing and retrieving any amount of data.
  - **Amazon Elastic File System (EFS)**: Provides simple, scalable elastic file storage for use with AWS services and resources.
  - **Amazon Elastic Block Store (EBS)**: Provides persistent block-level storage volumes for EC2 instances.
- **Relational Database Services**:
  - **Amazon Relational Data Store (RDS)**: Managed relational database service that automates time-consuming tasks like hardware provisioning, patching, and backups.
  - **Amazon ElastiCache**: In-memory caching service to deploy, run, and scale popular open source compatible in-memory caches.
- **Non-Relational Database Services**:
  - **Amazon DynamoDB**: A fast, fully managed NoSQL database service that provides seamless scalability and proven performance.
  - **AWS DocumentDB**: A fast, scalable, highly available, and fully managed document database service that supports MongoDB workloads.
  - **AWS Neptune**: A fully managed graph database service that makes it easy to build and run applications that work with highly connected datasets.
- **Serverless Computing**:
  - **AWS Lambda**: Runs code in response to events and automatically manages compute resources.
- **Security Services**:
  - **AWS Identity and Access Management (IAM)**: Enables centralized access

control and management of AWS services and resources.
- **AWS Key Management Service (KMS)**: Manages encryption keys for encrypting AWS resources.

- **Other Services**:
  - **Amazon Route 53**: Highly available and scalable Domain Name System (DNS) service.
  - **Amazon CloudFront**: Content delivery network (CDN) for faster delivery of static and dynamic content.
  - **Amazon SNS**: Managed pub-sub messaging service for coordinating distributed systems and serverless applications.

5.2 Compute Services

Compute services provide dynamically scalable compute capacity in the cloud. Compute resources can be provisioned on-demand in the form of virtual machines. Virtual machines can be created from standard images provided by the cloud service provider (such as Linux or Windows images) or custom images created by the users. A machine image is a template that contains a software configuration (operating system, application server, and applications). Compute services can be accessed from the web consoles of these services that provide graphical user interfaces for provisioning, managing, and monitoring these services. Cloud service providers also provide APIs for various programming languages (such as Java, Python, Go, Ruby, etc.) that allow developers to access and manage these services programmatically.

Features
- **Scalable**: Compute services allow rapidly provisioning as many virtual machine instances as required. The provisioned capacity can be scaled up or down based on the workload levels. Auto-scaling policies can be defined for compute services that are triggered when the monitored metrics (such as CPU usage and memory usage) go above predefined thresholds.
- **Flexible**: Compute services offer a wide range of options for virtual machines with multiple instance types, operating systems, and zones/regions.
- **Secure**: Compute services provide various security features that control access to the virtual machine instances, such as security groups, access control lists and network firewalls. Users can securely connect to the instances with SSH using authentication mechanisms such as OAuth or security certificates and key pairs.
- **Cost effective**: Cloud service providers offer various billing options such as on-demand instances, which are billed per hour, reserved instances which are reserved after a one-time initial payment, and spot instances for which users can place bids.

5.3 Amazon EC2

Amazon EC2 is an Infrastructure-as-a-Service (IaaS) provided by Amazon. EC2 delivers scalable, pay-as-you-go compute capacity in the cloud. EC2 provides computing capacity in the form of virtual machines that are launched in Amazon's cloud computing environment.

5.3.1 EC2 Instance Types

An instance type defines the hardware that is used for an instance. Amazon EC2 supports various instance types, which vary in the compute capacity (virtual CPUs), memory, storage, and networking performance. For each instance type, there are multiple instance families.

EC2 offers the following instance types:

*   **General Purpose**: The general-purpose instances provide a balance of compute, memory, and network resources and are well-suited for a wide range of applications. Within the general-purpose type, there are various families such as M5, M6a, M6i, M7a, M7g, M7gd, T3, T3a, and T4g.
*   **Compute Optimized**: The compute-optimized instances are optimized for compute-intensive workloads and deliver cost-effective high performance at a low price per compute ratio. Within the compute-optimized type, there are various families such as C5, C6a, C6i, C6g, C7a, C7g, and C7gd.
*   **Memory Optimized**: The memory-optimized instances are optimized for memory-intensive applications. Within the memory-optimized type, there are various families such as R5, R6a, R6i, R7a, R7g, X1, X2gd, X2idn, X2iedn, and z1d.
*   **Accelerated Computing**: The accelerated computing instances are intended for graphics and general-purpose GPU compute applications. Within the accelerated computing type, there are various families such as P3, P4, P5, G4dn, G5, Inf1, Inf2, Trn1, and VT1.
*   **Storage Optimized**: The storage-optimized instances are optimized for workloads that require high disk throughput. Within the storage-optimized type, there are various families such as D3, D3en, H1, I3, I3en, I4g, I4i, Im4gn, and Is4gen.

5.3.2 Amazon Machine Image

Amazon Machine Image (AMI) is an instance template that contains the software configuration (including operating system and applications) required to launch an instance. AMIs are based on Linux or Windows operating systems. AMIs can come from different sources such as (1) AMIs published by AWS, (2) AWS Marketplace, (3) Community AMIs, or (4) your own AMIs created from existing instances.

5.3.3 Security Groups

A security group is like a virtual firewall that allows you to control the traffic coming in and going out of your instances. By default, all incoming traffic is denied for an instance. Within a security group, you can define rules to allow traffic based on port, protocol, source, or destination. For example, if you are running a web server on an EC2 instance, you can allow incoming HTTP traffic from any source by adding a rule with the protocol as HTTP, port as 80, and source as 0.0.0.0/0. The source/destination can be defined either using a single IP address, IP address range as a Classless Inter-Domain Routing (CIDR) block, or the ID of another security group. Security groups allow all outgoing traffic by default. Security groups are stateful in nature; therefore, if you send a request from your instance, the response traffic for that request is allowed to flow in regardless of inbound security group rules. The security group rules are always permissive in nature; therefore, you cannot define a rule to deny certain types of traffic.

5.3.4 Tenancy Options

Amazon EC2 supports the following tenancy options for the instances:

- **Shared Tenancy**: Shared tenancy is the default tenancy model for all EC2 instances. In this model, the instances run on shared hardware. Therefore, a single host can host instances from different customers.
- **Dedicated Instances**: Dedicated instances run on a single-tenant hardware, which means that the hardware is dedicated to a single customer.
- **Dedicated Hosts**: In the dedicated hosts model, the instance runs on a Dedicated Host, which is an isolated physical server solely dedicated to a single customer.

5.3.5 Pricing Options

- **On-Demand Instances**: On-demand instances do not have any upfront costs or commitments. Users are charged for the running instances on an hourly basis. The price per hour for different instance types in different AWS regions is published on the AWS website.
- **Reserved Instances**: Reserved Instances are recommended for long-term use or predictable workloads where you can save significantly on the costs of running the instances by purchasing reserved instances. By purchasing reserved instances for a 1-year or 3-year term, you can save between 20% to 75% on the hourly rate as compared to the on-demand instances. For reserved instances, the payment can be made either all-upfront for the entire term, partial-upfront, or no-upfront.
- **Spot Instances**: With spot instances, you can specify the price that you are willing to pay for a certain instance type. When a bid is over the current spot price, the instance is provisioned. Spot instances run until you terminate them or until your bid price is above the current spot price. Since spot instances can get terminated anytime, they are not recommended for critical workloads where interruption cannot be tolerated.

5.3.6 Placement Groups

Placement Groups allow you to define how your instances are placed on the underlying hardware. A placement group is a logical grouping of instances. EC2 supports the following placement strategies:

- **Cluster**: A cluster placement group clusters instances into a low-latency group in a single availability zone. The instances in a cluster placement group can use the low-latency 10 Gbps network for communicating with other instances in the group. Cluster placement groups are recommended for applications that benefit from low network latency and high network throughput.
- **Partition**: A partition placement group spreads instances across logical partitions, ensuring that instances in one partition do not share underlying hardware with instances in other partitions. When you use a partition placement group, you can either allow EC2 to distribute the instances evenly across the partitions or launch instances into a specific partition. Partition placement groups are recommended for large distributed and replicated workloads such as HDFS or HBase.
- **Spread**: A spread placement group spreads instances across underlying hardware. Each instance in the spread placement group is placed on the distinct underlying

hardware. Spread placement groups are recommended for applications that have a small number of critical instances that should be kept separate from each other.

Let us now look at the steps involved in setting up an EC2 instance. From the Amazon EC2 console, create a key pair as shown in Figure 5.1. Save the key pair (.pem) file. You will require this file later for securely connecting to the EC2 instance. Next, from the EC2 console, click on the instance launch button to open the wizard.

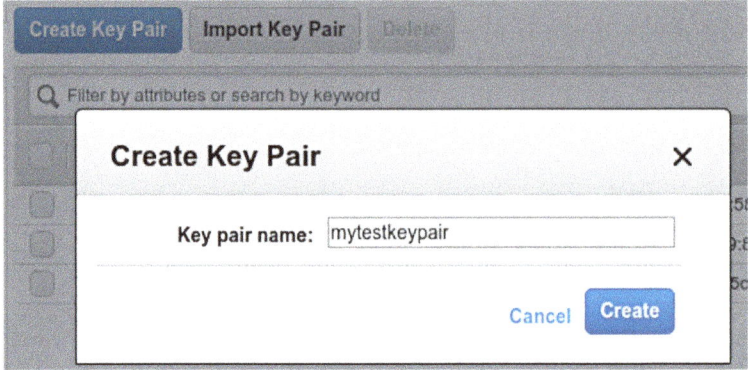

Figure 5.1: Creating a new key-pair

Next, choose an Amazon Machine Image (AMI) as shown in Figure 5.2.

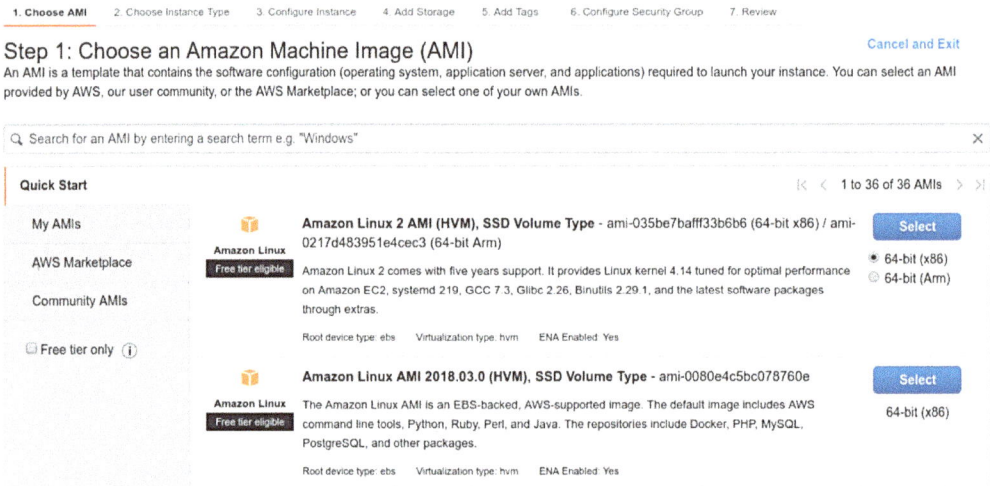

Figure 5.2: Launching an EC2 instance - step 1

Next, choose the instance type as shown in Figure 5.3.

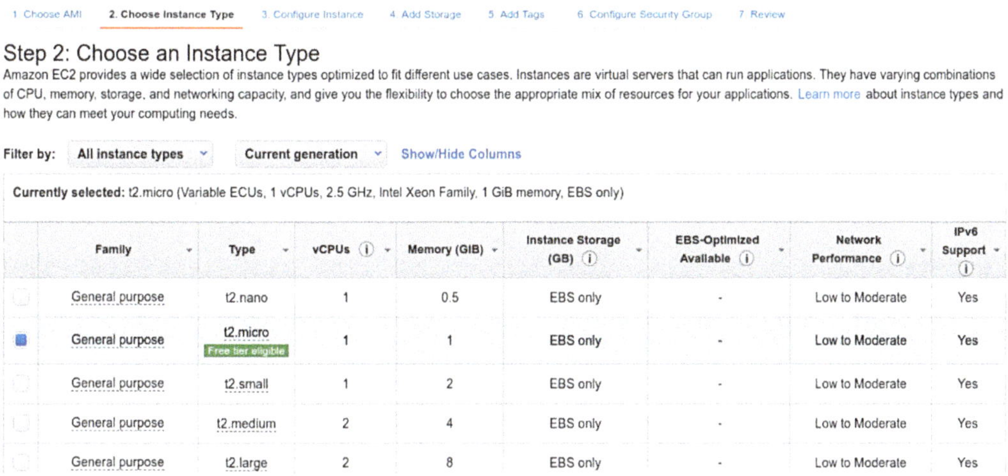

Figure 5.3: Launching an EC2 instance - step 2

Next, configure the instance, as shown in Figure 5.4.

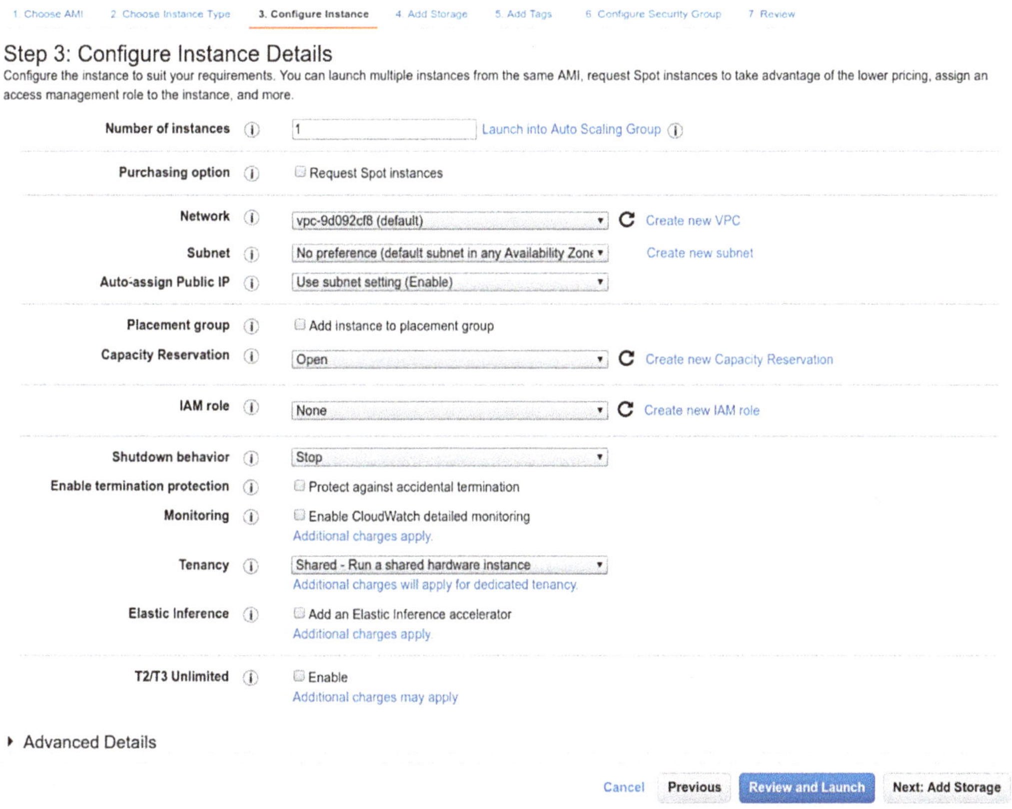

Figure 5.4: Launching an EC2 instance - step 3

Next, configure the instance storage, as shown in Figure 5.5.

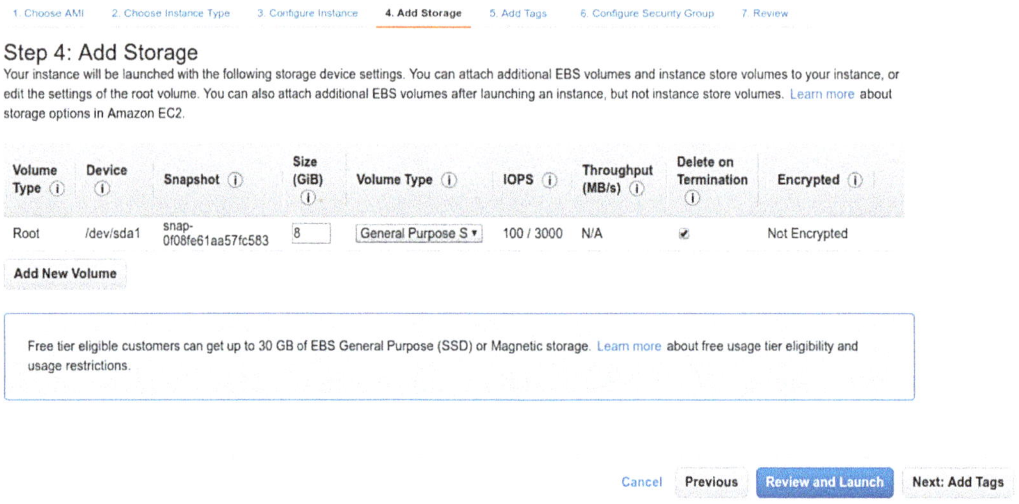

Figure 5.5: Launching an EC2 instance - step 4

Next, add tags to identify the instance, as shown in Figure 5.6.

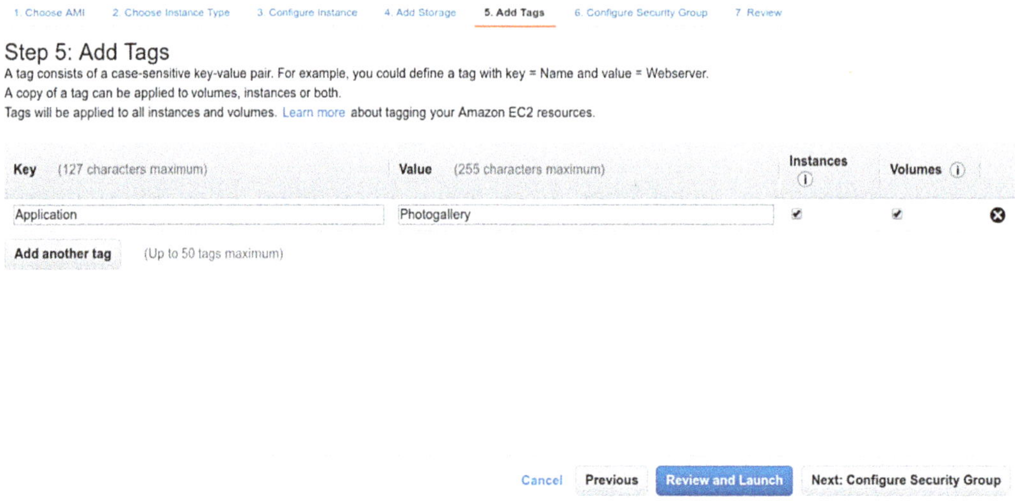

Figure 5.6: Launching an EC2 instance - step 5

Next, create a new security group, as shown in Figure 5.7. A security group is a set of firewall rules that control the traffic to your instance. For example, if you want to set up a web server on your instance, then add rules to allow HTTP and HTTPS traffic to your instance.

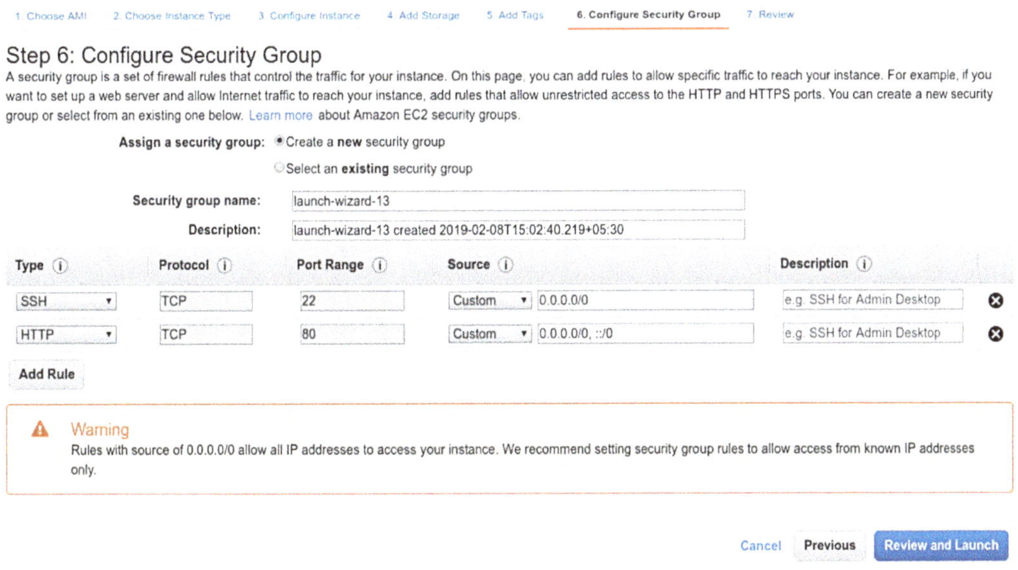

Figure 5.7: Launching an EC2 instance - step 6

Finally, review the instance launch details and click the launch button. Wait for the instance to come into 'running' state. Note down the public IP address of the instance from the EC2 console. From a terminal on your local machine, connect to the instance via SSH as follows:

```
#Connecting to an EC2 Ubuntu instance with SSH
ssh -i mytestkeypair.pem ububtu@<Public-IP-Address>
```

Box 5.1 shows the Python code for launching an EC2 instance. In this example, we create an EC2 client connection by calling *boto3.client* function. The EC2 region, AWS access key, and AWS secret key are passed to this function. After connecting to EC2, a new instance is launched using the *run_instances* function of the EC2 client. The AMI-ID, instance type, EC2 key handle, and security group are passed to this function. The program waits until the status of the newly launched instance becomes 'running' and then prints the instance details such as public DNS, instance IP, and launch time.

■ **Box 5.1: Python program for launching an EC2 instance**

```
import boto3
from time import sleep

AWS_KEY="<enter>"
AWS_SECRET="<enter>"
```

```python
REGION="us-east-1"
AMI_ID = "ami-80861296"
EC2_KEY_HANDLE = "cloud"
INSTANCE_TYPE="t2.nano"
SECGROUP_ID="sg-1f25617b"

ec2 = boto3.client('ec2', aws_access_key_id=AWS_KEY,
                aws_secret_access_key=AWS_SECRET,
                region_name=REGION)

print "Launching instance with AMI-ID %s, with keypair %s, \
      instance type %s, security group \
      %s"%(AMI_ID,EC2_KEY_HANDLE,INSTANCE_TYPE,SECGROUP_ID)

response =  ec2.run_instances(ImageId=AMI_ID,
                KeyName=EC2_KEY_HANDLE,
                InstanceType=INSTANCE_TYPE,
                SecurityGroupIds = [ SECGROUP_ID, ],
                MinCount=1,
                MaxCount=1)

print response
Instance_ID=response['Instances'][0]['InstanceId']

print "Waiting for instance to be up and running"

response = ec2.describe_instances(InstanceIds=[Instance_ID])
status=response['Reservations'][0]['Instances'][0]['State']['Name']
print "Status: "+str(status)

while status == 'pending':
  sleep(10)
  response = ec2.describe_instances(InstanceIds=[Instance_ID])
  status=response['Reservations'][0]['Instances'][0]['State']['Name']
  print "Status: "+str(status)

if status == 'running':
  response = ec2.describe_instances(InstanceIds=[Instance_ID])
  print "\nInstance is now running. Instance details are:"
  print "Intance Type: " + \
    str(response['Reservations'][0]['Instances'][0]['InstanceType'])
  print "Intance State: " + \
    str(response['Reservations'][0]['Instances'][0]['State']['Name'])
  print "Intance Launch Time: " + \
    str(response['Reservations'][0]['Instances'][0]['LaunchTime'])
  print "Intance Public DNS: " + \
    str(response['Reservations'][0]['Instances'][0]['PublicDnsName'])
  print "Intance Private DNS: " + \
    str(response['Reservations'][0]['Instances'][0]['PrivateDnsName'])
  print "Intance IP: " + \
    str(response['Reservations'][0]['Instances'][0]['PublicIpAddress'])
  print "Intance Private IP: " + \
    str(response['Reservations'][0]['Instances'][0]['PrivateIpAddress'])
```

Box 5.2 shows the Python code for viewing details of running instances. In this example, the *describe_instances* function of the EC2 client is used to get information on all running instances.

■ Box 5.2: Python program for viewing details of running instances

```
import boto3

AWS_KEY="<enter>"
AWS_SECRET="<enter>"
REGION="us-east-1"

print "Connecting to EC2"
ec2 = boto3.client('ec2', aws_access_key_id=AWS_KEY,
                          aws_secret_access_key=AWS_SECRET,
                          region_name=REGION)

response = ec2.describe_instances()
for instance in response['Reservations'][0]['Instances']:
    print "Intance Type: " + str(instance['InstanceType'])
    print "Intance State: " + str(instance['State']['Name'])
    print "Intance Launch Time: " + str(instance['LaunchTime'])
    print "Intance Public DNS: " + str(instance['PublicDnsName'])
    print "Intance Private DNS: " + str(instance['PrivateDnsName'])
    print "Intance IP: " + str(instance['PublicIpAddress'])
    print "Intance Private IP: " + str(instance['PrivateIpAddress'])
```

5.4 AWS EC2 Auto Scaling

AWS EC2 Auto Scaling service allows automatic scaling of Amazon EC2 capacity up or down according to user-defined conditions. Therefore, with AutoScaling users can increase the number of EC2 instances running their applications seamlessly during spikes in the application workloads to meet the application performance requirements, and scale down capacity when the workload is low to save costs.

5.4.1 Launch Configuration

A Launch Configuration is a template that is used by the Auto Scaling service to launch new instances within an Auto Scaling Group. A Launch Configuration comprises AMI, instance type, security group, and key-pair.

5.4.2 Auto Scaling Group

An Auto Scaling Group is a collection of instances that are managed by the Auto Scaling service. An Auto Scaling Group comprises a configuration such as a launch configuration to launch new instances within the group, desired capacity, maximum capacity, and scaling policies.

5.4.3 Scaling Policy

Scaling policies can be defined for an Auto Scaling Group which define how to adjust the capacity dynamically.

Amazon EC2 Auto Scaling supports the following types of scaling policies:

- **Target tracking scaling**: With this policy, you can increase or decrease the current capacity of the group based on a target value for a specific metric.
- **Step scaling**: With this policy, you can increase or decrease the current capacity of the group based on a set of scaling adjustments, known as step adjustments, that vary based on the size of the alarm breach.
- **Simple scaling**: With this policy, you can increase or decrease the current capacity of the group based on a single scaling adjustment.

To use the Auto Scaling service, you have to create an EC2 Auto Scaling Group from the Auto Scaling console. There are two steps involved in setting up an Auto Scaling Group. The first step is to create or select a launch template that your Auto Scaling group uses to launch your EC2 instances. The second step is to create an Auto Scaling group. In this step, you have to give the Auto Scaling group a name and specify the number of instances you want to run in the group. The Auto Scaling Group maintains the number of instances specified and replaces any instances that become unhealthy or impaired. You can optionally configure your group to adjust the capacity according to demand, in response to Amazon CloudWatch metrics.

The steps for creating a launch template are similar to the steps for launching a new instance. EC2 Auto Scaling provides a wizard to create a launch template where you can specify information such as the AMI ID, instance type, key pair, security groups, and block device mapping for your instances. EC2 Auto Scaling uses groups to organize EC2 instances. The instances in an Auto Scaling group are treated as a logical unit for scaling and management. When creating an Auto Scaling Group, you can specify the minimum, maximum, and desired number of EC2 instances. You can optionally add the scaling policies to scale up or scale down the size of the group automatically. Let us look at the steps involved in creating an Auto Scaling Group in more detail. To create an Auto Scaling Group, you have to provide a group name and a group size, as shown in Figure 5.8.

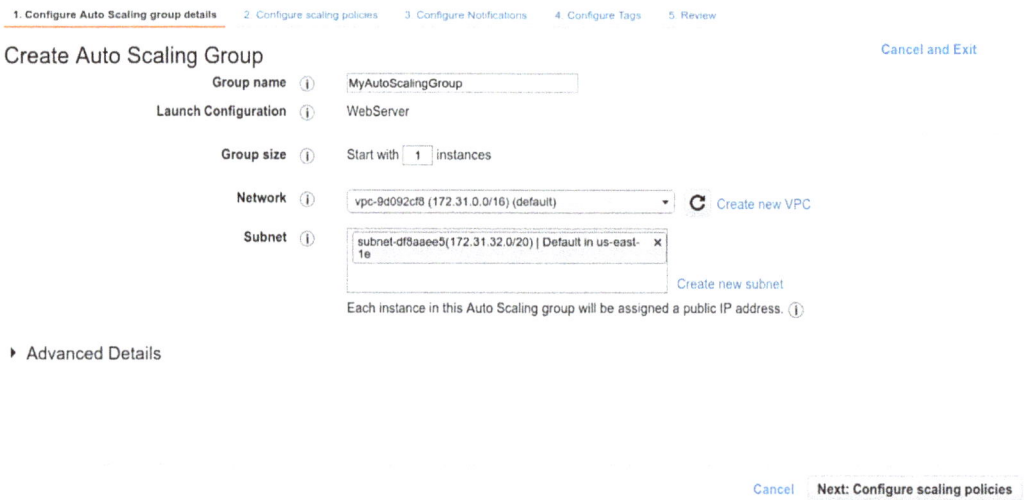

Figure 5.8: Creating an AutoScaling Group - step 1

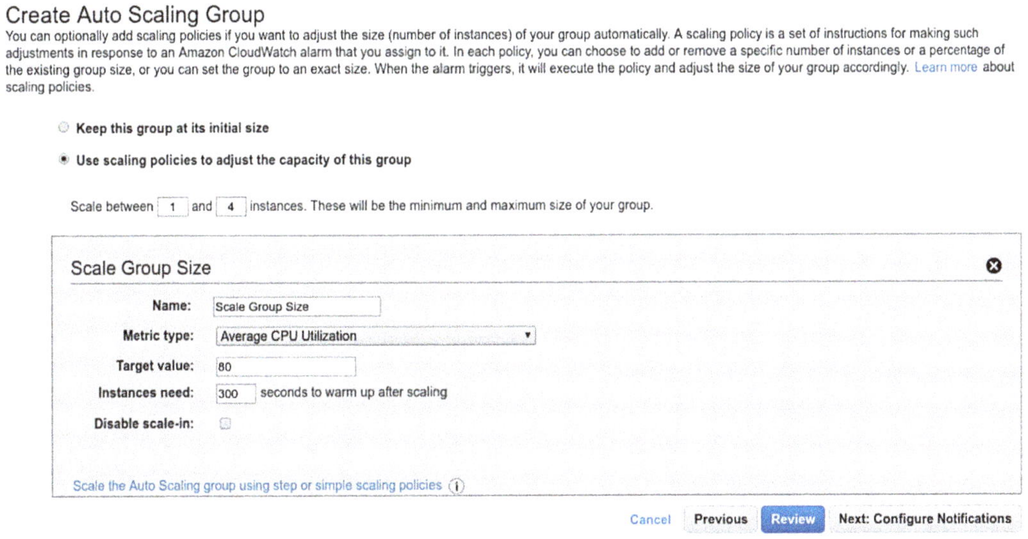

Create Auto Scaling Group

You can optionally add scaling policies if you want to adjust the size (number of instances) of your group automatically. A scaling policy is a set of instructions for making such adjustments in response to an Amazon CloudWatch alarm that you assign to it. In each policy, you can choose to add or remove a specific number of instances or a percentage of the existing group size, or you can set the group to an exact size. When the alarm triggers, it will execute the policy and adjust the size of your group accordingly. Learn more about scaling policies.

○ Keep this group at its initial size

● Use scaling policies to adjust the capacity of this group

Scale between [1] and [4] instances. These will be the minimum and maximum size of your group.

Scale Group Size   ⊗

Name: [Scale Group Size]
Metric type: [Average CPU Utilization ▼]
Target value: [80]
Instances need: [300] seconds to warm up after scaling
Disable scale-in: ☐

Scale the Auto Scaling group using step or simple scaling policies ⓘ

Cancel Previous **Review** Next: Configure Notifications

Figure 5.9: Creating an AutoScaling Group - step 2

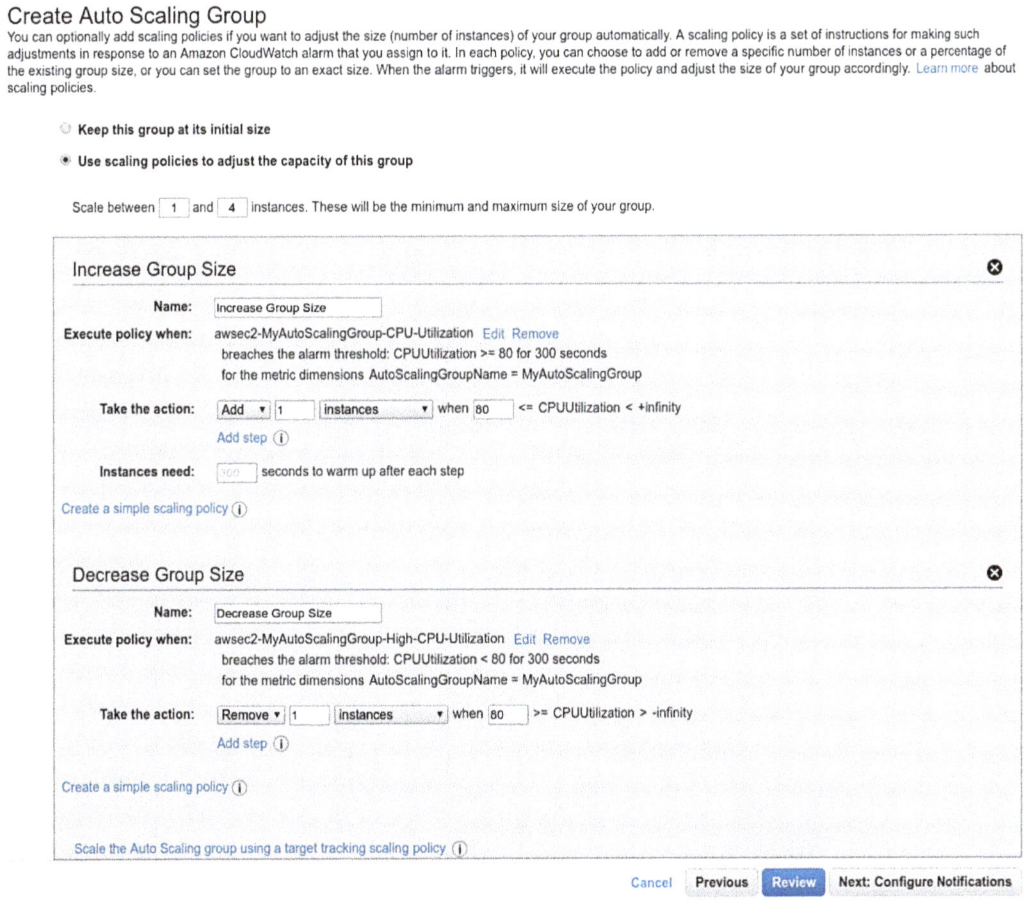

Create Auto Scaling Group

You can optionally add scaling policies if you want to adjust the size (number of instances) of your group automatically. A scaling policy is a set of instructions for making such adjustments in response to an Amazon CloudWatch alarm that you assign to it. In each policy, you can choose to add or remove a specific number of instances or a percentage of the existing group size, or you can set the group to an exact size. When the alarm triggers, it will execute the policy and adjust the size of your group accordingly. Learn more about scaling policies.

○ Keep this group at its initial size

● Use scaling policies to adjust the capacity of this group

Scale between [1] and [4] instances. These will be the minimum and maximum size of your group.

Increase Group Size   ⊗

Name: [Increase Group Size]
Execute policy when: awsec2-MyAutoScalingGroup-CPU-Utilization Edit Remove
breaches the alarm threshold: CPUUtilization >= 80 for 300 seconds
for the metric dimensions AutoScalingGroupName = MyAutoScalingGroup
Take the action: [Add ▼] [1] [instances ▼] when [80] <= CPUUtilization < +infinity
Add step ⓘ
Instances need: [300] seconds to warm up after each step

Create a simple scaling policy ⓘ

Decrease Group Size   ⊗

Name: [Decrease Group Size]
Execute policy when: awsec2-MyAutoScalingGroup-High-CPU-Utilization Edit Remove
breaches the alarm threshold: CPUUtilization < 80 for 300 seconds
for the metric dimensions AutoScalingGroupName = MyAutoScalingGroup
Take the action: [Remove ▼] [1] [instances ▼] when [80] >= CPUUtilization > -infinity
Add step ⓘ

Create a simple scaling policy ⓘ

Scale the Auto Scaling group using a target tracking scaling policy ⓘ

Cancel Previous **Review** Next: Configure Notifications

Figure 5.10: Creating an AutoScaling Group - step 3

At the next step, you can optionally define the scaling policies to adjust the size of the group. Figure 5.9 shows an example of creating a target tracking scaling policy. You can define a target value for a metric such as average CPU utilization, average network in (bytes), average network out (bytes), and application load balancer request count per target.

Figure 5.10 shows an example of creating a step scaling policy. Here, we define the scaling adjustments for increasing and decreasing the group size and the alarms which trigger the adjustment actions. Figure 5.11 shows how to create a CloudWatch alarm for scale-up adjustment. Here, we create an alarm for average CPU utilization greater than or equal to 80% for at least 1 consecutive period of 5 minutes. Figure 5.12 shows how to create an alarm for scale-down adjustment. Here we create an alarm for average CPU utilization less than 80% for at least 1 consecutive period of 5 minutes.

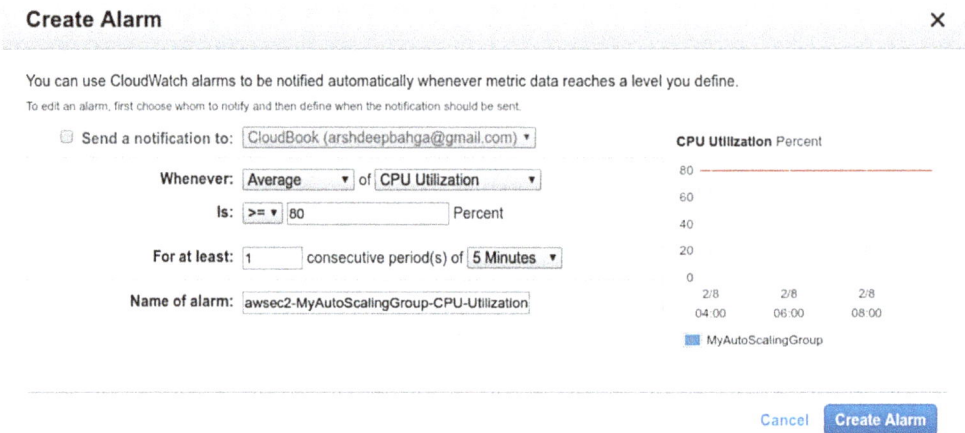

Figure 5.11: Creating a CloudWatch alarm to be used for scaling up policy

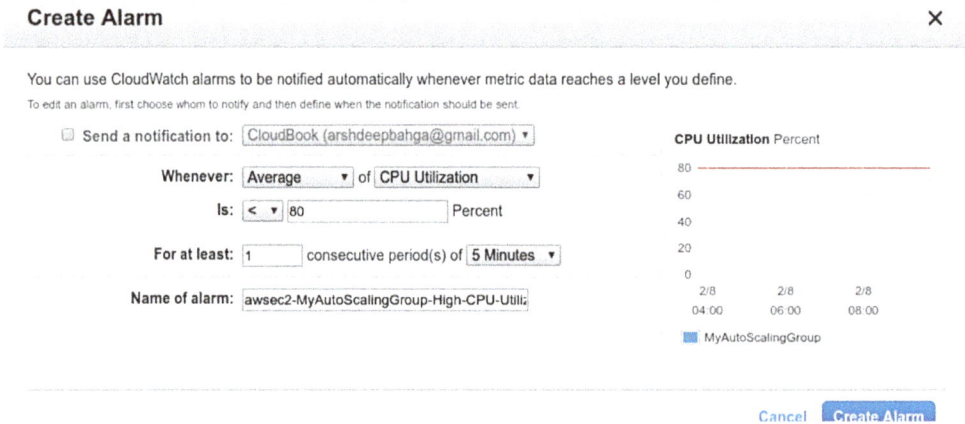

Figure 5.12: Creating a CloudWatch alarm to be used for scaling down policy

5.5   AWS Elastic Load Balancing

AWS Elastic Load Balancing (ELB) is a managed service that allows you to create load balancers for distributing traffic across a group of EC2 instances. With ELB, you can load balance HTTP, HTTPS, TCP, and SSL traffic to EC2 instances. ELB supports three types of load balancers as follows:

- **Application Load Balancer**: Application Load Balancers are meant for web applications with HTTP and HTTPS traffic. Application Load Balancers operate at the request level and provide advanced routing and visibility features.
- **Network Load Balancer**: Network Load Balancers are meant for TCP and TLS connections. Network Load Balancers operate at the connection level and can handle millions of requests per second securely while maintaining ultra-low latencies. You can use a Network Load Balancer when you need ultra-high performance, the ability to terminate TLS connections at scale, centralize certificate deployment, and static IP addresses for your application.
- **Classic Load Balancer**: Classic Load Balancer is the previous generation of the load balancer that supports HTTP, HTTPS, and TCP traffic.

5.5.1   Internet-Facing or Internal Load Balancers

An Elastic Load Balancer can either be Internet-facing or internal. An Internet-facing load balancer can receive requests from clients over the Internet and distribute the requests among the EC2 instances that are registered with the load balancer. An Internet-facing load balancer is assigned a public DNS that clients can use to send the requests. An internal load balancer routes requests from clients to targets using private IP addresses.

5.5.2   Listeners

A Listener is a process that checks for the connection requests using the protocol and port specified. For each load balancer, you can configure one or more listeners. ELB supports HTTP, HTTPS, TCP, and SSL protocols.

5.5.3   Health Checks

ELB uses health checks to detect unhealthy targets, stop sending traffic to them, and then spread the load across the remaining healthy targets. An elastic load balancer performs the health check for registered instances using the protocol and path specified for the health check. You can set the time interval for health checks, a timeout period, the number of consecutive health check failures for an instance to be marked as unhealthy (unhealthy threshold), and the number of consecutive successful health checks for an instance to be marked as healthy (healthy threshold).

5.5.4   Sticky Sessions

Elastic Load Balancers route requests independently to the registered targets. For session-based applications, you can use the sticky sessions feature to route requests from the same user session to the same instance. A sticky session ensures that all requests coming from a user in a session are routed to the same instance. If your application doesn't use session cookies, you can create a session cookie by specifying a stickiness duration. ELB uses a cookie named

AWSELB that is used to map the session to the instance. If your application has its session cookie, then you can configure ELB so that the session cookie follows the duration specified by the application's session cookie.

5.5.5 Connection Draining

You can enable the Connection Draining feature to stop sending requests to instances that are deregistering or unhealthy while keeping the existing connections open. This enables the load balancer to complete in-flight requests made to instances that are deregistering or unhealthy. While enabling connection draining, you have to specify the maximum timeout value between 1 and 3600 seconds. When the maximum timeout is reached, the load balancer forcibly closes connections to the deregistering instance.

5.5.6 Using an Application Load Balancer

Let us look at an example of setting up and using an application load balancer. For testing the application load balancer, we will use a simple Flask web application that displays the details of the instance on which it is deployed. Amazon EC2 provides the following URL to view instance metadata from within a running instance:
http://169.254.169.254/latest/meta-data/

The Flask web application shown in Box 5.3 uses the above URL to get details of the instance such as the hostname, instance ID, and public IP address. When you run this Flask web application, you can view the details of the instance on which it is running by opening the URL: http://<public-IP>:5000 in a browser where *public-IP* is the IP address of the instance. Figure 5.13 shows a screenshot of this Flask web application. Set up two EC2 instances and deploy this Flask application on them.

■ **Box 5.3: Source code of Flask web application for displaying instance details**

```
from flask import Flask
import urllib2
app = Flask(__name__)

@app.route('/')
def hello_world():
    BASEURL='http://169.254.169.254/latest/meta-data/'
  response = urllib2.urlopen(BASEURL+'hostname')
  hostname = response.read()
  response = urllib2.urlopen(BASEURL+'instance-id')
  instanceid = response.read()
  response = urllib2.urlopen(BASEURL+'public-ipv4')
  publicipv4 = response.read()

  html = 'Hostname: '+hostname+'<br>'+'Instance-ID: '+\
          instanceid+'<br>'+'Public-IP: '+publicipv4
  return html

if __name__ == '__main__':
    app.run(host='0.0.0.0')
```

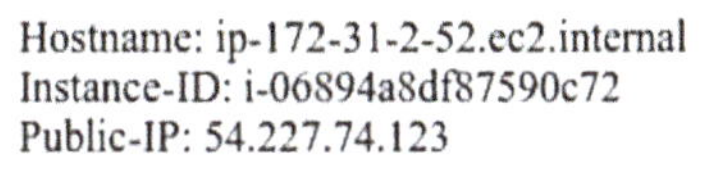

Hostname: ip-172-31-2-52.ec2.internal
Instance-ID: i-06894a8df87590c72
Public-IP: 54.227.74.123

Figure 5.13: Screenshot of Flask web application for displaying instance details

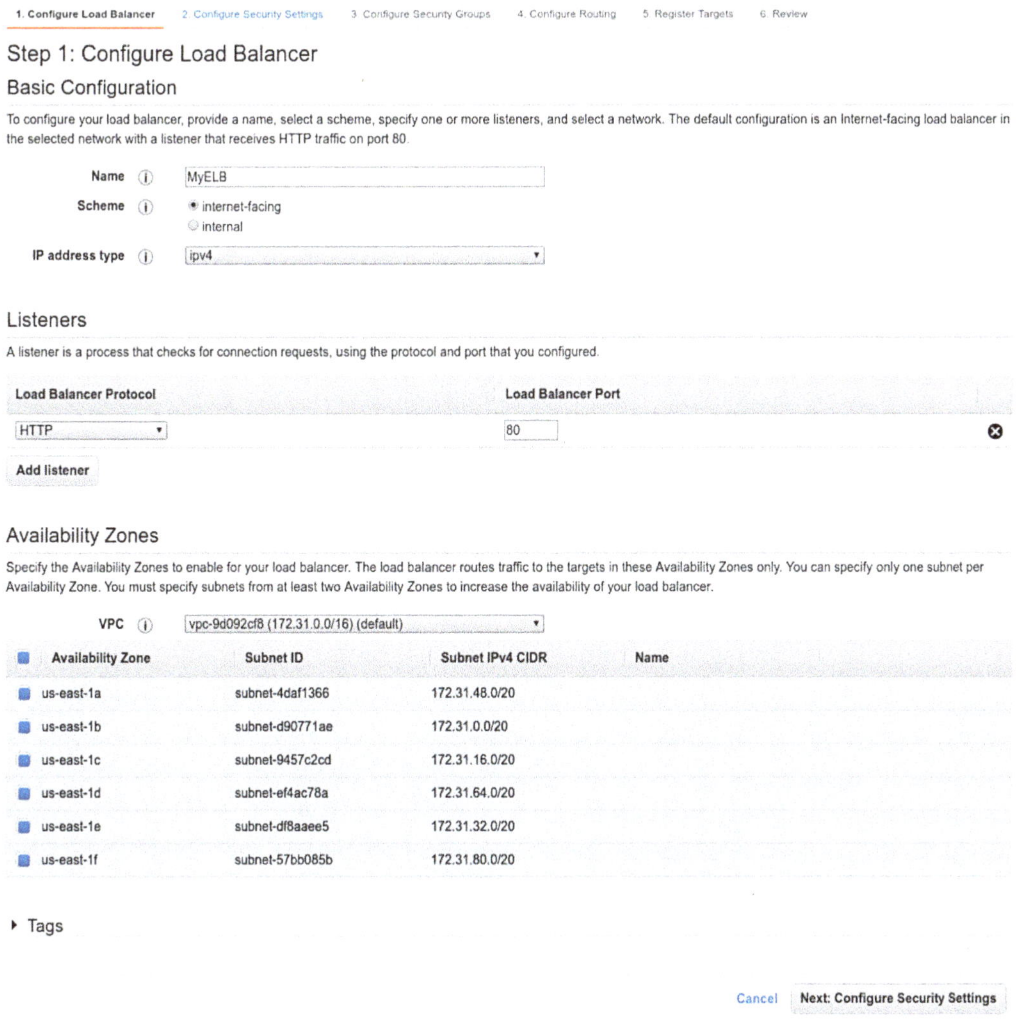

1. Configure Load Balancer   2. Configure Security Settings   3 Configure Security Groups   4. Configure Routing   5. Register Targets   6. Review

Step 1: Configure Load Balancer

Basic Configuration

To configure your load balancer, provide a name, select a scheme, specify one or more listeners, and select a network. The default configuration is an Internet-facing load balancer in the selected network with a listener that receives HTTP traffic on port 80.

Name (i)	MyELB
Scheme (i)	● internet-facing ○ internal
IP address type (i)	ipv4 ▼

Listeners

A listener is a process that checks for connection requests, using the protocol and port that you configured.

Load Balancer Protocol	Load Balancer Port	
HTTP ▼	80	✖

Add listener

Availability Zones

Specify the Availability Zones to enable for your load balancer. The load balancer routes traffic to the targets in these Availability Zones only. You can specify only one subnet per Availability Zone. You must specify subnets from at least two Availability Zones to increase the availability of your load balancer.

	VPC (i)	vpc-9d092cf8 (172.31.0.0/16) (default) ▼		
	Availability Zone	**Subnet ID**	**Subnet IPv4 CIDR**	**Name**
▣	us-east-1a	subnet-4daf1366	172.31.48.0/20	
▣	us-east-1b	subnet-d90771ae	172.31.0.0/20	
▣	us-east-1c	subnet-9457c2cd	172.31.16.0/20	
▣	us-east-1d	subnet-ef4ac78a	172.31.64.0/20	
▣	us-east-1e	subnet-df8aaee5	172.31.32.0/20	
▣	us-east-1f	subnet-57bb085b	172.31.80.0/20	

▸ Tags

Cancel   **Next: Configure Security Settings**

Figure 5.14: Creating an Application Load Balancer - step 1

Next, from the EC2 dashboard, open the load balancer page and select the option to create a new application load balancer. At step-1, as shown in Figure 5.14, provide the basic configuration for the load balancer such as the load balancer name, scheme, IP address type, and listeners. Here we define an HTTP listener which listens on port 80 of the load balancer. Next, select the availability zones for the load balancer.

At step-2, we configure the security settings, as shown in Figure 5.15. As we didn't define an HTTPS listener in the previous step, we can skip this step.

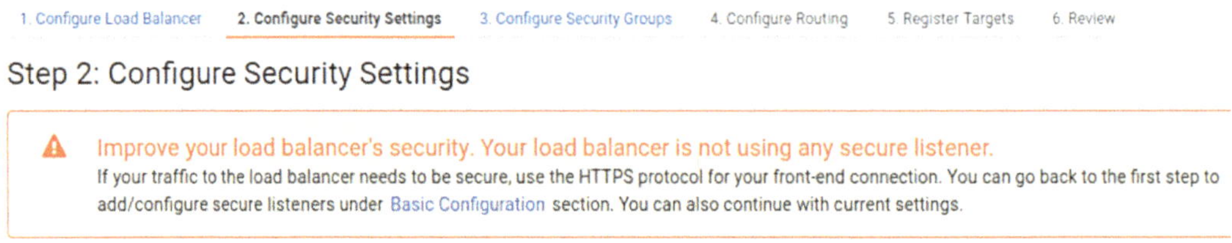

1. Configure Load Balancer   **2. Configure Security Settings**   3. Configure Security Groups   4. Configure Routing   5. Register Targets   6. Review

Step 2: Configure Security Settings

> ⚠ Improve your load balancer's security. Your load balancer is not using any secure listener.
> If your traffic to the load balancer needs to be secure, use the HTTPS protocol for your front-end connection. You can go back to the first step to add/configure secure listeners under Basic Configuration section. You can also continue with current settings.

Figure 5.15: Creating an Application Load Balancer - step 2

At step-3, we configure the security groups, as shown in Figure 5.16. Here we open port 80.

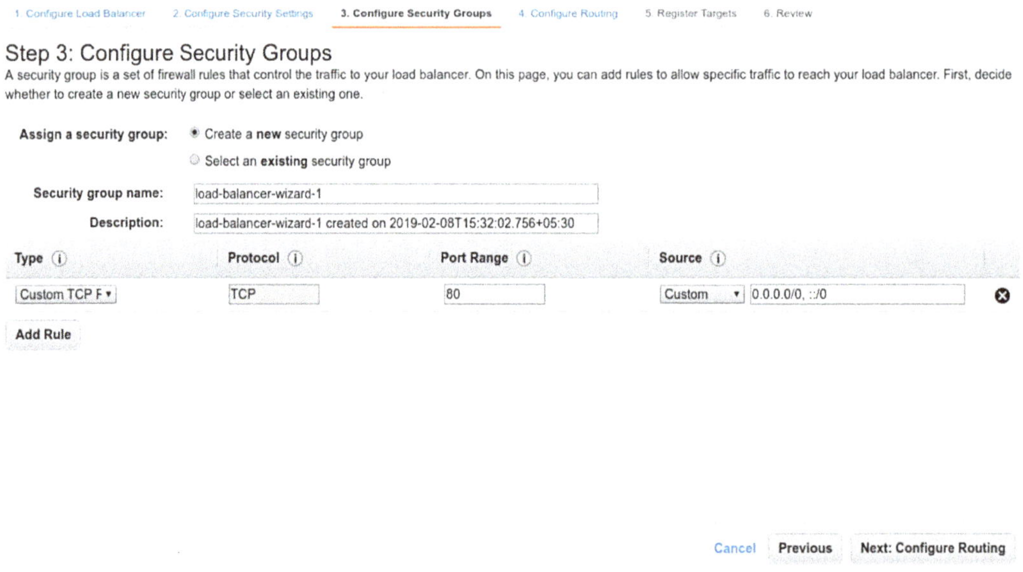

1. Configure Load Balancer   2. Configure Security Settings   **3. Configure Security Groups**   4. Configure Routing   5. Register Targets   6. Review

Step 3: Configure Security Groups
A security group is a set of firewall rules that control the traffic to your load balancer. On this page, you can add rules to allow specific traffic to reach your load balancer. First, decide whether to create a new security group or select an existing one.

| Assign a security group: | ⦿ Create a **new** security group |
| | ○ Select an **existing** security group |

| Security group name: | load-balancer-wizard-1 |
| Description: | load-balancer-wizard-1 created on 2019-02-08T15:32:02.756+05:30 |

Type ⓘ	Protocol ⓘ	Port Range ⓘ	Source ⓘ	
Custom TCP F ▾	TCP	80	Custom ▾	0.0.0.0/0, ::/0	✖

Add Rule

Cancel   **Previous**   **Next: Configure Routing**

Figure 5.16: Creating an Application Load Balancer - step 3

At step-4, we configure the routing, as shown in Figure 5.17. Here we create a new target group and provide the target name, type, protocol, and port. The load balancer routes requests to targets in a target group using the protocol and port specified. At this step, we also define the health check settings, which are used by the load balancer to check if a target is in a healthy state or not.

At step-5, we register the targets, as shown in Figure 5.18. Here you can select the two EC2 instances where you previously deployed the Flask web application to display the instance details.

At the next step, you can review the load balancer configuration and create the load balancer. Once the load balancer becomes operational, note down the public DNS of the load balancer from the ELB console and access the same in a browser. You can see the Flask web application with the details of the instance which served the request. Next, refresh the web page, and you can see the details of the other instance. The load balancer routes the requests to the two instances in a round-robin fashion.

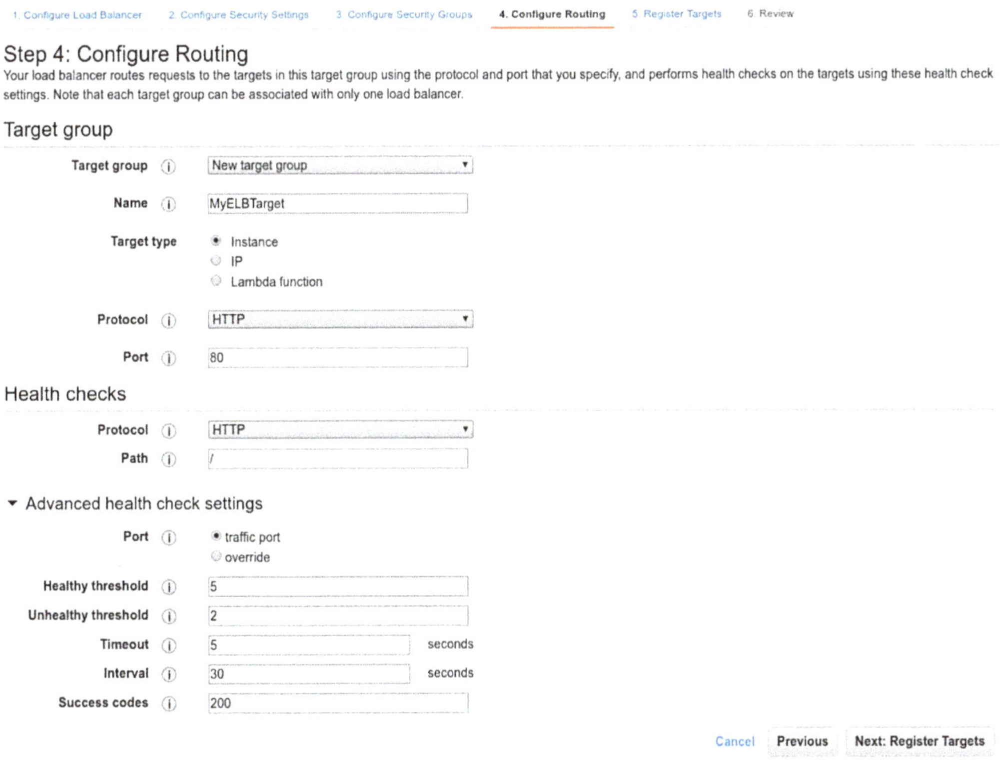

1. Configure Load Balancer   2. Configure Security Settings   3. Configure Security Groups   **4. Configure Routing**   5. Register Targets   6. Review

Step 4: Configure Routing

Your load balancer routes requests to the targets in this target group using the protocol and port that you specify, and performs health checks on the targets using these health check settings. Note that each target group can be associated with only one load balancer.

Target group

Target group ⓘ	New target group ▼
Name ⓘ	MyELBTarget
Target type	● Instance ○ IP ○ Lambda function
Protocol ⓘ	HTTP ▼
Port ⓘ	80

Health checks

Protocol ⓘ	HTTP ▼
Path ⓘ	/

▼ Advanced health check settings

Port ⓘ	● traffic port ○ override
Healthy threshold ⓘ	5
Unhealthy threshold ⓘ	2
Timeout ⓘ	5 seconds
Interval ⓘ	30 seconds
Success codes ⓘ	200

Cancel   **Previous**   **Next: Register Targets**

Figure 5.17: Creating an Application Load Balancer - step 4

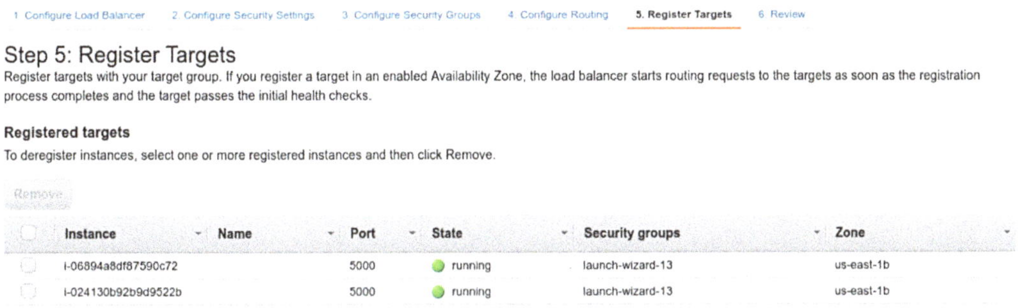

1. Configure Load Balancer   2. Configure Security Settings   3. Configure Security Groups   4. Configure Routing   **5. Register Targets**   6. Review

Step 5: Register Targets

Register targets with your target group. If you register a target in an enabled Availability Zone, the load balancer starts routing requests to the targets as soon as the registration process completes and the target passes the initial health checks.

Registered targets

To deregister instances, select one or more registered instances and then click Remove.

Remove

	Instance	Name	Port	State	Security groups	Zone
☐	i-06894a8df87590c72		5000	🟢 running	launch-wizard-13	us-east-1b
☐	i-024130b92b9d9522b		5000	🟢 running	launch-wizard-13	us-east-1b

Figure 5.18: Creating an Application Load Balancer - step 5

By leveraging Amazon Application Load Balancer, microservices applications can benefit from improved availability, scalability, and efficient traffic management, allowing developers to focus on building and deploying their services without worrying about the underlying infrastructure. ALB automatically distributes incoming traffic across multiple targets, ensuring high availability and fault tolerance. If one target fails, ALB routes traffic to healthy targets, reducing the impact of failures on the overall application. ALB supports advanced request routing, allowing you to route traffic based on various rules, such as URL path, host header, and HTTP headers. This flexibility enables efficient traffic management and content-based routing for microservices applications.

5.6   Storage Services

In this section, we describe the different types of cloud storage services. In cloud computing environments, three types of storage solutions are offered: (1) Block storage, (2) File storage, (3) Object storage. Block storage operates at the operating system kernel level, and the data is stored and organized as an array of unrelated blocks. In Block storage, the data is stored without any concept of data format or type. Block storage is accessed over the network as a Storage Area Network (SAN) using protocols such as iSCSI. File storage operates at the operating system user level, and the data is stored as data blocks which are managed by a file system. In file storage, data is managed as a named hierarchy of files and folders. Files have metadata associated with them (such as file name, type, and creation date). File storage is accessed over the network as a Network Attached Storage (NAS) using protocols such as Network File System (NFS) or Common Internet File System (CIFS). Object storage operates at the application level, and the data is stored as objects. Each object consists of an object identifier (OID), data, and metadata. Object storage is accessed with protocols such as HTTP using REST APIs. Figure 5.19 shows a representation of the three types of storage and the protocols used.

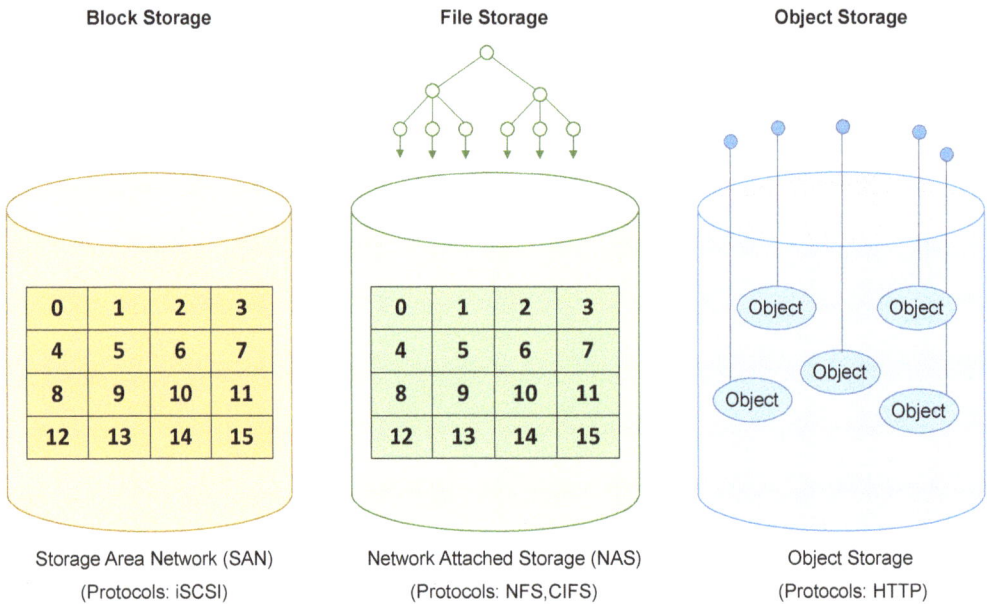

Figure 5.19: Storage types: Block, File and Object Storage

5.7   Amazon Simple Storage Service (S3)

Amazon Simple Storage Service (S3) is an online cloud-based data storage infrastructure for storing and retrieving any amount of data. S3 provides a highly reliable, scalable, fast, fully redundant, and affordable storage infrastructure. S3 is a cloud object storage service. Data stored on S3 is organized in the form of buckets. You must create a bucket before you can store data on S3. S3 console provides simple wizards for creating a new bucket and uploading files. You can upload any type of file to S3. While uploading a file, you can specify the redundancy and encryption options and access permissions. Data stored on S3 is independent of any server and is accessed over the Internet using the S3 web interface or console, S3 REST APIs, or using the AWS SDKs.

5.7.1 Buckets

Figures 5.20 to 5.22 show the steps for creating a bucket from the Amazon S3 console. While creating a bucket, a bucket name is provided. The bucket name has to be unique across all AWS accounts, and not just within your AWS account. An S3 bucket is created for a specific region. By selecting a region for the bucket, you can control where your data is stored. Typically, you would want to store your data in the region closest to you or your customers. For disaster recovery purposes, you may want to choose a region that is far away from your location. While creating a bucket, you can enable features such as versioning, logging, and encryption.

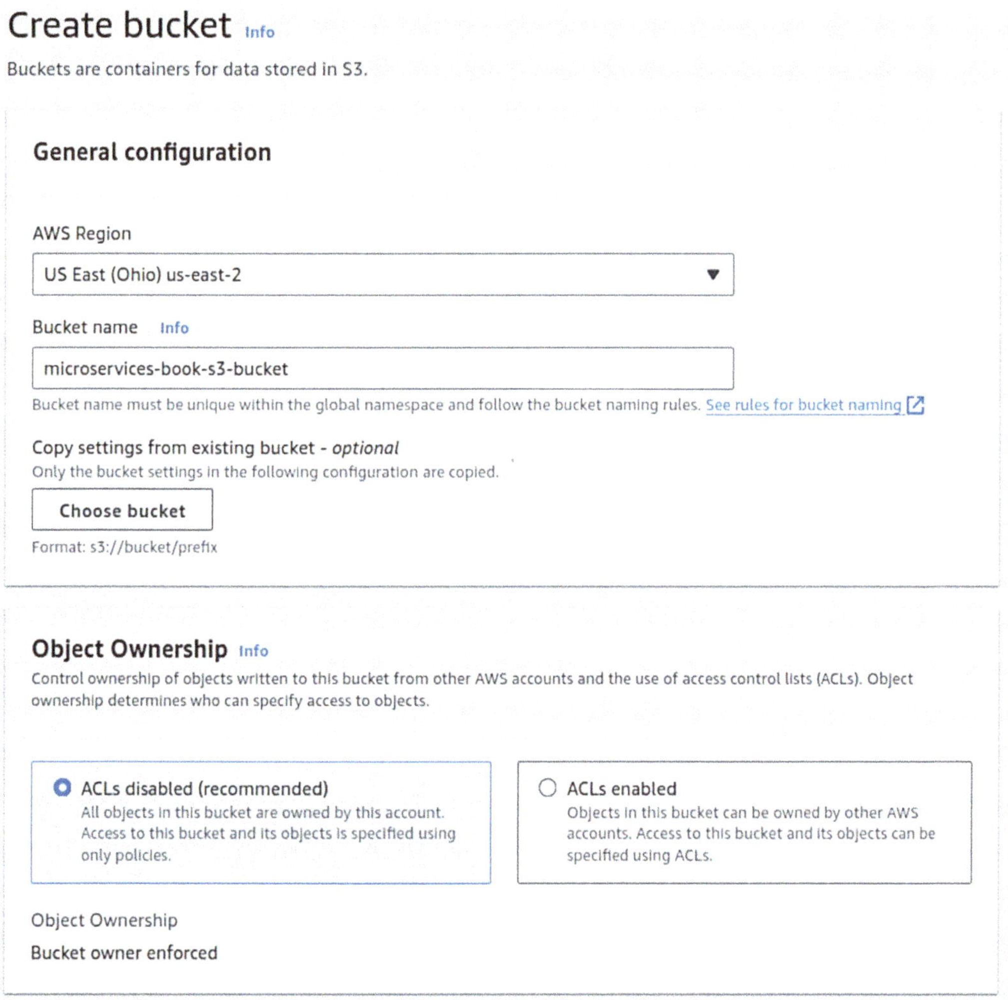

Create bucket Info

Buckets are containers for data stored in S3.

General configuration

AWS Region

US East (Ohio) us-east-2   ▼

Bucket name   Info

microservices-book-s3-bucket

Bucket name must be unique within the global namespace and follow the bucket naming rules. See rules for bucket naming ↗

Copy settings from existing bucket - *optional*
Only the bucket settings in the following configuration are copied.

Choose bucket

Format: s3://bucket/prefix

Object Ownership Info

Control ownership of objects written to this bucket from other AWS accounts and the use of access control lists (ACLs). Object ownership determines who can specify access to objects.

🔘 ACLs disabled (recommended)
All objects in this bucket are owned by this account. Access to this bucket and its objects is specified using only policies.

⭕ ACLs enabled
Objects in this bucket can be owned by other AWS accounts. Access to this bucket and its objects can be specified using ACLs.

Object Ownership

Bucket owner enforced

Figure 5.20: Creating an S3 bucket - part 1

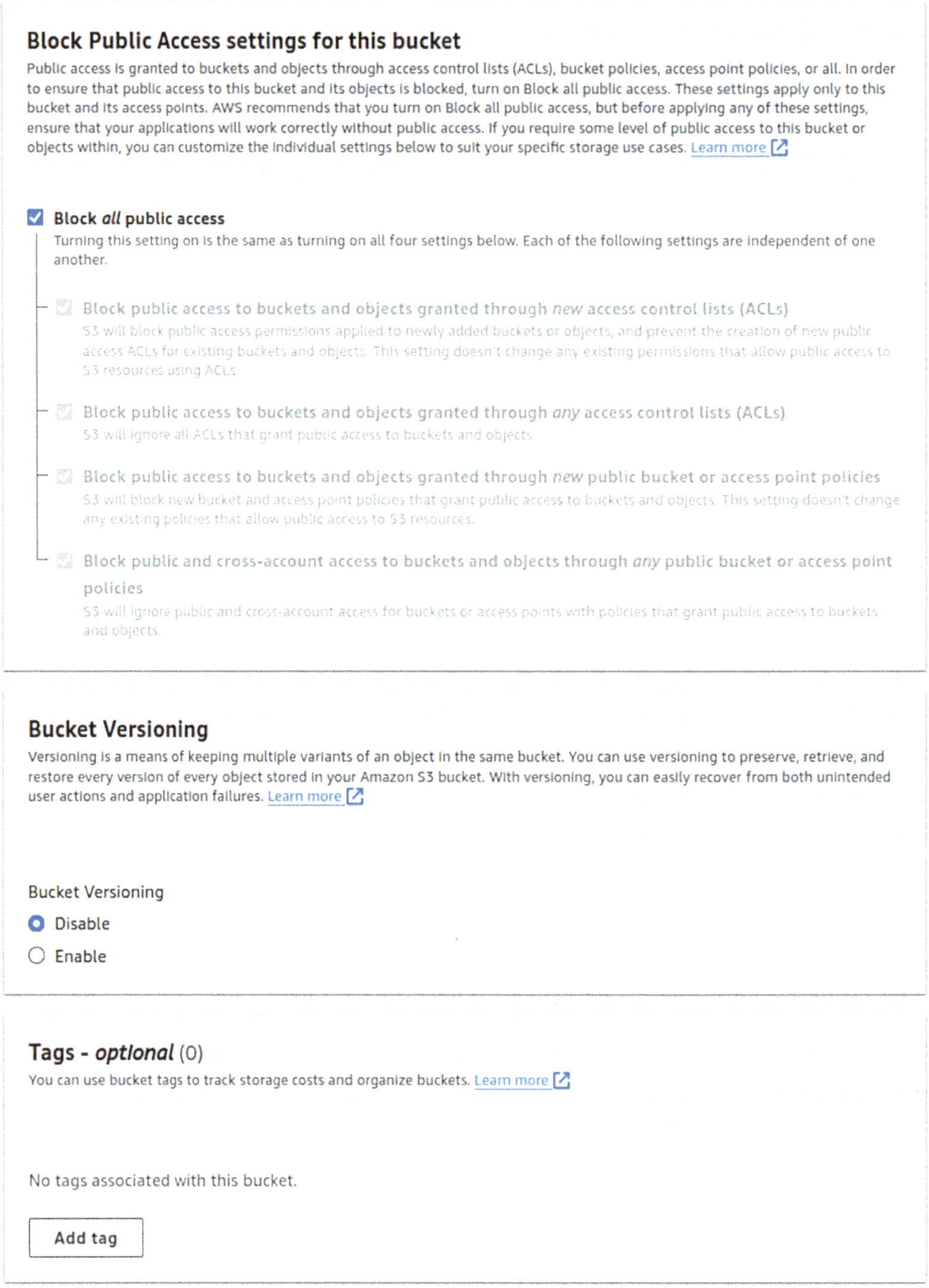

Block Public Access settings for this bucket

Public access is granted to buckets and objects through access control lists (ACLs), bucket policies, access point policies, or all. In order to ensure that public access to this bucket and its objects is blocked, turn on Block all public access. These settings apply only to this bucket and its access points. AWS recommends that you turn on Block all public access, but before applying any of these settings, ensure that your applications will work correctly without public access. If you require some level of public access to this bucket or objects within, you can customize the individual settings below to suit your specific storage use cases. Learn more [↗]

☑ **Block *all* public access**
Turning this setting on is the same as turning on all four settings below. Each of the following settings are independent of one another.

- ☑ Block public access to buckets and objects granted through *new* access control lists (ACLs)
  S3 will block public access permissions applied to newly added buckets or objects, and prevent the creation of new public access ACLs for existing buckets and objects. This setting doesn't change any existing permissions that allow public access to S3 resources using ACLs

- ☑ Block public access to buckets and objects granted through *any* access control lists (ACLs)
  S3 will ignore all ACLs that grant public access to buckets and objects

- ☑ Block public access to buckets and objects granted through *new* public bucket or access point policies
  S3 will block new bucket and access point policies that grant public access to buckets and objects. This setting doesn't change any existing policies that allow public access to S3 resources.

- ☑ Block public and cross-account access to buckets and objects through *any* public bucket or access point policies
  S3 will ignore public and cross-account access for buckets or access points with policies that grant public access to buckets and objects.

Bucket Versioning

Versioning is a means of keeping multiple variants of an object in the same bucket. You can use versioning to preserve, retrieve, and restore every version of every object stored in your Amazon S3 bucket. With versioning, you can easily recover from both unintended user actions and application failures. Learn more [↗]

Bucket Versioning

🔘 Disable

⚪ Enable

Tags - *optional* (0)

You can use bucket tags to track storage costs and organize buckets. Learn more [↗]

No tags associated with this bucket.

[Add tag]

Figure 5.21: Creating an S3 bucket - part 2

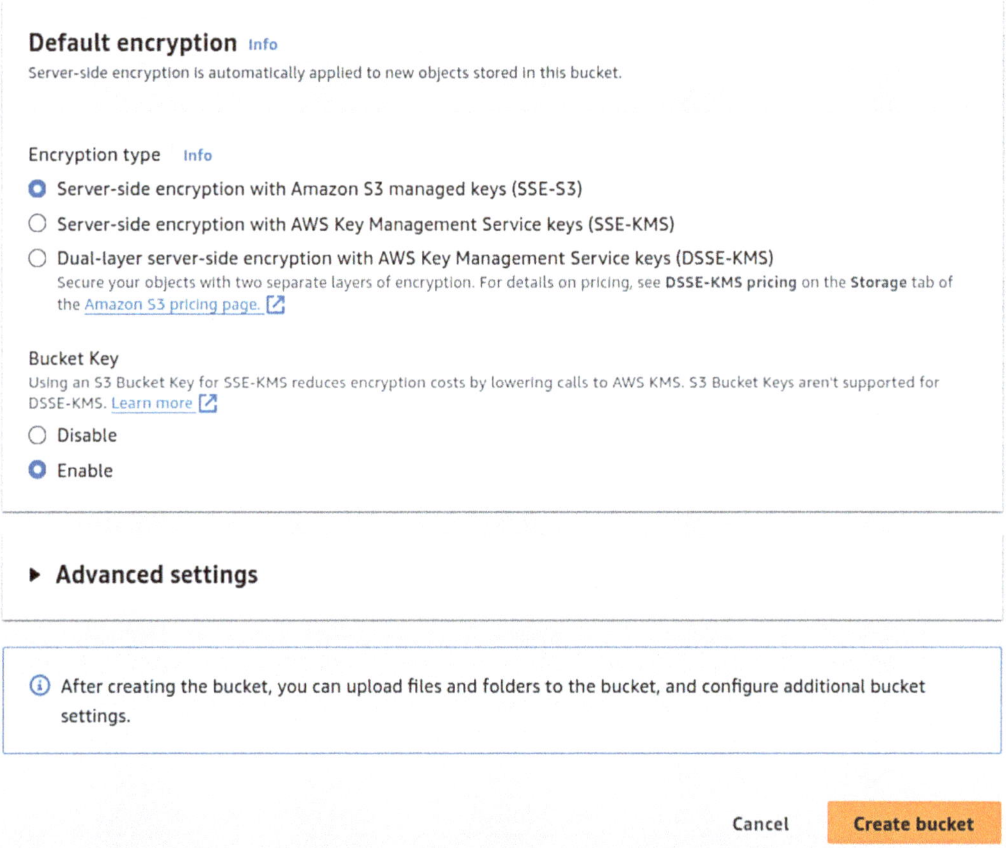

Default encryption Info

Server-side encryption is automatically applied to new objects stored in this bucket.

Encryption type   Info

🔘 Server-side encryption with Amazon S3 managed keys (SSE-S3)

⭘ Server-side encryption with AWS Key Management Service keys (SSE-KMS)

⭘ Dual-layer server-side encryption with AWS Key Management Service keys (DSSE-KMS)

Secure your objects with two separate layers of encryption. For details on pricing, see **DSSE-KMS pricing** on the **Storage** tab of the Amazon S3 pricing page. 🔗

Bucket Key

Using an S3 Bucket Key for SSE-KMS reduces encryption costs by lowering calls to AWS KMS. S3 Bucket Keys aren't supported for DSSE-KMS. Learn more 🔗

⭘ Disable

🔘 Enable

▶ **Advanced settings**

ⓘ After creating the bucket, you can upload files and folders to the bucket, and configure additional bucket settings.

Cancel   Create bucket

Figure 5.22: Creating an S3 bucket - part 3

Box 5.4 shows a Python program for creating an S3 bucket. In this program, we initialize an S3 client by passing the AWS access key and AWS secret key to the *boto3.client* function. Next, we use the S3 client's *create_bucket* function for creating a new bucket.

■ **Box 5.4: Python program for creating an S3 bucket**

```
import boto3
import json

AWS_KEY="<enter>"
AWS_SECRET="<enter>"
REGION="us-east-1"

s3 = boto3.client('s3', aws_access_key_id=AWS_KEY,
                        aws_secret_access_key=AWS_SECRET)

s3.create_bucket(Bucket='cloudcomputingcourse2019')
```

Box 5.5 shows a Python program for listing all S3 buckets in an AWS account.

■ **Box 5.5: Python program for listing S3 buckets in an AWS account**

```
import boto3
import json

AWS_KEY="<enter>"
AWS_SECRET="<enter>"
REGION="us-east-1"

s3 = boto3.client('s3', aws_access_key_id=AWS_KEY,
                        aws_secret_access_key=AWS_SECRET)


response = s3.list_buckets()

buckets = [bucket['Name'] for bucket in response['Buckets']]

print("Bucket List: %s" % buckets)
```

5.7.2 Objects

Objects are the entities that are stored in Amazon S3. Objects have object data and metadata. Objects can store data in any format, and the data stored is opaque to S3. Objects' size can range from 0 bytes to 5TB. An object consists of a Key, Version ID, Value, Metadata, Subresources, and Access Control Information. Each object is uniquely identified by a combination of Bucket, Key, and an optional Version ID. Key is the name that is assigned to the object. You can use versioning to keep multiple versions of the same object in a bucket. Version ID allows you to identify a specific version of an object. The Value of an object is the actual content that you store. Value is a sequence of bytes. The Metadata for an object consists of a set of key-value pairs that provide information regarding the object (such as Date, Content-Length, Last-Modified, and Content-MD5). The subresources for an object are used to store object-specific additional information. For example, the ACL subresource contains a list of grants, including the grantees and the permissions granted. Similarly, the Torrent subresource is used to return the torrent file associated with an object.

Box 5.6 shows the Python code for storing data on S3 from a string using the *put_object* function of the S3 client.

■ **Box 5.6: Python program for putting an object in an S3 bucket**

```
import boto3

AWS_KEY="<enter>"
AWS_SECRET="<enter>"
REGION="us-east-1"
BUCKET = "cloudcomputingcourse2019"

s3 = boto3.client('s3', aws_access_key_id=AWS_KEY,
                        aws_secret_access_key=AWS_SECRET)
```

```
s3.put_object(Bucket=BUCKET,
              Key='data.txt',
              Body='Hello world')
```

Box 5.7 shows the Python code for getting the contents of an object from S3 using the *get_object* function of the S3 client.

■ **Box 5.7: Python program for getting an object from an S3 bucket**

```
import boto3
import json

AWS_KEY="<enter>"
AWS_SECRET="<enter>"
REGION="us-east-1"
BUCKET = "cloudcomputingcourse2019"

s3 = boto3.client('s3', aws_access_key_id=AWS_KEY,
                         aws_secret_access_key=AWS_SECRET)


response = s3.get_object(Bucket=BUCKET,
                         Key='data.txt')

data = json.loads(response['Body'].read())
print data
```

Box 5.8 shows the Python code for uploading a file to S3 using the *upload_file* function of the S3 client.

■ **Box 5.8: Python program for uploading a file to an S3 bucket**

```
import boto3

AWS_KEY="<enter>"
AWS_SECRET="<enter>"
REGION="us-east-1"
BUCKET = "cloudcomputingcourse2019"

s3 = boto3.client('s3', aws_access_key_id=AWS_KEY,
                         aws_secret_access_key=AWS_SECRET)


filenameWithPath = "/home/ubuntu/s3/pic.png"
path_filename='pic.png'

s3.upload_file(filenameWithPath, BUCKET, path_filename)

s3.put_object_acl(ACL='public-read', Bucket=BUCKET, Key=path_filename)
```

Box 5.9 shows the Python code for downloading a file stored on S3 using the *download_file* function of the S3 client.

■ Box 5.9: Python program for downloading a file stored on S3

```
import boto3

AWS_KEY="<enter>"
AWS_SECRET="<enter>"
REGION="us-east-1"
BUCKET = "cloudcomputingcourse2019"

s3 = boto3.client('s3', aws_access_key_id=AWS_KEY,
                       aws_secret_access_key=AWS_SECRET)
path_filename='pic.png'
s3.download_file(BUCKET, path_filename, "pic1.png")
```

5.7.3 Managing Access with Bucket Policies and ACLs

By default, access to all resources in S3, including buckets and objects, is private. You can manage access to the S3 resources using resource-based policies or user-based policies. Resource-based policies include bucket policies and access control lists (ACLs)). User-based policies include AWS Identity and Access Management (IAM) policies attached to users in an AWS account.

Access Control Lists (ACLs) allow you to grant permissions such as read or write at the level of a bucket or object. With ACLs, you can give read or write permissions to other AWS accounts or to the public. Each bucket and object has an ACL attached to it as a subresource. An ACL defines which AWS accounts or groups are granted access and the type of access such as READ, WRITE, READ_ACP, WRITE_ACP, and FULL_CONTROL. For each request received against an S3 resource, the corresponding ACL is checked to verify that the requester has the necessary access permissions. Box 5.10 shows the Python code for changing the ACL for an object in an S3 bucket using the *put_object_acl* function of the S3 client.

■ Box 5.10: Python program for changing the ACL for an object in an S3 bucket

```
import boto3
import json

AWS_KEY="<enter>"
AWS_SECRET="<enter>"
REGION="us-east-1"
BUCKET = "cloudcomputingcourse2019"

s3 = boto3.client('s3', aws_access_key_id=AWS_KEY,
                       aws_secret_access_key=AWS_SECRET)

s3.put_object_acl(ACL='private', Bucket=BUCKET, Key='pic1.png')
s3.put_object_acl(ACL='public-read', Bucket=BUCKET, Key='pic2.png')
```

Bucket Policies allow more fine-grained control for managing access as compared to ACLs. Using bucket policies, you can specify who can access an S3 resource and the allowed actions. You can select specific resources for which the policy is applied, limit access to specific IP addresses, grant cross-account permissions, grant read-only permissions to an anonymous user, and other such advanced access control options. Box 5.11 shows an example of a bucket policy. Box 5.12 shows the Python code for applying a bucket policy to an S3 bucket.

■ Box 5.11: Example of an S3 bucket policy

```
{
  "Id": "Policy1542777988665",
  "Version": "2012-10-17",
  "Statement": [
    {
      "Sid": "Stmt1542777985222",
      "Action": [
        "s3:GetObject",
        "s3:PutObject"
      ],
      "Effect": "Allow",
      "Resource": "arn:aws:s3:::cloudcomputingcourse2018",
      "Principal": "*"
    }
  ]
}
```

■ Box 5.12: Python program for applying a bucket policy to an S3 bucket

```
import boto3
import json

AWS_KEY="<enter>"
AWS_SECRET="<enter>"
REGION="us-east-1"
BUCKET = "cloudcomputingcourse2019"

s3 = boto3.client('s3', aws_access_key_id=AWS_KEY,
                        aws_secret_access_key=AWS_SECRET)
bucket_policy = {
    'Version': '2012-10-17',
    'Statement': [{
        'Sid': 'AddPerm',
        'Effect': 'Allow',
        'Principal': '*',
        'Action': ['s3:GetObject'],
        'Resource': "arn:aws:s3:::%s/*" % BUCKET
    }]
}
s3.put_bucket_policy(Bucket=BUCKET, Policy=json.dumps(bucket_policy))
```

5.7.4 Cross-Origin Resource Sharing (CORS)

Cross-Origin Resource Sharing (CORS) is a mechanism that allows a client application running at one origin (domain) to have permission to access selected resources from a different origin (domain). You can enable CORS for an S3 bucket using the Amazon S3 console, or by using the Amazon S3 REST API and the AWS SDKs. To allow cross-origin requests, a CORS configuration is created as shown in Box 5.13. A CORS configuration specifies rules such as the origins which are allowed to access a bucket, the allowed operations, or HTTP methods, and other operation-specific information. Box 5.14 shows a Python program for setting a CORS configuration for a bucket.

■ **Box 5.13: Example of a CORS Configuration for an S3 bucket**

```
<CORSConfiguration>
 <CORSRule>
   <AllowedOrigin>http://www.example.com</AllowedOrigin>
   <AllowedMethod>GET</AllowedMethod>
   <AllowedMethod>POST</AllowedMethod>
   <AllowedMethod>PUT</AllowedMethod>
   <AllowedHeader>*</AllowedHeader>
 </CORSRule>
</CORSConfiguration>
```

■ **Box 5.14: Python program for setting a CORS configuration for an S3 bucket**

```
import boto3
import json
AWS_KEY="<enter>"
AWS_SECRET="<enter>"
REGION="us-east-1"
BUCKET = "cloudcomputingcourse2019"
s3 = boto3.client('s3', aws_access_key_id=AWS_KEY,
                  aws_secret_access_key=AWS_SECRET)

cors_configuration={
        'CORSRules': [
            {
                'AllowedHeaders': [
                    '*',
                ],
                'AllowedMethods': [
                    'PUT','POST','DELETE'
                ],
                'AllowedOrigins': [
                    'http://www.example.com',
                ],
                'ExposeHeaders': [
                    'x-amz-server-side-encryption',
                    'x-amz-request-id', 'x-amz-id-2'
                ],
                'MaxAgeSeconds': 3000
```

```
            },
        ]

s3.put_bucket_cors(Bucket=BUCKET, CORSConfiguration=cors_configuration)
```

5.7.5 Versioning

S3 allows you to enable versioning for a bucket. When versioning is enabled, you can have multiple versions of an object in one bucket. Versioning helps in protecting your data from accidental or malicious updates or deletes. Each version is identified by a version ID. You can retrieve and restore every version of every object stored in a bucket for which versioning is enabled. Versioning is enabled at the bucket level and once enabled, it cannot be disabled, but can only be suspended. A bucket in which versioning is enabled maintains one current and zero or more noncurrent object versions.

5.7.6 Encryption

You can protect sensitive data stored in S3 using encryption. You can either use Server-Side Encryption (SSE) or Client-Side Encryption for protecting data at rest in S3. With server-side encryption, S3 encrypts the data at the object level before saving it on disks in its data centers and decrypts it when you download the objects. S3 provides three options for SSE depending on how you choose to manage the encryption keys: (1) SSE-S3, (2) SSE-KMS, and (3) SSE-C. In the SSE-S3 option (Server-Side Encryption with Amazon S3-Managed Keys) the encryption key management and key protection are handled by Amazon S3. Each object is encrypted with a unique key using the 256-bit Advanced Encryption Standard (AES-256). The SSE-KMS option (Server-Side Encryption with AWS KMS-Managed Keys), is similar to SSE-S3 but gives you additional flexibility to create and manage encryption keys yourself and keep an audit trail of when your key was used, and by whom. The SSE-C option (Server-Side Encryption with Customer-Provided Keys) is used when you want to maintain your encryption keys and allows Amazon S3 to manage the encryption/decryption of objects. With client-side encryption, you encrypt the data at the client side before uploading the data to S3.

5.7.7 Static Website Hosting

Amazon S3 buckets can be used for hosting static websites that don't require a full web server. A static website includes only static HTML web pages, and static resources such as images, stylesheets (CSS files), and JavaScript files. By hosting a static website on S3, you can leverage the scalability, availability, durability, and security offered by S3. To host a static website on S3, create a bucket with a name that matches the desired website hostname (for example, www.example.com). Next, upload the static files to the S3 bucket and make the files public. Next, enable static website hosting for the bucket from the S3 console and specify an index document (for example, index.html) and an error document (for example, error.html). When you enable static website hosting for a bucket you get an S3 website URL like *<bucket-name>.s3-website.<AWS-region>.amazonaws.com*. Open this URL in a browser to check if the website is working. If you wish to use a more user-friendly URL for the website, you can register a domain name and then add a CNAME record in the DNS settings for the domain or an Amazon Route 53 alias to resolve the domain to the S3 website URL.

5.7.8 Transfer Acceleration

You can enable Transfer Acceleration for a bucket to enable fast, easy, and secure transfers of files over long distances between your client and the S3 bucket. Transfer Acceleration feature in S3 uses the globally distributed edge locations of Amazon CloudFront to route data from an edge location to S3 over an optimized path.

5.7.9 Durability and Availability

Durability and availability are two essential aspects of data accessibility. While durability refers to long-term data protection, availability refers to system uptime. A durable storage system ensures that the data stored is not lost due to corruption or degradation. An available storage system is one that continues to remain operational and can deliver data when requested. Amazon S3 is designed for both high durability and high availability. S3 is designed for 99.999999999% (eleven nines) of durability and 99.99% availability. S3 provides such high durability of data by storing data redundantly on multiple systems in multiple facilities within a region.

5.7.10 Consistency

S3 provides read-after-write consistency for PUTs of new objects. Whereas for PUTs to existing objects and for object DELETEs, S3 offers eventual consistency. Eventual consistency for overwrite PUTs means that if you update an object with a PUT request, and then read the object with a GET request, you can either get the old data or updated data. Similarly, eventual consistency for DELETE means that if you delete an object and then read the object with a GET request, you may still be able to read the deleted object. However, updates to a single key are atomic, which means that if you update an object and then read the object, you either get the new data or old data, but you never get partially updated or inconsistent data.

5.7.11 Storage Classes

S3 offers various storage classes which are designed for different use cases and differ in the durability and availability. The storage classes offered are as follows:
- **Standard**: Standard storage class is designed for frequently accessed data and offers high durability (99.999999999%), high availability (99.99%), low latency, and high throughput. There is no minimum storage duration or minimum billable object size for this storage class.
- **Standard - Infrequently Accessed**: Standard - Infrequently Accessed (IA) storage class offers the high durability (99.999999999%) and availability (99.9%) like the Standard storage class, but it is designed for long-lived and infrequently accessed data. The Standard-IA storage class has a lower GB-month storage cost than the Standard class; however, the minimum storage duration is 30 days, the minimum billable object size is 128 KB, and a per-GB retrieval fee applies.

- **Intelligent Tiering**: Intelligent Tiering storage class offers high durability (99.999999999%) and availability (99.9%) and is designed for long-lived data with changing or unknown access patterns. The minimum storage duration is 30 days, and monitoring and automation fees per object apply. There is no minimum billable object size or retrieval fee for this storage class.
- **One Zone - Infrequently Accessed**: One Zone - Infrequently Accessed (IA) storage class offers high durability (99.999999999%) and a slightly lower availability (99.5%). One Zone-IA storage class is designed for long-lived, infrequently accessed, and non-critical data. Data is stored in one availability zone only, so this storage class is not resilient to the loss of the availability zone. The minimum storage duration for this storage class is 30 days, the minimum billable object size is 128 KB, and a per-GB retrieval fee applies.
- **Glacier**: Glacier storage class offers the same durability and availability as the Standard storage class but at an extremely low cost. Glacier is designed for long-term data archiving with retrieval times ranging from minutes to hours. The minimum storage duration for this storage class is 90 days, and a per-GB retrieval fee applies. Data archived on Glacier is not available for real-time access. To retrieve an object archived in Glacier, a restore command is issued which creates a temporary copy of the object that is available for the duration specified.
- **Reduced Redundancy**: Reduced Redundancy storage class offers slightly lower durability (99.99%) and high availability (99.99%). This storage class is designed for frequently accessed and non-critical data.

5.7.12   Object Lifecycle Management

S3 allows you to define lifecycle rules for a group of objects to ensure that the objects are stored cost-effectively throughout their lifecycle. A lifecycle configuration can be attached to an S3 bucket such that it applies to all objects in the bucket or to a group of objects specified by a prefix. There are two types of actions that can be defined in a lifecycle configuration: (1) transition action, (2) expiration action. A transition action is defined when the objects have to be transitioned to another storage class. For example, newly created objects can be stored in Standard storage class and then transitioned to Standard-IA class after 60 days and then transitioned to Glacier after 120 days. Expiration actions define when the objects expire. The expired objects are automatically deleted by S3. For example, an expiration action can be defined to delete objects older than 2 years.

5.7.13   Cross-Region Replication

Cross-region replication allows you to copy objects from a source bucket in one AWS region to a destination bucket in another region, automatically and asynchronously. Cross-region replication is enabled at the bucket-level by providing the destination bucket where you want S3 to replicate the objects and an AWS IAM role that Amazon S3 can assume to replicate objects on your behalf. To enable cross-region replication, you must have versioning enabled for the source and destination buckets. When an object is copied from a source to destination bucket, the metadata and ACLs associated with the object are also replicated in the destination. If any change is made to the metadata or ACLs for an object in the source bucket, a new replication is triggered.

5.8 Amazon Elastic File System (EFS)

Amazon Elastic File System (EFS) provides a highly scalable, available, and durable file storage that can be used with EC2 instances. The storage capacity in an EFS file system is elastic and grows or shrinks as you add or delete files. EFS supports the Network File System protocols (NFSv4.1 and NFSv4.0). EFS file systems are distributed across several storage servers, which enables the file system to grow elastically and support parallel access from multiple EC2 instances. EFS is designed for use cases such as Big Data and Analytics workloads, Media Processing workflows, Content Management, and Web Serving. EFS can provide high throughput coupled with read-after-write consistency, low-latency file operations, and shared file access, which is required for such use cases.

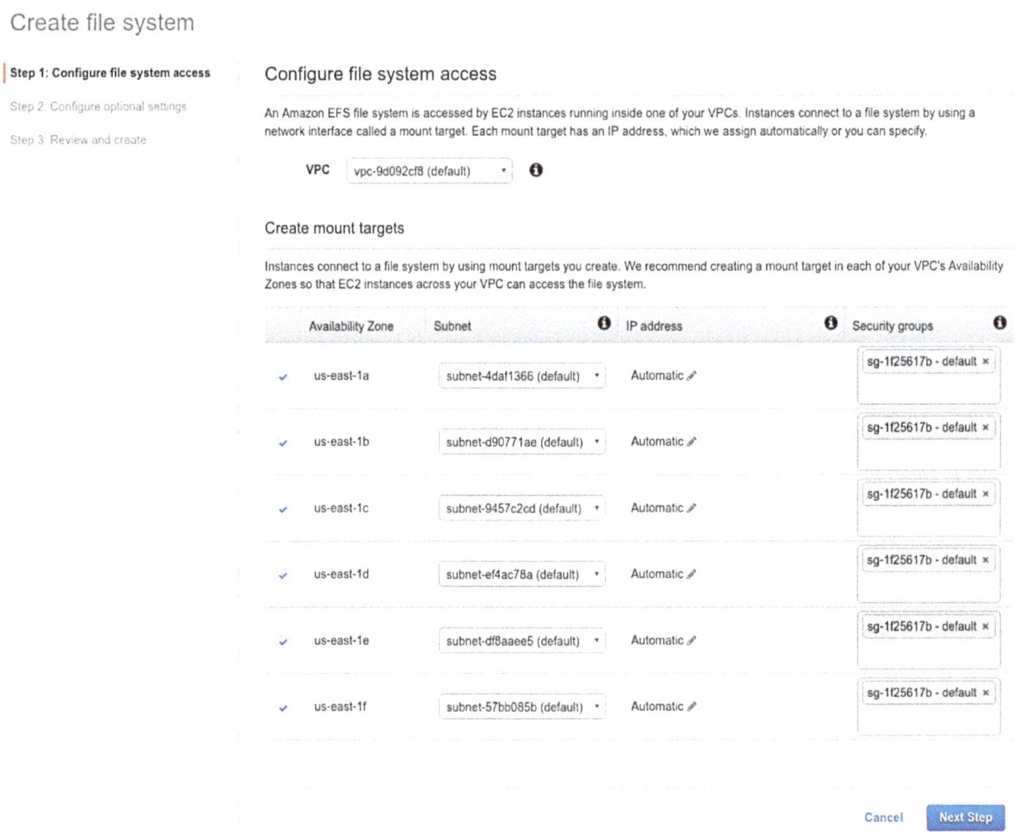

Figure 5.23: Creating an EFS file system - step 1

EFS offers several benefits for microservices applications. Firstly, it provides a scalable and highly available file storage service, ensuring that your microservices can access shared data concurrently without performance bottlenecks. EFS seamlessly scales file system capacity on-demand, eliminating the need for provisioning and managing storage capacity. Additionally, EFS supports the NFS protocol, allowing microservices running on various instances or containers to access the same file system simultaneously. This facilitates easy data sharing and collaboration among different components of your application. Furthermore, EFS offers data replication across multiple Availability Zones, providing built-in redundancy

Create file system

Step 1: Configure file system access

Step 2: Configure optional settings

Step 3: Review and create

Configure optional settings

Add tags

You can add tags to describe your file system. A tag consists of a case-sensitive key-value pair. (For example, you can define a tag with key-value pair with key = Corporate Department and value = Sales and Marketing.) At a minimum, we recommend a tag with key = Name.

Key	Value	Remove
Name	Add New Value	⊗
Add New Key		

Choose performance mode

We recommend **General Purpose** performance mode for most file systems. **Max I/O** performance mode is optimized for applications where tens, hundreds, or thousands of EC2 instances are accessing the file system — it scales to higher levels of aggregate throughput and operations per second with a tradeoff of slightly higher latencies for file operations.

  ● **General Purpose**
  ○ **Max I/O**

Choose throughput mode

We recommend **Bursting** throughput mode for most file systems. Use **Provisioned** throughput mode for applications that require more throughput than allowed by **Bursting** throughput. ☑ Learn more

  ● **Bursting**
  ○ **Provisioned**

Enable encryption

If you enable encryption for your file system, all data on your file system will be encrypted at rest. You can select a KMS key from your account to protect your file system, or you can provide the ARN of a key from a different account. Encryption of data at rest can only be enabled during file system creation. Encryption of data in transit is configured when mounting your file system. Learn more

  ☐ **Enable encryption of data at rest**

Cancel   Previous   Next Step

Figure 5.24: Creating an EFS file system - step 2

and data durability, ensuring your data remains accessible even in the event of an Availability Zone failure. With its pay-as-you-go pricing model, EFS allows you to optimize costs by only paying for the storage you actually use.

You can mount an EFS file system to any number of EC2 instances at the same time. To get started with using EFS, create an EFS file system from the EFS console as shown in Figures 5.23 to 5.25. At the first step, choose the VPC and then select the availability zones as shown in Figure 5.23. Next, you can configure optional settings and add tags, choose a performance mode (such as General Purpose or Max I/O), choose a throughput mode (such as Bursting or Provisioned), and enable encryption, as shown in Figure 5.24. Finally, you can review and create the file system, as shown in Figure 5.25.

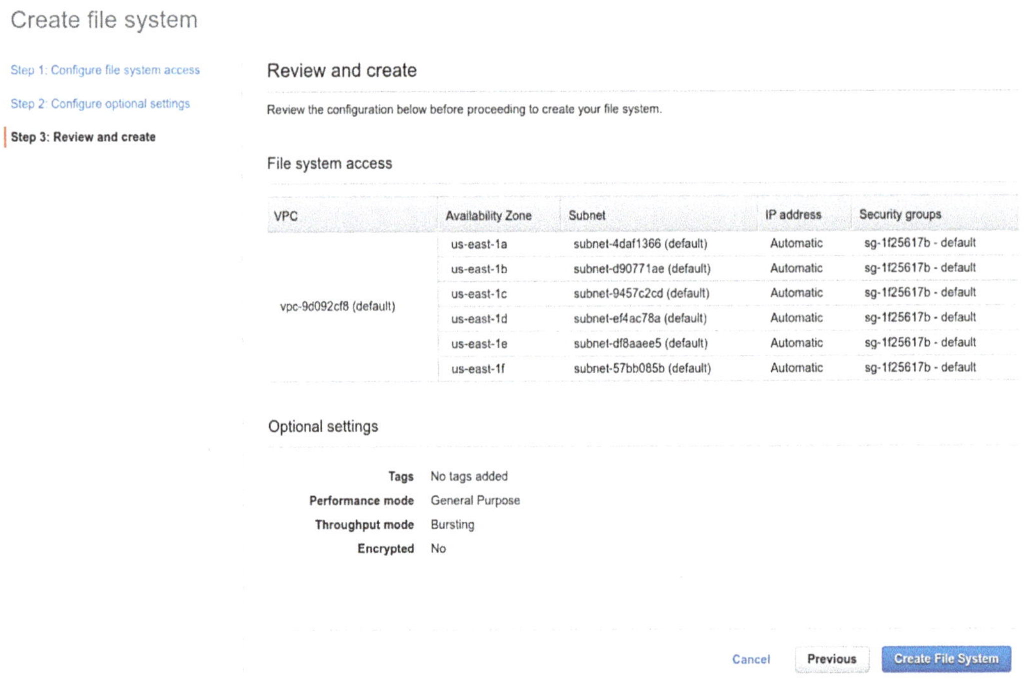

Create file system

Step 1: Configure file system access

Review and create

Step 2: Configure optional settings

Review the configuration below before proceeding to create your file system.

Step 3: Review and create

File system access

VPC	Availability Zone	Subnet	IP address	Security groups
vpc-9d092cf8 (default)	us-east-1a	subnet-4daf1366 (default)	Automatic	sg-1f25617b - default
	us-east-1b	subnet-d90771ae (default)	Automatic	sg-1f25617b - default
	us-east-1c	subnet-9457c2cd (default)	Automatic	sg-1f25617b - default
	us-east-1d	subnet-ef4ac78a (default)	Automatic	sg-1f25617b - default
	us-east-1e	subnet-df8aaee5 (default)	Automatic	sg-1f25617b - default
	us-east-1f	subnet-57bb085b (default)	Automatic	sg-1f25617b - default

Optional settings

Tags	No tags added
Performance mode	General Purpose
Throughput mode	Bursting
Encrypted	No

Cancel   **Previous**   **Create File System**

Figure 5.25: Creating an EFS file system - step 3

You can also create an EFS file system programmatically using the AWS SDKs. Box 5.15 shows a Python program for creating an EFS file system.

■ Box 5.15: Python program for creating an EFS file system

```python
import boto3

AWS_KEY="<enter>"
AWS_SECRET="<enter>"
REGION="us-east-1"

client = boto3.client('efs', aws_access_key_id=AWS_KEY,
                      aws_secret_access_key=AWS_SECRET)


response = client.create_file_system(
    CreationToken='myfs',
    PerformanceMode='generalPurpose',
    Encrypted=False,
    ThroughputMode='bursting'
)
```

Once the Amazon EFS file system is created, you can mount the file system to an EC2 instance using the commands as shown in Box 5.16.

> ■ **Box 5.16: Commands for mounting an EFS**
>
> ```
> sudo apt-get install nfs-common
>
> sudo mkdir efs
>
> sudo mount -t nfs4 -o nfsvers=4.1,rsize=1048576,\
>         wsize=1048576,hard,timeo=600,retrans=2,\
>         noresvport fs-4996ba03.efs.us-east-1.amazonaws.com:/ efs
>
> cd efs
>
> touch test.txt
> ```

5.8.1 EFS Performance Modes

EFS provides two performance modes: (1) General Purpose and (2) Max I/O. The General Purpose performance mode is suitable for applications requiring low latency such as web serving, content management, and file serving. The Max I/O performance mode is optimized for applications where a large number of EC2 instances are accessing the file system. The Max I/O mode scales to higher levels of aggregate throughput and operations per second with a tradeoff of slightly higher latencies for file operations.

5.8.2 EFS Throughput Modes

EFS provides two throughput modes: (1) Bursting throughput and (2) Provisioned throughput. When Bursting throughput mode is used for an EFS file system, the throughput scales as a file system grows. Bursting throughput mode is useful for file-based workloads that require low levels of throughput for most of the time and high levels of throughput occasionally. Provisioned throughput mode is useful for applications requiring higher levels of throughput than those allowed by the Bursting throughput mode. With provisioned throughput mode, you can provision throughput in the range of 1-1024 MiB/s.

5.8.3 Encryption

EFS supports both encryption of data in transit and encryption of data at rest. The encryption of data at rest can be enabled when creating an Amazon EFS file system. While enabling the encryption of data at rest, you can select a Key Management Service (KMS) key from your AWS account to protect your file system, or you can provide the ARN of a key from a different AWS account. The encryption of data in transit can be enabled when you mount the file system. Encryption of data in transit is enabled by connecting to Amazon EFS using TLS.

5.9 Amazon Elastic Block Store (EBS)

Amazon Elastic Block Store (EBS) provides block-level storage volumes for use with EC2 instances. EBS is designed for high availability and durability, and the EBS volumes are automatically replicated within an availability zone. You can attach multiple EBS volumes to an EC2 instance; however, a volume can be attached to only one instance at a time.

5.9.1 Volumes

An EBS Volume is a block-level storage device that can be attached to an EC2 instance. The benefit of using an EBS volume with an EC2 instance is that it can persist independently from the life of the instance. A volume attached to an EC2 instance can be used like any other physical hard drive. EBS volumes can be used for various purposes such as system boot volumes, database storage, and throughput-intensive applications. EBS provides various types of volumes that differ in performance characteristics and cost. The volume types are as follows:

- **Magnetic (standard)**: Magnetic volumes have low-performance characteristics. A magnetic volume can range in size from 1 GB to 1 TB. A magnetic volume can deliver approximately 100 IOPS on average, with burst capability of up to hundreds of IOPS. Magnetic volumes are suited for workloads where data is accessed infrequently or for applications where low storage cost is a requirement.
- **General Purpose SSD (gp2)**: General Purpose SSD volumes offer cost-effective storage that balances price and performance for a wide variety of workloads. The volume size can vary from 1 GB to 16 TB. These volumes can provide a baseline performance of 3 IOPS per GB with a minimum of 100 IOPS and burstable to 3000 IOPS. General Purpose SSD volumes are suitable for use cases such as system boot volumes, virtual desktops, low-latency interactive applications, and for development and test environments.
- **Provisioned IOPS SSD (io1)**: Provisioned IOPS SSD volumes are the highest-performance volumes designed for mission-critical low-latency or high-throughput workloads. The volume size can vary from 4 GB to 16 TB, with a maximum IOPS of 64000, and maximum throughput of 1000 MB/s. Provisioned IOPS SSD volumes are suitable for use cases such as critical business applications that require sustained IOPS performance and large database workloads.
- **Cold HDD (sc1)**: Cold HDD volumes are designed for less frequently accessed workloads. The volume size can vary from 500 GB to 16 TB, with a maximum IOPS of 250 and a maximum throughput of 250 MB/s. Cold HDD volumes are suitable for throughput-oriented storage for large volumes of data that is infrequently accessed.
- **Throughput Optimized HDD (st1)**: Throughput-Optimized HDD volumes are designed for frequently accessed, throughput-intensive workloads. The volume size can vary from 500 GB to 16 TB, with a maximum IOPS of 500 and a maximum throughput of 500 MB/s. Throughput-Optimized HDD volumes are suitable for use cases such as streaming workloads requiring consistent and fast throughput at a low price, big data, data warehouses, and log processing.

You can create an EBS volume from the Amazon EC2 console, as shown in Figure 5.26. To create a volume, select a volume type, enter a volume size, and select an availability zone.

You can optionally select a snapshot from which the volume has to be created. You can choose to encrypt the volume.

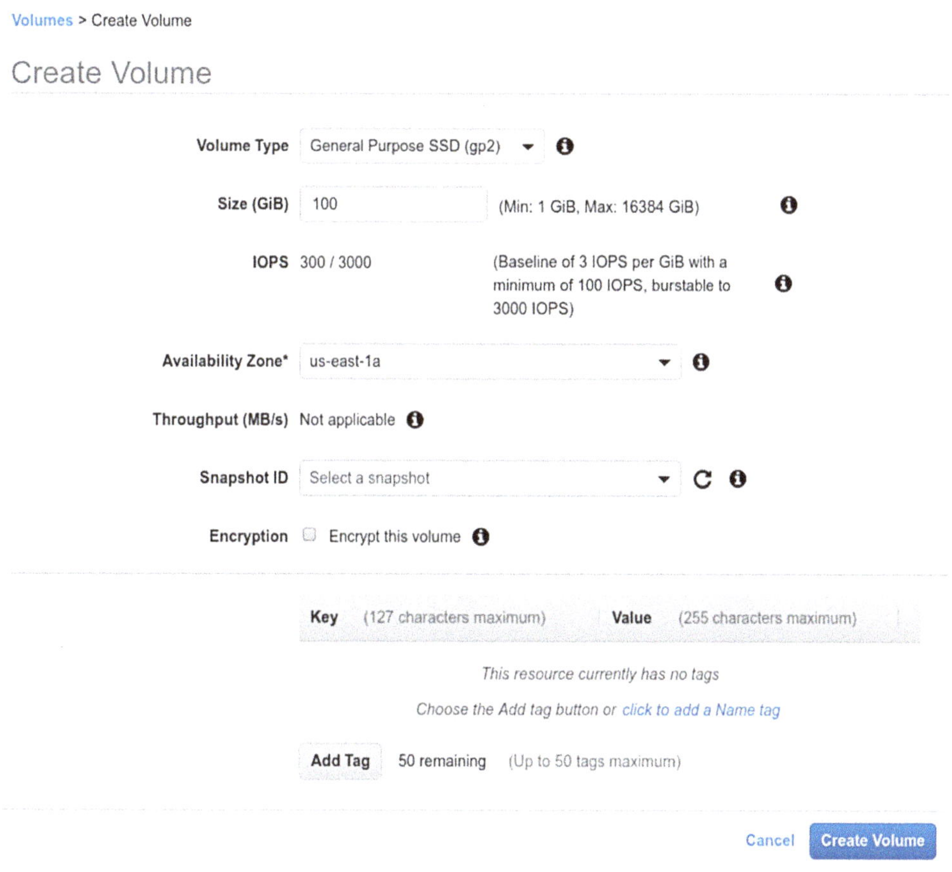

Volumes > Create Volume

Create Volume

Volume Type	General Purpose SSD (gp2) ▼ ❶
Size (GiB)	100 (Min: 1 GiB, Max: 16384 GiB) ❶
IOPS	300 / 3000 (Baseline of 3 IOPS per GiB with a minimum of 100 IOPS, burstable to 3000 IOPS) ❶
Availability Zone*	us-east-1a ▼ ❶
Throughput (MB/s)	Not applicable ❶
Snapshot ID	Select a snapshot ▼ ⟳ ❶
Encryption	☐ Encrypt this volume ❶

Key (127 characters maximum)	**Value** (255 characters maximum)

This resource currently has no tags
Choose the Add tag button or click to add a Name tag

Add Tag   50 remaining   (Up to 50 tags maximum)

Cancel   **Create Volume**

Figure 5.26: Creating an EBS volume

Volumes can also be created programmatically using AWS SDKs. Box 5.17 shows a Python program for creating an EBS volume.

■ **Box 5.17: Python program for creating an EBS volume**

```
import boto3
AWS_KEY="<enter>"
AWS_SECRET="<enter>"
REGION="us-east-1"
client = boto3.client('ec2', aws_access_key_id=AWS_KEY,
                      aws_secret_access_key=AWS_SECRET,
                      region_name=REGION)
response = client.create_volume(
    AvailabilityZone='us-east-1a',
    Encrypted=False, Size=50,
    VolumeType= 'gp2'  #'standard'|'io1'|'gp2'|'sc1'|'st1',
)
```

5.9.2 Snapshots

You can create a snapshot of an EBS volume from the Amazon EC2 console, as shown in Figure 5.27. Snapshots can also be created programmatically using AWS SDKs.

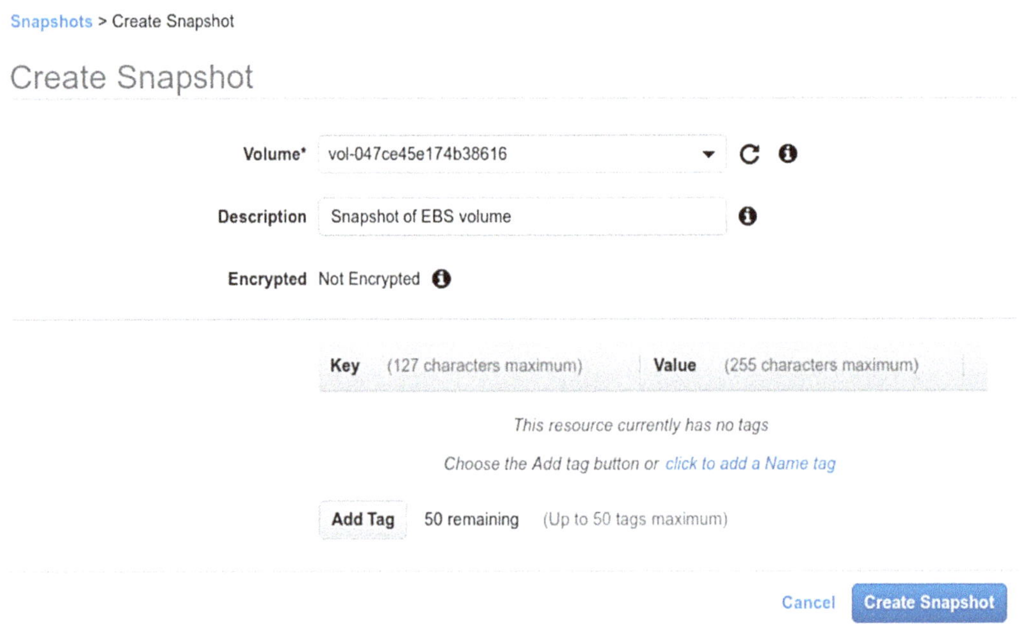

Snapshots > Create Snapshot

Create Snapshot

Volume*	vol-047ce45e174b38616 ▾ C ❶
Description	Snapshot of EBS volume ❶
Encrypted	Not Encrypted ❶

Key (127 characters maximum)	Value (255 characters maximum)

This resource currently has no tags

Choose the Add tag button or click to add a Name tag

Add Tag   50 remaining   (Up to 50 tags maximum)

Cancel   **Create Snapshot**

Figure 5.27: Creating a Snapshot of an EBS volume

5.9.3 Encryption

While creating a new EBS volume, you can choose to encrypt the volume. Volumes created from encrypted snapshots are automatically encrypted, and the volumes created from unencrypted snapshots are automatically unencrypted. If you choose to encrypt a volume, you have to select a Master Key. Amazon uses the AWS Key Management Service (KMS) for managing the keys. A unique customer master key (CMK) is automatically created for each region in your account, and this key is used for encrypting EBS volumes. You can also specify a customer-managed CMK that you created separately using AWS KMS. The data on an encrypted volume is encrypted using the industry-standard AES-256 algorithm.

EBS offers persistent block-level storage volumes that can be attached to EC2 instances or used as root device volumes. In a microservices architecture, each service can have its own EBS volume attached, allowing for data isolation and independent scaling of storage capacity for each service. EBS volumes are highly available and durable, with built-in replication across multiple Availability Zones, ensuring data redundancy. Additionally, EBS supports creating snapshots, which can be used for data backup and recovery purposes, enabling easy rollback or cloning of microservices environments. By leveraging EBS, microservices can benefit from persistent, scalable, and reliable storage tailored to their specific needs.

5.10   Relational Databases

A relational database or SQL database is a database that conforms to the relational model that was popularized by IBM's Edgar Codd in 1970 [16]. A relational database has a collection of relations (or tables). A relation is a set of tuples (or rows). Each relation has a fixed schema that defines the set of attributes (or columns in a table) and the constraints on the attributes. Each tuple in a relation has the same attributes (columns). The tuples in a relation can have any order, and the relation is not sensitive to the ordering of the tuples. Each attribute has a domain, which is the set of possible values for the attribute. Relations can be modified using insert, update, and delete operations. Every relation has a primary key that uniquely identifies each tuple in the relation. An attribute can be made a primary key if it does not have repeated values in different tuples. That is, no two tuples can have the same value for the primary key attribute. Figure 5.28 shows the pros and cons of using relational databases.

Pros	Cons
Well-defined consistency model. An application that runs on one relational database (such as MySQL) can be easily changed to run on other relational databases (e.g., Microsoft SQL server). The underlying model remains unchanged.	Performance is the major constraint for relational databases. The performance depends on the number of relations and the size of the relations. Scaling out relational database deployments is difficult.
Provide ACID guarantees.	Limited support for complex data structures. Eg. if the data is naturally organized hierarchically and stored as such, the hierarchical approach can allow quick analysis of data.
Relational integrity maintained through entity and referential integrity constraints.	A complete knowledge of the database structure is required to create ad hoc queries.
Well suited for Online Transaction Processing (OLTP) applications.	Setting up and maintaining a relational database system can be expensive.
Sound theoretical foundation (based on relational model) which has been tried and tested for several years. Stable and standardized databases available.	Some relational databases have limits on the size of the fields.
The database design and normalization steps are well defined, and the underlying structure is well understood.	Integrating data from multiple relational database systems can be cumbersome.

Figure 5.28: Pros and Cons of relational databases

A relational database has various constraints described as follows:
- **Domain Constraint:** Domain constraints restrict the domain of each attribute or the set of possible values for the attribute. Domain constraints specify that the value of each attribute must be a value from the domain of the attribute.
- **Entity Integrity Constraint:** Entity integrity constraint states that no primary key value can be null. Since the primary key is used to identify each tuple uniquely in a

relation, having a null value for a primary key value makes it impossible to identify tuples in the relation.

- **Referential Integrity Constraint:** Referential integrity constraints are required to maintain consistency among the tuples in two relations. Referential integrity requires every value of one attribute of a relation to exist as a value of another attribute in another relation. In other words, tuples in a relation that refers to another relation must refer to tuples that exist in the other relation.
- **Foreign Key:** For cross-referencing between multiple relations, foreign keys are used. A foreign key is a key in a relation that matches the primary key of another relation.

Relational databases support at least one comprehensive sublanguage, the most popular being the Structured Query Language (SQL). Relational databases provide ACID guarantees that are a set of properties that guarantee that a database transactions are processed reliably. ACID guarantees are described as follows:

- **Atomicity:** Atomicity property ensures that each transaction is either 'all or nothing'. In other words, an atomic transaction ensures that all parts of the transaction complete or the database state is left unchanged. Partially completed transactions in the event of system outages can lead to an invalid state. Atomicity ensures that the transaction is indivisible and is either committed or aborted.
- **Consistency:** Consistency property ensures that each transaction brings the database from one valid state to another. In other words, the data in a database always conforms to the defined schema and constraints.
- **Isolation:** Isolation property ensures that the database state obtained after a set of concurrent transactions is the same as would have been if the transactions were executed serially. This provides concurrency control, i.e., the results of incomplete transactions are not visible to other transactions. The transactions are isolated from each other until they finish.
- **Durability:** Durability property ensures that once a transaction is committed, the data remains as it is, i.e., it is not affected by system outages such as power loss. Durability guarantees that the database can keep track of changes and can recover from abnormal terminations.

5.10.1 OLTP vs OLAP

Relational databases can be categorized into two categories: (1) Online Transaction Processing (OLTP), (2) Online Analytical Processing (OLAP). OLTP involves several short online transactions. OLTP systems are suitable for transaction-oriented applications such as an E-Commerce application which require frequently writing new data, updating, or deleting existing data, while maintaining the integrity of the data. OLTP systems are designed for large numbers of short online transactions where the queries typically involve INSERT, UPDATE, DELETE operations. The query response time is in milliseconds, and transaction throughput is used as a performance metric of OLTP systems. Amazon RDS is a relational database service that is suitable for OLTP use cases.

OLAP systems are referred to as data warehouses, which allow the analysis of data for making business decisions. OLAP systems have a lower volume of transactions as compared to OLTP systems; however, the queries are more complex. An OLAP system is typically used to collect data from several OLTP systems within an organization and query the data for data mining, analytics, and decision-making. OLAP systems are designed for online analysis of large volumes of data where the queries typically involve a SELECT operation. The query response time is in seconds to minutes, and query throughput is used as a performance metric of OLAP systems. Amazon Redshift is a data warehouse service that is suitable for OLAP use cases.

5.11 MySQL

MySQL is an open-source Relational Database Management System (RDBMS). MySQL is one of the most widely used RDBMS and a good choice for microservices applications where the data is structured.

Let us look at an example of using MySQL for a reference application that maintains records of employees in a company. An entity-relationship (ER) diagram is a graphical representation of the logical structure of a database. ER diagrams provide a clear and intuitive visualization of the relationships between entities, attributes, and cardinalities, making it easier to understand and maintain the database design. Figure 5.29 shows the Entity-Relationship (ER) diagram for the reference application. The ER diagram shows three entities - Employee, Department, and Project. Note that a one-to-one relationship exists between Employee and Department entities, whereas a many-to-many relationship exists between Employee and Project. The attributes for the Employee, Department, and Project entities are also shown in the ER diagram.

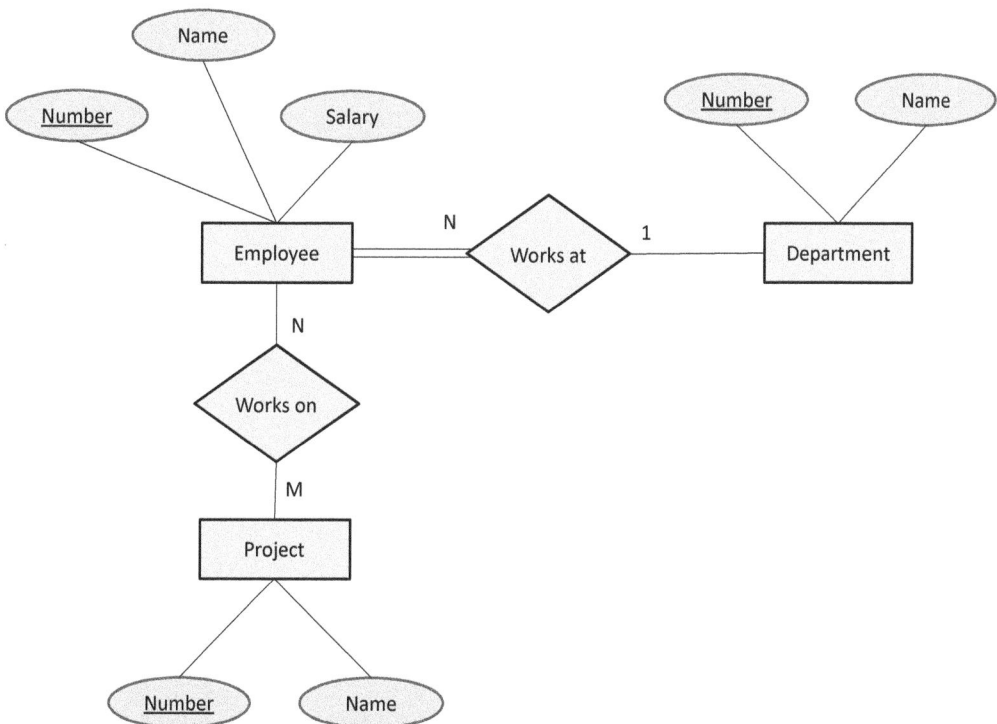

Figure 5.29: Entity-relationship (ER) diagram for the reference application

To map the ER model represented in the ER diagram to a relational model, we follow the following rules:

- For each regular entity in the ER model, create a relation (table).
- Make the attributes of the entity as the attributes of the table (or columns in a table). Choose one of the key attributes of the entity as the primary key for the relation.
- For a 1:1 relationship between two entities (say P and Q), include as a foreign key in one of the relations, say the relation for entity P, the primary key of the other relation Q.
- For a 1:N relationship between two entities (say R and S), include as a foreign key in the relation for entity S (where S is the entity on the N side of the relationship), the primary key of the relation for entity R.
- For a M:N relationship between two entities (say U and V), create a new relation and in that relation include as foreign keys, the primary keys of the relations for entities U and V. If the M:N relationship has any simple attributes, include those as well in the new relation.

Following the above rules, we come up with the relations (tables) and their attributes (columns in the tables). Box 5.18 shows the 'CREATE TABLE' SQL statements for creating the tables.

■ Box 5.18: SQL statements for creating tables

```
CREATE TABLE department(
number varchar(50) NOT NULL PRIMARY KEY,
name varchar(200) NULL
);

CREATE TABLE employee (
number varchar(100) NOT NULL PRIMARY KEY,
name varchar(100) NOT NULL,
salary varchar(20) NOT NULL,
department_id varchar(20) REFERENCES department (number),
);

CREATE TABLE project (
number varchar(20) NOT NULL PRIMARY KEY,
name varchar(100) NOT NULL
);

CREATE TABLE workson (
id INT(6) UNSIGNED AUTO_INCREMENT PRIMARY KEY,
employee_id varchar(20) NOT NULL REFERENCES employee (number),
project_id varchar(20) NOT NULL REFERENCES project (number)
);
```

After creating the tables, data can be inserted into the tables using the 'INSERT INTO' SQL statements as shown in Box 5.19.

■ Box 5.19: SQL statements for inserting data into tables

```
INSERT INTO department VALUES ("1001", "ECE");
```

```
INSERT INTO employee (number, name,
salary,department_id) VALUES ("5001",
"Alex", "50000", "1001");

INSERT INTO project VALUES ("201", "Cloud");

INSERT INTO workson(employee_id,project_id)
VALUES ("5001", "201");
```

Finally, the data can be queried using the SELECT statements as shown in Box 5.20.

■ Box 5.20: SQL statements for querying tables

```
# Retrieve all employees
SELECT * FROM employee;

# Retrieve top 3 employees with highest salary
SELECT * FROM employee ORDER BY salary DESC LIMIT 3;

# Retrieve all employees in department 'ECE'
SELECT e.name, e.number, d.name FROM
employee e, department d WHERE d.name='ECE' ;

# Count the number of employees working on 'IoT' project
SELECT COUNT(*) FROM project p, workson w WHERE p.name='IoT' ;
```

5.12 Amazon Relational Data Store

Amazon Relational Database Service (RDS) is a web service that makes it easy to set up, operate, and scale a relational database in the cloud. The benefit of using a managed relational database service such as RDS over your own on-premises database server or a database server running on a cloud instance (such as MySQL database server running on EC2), is that with a managed service, you do not need to worry about operating system installation and patches, software installation, database engine patches, server maintenance, scalability, and backups. RDS service takes care of all these tasks while you can focus on your application development.

Unlike an on-premises database server or a database server running on a cloud instance, you do not get shell access to an RDS database instance. You can use the same tools and software to manage, administer, query, and analyze a database on RDS as you use with an on-premises database or database on a cloud instance. So while you cannot connect to a DB instance using SSH, you can use an SQL administrator tool to connect to a database and run SQL queries.

To use Amazon RDS for a cloud application, a database instance can be created from the AWS RDS console or using the RDS API. You can choose any DB instance size based on the application requirements, starting from db.t2.micro with 1 virtual CPU (vCPU) and 1 GB RAM, up to db.m5.24xlarge with 96 vCPU and 384 GB RAM. You can choose a minimum storage size of 20 GB and a maximum of 16384 GB. RDS supports three storage types: (1) General Purpose SSD, (2) Provisioned IOPS, and (3) Magnetic. The General Purpose SSD (gp2) is cost-effective storage which is suitable for a wide range of workloads.

General Purpose SSD provides low latency with the ability to burst performance up to 3000 IOPS (Input/Output Operations Per Second). The Provisioned IOPS storage is designed for I/O intensive workloads that require low I/O latency and consistent I/O throughput. RDS supports a range of IOPS from 1000-4000 IOPS for provisioned storage. The Magnetic storage option is provided for backward compatibility, and it is recommended that you choose General Purpose SSD over magnetic storage for new applications.

RDS supports various database engines, including Amazon Aurora, MySQL, MariaDB, PostgreSQL, Oracle, and Microsoft SQL Server. RDS supports two licensing models: *License Included* and *Bring Your Own License (BYOL)*.

RDS supports automated database backups and creates a storage volume snapshot of your DB instance, backing up the entire DB instance and not just individual databases. You can configure the backup retention period up to a maximum of 35 days. Automated backups are deleted when you delete your database instance. RDS also supports manual snapshots of a database which persist even after the database instance is deleted. Manual DB snapshots can be initiated from the RDS console or using the RDS API. RDS allows you to recover a database from automated backups or manual snapshots. When automated backups are used for recovery, RDS combines the daily backups with the transaction log to restore a database to any point during the retention window. When manual snapshots are used to recover a database, you can launch a new DB instance from a snapshot.

RDS supports Multi-AZ deployments where a database cluster can be created that spans across multiple Availability Zones. If you choose the Multi-AZ deployment option while creating a DB instance, RDS creates a replica in a different availability zone to provide data redundancy, eliminate I/O freezes, and minimize latency spikes during system backups. A primary instance is created in one availability zone, and a secondary instance is created in another availability zone. RDS automatically replicates data from the primary instance to the secondary instance using synchronous replication. RDS provides automatic failovers and switches over the primary DB instance automatically in the case of a failover event such as an availability zone outage, failure of the primary DB instance, change in server type of DB instance, operating system patching of DB instance in progress, or when a manual failover of the DB instance is initiated.

RDS databases can be scaled either vertically or horizontally. In vertical scaling, you can choose a different DB instance size/class to scale up or scale down a database based on the application's workload requirements. You can also increase the amount of storage or change the storage type and performance for a DB instance. Horizontal scaling of a database can be achieved with sharding or read replicas. Sharding involves partitioning a large database into multiple database instances or shards. When sharding is used, the application needs to be aware of how the data is partitioned to route the queries to the correct shard. Another approach for horizontal scaling is using read replicas where one or more replicas of a database are created for read transactions. All the write transactions go to a primary database, and the read transactions are served from the read replicas. Updates made to the primary database are asynchronously copied to the read replicas.

Amazon RDS provides several benefits for microservices applications, including high availability, scalability, and managed database administration. With RDS, developers can focus on building their applications without worrying about database management tasks such as patching, backups, and failover.

5.12.1 Setting up an RDS Database Instance

Figures 5.30 to 5.34 show screenshots of the database creation wizard in the Amazon RDS console.

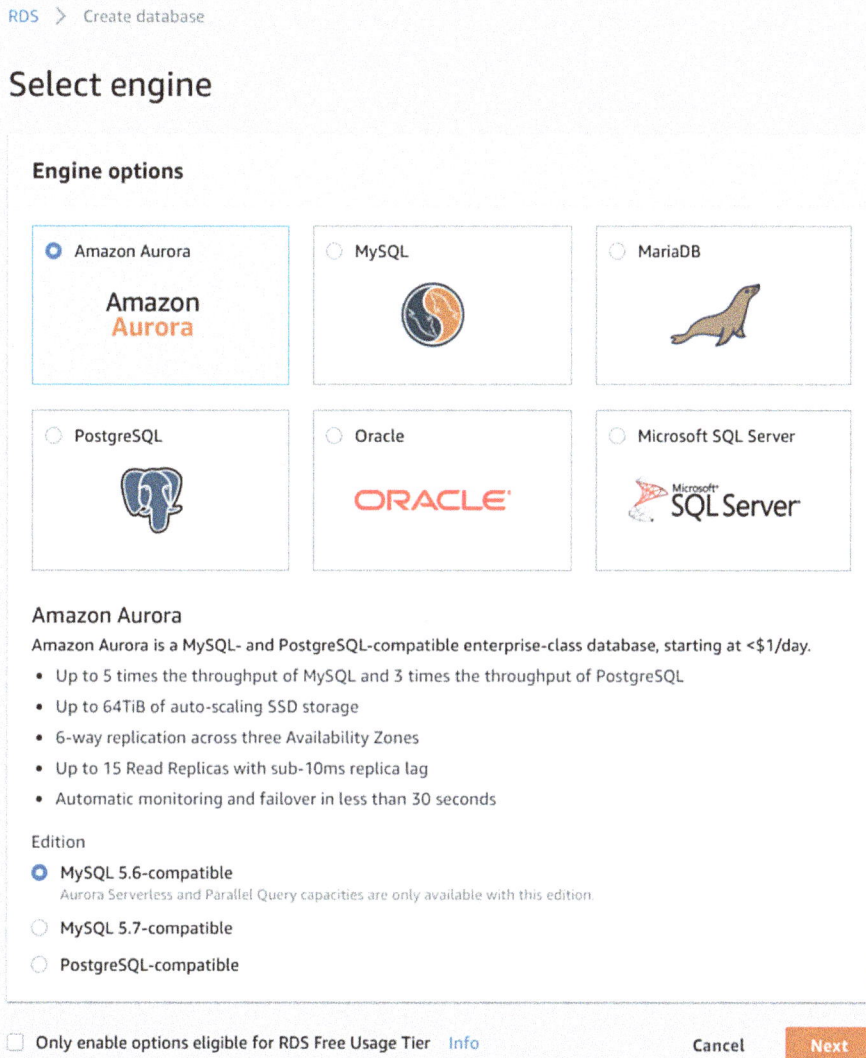

Figure 5.30: Amazon RDS create database wizard - step 1

At the first step, you can select the type of database to create (Amazon Aurora, MySQL, MariaDB, PostgreSQL, Oracle, or Microsoft SQL Server). You can select the type of deployment (such as production or dev/test). Production deployment is a multi-availability zone (multi-AZ) deployment, where database instances are launched in multiple availability zones. Moreover, for production deployment, a provisioned IOPS (Input/Output Operations Per Second) storage is used. Next, you can select a database instance class, storage type (general-purpose SSD or provisioned IOPS), allocated storage, DB instance identifier, DB username, and password. Finally, you can configure advanced settings such as network and security options (including VPC, subnet group, public accessibility, availability zone, and security groups), database options (such as DB name, port, parameter group, option group), encryption, backup options (including backup retention period and backup window), monitoring, and logging options.

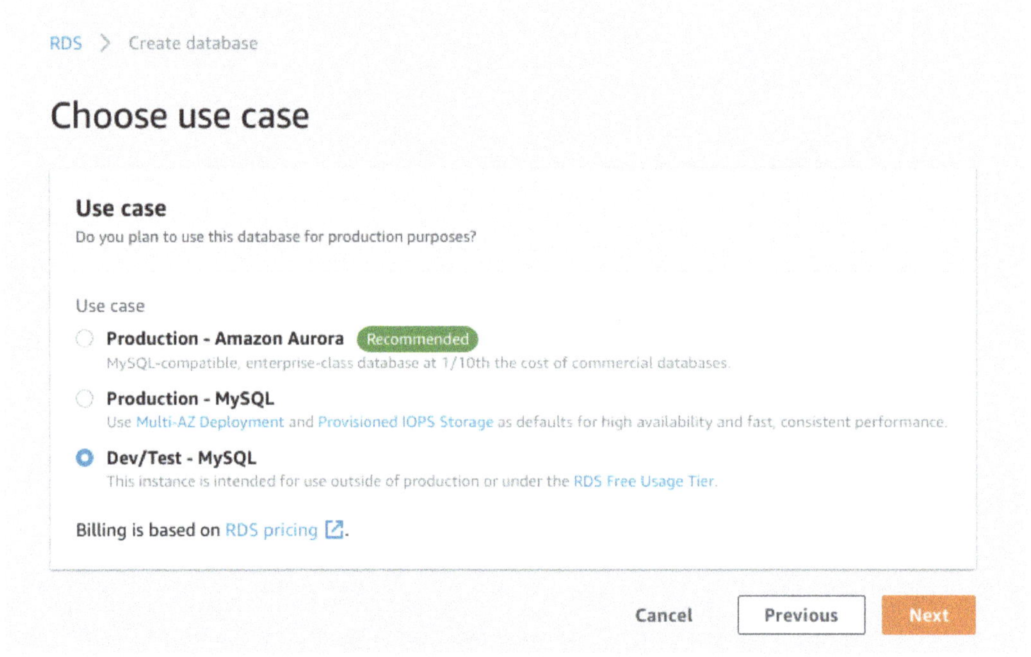

Figure 5.31: Amazon RDS create database wizard - step 2

The status of the launched DB instances in Amazon RDS can be conveniently monitored from the AWS Management Console. It typically takes a few minutes for a newly launched instance to transition from the 'creating' state to the 'available' state. During this brief period, Amazon RDS performs several background tasks, such as provisioning the necessary compute resources and configuring the database engine. Once the instance is reported as 'available', you can access its connection details, including the instance endpoint, from the instance properties tab. This endpoint is a secure, unique address that applications and clients can use to establish a connection to the database instance over an encrypted channel. It's important to note that RDS instances are typically launched within a Virtual Private Cloud (VPC) for enhanced security and network isolation, so proper network configuration and security group rules may need to be set up to allow incoming connections to the instance endpoint.

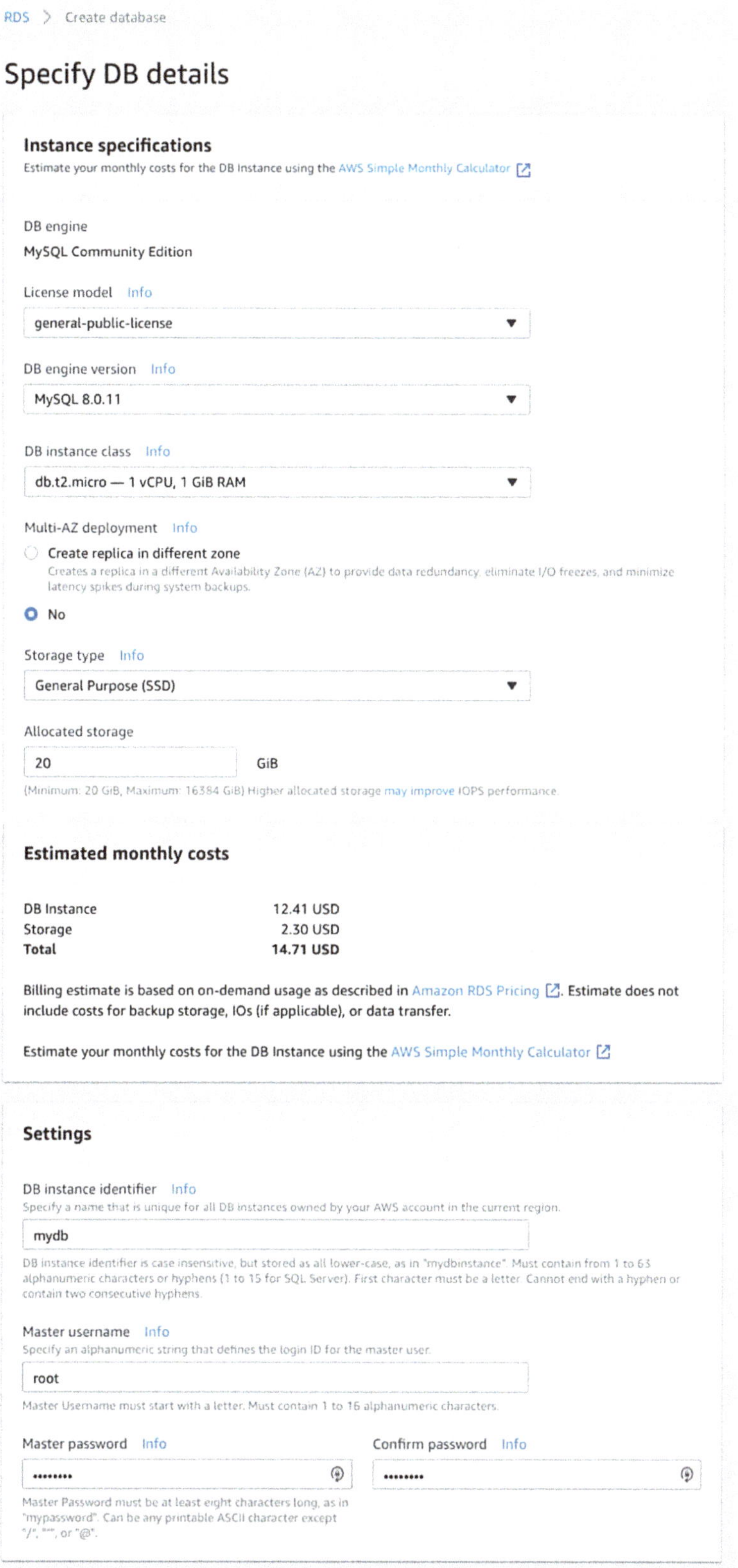

RDS > Create database

Specify DB details

Instance specifications

Estimate your monthly costs for the DB Instance using the AWS Simple Monthly Calculator ⬈

DB engine
MySQL Community Edition

License model   Info

| general-public-license   ▼ |

DB engine version   Info

| MySQL 8.0.11   ▼ |

DB instance class   Info

| db.t2.micro — 1 vCPU, 1 GiB RAM   ▼ |

Multi-AZ deployment   Info

○ **Create replica in different zone**
  Creates a replica in a different Availability Zone (AZ) to provide data redundancy, eliminate I/O freezes, and minimize
  latency spikes during system backups.

🔘 **No**

Storage type   Info

| General Purpose (SSD)   ▼ |

Allocated storage

| 20 | GiB

(Minimum: 20 GiB, Maximum: 16384 GiB) Higher allocated storage may improve IOPS performance.

Estimated monthly costs

DB Instance	12.41 USD
Storage	2.30 USD
Total	**14.71 USD**

Billing estimate is based on on-demand usage as described in Amazon RDS Pricing ⬈. Estimate does not
include costs for backup storage, IOs (if applicable), or data transfer.

Estimate your monthly costs for the DB Instance using the AWS Simple Monthly Calculator ⬈

Settings

DB instance identifier   Info
Specify a name that is unique for all DB instances owned by your AWS account in the current region.

| mydb |

DB instance identifier is case insensitive, but stored as all lower-case, as in "mydbinstance". Must contain from 1 to 63
alphanumeric characters or hyphens (1 to 15 for SQL Server). First character must be a letter. Cannot end with a hyphen or
contain two consecutive hyphens.

Master username   Info
Specify an alphanumeric string that defines the login ID for the master user.

| root |

Master Username must start with a letter. Must contain 1 to 16 alphanumeric characters.

Master password   Info   Confirm password   Info

| ••••••••   ⊚ | | ••••••••   ⊚ |

Master Password must be at least eight characters long, as in
"mypassword". Can be any printable ASCII character except
"/", """, or "@".

Figure 5.32: Amazon RDS create database wizard - step 3

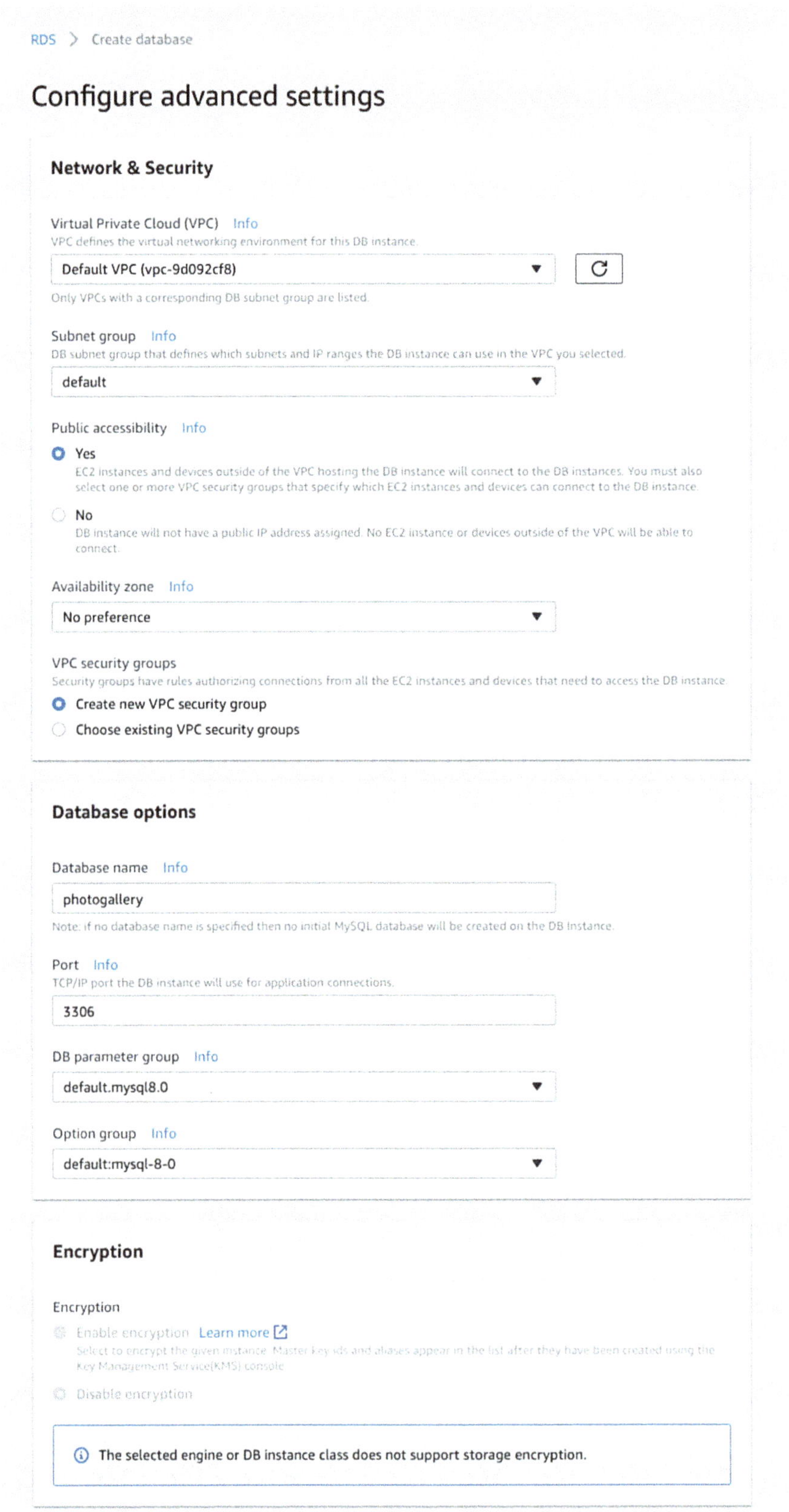

RDS > Create database

Configure advanced settings

Network & Security

Virtual Private Cloud (VPC)   Info
VPC defines the virtual networking environment for this DB instance.

| Default VPC (vpc-9d092cf8) ▼ | | C |

Only VPCs with a corresponding DB subnet group are listed.

Subnet group   Info
DB subnet group that defines which subnets and IP ranges the DB instance can use in the VPC you selected.

| default ▼ |

Public accessibility   Info

● Yes
    EC2 instances and devices outside of the VPC hosting the DB instance will connect to the DB instances. You must also
    select one or more VPC security groups that specify which EC2 instances and devices can connect to the DB instance.

○ No
    DB instance will not have a public IP address assigned. No EC2 instance or devices outside of the VPC will be able to
    connect.

Availability zone   Info

| No preference ▼ |

VPC security groups
Security groups have rules authorizing connections from all the EC2 instances and devices that need to access the DB instance.

● Create new VPC security group
○ Choose existing VPC security groups

Database options

Database name   Info

| photogallery |

Note: if no database name is specified then no initial MySQL database will be created on the DB instance.

Port   Info
TCP/IP port the DB instance will use for application connections.

| 3306 |

DB parameter group   Info

| default.mysql8.0 ▼ |

Option group   Info

| default:mysql-8-0 ▼ |

Encryption

Encryption

⚙ Enable encryption Learn more ↗
    Select to encrypt the given instance. Master key ids and aliases appear in the list after they have been created using the
    Key Management Service(KMS) console.

○ Disable encryption

| ⓘ The selected engine or DB instance class does not support storage encryption. |

Figure 5.33: Amazon RDS create database wizard - step 4

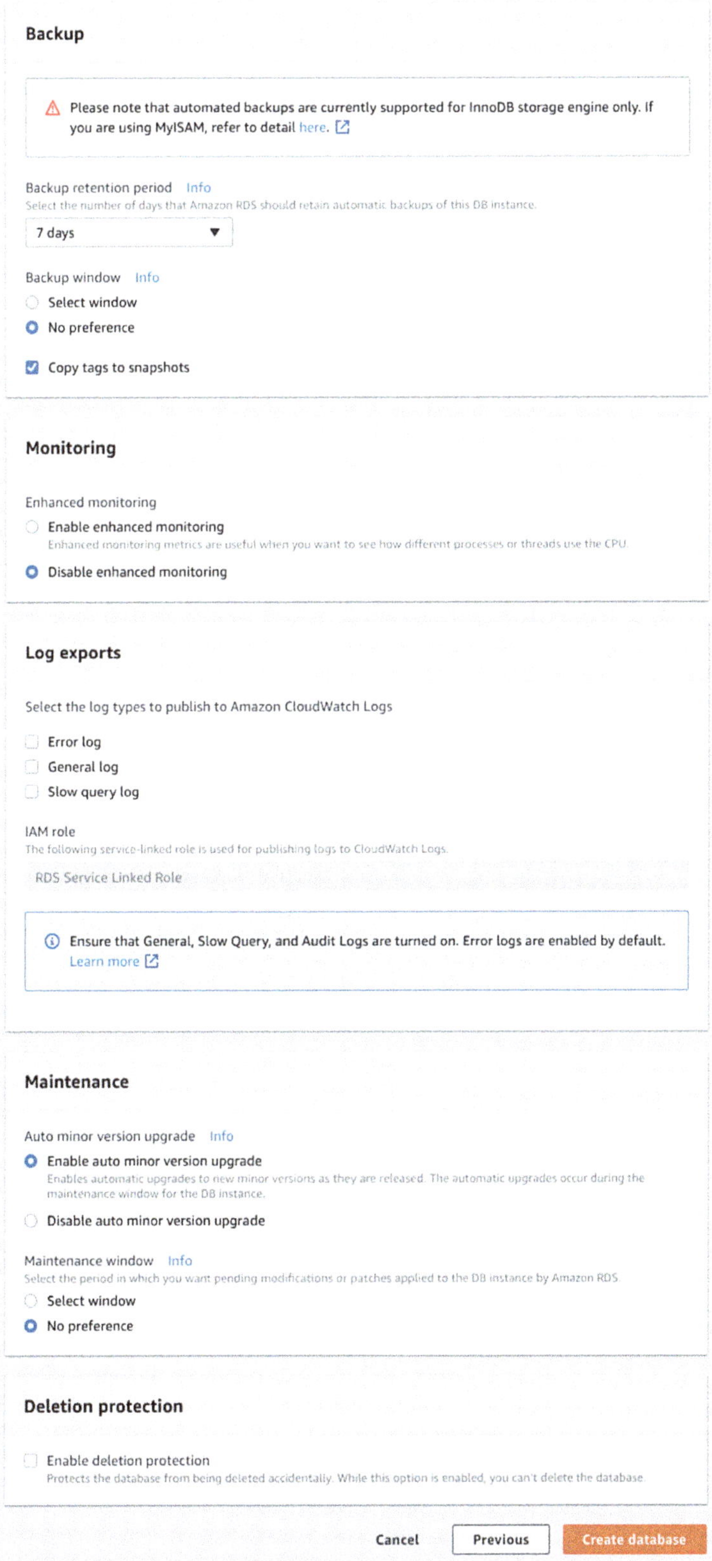

Backup

⚠ Please note that automated backups are currently supported for InnoDB storage engine only. If you are using MyISAM, refer to detail here. ⧉

Backup retention period   Info
Select the number of days that Amazon RDS should retain automatic backups of this DB instance.

7 days ▼

Backup window   Info
○ Select window
● No preference

☑ Copy tags to snapshots

Monitoring

Enhanced monitoring
○ Enable enhanced monitoring
   Enhanced monitoring metrics are useful when you want to see how different processes or threads use the CPU.
● Disable enhanced monitoring

Log exports

Select the log types to publish to Amazon CloudWatch Logs

☐ Error log
☐ General log
☐ Slow query log

IAM role
The following service-linked role is used for publishing logs to CloudWatch Logs.

RDS Service Linked Role

ⓘ Ensure that General, Slow Query, and Audit Logs are turned on. Error logs are enabled by default.
Learn more ⧉

Maintenance

Auto minor version upgrade   Info
● Enable auto minor version upgrade
   Enables automatic upgrades to new minor versions as they are released. The automatic upgrades occur during the maintenance window for the DB instance.
○ Disable auto minor version upgrade

Maintenance window   Info
Select the period in which you want pending modifications or patches applied to the DB instance by Amazon RDS.
○ Select window
● No preference

Deletion protection

☐ Enable deletion protection
   Protects the database from being deleted accidentally. While this option is enabled, you can't delete the database.

Cancel   Previous   Create database

Figure 5.34: Amazon RDS create database wizard - step 5

Box 5.21 shows the Python code for launching an Amazon RDS instance. In this example, an instance of the boto3 client for RDS is created using the *boto3.client* function. The RDS region, AWS access key, and AWS secret key are passed to this function. The RDS client is then used to create a new database instance using the *create_db_instance* function. The input parameters to this function include the database name, instance ID, database size, instance type, database username, database password, database port, database engine, database name, and security groups. The program waits until the status of the RDS instance becomes available and then prints the instance details such as instance ID, instance state, instance type, allocated storage, and instance endpoint.

■ **Box 5.21: Python program for launching an RDS instance**

```
import boto3
from time import sleep


AWS_KEY="<enter>"
AWS_SECRET="<enter>"
REGION="us-east-1"

INSTANCE_TYPE="db.t2.micro"
ID = "MySQL-db-instance"
USERNAME = 'root'
PASSWORD = 'password'
DB_PORT = 3306
DB_SIZE = 5
DB_ENGINE = 'mysql'
DB_NAME = 'mytestdb'
SECGROUP_ID="sg-1f25617b"

print "Connecting to RDS"

rds = boto3.client('rds', aws_access_key_id=AWS_KEY,
                        aws_secret_access_key=AWS_SECRET,
                        region_name=REGION)

print "Creating an RDS instance"

response = rds.create_db_instance(DBName=DB_NAME,
            DBInstanceIdentifier=ID,
            AllocatedStorage=DB_SIZE,
            DBInstanceClass=INSTANCE_TYPE,
            Engine=DB_ENGINE,
            MasterUsername=USERNAME,
            MasterUserPassword=PASSWORD,
            VpcSecurityGroupIds=[
                SECGROUP_ID,
            ],
            Port=DB_PORT)

print response
print "Waiting for instance to be up and running"
```

```
sleep(30)
response = rds.describe_db_instances(DBInstanceIdentifier=ID)
status = response['DBInstances'][0]['DBInstanceStatus']

while not status == 'available':
    sleep(10)
    response = rds.describe_db_instances(DBInstanceIdentifier=ID)
    status = response['DBInstances'][0]['DBInstanceStatus']
    print "Status: "+str(status)

if status == 'available':
    response = rds.describe_db_instances(DBInstanceIdentifier=ID)
    print "\nRDS Instance is now running. Instance details are:"
    print "Intance ID: " + \
        str(response['DBInstances'][0]['DBInstanceIdentifier'])
    print "Intance State: " + \
        str(response['DBInstances'][0]['DBInstanceStatus'])
    print "Instance Type: " + \
        str(response['DBInstances'][0]['DBInstanceClass'])
    print "Engine: " + str(response['DBInstances'][0]['Engine'])
    print "Allocated Storage: " + \
    str(response['DBInstances'][0]['AllocatedStorage'])
    print "Endpoint: " + str(response['DBInstances'][0]['Endpoint'])
```

Box 5.22 shows the Python code for creating a MySQL table, writing, and reading from the table. This example uses the MySQLdb Python package. To connect to the MySQL RDS instance, the *MySQLdb.connect* function is called, and the endpoint of the RDS instance, database username, password, and port are passed to this function. After the connection to the RDS instance is established, a cursor to the database is obtained by calling *conn.cursor*. Next, a new database table named *Student* is created with *Id* as the primary key and other columns. After creating the table, some values are inserted. To execute the SQL commands for database manipulation, the commands are passed to the *cursor.execute* function.

■ Box 5.22: Python program for creating a MySQL table, writing, and reading from the table

```
import MySQLdb

USERNAME = 'root'
PASSWORD = 'password'
DB_NAME = 'mytestdb'

print "Connecting to RDS instance"

conn = MySQLdb.connect (host = "<enter>",
                        user = USERNAME,
                        passwd = PASSWORD,
                        db = DB_NAME,
        port = 3306)

print "Connected to RDS instance"
```

```
cursor = conn.cursor ()
cursor.execute ("SELECT VERSION()")
row = cursor.fetchone ()
print "server version:", row[0]

cursor.execute ("CREATE TABLE \
    Student(Id INT PRIMARY KEY, Name TEXT, Major TEXT, Grade FLOAT) ")
cursor.execute ("INSERT INTO Student VALUES(100, 'John', 'CS', 3)")
cursor.execute ("INSERT INTO Student VALUES(101, 'David', 'ECE', 3.5)")
cursor.execute ("INSERT INTO Student VALUES(102, 'Bob', 'CS', 3.9)")
cursor.execute ("INSERT INTO Student VALUES(103, 'Alex', 'CS', 3.6)")
cursor.execute ("INSERT INTO Student VALUES(104, 'Martin', 'ECE', 3.1)")

cursor.execute("SELECT * FROM Student")
rows = cursor.fetchall()

for row in rows:
  print row

cursor.close ()
conn.close ()
```

5.13   Amazon ElastiCache

Amazon ElastiCache is a managed service that makes it easier to launch, manage, and scale
a distributed in-memory cache in the AWS cloud. With ElastiCache, you can set up an
in-memory caching environment to improve the response time of your cloud applications
by caching frequently-used data. In-memory cache stores frequently accessed data items
in memory and improves the application performance, as fetching a cached data item from
an in-memory cache is much faster than a database read query. A cache acts as a memory
buffer between your application and the database and decreases the access latency, increases
throughput, and reduces the load on the database. While you can set up your caching cluster
on EC2, ElastiCache makes it easier to set up and scale a caching cluster as it is a managed
service and takes care of installation, updates, and patches.

When deciding which data items to cache in your application, you should evaluate the
data access patterns. The data items that are more frequently accessed or less frequently
updated can be cached. For example, in an E-Commerce application, the list of products
can be cached. When the users search for a specific category of products, the results can be
returned from a cache.

ElastiCache provides a cost-effective and scalable caching solution for microservices
applications. By offloading read-heavy workloads from databases to ElastiCache, the
microservices can significantly improve response times and reduce the load on the underlying
database infrastructure. ElastiCache supports popular caching engines like Redis and
Memcached, making it easy to integrate with existing applications. Additionally, ElastiCache
offers features like clustering, replication, and automatic failover, ensuring high availability
and durability for mission-critical microservices applications. Figure 5.35 shows an example
of using ElastiCache Redis cluster for an application.

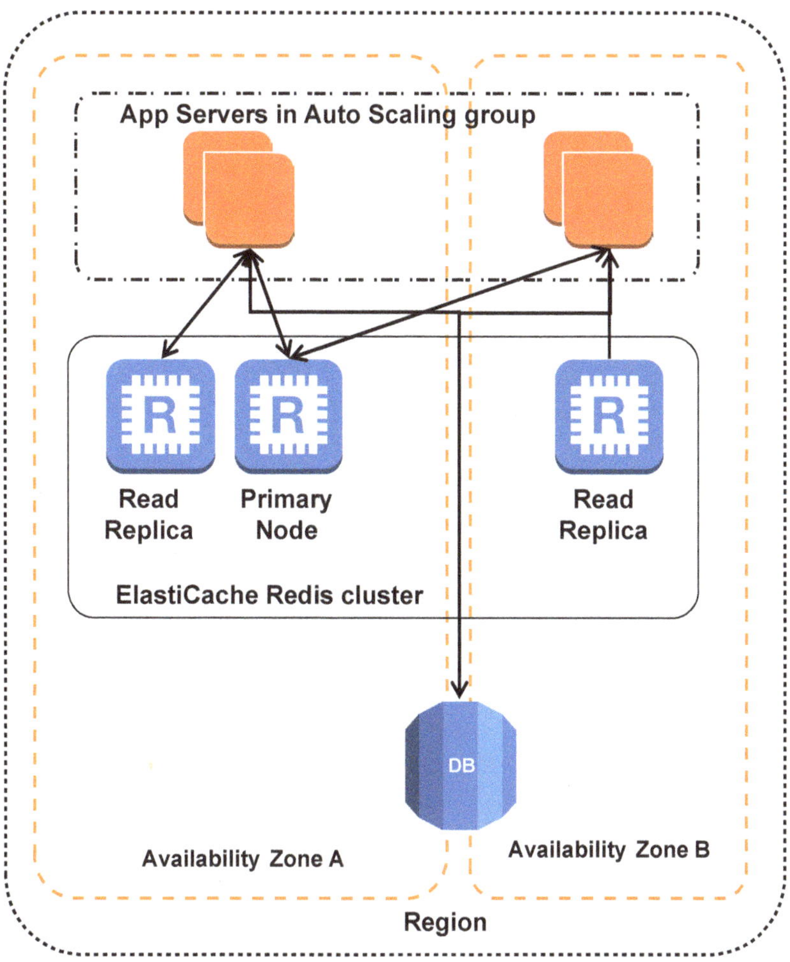

Figure 5.35: Redis cluster with Multi-AZ deployment

ElastiCache works with both the Redis and Memcached engines. Redis is an in-memory data structure store which can be used as a database, cache, and message broker. Memcached is a high-performance, distributed memory object caching system, which can be used for speeding up dynamic web applications. While both Redis and Memcached are in-memory key-value stores, their functionalities differ. You can choose Memcached if you want to cache objects such as a database, want a simple data model, and the ability to scale out and scale in the capacity of the cluster based on demand. You can choose Redis if you want complex data types (such as strings, hashes, lists, sets, sorted sets, and bitmaps), the ability to sort and rank in-memory datasets, and persist the in-memory data onto the disk. While Memcached clusters are in-memory only, the Redis cluster can be persisted to disk, and you can create snapshots and recover from failures.

ElastiCache for Redis provides automatic detection and recovery from cache node failure. A Redis cluster is a logical grouping of one or more shards. If cluster mode is disabled, a Redis cluster consists of a single cache node that handles both read and write transactions. If you enable cluster mode for Redis, you can create up to 90 shards in the cluster where each shard is a grouping of one to six related nodes. When a shard has multiple nodes, one of the nodes acts as the read/write primary node, and the other nodes act as read-only replica nodes. A Redis cluster can have a Multi-AZ (multiple availability zones) deployment where the primary node can be in one availability zone, and the read replicas can be in multiple availability zones. In the event of failure of the primary node, one of the read replicas is selected to become the new primary node. ElastiCache for Redis supports automatic failover of a failed primary cluster to a read replica in a Redis cluster that supports replication.

5.14 Non-Relational Databases

Non-relational databases (or NoSQL databases) are becoming popular with the increasing use of cloud computing services. Non-relational databases have better horizontal scaling capability and improved performance at the cost of having less rigorous consistency models.

Definition of NoSQL
NoSQL databases are modern, non-relational database management systems designed for handling large volumes of structured, semi-structured, and unstructured data.
They prioritize horizontal scalability, high availability, partition tolerance, and eventual consistency over traditional ACID properties, and typically feature schema-less or flexible schema, simple APIs, and open-source and distributed architectures.

Unlike relational databases, NoSQL databases do not provide ACID guarantees. Most NoSQL databases offer 'eventual' consistency, which means that given a sufficiently long period over which no updates are made, all updates can be expected to propagate eventually through the system and the replicas are consistent. Some authors have referred to the term BASE (Basically Available, Soft state, Eventual consistency) guarantees for NoSQL databases as opposed to ACID guarantees provided by relational databases, as shown in Figure 5.36.

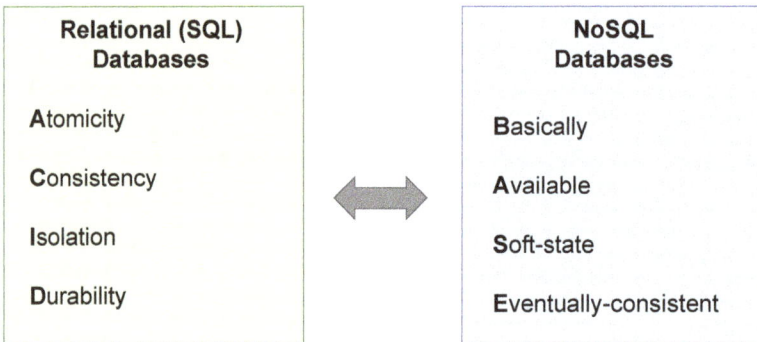

Figure 5.36: ACID vs BASE guarantees for SQL and NoSQL databases

The driving force behind the NoSQL databases is the need for databases that can achieve the performance-related measures of high scalability, fault tolerance, and availability. These databases can be distributed on a large cluster of machines. Fault tolerance is provided by storing multiple replicas of data on different machines. Figure 5.37 lists some pros and cons of non-relational databases.

Pros	Cons
Easy to scale-out. Higher performance for massive scale data as compared to relational databases. Allows sharing of data across multiple servers.	Do not provide ACID guarantees, therefore less suitable for applications such as transaction processing that require strong consistency.
Most solutions are either open-source or cheaper as compared to relational databases.	No fixed schema. There is no common data storage model. Different solutions have different data storage models.
High availability and fault tolerance provided by data replication.	Limited support for aggregation (SUM, AVG, COUNT, GROUP BY) as compared to relational databases.
Support complex data structures and native programming objects.	Performance for complex joins is poor as compared to relational databases.
No fixed schema. Support unstructured data.	No well defined approach for database design, since different solutions have different data storage models.
Very fast retrieval of data. Suitable for real-time applications.	Lack of a consistent model can lead to solution lock-in, i.e., migrating from one solution to other may require significant remodeling of the application.

Figure 5.37: Pros and Cons of non-relational databases

NoSQL databases provide significant advantages for microservices architectures that demand high scalability, flexibility, and performance when handling large volumes of data. Unlike relational databases, NoSQL solutions are optimized for distributed, unstructured, and semi-structured data models.

A key strength is horizontal scalability, allowing data to be distributed across multiple nodes or servers. This enables microservices to seamlessly scale to handle rapidly increasing data volumes and user traffic without degrading performance. NoSQL databases also offer schema flexibility with dynamic or schema-less data models, aligning with microservices' evolving data requirements. High availability and partition tolerance are built into many NoSQL databases through replication and sharding mechanisms. This ensures individual microservices remain operational despite failures in other components. Real-time performance is another major benefit, with optimizations for rapid read/write operations and low-latency data access for real-time analytics, streaming, and event-driven architectures. NoSQL solutions support polyglot persistence with varied data models like key-value, document, column-family, and graph databases. This allows using the ideal data store for each microservice's needs. Simple and intuitive data models also increase developer productivity for microservices teams.

5.15   Consistency, Availability & Partition Tolerance (CAP)

For distributed data systems, a trade-off exists between consistency and availability. These trade-offs are explained with the CAP theorem, which states that under partitioning, a distributed data system can either be consistent or available but not both at the same time. Figure 5.38 shows a representation of the CAP theorem.

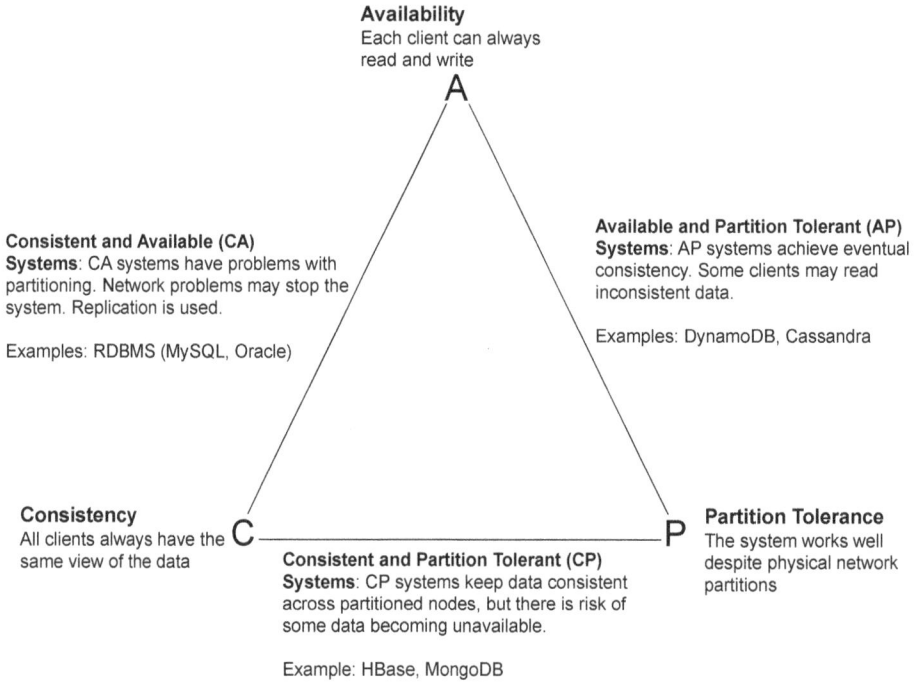

Availability
Each client can always
read and write

A

Consistent and Available (CA)
Systems: CA systems have problems with
partitioning. Network problems may stop the
system. Replication is used.

Examples: RDBMS (MySQL, Oracle)

Available and Partition Tolerant (AP)
Systems: AP systems achieve eventual
consistency. Some clients may read
inconsistent data.

Examples: DynamoDB, Cassandra

Consistency
All clients always have the **C**
same view of the data

P **Partition Tolerance**
The system works well
despite physical network
partitions

Consistent and Partition Tolerant (CP)
Systems: CP systems keep data consistent
across partitioned nodes, but there is risk of
some data becoming unavailable.

Example: HBase, MongoDB

Figure 5.38: Consistency, Availability & Partition Tolerance (CAP)

A consistent system is one in which all reads are guaranteed to incorporate the previous writes. In a consistent system, after an update operation is performed by a writer, it is seen by all the readers. Availability refers to the ability of the system to respond to all the queries without being unavailable. A distributed data system is called available when it can continue to perform its operations even in the event of failure of some of the nodes. Partition tolerance refers to the ability of the system to continue performing its operations in the event of network partitions. Network partitions can occur when two (or more) sets of nodes are unable to connect.

The CAP theorem states that the system can either favor consistency and partition tolerance over availability, or favor availability and partition tolerance over consistency. Let us take the example of NoSQL databases such as Amazon DynamoDB and Cassandra. These databases prefer consistency and partition tolerance over availability. Such systems are said to be 'eventually consistent' as all the writes are eventually (not immediately) seen by all the nodes. In an eventually consistent system, clients can experience an inconsistent state of the system while the updates are being propagated to all the nodes, and the system has not yet reached a steady state. In the event of network partitions, all the nodes may not have the most recent updates and may return inconsistent or outdated information. When the network partitions are resolved, all the nodes eventually see the updates.

HBase, in contrast to DynamoDB and Cassandra, prefers consistency and partition tolerance over availability. By adopting strong consistency, HBase ensures that updates are immediately available to all clients. In the event of network partitions, the system can become unavailable to ensure consistency.

5.16   Key-Value Databases

Key-value databases are the simplest form of NoSQL databases. These databases store data in the form of key-value pairs. The keys are used to uniquely identify the values stored in the database. Applications that want to store data generate unique keys and submit the key-value pairs to the database. The database uses the key to determine where the value should be stored. Most key-value databases have distributed architectures comprising of multiple storage nodes. The data is partitioned across the storage nodes by the keys. For determining the partitions for the keys, hash functions are used. The partition number for a key is obtained by applying a hash function to the key. The hash functions are chosen such that the keys are evenly distributed across the partitions.

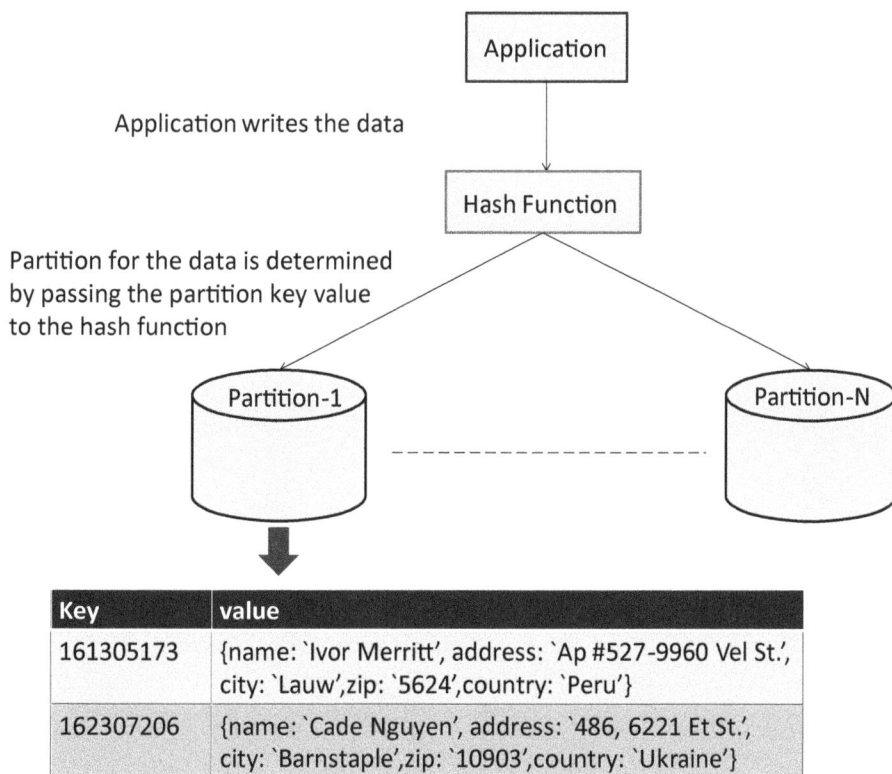

Key	value
161305173	{name: `Ivor Merritt', address: `Ap #527-9960 Vel St.', city: `Lauw',zip: `5624',country: `Peru'}
162307206	{name: `Cade Nguyen', address: `486, 6221 Et St.', city: `Barnstaple',zip: `10903',country: `Ukraine'}

Figure 5.39: Using key-value database for storing customer records

Key-value databases provide greater flexibility in terms of the type of values that can be stored. The values can be of any type (such as strings, integers, floats, and binary large object

(BLOB)). Most key-value stores have support for native programming language data types. There are limits on the size of the values that can be stored.

Unlike relational databases in which the tables have fixed schemas and there are constraints on the columns, in key-value databases, there are no such constraints. Key-value databases do not have tables like in relational databases. However, some key-value databases support tables, buckets, or collections to create separate namespaces for the keys. Keys within a table, bucket, or collection are unique.

Key-value databases are suited for applications that require storing unstructured data without a fixed schema. These databases can be scaled up horizontally and can store a large number of key-value pairs. Unlike relational databases that provide specialized query languages (such as SQL), the key-value databases only provide basic querying and searching capabilities. Key-value databases are suitable for applications for which the ability to store and retrieve data in a fast and efficient manner is more important than imposing structure or constraints on the data. For example, key-value databases can be used to store configuration data, user data, transient or intermediate data (such as shopping cart data), item-attributes, and BLOBs (such as audio and images). Figure 5.39 shows an example of using a key-value database for storing customer records.

5.16.1 Amazon DynamoDB

Amazon DynamoDB is a fully-managed, serverless NoSQL database service from Amazon, making it an ideal choice for microservices applications. With DynamoDB, you can offload the operational overhead of managing databases, allowing you to focus on building and scaling your microservices. Its seamless scalability enables your applications to handle any traffic volume, automatically adjusting the provisioned throughput to meet performance demands. DynamoDB offers low-latency, predictable performance, ensuring consistent and fast data access for your microservices. Additionally, its built-in replication across multiple Availability Zones ensures high availability and reliability, which is crucial for distributed microservices architectures. With DynamoDB, you can easily store and retrieve data of any size, enabling your microservices to handle various workloads efficiently.

DynamoDB's data model includes Tables, Items, and Attributes. A table is a collection of items, and each item is a collection of attributes. DynamoDB supports three categories of data types for the attributes: (1) Scalar Types including number, string, binary, Boolean, and null, (2) Document Types including list and map, (3) Set Types including string set, number set, and binary set. There is no limit on the number of attributes for an item; however, there is an item size limit of 400 KB.

Tables in DynamoDB do not have a fixed schema. When creating a table, only the primary key needs to be specified. The primary key uniquely identifies the items in a table. The primary key is a combination of a partition key and an optional sort key. The partition key is hashed using a hash function to determine the partition where the item should be stored. The partition key value must be unique across all items if no sort is specified. An optional sort key can be specified, which is used to sort items within a partition. If the primary key used is a combination of the hash key and sort key, then it is possible for two items to have the same value of the partition key, but the sort key must have different values. Items are composed of attributes. The attributes can be added at runtime. The items in a table can have different attributes. Each attribute is a key-value pair.

When you create a DynamoDB table, you have to specify the amount of read and write capacity units that you want to provision for the table. One read capacity unit represents one strongly consistent read per second, or two eventually consistent reads per second, for an item up to 4 KB in size. One write capacity unit represents one write per second for an item up to 1 KB in size. The minimum provisioned capacity is 5 units for read and 5 units for write. You can provision a maximum of up to 40,000 units of read and write capacity. You can set up auto-scaling for a table to scale up the read or write capacity when the target utilization reaches a threshold.

Create DynamoDB table

Tutorial

DynamoDB is a schema-less database that only requires a table name and primary key. The table's primary key is made up of one or two attributes that uniquely identify items, partition the data, and sort data within each partition.

Table name* customers

Primary key* Partition key

customerID   String

☑ Add sort key

name| String

Table settings

Default settings provide the fastest way to get started with your table. You can modify these default settings now or after your table has been created.

☑ Use default settings

- No secondary indexes.
- Provisioned capacity set to 5 reads and 5 writes.
- Basic alarms with 80% upper threshold using SNS topic "dynamodb".

Additional charges may apply if you exceed the AWS Free Tier levels for CloudWatch or Simple Notification Service. Advanced alarm settings are available in the CloudWatch management console.

Cancel   **Create**

Figure 5.40: Creating a DynamoDB table

When you write data to a DynamoDB table, the data is eventually consistent across all storage locations. DynamoDB supports eventually consistent and strongly consistent reads. For eventually consistent reads, when you read data, the results may not reflect the most recent write operation completed. Whereas, for strongly consistent reads, the results reflect all prior write operations that were successful.

DynamoDB allows you to define secondary indexes for a table, which let you query a table using an alternate key. DynamoDB supports two kinds of indexes: (1) Global secondary index, which is an index with a partition key and sort key that can be different from those on the table, and (2) Local secondary index, which is an index that has the same partition key as the table, but a different sort key. You can define up to 5 global secondary indexes and 5 local secondary indexes per table.

For reading items, DynamoDB provides scan and query operations. The scan operation is used to retrieve all items in the table. You can specify optional filtering criteria. The filtering criteria can look for specific values of attributes or a range of values. The query operation is used to query for items with the primary key (either only the partition key or the partition key and the sort key). To query the table using attributes other than the primary key, secondary indexes can be added.

Let us look at an example of using DynamoDB to store customer information for an E-Commerce application. The first step is to create a DynamoDB table. You can either create a table from the DynamoDB dashboard or using the DynamoDB APIs. Figure 5.40 shows an example of creating a DynamoDB table. In this example, the customerID is specified as the partition key and the customer name as the sort key. We use the rest of the default settings for secondary indexes, provisioned capacity, and alarms.

Box 5.23 shows a Python example of writing data to a DynamoDB table. For this example, we created synthetic customer data from www.generatedata.com and saved the data in a CSV file. In the Python example, each row of the CSV file is read one by one in a loop, and the customer data is written to the DynamoDB table.

■ Box 5.23: Writing data to DynamoDB table

```python
import boto3
import csv

AWS_KEY="<enter>"
AWS_SECRET="<enter>"
REGION="us-east-1"

dynamodb = boto3.resource('dynamodb', aws_access_key_id=AWS_KEY,
                          aws_secret_access_key=AWS_SECRET,
                          region_name=REGION)
table = dynamodb.Table('customers')

reader = csv.reader(open("customers.csv","r"))
header=reader.next()

for row in reader:
    print row
    item = table.put_item(
        Item={
          "customerID":row[0],
          "name":row[1],
          "address": row[2],
          "city": row[3],
          "zip": row[4],
          "country": row[5],
          "createdAt": row[6]
        })
```

Box 5.24 shows a Python example of reading data from DynamoDB using scan and query operations.

■ Box 5.24: Reading data from DynamoDB table with query and scan operations

```python
import boto3
from boto3.dynamodb.conditions import Key, Attr

AWS_KEY="<enter>"
AWS_SECRET="<enter>"
REGION="us-east-1"

dynamodb = boto3.resource('dynamodb', aws_access_key_id=AWS_KEY,
                          aws_secret_access_key=AWS_SECRET,
                          region_name=REGION)
client = boto3.client('dynamodb', aws_access_key_id=AWS_KEY,
                          aws_secret_access_key=AWS_SECRET,
                          region_name=REGION)

table = dynamodb.Table('customers')

#Describe table
response = client.describe_table(TableName='customers')
print response

#Scan table
response=table.scan()
items = response['Items']
for item in items:
    print item

#Scan table with filter
response = table.scan(FilterExpression=Attr('country').eq('India'))
items = response['Items']
for item in items:
    print item

#Scan table with filters
response = table.scan(
  FilterExpression=Attr('createdAt').between('2012-03-26T00:00:00-00:00',
        '2013-03-26T00:00:00-00:00'))
items = response['Items']
for item in items:
    print item

#Query table with partition key
response = table.query(
  KeyConditionExpression=Key('customerID').eq('1623072020799'))
items = response['Items']
for item in items:
    print item
```

5.17   Document Databases

Document store databases store semi-structured data in the form of documents which are encoded in different standards such as JSON, XML, BSON or YAML. By semi-structured data, we mean that the documents stored are similar to each other (similar fields, keys, or attributes), but there are no strict requirements for a schema. Documents are organized in different ways in different document databases such as collections, buckets, or tags.

ID	Document

56fd4f59849f6367af489537	```
	{
	    "title" : "Motorola Moto G (3rd Generation)",
	    "features" : [
	        "Advanced water resistance",
	        "13 MP camera",
	        "5in HD display",
	        "Quad core processing power",
	        "5MP rear camera",
	        "Great 24hr battery",
	        "4G LTE Speed"
	    ],
	    "specifications" : {
	        "Color" : "Black",
	        "Size" : "16 GB",
	        "Dimensions" : "0.2 x 2.9 x 5.6 inches",
	        "Weight" : "5.4 ounces"
	    },
	    "price" : 219.99
	}
	``

56fd504d849f6367af489538	```
	{
	    "title" : "Canon EOS Rebel T5",
	    "features" : [
	        "18 megapixel CMOS (APS-C) sensor",
	        "EF-S 18-55mm IS II standard zoom lens",
	        "3-inch LCD TFT color, liquid-crystal monitor",
	        "EOS 1080p full HD movie mode"
	    ],
	    "specifications" : {
	        "Color" : "Black",
	        "MaximumAperture" : "f/3.5",
	        "Dimensions" : "3.94 x 3.07 x 5.12 inches",
	        "Weight" : "1.06 pounds"
	    },
	    "price" : 399
	}
	``

Figure 5.41: Using document database for storing product records

Each document stored in a document database has a collection of named fields and their values. Each document is identified by a unique key or ID. There is no need to define any schema for the documents before storing them in the database. While it is possible to store JSON or XML-like documents as values in a key-value database, the benefit of using document databases over key-value databases is that these databases allow efficiently querying the documents based on the attribute values in the documents. Document databases are useful for applications that want to store semi-structured data.

While in relational databases, the data is stored in a normalized form to eliminate duplicates, in document databases, data is stored in denormalized form. Document databases do not provide the join functionality provided by relational databases. Therefore, all data that needs to be retrieved together is stored in a document. For example, in an E-Commerce application, all data related to a particular product is usually retrieved together. In this case, a document can be created for each product. Each document comprises the data on the product features and attributes. Figure 5.41 shows an example of using a document database for storing product records.

5.17.1 MongoDB

MongoDB is a document-oriented, non-relational database system. Unlike traditional relational databases that store data in tables with fixed schemas, MongoDB stores data in flexible, JSON-like documents with dynamic schemas. This approach provides a more natural way of representing data objects used in web applications and other modern software systems.

> **■ Box 5.25: Commands for setting up and running MongoDB**
>
> ```
> #Import the public key used by the package management system
> sudo apt-key adv -keyserver hkp://keyserver.ubuntu.com:80 -recv 7F0CEB10
>
> #Create a list file for MongoDB
> echo "deb http://repo.mongodb.org/apt/ubuntu trusty/mongodb-org/3.0
> multiverse" | sudo tee /etc/apt/sources.list.d/mongodb-org-3.0.list
>
> #Reload local package database
> sudo apt-get update
>
> #Install MongoDB
> sudo apt-get install -y mongodb-org
>
> #Start MongoDB service
> sudo service mongod start
> ```

The basic unit of data storage in MongoDB is a document, which is a collection of key-value pairs. Documents are organized into collections, which can be thought of as analogous to tables in a relational database. However, unlike tables, collections in MongoDB do not enforce a rigid schema. This means that documents within the same collection can have different sets of fields, allowing for greater flexibility and easier schema evolution as application requirements change over time.

One of the key advantages of MongoDB is its scalability. It is designed to scale horizontally across multiple servers, a feature known as sharding. Sharding allows data to be partitioned across multiple servers, enabling MongoDB to handle large datasets and high throughput workloads. Additionally, MongoDB supports replication, which provides data redundancy and high availability by maintaining multiple copies of data across different servers. MongoDB also offers a rich query language that supports a wide range of operations, including complex queries, indexing, aggregation, and geospatial queries. The query language is designed to be intuitive and easy to learn for developers.

Box 5.25 shows the commands for setting up and running MongoDB. Box 5.26 shows examples of using the MongoDB shell commands for writing data to a MongoDB database and querying the data. The data used in this example is the products data for an E-Commerce application. Data for each product is stored as a single document.

■ Box 5.26: Using MongoDB shell commands

```
#Launch MongoDB shell
mongo localhost:27017

#Switch to new database named storedb
> use storedb
switched to db storedb

post = {
 "title" :  "Motorola Moto G (3rd Generation)",
 "features" :  [
 "Advanced water resistance",
 "13 MP camera which includes a color-balancing dual LED Flash",
 "5in HD display",
 "Quad core processing power",
 "5MP rear camera",
 "Great 24hr battery performance with a 2470mAh battery",
 "4G LTE Speed"
 ],
 "specifications" :  {
 "Color" :  "Black",
 "Size" :  "16 GB",
 "Dimensions" :  "0.2 x 2.9 x 5.6 inches",
 "Weight" :  "5.4 ounces"
 },
 "price" :  219.99
}

> db.collection.insert(post)
WriteResult({ "Inserted" :  1 })

#Get all documents
> db.collection.find()
{ "_id" :  ObjectId("56fd4f59849f6367af489537"),
"title" :  "Motorola Moto G (3rd Generation)",
"features" :  [ "Advanced water resistance",
"13 MP camera which includes a color-balancing dual LED Flash",
"5in HD display", "Quad core processing power", "5MP rear camera",
"Great 24hr battery performance with a 2470mAh battery","4G LTE Speed"],
"specifications" :  { "Color" :  "Black", "Size" :  "16 GB",
"Dimensions" :  "0.2 x 2.9 x 5.6 inches", "Weight" :  "5.4 ounces" },
"price" :  219.99 }

{ "_id" :  ObjectId("56fd504d849f6367af489538"),
"title" :  "Canon EOS Rebel T5",
"features" :  [ "18 megapixel CMOS (APS-C) sensor",
"EF-S 18-55mm IS II standard zoom lens",
```

```
"3-inch LCD TFT color, liquid-crystal monitor",
"EOS 1080p full HD movie mode" ],
"specifications" :  { "Color" :  "Black",
"MaximumAperture" :  "f3.5", "Dimensions" :  "3.94 x 3.07 x 5.12 inches",
"Weight" :  "1.06 pounds" }, "price" :  399 }

#Get documents with specific attribute values
> db.collection.find({"title" :  "Canon EOS Rebel T5"})
{ "_id" :  ObjectId("56fd504d849f6367af489538"),
"title" :  "Canon EOS Rebel T5",
"features" :  [ "18 megapixel CMOS (APS-C) sensor",
"EF-S 18-55mm IS II standard zoom lens",
"3-inch LCD TFT color, liquid-crystal monitor",
"EOS 1080p full HD movie mode" ],
"specifications" :  { "Color" :  "Black",
"MaximumAperture" :  "f3.5", "Dimensions" :  "3.94 x 3.07 x 5.12 inches",
"Weight" :  "1.06 pounds" }, "price" :  399 }
```

Box 5.27 shows a Python program for writing data to MongoDB and reading the data. For this example, we use the pyMongo Python library.

■ Box 5.27: Python program for writing data to MongoDB and reading the data

```python
from datetime import date
import datetime, time, cPickle
from pymongo import MongoClient
client = MongoClient()
db = client['storedb']
collection = db['current']

item = {
 "title" :  "Motorola Moto G (3rd Generation)",
 "features" :  [
  "Advanced water resistance",
  "13 MP camera which includes a color-balancing dual LED Flash",
  "5in HD display",
  "Quad core processing power",
  "5MP rear camera",
  "Great 24hr battery performance with a 2470mAh battery",
  "4G LTE Speed"
 ],
 "specifications" :  {
  "Color" :  "Black",
  "Size" :  "16 GB",
  "Dimensions" :  "0.2 x 2.9 x 5.6 inches",
  "Weight" :  "5.4 ounces"
 },
 "price" :  219.99
}
#Insert an item
collection.insert_one(item)
#Retrieve all items
results=db.collection.find()
for item in results:
```

Overview of Amazon Web Services


```
 print item

#Find an item
results = collection.find({"title" :  "Motorola Moto G"})
for item in results:
 print item
```

5.17.2 Amazon DocumentDB

Amazon DocumentDB is a fully managed document database service that supports MongoDB workloads. It is designed to be compatible with MongoDB, allowing developers to use the same MongoDB drivers and tools they are familiar with. The service automatically provisions, patches, and scales compute resources, as well as provides backup and restore capabilities. Amazon DocumentDB provides high availability and durability by replicating data across multiple Availability Zones (AZs) within an AWS Region. It is designed to handle the majority of MongoDB workloads, making it a cost-effective and scalable solution for running MongoDB-compatible applications on AWS.

Some key benefits of using Amazon DocumentDB over MongoDB are as follows:

- Fully Managed Service: Amazon DocumentDB is a fully managed database service, relieving users from the burden of provisioning hardware, managing replicas, applying patches, and other administrative tasks. MongoDB, on the other hand, requires self-management or using a third-party managed service.
- Cost Optimization: DocumentDB's on-demand pricing model and automatic scaling capabilities can help optimize costs by only paying for the resources you need. Running MongoDB clusters can be more expensive, especially for over-provisioned or under-utilized deployments.
- High Availability and Durability: DocumentDB provides built-in replication across multiple Availability Zones, ensuring high availability and data durability. With MongoDB, you need to set up and manage your own replica sets for high availability.
- Automated Backups and Point-in-Time Recovery: DocumentDB provides automatic backups and point-in-time recovery, simplifying data protection and recovery processes. With MongoDB, you need to set up and manage your own backup and recovery processes.
- Security and Compliance: DocumentDB offers encryption at rest using AWS Key Management Service (KMS), as well as integration with AWS Identity and Access Management (IAM) for access control. It is also compliant with various security standards and regulations.
- AWS Integration: As a native AWS service, DocumentDB seamlessly integrates with other AWS services like VPC, Lambda, CloudTrail, and more. This integration can be more complex with self-managed MongoDB deployments.
- Performance and Scalability: DocumentDB provides in-memory performance and can automatically scale storage and compute resources based on workload demands, ensuring consistent performance as your application grows.

While MongoDB offers more flexibility in terms of configurations and features, Amazon DocumentDB provides a more streamlined, managed, and AWS-integrated experience, making it a good choice for microservices applications deployed in the AWS ecosystem.

5.18 Graph Databases

Graph stores are NoSQL databases designed for storing data that has graph structure with nodes and edges. While relational databases model data in the form of rows and columns, the graph databases model data in the form of nodes and relationships. Nodes represent the entities in the data model. Nodes have a set of attributes. A node can represent different types of entities, for example, a person, place (such as a city, a restaurant, or a building) or an object (such as a car). The relationships between the entities are represented in the form of links between the nodes. Links also have a set of attributes. Links can be directed or undirected. Directed links denote that the relationship is unidirectional. For example, for two entities, author and book, a unidirectional relationship called 'writes' exists between them, such that an author writes a book. Whereas for two friends, say A and B, the friendship relationship between A and B is bidirectional. In the graph theory terminology, the vertices in a graph are the nodes representing the entities, and the edges between the vertices are the links between the nodes representing the relationships between the entities. A set of nodes, along with the links between them, form a path.

Graph databases are useful for a wide range of applications, where you may need to model entities and the relationships between them, such as social media, financial, networking, or various types of enterprise applications. In relational databases, the relationships between entities are modeled in the form of different tables with primary keys and foreign keys. Computing relationships and querying related entities in relational databases require complex join operations between the database tables. Graph databases, in contrast to relational databases, model relationships in the form of links between the nodes. Since the relationships between the entities are explicitly stored in the form of links, querying for related entities in graph databases is much simpler and faster than relational databases as the complex join operations are avoided. Graph databases are suitable for applications in which the primary focus is on querying for relationships between entities and analyzing the relationships.

5.18.1 Amazon Neptune

Amazon Neptune is a managed graph database service offered by AWS that provides a robust and scalable solution for storing and querying highly interconnected data. Designed with performance and reliability in mind, Neptune is capable of handling billions of relationships and executing complex graph queries with millisecond latency.

One of the key advantages of Neptune is its support for widely adopted graph query languages, such as Apache TinkerPop Gremlin and W3C's SPARQL. Gremlin, a graph traversal language, enables developers to efficiently navigate and manipulate graph data structures, while SPARQL, a standardized query language for RDF data, facilitates the integration of Neptune with existing semantic web technologies.

A Neptune cluster can be set up from the Neptune console, as shown in Figure 5.42. To set up a cluster, choose a DB engine version, DB instance class, and enter a DB instance identifier. Next, complete the advanced configuration, where you can choose the VPC that hosts the DB cluster, choose VPC security groups to secure network access to the DB cluster, enable IAM DB authentication, enable encryption, and choose a backup retention period. Once the cluster is launched, you can view the DB cluster and DB instance details as shown in Figure 5.43.

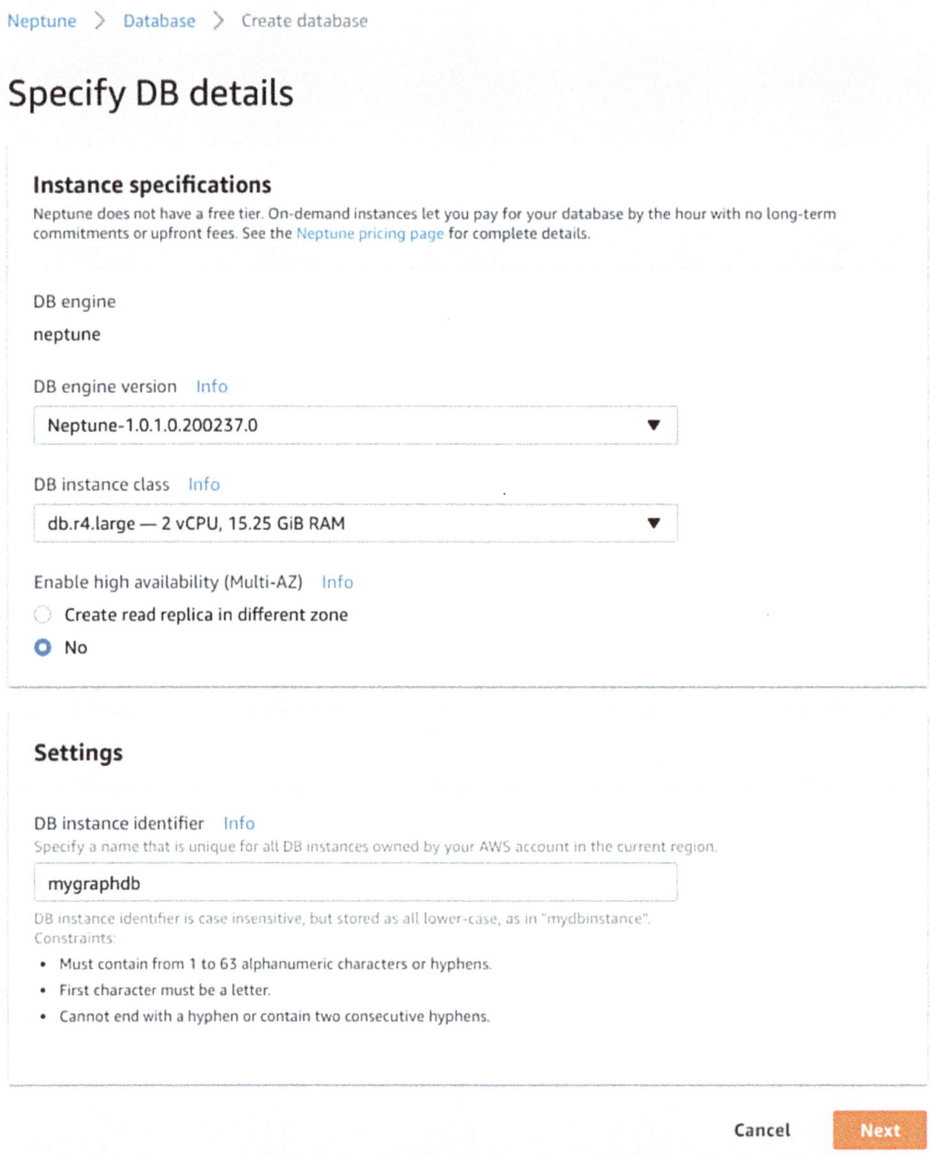

Neptune > Database > Create database

Specify DB details

Instance specifications

Neptune does not have a free tier. On-demand instances let you pay for your database by the hour with no long-term commitments or upfront fees. See the Neptune pricing page for complete details.

DB engine

neptune

DB engine version   Info

Neptune-1.0.1.0.200237.0 ▼

DB instance class   Info

db.r4.large — 2 vCPU, 15.25 GiB RAM ▼

Enable high availability (Multi-AZ)   Info

○ Create read replica in different zone

🔘 No

Settings

DB instance identifier   Info

Specify a name that is unique for all DB instances owned by your AWS account in the current region.

mygraphdb

DB instance identifier is case insensitive, but stored as all lower-case, as in "mydbinstance".
Constraints:

- Must contain from 1 to 63 alphanumeric characters or hyphens.
- First character must be a letter.
- Cannot end with a hyphen or contain two consecutive hyphens.

Cancel   **Next**

Figure 5.42: Creating a Neptune cluster

Let us look at an example of using a Graph database for an E-Commerce application. Figure 5.44 shows a labeled property graph model for an E-Commerce application. In this graph, we have two types of nodes: *Customer* and *Product*. The *Customer* nodes have attributes such as customer name, address, city, country, and zip code. The *Product* nodes have attributes such as product title, price, and various other product-specific properties (such as color, size, and weight). There are two types of relationships between the customer and product nodes: *Orders* or *Rates*. The *Order* relationship between a customer and product has properties such as the order date and quantity. The *Rates* relationship between a customer and a product has a single property to capture the customer rating.

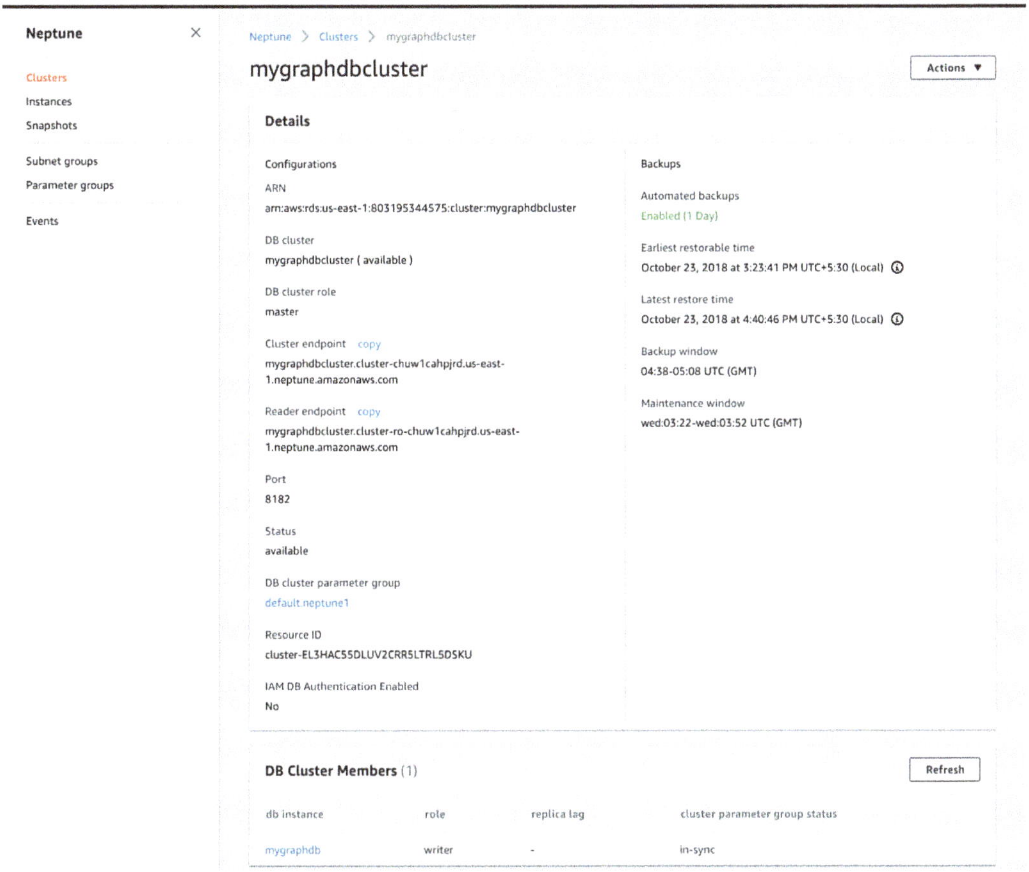

Figure 5.43: Viewing Neptune cluster details

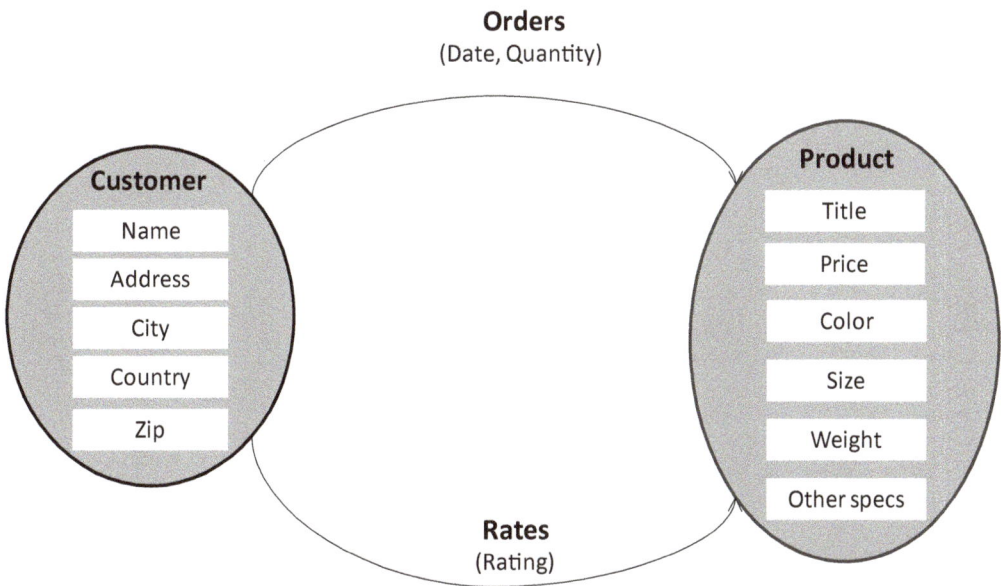

Orders
(Date, Quantity)

Customer

Name

Address

City

Country

Zip

Product

Title

Price

Color

Size

Weight

Other specs

Rates
(Rating)

Figure 5.44: Labeled property graph example

Box 5.28 shows an example of accessing Neptune using Apache TinkerPop Gremlin graph traversal language. This example uses *gremlinpython* package. In this example, we connect to the Neptune DB instance and then use Gremlin queries to add vertices for customers and products, and then add edges between the customers and products (for orders and ratings).

■ **Box 5.28: Accessing Neptune with Gremlin Python client**

```
from __future__ import print_function
from gremlin_python import statics
from gremlin_python.structure.graph import Graph
from gremlin_python.process.graph_traversal import __
from gremlin_python.process.strategies import *
from gremlin_python.driver.driver_remote_connection import \
        DriverRemoteConnection
from gremlin_python.process.traversal import Order
from gremlin_python.process.traversal import P
statics.load_statics(globals())

graph = Graph()

g = graph.traversal().withRemote(DriverRemoteConnection(
  'ws://mydb.cluster.us-east-1.neptune.amazonaws.com:8182/gremlin','g'))

#Add a vertex for a customer
c1 = g.addV('CUSTOMER').property('name', 'Bradley Russo').\
  property('address', '486, 6221 Et St.,Barnstaple').\
  property('country', 'Ukraine').\
  property('zipcode', '10903').next()

#Add a vertex for a customer
c2 = g.addV('CUSTOMER').property('name', 'Jarrod Nieves').\
  property('address', '198-550 At, Rd.,Hines Creek').\
  property('country', 'Greece').\
  property('zipcode', '20587').next()

#Add a vertex for a customer
c3 = g.addV('CUSTOMER').property('name', 'Ivor Merritt').\
  property('address', '527-9960 Vel Street,Lauw').\
  property('country', 'Peru').\
  property('zipcode', '5624').next()

#Add a vertex for a product
p1 = g.addV('PRODUCT').property('title', \
  'Motorola Moto G (3rd Generation)').\
  property('features', "Advanced water resistance,\
  13 MP camera, 5in HD display, \
  Quad core processing power, 5MP rear camera, \
  4G LTE Speed").\
  property('Color', 'Black').\
  property('Size', '16GB').\
  property('Dimensions', '0.2 x 2.9 x 5.6 inches').\
  property('Weight', '5.4 ounces').\
```

```
   property('price', 219.99).next()

#Add a vertex for a product
p2 = g.addV('PRODUCT').property('title', \
   'Canon EOS Rebel T5').property('features', \
   "18 megapixel CMOS (APS-C) sensor, \
   EF-S 18-55mm IS II standard zoom lens, \
   3-inch LCD TFT color,liquid-crystal monitor, \
   EOS 1080p full HD movie mode").\
   property('Color', 'Black').\
   property('MaximumAperture', 'f3.5').\
   property('Dimensions', '3.94 x 3.07 x 5.12 inches').\
   property('Weight', '1.06 pounds').\
   property('price', 399).next()

#Add edges for customers ordering products
r1 =  g.V(c1).addE('ORDERS').to(p1).\
   property('date',"2015-11-03").\
   property('quantity',2).next()

r2 =  g.V(c2).addE('ORDERS').to(p1).\
   property('date',"2015-11-03").\
   property('quantity',1).next()

r3 =  g.V(c1).addE('ORDERS').to(p2).\
   property('date',"2015-11-03").\
   property('quantity',1).next()

r4 =  g.V(c2).addE('ORDERS').to(p2).\
   property('date',"2015-11-03").\
   property('quantity',1).next()

#Add edges for customers rating products
r5 =  g.V(c1).addE('RATES').to(p1).\
   property('rating',4.8).next()

r6 =  g.V(c2).addE('RATES').to(p2).\
   property('rating',4.5).next()

#Print list of all vertices
print(g.V().toList())

#Print list of all customers
print(g.V().hasLabel('CUSTOMER').toList())
print(g.V().hasLabel('CUSTOMER').name.toList())

#Print list of all products
print(g.V().hasLabel('PRODUCT').toList())
print(g.V().hasLabel('PRODUCT').title.toList())

#Print list of all customers from the country Greece
print(g.V().hasLabel('CUSTOMER').\
   has('country','Greece').toList())
```

5.19   Serverless Computing

Serverless Computing is an execution model for cloud computing environments where the cloud provider executes a piece of code (a function) by dynamically allocating resources. The cloud provider manages the provisioning and scaling of the infrastructure required to run the functions. Cloud providers charge for the amount of resources used to run the code, which makes serverless computing much more cost-effective than server-based computing where servers have to run continuously.

Serverless computing, also known as Functions-as-a-Service (FaaS), is a cloud computing execution model where the cloud provider dynamically manages the allocation and provisioning of resources. With serverless computing, developers don't have to worry about provisioning, maintaining, or administering servers. Instead, they deploy individual functions or code snippets that are triggered by specific events or requests.

In the serverless model, the code is structured into small, separate functions that are executed in response to events or triggers, such as an HTTP request, a database update, a file upload, or a scheduled event. When a function is triggered, the cloud provider automatically allocates the necessary compute resources, executes the function, and then de-allocates the resources when the function finishes running.

One of the key benefits of serverless computing is that it allows developers to focus solely on writing code without worrying about server management tasks like provisioning, patching, scaling, or load balancing. The cloud provider handles all of these infrastructure-related tasks automatically, making it easier to build and deploy applications quickly and efficiently.

Serverless functions are typically designed to be stateless, meaning they don't maintain any long-lasting state between executions. If state needs to be maintained, it must be stored in external services like databases or object storage. This stateless nature allows functions to be easily scaled and executed in parallel, making them well-suited for event-driven architectures and microservices.

Popular serverless platforms include AWS Lambda, Google Cloud Functions, and Azure Functions. These services provide a highly scalable and cost-effective way to run code, as users only pay for the compute resources consumed during the execution of their functions, rather than maintaining always-on servers.

5.20   AWS Lambda

AWS Lambda is a serverless offering from Amazon Web Services (AWS). AWS describes Lambda as a compute service that lets you run code without provisioning or managing servers. Using Lambda, you can deploy your code as Lambda functions which are executed only when needed. Lambda handles the provisioning and scaling of the compute infrastructure required to execute the functions. Lambda also takes care of the maintenance of computing infrastructure, operating system patching, code monitoring, and logging. You are charged only for the compute time consumed by the functions. With Lambda, you can achieve thousands of executions per second for your functions and that too with zero administration. Lambda supports code implemented in Node.js, Java, C#, Go, and Python programming languages.

Figure 5.45 shows the triggers for Lambda. The execution of Lambda functions is triggered in response to events. For example, an HTTP request sent to the API Gateway, a record written to DynamoDB table, a new file uploaded to Amazon S3, a new message inserted into an Amazon SQS queue, a notification from Amazon SNS, a scheduled event from CloudWatch, etc. When a Lambda function is executed, it can either interact with other AWS services (for example, other Lambda functions, CloudWatch, DynamoDB, EC2, S3, SNS, RDS, and Kinesis) or return a response. The AWS resources or services which a Lambda function can access are defined in an IAM role which is associated with the Lambda function. The IAM role (execution role) defines the permissions of a Lambda function. For example, if a Lambda function is reading an object in an S3 bucket or writing a record to a DynamoDB table, then you have to grant permissions for the relevant actions to the execution role.

5.20.1 Triggers

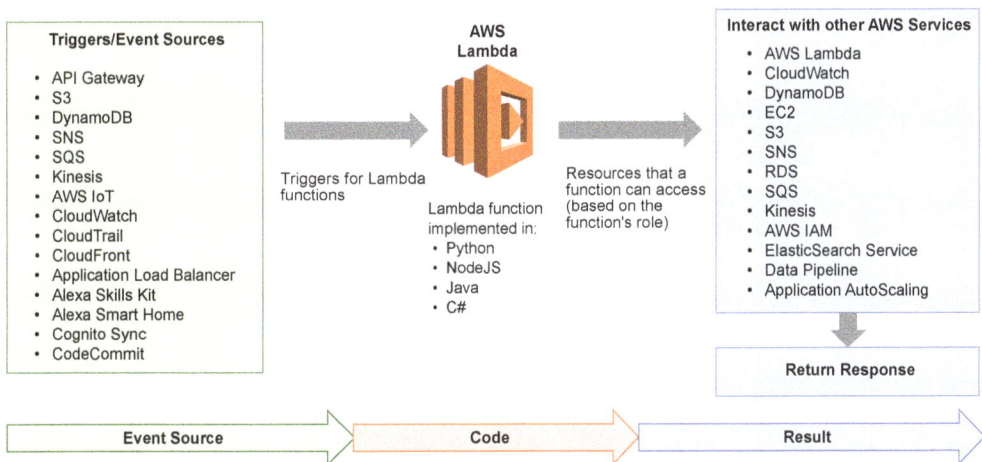

Figure 5.45: Triggers and resources for Lambda

- **API Gateway**: Lambda functions can be invoked in response to an HTTPS request received by a REST API endpoint implemented using API Gateway. While defining a REST API endpoint within API Gateway, you can map individual HTTP methods such as GET, PUT, POST, and DELETE to specific Lambda functions. When an HTTPS request is sent to the API endpoint, the Lambda function corresponding to the request method is invoked. The data in the request body is passed as a parameter to the Lambda function. A Lambda function can respond with valid HTTP status codes so that the caller of the REST endpoint receives the HTTP status codes in the response. You can also configure a custom Integration Response within API Gateway, which maps the output from your Lambda function to the headers and output model of the method response.
- **S3**: Lambda functions can be invoked by events published by S3. For example, you can configure an event notification for an S3 bucket to publish an event whenever a file is added, removed, or changed, to trigger a Lambda function. Supported event types are as follows: PUT, POST, COPY, Multipart upload completed, All object create events, Object in RRS lost, Permanently deleted, Delete marker created, All object

delete events, Restore from Glacier initiated, and Restore from Glacier completed. You can optionally define a prefix and suffix to limit the event notification to objects with keys that start with or end with the matching characters.

- **DynamoDB**: Lambda functions can be triggered in response to updates made to DynamoDB tables. To use this feature, you have to enable DynamoDB Streams for a DynamoDB table. The Lambda runtime polls shards in a DynamoDB Streams stream for records and invokes the Lambda function to process the data when records are available.

- **SNS**: Lambda functions can be triggered in response to notifications received from Amazon Simple Notification Service (SNS). You can configure a Lambda function to subscribe to an SNS topic. When a message is published to the SNS topic, the message is sent to the AWS Lambda function with the message as the payload, which invokes the Lambda function.

- **SQS**: Lambda functions can be configured to process messages pushed to an Amazon Simple Queue Service (SQS) queue. The Lambda runtime polls the SQS queue and invokes the Lambda function synchronously with an event that contains queue messages. Messages are read in batches, and the Lambda function is invoked once for each batch. When the function execution for a batch of messages completes successfully, Lambda deletes the messages from the queue.

- **Kinesis**: Lambda functions can be configured to process records in an Amazon Kinesis data stream. The Lambda runtime polls the Kinesis data stream and invokes the Lambda function synchronously with an event that contains stream records. You can configure a batch size to process records from the Kinesis data stream in batches and the position in the stream to start reading the messages from (such as Latest, At timestamp, or Trim horizon).

- **AWS IoT**: You can configure a Lambda function to be triggered by a custom AWS IoT rule or an AWS IoT Button. To create a new AWS IoT Rule, you have to provide a rule name, description, and the rule query statement (in SQL). To configure an AWS IoT Button trigger for a Lambda function, you have to provide the device serial number (DSN) of your button.

- **CloudWatch**: Lambda functions can be triggered in response to CloudWatch Events. CloudWatch events are emitted when any changes occur in the AWS resources. Within CloudWatch, you can create rules to filter the CloudWatch events by selecting a service name and the event type. For example, you can create a CloudWatch rule to filter all PutObject events for an S3 bucket and then add a Lambda function as the target for the rule to process the message and take action. Lambda functions can also be configured to process CloudWatch logs by creating a log subscription. The log events sent to the log group trigger your Lambda function with the contents of the logs received. You can optionally define a filter pattern to filter the logs.

- **CloudFront**: Lambda functions can be triggered in response to CloudFront events. AWS Lambda has a feature called Lambda@Edge, which lets you run Lambda functions to customize content that CloudFront delivers at AWS edge locations which are closer to your application's users. Lambda functions can be used to change CloudFront requests and responses by invoking functions at the following points: (1) right after the CloudFront service receives a request from the user, (2) right before the

CloudFront service forwards the request to the origin (your application), (3) right after the origin has responded to the request, (4) right before the response is sent back to the user.

- **Application Load Balancer**: Lambda functions can be used to process requests from an AWS Application Load Balancer. Rules defined in the load balancer can route HTTP requests to a Lambda function, which can process the requests and return HTTP responses.
- **Alexa Skills Kit**: Amazon Alexa is a smart virtual assistant that works on Amazon Echo devices. Alexa provides a set of built-in capabilities which are referred to as 'skills'. You can implement your custom skills for Alexa. For example, a skill to look up the current weather in your city. Custom skills can be implemented using Lambda functions. The Lambda functions are executed in response to Alexa voice interactions.
- **Alexa Smart Home**: With Alexa's Smart Home skills, you can enable voice interactions to control and check the status of cloud-connected devices such as lights, sensors, thermostats, cameras, locks, cooking, and entertainment devices. Lambda functions can be used to implement Smart Home skills for Alexa.
- **Cognito Sync**: Lambda functions can be invoked in response to Amazon Cognito sync events. The Cognito Sync trigger is invoked whenever a Cognito identity pool dataset is synced.
- **CodeCommit**: Lambda functions can be triggered in response to Amazon CodeCommit repository events. For example, a Lambda function can be invoked when a new branch or tag is created, a branch or tag is deleted, or a commit is pushed to an existing branch.

5.20.2 Lambda Function Example

Let us look at an example of creating a Lambda function for resizing images uploaded to an S3 bucket. The Lambda function is triggered every time a new image is uploaded to an S3 bucket. The function resizes the image and saves it to another S3 bucket. Before we create a Lambda function, we need to create an execution role that gives the function the permissions required to access AWS resources. In this example, we want to grant the Lambda function permissions to read files from an S3 bucket and write files to an S3 bucket. Figures 5.46 to 5.48 show the steps for creating an IAM role that gives Lambda full access to S3.

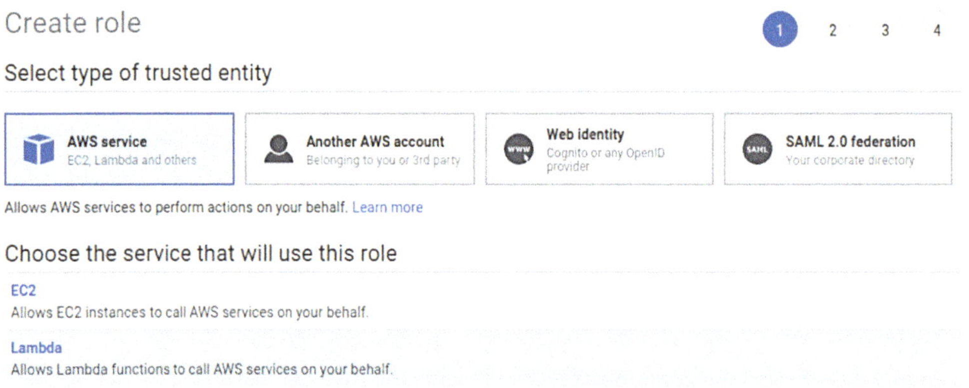

Create role   **1**   2   3   4

Select type of trusted entity

AWS service	Another AWS account	Web identity	SAML 2.0 federation
EC2, Lambda and others	Belonging to you or 3rd party	Cognito or any OpenID provider	Your corporate directory

Allows AWS services to perform actions on your behalf. Learn more

Choose the service that will use this role

EC2
Allows EC2 instances to call AWS services on your behalf.

Lambda
Allows Lambda functions to call AWS services on your behalf.

Figure 5.46: Creating IAM role for Lambda function - step 1

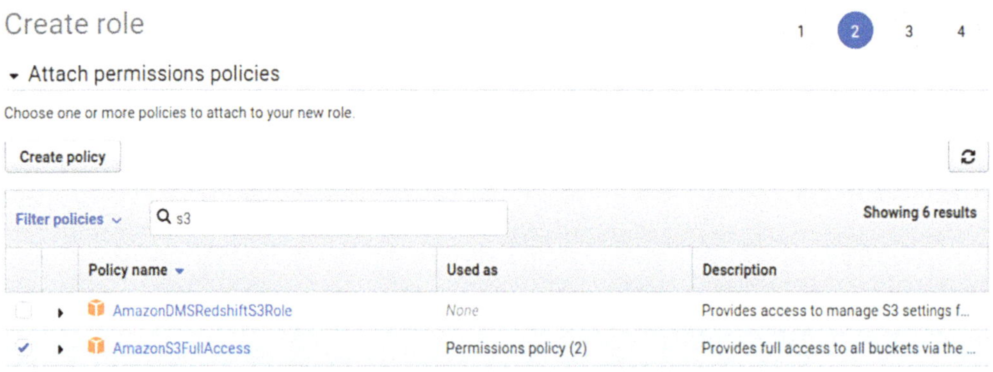

Create role   1   **2**   3   4

▾ Attach permissions policies

Choose one or more policies to attach to your new role.

Create policy   ⟳

Filter policies ⌄   🔍 s3   Showing 6 results

		Policy name ▾	Used as	Description
☐	▸	🛡 AmazonDMSRedshiftS3Role	None	Provides access to manage S3 settings f...
✓	▸	🛡 AmazonS3FullAccess	Permissions policy (2)	Provides full access to all buckets via the ...

Figure 5.47: Creating IAM role for Lambda function - step 2

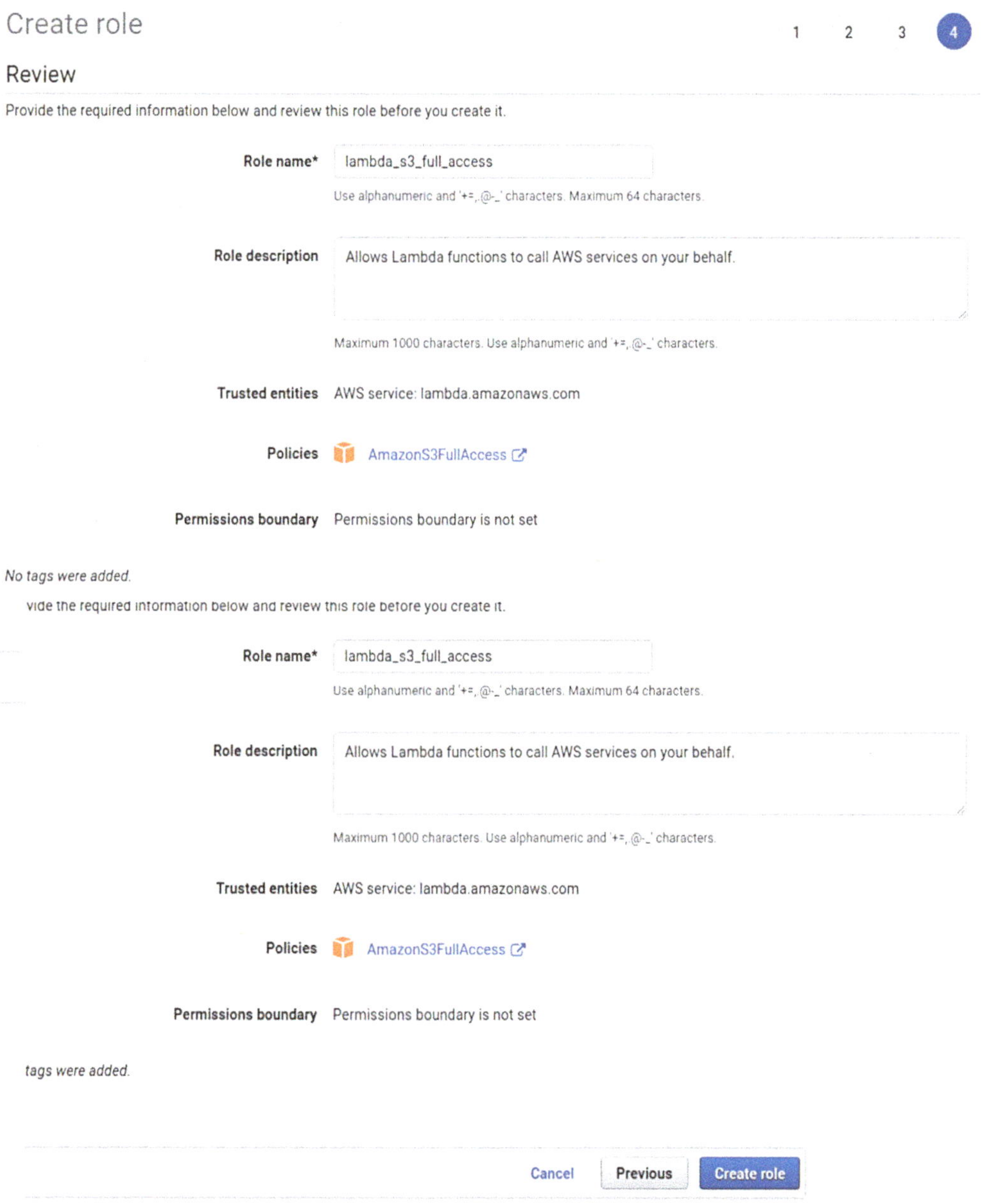

Create role

1 2 3 **4**

Review

Provide the required information below and review this role before you create it.

Role name* | lambda_s3_full_access
Use alphanumeric and '+=,.@-_' characters. Maximum 64 characters.

Role description | Allows Lambda functions to call AWS services on your behalf.

Maximum 1000 characters. Use alphanumeric and '+=,.@-_' characters.

Trusted entities AWS service: lambda.amazonaws.com

Policies 📦 AmazonS3FullAccess ☑

Permissions boundary Permissions boundary is not set

No tags were added.

vide the required information below and review this role before you create it.

Role name* | lambda_s3_full_access
Use alphanumeric and '+=, @-_' characters. Maximum 64 characters.

Role description | Allows Lambda functions to call AWS services on your behalf.

Maximum 1000 characters. Use alphanumeric and '+=, @-_' characters.

Trusted entities AWS service: lambda.amazonaws.com

Policies 📦 AmazonS3FullAccess ☑

Permissions boundary Permissions boundary is not set

tags were added.

Cancel   **Previous**   **Create role**

Figure 5.48: Creating IAM role for Lambda function - step 3

Next, from the Lambda console, create a new function, as shown in Figure 5.49. Enter a function name, select the Python runtime, and choose the IAM role created previously. Next, configure an S3 trigger for the Lambda function as shown in Figures 5.50 and 5.51, and then save the function.

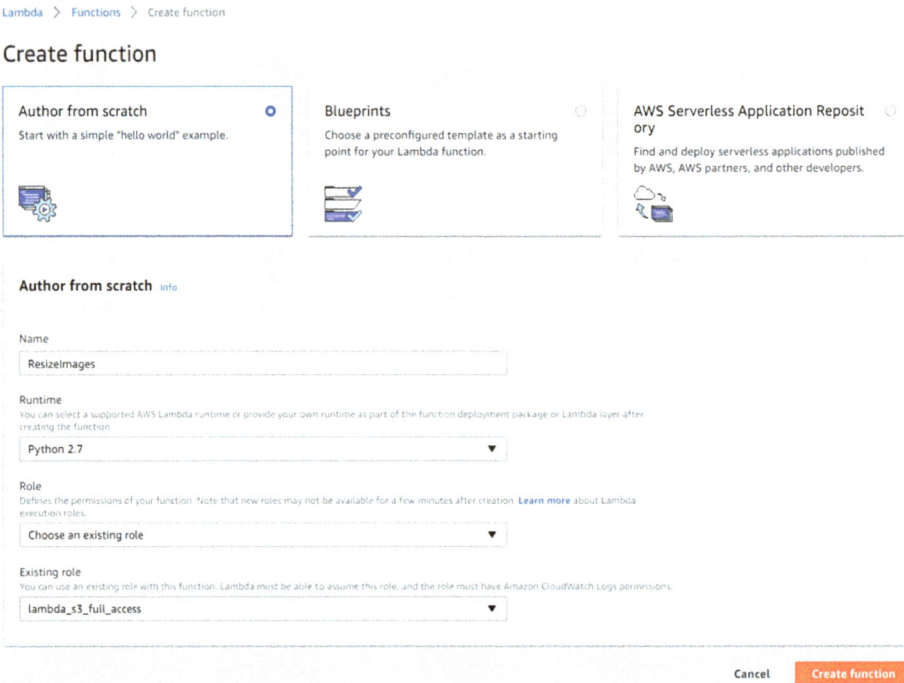

Figure 5.49: Creating Lambda function for resizing images - step 1

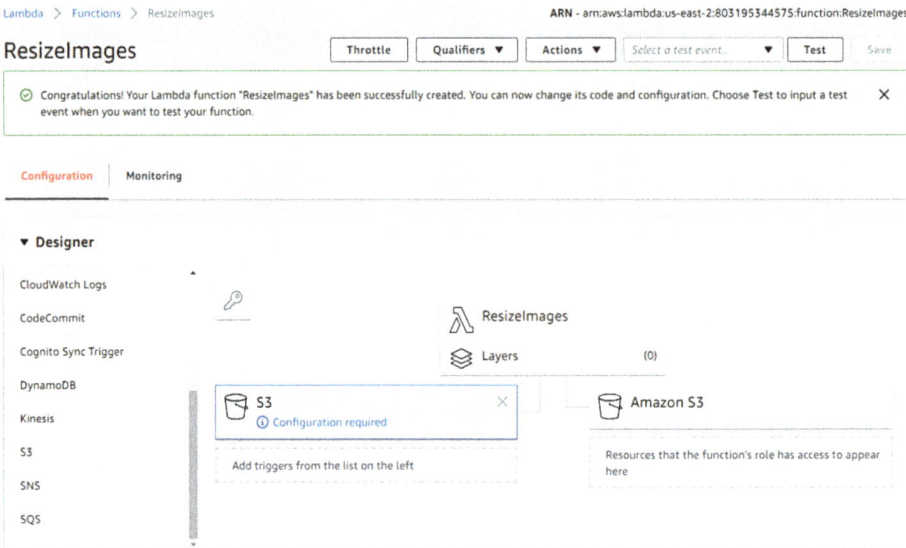

Figure 5.50: Creating Lambda function for resizing images - step 2

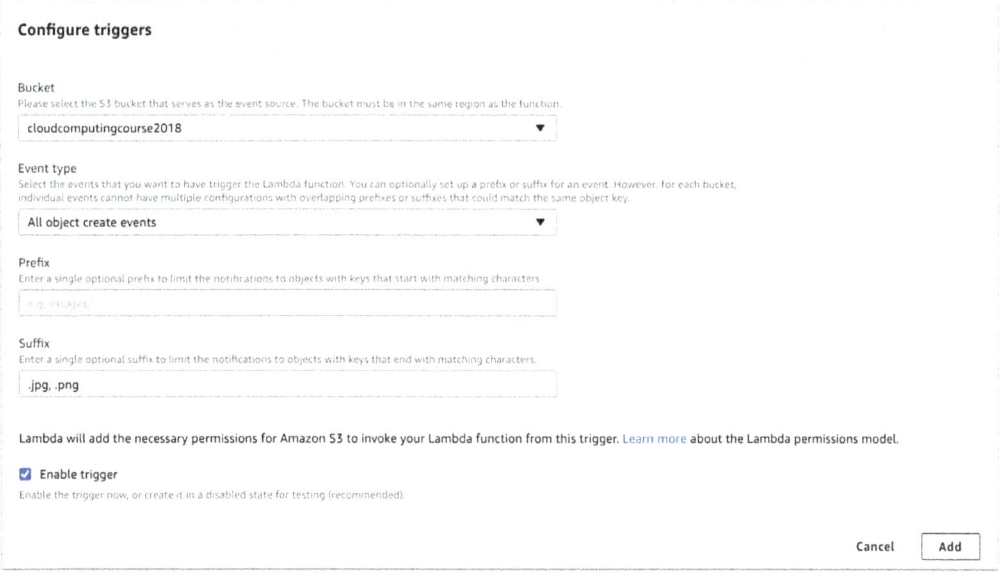

Configure triggers

Bucket
Please select the S3 bucket that serves as the event source. The bucket must be in the same region as the function.

cloudcomputingcourse2018	▼

Event type
Select the events that you want to have trigger the Lambda function. You can optionally set up a prefix or suffix for an event. However, for each bucket, individual events cannot have multiple configurations with overlapping prefixes or suffixes that could match the same object key.

All object create events	▼

Prefix
Enter a single optional prefix to limit the notifications to objects with keys that start with matching characters

e.g. images/	

Suffix
Enter a single optional suffix to limit the notifications to objects with keys that end with matching characters.

.jpg, .png	

Lambda will add the necessary permissions for Amazon S3 to invoke your Lambda function from this trigger. Learn more about the Lambda permissions model.

☑ Enable trigger
Enable the trigger now, or create it in a disabled state for testing (recommended).

Cancel **Add**

Figure 5.51: Configuring S3 trigger for the Lambda function for resizing images

Box 5.29 shows the implementation of the Lambda function for resizing images.

■ **Box 5.29: Lambda function for resizing images - lambda_function.py**

```python
import boto3
import uuid
import traceback
from PIL import Image
import PIL.Image
from resizeimage import resizeimage
import os

THUMBNAIL_SIZE = [250, 250]

def image_resize(image_source_path, resized_cover_path):
    with Image.open(image_source_path) as image:
        cover = resizeimage.resize_cover(image, THUMBNAIL_SIZE)
        cover.save(resized_cover_path, image.format)

def handler(event, context):
    s3_client = boto3.client('s3')
    try:
        for record in event['Records']:
            bucket = record['s3']['bucket']['name']
            key = record['s3']['object']['key']
            item_uuid=uuid.uuid4()
            os.mkdir('/tmp/{}'.format(item_uuid))
            download_path = '/tmp/{}/{}'.format(item_uuid, key)
            upload_path_thumbnail = '/tmp/resized-{}'.format(key)
            uploadToBucket = 'cloudcomputingcourse2018output'
            uploadFilename = 'resized/resized-'+key
```

```
            s3_client.download_file(bucket, key, download_path)
            image_resize(download_path, upload_path_thumbnail)
            s3_client.upload_file(upload_path_thumbnail,
                            uploadToBucket, uploadFilename)
    except Exception:
        print(traceback.format_exc())
```

In this function, we use two Python packages - *pillow* and *python-resize-image*, which are not available by default in the Lambda Python runtime environment. Therefore, we have to create a deployment package for the Lambda function by including the Python packages used in the Lambda function. You can create the deployment package for the Lambda function with the commands shown in the box below:

```
■ #Setting up Lambda function package
cd  /
mkdir imgresize
cd imgresize
pip install pillow -t /home/ubuntu/imgresize/
pip install python-resize-image -t /home/ubuntu/imgresize/
pip install boto3 -t /home/ubuntu/imgresize/
```

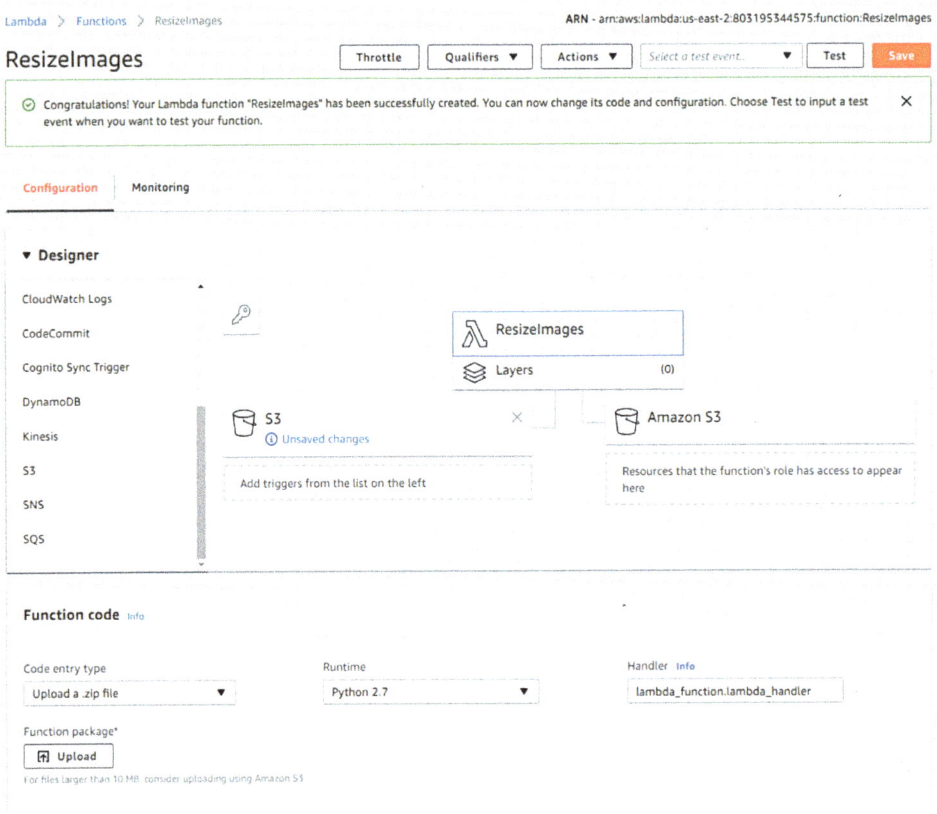

Figure 5.52: Uploading the code for the Lambda function

Next, create a zip file of the deployment package of the Lambda function and upload the code zip file to the Lambda function, as shown in Figure 5.52. Finally, you can test the Lambda function by uploading an image file to the source S3 bucket configured in the S3 trigger for the Lambda function. You can see the resized image in the destination S3 bucket specified in the Lambda function.

5.21   Identity & Access Management

Identity and Access Management (IAM) is a framework that deals with identifying individuals in a system and controlling their access to resources within that system based on predetermined rules and policies. It encompasses two main components: Identity Management and Access Management.

Identity Management deals with the processes of establishing, maintaining, and terminating digital identities for individuals or entities within a system. It involves activities such as user provisioning, account management, identity lifecycle management, and identity federation.

Access Management, on the other hand, deals with controlling and managing the access privileges of authenticated identities to various resources within a system. It includes authentication mechanisms (verifying identities), authorization processes (determining what resources an identity can access), and access control enforcement.

There are two common access control models used in IAM:

1. **Role-Based Access Control (RBAC)**: RBAC is a widely used access control model that restricts system access based on the roles assigned to users within an organization. It simplifies access management by associating permissions (or access rights) with roles rather than individual users. Users are assigned one or more roles, and each role is granted specific permissions to perform certain operations or access certain resources. RBAC provides a logical way to manage access control by aligning roles with job functions or responsibilities within an organization.

2. **Attribute-Based Access Control (ABAC)**: ABAC is a more flexible and dynamic access control model that evaluates access requests based on various attributes associated with subjects (users or entities), objects (resources), and environmental conditions. Instead of relying solely on roles, ABAC considers a wide range of attributes, such as user properties (e.g., department, clearance level), resource attributes (e.g., data classification, location), and contextual attributes (e.g., time of day, IP address). Access decisions are made by evaluating policies that combine these attributes through logical rules or conditions. ABAC provides a more granular and context-aware access control mechanism, allowing for fine-grained access control decisions.

Both RBAC and ABAC have their strengths and weaknesses, and the choice between them depends on the specific requirements and complexity of the organization's access control needs. RBAC is simpler to implement and manage, while ABAC offers more flexibility and granularity but can be more complex to configure and maintain.

Modern IAM solutions often combine elements of both RBAC and ABAC, leveraging the advantages of each approach to provide comprehensive and tailored access control solutions.

5.22   AWS Identity and Access Management (IAM)

AWS Identity and Access Management (IAM) is a core service provided by AWS that allows you to securely control access to AWS resources. With IAM, you can manage user identities, grant permissions, and enforce access policies across your entire AWS account or individual resources. IAM plays a crucial role in ensuring that only authorized users, applications, and services can access and interact with your AWS resources, thereby enhancing security and compliance within your AWS environment.

IAM operates on the fundamental principles of identities, permissions, and policies. Identities represent the entities that require access to AWS resources, such as users, applications, or services. Permissions define the actions that these identities are allowed to perform on specific AWS resources. Policies are JSON documents that define and enforce these permissions, specifying which identities have access to which resources and what actions they can perform.

The key concepts related to AWS IAM are as follows:

- **Users**: IAM users represent individual identities within your AWS account. These can be actual users, applications, or services that require access to AWS resources. Each IAM user has unique security credentials (access keys or password) and can be assigned specific permissions through policies.
- **Groups**: IAM groups are collections of IAM users. By organizing users into groups, you can more easily manage and apply permissions to multiple users at once, simplifying access management across your organization.
- **Roles**: IAM roles are similar to IAM users in that they are granted permissions through policies. However, roles are intended to be assumed by trusted entities, such as AWS services, applications, or external identities. This allows you to grant temporary, limited access to resources without having to share long-term credentials.
- **Policies**: IAM policies are JSON documents that define the permissions for identities (users, groups, or roles). Policies specify the actions that can be performed on specific AWS resources, as well as any conditions or restrictions that apply. IAM supports two types of policies: managed policies (predefined by AWS or created by you) and inline policies (embedded directly on a user, group, or role).
- **Multi-Factor Authentication (MFA)**: IAM supports MFA, which adds an extra layer of security by requiring users to provide a one-time code in addition to their regular credentials when accessing AWS resources. This code can be generated from a hardware or software token, providing enhanced protection against unauthorized access.

One of the key benefits of IAM is its adherence to the principle of least privilege. This means that users, groups, and roles are granted only the minimum permissions required to perform their intended tasks, reducing the risk of accidental or malicious actions. IAM allows you to define granular permissions that control not only what actions can be performed but also on which specific resources and under what conditions.

IAM integrates seamlessly with other AWS services, enabling you to manage access control across your entire AWS environment. For example, you can use IAM roles to grant temporary access to AWS resources for applications running on Amazon EC2 instances or AWS Lambda functions, without having to embed long-term credentials within your code.

Additionally, IAM supports resource-based policies, which allow you to define permissions directly on specific AWS resources, such as S3 buckets or DynamoDB tables. This provides an additional layer of access control, ensuring that only authorized identities can interact with those resources, even if they have broader permissions within your AWS account.

IAM also supports federated access, which allows you to grant temporary access to AWS resources to external identities, such as users from your corporate directory or other identity providers (IdPs). This enables seamless integration between your existing identity management systems and AWS, simplifying access management and reducing the need to manage separate sets of credentials.

To further enhance security, IAM provides detailed logging and auditing capabilities, allowing you to monitor and track all actions performed by identities within your AWS account. This log data can be analyzed for security and compliance purposes, providing visibility into potential misconfigurations or unauthorized access attempts.

AWS IAM offers several benefits for microservices applications, making it well-suited for managing access and permissions in a decentralized, distributed architecture. By leveraging IAM roles, you can grant temporary, least-privilege access to specific AWS resources required by each microservice, without embedding long-term credentials within the application code. This approach aligns with the principle of least privilege and enhances security by minimizing the potential attack surface. Additionally, IAM's integration with other AWS services allows for seamless access management across your microservices infrastructure, enabling you to consistently enforce access policies and audit trails across your entire application ecosystem.

5.22.1 Users

AWS recommends creating individual IAM users to provide shared access to your AWS account instead of using the root account credentials. This approach follows the security best practice of least privilege and minimizes the risk of unintended access or accidental changes to your AWS resources. Creating IAM users allows you to grant specific permissions tailored to each user's or application's needs, enhancing the overall security posture of your AWS environment.

Let us look at the steps involved in creating an IAM user. From the IAM console, launch the user creation wizard, as shown in Figure 5.53. Provide a username and select the access type for the user. You can enable Programmatic access or AWS Management Console access or both. The programmatic access enables an access key ID and secret access key for the user you create, which can be used with the AWS API, CLI, SDK, and other development tools. The console access enables a password for the user you create that allows the user to sign in to the AWS Management Console. At the next step, add the user to an existing group or create a new group. Here we select an existing group, as shown in Figure 5.54. If you choose to add the user to an existing group, the user will inherit the permissions and policies associated with that group. This is a convenient way to manage permissions for multiple users with similar access requirements. IAM allows you to attach metadata tags to users for better organization and resource tracking, as shown in Figure 5.55. Tags can be used for various purposes, such as cost allocation, access control, or identifying ownership. Next, review your choices and create the user, as shown in Figure 5.56. When the user is created, you can view and download the security credentials, as shown in Figure 5.57.

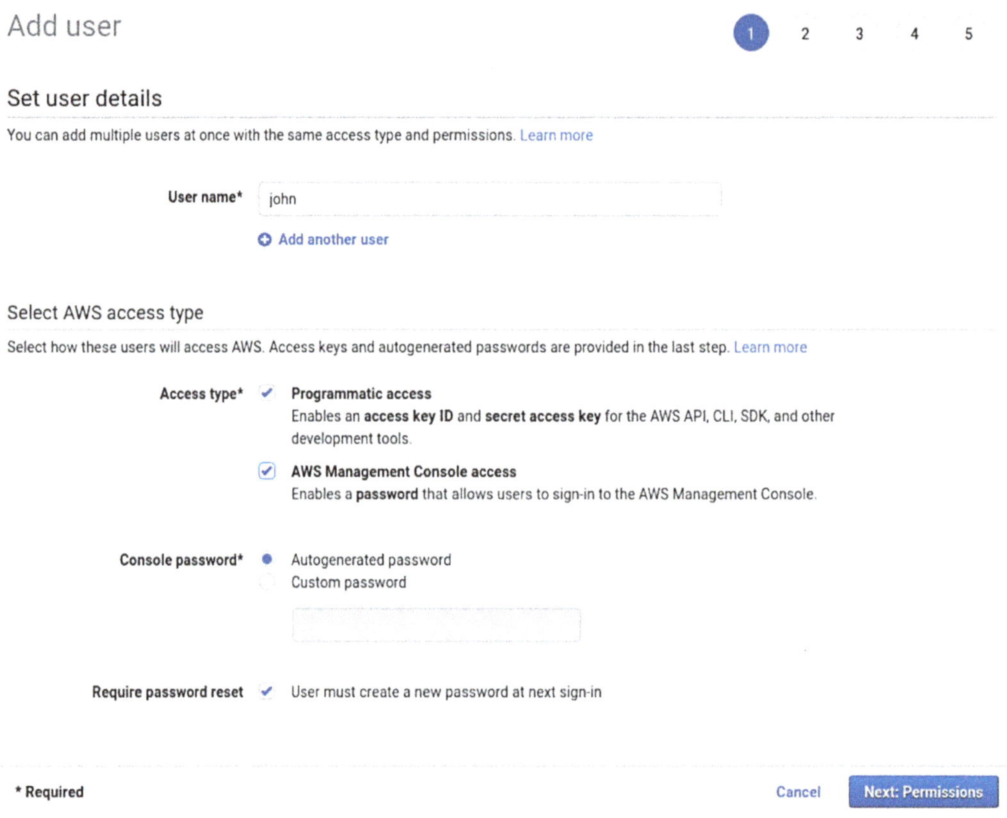

Add user   ① 2 3 4 5

Set user details

You can add multiple users at once with the same access type and permissions. Learn more

User name*   john

⊕ Add another user

Select AWS access type

Select how these users will access AWS. Access keys and autogenerated passwords are provided in the last step. Learn more

Access type*   ✓   **Programmatic access**
Enables an **access key ID** and **secret access key** for the AWS API, CLI, SDK, and other development tools.

☑   **AWS Management Console access**
Enables a **password** that allows users to sign-in to the AWS Management Console.

Console password* ● Autogenerated password
○ Custom password

Require password reset ✓ User must create a new password at next sign-in

* Required   Cancel   Next: Permissions

Figure 5.53: Creating an IAM user - step 1

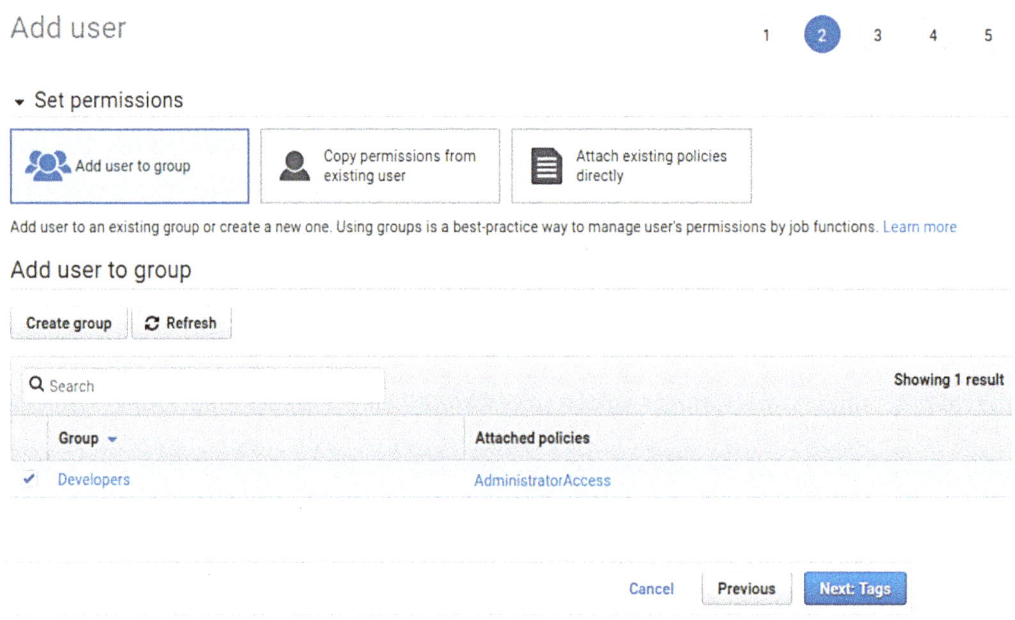

Add user   1 ② 3 4 5

▾ Set permissions

| Add user to group | Copy permissions from existing user | Attach existing policies directly |

Add user to an existing group or create a new one. Using groups is a best-practice way to manage user's permissions by job functions. Learn more

Add user to group

Create group   ⟳ Refresh

Q Search   Showing 1 result

Group ▾	Attached policies
✓ Developers	AdministratorAccess

Cancel   Previous   Next: Tags

Figure 5.54: Creating an IAM user - step 2

Add user

1   2   3   4   5

Add tags (optional)

IAM tags are key-value pairs you can add to your user. Tags can include user information, such as an email address, or can be descriptive, such as a job title. You can use the tags to organize, track, or control access for this user. Learn more

Key		Value (optional)	Remove
title		developer	✕
Add new key			

You can add 49 more tags.

Figure 5.55: Creating an IAM user - step 3

Add user

1   2   3   4   5

Review

Review your choices. After you create the user, you can view and download the autogenerated password and access key.

User details

User name	john
AWS access type	Programmatic access and AWS Management Console access
Console password type	Autogenerated
Require password reset	Yes
Permissions boundary	Permissions boundary is not set

Permissions summary

The user shown above will be added to the following groups.

Type	Name
Group	Developers

Cancel   Previous   Create user

Figure 5.56: Creating an IAM user - step 4

Add user

1   2   3   4   5

✓ **Success**

You successfully created the users shown below. You can view and download user security credentials. You can also email users instructions for signing in to the AWS Management Console. This is the last time these credentials will be available to download. However, you can create new credentials at any time.

Users with AWS Management Console access can sign-in at: https://803195344575.signin.aws.amazon.com/console

⬇ Download .csv

	User	Access key ID	Secret access key	Password	Email login instructions
▸ ✓	john	AKIA3WARMK27SGVFUXF2	********* Show	********* Show	Send email ↗

Figure 5.57: Creating an IAM user - step 5

5.22.2   Groups

An IAM group is a collection of IAM users. Groups allow you to specify permissions that
are applied to multiple users. Groups make permission management easier as you can apply
a set of permissions to multiple users by adding them to a group. You can use IAM groups to
assign different permissions to different users within an organization. For example, you can
create IAM groups for administrators, developers, and testers, and then add IAM users to
these groups. Let us look at the steps involved in creating a group. From the IAM console,
launch the group creation wizard as shown in Figure 5.58 and provide a group name. Next,
attach one or more policies to the group, as shown in Figure 5.59. Next, review your choices
and create the group, as shown in Figure 5.60.

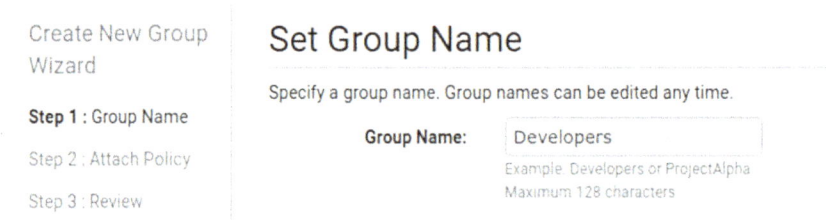

Figure 5.58: Creating an IAM group - step 1

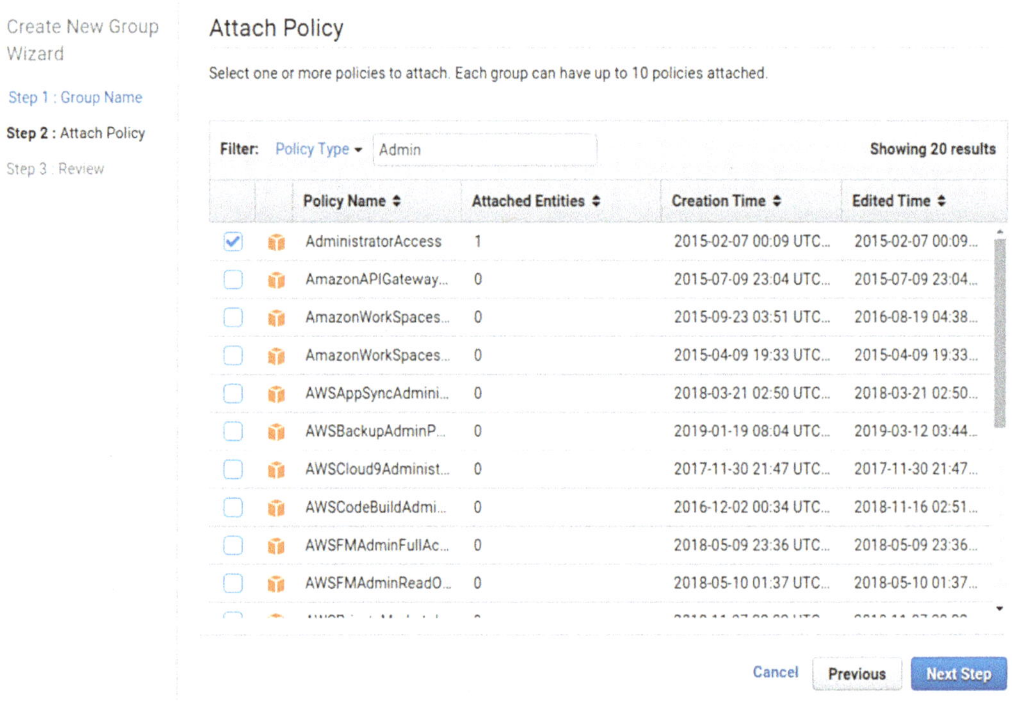

Figure 5.59: Creating an IAM group - step 2

Create New Group
Wizard

Step 1 : Group Name

Step 2 : Attach Policy

Step 3 : Review

Review

Review the following information, then click **Create Group** to proceed.

Group Name   Developers   Edit Group Name

Policies   arn:aws:iam::aws:policy/AdministratorAccess   Edit Policies

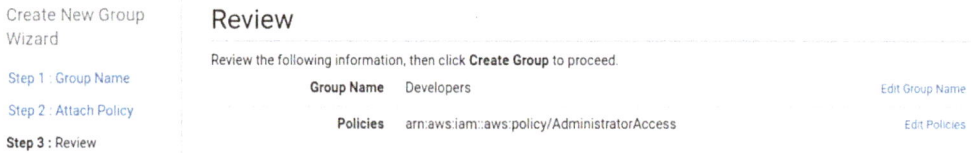

Figure 5.60: Creating an IAM group - step 3

5.22.3   Policies

A policy defines the AWS permissions that you can assign to a user, group, or role. Figure 5.61 shows an example of a policy for full access to S3 resources. Policies are stored as JSON documents. The policies are evaluated when a principal (user or role) requests an AWS resource. A policy document contains one or more permissions where each permission defines an Effect, Service, Resource, Action, and Condition. Effect can be Allow or Deny. Service specifies the AWS service to which the permission applies. Resource specifies the Amazon Resource Name (ARN) of the resource to which the permission applies. The ARN format is as follows: *arn:aws:service:region:account-id:[resourcetype:]resource*. For example, for an S3 bucket named 'mytestbucket' within AWS region us-east-1 and AWS account number 87654321, the ARN would be *arn:aws:s3:us-east-1:87654321:mytestbucket/**. An Action specifies the subset of actions within a service that the permission allows or denies. For example, an action 's3:ListBucket' allows listing an S3 bucket. An optional Condition can be used to specify the circumstances under which the policy grants permission.

AWS supports six types of policies: identity-based policies, resource-based policies, permissions boundaries, Organizations Service Control Policies (SCPs), Access Control Policies (ACLs), and session policies. Identity-based policies grant permissions to identities such as users, groups, or roles. Resource-based policies grant permissions to a principal entity that is specified in the policy. For example, an Amazon S3 bucket policy is a resource-based policy. A permissions boundary allows you to set the maximum permissions that an identity-based policy can grant to an IAM entity. AWS Organizations service control policies (SCPs) allow you to specify the maximum permissions for an organization or organizational unit. Access control policies (ACLs) allow you to control which principals in another account can access a resource. Session policies are policies that are passed as a parameter when you use the AWS CLI or AWS API to assume a role or a federated user.

5.22.4   Roles

An IAM role is an IAM identity that you can create in your account. Similar to an IAM user, a role has specific permissions. However, unlike an IAM user, which is uniquely associated with one person, a role can be assumed by anyone who needs it. While an IAM user has long-term credentials such as a password or access keys associated with it, in the case of a role, when a role is assumed, it provides you with temporary security credentials for the role session. A role grants specific privileges to specific actors for a set duration of time. When an actor assumes a role, a temporary security token is provided from the AWS Security Token Service (STS) that the actor can use to access AWS Cloud services. Roles can be used to delegate access to users, applications, or services that don't have access to your AWS resources.

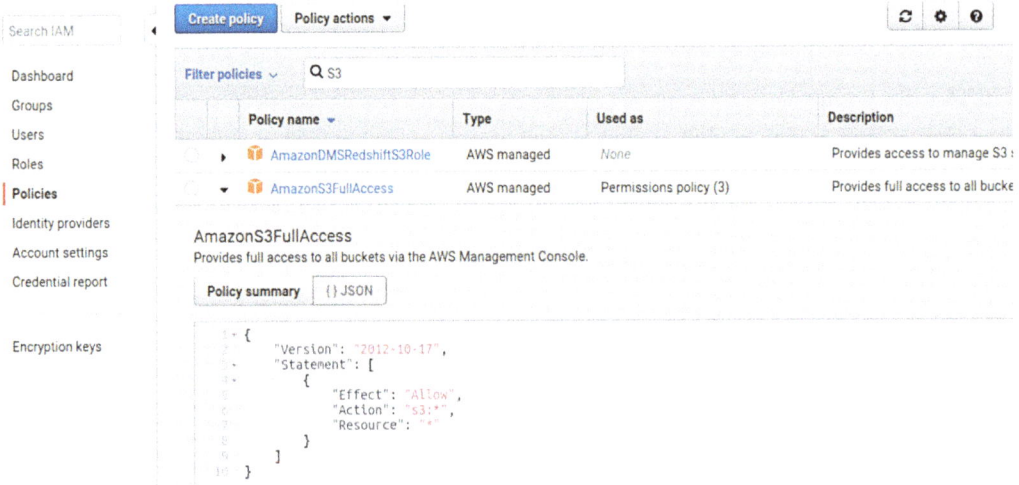

Figure 5.61: IAM policies

A role can be used by the following:
- An IAM user in the same AWS account as the role
- An IAM user in a different AWS account than the role
- An AWS service such as EC2, Lambda, and others
- An external user authenticated by an external identity provider (IdP) service that is compatible with SAML 2.0 or OpenID Connect, or a custom-built identity broker.

Let us look at an example of creating a role that can be used by the EC2 service to read and write files within S3. From the IAM console, launch the role creation wizard, as shown in Figure 5.62. Here we select the type of entity as AWS service and EC2 service from the list of services. Next, we select one or more policies to attach to the role, as shown in Figure 5.63. Here we select the *AmazonS3FullAccess* policy. Next, provide a role name and description, as shown in Figure 5.64.

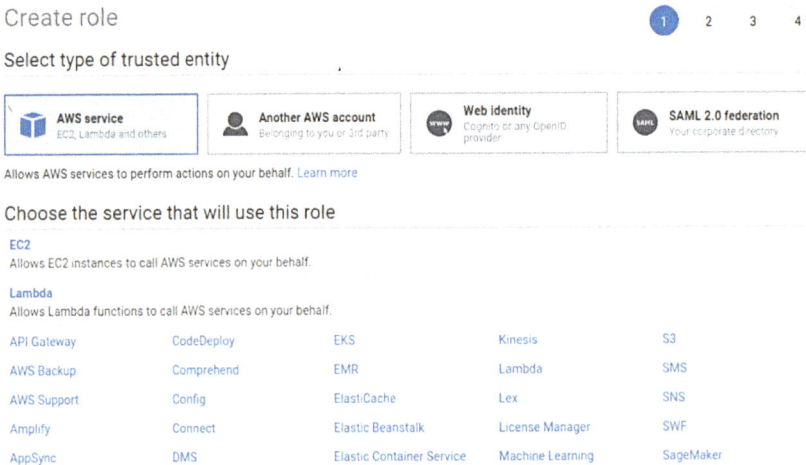

Figure 5.62: Creating an IAM role - step 1

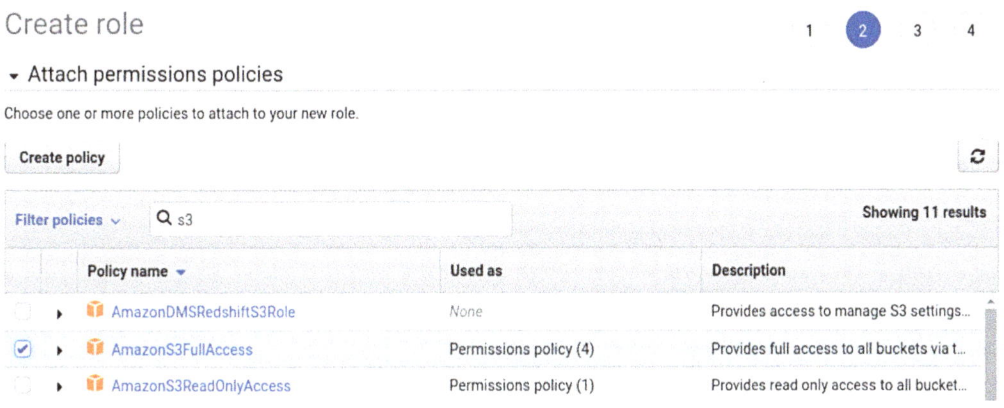

Figure 5.63: Creating an IAM role - step 2

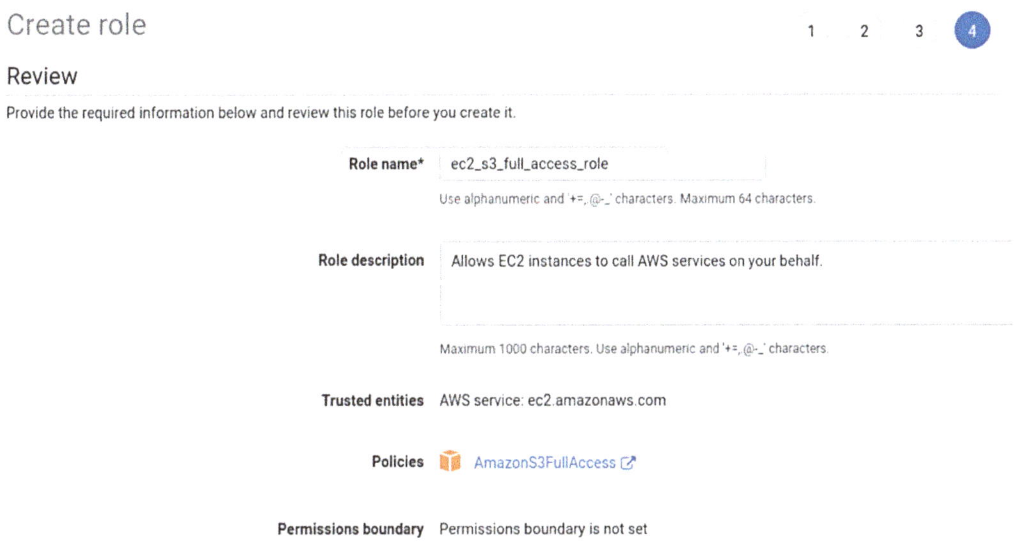

Figure 5.64: Creating an IAM role - step 3

5.23 Key Management

Management of encryption keys is critical to ensure the security of encrypted data. The key management lifecycle involves different phases, including:

- **Creation**: Creation of keys is the first step in the key management lifecycle. Keys must be created in a secure environment and must have adequate strength. It is recommended to encrypt the keys themselves with a separate master key.
- **Backup**: Backup of keys must be made before putting them into production because, in the event of loss of keys, all encrypted data can become useless.
- **Deployment**: In this phase, the new key is deployed for encrypting the data. Deployment of a new key involves rekeying existing data.

- **Monitoring**: After a key has been deployed, monitoring the performance of the encryption environment is done to ensure that the key has been deployed correctly.
- **Rotation**: Key rotation involves creating a new key and re-encrypting all data with the new key.
- **Expiration**: Key expiration phase begins after the key rotation is complete. It is recommended to complete the key rotation process before the expiry of the existing key.
- **Archival**: Archival is the phase before the key is finally destroyed. It is recommended to archive old keys for some time to account for scenarios where there is still some data in the system that is encrypted with the old key.
- **Destruction**: Expired keys are finally destroyed after ensuring that there is no data encrypted with the expired keys.

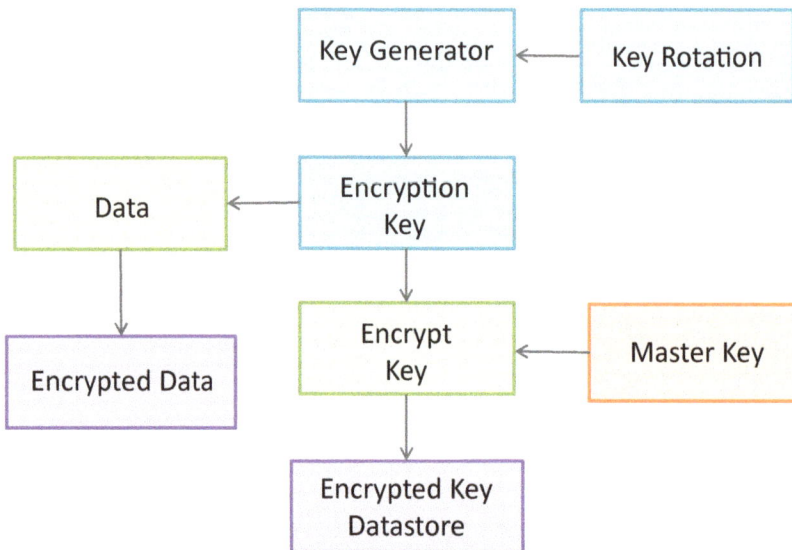

Figure 5.65: Example of a key management approach

Figure 5.65 shows an example of a key management approach. All keys for encryption must be stored in a data store that is separate and distinct from the actual data store. Additional security features such as key rotation and key encrypting keys can be used. Keys can be automatically or manually rotated. In the automated key change approach, the key is changed after a certain number of transactions. All keys can themselves be encrypted using a master key.

5.24　AWS Key Management Service (KMS)

AWS Key Management Service (AWS KMS) is a managed service that makes it easy for you to create and control the encryption keys used to encrypt your data. KMS is integrated with various AWS services that encrypt the data using the encryption keys managed by KMS. With KMS, you can perform various key management actions such as creating and listing master keys, enabling and disabling master keys, creating and viewing grants and access control policies for master keys, deleting master keys, and other actions.

KMS uses a type of key called a customer master key (CMK). CMKs are not used to directly encrypt or decrypt data. Instead, they are used to generate, encrypt, and decrypt data keys that are then used to encrypt and decrypt your application data outside of AWS KMS.

KMS supports three types of CMKs: customer-managed CMKs, AWS-managed CMKs, and AWS-owned CMKs. Customer-managed CMKs are CMKs in your AWS account that you create, own, and manage. AWS-managed CMKs are CMKs in your account that are created, managed, and used on your behalf by an AWS service that integrates with AWS KMS. AWS-owned CMKs are part of a collection of CMKs that AWS owns and manages for use in multiple AWS accounts.

CMKs reside within KMS and never leave KMS unencrypted. To use a CMK, you request KMS to generate a data key. KMS generates the data key, encrypts it under the CMK, and returns the encrypted data key along with a plaintext copy of the data key. You can use the plaintext data key to encrypt data within your application outside of KMS. The encrypted data key is typically stored along with the encrypted data, while the plaintext data key should be securely managed and removed from memory after encrypting the data.

To decrypt data, you pass the encrypted data key to KMS. KMS then uses the corresponding CMK to decrypt the data key and returns the plaintext data key. You can use this plaintext data key to decrypt the data, and then securely remove the plaintext key from memory.

This strategy of encrypting the data with a data key and then encrypting the data key with a CMK is called envelope encryption. Envelope encryption protects your data keys by encrypting them with a master key (CMK) which is stored and managed securely by KMS. The benefit of envelope encryption is that you can safely store the encrypted data key alongside the encrypted data without exposing the data key in plaintext form.

5.25 Amazon Route 53

Amazon Route 53 is a managed Domain Name System (DNS) service from AWS which can be used for domain registration, DNS routing, and health checking of web resources.

Let us briefly look at what DNS is and the types of DNS records. DNS is a distributed directory that resolves human-readable hostnames into machine-readable IP addresses. DNS translates the domain names of websites (which we type in a browser) into IP addresses of the web servers on which the websites are hosted. DNS record types include:

- **Start of Authority (SOA)**: The SOA record specifies authoritative information about a DNS zone, including the primary name server, the email of the domain administrator, the domain serial number, and timers relating to refreshing the zone.
- **Address Record (A and AAAA)**: The address record maps a hostname to the IP address of the host. The A record returns a 32-bit IPv4 address whereas the AAAA record returns a 128-bit IPv6 address.
- **Canonical Name (CNAME)**: CNAME is an alias of a hostname (defined in an A or AAAA record).
- **Mail Exchange (MX)**: MX records are used to define the mail servers used for a domain.
- **Name Server (NS)**: NS records delegate a DNS zone to use the given authoritative name servers

- **Text (TXT)**: TXT records are used to store arbitrary text information.
- **Pointer (PTR)**: Pointer record is a pointer to a CNAME and is used for implementing reverse DNS lookups (address to name translation).
- **Sender Policy Framework (SPF)**: SPF records identify mail servers used for sending emails from your domain and are used for spam protection.
- **Service (SRV)**: SRV records give the locations of well-known services and are used for newer protocols instead of using protocol-specific records.
- **Naming Authority Pointer (NAPTR)**: NAPTR record specifies a regular expression-based rewrite rule that, when applied to an existing string, produces a new domain label or URI.
- **Certification Authority Authorization (CAA)**: CAA lets the owner of a domain name authorize designated and specific Certification Authorities (CAs) to issue SSL/TLS certificates for their domain name.

You can use Route 53 to register domain names for your websites or web applications. Route 53 also allows you to create hosted zones for domains. A hosted zone is a container for DNS records which contain information about how to route traffic for a specific domain and its subdomains. Route 53 supports two types of hosted zones: public and private. Public hosted zones contain records that specify how to route traffic to the Internet. Whereas private hosted zones contain records that specify how to route traffic in an Amazon VPC. If you register a domain with Route 53, a hosted zone is automatically created. Within a hosted zone, Route 53 automatically creates a name server (NS) record and a start of authority (SOA) record for the zone. You can create record sets within a hosted zone to tell the Domain Name System (DNS) how you want traffic to be routed for your domain. Route 53 supports the DNS record types described above. When you create a resource record set, you can specify whether it is an Alias or Non-Alias record. Route 53 alias records are used to route traffic to selected AWS resources such as a CloudFront distribution, S3 bucket, ELB load balancer, VPC interface endpoint, and Elastic Beanstalk environment.

When you create a resource record set, you choose a routing policy. Route 53 supports the following routing policies:

- **Simple**: Simple routing policy maps a domain to one URL. When simple routing policy is selected, Route 53 responds to queries based only on the values in a record. Use a simple routing policy when you need to redirect to a single resource.
- **Weighted**: Weighted routing policy allows you to control the percentage of the requests that go to a specific endpoint. When the weighted routing policy is selected, Route 53 responds to queries based on weighting that you specify in this and other record sets that have the same name and type.
- **Latency**: Latency routing policy redirects a user to the server that has the least latency to the user. When latency routing policy is selected, Route 53 responds to queries based on regions that you specify in this and other record sets that have the same name and type.
- **Failover**: Failover routing policy is used for disaster recovery purposes. When failover routing policy is selected, Route 53 responds to queries using primary record sets if any are healthy or using secondary record sets otherwise.
- **Geolocation**: Geolocation routing policy routes requests based on the user's location. When geolocation routing policy is selected, Route 53 responds to queries based on

the locations from which DNS queries originate.

- **Multi-Value**: Multi-Value routing policy allows you to route traffic to multiple resources. When the multi-value routing policy is selected, Route 53 responds to DNS queries with up to eight healthy records selected at random.

Route 53 has a health checks functionality that allows you to monitor the health and performance of your application's servers, or endpoints, from a network of health checkers in locations around the world. You can specify either a domain name or an IP address and a port to create HTTP, HTTPS, and TCP health checks that check the health of the endpoint. Each health check provides CloudWatch metrics that you can view and set alarms on. Route 53 health checks can also be used for DNS failover by associating health checks with any Route 53 DNS resource recordset.

5.26   Amazon CloudFront

Amazon CloudFront is a content delivery network (CDN) service from Amazon. CloudFront can be used to deliver dynamic, static, and streaming content using a global network of edge locations. The content in CloudFront is organized into distributions. Each distribution specifies the original location of the content to be delivered, which can be an Amazon S3 bucket, an Amazon EC2 instance, or your origin server. Distributions can be accessed by their domain names. When a user requests some content that is served through a CloudFront distribution, the request is routed to the edge location that provides the lowest latency. If the content is already in the edge location, CloudFront delivers it immediately. However, if the content is not in the edge location, CloudFront retrieves it from the origin server.

To create a CloudFront distribution, you have to select the delivery method of your content, which can either be Web (HTTP, HTTPS) or RTMP. Web distribution is used to speed up the distribution of static and dynamic content such as .html, .css, .php, and graphics files. For a web distribution, the origin is either an Amazon S3 bucket or a web server. An RTMP distribution is used to speed up the distribution of your streaming media files using Adobe Flash Media Server's RTMP protocol. For an RTMP distribution, the origin is an Amazon S3 bucket.

To create a web distribution, you have to specify the domain name for your origin (such as the Amazon S3 bucket or web server from which you want CloudFront to get your web content) and an origin path. Next, you have to specify the cache behavior settings such as the viewer protocol policy, allowed HTTP methods, minimum, maximum, and default TTL, and other settings. Next, you have to specify distribution settings such as price class, alternate domain names, SSL certificate to use, supported HTTP versions, IPv6 support, and logging options. When the distribution is created, CloudFront assigns a domain name to your distribution. A CloudFront domain name looks like d123456abcdef.cloudfront.net. If you created a distribution for an S3 bucket as the origin, you can access the files in the S3 bucket using a URL like *http://d123456abcdef.cloudfront.net/image.jpg*. If you have configured CloudFront distribution to use your domain name, you can access the files in the S3 bucket using a URL like *http://www.example.com/image.jpg*.

CloudFront can provide significant benefits for microservices applications. By caching and serving static and dynamic content from edge locations closer to end-users, CloudFront can improve the performance and responsiveness of microservices applications. It can reduce latency, offload traffic from the origin servers, and enhance the overall user experience. Additionally, CloudFront's built-in security features, such as HTTPS support, field-level encryption, and geo-restriction, can help secure microservices applications from various threats. With its pay-as-you-go pricing model and seamless integration with other AWS services, CloudFront can be a valuable asset for scaling and optimizing microservices architectures.

5.27 Amazon SNS

Amazon Simple Notification Service (SNS) is a highly available, durable, secure, fully managed pub-sub messaging service that enables you to decouple microservices, distributed systems, and event-driven serverless applications. SNS has two types of clients - publishers and subscribers. Publishers communicate asynchronously with subscribers by producing and sending messages to topics. A topic is a logical access point and a communication channel. SNS topics support high-throughput, push-based, many-to-many messaging. Subscribers are the consumers who subscribe to topics to receive notifications. When a publisher publishes a message to a topic, it is forwarded to all the subscribers of the topic using the communication method configured for the subscriber. SNS can deliver notifications using supported protocols, including Amazon SQS, HTTP/S, email, SMS, and Lambda. To create a topic, you have to specify a topic name. You can control access to the topic by defining an access policy that determines which publishers and subscribers can communicate with the topic. By default, only the topic owner can publish or subscribe to the topic. You can optionally enable server-side encryption for a topic. SNS encrypts your message as soon as it is received. The message is decrypted immediately before delivery. You can optionally enable delivery status logging to log delivery status for protocols including AWS Lambda, Amazon SQS, HTTP/S, and platform application endpoints. To subscribe to a topic, you have to provide a topic ARN and choose a protocol (such as HTTP, HTTPS, Email, Email-JSON, Amazon SQS, AWS Lambda, SMS, or platform application endpoint). You can optionally specify a subscription filter to filter the messages. SNS can be used for a variety of scenarios such as user notifications and system-to-system messaging. With SNS, you can send push notifications to mobile apps, text messages to mobile phone numbers, and plain-text emails to email addresses. You can also fan out messages with a topic or publish them to mobile endpoints directly. SNS is also useful for system-to-system messaging for microservices, distributed architectures, and serverless applications.

Summary

In this chapter, we covered various compute and storage services offered by Amazon Web Services (AWS). We started by describing the AWS Compute Services, which provide dynamically scalable virtual machines. We explained Amazon Elastic Compute Cloud (EC2), an Infrastructure-as-a-Service (IaaS) offering, including instance types, Amazon Machine Images (AMIs), security groups, and pricing models. We provided guidance on launching and managing EC2 instances through the console and programmatically using Python. We covered AWS EC2 Auto Scaling, which automatically scales EC2 capacity based on user-defined conditions, and we explained AWS Elastic Load Balancing (ELB), a service for distributing traffic across EC2 instances. We described the different types of load balancers and setting up an Application Load Balancer with a sample Flask web application. In the storage services section, we introduced block storage, file storage, and object storage. We provided a detailed explanation of Amazon Simple Storage Service (S3), an object storage service, covering buckets, objects, access management, versioning, encryption, static website hosting, durability, availability, storage classes, and more. We described Amazon Elastic File System (EFS) and Amazon Elastic Block Store (EBS), highlighting the different types of EBS volumes, snapshots, and encryption options. We covered relational databases and their key concepts like tables, rows, columns, keys, constraints, and ACID properties. We explained Amazon Relational Database Service (RDS), a managed relational database service offered by AWS, and how to set up and use it for various use cases. We introduced non-relational databases (NoSQL) and their driving forces, such as the need for high scalability, fault tolerance, and availability. We covered the CAP theorem, which explains the trade-off between consistency, availability, and partition tolerance in distributed systems. We described different types of NoSQL databases, including key-value stores like Amazon DynamoDB, document databases like MongoDB and Amazon DocumentDB, and graph databases like Amazon Neptune. We explained in-memory caching with Amazon ElastiCache and its Redis and Memcached engines. We covered serverless computing and AWS Lambda, which allows running code without provisioning servers. We discussed Identity and Access Management (IAM), covering users, groups, roles, and policies, and how AWS IAM allows secure control over AWS resources. We covered key management and the AWS Key Management Service (KMS) for creating and controlling encryption keys. We described Amazon Route 53, a managed Domain Name System (DNS) service, covering domain registration, DNS routing, and health checking. We explained Amazon CloudFront, a content delivery network (CDN) service for delivering dynamic, static, and streaming content. Finally, we covered Amazon Simple Notification Service (SNS), a pub-sub messaging service for decoupling microservices, distributed systems, and event-driven serverless applications, explaining publishers, subscribers, topics, and use cases like user notifications, and system-to-system messaging. This chapter provided an overview of the essential AWS cloud services that readers will need to understand for the microservices implementation examples covered in the following chapters. The compute, storage, database, networking, security, and messaging services described here form the building blocks for deploying and managing microservices architectures on the AWS cloud platform. Having this foundational knowledge will enable readers to effectively follow along with the hands-on microservices examples demonstrated in the upcoming chapters.

6

DEVELOPING MICROSERVICES WITH FLASK ON EC2

THIS CHAPTER COVERS

- Key concepts for developing and deploying microservices
- Monolithic implementation of E-Commerce application
- Microservices implementation of E-Commerce application
- Deploying microservices application on Amazon EC2
- Configuring a Domain with Route 53

6.1 Introduction

In this chapter, we will cover the development of microservices and deployment on Amazon EC2. We will use a running example of an E-Commerce application throughout this chapter.

The domain model of an application represents the different business entities, their attributes, and relationships that are meaningful from the application perspective. A common approach to visualize and design the target domain model uses entity-relationship diagrams that map out the key entities, properties, and connections.

Figure 6.1 shows the Entity-Relationship (ER) diagram of an E-Commerce application. We will use the ER diagram to craft the data schema of the application. The main entities identified for the E-Commerce domain are User, Product, Order, OrderItem, and Review. The attributes of each entity are shown. The User and Order entities have a 1:N relationship, User and Review have a 1:N relationship, Product and Review have a 1:N relationship, Product and OrderItem have a 1:1 relationship, and Order and OrderItem have a 1:N relationship.

The E-Commerce application allows customers to purchase products online through a browser. In this chapter, we will build an online shopping store where users can browse products, add items to a cart, and submit orders. The key components will include user accounts, product listings and details, shopping cart management, and order processing workflow.

We will use Python and the Flask framework to develop this application. Python is a very popular high-level programming language used widely for web development thanks to its simple, easy-to-read syntax. Flask provides a lightweight web application framework that makes building web apps in Python quicker and easier. Flask provides flexibility to add functions as needed, has availability of many extensions, and a fully-featured toolset for aspects like authentication and database integration.

6.2 Key Concepts

Let us review the key concepts and technologies involved in building the E-Commerce application.

6.2.1 Flask

Flask is a popular Python web framework that provides tools, libraries, and technologies needed to build web applications in Python. It is considered a "microframework" as it keeps the core simple but extensible. Flask provides important functionalities for building web applications and services such as:

- **Routing**: Maps URL paths to Python functions that handle requests. Allows calling APIs via HTTP.
- **Request & Response**: Gets details of HTTP requests and creates responses.
- **Templates**: Used for dynamically generating HTML to serve webpages. Supports Jinja templating language.
- **Configuration**: Stores application configs and secrets securely.
- **Blueprints**: Used to create components/services. Helpful for building a modular app.
- **Extensions Ecosystem**: Has rich ecosystem of extensions for database (SQLAlchemy), user auth (Flask-Login), etc.

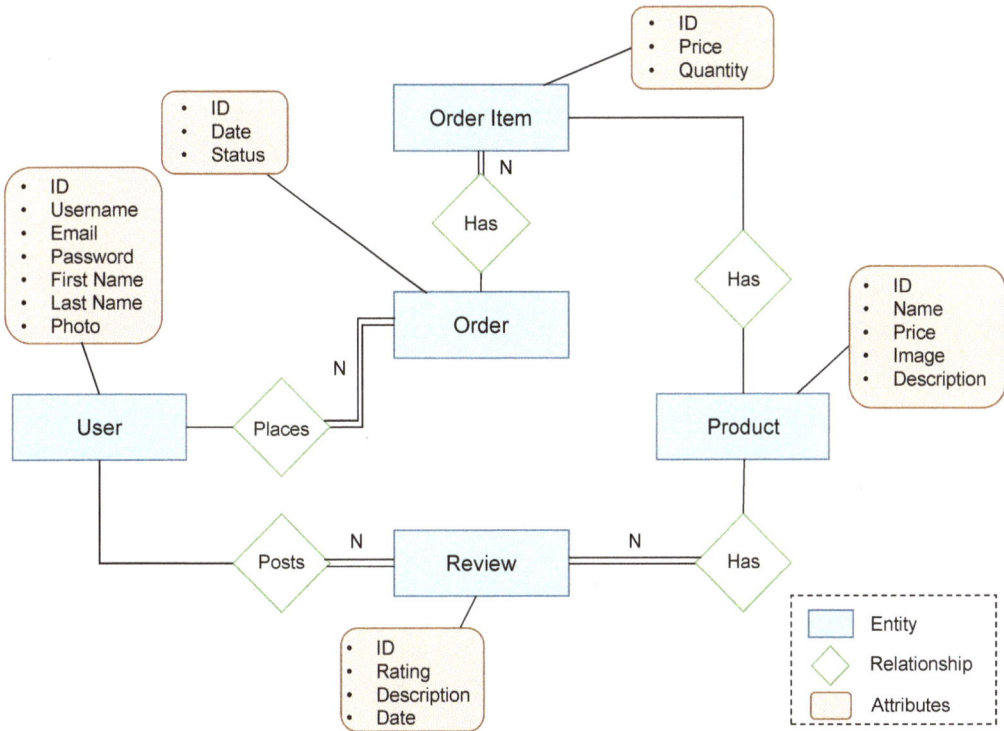

Figure 6.1: Entity-Relationship (ER) diagram of an E-Commerce application

The advantages of using Flask for microservices development are as follows:
- Easy to get started as Flask apps have minimal boilerplate code compared to other frameworks
- Embedded development server allows testing during development
- Use of Jinja templates to generate HTML pages by injecting data
- Integrates with libraries like SQLAlchemy and WTForms for database and forms
- Lightweight and modular architecture, easy to add functionality
- Backed by a large community and ecosystem of extension libraries

6.2.2   CRUD functionality

CRUD stands for Create, Read, Update, and Delete - the four basic functions when manipulating records in a database. For example, for an E-Commerce application:
- **Create**: Add new users, products, orders into respective database tables
- **Read** Fetch users, products, orders from the database to display
- **Update** Edit existing records such as order status or user profiles
- **Delete** Remove obsolete products or users

6.2.3   SQLAlchemy and Object-Relational Mapping (ORM)

SQLAlchemy is the Python SQL toolkit that provides a high-level Object-Relational Mapping (ORM) layer using mapper classes to abstract and wrap database tables into Python objects. We will use the Flask-SQLAlchemy extension to execute the CRUD operations.

The benefits of using an ORM like SQLAlchemy are:
- Avoid writing manual SQL code for common queries
- Manipulate database records as Python objects instead of rows
- Handles object-to-table mapping, relationships, and persistence
- Database vendor agnostic - can switch underlying database
- Migrations help manage schema changes

So instead of SQL, we will use Flask-SQLAlchemy wrapper and mapper classes for the User, Product, and Order entities to interface with the backend.

6.2.4 Database Migrations

As the application evolves, the database schema will require changes to models like adding columns or new tables. Tracking these changes manually can be tedious and error-prone. We will use the Flask-Migrate extension to handle database migrations. Scripts for incremental versions are used to progress the database schema to the current application state starting from the initial structure.

6.2.5 Authentication and Authorization

Creating user accounts for an E-Commerce application requires various authentication and authorization capabilities. We will incorporate the following functions using Flask extensions like Flask-Login combined with password hashing and role-based access:
- User session management via Flask-Login to track logged-in state
- Password hashing for account security rather than plain text passwords
- Protecting access with @*login_required* decorator
- Role-based authorization, for example, admin and customer accounts

6.2.6 Routing

Routing refers to mapping URLs to functions that handle requests made to those URLs. Flask provides a simple, powerful routing system that makes it easy to bind URL paths to Python view functions, while also offering flexibility to handle more complex applications and URLs. The routing becomes the foundation for building the logic of the web application.

Flask uses the @*app.route* decorator to register routes in the application. The @*app.route* decorator binds a function to a URL path so that when a user visits that path, Flask knows which function to call to handle the request.

You can also specify the allowed HTTP methods (such as GET and POST) for a route using 'methods' argument. Flask route paths can also contain variable rules that match certain patterns. For example, for a route like @*app.route('/product/<product_id>')*, when a user visits the URL */product/123*, the *product_id* will be 123. This avoids having to create separate routes for each product.

The order of route registration is also important in Flask. The first route that matches a request is executed. So more specific routes should be registered first before broader routes.

The key benefits of Flask's routing are as follows:
- Flexible routes with variable rules and HTTP method support
- Bind URLs to Python functions easily with decorators

- Modular design allowing splitting routes across files/modules
- Generate URLs to routes using the function *url_for( )* based on function name
- Integration with WSGI servers, unit testing frameworks, etc.

6.2.7 Sessions Management

Flask uses sessions to allow users to log in and maintain state across requests. Sessions are implemented in Flask using signed cookies. When a user logs in or a new session is created, Flask generates a cryptographically signed cookie with a random session ID. This session ID is used to identify the session and is sent back to the browser. On subsequent requests, the browser sends back the cookie with the session ID. Flask uses this to fetch the session data from the backend session store and make it available for that request.

By default, Flask uses a simple in-memory dictionary as the session store. But this can be configured to use server-side databases like Redis for multi-server setups. The session data itself is serialized and stored on the server, while the client only gets the session ID cookie. This allows robust session management while keeping sensitive data only on the server.

Flask signs the session cookies cryptographically to prevent tampering. It uses a secret key defined in the app config to create a hash signature and validate the cookie on each request.

6.2.8 HTML Templating with Jinja

Flask uses the Jinja template engine to generate HTML pages by substituting placeholders with data through Python dictionaries and objects passed in from the routes and controllers. The benefits of using a template engine are:
- HTML template separation from business logic
- Common page elements using template inheritance
- Secure against injection attacks
- Renders views and pages after merging data

We will use Jinja templates to render the home page, product page, cart, and orders pages by pulling data from the database and filling the templates.

6.2.9 Forms and Validation

Web forms are used to accept user input. Validation is required for forms to filter bad data and convert types. We will use the forms package WTForms for form rendering and validation features including:
- Form fields for HTML5 input widgets
- Data validation functions like length, required
- Cross-Site Request Forgery (CSRF) protection against attacks
- Processing form submissions in route handlers
- Integration with ORM models

6.2.10 Responsive Design

To provide a responsive design and good user experience across desktop and mobile devices, we will use the Bootstrap frontend framework. Bootstrap provides responsive styling out of the box for designing access-friendly pages through features such as:

- Mobile-friendly grid system
- Toggles and accordions for content
- Styling for buttons, tables, images
- Responsiveness without custom media queries

6.2.11 File Uploads

Flask provides the tools to securely handle file uploads. Flask uses the Werkzeug library to handle file uploads. When a form contains a file input, the submitted file data ends up in the *request.files* attribute of the request object. The *request.files* attribute is a dictionary-like object that maps the name of the file input to a *FileStorage* object containing the uploaded file data.

Flask provides a *secure_filename()* function to sanitize filenames before saving to avoid directory traversal attacks. For images specifically, a library like Pillow can be used to further process and validate the uploaded image before saving it.

In the E-Commerce application, we will use the file uploading functionality of Flask to handle uploads of product and user profile images.

6.3 Monolithic Implementation of E-Commerce application

In this section, we will describe a monolithic implementation of an E-Commerce application. Figure 6.2 shows the three-tier architecture of the monolithic E-Commerce application comprising UI Layer, Business Logic Layer, and Data Layer.

6.3.1 Application Architecture

UI or Presentation Layer

The UI Layer consists of the frontend code written in HTML, CSS, and Javascript that renders the user interface. The main templates are home.html, product.html, cart.html, orders.html, login.html, and register.html which display the home, product, cart, orders, login, and register pages respectively. Flask is used to render these templates and provide the routing between the different pages.

Business Logic or Application Layer

The Business Logic Layer contains the main Python application logic written using the Flask framework. The 'app.py' serves as the entry point and initializes Flask, database, and other configurations. It contains the view functions that handle the routes and perform CRUD operations.

Data Layer

The Data Layer consists of SQLAlchemy models and SQLite database to persist data. The main models are User, Product, Order, OrderItem, and Review. SQLAlchemy ORM is used to perform database operations like create, read, update, and delete seamlessly.

The application follows a layered architecture for separation of concerns. Routes and view functions handle flow and calls service layer methods. Service layer methods contain business logic for use cases. Data layer models handle persistence and database operations.

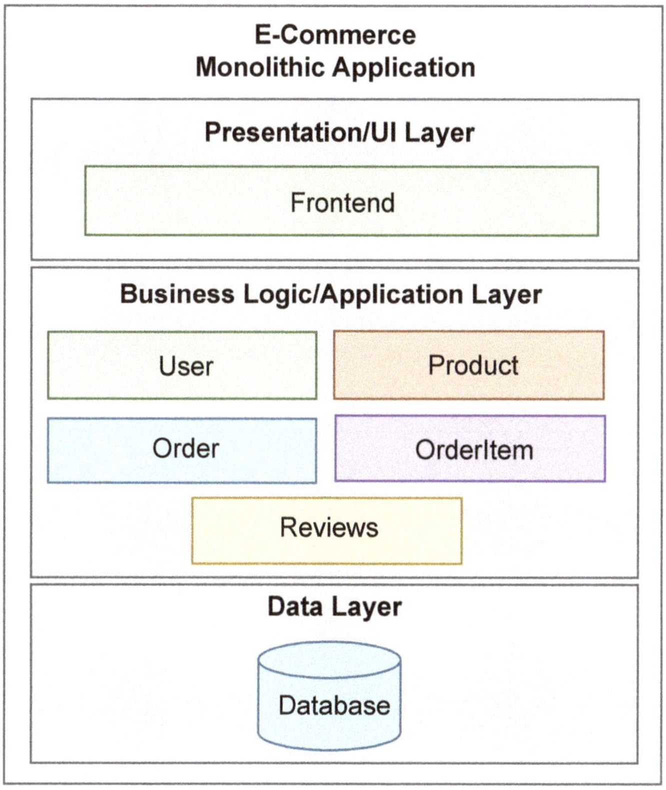

Figure 6.2: Monolithic E-Commerce application architecture

This monolithic structure keeps UI, business logic, and data access together in one codebase. All components are deployed together as a single application. While keeping everything in one codebase simplifies development, it lacks flexibility for complex applications.

6.3.2 Data Modeling

The data models provide the core structure for information used throughout the application. Key aspects that need persistent storage are user accounts, products in the catalog, orders, and reviews. Figure 6.1 shows the Entity-Relationship (ER) diagram of an E-Commerce application. We will use the ER diagram to design the database schema.

With the ER diagram available, we can map it more concretely to an application by translating it to relational database tables with foreign key constraints, and then to Flask ORM model classes.

Based on the ER to Relational mapping principles, the schema derived from the ER diagram is shown in Figure 6.3.

User Table

ID	First Name	Last Name	Username	Email	Password	Photo	Creation Date

Product Table

ID	Name	Description	Image	Price	Creation Date

Order Table

ID	User ID	Is Open	Creation Date

Order Item Table

ID	Product ID	Quantity	Price	Creation Date

Review Table

ID	User ID	Product ID	Rating	Description	Creation Date

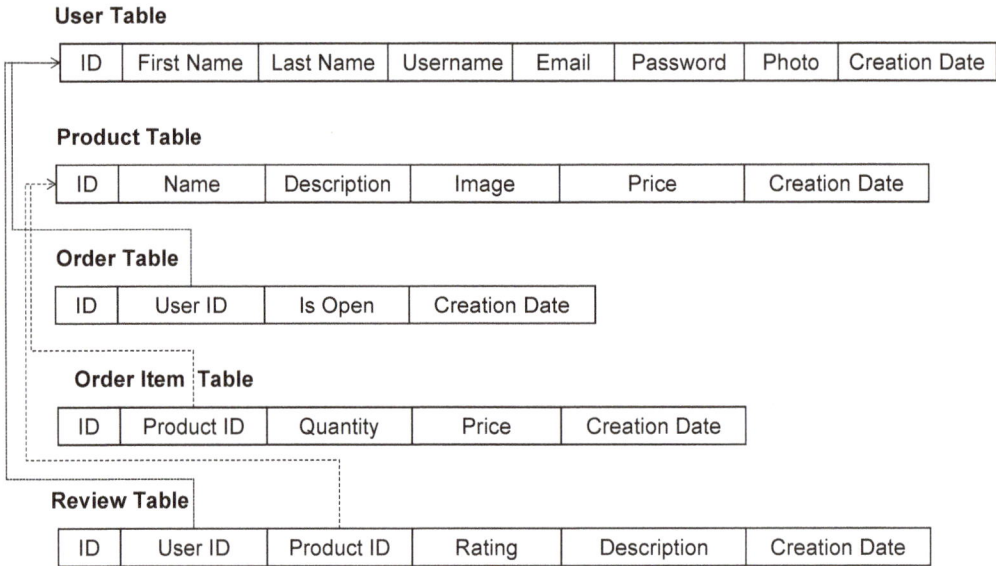

Figure 6.3: Database schema

6.3.3 Application Flow and UI

The application flow starts with the user registering on the application and then logging in. Figures 6.4 and 6.5 show the screenshots of the register and login pages. Account registration uses WTForms to validate submission of required fields (name, email, and password) before writing a new User object to the database. Upon successful registration, the user is prompted to login. When the user logs in, it verifies the password and creates a user session.

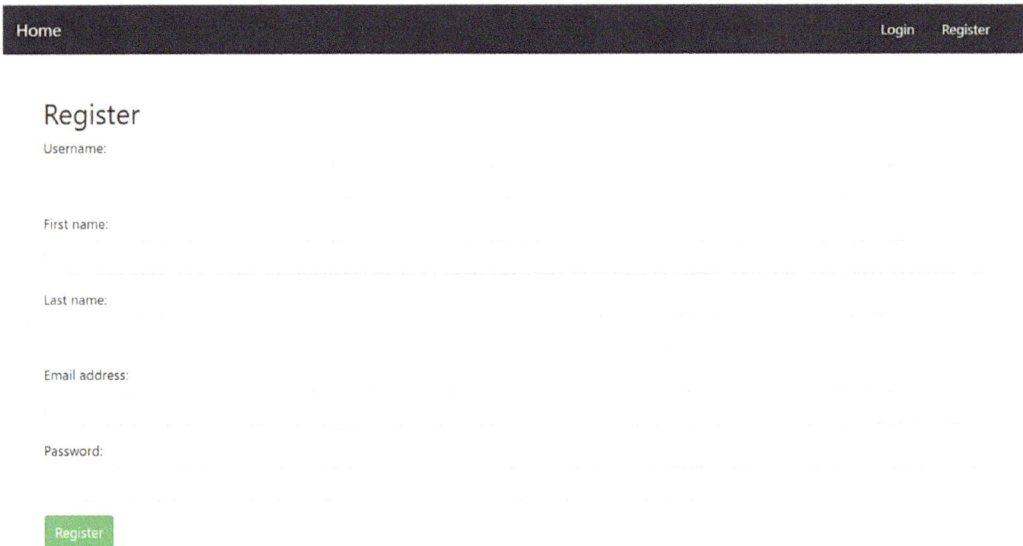

Home	Login	Register

Register

Username:

First name:

Last name:

Email address:

Password:

Register

Figure 6.4: Screenshot of the register page of the E-Commerce application

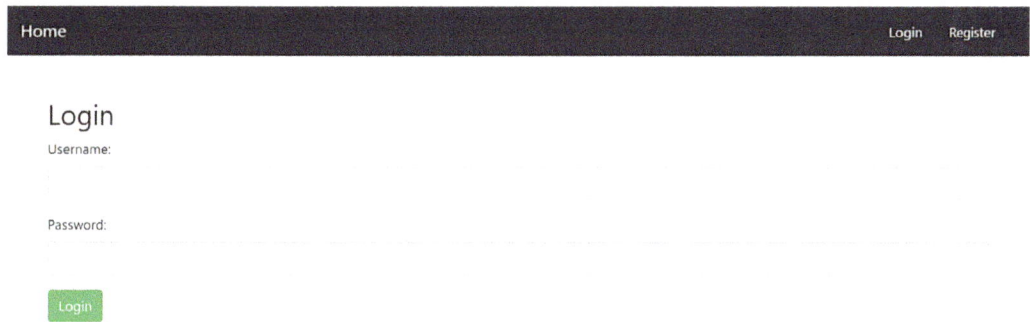

Figure 6.5: Screenshot of the login page of the E-Commerce application

The user then accesses the home page, which displays the available products. For each product, the product image, name, and price are shown. This data rendered on the template comes from ORM Product queries. Figure 6.6 shows the screenshot of the home page.

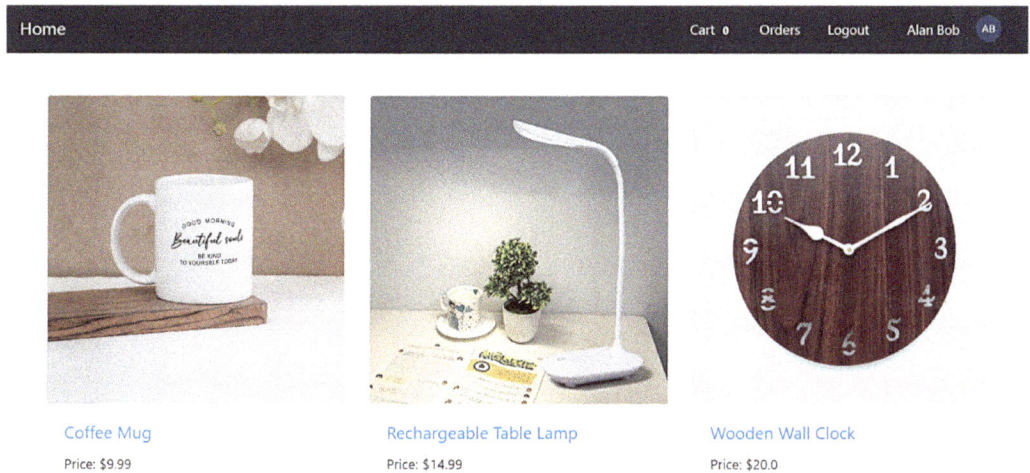

Figure 6.6: Screenshot of the home page of the E-Commerce application

In the product page, the user can view the product details like product image, name, description, and price. An 'Add to Cart' button is shown. At the bottom of the product page, the reviews section is shown. User can give a star rating and write a review for the product. Figure 6.7 shows the screenshot of the product page.

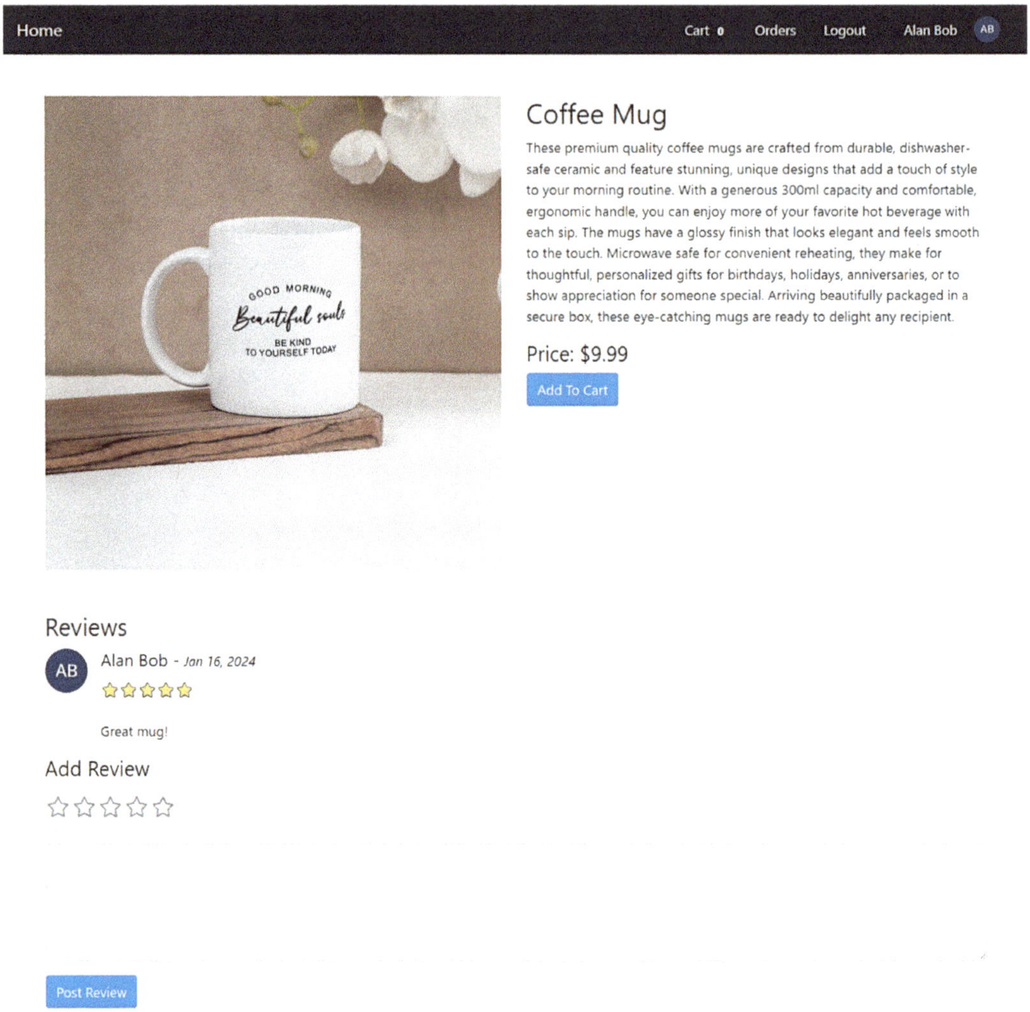

Figure 6.7: Screenshot of the product page of the E-Commerce application

When products are added to the cart, an open order is created. Users can add multiple products to the cart. Figure 6.8 shows the screenshot of the shopping cart page.

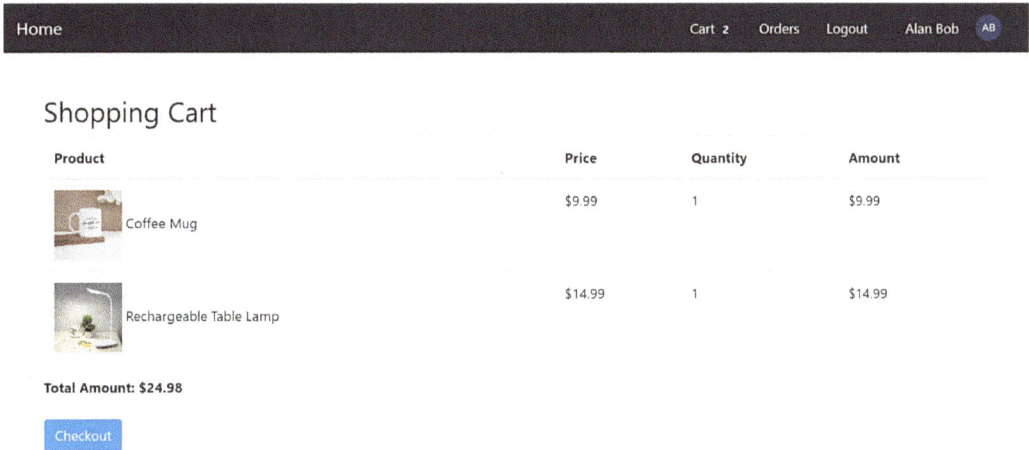

Figure 6.8: Screenshot of the shopping cart page of the E-Commerce application

On checkout, the cart is saved as a closed order. Figure 6.9 shows the screenshot of the 'thank you' page, which is shown after an order is placed.

Figure 6.9: Screenshot of the thank you page of the E-Commerce application

User can view the list of orders placed along with the items in each order, order ID, date, and total amount on the orders page. Figure 6.10 shows the screenshot of the orders page.

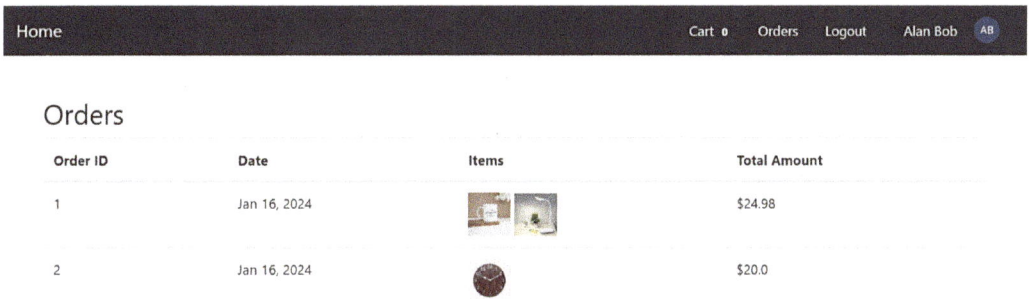

Figure 6.10: Screenshot of the orders page of the E-Commerce application

The application UX combines rendered HTML output from view functions and templates.

Common elements like header and footer are embedded via template inheritance, reducing duplication. Forms, validation, and handler workflows process input, while flash messaging provides feedback.

6.3.4 Flask Application Implementation

The monolithic E-Commerce Flask application is implemented in a single 'app.py' file which brings together the UI layer, business logic, and data access using Flask. For a better explanation of the implementation details, we have broken down this file into configuration, models, utility functions, forms, and routes sections.

Box 6.1 shows the code of the configuration and imports section. We begin with importing Flask, SQLAlchemy, Flask extensions like Migrate, Bootstrap, LoginManager, and other Python packages. Subsequently, we configure the Flask app, database URI, secret keys, upload folder, and other aspects of the application. The configuration helps initialize Flask and extensions.

■ **Box 6.1: Flask application configuration**

```
import os
import requests
from flask import Flask, send_from_directory
from flask_migrate import Migrate
from flask import render_template, session, redirect, url_for,
from flask import flash, request, jsonify
from flask_wtf import FlaskForm
from wtforms import StringField, PasswordField,
from wtforms import SubmitField, HiddenField, IntegerField
from wtforms.validators import DataRequired, Email
from flask_bootstrap import Bootstrap
from flask_login import LoginManager, current_user, login_user,
from flask_login import logout_user, login_required
from passlib.hash import sha256_crypt
import time, random
import avinit
from werkzeug.utils import secure_filename
from datetime import datetime
from flask_sqlalchemy import SQLAlchemy
from flask_login import UserMixin

app = Flask(__name__, static_folder='static')
app.config['SECRET_KEY'] = "DoWgTDq87Kmne3TsCjNFabP"
app.config['WTF_CSRF_SECRET_KEY'] = "sEWQkE9oYBiF5fVJnm278i7"
app.config['ENV'] = "development"
app.config['DEBUG'] = True
app.config['SQLALCHEMY_TRACK_MODIFICATIONS'] = False
basedir = os.path.abspath(os.path.dirname(__file__))
app.config['SQLALCHEMY_DATABASE_URI']  = 'sqlite:///' +
                    os.path.join(basedir, 'app.sqlite')
app.config['SQLALCHEMY_ECHO'] = True
app.config['UPLOAD_FOLDER'] = 'uploads'

db = SQLAlchemy()
```

```
db.init_app(app)
login_manager = LoginManager()
login_manager.init_app(app)
login_manager.login_message = "Please login"
login_manager.login_view = "login"

bootstrap = Bootstrap()
migrate = Migrate(app, db)
```

Box 6.2 shows the code of the models section. The Flask-SQLAlchemy extension wraps the SQLAlchemy ORM that connects the Python code to databases. This requires mapping the database schema to equivalent Python model classes defining the properties. The models User, Product, Order, OrderItem, and Review are defined by extending *db.Model*. This creates ORM mapped classes. Key fields (such as username, product name, price, etc.) are defined as *db.Columns*. Relationships between models are defined using foreign keys. Bidirectional relationships can also be defined between the classes. With the schema mapped as models, SQLAlchemy ORM handles the database operations behind the scenes. Migrations script out schema changes over time, enabling easy modifications. This ORM approach reduces manual SQL work significantly.

■ Box 6.2: Flask application models

```
class User(UserMixin, db.Model):
    id = db.Column(db.Integer, primary_key=True)
    username = db.Column(db.String(255), unique=True, nullable=False)
    email = db.Column(db.String(255), unique=True, nullable=False)
    first_name = db.Column(db.String(255), unique=False, nullable=True)
    last_name = db.Column(db.String(255), unique=False, nullable=True)
    password = db.Column(db.String(255), unique=False, nullable=False)
    photo = db.Column(db.String(255), unique=False, nullable=True)
    is_admin = db.Column(db.Boolean, default=False)
    authenticated = db.Column(db.Boolean, default=False)
    api_key = db.Column(db.String(255), unique=True, nullable=True)
    date_added = db.Column(db.DateTime, default=datetime.utcnow)
    date_updated = db.Column(db.DateTime, onupdate=datetime.utcnow)

    def encode_api_key(self):
        self.api_key = sha256_crypt.hash(self.username +
                        str(datetime.utcnow))

    def encode_password(self):
        self.password = sha256_crypt.hash(self.password)

    def __repr__(self):
        return '<User %r>' % (self.username)

    def to_json(self):
        return {
            'first_name': self.first_name,
            'last_name': self.last_name,
            'username': self.username,
```

```python
                'email': self.email,
                'photo': '/uploads/'+self.photo,
                'id': self.id,
                'api_key': self.api_key,
                'is_active': True,
                'is_admin': self.is_admin
        }

class Product(db.Model):
    id = db.Column(db.Integer, primary_key=True)
    name = db.Column(db.String(255), unique=True, nullable=False)
    slug = db.Column(db.String(255), unique=True, nullable=False)
    price = db.Column(db.Float, default=0)
    image = db.Column(db.String(255), unique=False, nullable=True)
    description = db.Column(db.Text)
    date_added = db.Column(db.DateTime, default=datetime.utcnow)
    date_updated = db.Column(db.DateTime, onupdate=datetime.utcnow)

    def to_json(self):
        return {
            'id': self.id,
            'name': self.name,
            'description': self.description,
            'slug': self.slug,
            'price': self.price,
            'image': "/uploads/"+self.image
        }

class Order(db.Model):
    id = db.Column(db.Integer, primary_key=True)
    user_id = db.Column(db.Integer, db.ForeignKey('user.id'))
    items = db.relationship('OrderItem', backref='orderItem')
    is_open = db.Column(db.Boolean, default=True)
    date_added = db.Column(db.DateTime, default=datetime.utcnow)
    date_updated = db.Column(db.DateTime, onupdate=datetime.utcnow)

    def create(self, user_id):
        self.user_id = user_id
        self.is_open = True
        return self

    def to_json(self):
        items = []
        amount=0
        for i in self.items:
            items.append(i.to_json())
            amount=amount+i.price*i.quantity
            amount=round(amount,2)

        return {
            'id': self.id,
            'items': items,
            'is_open': self.is_open,
            'user_id': self.user_id,
```

```
                        'date_added': self.date_added.strftime("%b %d, %Y"),
                        'amount': amount
                }


class OrderItem(db.Model):
    id = db.Column(db.Integer, primary_key=True)
    order_id = db.Column(db.Integer, db.ForeignKey('order.id'))
    product_id = db.Column(db.Integer, db.ForeignKey('product.id'))
    price = db.Column(db.Float, default=0)
    quantity = db.Column(db.Integer, default=1)
    date_added = db.Column(db.DateTime, default=datetime.utcnow)
    date_updated = db.Column(db.DateTime, onupdate=datetime.utcnow)

    def __init__(self, product_id, quantity, price):
        self.product_id = product_id
        self.quantity = quantity
        self.price = price

    def to_json(self):
        return {
            'price': self.price,
            'product': self.product_id,
            'quantity': self.quantity
        }

class Review(db.Model):
    id = db.Column(db.Integer, primary_key=True)
    user_id = db.Column(db.Integer)
    product_id = db.Column(db.Integer)
    rating = db.Column(db.Float, default=0)
    description = db.Column(db.Text)
    date_added = db.Column(db.DateTime, default=datetime.utcnow)
    date_updated = db.Column(db.DateTime, onupdate=datetime.utcnow)

    def to_json(self):
        return {
            'id': self.id,
            'user_id': self.user_id,
            'product_id': self.product_id,
            'rating': self.rating,
            'description': self.description,
            'date_added': self.date_added.strftime("%b %d, %Y")
        }
```

Box 6.3 shows the code of the forms section. Forms help validate and sanitize the input and encapsulate the processing. For example, the *RegistrationForm* validates fields for registration, and *ItemForm* handles add-to-cart actions.

■ Box 6.3: Flask application forms

```
class LoginForm(FlaskForm):
    username = StringField('Username', validators=[DataRequired()])
```

```
    password = PasswordField('Password', validators=[DataRequired()])
    submit = SubmitField('Login')

class RegistrationForm(FlaskForm):
    username = StringField('Username', validators=[DataRequired()])
    first_name = StringField('First name', validators=[DataRequired()])
    last_name = StringField('Last name', validators=[DataRequired()])
    email = StringField('Email address',
                        validators=[DataRequired(), Email()])
    password = PasswordField('Password', validators=[DataRequired()])
    submit = SubmitField('Register')

class ItemForm(FlaskForm):
    product_id = HiddenField(validators=[DataRequired()])
    quantity = HiddenField(validators=[DataRequired()], default=1)
```

Box 6.4 shows the code of the utility functions section. Reusable utility functions help avoid duplicating logic. For example, *get_user()* returns the logged-in user, *get_cart* returns the items in the cart, and *get_orders* returns the order history. The *user_loader* callback loads the user from the session.

■ Box 6.4: Flask application utility functions

```
#User related utility functions
@login_manager.user_loader
def load_user(user_id):
    return User.query.filter_by(id=user_id).first()

@login_manager.request_loader
def load_user_from_request(request):
    api_key = request.headers.get('Authorization')
    if api_key:
        api_key = api_key.replace('Basic ', '', 1)
        user = User.query.filter_by(api_key=api_key).first()
        if user:
            return user
    return None

@user_loaded_from_header.connect
def user_loaded_from_header(self, user=None):
    g.login_via_header = True

def get_user():
    if current_user.is_authenticated:
        return current_user.to_json()
    else:
        return {'message': 'Not logged in'}

def get_user_with_id(id):
    item = User.query.filter_by(id=id).first()
    if item is not None:
        response = item.to_json()
    else:
```

```python
        response = {'message': 'Cannot find user'}
    return response

def get_user_name_photo():
    try:
        user = get_user()
        user_name = user['first_name']+" "+user['last_name']
        user_photo = user['photo']
    except:
        user_name=''
        user_photo=''
    return user_name, user_photo

#Order related utility functions
def get_order():
    user = get_user()
    open_order = Order.query.filter_by(user_id=user['id'],
                    is_open=1).first()
    if open_order is None:
        return {'result':False, 'message': 'No order found'}
    else:
        return {'result': open_order.to_json()}

def get_order_from_session():
    default_order = {
        'items': {},
        'total': 0,
    }
    return session.get('order', default_order)

def get_orders():
    user = get_user()
    if not 'id' in user:
        return []
    orders = Order.query.filter_by(user_id=user['id'], is_open=0)
    if orders is None:
        response = []
    else:
        items=[]
        for item in orders:
            items.append(item.to_json())
        response = items
    return response

def post_add_to_cart(product_id, price, qty=1):
    user = get_user()
    p_id = int(product_id)
    qty = int(qty)
    price = float(price)
    u_id = int(user['id'])
    known_order = Order.query.filter_by(user_id=u_id,
                          is_open=1).first()
    if known_order is None:
        known_order = Order()
```

```python
            known_order.is_open = True
            known_order.user_id = u_id
            order_item = OrderItem(p_id, qty, price)
            known_order.items.append(order_item)
        else:
            found = False
            for item in known_order.items:
                if item.product_id == p_id:
                    found = True
                    item.quantity += qty
            if found is False:
                order_item = OrderItem(p_id, qty, price)
                known_order.items.append(order_item)
        db.session.add(known_order)
        db.session.commit()
        response = known_order.to_json()
        return response


def post_checkout():
    user = get_user()
    if not 'id' in user:
        return {'message': 'Not logged in'}
    order_model = Order.query.filter_by(user_id=user['id'],
                                        is_open=1).first()
    order_model.is_open = 0
    db.session.add(order_model)
    db.session.commit()
    response = order_model.to_json()
    return response


def get_cart():
    user = get_user()
    if not 'id' in user:
        return []
    open_order = Order.query.filter_by(user_id=user['id'],
                            is_open=1).first()
    if open_order is None:
        response = []
    else:
        items=[]
        for item in open_order.items:
            items.append(item.to_json())
        response = items
    return response


#Review related utility functions
def post_review(user_id, product_id, rating,
                description):
    item = Review()
    item.product_id = product_id
    item.user_id = user_id
    item.rating = rating
    item.description=description
    db.session.add(item)
```

```
        db.session.commit()
        response = jsonify({'message': 'Review added',
                      'review': item.to_json()})
        return response

def get_reviews(product_id):
    reviews = Review.query.filter_by(product_id=product_id)
    if reviews is None:
        response = []
    else:
        items=[]
        for item in reviews:
            items.append(item.to_json())
        response = items
    return response
```

Box 6.5 shows the code of the routes section. The *@app.route* decorator is used to create endpoints. For example, the endpoint '/' maps to the home page and '/product/<slug>' renders the product page. View functions use utility functions to retrieve data and render the templates.

■ Box 6.5: Flask application routes

```
@app.route('/', methods=['GET'])
def home():
    if current_user.is_authenticated:
        session['order'] = get_order_from_session()
    try:
        items = []
        for row in Product.query.all():
            items.append(row.to_json())
        products = {'results': items}
    except requests.exceptions.ConnectionError:
        products = {
            'results': []
        }
    user_name, user_photo = get_user_name_photo()
    return render_template('home.html', products=products,
        user_name = user_name, user_photo=user_photo)

@app.route('/register', methods=['GET', 'POST'])
def register():
    form = RegistrationForm(request.form)
    if request.method == "POST":
        if form.validate_on_submit():
            username = form.username.data
            item = User.query.filter_by(username=username).first()
            if item is not None:
                flash('Please try another username', 'error')
                return render_template('register/index.html', form=form)
            else:
                user = False
                first_name = form.first_name.data
```

```
                  last_name = form.last_name.data
                  email = form.email.data
                  username = form.username.data
                  password = sha256_crypt.hash(form.password.data)
                  user = User()
                  user.email = email
                  user.first_name = first_name
                  user.last_name = last_name
                  user.password = password
                  user.username = username
                  user.authenticated = True
                  name=first_name+' '+ last_name
                  filename = "user"+str(int(time.time()*1000))+".png"
                  imgpath=os.path.join(app.config['UPLOAD_FOLDER'],
                          filename)
                  r = lambda: random.randint(0,255)
                  colors=[]
                  colors.append('#%02X%02X%02X' % (r(),r(),r()))
                  avinit.get_png_avatar(name, output_file=imgpath,
                                     colors=colors)
                  user.photo = filename
                  db.session.add(user)
                  db.session.commit()
                  if user:
                      flash('Please login', 'success')
                      return redirect(url_for('login'))
          else:
              flash('Errors found', 'error')

      return render_template('register.html', form=form)

@app.route('/login', methods=['GET', 'POST'])
def login():
    if current_user.is_authenticated:
        return redirect(url_for('home'))
    form = LoginForm()
    if request.method == "POST":
        if form.validate_on_submit():
            username = request.form['username']
            user = User.query.filter_by(username=username).first()
            api_key=None
            if user:
                if sha256_crypt.verify(str(request.form['password']),
                              user.password):
                    user.encode_api_key()
                    db.session.commit()
                    login_user(user)
                    api_key = user.api_key
                if api_key:
                    session['user_api_key'] = api_key
                    userjson = user.to_json()
                    session['user'] = userjson
                    order = get_order()
                    if order['result']:
```

```
                            session['order'] = order
                    flash('Welcome back, ' +
                        userjson['first_name'], 'success')
                    return redirect(url_for('home'))
            else:
                flash('Cannot login', 'error')
        else:
            flash('Errors found', 'error')
    return render_template('login.html', form=form)

@app.route('/logout', methods=['GET'])
def logout():
    if current_user.is_authenticated:
        logout_user()
    session.clear()
    return redirect(url_for('home'))

@app.route('/api/product/create', methods=['POST'])
def post_create():
    name = request.form.get('name')
    slug = request.form.get('slug')
    description = request.form.get('description')
    price = request.form.get('price')
    image = request.files.get('image')
    filename = secure_filename(image.filename)
    image.save(os.path.join(app.config['UPLOAD_FOLDER'], filename))
    item = Product()
    item.name = name
    item.slug = slug
    item.image = image
    item.price = price
    item.image = filename
    item.description=description
    db.session.add(item)
    db.session.commit()
    response = jsonify({'message': 'Product added',
                'product': item.to_json()})
    return response

@app.route('/product/<slug>', methods=['GET', 'POST'])
def product(slug):
    product = Product.query.filter_by(slug=slug).first()
    if product is not None:
        item = product.to_json()
        form = ItemForm(product_id=item['id'])
        reviews=get_reviews(item['id'])
        reviewslist=[]
        for review in reviews:
            try:
                reviewdict={}
                reviewdict['rating']=review['rating']
                reviewdict['description']=review['description']
                reviewdict['date_added']=review['date_added']
                reviewer=get_user_with_id(review['user_id'])
```

```
                    reviewdict['photo']=reviewer['photo']
                    reviewdict['user_name']=reviewer['first_name']+' '+
                                    reviewer['last_name']
                    reviewslist.append(reviewdict)
            except:
                pass
    if request.method == "POST":
        if 'user' not in session:
            flash('Please login', 'error')
            return redirect(url_for('login'))
        order = post_add_to_cart(product_id=item['id'],
            price=item['price'], qty=1)
        session['order'] = order
        flash('Item has been added to cart', 'success')
    user_name, user_photo = get_user_name_photo()
    return render_template('product.html', product=item,
            form=form, reviews=reviewslist,
        user_name = user_name, user_photo=user_photo)


@app.route('/checkout', methods=['GET'])
def summary():
    if 'user' not in session:
        flash('Please login', 'error')
        return redirect(url_for('login'))
    if 'order' not in session:
        flash('No order found', 'error')
        return redirect(url_for('home'))
    order = get_order()
    if len(order['result']['items']) == 0:
        flash('No order found', 'error')
        return redirect(url_for('home'))
    post_checkout()
    return redirect(url_for('thank_you'))


@app.route('/order/thank-you', methods=['GET'])
def thank_you():
    if 'user' not in session:
        flash('Please login', 'error')
        return redirect(url_for('login'))
    if 'order' not in session:
        flash('No order found', 'error')
        return redirect(url_for('home'))
    session.pop('order', None)
    flash('Thank you for your order', 'success')
    user_name, user_photo = get_user_name_photo()
    return render_template('thanks.html', user_name = user_name,
                    user_photo=user_photo)


@app.route('/cart', methods=['GET'])
def cart():
    if 'user' not in session:
        flash('Please login', 'error')
        return redirect(url_for('login'))
    try:
```

```
            products = get_cart()
            productsInCart=[]
            totalamount=0
            for p in products:
                item = Product.query.filter_by(id=str(p['product'])).first()
                resp=item.to_json()
                itemdict={}
                itemdict['quantity']=p['quantity']
                itemdict['name']=resp['name']
                itemdict['description']=resp['description']
                itemdict['id']=resp['id']
                itemdict['slug']=resp['slug']
                itemdict['price']=resp['price']
                itemdict['image']=resp['image']
                itemdict['total']=p['quantity']*resp['price']
                totalamount=totalamount+itemdict['total']
                totalamount=round(totalamount,2)
                productsInCart.append(itemdict)
        except requests.exceptions.ConnectionError:
            productsInCart=[]
        user_name, user_photo = get_user_name_photo()
        return render_template('cart.html', products=productsInCart,
            totalamount=totalamount, user_name = user_name,
            user_photo=user_photo)

@app.route('/orders', methods=['GET'])
def orders():
    if 'user' not in session:
        flash('Please login', 'error')
        return redirect(url_for('login'))
    try:
        orders = get_orders()
        ordersPlaced=[]
        for p in orders:
            itemdict={}
            itemdict['itemscount']=len(p['items'])
            itemdict['id']=p['id']
            itemdict['date_added']=p['date_added']
            itemdict['amount']=p['amount']
            itemdict['productimages']=[]
            for q in p['items']:
                resp=get_product_with_id(q['product'])
                itemdict['productimages'].append(resp['image'])
            ordersPlaced.append(itemdict)
        except requests.exceptions.ConnectionError:
            ordersPlaced=[]
        user_name, user_photo = get_user_name_photo()
        return render_template('orders.html', orders=ordersPlaced,
            user_name = user_name, user_photo=user_photo)

@app.route('/postreview', methods=['POST'])
def postreview():
    ratinginput = request.form.get('ratinginput')
    reviewinput = request.form.get('reviewinput')
```

```
    productslug = request.form.get('productslug')
    user = get_user()
    user_id = int(user['id'])
    product_id = request.form.get('productid')
    post_review(user_id, product_id, ratinginput, reviewinput)
    flash('Thank you for your review', 'success')
    return redirect('/product/'+productslug)

@app.route('/uploads/<filename>')
def uploaded_file(filename):
    return send_from_directory(app.config['UPLOAD_FOLDER'], filename)
```

6.3.5 Flask Templates

Box 6.6 shows the code of the base template that all other templates extend. It contains the common HTML structure like <head>, <body>, and navigation bar. It implements Jinja blocks like {% block title %} and {% block content %} that child templates override to inject page-specific content. The navbar shows Login and Register links when the user is not logged in, and Cart, Orders, and Logout links when logged in.

■ **Box 6.6: Flask application base template**

```html
<!DOCTYPE html>
<html lang="en">
<head>
<meta charset="UTF-8">
<meta name="viewport" content="width=device-width,initial-scale=1.0">
<title>{% block title %} {% endblock %}</title>
{% block styles %}
<link href="/static/css/bootstrap.min.css" />
<link rel="stylesheet" href="/static/css/fontawesome.css">
<link href="/static/css/star-rating.css" />
<link href="/static/css/krajee-fas-theme.css"/>
{% endblock %}
{% block scripts %}
<script src="/static/js/jquery-3.5.1.min.js"></script>
<script src="/static/js/popper.min.js"></script>
<script src="/static/js/bootstrap.min.js"></script>
<script src="/static/js/star-rating.js"></script>
<script src="/static/js/krajee-fas-theme.js"></script>
{% endblock %}
<script>
//Remove flash messages after 4 seconds
setTimeout(function() {
  var el = document.querySelector('.alert-dismissible');
  el.style.opacity = 0;
  setTimeout(function() {
    el.style.display = 'none';
  }, 500);
}, 4000);
</script>
{% endblock %}
```

```
</head>
<body>
    <nav class="navbar navbar-expand-lg navbar-dark bg-dark">
        <a class="navbar-brand" href="/">Home</a>
        <button class="navbar-toggler" type="button"
        data-toggle="collapse" data-target="#navbarNav"
            aria-controls="navbarNav" aria-expanded="false"
            aria-label="Toggle navigation">
            <span class="navbar-toggler-icon"></span>
        </button>
        <div class="collapse navbar-collapse" id="navbarNav">
            <ul class="navbar-nav ml-auto">
            {% if not session['user'] %}
            <li class="nav-item">
                <a class="nav-link" href="/login">Login</a></li>
            <li class="nav-item">
                <a class="nav-link" href="/register">Register</a></li>
            {% else %}
            <li class="nav-item">
                <a class="nav-link" href="/cart">Cart <span
                class="badge">{{ count_items() }}</span></a></li>
            <li class="nav-item">
            <a class="nav-link" href="/orders">Orders</a></li>
            <li class="nav-item">
            <a class="nav-link" href="/logout">Logout</a></li>
            <span >{{user_name}}</span>
            <img src="{{user_photo}}" class="rounded-circle">
            {% endif %}
            </ul>
        </div>
    </nav>
{% for error_message in
get_flashed_messages(category_filter=["error"]) %}
  <div class="alert alert-danger
  alert-dismissible">{{ error_message }}</div>
{% endfor %}
{% for success_message in
get_flashed_messages(category_filter=["success"]) %}
  <div class="alert alert-success
  alert-dismissible">{{ success_message }}</div>
{% endfor %}
{% for info_message in
get_flashed_messages(category_filter=["info"]) %}
  <div class="alert alert-info
  alert-dismissible">{{ info_message }}</div>
{% endfor %}
{% block content %}{% endblock %}
</body>
</html>
```

Box 6.7 shows the code of the login page template. It extends base.html and displays a login form with username and password fields. The form is submitted to the /login route. Any error message from invalid login is displayed. On successful login, the user is redirected to the home page.

■ **Box 6.7: Flask application login page template**

```
{% extends "base.html" %}
{% from "macros.html" import render_field %}
{% from "macros.html" import count_items %}
{% block title %}Login{% endblock %}
{% block content %}
<div class="container mt-5">
  <h2>Login</h2>
  <strong>{{ message }}</strong>
  <form method="post">
    {{ form.hidden_tag() }}
    {{ render_field(form.username) }}
    {{ render_field(form.password) }}
    {{ form.submit(class_="btn btn-success pull-right") }}
  </form>
</div>
{% endblock %}
```

Box 6.8 shows the code of the register page template. It extends base.html and displays a registration form with fields like username, first name, last name, email, and password. The form is submitted to the /register route, which creates the new user account. Any registration error messages are displayed. Upon successful registration, the user is prompted to log in.

■ **Box 6.8: Flask application register page template**

```
{% extends "base.html" %}
{% from "macros.html" import render_field %}
{% from "macros.html" import count_items %}
{% block title %}Login{% endblock %}
{% block content %}
<div class="container mt-5">
    <h2>Register</h2>
    <strong>{{ message }}</strong>
    <form method="post">
        {{ form.hidden_tag() }}
        {{ render_field(form.username) }}
        {{ render_field(form.first_name) }}
        {{ render_field(form.last_name) }}
        {{ render_field(form.email) }}
        {{ render_field(form.password) }}
        {{ form.submit(class_="btn btn-success pull-right") }}
    </form>
</div>
{% endblock %}
```

Box 6.9 shows the code of the home page template that displays the product catalog. It loops through the list of products passed from the view. For each product, it displays the image, name, price, and a link to the product page.

■ **Box 6.9: Flask application home page template**

```
{% extends "base.html" %}
{% from "macros.html" import render_field %}
{% from "macros.html" import count_items %}
{% block title %}Home{% endblock %}
{% block content %}
<div class="container mt-5">
  <div class="row">
    {% if products | length > 0 %}
    {% for product in products.results %}
    {% set url = "/product/" + product.slug %}
    <div class="col-md-4">
      <div class="card mb-4">
        <a href="{{ url }}"><img src="{{product.image}}"
          class="card-img-top"></a>
        <div class="card-body">
          <a href="{{ url }}">
            <h5 class="card-title">{{ product.name }}</h5>
          </a>
          <p class="card-text">Price: ${{ product.price }}</p>
        </div>
      </div>
    </div>
    {% endfor %}
    {% else %}
    <strong>No products found.</strong>
    {% endif %}
  </div>
</div>
{% endblock %}
```

Box 6.10 shows the code of the product page template that displays details of a single product. It shows the product image, name, description, and price. It allows adding the product to the cart. It also displays reviews for the product posted by users. A form allows the logged-in user to post a new review along with a star rating for the product.

■ **Box 6.10: Flask application product page template**

```
{% extends "base.html" %}
{% from "macros.html" import render_field %}
{% from "macros.html" import count_items %}
{% block title %}Home{% endblock %}
{% block content %}
{% set url = "/product/" + product.slug %}
<div class="container mt-5">
  <div class="row">
    <div class="col-md-6">
      <img src="{{product.image}}" width="100%">
    </div>
    <div class="col-md-6">
      <h2>{{ product.name }}</h2>
```

```
      <p>{{ product.description }}
      </p>
      <h4>Price: ${{ product.price }}</h4>
      <form method="POST">
        {{ form.hidden_tag() }}
        <button type="submit" class="btn btn-primary"
        id="buy-now">Add To Cart</button>
    </form>
    </div>
  </div>
</div>

<div class="container mt-5">
  <h3>Reviews</h3>
  {% for review in reviews %}
  <div class="media mb-3">
    <img src="{{review.photo}}" class="mr-3 rounded-circle" width="50">
    <div class="media-body">
      <h5 class="mt-0">{{review.user_name}} - <small>
        <i> {{review.date_added}}</i></small></h5>
      <input required class="rating" type="number"
      value="{{review.rating}}" title=""  data-theme="krajee-fas"
      data-min=0 data-max=5 data-step=0.5 data-size="xs"
      data-show-caption="false" data-show-clear="false"
      data-display-only="true">
      {{review.description}}
    </div>
  </div>
  {% endfor %}

  <form action="/postreview" method="post">
    <input type="hidden" name="productid" value="{{product.id}}">
    <input type="hidden" name="productslug" value="{{product.slug}}">
    <div class="form-group">
      <h4>Add Review</h4>
      <input required class="rating" id="ratinginput"
      name="ratinginput" type="number" value="0" title=""
      data-theme="krajee-fas" data-min=0 data-max=5 data-step=1
      data-size="sm"  data-show-caption="false"
      data-show-clear="false" data-display-only="false">
      <textarea class="form-control" rows="5" id="reviewinput"
      name="reviewinput"></textarea>
    </div>
    <button type="submit" class="btn btn-primary">Post Review</button>
  </form>
  <br><br>
</div>
{% endblock %}
```

Box 6.11 shows the code of the cart page template that displays the user's shopping cart. It displays a table of products added to the cart with details like name, price, quantity, and total amount. A Checkout button is shown to place the order.

■ Box 6.11: Flask application cart page template

```
{% extends "base.html" %}
{% from "macros.html" import render_field %}
{% from "macros.html" import count_items %}
{% block title %}Shopping Cart{% endblock %}
{% block content %}
<div class="container mt-5">
  <h2>Shopping Cart</h2>
  {% if products | length > 0 %}
  <table class="table">
    <thead>
      <tr>
        <th>Product</th>
        <th>Price</th>
        <th>Quantity</th>
        <th>Amount</th>
      </tr>
    </thead>
    <tbody>
      {% for product in products %}
      <tr>
        <td><img src="{{product.image}}" style="max-width: 80px;">
        {{product.name}}</td>
        <td>${{product.price}}</td>
        <td>{{product.quantity}}</td>
        <td>${{product.total}}</td>
      </tr>
      {% endfor %}
    </tbody>
  </table>
  <strong>Total Amount: ${{totalamount}}</strong><br><br>
  <a href="/checkout">
    <button class="btn btn-primary">Checkout</button></a>
  {% else %}
    <strong><p class="mt-5">Cart is empty!</p></strong>
    {% endif %}
</div>
{% endblock %}
```

Box 6.12 shows the code of the orders page template that displays a table of the user's order history. It loops through the orders passed from the view and displays details like order ID, date, product images, and total amount.

■ Box 6.12: Flask application orders page template

```
{% extends "base.html" %}
{% from "macros.html" import render_field %}
{% from "macros.html" import count_items %}
{% block title %}Orders{% endblock %}
{% block content %}
<div class="container mt-5">
```

```
<h2>Orders</h2>
{% if orders | length > 0 %}
<table class="table">
  <thead>
    <tr>
      <th>Order ID</th>
      <th>Date</th>
      <th>Items</th>
      <th>Total Amount</th>
    </tr>
  </thead>
  <tbody>
    {% for order in orders %}
    <tr>
      <td>{{order.id}}</td>
      <td>{{order.date_added}}</td>
      <td>
          {% for image in order.productimages %}
          <img src="{{image}}" style="max-width: 50px;">
          {% endfor %}
      </td>
      <td>${{order.amount}}</td>
    </tr>
    {% endfor %}
  </tbody>
</table>
{% else %}
  <strong><p class="mt-5">No orders!</p></strong>
  {% endif %}
</div>
{% endblock %}
```

6.4   Microservices Implementation of E-Commerce application

The monolithic E-Commerce application described in the previous section consisted of a single Flask codebase that handled user management, product catalog, shopping cart, ordering, and reviews. The models, views, and route logic were all contained in a single application module.

In this section, we will describe how to transition this application into microservices and then provide the implementation details. The first step in transitioning involves identifying bounded contexts that can be logically separated.

Following the decomposition by business subdomain and database per service patterns, we decompose the functionality out of the monolithic Flask application into separate microservices. For the E-Commerce app, the core domains include user management, product catalog, ordering, reviews, and the frontend. These are extracted into the following microservices:

- **Frontend Service**: The Frontend service serves the HTML pages and delegates requests to backend services. Frontend has no storage capabilities and performs only presentation responsibilities.
- **User Service**: The User service handles user registration, authentication, and account

management. It is backed by its own dedicated User database containing profile data such as the user's first name, last name, username, email, hashed password, and photo.

- **Product Service**: The Product service handles the product catalog. It is backed by its own dedicated Product database containing product names, descriptions, pricing, and photos.
- **Order Service**: The Order service handles the shopping cart and order processing workflow. It is backed by its own dedicated Order database containing the Order and Order Item tables.
- **Review Service**: The Review service handles the product reviews and ratings. It is backed by its own dedicated Review database containing customer reviews associated with product IDs.

The application flow, user interface, and the implementations of the Flask templates for the frontend remain the same as in the monolithic implementation described in the previous section.

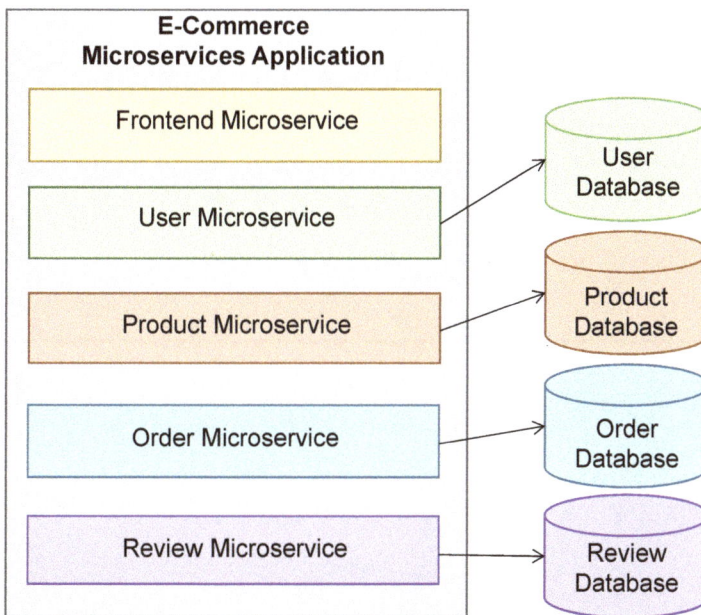

Figure 6.11: Microservices E-Commerce application architecture

6.4.1 Microservices Implementation

The frontend microservice is implemented in a single 'frontend.py' file. For better explanation, we break it down into three parts - configuration and API clients, forms, and routes.

Box 6.13 shows the code of the frontend microservice configuration and API clients. The frontend microservice handles UI rendering and calls backend microservices for data and actions via API clients. The following API clients are implemented:

- **UserClient**: Calls the user service for user management, login, registration, and getting user details.

- **ProductClient**: Calls the product service to get all products, get details of a product, and create a product.
- **OrderClient**: Calls the order service for cart and order management.
- **ReviewClient**: Calls the review service to add and retrieve reviews.

■ Box 6.13: Frontend microservice configuration and API clients

```
import os
import requests
from flask import Flask
from flask_migrate import Migrate
from flask import render_template, session, redirect
from flask import url_for, flash, request, jsonify
from flask_login import current_user
from flask_wtf import FlaskForm
from wtforms import StringField, PasswordField
from wtforms import SubmitField, HiddenField, IntegerField
from wtforms.validators import DataRequired, Email
from flask_bootstrap import Bootstrap
from flask_login import LoginManager
from flask import session, request

login_manager = LoginManager()
bootstrap = Bootstrap()

app = Flask(__name__, static_folder='static')
app.config['UPLOAD_FOLDER'] = 'static/images'
app.config['SECRET_KEY'] = "DoWgTDq87Kmne3TsCjNFabP"
app.config['WTF_CSRF_SECRET_KEY'] = "sEWQkE9oYBiF5fVJnm278i7"
app.config['ENV'] = "development"
app.config['DEBUG'] = True

USER_SERVICE_URL='http://172.31.25.162:5000'
PRODUCT_SERVICE_URL='http://172.31.16.52:5000'
ORDER_SERVICE_URL='http://172.31.28.134:5000'
REVIEW_SERVICE_URL='http://172.31.19.31:5000'

login_manager.init_app(app)
login_manager.login_message = "Please login"
login_manager.login_view = "login"

#API clients
class UserClient:
    @staticmethod
    def post_login(form):
        api_key = False
        payload = {
            'username': form.username.data,
            'password': form.password.data
        }
        url = USER_SERVICE_URL+'/api/user/login'
        response = requests.request("POST", url=url, data=payload)
        if response:
```

```python
            d = response.json()
            #print("This is response from user api: " + str(d))
            if d['api_key'] is not None:
                api_key = d['api_key']
        return api_key

    @staticmethod
    def get_user():
        headers = {
            'Authorization': 'Basic ' + session['user_api_key']
        }
        url = USER_SERVICE_URL+'/api/user'
        response = requests.request(method="GET",
                        url=url, headers=headers)
        user = response.json()
        return user

    @staticmethod
    def get_user_with_id(id):
        response = requests.request(method="GET",
            url=USER_SERVICE_URL+'/api/userid/' + str(id))
        user = response.json()
        return user

    @staticmethod
    def post_user_create(form):
        user = False
        payload = {
            'email': form.email.data,
            'password': form.password.data,
            'first_name': form.first_name.data,
            'last_name': form.last_name.data,
            'username': form.username.data
        }
        url = USER_SERVICE_URL+'/api/user/create'
        response = requests.request("POST", url=url, data=payload)
        if response:
            user = response.json()
        return user

    @staticmethod
    def does_exist(username):
        url = USER_SERVICE_URL+'/api/user/' + username + '/exists'
        response = requests.request("GET", url=url)
        return response.status_code == 200


class ProductClient:
    @staticmethod
    def get_products():
        r = requests.get(PRODUCT_SERVICE_URL+'/api/products')
        products = r.json()
        return products
```

```
    @staticmethod
    def get_product(slug):
        response = requests.request(method="GET",
            url=PRODUCT_SERVICE_URL+'/api/product/' + slug)
        product = response.json()
        return product

    @staticmethod
    def get_product_with_id(id):
        response = requests.request(method="GET",
            url=PRODUCT_SERVICE_URL+'/api/productid/' + str(id))
        product = response.json()
        return product

class OrderClient:
    @staticmethod
    def get_order():
        headers = {
            'Authorization': 'Basic ' + session['user_api_key']
        }
        url = ORDER_SERVICE_URL+'/api/order'
        response = requests.request(method="GET",
                    url=url, headers=headers)
        order = response.json()
        return order

    @staticmethod
    def post_add_to_cart(product_id, price, qty=1):
        payload = {
            'product_id': product_id,
            'qty': qty,
            'price': price
        }
        url = ORDER_SERVICE_URL+'/api/order/add-item'

        headers = {
            'Authorization': 'Basic ' + session['user_api_key']
        }
        response = requests.request("POST", url=url,
            data=payload, headers=headers)
        if response:
            order = response.json()
            return order

    @staticmethod
    def post_checkout():
        url = ORDER_SERVICE_URL+'/api/order/checkout'

        headers = {
            'Authorization': 'Basic ' + session['user_api_key']
        }
        response = requests.request("POST", url=url, headers=headers)
        order = response.json()
        return order
```

```python
    @staticmethod
    def get_order_from_session():
        default_order = {
            'items': {},
            'total': 0,
        }
        return session.get('order', default_order)

    @staticmethod
    def get_cart():
        headers = {
            'Authorization': 'Basic ' + session['user_api_key']
        }
        r = requests.get(ORDER_SERVICE_URL+'/api/cart', headers=headers)
        products = r.json()
        return products

    @staticmethod
    def get_orders():
        headers = {
            'Authorization': 'Basic ' + session['user_api_key']
        }
        r = requests.get(ORDER_SERVICE_URL+'/api/orders',
                        headers=headers)
        orders = r.json()
        return orders


class ReviewClient:
    @staticmethod
    def post_review(user_id, product_id, rating, review):
        payload = {
            'user_id': user_id,
            'product_id': product_id,
            'rating': rating,
            'review': review
        }
        url = REVIEW_SERVICE_URL+'/api/review/add'

        headers = {
            'Authorization': 'Basic ' + session['user_api_key']
        }
        response = requests.request("POST", url=url,
                        data=payload, headers=headers)
        if response:
            order = response.json()
            return order

    @staticmethod
    def get_reviews(product_id):
        headers = {
            'Authorization': 'Basic ' + session['user_api_key']
        }
```

```
        r = requests.get(REVIEW_SERVICE_URL+'/api/reviews/'+
                    str(product_id), headers=headers)
        orders = r.json()
        return orders

@login_manager.user_loader
def load_user(user_id):
    return None

def get_user_name_photo():
    try:
        response = UserClient.get_user()
        user = response['result']
        #user_id = int(user['id'])
        user_name = user['first_name']+" "+user['last_name']
        user_photo = user['photo']
    except:
        user_name=''
        user_photo=''

    return user_name, user_photo
```

Box 6.14 shows the code of the frontend microservice forms. Forms are used to submit data for actions like login, registration, and adding items to the cart. The following forms are implemented:

- **LoginForm**: Form with fields for username and password to log in user.
- **RegistrationForm**: Form to register a new user with fields for username, name, email, and password.
- **ItemForm**: Hidden form to add items to cart by passing the product ID.

■ **Box 6.14: Frontend microservice forms**

```
class LoginForm(FlaskForm):
    username = StringField('Username', validators=[DataRequired()])
    password = PasswordField('Password', validators=[DataRequired()])
    submit = SubmitField('Login')

class RegistrationForm(FlaskForm):
    username = StringField('Username', validators=[DataRequired()])
    first_name = StringField('First name', validators=[DataRequired()])
    last_name = StringField('Last name', validators=[DataRequired()])
    email = StringField('Email address',
                    validators=[DataRequired(), Email()])
    password = PasswordField('Password', validators=[DataRequired()])
    submit = SubmitField('Register')

class ItemForm(FlaskForm):
    product_id = HiddenField(validators=[DataRequired()])
    quantity = HiddenField(validators=[DataRequired()], default=1)
```

Box 6.15 shows the code of the frontend microservice routes. The frontend handles UI using Jinja templates and Flask routes. The following routes are implemented:

- **Home**: The route '/' renders the home page which shows the products. It calls the product service using the ProductClient to retrieve the product catalog.
- **Login**: The route '/login' renders the LoginForm and calls the user service using the UserClient to log the user in and create a session.
- **Register**: The route '/register' renders the RegistrationForm and calls the user service using the UserClient to create a new user.
- **Logout**: The route '/logout' logs the user out and clears the session.
- **Product**: The route '/product/<slug>' renders the product detail page. It calls the product service using the ProductClient to retrieve the product details. It calls the review service using the ReviewClient to retrieve the product reviews. It uses the ItemForm to add a product to the cart.
- **Cart**: The route '/cart' renders the shopping cart page. It calls the order service using the OrderClient.
- **Orders**: The route '/orders' renders the order page. It calls the order service using the OrderClient.
- **Checkout**: The route '/checkout' checks out an order. It calls the order service using the OrderClient.
- **Thank You**: The route '/order/thank-you' renders the order completion page.
- **Review**: The route '/postreview' submits the review form. It calls the review service using the ReviewClient.

■ **Box 6.15: Frontend microservice routes**

```
@app.route('/', methods=['GET'])
def home():
    if current_user.is_authenticated:
        session['order'] = OrderClient.get_order_from_session()
    try:
        products = ProductClient.get_products()
    except requests.exceptions.ConnectionError:
        products = {
            'results': []
        }
    user_name, user_photo = get_user_name_photo()
    return render_template('home.html', products=products,
        user_name = user_name, user_photo=user_photo)

@app.route('/register', methods=['GET', 'POST'])
def register():
    form = RegistrationForm(request.form)
    if request.method == "POST":
        if form.validate_on_submit():
            username = form.username.data
            user = UserClient.does_exist(username)
            if user:
                flash('Please try another username', 'error')
                return render_template('register/index.html', form=form)
            else:
                user = UserClient.post_user_create(form)
```

```
                     if user:
                         flash('Please login', 'success')
                         return redirect(url_for('login'))
             else:
                 flash('Errors found', 'error')
         return render_template('register.html', form=form)

@app.route('/login', methods=['GET', 'POST'])
def login():
    if current_user.is_authenticated:
        return redirect(url_for('home'))
    form = LoginForm()
    if request.method == "POST":
        if form.validate_on_submit():
            api_key = UserClient.post_login(form)
            if api_key:
                session['user_api_key'] = api_key
                user = UserClient.get_user()
                sessiondict={}
                sessiondict['first_name'] = user['result']['first_name']
                sessiondict['last_name'] = user['result']['last_name']
                sessiondict['id'] = user['result']['id']
                sessiondict['username'] = user['result']['username']
                sessiondict['email'] = user['result']['email']
                sessiondict['api_key'] = user['result']['api_key']
                session['user'] = sessiondict
                order = OrderClient.get_order()
                if order.get('result', False):
                    session['order'] = order['result']
                return redirect(url_for('home'))
            else:
                flash('Cannot login', 'error')
        else:
            flash('Errors found', 'error')
    return render_template('login.html', form=form)

@app.route('/logout', methods=['GET'])
def logout():
    session.clear()
    return redirect(url_for('home'))

@app.route('/product/<slug>', methods=['GET', 'POST'])
def product(slug):
    response = ProductClient.get_product(slug)
    item = response['result']
    form = ItemForm(product_id=item['id'])
    result=ReviewClient.get_reviews(item['id'])
    reviews=result['result']
    reviewslist=[]
    for review in reviews:
        try:
            reviewdict={}
            reviewdict['rating']=review['rating']
            reviewdict['description']=review['description']
```

```
                reviewdict['date_added']=review['date_added']
                reviewer=UserClient.get_user_with_id(review['user_id'])
                reviewdict['photo']=reviewer['result']['photo']
                reviewdict['user_name']=reviewer['result']['first_name']+' '+
                                reviewer['result']['last_name']
                reviewslist.append(reviewdict)
        except:
            pass
    if request.method == "POST":
        if 'user' not in session:
            flash('Please login', 'error')
            return redirect(url_for('login'))
        order = OrderClient.post_add_to_cart(product_id=item['id'],
                                price=item['price'], qty=1)
        session['order'] = order['result']
        flash('Item has been added to cart', 'success')
    user_name, user_photo = get_user_name_photo()
    return render_template('product.html', product=item,
                form=form, reviews=reviewslist,
                user_name = user_name, user_photo=user_photo)


@app.route('/checkout', methods=['GET'])
def summary():
    if 'user' not in session:
        flash('Please login', 'error')
        return redirect(url_for('login'))
    if 'order' not in session:
        flash('No order found', 'error')
        return redirect(url_for('home'))
    order = OrderClient.get_order()
    if len(order['result']['items']) == 0:
        flash('No order found', 'error')
        return redirect(url_for('home'))
    OrderClient.post_checkout()
    return redirect(url_for('thank_you'))


@app.route('/order/thank-you', methods=['GET'])
def thank_you():
    if 'user' not in session:
        flash('Please login', 'error')
        return redirect(url_for('login'))
    if 'order' not in session:
        flash('No order found', 'error')
        return redirect(url_for('home'))
    session.pop('order', None)
    flash('Thank you for your order', 'success')
    user_name, user_photo = get_user_name_photo()
    return render_template('thanks.html', user_name = user_name,
                user_photo=user_photo)


@app.route('/cart', methods=['GET'])
def cart():
    if 'user' not in session:
        flash('Please login', 'error')
```

```python
            return redirect(url_for('login'))
    try:
        result = OrderClient.get_cart()
        products=result['result']
        productsInCart=[]
        totalamount=0
        for p in products:
            resp = ProductClient.get_product_with_id(str(p['product']))
            itemdict={}
            itemdict['quantity']=p['quantity']
            itemdict['name']=resp['result']['name']
            itemdict['description']=resp['result']['description']
            itemdict['id']=resp['result']['id']
            itemdict['slug']=resp['result']['slug']
            itemdict['price']=resp['result']['price']
            itemdict['image']=resp['result']['image']
            itemdict['total']=p['quantity']*resp['result']['price']
            totalamount=totalamount+itemdict['total']
            totalamount=round(totalamount,2)
            productsInCart.append(itemdict)
    except requests.exceptions.ConnectionError:
        productsInCart=[]
    user_name, user_photo = get_user_name_photo()
    return render_template('cart.html', products=productsInCart,
                totalamount=totalamount, user_name = user_name,
                user_photo=user_photo)


@app.route('/orders', methods=['GET'])
def orders():
    if 'user' not in session:
        flash('Please login', 'error')
        return redirect(url_for('login'))
    try:
        result = OrderClient.get_orders()
        orders=result['result']
        ordersPlaced=[]
        for p in orders:
            itemdict={}
            itemdict['itemscount']=len(p['items'])
            itemdict['id']=p['id']
            itemdict['date_added']=p['date_added']
            itemdict['amount']=p['amount']
            itemdict['productimages']=[]
            for q in p['items']:
                resp=ProductClient.get_product_with_id(q['product'])
                itemdict['productimages'].append(resp['result']['image'])
            ordersPlaced.append(itemdict)
    except requests.exceptions.ConnectionError:
        ordersPlaced=[]
    user_name, user_photo = get_user_name_photo()
    return render_template('orders.html', orders=ordersPlaced,
        user_name = user_name, user_photo=user_photo)


@app.route('/postreview', methods=['POST'])
```

```
def postreview():
    ratinginput = request.form.get('ratinginput')
    reviewinput = request.form.get('reviewinput')
    productslug = request.form.get('productslug')
    response = UserClient.get_user()
    user = response['result']
    user_id = int(user['id'])
    product_id = request.form.get('productid')
    ReviewClient.post_review(user_id, product_id,
                              ratinginput, reviewinput)
    flash('Thank you for your review', 'success')
    return redirect('/product/'+productslug)

if __name__ == '__main__':
    app.run(host='0.0.0.0', port=5000)
```

Box 6.16 shows the code of the user microservice which handles user management functionality. The goal is to keep it focused on user management and authentication functionality that can be reused across different services. It implements the User model, login manager, and routes. The User model is defined using Flask-SQLAlchemy and includes fields like id, first name, last name, username, email, password, and photo. It has methods like *encode_password()* to hash the password before storing and *to_json()* to serialize a user object to JSON. The login manager is used to manage user sessions and is implemented using Flask-Login. It has a *user_loader* callback to reload the user object from the ID stored in session. It has a *request_loader* to load a user from the API key in the request header. The API key is hashed so it can be used for authentication instead of username and password.

The following routes are implemented in the user service:

- **Get all Users**: The route '/api/users' returns the list of all users.
- **Create User**: The route '/api/user/create' registers a new user by taking data in the request body.
- **Check if User Exists**: The route '/api/user/<name>/exists' checks if a username already exists.
- **Login**: The route '/api/user/login' logs in a user by validating the username and password and returns an API key.
- **Logout**: The route '/api/user/logout' logs out the user and clears the session.
- **Get User**: The route '/api/user' retrieves the logged-in user.
- **Serve User Photo**: The route '/uploads/<file>' serves the uploaded user profile image.

■ **Box 6.16: User microservice**

```
import os
from flask import Flask, send_from_directory
from flask_login import LoginManager
from flask_migrate import Migrate
from flask.sessions import SecureCookieSessionInterface
from flask import g
from flask_sqlalchemy import SQLAlchemy
from datetime import datetime
from flask_login import UserMixin
```

```python
from passlib.hash import sha256_crypt
from flask import make_response, request, jsonify
from flask_login import current_user, login_user
from flask_login import logout_user, login_required
from passlib.hash import sha256_crypt
from flask.sessions import SecureCookieSessionInterface
from flask_login import user_loaded_from_header
import time, random
import avinit
import imghdr
import base64


db = SQLAlchemy()
login_manager = LoginManager()
basedir = os.path.abspath(os.path.dirname(__file__))
app = Flask(__name__)
app.config['SECRET_KEY'] = "DoWgTDq87Kmne3TsCjNFabP"
app.config['SQLALCHEMY_TRACK_MODIFICATIONS'] = False
app.config['ENV'] = "development"
app.config['DEBUG'] = True
app.config['SQLALCHEMY_DATABASE_URI']  = 'sqlite:///' +
                 os.path.join(basedir, 'user.sqlite')
app.config['SQLALCHEMY_ECHO'] = True
app.config['UPLOAD_FOLDER'] = 'uploads'
db.init_app(app)
login_manager.init_app(app)
migrate = Migrate(app, db)

class User(UserMixin, db.Model):
    id = db.Column(db.Integer, primary_key=True)
    username = db.Column(db.String(255), unique=True, nullable=False)
    email = db.Column(db.String(255), unique=True, nullable=False)
    first_name = db.Column(db.String(255), unique=False, nullable=True)
    last_name = db.Column(db.String(255), unique=False, nullable=True)
    password = db.Column(db.String(255), unique=False, nullable=False)
    photo = db.Column(db.String(255), unique=False, nullable=True)
    is_admin = db.Column(db.Boolean, default=False)
    authenticated = db.Column(db.Boolean, default=False)
    api_key = db.Column(db.String(255), unique=True, nullable=True)
    date_added = db.Column(db.DateTime, default=datetime.utcnow)
    date_updated = db.Column(db.DateTime, onupdate=datetime.utcnow)

    def encode_api_key(self):
        self.api_key = sha256_crypt.hash(self.username +
                     str(datetime.utcnow))

    def encode_password(self):
        self.password = sha256_crypt.hash(self.password)

    def __repr__(self):
        return '<User %r>' % (self.username)

    def to_json(self):
        img_path = 'uploads/'+self.photo
```

```
            img_type = imghdr.what(img_path)
            with open(img_path, "rb") as image_file:
                encoded_string = base64.b64encode(image_file.read())
            if img_type == 'jpeg':
                prefix = 'data:image/jpeg;base64,'
            elif img_type == 'png':
                prefix = 'data:image/png;base64,'
            img_data = prefix + encoded_string.decode('utf-8')

            return {
                'first_name': self.first_name,
                'last_name': self.last_name,
                'username': self.username,
                'email': self.email,
                'photo': img_data,
                'id': self.id,
                'api_key': self.api_key,
                'is_active': True,
                'is_admin': self.is_admin
            }

@login_manager.user_loader
def load_user(user_id):
    return User.query.filter_by(id=user_id).first()

@login_manager.request_loader
def load_user_from_request(request):
    api_key = request.headers.get('Authorization')
    if api_key:
        api_key = api_key.replace('Basic ', '', 1)
        user = User.query.filter_by(api_key=api_key).first()
        if user:
            return user
    return None

@app.route('/api/users', methods=['GET'])
def get_users():
    data = []
    for row in User.query.all():
        data.append(row.to_json())
    response = jsonify(data)
    return response

@app.route('/api/user/create', methods=['POST'])
def post_register():
    first_name = request.form['first_name']
    last_name = request.form['last_name']
    email = request.form['email']
    username = request.form['username']
    password = sha256_crypt.hash((str(request.form['password'])))
    user = User()
    user.email = email
    user.first_name = first_name
    user.last_name = last_name
```

```
        user.password = password
        user.username = username
        user.authenticated = True
        name=first_name+' '+ last_name
        filename = "user"+str(int(time.time()*1000))+".png"
        imgpath=os.path.join(app.config['UPLOAD_FOLDER'], filename)
        r = lambda: random.randint(0,255)
        colors=[]
        colors.append('#%02X%02X%02X' % (r(),r(),r()))
        avinit.get_png_avatar(name, output_file=imgpath, colors=colors)
        user.photo = filename
        db.session.add(user)
        db.session.commit()
        response = jsonify({'message': 'User added',
                'result': user.to_json()})
        return response

@app.route('/api/user/login', methods=['POST'])
def post_login():
    username = request.form['username']
    user = User.query.filter_by(username=username).first()
    if user:
        if sha256_crypt.verify(str(request.form['password']),
                            user.password):
            user.encode_api_key()
            db.session.commit()
            login_user(user)
            return make_response(jsonify({'message': 'Logged in',
                        'api_key': user.api_key}))
    return make_response(jsonify({'message': 'Not logged in'}), 401)

@app.route('/api/user/logout', methods=['POST'])
def post_logout():
    if current_user.is_authenticated:
        logout_user()
        return make_response(jsonify({'message': 'You are logged out'}))
    return make_response(jsonify({'message': 'You are not logged in'}))

@app.route('/api/user/<username>/exists', methods=['GET'])
def get_username(username):
    item = User.query.filter_by(username=username).first()
    if item is not None:
        response = jsonify({'result': True})
    else:
        response = jsonify({'message': 'Cannot find username'}), 404
    return response

@login_required
@app.route('/api/user', methods=['GET'])
def get_user():
    if current_user.is_authenticated:
        return make_response(jsonify({'result': current_user.to_json()}))

    return make_response(jsonify({'message': 'Not logged in'})), 401
```

```
@app.route('/api/userid/<id>', methods=['GET'])
def userid(id):
    item = User.query.filter_by(id=id).first()
    if item is not None:
        response = jsonify({'result': item.to_json()})
    else:
        response = jsonify({'message': 'Cannot find user'}), 404
    return response

@app.route('/uploads/<filename>')
def uploaded_file(filename):
    return send_from_directory(app.config['UPLOAD_FOLDER'], filename)

@user_loaded_from_header.connect
def user_loaded_from_header(self, user=None):
    g.login_via_header = True

if __name__ == '__main__':
    app.run(host='0.0.0.0', port=5000)
```

Box 6.17 shows the code of the product microservice. The product microservice handles product data and operations. The Product model is defined using Flask-SQLAlchemy and includes fields like product ID, name, description, price, slug, and image. The slug field is used for a unique, URL-friendly name. The Product model uses the *to_json()* method to serialize the product data to JSON. The following routes are implemented in the product service:

- **Get all Products**: The route '/api/products' returns a JSON list of all products.
- **Get Product with Slug**: The route '/api/product/<slug>' retrieves a single product using slug.
- **Get Product with ID**: The route '/api/productid/<id>' retrieves a single product using ID.
- **Create Product**: The route '/api/product/create' creates a new product by taking data in the request body.
- **Serve Product Image**: The route '/uploads/<file>' serves the uploaded product image.

■ Box 6.17: Product microservice

```
import os
from flask import Flask, send_from_directory
from flask_migrate import Migrate
from flask import jsonify, request
from flask_sqlalchemy import SQLAlchemy
from datetime import datetime
from flask_migrate import Migrate
from werkzeug.utils import secure_filename
import imghdr
import base64

db = SQLAlchemy()
```

```python
basedir = os.path.abspath(os.path.dirname(__file__))
app = Flask(__name__)
app.config['SECRET_KEY'] = "DoWgTDq87Kmne3TsCjNFabP"
app.config['SQLALCHEMY_TRACK_MODIFICATIONS'] = False
app.config['ENV'] = "development"
app.config['DEBUG'] = True
app.config['SQLALCHEMY_DATABASE_URI'] = 'sqlite:///' + \
                os.path.join(basedir, 'product.sqlite')
app.config['SQLALCHEMY_ECHO'] = True
app.config['UPLOAD_FOLDER'] = 'uploads'
db.init_app(app)
migrate = Migrate(app, db)

class Product(db.Model):
    id = db.Column(db.Integer, primary_key=True)
    name = db.Column(db.String(255), unique=True, nullable=False)
    slug = db.Column(db.String(255), unique=True, nullable=False)
    price = db.Column(db.Float, default=0)
    image = db.Column(db.String(255), unique=False, nullable=True)
    description = db.Column(db.Text)
    date_added = db.Column(db.DateTime, default=datetime.utcnow)
    date_updated = db.Column(db.DateTime, onupdate=datetime.utcnow)

    def to_json(self):
        img_path = 'uploads/'+self.image
        img_type = imghdr.what(img_path)
        with open(img_path, "rb") as image_file:
            encoded_string = base64.b64encode(image_file.read())
        if img_type == 'jpeg':
            prefix = 'data:image/jpeg;base64,'
        elif img_type == 'png':
            prefix = 'data:image/png;base64,'
        img_data = prefix + encoded_string.decode('utf-8')

        return {
            'id': self.id,
            'name': self.name,
            'description': self.description,
            'slug': self.slug,
            'price': self.price,
            'image': img_data
        }

@app.route('/api/products', methods=['GET'])
def products():
    items = []
    for row in Product.query.all():
        items.append(row.to_json())
    response = jsonify({'results': items})
    return response

@app.route('/api/product/create', methods=['POST'])
def post_create():
    name = request.form.get('name')
```

```
        slug = request.form.get('slug')
        description = request.form.get('description')
        price = request.form.get('price')
        image = request.files.get('image')
        filename = secure_filename(image.filename)
        image.save(os.path.join(app.config['UPLOAD_FOLDER'], filename))
        item = Product()
        item.name = name
        item.slug = slug
        item.image = image
        item.price = price
        item.image = filename
        item.description=description
        db.session.add(item)
        db.session.commit()
        response = jsonify({'message': 'Product added',
                    'product': item.to_json()})
        return response

@app.route('/api/product/<slug>', methods=['GET'])
def product(slug):
    item = Product.query.filter_by(slug=slug).first()
    if item is not None:
        response = jsonify({'result': item.to_json()})
    else:
        response = jsonify({'message': 'Cannot find product'}), 404
    return response

@app.route('/api/productid/<id>', methods=['GET'])
def productid(id):
    item = Product.query.filter_by(id=id).first()
    if item is not None:
        response = jsonify({'result': item.to_json()})
    else:
        response = jsonify({'message': 'Cannot find product'}), 404
    return response

@app.route('/uploads/<filename>')
def uploaded_file(filename):
    return send_from_directory(app.config['UPLOAD_FOLDER'], filename)

if __name__ == '__main__':
    app.run(host='0.0.0.0', port=5000)
```

Box 6.18 shows the code of the order microservice. The order microservice handles shopping cart and order management functionality. This service defines the Order and OrderItem models. The Order model contains fields like user ID, is-open and order date. It has a one-to-many relationship with the OrderItem model. OrderItem contains fields like product ID, quantity, and price. Both models implement *to_json()* methods to serialize the model data to JSON. The following routes are implemented in the order service:

- **Get Order**: The route '/api/order' retrieves the current open order for a user.
- **Add to Cart**: The route '/api/order/add-item' adds an item to the cart by passing the product ID and quantity in the request.

- **Checkout**: The route '/api/order/checkout' closes an open order.
- **Get Cart**: The route '/api/cart' retrieves the cart items in an open order.
- **Get all Orders**: The route '/api/orders' retrieves the list of closed orders for a user.

■ **Box 6.18: Order microservice**

```
import os
from flask import Flask
from flask_migrate import Migrate
from flask import jsonify, request, make_response
from flask import Flask
from flask_sqlalchemy import SQLAlchemy
from datetime import datetime
import requests


db = SQLAlchemy()
basedir = os.path.abspath(os.path.dirname(__file__))
app = Flask(__name__)
app.config['SECRET_KEY'] = "DoWgTDq87Kmne3TsCjNFabP"
app.config['SQLALCHEMY_TRACK_MODIFICATIONS'] = False
app.config['ENV'] = "development"
app.config['DEBUG'] = True
app.config['SQLALCHEMY_DATABASE_URI']  = 'sqlite:///' +
                os.path.join(basedir, 'order.sqlite')
app.config['SQLALCHEMY_ECHO'] = True
USER_SERVICE_URL='http://127.0.0.1:5000'

db.init_app(app)
migrate = Migrate(app, db)

class Order(db.Model):
    id = db.Column(db.Integer, primary_key=True)
    user_id = db.Column(db.Integer)
    items = db.relationship('OrderItem', backref='orderItem')
    is_open = db.Column(db.Boolean, default=True)
    date_added = db.Column(db.DateTime, default=datetime.utcnow)
    date_updated = db.Column(db.DateTime, onupdate=datetime.utcnow)

    def create(self, user_id):
        self.user_id = user_id
        self.is_open = True
        return self

    def to_json(self):
        items = []
        amount=0
        for i in self.items:
            items.append(i.to_json())
            amount=amount+i.price*i.quantity
            amount=round(amount,2)

        return {
            'id': self.id,
            'items': items,
```

```
            'is_open': self.is_open,
            'user_id': self.user_id,
            'date_added': self.date_added.strftime("%b %d, %Y"),
            'amount': amount
        }

class OrderItem(db.Model):
    id = db.Column(db.Integer, primary_key=True)
    order_id = db.Column(db.Integer, db.ForeignKey('order.id'))
    product_id = db.Column(db.Integer)
    price = db.Column(db.Float, default=0)
    quantity = db.Column(db.Integer, default=1)
    date_added = db.Column(db.DateTime, default=datetime.utcnow)
    date_updated = db.Column(db.DateTime, onupdate=datetime.utcnow)

    def __init__(self, product_id, quantity, price):
        self.product_id = product_id
        self.quantity = quantity
        self.price = price

    def to_json(self):
        return {
            'price': self.price,
            'product': self.product_id,
            'quantity': self.quantity
        }

class UserClient:
    @staticmethod
    def get_user(api_key):
        headers = {
            'Authorization': api_key
        }
        response = requests.request(method="GET",
            url=USER_SERVICE_URL+'/api/user', headers=headers)
        if response.status_code == 401:
            return False
        user = response.json()
        return user

@app.route('/api/order/add-item', methods=['POST'])
def order_add_item():
    api_key = request.headers.get('Authorization')
    response = UserClient.get_user(api_key)
    if not response:
        return make_response(jsonify({'message': 'Not logged in'}),401)
    user = response['result']
    p_id = int(request.form['product_id'])
    qty = int(request.form['qty'])
    price = float(request.form['price'])
    u_id = int(user['id'])
    known_order = Order.query.filter_by(user_id=u_id, is_open=1).first()
    if known_order is None:
        known_order = Order()
```

```python
            known_order.is_open = True
            known_order.user_id = u_id
            order_item = OrderItem(p_id, qty, price)
            known_order.items.append(order_item)
        else:
            found = False
            for item in known_order.items:
                if item.product_id == p_id:
                    found = True
                    item.quantity += qty
            if found is False:
                order_item = OrderItem(p_id, qty, price)
                known_order.items.append(order_item)
        db.session.add(known_order)
        db.session.commit()
        response = jsonify({'result': known_order.to_json()})
        return response


@app.route('/api/order', methods=['GET'])
def order():
    api_key = request.headers.get('Authorization')
    response = UserClient.get_user(api_key)
    if not response:
        return make_response(jsonify({'message': 'Not logged in'}),401)
    user = response['result']
    open_order = Order.query.filter_by(user_id=user['id'],
                                       is_open=1).first()
    if open_order is None:
        response = jsonify({'message': 'No order found'})
    else:
        response = jsonify({'result': open_order.to_json()})
    return response


@app.route('/api/order/checkout', methods=['POST'])
def checkout():
    api_key = request.headers.get('Authorization')
    response = UserClient.get_user(api_key)
    if not response:
        return make_response(jsonify({'message': 'Not logged in'}),401)
    user = response['result']
    order_model = Order.query.filter_by(user_id=user['id'],
                                        is_open=1).first()
    order_model.is_open = 0
    db.session.add(order_model)
    db.session.commit()
    response = jsonify({'result': order_model.to_json()})
    return response


@app.route('/api/cart', methods=['GET'])
def cart():
    api_key = request.headers.get('Authorization')
    response = UserClient.get_user(api_key)
    if not response:
        return make_response(jsonify({'message': 'Not logged in'}), 401)
```

```
        user = response['result']
        open_order = Order.query.filter_by(user_id=user['id'],
                                    is_open=1).first()
        if open_order is None:
            response = jsonify({'message': 'No order found', 'result': []})
        else:
            items=[]
            for item in open_order.items:
                items.append(item.to_json())
            response = jsonify({'result': items})
        return response

@app.route('/api/orders', methods=['GET'])
def orders():
    api_key = request.headers.get('Authorization')
    response = UserClient.get_user(api_key)
    if not response:
        return make_response(jsonify({'message': 'Not logged in'}), 401)
    user = response['result']
    orders = Order.query.filter_by(user_id=user['id'], is_open=0)
    if orders is None:
        response = jsonify({'message': 'No order found', 'result': []})
    else:
        items=[]
        for item in orders:
            items.append(item.to_json())
        response = jsonify({'result': items})
    return response

if __name__ == '__main__':
    app.run(host='0.0.0.0', port=5000)
```

Box 6.19 shows the code of the review microservice. The review microservice handles product reviews and ratings functionality. The review service defines the Review model which contains fields like review ID, user ID, product ID, rating, and description. It uses the *to_json()* method to serialize the review object to JSON. The following routes are implemented in the review service:

- **Add Review**: The route '/api/review/add' creates a new review by taking data in the request body.
- **Get Review**: The route '/api/reviews/<product_id>' retrieves all reviews for a product.

■ Box 6.19: Review microservice

```
import os
from flask import Flask, send_from_directory
from flask_migrate import Migrate
from flask import jsonify, request
from flask_sqlalchemy import SQLAlchemy
from datetime import datetime
from flask_migrate import Migrate
from werkzeug.utils import secure_filename
```

```python
db = SQLAlchemy()
basedir = os.path.abspath(os.path.dirname(__file__))


app = Flask(__name__)
app.config['SECRET_KEY'] = "DoWgTDq87Kmne3TsCjNFabP"
app.config['SQLALCHEMY_TRACK_MODIFICATIONS'] = False
app.config['ENV'] = "development"
app.config['DEBUG'] = True
app.config['SQLALCHEMY_DATABASE_URI']  = 'sqlite:///' +
            os.path.join(basedir, 'review.sqlite')
app.config['SQLALCHEMY_ECHO'] = True
app.config['UPLOAD_FOLDER'] = 'uploads'

db.init_app(app)
migrate = Migrate(app, db)

class Review(db.Model):
    id = db.Column(db.Integer, primary_key=True)
    user_id = db.Column(db.Integer)
    product_id = db.Column(db.Integer)
    rating = db.Column(db.Float, default=0)
    description = db.Column(db.Text)
    date_added = db.Column(db.DateTime, default=datetime.utcnow)
    date_updated = db.Column(db.DateTime, onupdate=datetime.utcnow)

    def to_json(self):
        return {
            'id': self.id,
            'user_id': self.user_id,
            'product_id': self.product_id,
            'rating': self.rating,
            'description': self.description,
            'date_added': self.date_added.strftime("%b %d, %Y")
        }

@app.route('/api/review/add', methods=['POST'])
def post_create():
    user_id = request.form.get('user_id')
    product_id = request.form.get('product_id')
    rating = request.form.get('rating')
    description = request.form.get('review')
    item = Review()
    item.product_id = product_id
    item.user_id = user_id
    item.rating = rating
    item.description=description
    db.session.add(item)
    db.session.commit()
    response = jsonify({'message': 'Review added',
        'review': item.to_json()})
    return response

@app.route('/api/reviews/<productid>', methods=['GET'])
def reviews(productid):
```

```
    reviews = Review.query.filter_by(product_id=productid)
    if reviews is None:
        response = jsonify({'message': 'No reviews found',
            'result': []})
    else:
        items=[]
        for item in reviews:
            items.append(item.to_json())

        response = jsonify({'result': items})
    return response

if __name__ == '__main__':
    app.run(host='0.0.0.0', port=5000)
```

6.5 Deploying Microservices Application on Amazon EC2

In this section, we will explain how to deploy the microservices application on Amazon EC2. Figure 6.12 shows the EC2 deployment architecture. Separate EC2 instances are launched for each microservice - frontend, user, product, order, and review. The frontend EC2 instance is public-facing and runs Nginx as a reverse proxy. The other microservice instances are not public-facing and can be accessed only by the frontend instance. The user, product, order, and review microservices have their own SQLite databases. The services are decoupled from each other and communicate via REST APIs. The source code of the microservices is the same as explained in the previous section. Only minor configuration changes are required, such as updating the IP addresses of the instances in the Flask configurations.

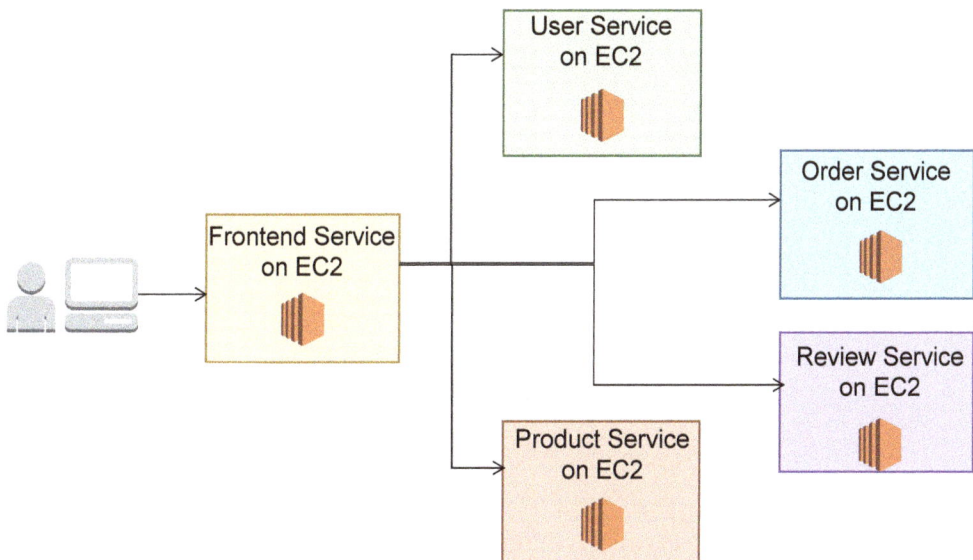

Figure 6.12: EC2 deployment architecture for the E-Commerce microservices application

6.5.1 Nginx Reverse Proxy

Nginx is run on the frontend EC2 instance to act as a reverse proxy. It receives all public traffic and routes requests to appropriate microservices based on the URL path. Nginx provides benefits like security, load balancing, and SSL termination. It also serves static files directly. The Nginx config defines upstream targets for each service, SSL certificate locations, proxy headers, URI rewrite rules, and static files configuration.

Box 6.20 shows the Nginx configuration file which defines a server block that listens on port 80 and 443 for HTTP and HTTPS traffic. It redirects all HTTP requests to HTTPS for security. The SSL certificate and key locations are specified for HTTPS encryption. Location blocks define routes for static files, and proxy pass to the Flask app running on Gunicorn. Additional headers like P3P are set for browser compatibility. This provides a reverse proxy with SSL termination and routing to the Flask app with static files hosted directly by Nginx.

■ Box 6.20: Nginx configuration

```
server {
    listen 80;
    server_name app.study411.com;
    return 301 https://app.study411.com$request_uri;
}

server {
    listen 443 default_server ssl;
    server_name app.study411.com;

    access_log /var/log/nginx/access.log;
    error_log /var/log/nginx/error.log;

    location /static {
            alias /home/ubuntu/frontend/static;
    }

    ssl_certificate /etc/letsencrypt/live/
                app.study411.com/fullchain.pem ;
    ssl_certificate_key /etc/letsencrypt/live/
                app.study411.com/privkey.pem;

    location / {
            proxy_pass http://0.0.0.0:5000;
            proxy_set_header X-Forwarded-Host $server_name;
            proxy_set_header X-Real-IP $remote_addr;
            proxy_set_header Host $http_host;
            add_header P3P 'CP="ALL DSP COR PSAa
                    PSDa OUR NOR ONL UNI COM NAV"';
    }
}
```

6.5.2 Web Server Gateway Interface (WSGI)

WGSI is the protocol used in Python for communication between web servers and applications. It defines a standard interface for web servers like Nginx to forward requests to applications written in Python like Flask. Gunicorn implements the WSGI server, and Flask provides the WSGI application. This enables Nginx to route requests to Flask via Gunicorn as per the WSGI standard.

Box 6.21 shows the WSGI file, which is used to serve the Flask application using the WSGI protocol. It makes the Flask app importable and runnable by the WSGI server in a standardized way following the WSGI protocol. It provides an entry point for a production WSGI server like Gunicorn to load and serve the Flask app. It imports the Flask app instance from the application module. This would be something like 'app.py' which has the *app = Flask(name)* initialization.

The *if name == 'main'* block allows running the app directly with python wsgi.py when needed for testing. However, in production, Gunicorn or some other WSGI server runs this 'wsgi.py' file, which loads the application. The WSGI server handles the actual HTTP server capabilities and WSGI protocol.

■ **Box 6.21: WSGI application**

```
from app import app

if __name__ == '__main__':
    app.run(debug=False)
```

6.5.3 Gunicorn

Gunicorn is a Python WSGI HTTP server that runs each Flask application on the EC2 instance. Nginx forwards requests to Gunicorn, which runs the Flask application. This provides application server capabilities like load balancing, request handling, and process management. Gunicorn binds to a socket, and Nginx routes traffic to this socket on the localhost. This avoids an extra network hop.

Box 6.22 shows the Gunicorn configuration file which defines the number of workers, timeouts, and other configuration. Each service has its own Gunicorn instance. When Gunicorn starts and loads wsgi.py, it will import the app instance from the app module and use it to handle requests coming to the server.

■ **Box 6.22: Gunicorn configuration**

```
bind = '0.0.0.0:5000'
workers = 1
timeout=1000
```

6.5.4 Supervisor

Supervisor is used to monitor and control the Gunicorn processes as a service. The supervisor configuration for each service starts Gunicorn on boot, restarts on failure, and redirects logs. This provides a way to run the Flask apps in production with process management.

Box 6.23 shows the Supervisor configuration which specifies the running Gunicorn for the frontend application. It sets the app directory, command to start Gunicorn, runs as root user, starts on boot, restarts on crashes, and redirects stderr to stdout. This allows starting the Flask app with Gunicorn automatically on system boot and restarting it if the process crashes.

■ Box 6.23: Supervisor configuration

```
[program:frontend-supervisor]
directory=/home/ubuntu/frontend
command=/usr/local/bin/gunicorn wsgi:app -c
        /home/ubuntu/frontend/gunicorn.py

user=root
autostart=true
autorestart=true
redirect_stderr=true
```

6.5.5 SSL Certificate

An SSL certificate issued by Let's Encrypt is installed on the frontend instance using Certbot. Nginx uses this certificate to enable HTTPS traffic from clients. Certbot automatically obtains and renews SSL certificates from Let's Encrypt CA. This allows the application to be accessed securely via HTTPS using trusted certificates.

6.5.6 EC2 Security Groups

Security groups act as a firewall to allow selective traffic. Figure 6.13 shows the security group 'Microservice-Frontend' for the frontend service. It allows HTTP, HTTPS, and SSH traffic from the public Internet. Figure 6.14 shows the security group 'Microservice-Backend' for the backend services (user, order, product and review). It allows traffic only from the frontend security group on port 5000. In addition to this, SSH traffic is also allowed. This provides network-level security with minimal attack surface on backend services.

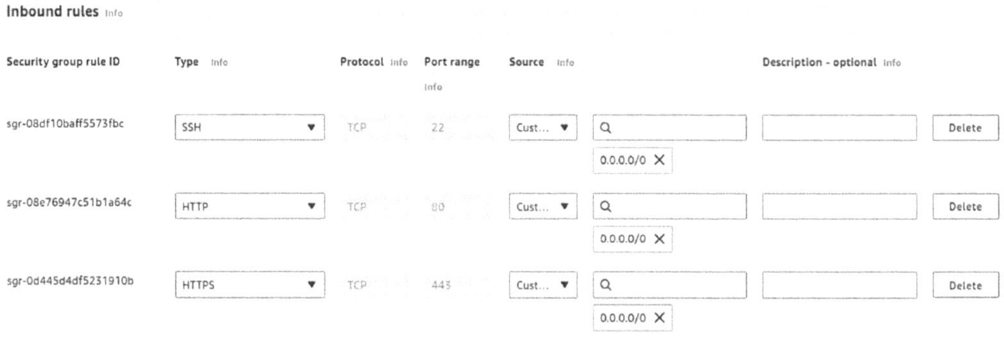

Inbound rules Info

Security group rule ID	Type Info	Protocol Info	Port range Info	Source Info		Description - optional Info	
sgr-08df10baff5573fbc	SSH ▼	TCP	22	Cust... ▼	Q 0.0.0.0/0 ✕		Delete
sgr-08e76947c51b1a64c	HTTP ▼	TCP	80	Cust... ▼	Q 0.0.0.0/0 ✕		Delete
sgr-0d445d4df5231910b	HTTPS ▼	TCP	443	Cust... ▼	Q 0.0.0.0/0 ✕		Delete

Figure 6.13: Security Group for frontend service

Inbound rules Info

Security group rule ID	Type		Protocol Info	Port range Info	Source Info			Description - optional Info		
sgr-0060354b73de15d2f	SSH	▼	TCP	22	Cust... ▼	Q 0.0.0.0/0 ✕				Delete
sgr-0a38641e342e05079	Custom TCP	▼	TCP	5000	Cust... ▼	Q sg-0b6fec4a9e73220c9 ✕				Delete
sgr-06da09668530204f1	Custom TCP	▼	TCP	5000	Cust... ▼	Q sg-06d1917a54e27c150 ✕				Delete

Figure 6.14: Security Group for other backend services

6.5.7 Setting Up and Configuring EC2 Instances

Figures 6.15, 6.16, 6.17, and 6.18 show the steps to launch an EC2 instance for the frontend. Note that we have used the security group 'Microservice-Frontend' (explained in the previous step - Figure 6.13) for this instance. Similarly, launch four more EC2 instances for the backend services. Use the security group 'Microservice-Backend' (explained in the previous step - Figure 6.14) for the backend instances.

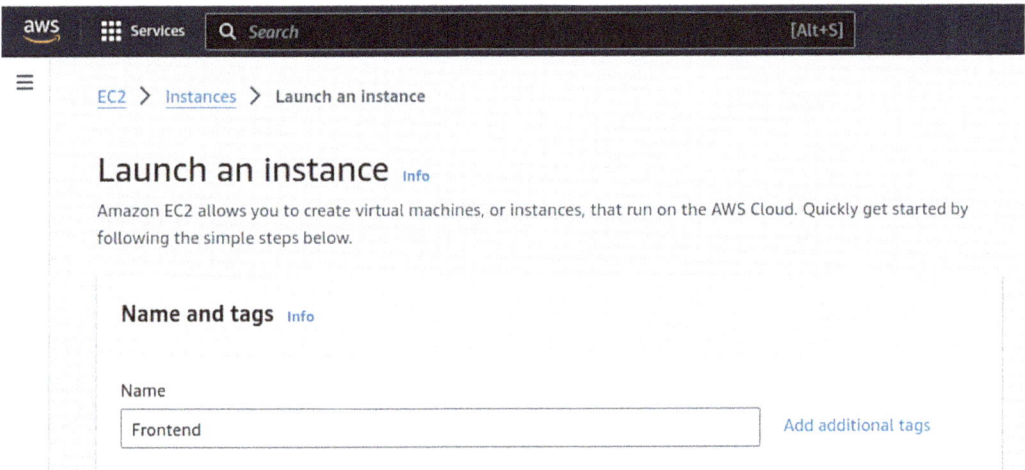

Figure 6.15: Launching an EC2 instance - part 1

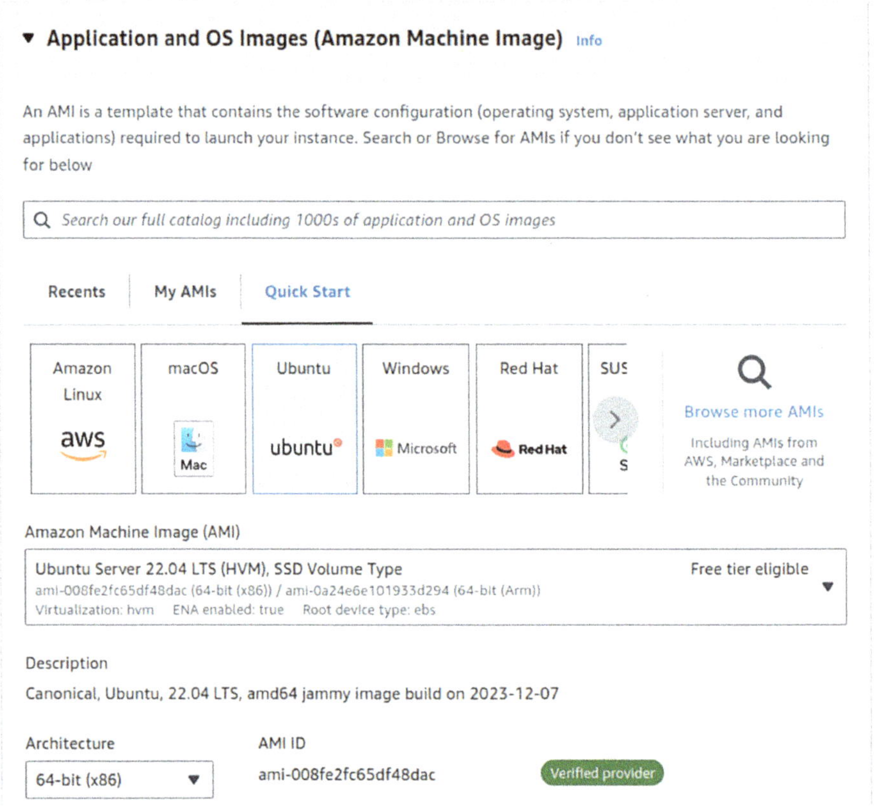

Figure 6.16: Launching an EC2 instance - part 2

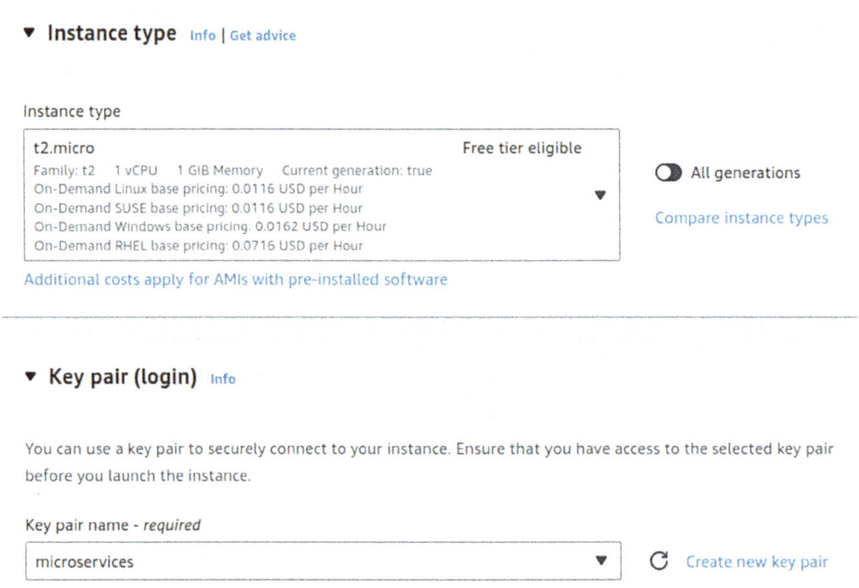

Figure 6.17: Launching an EC2 instance - part 3

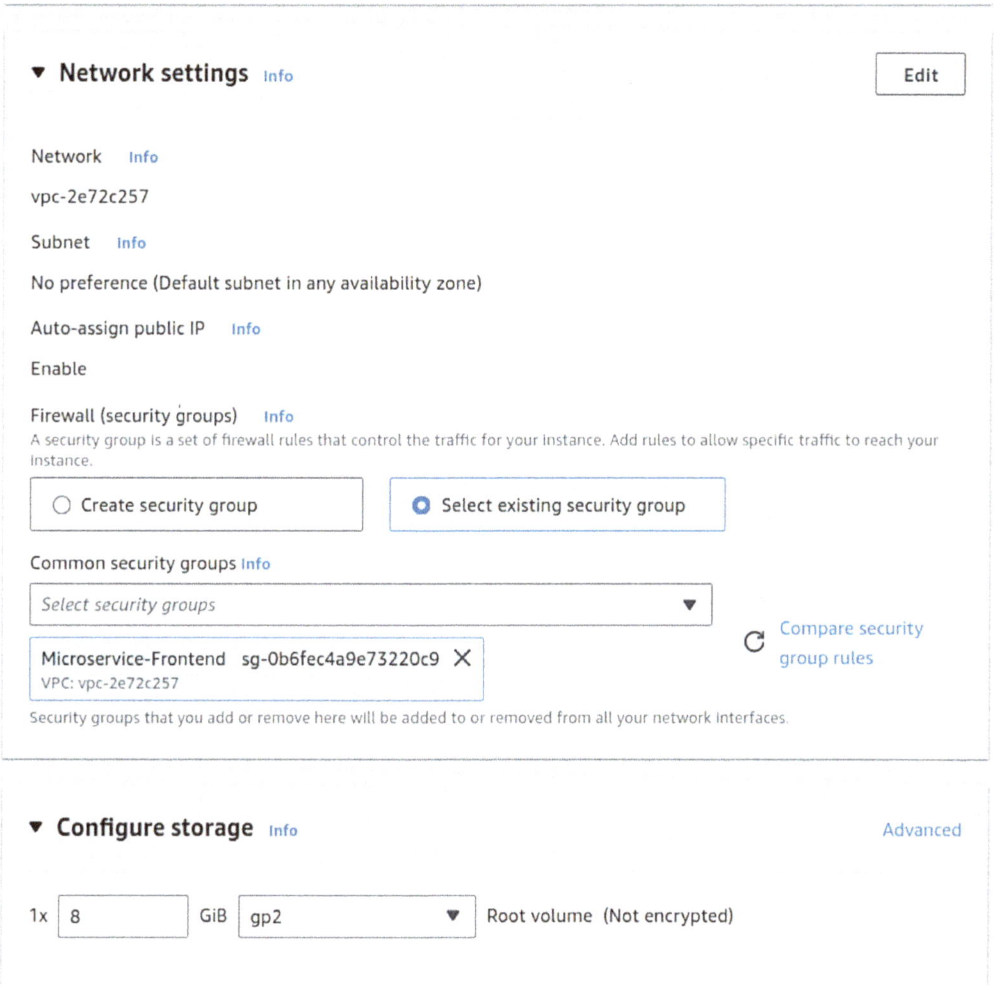

Figure 6.18: Launching an EC2 instance - part 4

Box 6.24 shows a readme file containing the steps to install required packages, set up the application, database, web server, and SSL certificates on an Ubuntu EC2 instance. It starts with installing Python, Flask, database, and other dependencies using pip and apt. Next, it initializes the Flask database, runs migrations to create tables, and starts the application. For setting up the web server, it copies the Nginx config file, links it to sites-enabled, and restarts Nginx. Supervisor is configured by copying the config file, reloading config, and restarting processes. To get an SSL certificate, it installs Certbot and stops Nginx to avoid port conflicts. Certbot then fetches and installs SSL certificates automatically. Finally, it shows a sample curl command to create a product by calling the product service API.

■ **Box 6.24: Setup commands**

```
#Install the required packages
sudo apt update
sudo apt install python3-pip python3-dev nginx supervisor
```

```
sudo apt install libcairo-5c-dev

#Install the python packages
sudo pip3 install -r requirements.txt

#Setup the DB
flask db init
flask db migrate
flask db upgrade

#Run the app
python3 app.py

#Setup Nginx
sudo cp nginx-flask.conf /etc/nginx/sites-available/
cd /etc/nginx/sites-enabled/
sudo ln -s ../sites-available/nginx-flask.conf .
sudo service nginx restart

#Setup Supervisor
sudo cp frontend-supervisor.conf /etc/supervisor/conf.d/
sudo supervisorctl reread
sudo supervisorctl update
sudo supervisorctl restart all

#Getting SSL Certificate
sudo apt install certbot
sudo service nginx stop
sudo certbot certonly --standalone -d app.study411.com

#Create products (replace localhost with private IP of product service)
curl -X POST -F "name=Coffee Mug" -F "slug=mug-1" -F "description=Mug"
    -F "price=9.99" -F "image=@mug.jpg"
    http://localhost:5000/api/product/create
```

The benefits of this deployment architecture on EC2 are as follows:

- Microservices allow independent scaling.
- Nginx provides security and reverse proxy capabilities.
- Gunicorn and Supervisor help run Flask apps in production.
- Following the WSGI standard enables using Nginx with Flask/Python.
- Security groups and SSL provide network and application security.

This deployment architecture can be improved further as follows:

- High availability can be added using an Elastic Load Balancer (ELB).
- Services can be migrated to containers and orchestrators like ECS.
- Instead of using SQLite database, a production-ready database like MySQL or PostgreSQL can be used.
- User photos and product images can be stored on a cloud storage solution like S3.

We will cover the above points for improvement in the subsequent chapters.

6.6   Configuring a Domain with Route 53

In this section, we will explain the steps to configure a domain using Route 53 for the frontend service hosted on EC2.

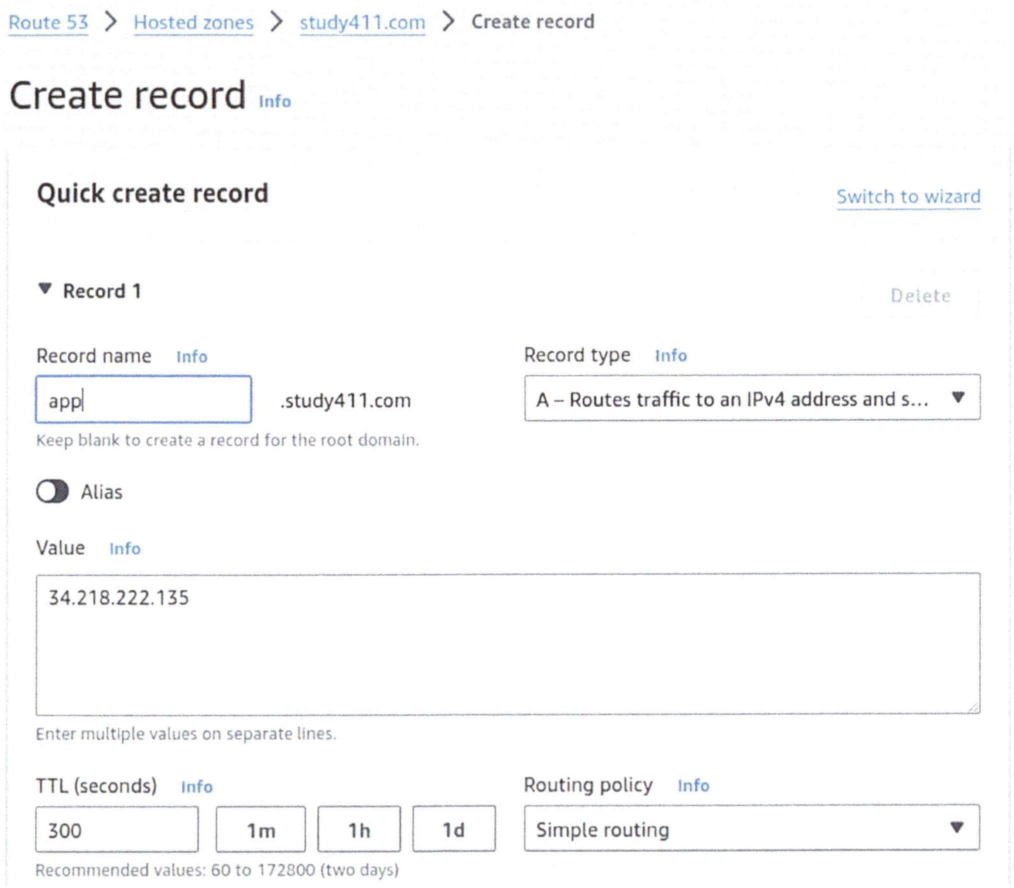

Route 53 ❯ Hosted zones ❯ study411.com ❯ Create record

Create record Info

Quick create record   Switch to wizard

▼ Record 1   Delete

Record name   Info   Record type   Info

| app| | .study411.com | A – Routes traffic to an IPv4 address and s... ▼ |

Keep blank to create a record for the root domain.

◯ Alias

Value   Info

| 34.218.222.135 |

Enter multiple values on separate lines.

TTL (seconds)   Info   Routing policy   Info

| 300 | 1m | 1h | 1d | | Simple routing   ▼ |

Recommended values: 60 to 172800 (two days)

Figure 6.19: Route 53 configuration

With this Route 53 configuration, you can have your custom domain pointing to the frontend EC2 server, so that the traffic to the domain will be routed seamlessly to the application. The steps to configure a domain are:

- **Register a domain name**: First, you need to register a domain name with a domain name registrar. This will allow you to own the domain name that you want to use for your frontend service.
- **Create a hosted zone in Route 53**: Once you have registered your domain, go to the Route 53 console in AWS and create a new Public Hosted Zone. Provide the domain name you registered as the Domain Name here. This will create a hosted zone in Route 53 corresponding to your domain. A hosted zone contains information about how you want to route traffic for that domain.
- **Create an A record set**: Within the hosted zone, create a new record set of type 'A'. Provide your domain name again in the Name field and in the Value field, provide the public IP address of your EC2 instance that is hosting the frontend service. This will

create an A record that routes traffic from your domain to the EC2 instance. Figure 6.19 shows how to configure an A record in Route 53.

- **Update domain registrar with Route 53 nameservers**: The final step is to configure your domain registrar to use the nameservers provided by the Route 53 hosted zone. Log into your registrar account and update the NS records for your domain to use the Route 53 nameservers. This delegates control of your domain to Route 53 for managing DNS records. This step is not required if the domain registrar is AWS itself.
- **Test the configuration**: It may take some time for the changes to propagate globally across DNS servers. You can use the 'dig' command to test and verify that your domain name is returning the correct IP address for your EC2 instance. Once propagated, accessing your domain should hit the frontend service hosted on that EC2 instance.

Summary

In this chapter, we covered the two different implementations of building an E-commerce web application using Python and the Flask framework. The two approaches we described and compared were - monolithic architecture and microservices architecture. In the monolithic implementation, we presented how all the functionality including user management, product catalog, shopping cart, order processing, and reviews is bundled into a single Flask codebase. We explained how the models, views, and routes live inside one application module that depends on a shared database accessed by all components. We then explored transitioning this monolithic approach into a microservices architecture. In the microservices design, we broke down the original coupled application into smaller, decoupled services like the user, product, order, review, and frontend. We described how each microservice owns its models, business logic, and routes. We presented how communication is handled via internal REST APIs instead of direct calls. Additionally, we adopted exclusive databases per service for increased encapsulation. We covered the deployment of the microservices application on Amazon EC2. We described an architecture where separate EC2 instances are launched for each microservice including the frontend, user, product, order, and review services. We explained that the frontend instance runs Nginx as a reverse proxy while the other instances are private-facing. Each microservice has its own database and they communicate via REST APIs. We explained how Nginx provides security, load balancing, SSL termination, and serves static files. We described how Gunicorn runs each Flask application on the instances and Supervisor manages and monitors the processes. We presented how security groups act as firewalls to allow selective traffic between services. We explained how SSL certificates from Let's Encrypt enable HTTPS traffic for security. We described how the deployment follows WSGI standards for communication between Nginx and Flask. Finally, we covered how Route 53 can be used to configure a custom domain name to route traffic to the frontend instance.

7 PERSISTING MICROSERVICES DATA WITH S3, RDS AND DYNAMODB

THIS CHAPTER COVERS

- Storing Files on Amazon S3
- Serving Files with CloudFront CDN
- Persisting Data with RDS
- Microservices app using EC2, S3, CloudFront & RDS
- Persisting Data with DynamoDB
- Microservices app using EC2, S3, CloudFront & DynamoDB

7.1   Introduction

In the previous chapter, we described the implementation of a microservices-based E-Commerce application. The E-Commerce application allowed users to register, login, browse products, add items to a cart, submit orders, and write reviews for products. The application had microservices such as Frontend, User, Product, Order and Review. We used SQLite as the database for persistence and the local file system for storing files like product images and user profile photos. While this setup is great for getting started and prototyping an application quickly, however, when it comes to deploying Flask applications to production, the SQLite and local storage approach has limitations in scalability, availability, and performance.

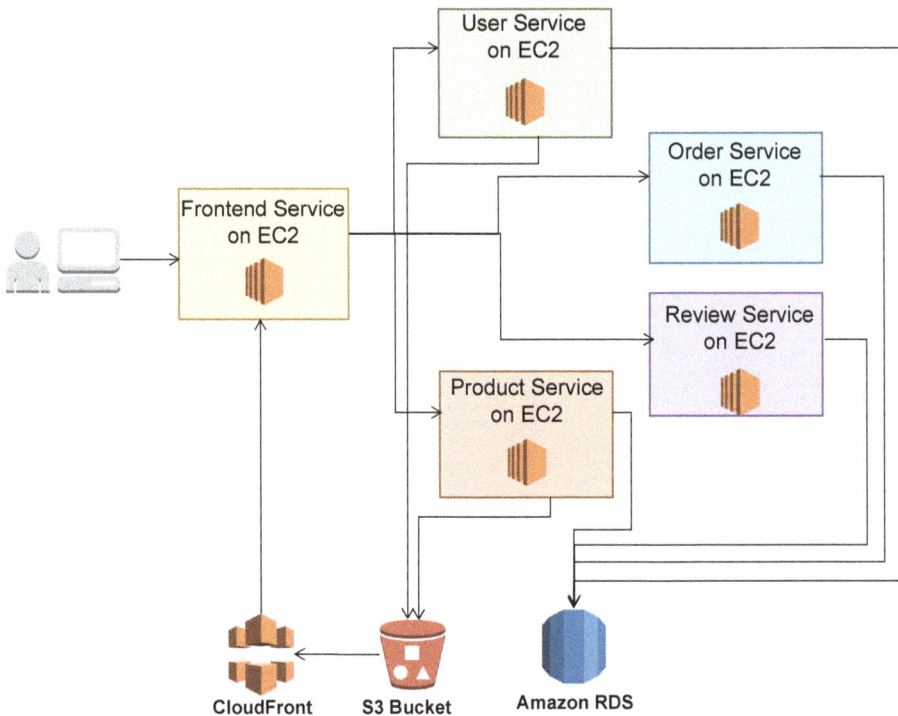

Figure 7.1: E-Commerce application using Flask, EC2, S3, CloudFront, and RDS

In this chapter, we will describe how the Flask application can be migrated from using local storage and SQLite to leveraging AWS services like S3, CloudFront, RDS, and DynamoDB. We will cover two versions of migrating the Flask application to AWS. In the first version as shown in Figure 7.1, we will use S3 for file storage, CloudFront CDN for serving files, and a MySQL RDS database instance. In the second version as shown in Figure 7.2, we will use S3 for file storage, CloudFront CDN, and DynamoDB for the database. DynamoDB is a fully managed NoSQL database provided by AWS. Using RDS and DynamoDB for the two versions of the application allows us to explore both relational and non-relational approaches for the application persistence layer.

The benefits of deploying the E-Commerce application on EC2 and using services like S3, CloudFront, RDS/DynamoDB are as follows:

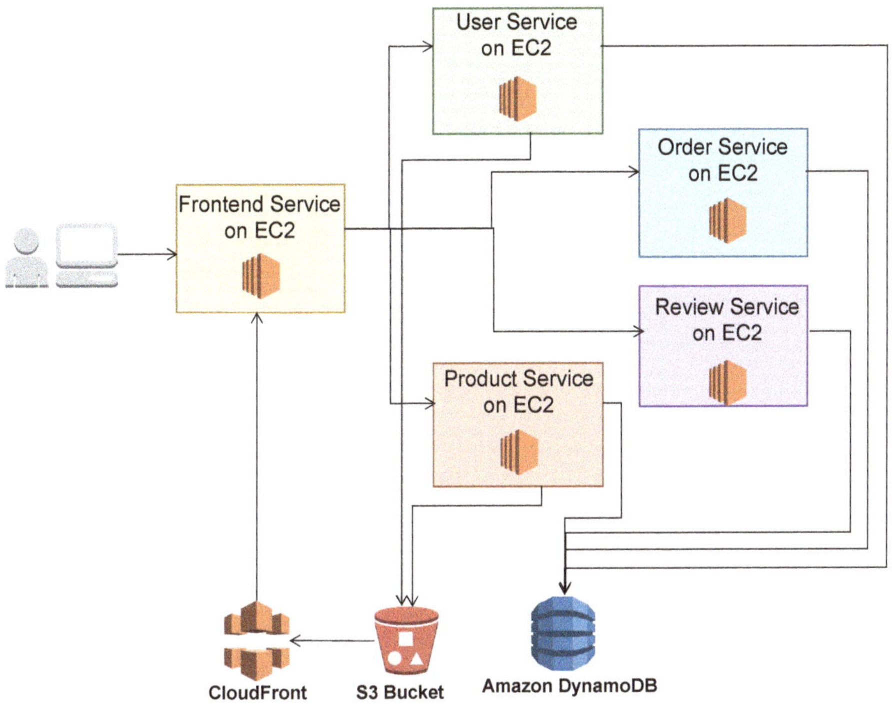

Figure 7.2: E-Commerce application using Flask, EC2, S3, CloudFront, and DynamoDB

- **EC2**: Amazon EC2 provides secure and resizable compute capacity in the AWS cloud. We can use EC2 to deploy our Flask application microservices. EC2 offers a wide range of instance types optimized for different performance needs like compute, memory, or storage. Auto Scaling groups allow automatically adding or removing EC2 instances based on demand to match capacity with load. EC2 is a fully managed service so we don't need to provision our own physical servers or data centers. We pay only for the compute resources we use on an hourly basis with no long-term commitments.

- **S3**: Amazon S3 offers highly durable and scalable object storage in the cloud. We leverage S3 to store user profile photos and product images. A key benefit of S3 is the virtually unlimited storage capacity that scales automatically based on usage. There is no need for capacity planning or managing storage infrastructure. S3 provides 99.999999999% durability for objects by replicating across multiple facilities. Objects are stored in S3 buckets which act as containers. Access permissions, encryption, and versioning can be configured on buckets for security and data retention needs. Objects can have metadata tagged and lifecycle policies enabled to transition them to lower cost tiers. S3 is integrated with CloudFront to provide low latency access using edge locations close to users.

- **CloudFront**: Amazon CloudFront is a content delivery network (CDN) that accelerates the delivery of static and dynamic content using edge locations around the world. We can use CloudFront in front of S3 origins to cache frequently accessed content like product images. This allows delivering content with lower latency by serving it from locations closest to the user. CloudFront seamlessly handles traffic spikes without overload. Additional features include DDoS mitigation using AWS Shield, geo-restriction to control access by location, and HTTPS support. CloudFront provides capabilities like real-time logs and analytics that help gain insights into access patterns. By using CloudFront, we optimize the delivery of content to end-users while offloading traffic from the origin.

- **RDS**: Amazon RDS provides a fully managed relational database service with high availability, security, and scalability. We leverage RDS to run our MySQL databases instead of managing database servers ourselves. RDS handles time-consuming administrative tasks like backups, software patching, failure detection, recovery, and backups. We can create read replicas to scale database reads and multi-AZ deployments for high availability. RDS integrates with other AWS services like EC2, CloudWatch, S3, and IAM to provide a secure and monitored database environment. We don't need to worry about managing the underlying infrastructure or database software. RDS enables us to build applications faster with an enterprise-grade database backend.

- **DynamoDB**: Amazon DynamoDB is a fully managed NoSQL database service that provides fast and flexible access at scale. We can leverage DynamoDB as an alternative database option instead of RDS MySQL when requirements call for a non-relational data model. DynamoDB handles provisioning servers, partitioning data, and managing loads seamlessly, allowing massive scalability. Single-digit millisecond latency provides great performance for modern applications. DynamoDB replicates data across AZs for built-in high availability and durability. It offers capabilities like atomic counters, conditionals, indexing, and data streams for advanced use cases. Fine-grained access control integrated with IAM provides data security. DynamoDB is priced based on actual usage, not pre-provisioned capacity. Its flexibility and managed nature make DynamoDB a great database option for non-relational data.

7.2   Storing Files on Amazon S3

Amazon S3 provides secure, durable, and highly scalable object storage. In our E-commerce application, we will use S3 to store user profile photos and product images. Once uploaded, we only reference the images in our database by their S3 URL. This decouples the application from the storage layer.

Figures 7.3, 7.4, and 7.5 show the steps for creating an S3 bucket. Give the bucket a unique name and select the desired AWS region.

Create bucket Info

Buckets are containers for data stored in S3. Learn more [↗]

General configuration

AWS Region

US West (Oregon) us-west-2 ▼

Bucket type   Info

⦿ General purpose	○ Directory - *New*
Recommended for most use cases and access patterns. General purpose buckets are the original S3 bucket type. They allow a mix of storage classes that redundantly store objects across multiple Availability Zones.	Recommended for low-latency use cases. These buckets use only the S3 Express One Zone storage class, which provides faster processing of data within a single Availability Zone.

Bucket name   Info

microservices-ecommerce-app

Bucket name must be unique within the global namespace and follow the bucket naming rules. See rules for bucket naming [↗]

Copy settings from existing bucket - *optional*
Only the bucket settings in the following configuration are copied.

Choose bucket

Format: s3://bucket/prefix

Object Ownership   Info

Control ownership of objects written to this bucket from other AWS accounts and the use of access control lists (ACLs). Object ownership determines who can specify access to objects.

○ ACLs disabled (recommended)	⦿ ACLs enabled
All objects in this bucket are owned by this account. Access to this bucket and its objects is specified using only policies.	Objects in this bucket can be owned by other AWS accounts. Access to this bucket and its objects can be specified using ACLs.

> ⚠ We recommend disabling ACLs, unless you need to control access for each object individually or to have the object writer own the data they upload. Using a bucket policy instead of ACLs to share data with users outside of your account simplifies permissions management and auditing.

Object Ownership

⦿ **Bucket owner preferred**
   If new objects written to this bucket specify the bucket-owner-full-control canned ACL, they are owned by the bucket owner. Otherwise, they are owned by the object writer.

○ **Object writer**
   The object writer remains the object owner.

> ⓘ If you want to enforce object ownership for new objects only, your bucket policy must specify that the bucket-owner-full-control canned ACL is required for object uploads. Learn more [↗]

Figure 7.3: Creating S3 bucket - part 1

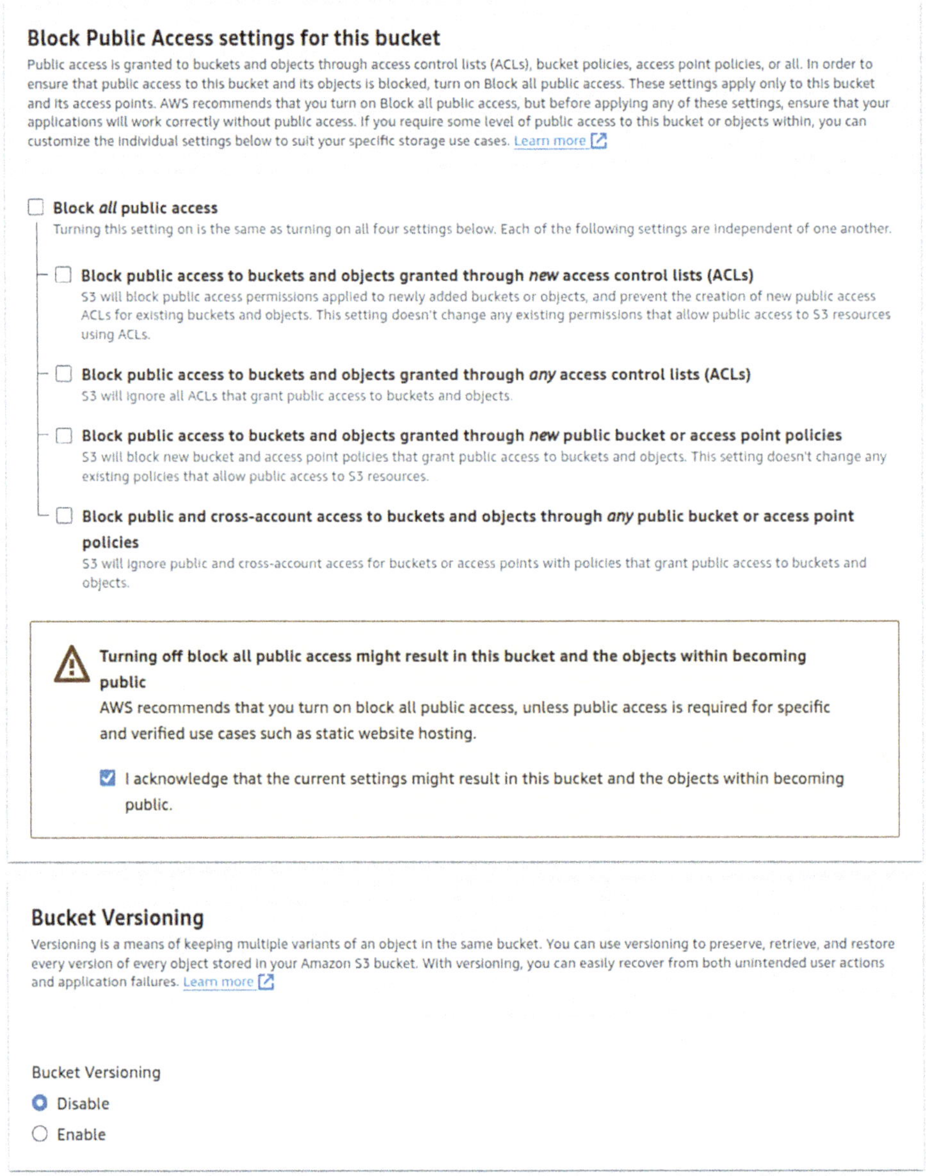

Block Public Access settings for this bucket

Public access is granted to buckets and objects through access control lists (ACLs), bucket policies, access point policies, or all. In order to ensure that public access to this bucket and its objects is blocked, turn on Block all public access. These settings apply only to this bucket and its access points. AWS recommends that you turn on Block all public access, but before applying any of these settings, ensure that your applications will work correctly without public access. If you require some level of public access to this bucket or objects within, you can customize the individual settings below to suit your specific storage use cases. Learn more 🔗

☐ **Block *all* public access**
   Turning this setting on is the same as turning on all four settings below. Each of the following settings are independent of one another.

   ☐ **Block public access to buckets and objects granted through *new* access control lists (ACLs)**
      S3 will block public access permissions applied to newly added buckets or objects, and prevent the creation of new public access ACLs for existing buckets and objects. This setting doesn't change any existing permissions that allow public access to S3 resources using ACLs.

   ☐ **Block public access to buckets and objects granted through *any* access control lists (ACLs)**
      S3 will ignore all ACLs that grant public access to buckets and objects.

   ☐ **Block public access to buckets and objects granted through *new* public bucket or access point policies**
      S3 will block new bucket and access point policies that grant public access to buckets and objects. This setting doesn't change any existing policies that allow public access to S3 resources.

   ☐ **Block public and cross-account access to buckets and objects through *any* public bucket or access point policies**
      S3 will ignore public and cross-account access for buckets or access points with policies that grant public access to buckets and objects.

> ⚠ **Turning off block all public access might result in this bucket and the objects within becoming public**
> AWS recommends that you turn on block all public access, unless public access is required for specific and verified use cases such as static website hosting.
>
> ☑ I acknowledge that the current settings might result in this bucket and the objects within becoming public.

Bucket Versioning

Versioning is a means of keeping multiple variants of an object in the same bucket. You can use versioning to preserve, retrieve, and restore every version of every object stored in your Amazon S3 bucket. With versioning, you can easily recover from both unintended user actions and application failures. Learn more 🔗

Bucket Versioning
🔘 Disable
⚪ Enable

Figure 7.4: Creating S3 bucket - part 2

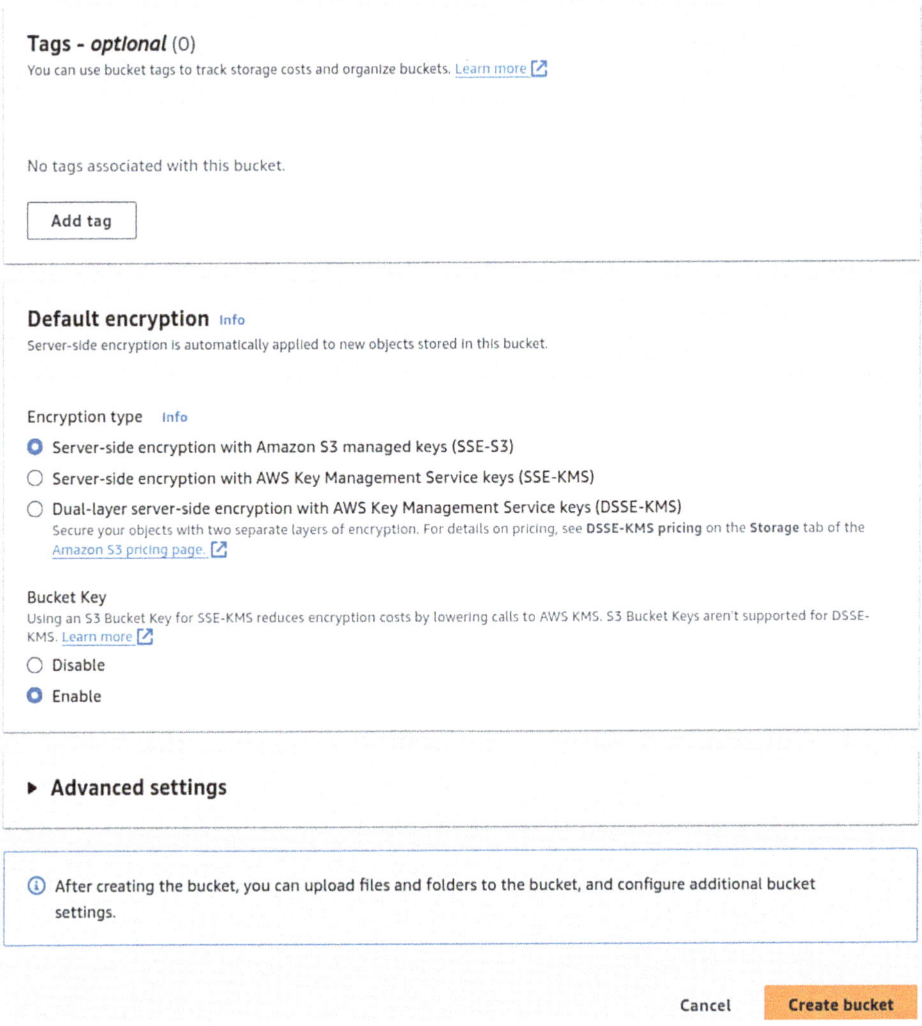

Tags - *optional* (0)
You can use bucket tags to track storage costs and organize buckets. Learn more ⧉

No tags associated with this bucket.

Add tag

Default encryption Info
Server-side encryption is automatically applied to new objects stored in this bucket.

Encryption type   Info
- ⦿ Server-side encryption with Amazon S3 managed keys (SSE-S3)
- ○ Server-side encryption with AWS Key Management Service keys (SSE-KMS)
- ○ Dual-layer server-side encryption with AWS Key Management Service keys (DSSE-KMS)
  Secure your objects with two separate layers of encryption. For details on pricing, see **DSSE-KMS pricing** on the **Storage** tab of the
  Amazon S3 pricing page. ⧉

Bucket Key
Using an S3 Bucket Key for SSE-KMS reduces encryption costs by lowering calls to AWS KMS. S3 Bucket Keys aren't supported for DSSE-KMS. Learn more ⧉
- ○ Disable
- ⦿ Enable

▶ **Advanced settings**

ⓘ After creating the bucket, you can upload files and folders to the bucket, and configure additional bucket
settings.

Cancel   **Create bucket**

Figure 7.5: Creating S3 bucket - part 3

By default, files uploaded to S3 are private. We need to configure a bucket policy to make the files public. Figure 7.6 shows the S3 bucket policy, which is required to make the objects public. Go to the bucket, choose Permissions > Bucket Policy, and apply the policy as shown in the figure.

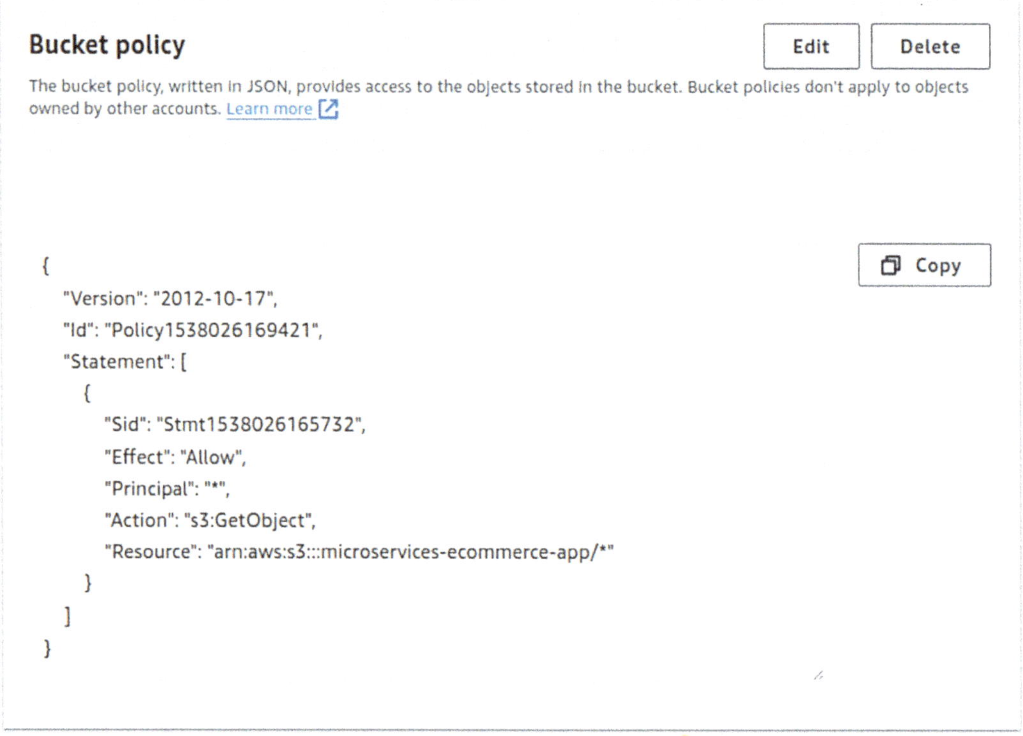

Bucket policy   Edit   Delete

The bucket policy, written in JSON, provides access to the objects stored in the bucket. Bucket policies don't apply to objects owned by other accounts. Learn more 🔗

                                                               📋 Copy

```
{
  "Version": "2012-10-17",
  "Id": "Policy1538026169421",
  "Statement": [
    {
      "Sid": "Stmt1538026165732",
      "Effect": "Allow",
      "Principal": "*",
      "Action": "s3:GetObject",
      "Resource": "arn:aws:s3:::microservices-ecommerce-app/*"
    }
  ]
}
```

Figure 7.6: S3 bucket policy

Figure 7.7 shows how to enable static website hosting for the S3 bucket. In the bucket settings, go to Properties > Static website hosting. Enter an index document and error document. With static website hosting enabled, objects can be accessed via the bucket website endpoint URL (like http://examplebucket.s3-website-us-east-1.amazonaws.com/photo.jpg).

By using S3, the E-Commerce application can scale to any number of users, products, and traffic without worrying about storage bottlenecks. We only pay for what we use with no upfront costs. The pay-as-you-go model provides cost optimization as application storage needs evolve.

S3 provides built-in features like versioning, encryption, and lifecycle policies. We can enable versioning to keep multiple variants of an image. With encryption, the image data is secured both in transit and at rest. Lifecycle policies can transition less accessed images to lower-cost storage tiers.

S3 provides enterprise-grade storage for our E-Commerce application. It handles replication, failover, access control, and optimizations like caching through CloudFront. S3 integration allows us to focus on the business logic and deliver better application performance.

Static website hosting

Use this bucket to host a website or redirect requests. Learn more ⧉

Static website hosting

○ Disable

● Enable

Hosting type

● Host a static website
 Use the bucket endpoint as the web address. Learn more ⧉

○ Redirect requests for an object
 Redirect requests to another bucket or domain. Learn more ⧉

> ⓘ For your customers to access content at the website endpoint, you must make all your content publicly readable. To do so, you can edit the S3 Block Public Access settings for the bucket. For more information, see Using Amazon S3 Block Public Access ⧉

Index document
Specify the home or default page of the website.

```
index.html
```

Error document - *optional*
This is returned when an error occurs.

```
error.html
```

Redirection rules – *optional*
Redirection rules, written in JSON, automatically redirect webpage requests for specific content. Learn more ⧉

```
1
```

JSON   Ln 1, Col 1   ⊗ Errors: 0   ⚠ Warnings: 0   ⚙

Figure 7.7: Enabling S3 static website hosting

7.3 Serving Files with CloudFront CDN

To optimize delivery of user profile photos and product images to customers across the globe, we leverage CloudFront as a content delivery network (CDN).

We configure an S3 bucket as the origin source for CloudFront. Rules are set up to cache read-only assets like user photos and product images with a long TTL. CloudFront copies these static assets to edge locations closer to end users.

Subsequent requests are served directly from the edge instead of the origin S3 bucket. This reduces latency as data is geographically closer to the user. Once CloudFront is set up, we use the CloudFront URL instead of the S3 URL to retrieve images in our application. This allows the CDN to optimize delivery with caching and compression. CloudFront also handles spikes in traffic gracefully.

Figures 7.8, 7.9, and 7.10 show the steps for creating a CloudFront distribution for the S3 bucket.

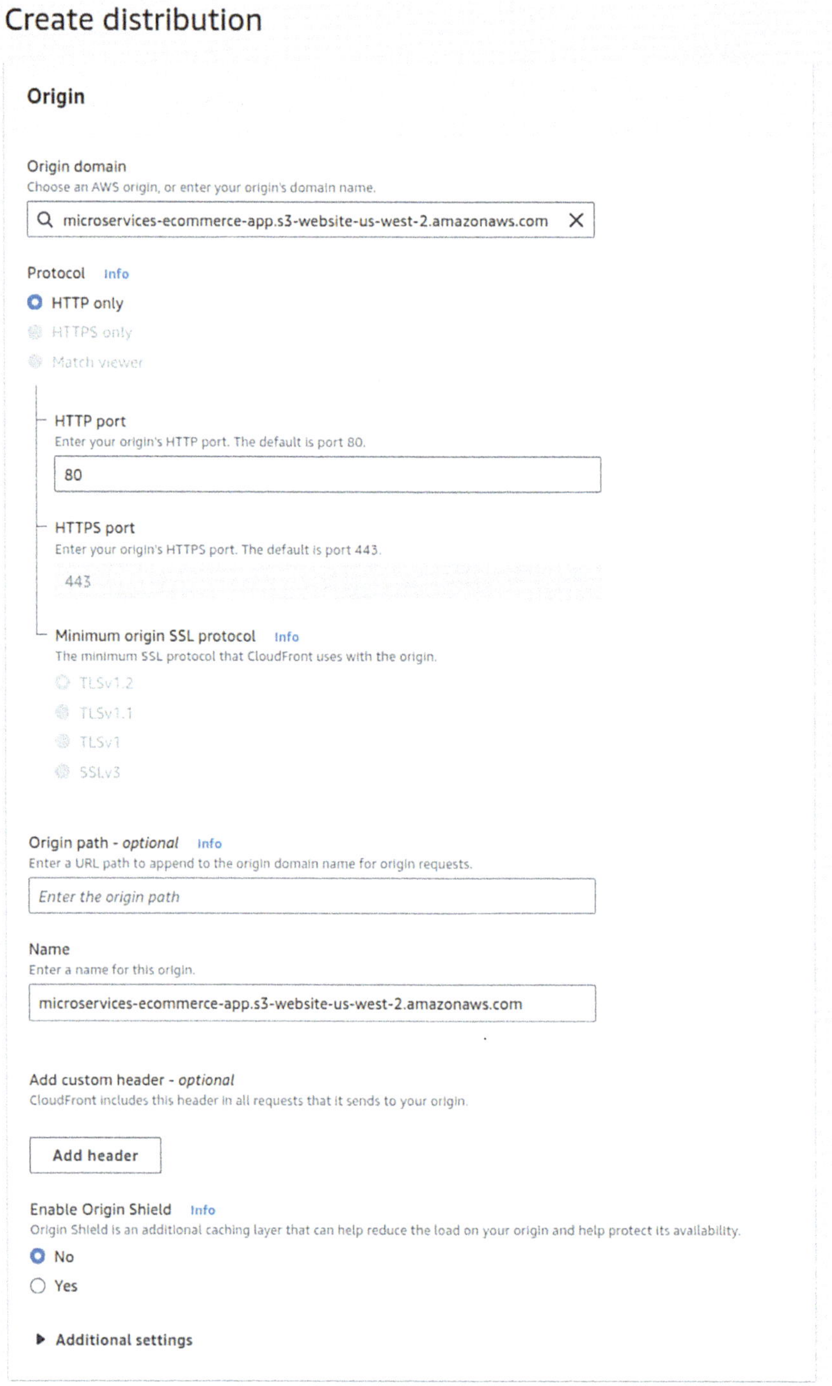

Figure 7.8: Creating CloudFront distribution - part 1

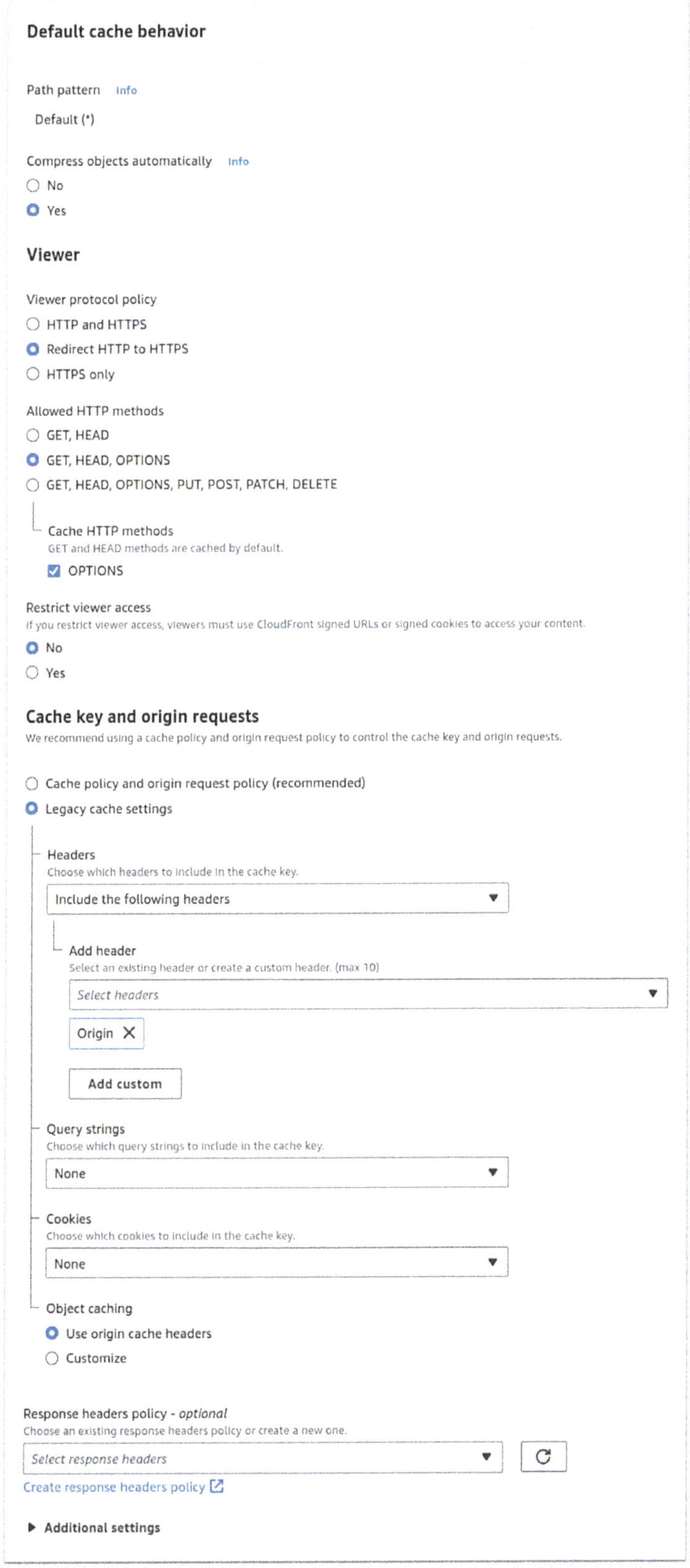

Default cache behavior

Path pattern   Info
  Default (*)

Compress objects automatically   Info
○ No
● Yes

Viewer

Viewer protocol policy
○ HTTP and HTTPS
● Redirect HTTP to HTTPS
○ HTTPS only

Allowed HTTP methods
○ GET, HEAD
● GET, HEAD, OPTIONS
○ GET, HEAD, OPTIONS, PUT, POST, PATCH, DELETE

  Cache HTTP methods
  GET and HEAD methods are cached by default.
  ☑ OPTIONS

Restrict viewer access
If you restrict viewer access, viewers must use CloudFront signed URLs or signed cookies to access your content.
● No
○ Yes

Cache key and origin requests
We recommend using a cache policy and origin request policy to control the cache key and origin requests.

○ Cache policy and origin request policy (recommended)
● Legacy cache settings

  Headers
  Choose which headers to include in the cache key.

  | Include the following headers   ▼ |

    Add header
    Select an existing header or create a custom header. (max 10)

    | Select headers   ▼ |

    | Origin ✕ |

    | Add custom |

  Query strings
  Choose which query strings to include in the cache key.

  | None   ▼ |

  Cookies
  Choose which cookies to include in the cache key.

  | None   ▼ |

  Object caching
  ● Use origin cache headers
  ○ Customize

Response headers policy - *optional*
Choose an existing response headers policy or create a new one.

| Select response headers   ▼ | | ⟳ |

Create response headers policy ↗

▶ Additional settings

Figure 7.9: Creating CloudFront distribution - part 2

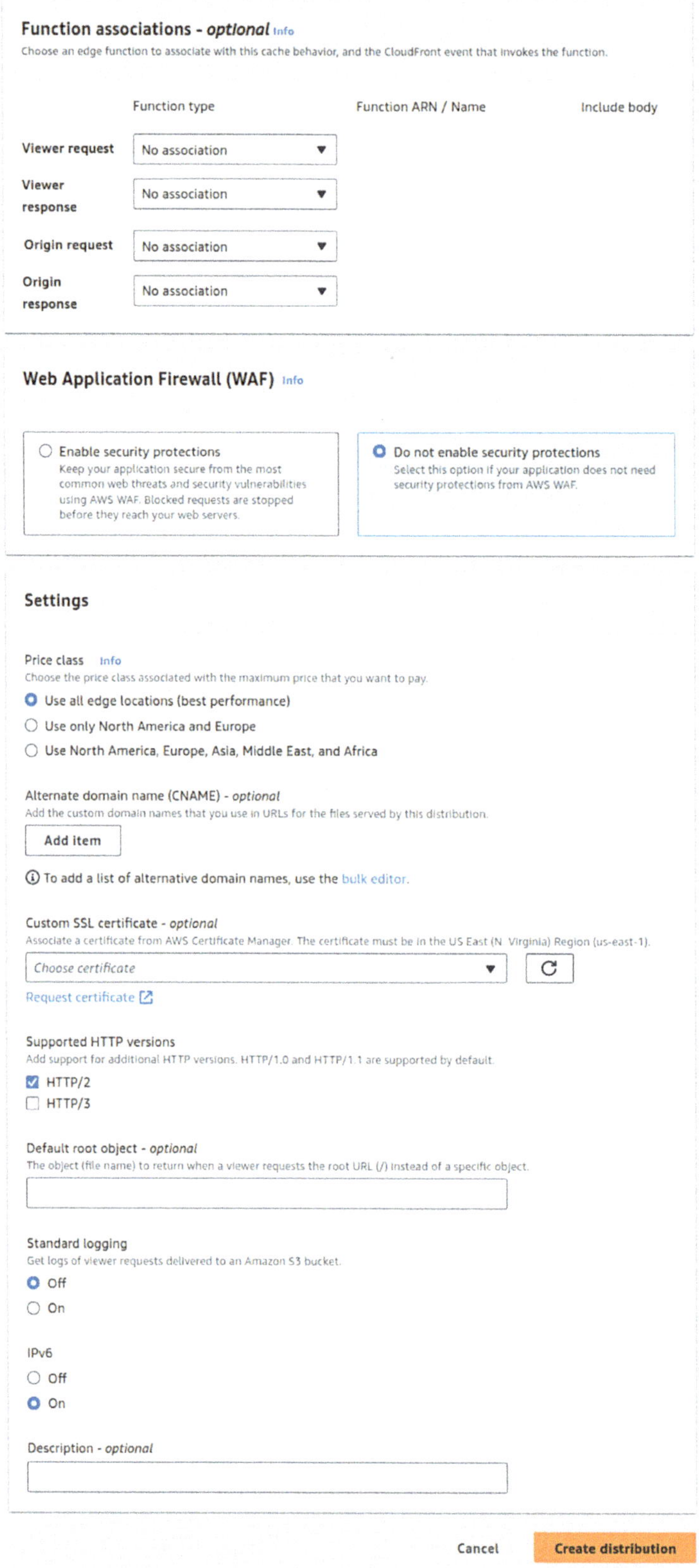

Function associations - *optional* Info

Choose an edge function to associate with this cache behavior, and the CloudFront event that invokes the function.

	Function type	Function ARN / Name	Include body
Viewer request	No association ▼		
Viewer response	No association ▼		
Origin request	No association ▼		
Origin response	No association ▼		

Web Application Firewall (WAF) Info

○ Enable security protections
Keep your application secure from the most common web threats and security vulnerabilities using AWS WAF. Blocked requests are stopped before they reach your web servers.

● Do not enable security protections
Select this option if your application does not need security protections from AWS WAF.

Settings

Price class   Info
Choose the price class associated with the maximum price that you want to pay.

● Use all edge locations (best performance)
○ Use only North America and Europe
○ Use North America, Europe, Asia, Middle East, and Africa

Alternate domain name (CNAME) - *optional*
Add the custom domain names that you use in URLs for the files served by this distribution.

[Add item]

ⓘ To add a list of alternative domain names, use the bulk editor.

Custom SSL certificate - *optional*
Associate a certificate from AWS Certificate Manager. The certificate must be in the US East (N. Virginia) Region (us-east-1).

[Choose certificate   ▼]   [↻]

Request certificate ↗

Supported HTTP versions
Add support for additional HTTP versions. HTTP/1.0 and HTTP/1.1 are supported by default.

☑ HTTP/2
☐ HTTP/3

Default root object - *optional*
The object (file name) to return when a viewer requests the root URL (/) instead of a specific object.

[   ]

Standard logging
Get logs of viewer requests delivered to an Amazon S3 bucket.
● Off
○ On

IPv6
○ Off
● On

Description - *optional*

[   ]

Cancel   [Create distribution]

Figure 7.10: Creating CloudFront distribution - part 3

To create a CloudFront distribution, log into the AWS Management Console and go to the CloudFront service. Click on 'Create Distribution' to start the process. Select "Web" as the delivery method. For the origin domain, select the S3 bucket you want CloudFront to pull from. Specify settings like distribution name, default root object, viewer protocol policy, allowed HTTP methods, caching settings, and origin request settings as shown in Figures 7.8-7.10. The rest of the settings can be left at their defaults initially. Scroll down and click 'Create Distribution' to complete the process. It will take some time for the distribution status to change from 'In Progress' to 'Deployed'. Once deployed, the S3 content will be available at the CloudFront domain name.

You can further customize caching, security policies, origins, and more in the distribution settings later on. Using CloudFront is an efficient way to improve access speed and add caching for your S3-hosted content.

For our E-Commerce application, CloudFront reduces the load off the origin servers by serving images globally. Users experience faster page loads as images are served from nearby edge locations. CloudFront logs provide insights into access patterns that help optimize application performance. By using CloudFront with S3, our Flask application can deliver low latency, highly secure content to customers all over the world.

7.4 Persisting Data with RDS

RDS provides a fully managed SQL database service with high availability. Automated backups, OS patching, failure detection, and recovery reduce operational overhead. Multi-AZ deployments provide high availability with automatic failover. Load balancing read replicas can be created to scale horizontal reads as traffic increases. With RDS managing database operations, developers can focus on the application instead of database administration.

Compared to self-managed databases, RDS provides enterprise-grade capabilities out-of-the-box. Point-in-time restore, read replicas, and backup capabilities aid disaster recovery. Audit logging helps meet regulatory requirements. By leveraging RDS, the application can scale capacity on demand to support growth. RDS optimizations reduce costs by using provisioned IOPS storage or spot instances. Automation and practices like infrastructure as code simplify RDS management.

We use a MySQL database on an RDS instance to store structured relational data for the User, Product, Order, and Review microservices of the E-Commerce application. Figures 7.11 and 7.12 show the steps for creating an RDS database. We configure the RDS instance type and storage suitable for the application. Installation and management of the database software are handled seamlessly by AWS.

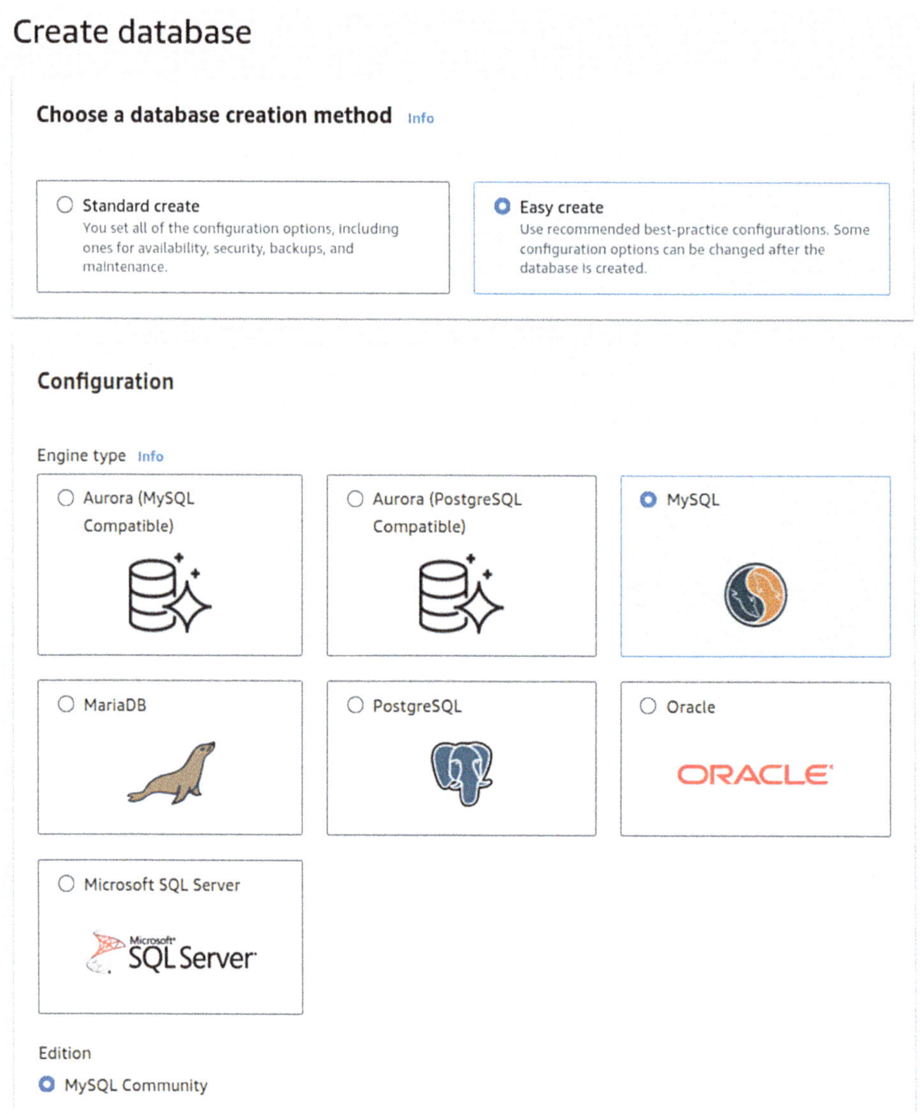

Create database

Choose a database creation method Info

○ **Standard create**
You set all of the configuration options, including ones for availability, security, backups, and maintenance.

● **Easy create**
Use recommended best-practice configurations. Some configuration options can be changed after the database is created.

Configuration

Engine type Info

○ Aurora (MySQL Compatible)

○ Aurora (PostgreSQL Compatible)

● MySQL

○ MariaDB

○ PostgreSQL

○ Oracle

○ Microsoft SQL Server

Edition
● MySQL Community

Figure 7.11: Creating RDS database - part 1

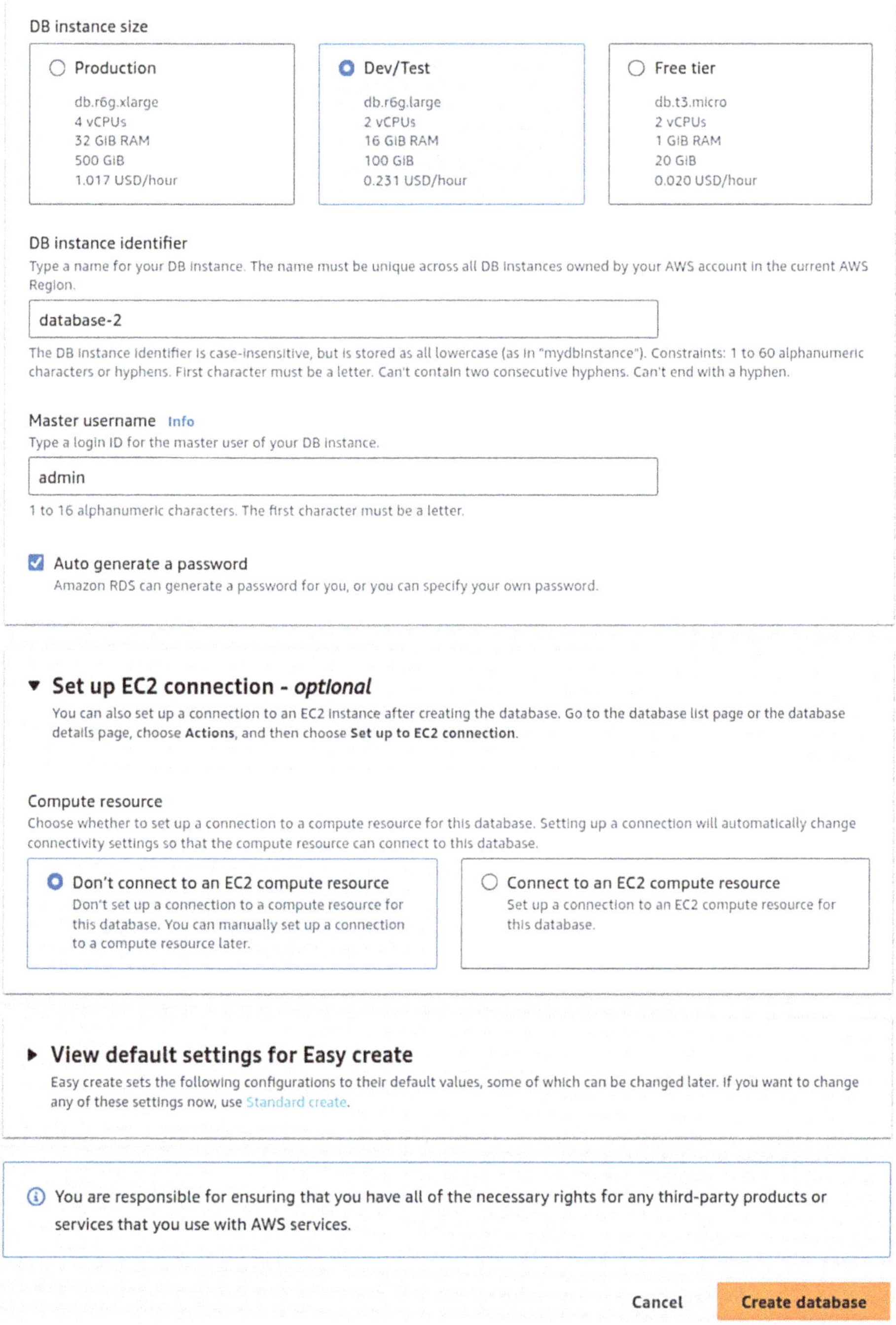

DB instance size

○ Production	● Dev/Test	○ Free tier
db.r6g.xlarge	db.r6g.large	db.t3.micro
4 vCPUs	2 vCPUs	2 vCPUs
32 GiB RAM	16 GiB RAM	1 GiB RAM
500 GiB	100 GiB	20 GiB
1.017 USD/hour	0.231 USD/hour	0.020 USD/hour

DB instance identifier

Type a name for your DB instance. The name must be unique across all DB instances owned by your AWS account in the current AWS Region.

```
database-2
```

The DB instance identifier is case-insensitive, but is stored as all lowercase (as in "mydbinstance"). Constraints: 1 to 60 alphanumeric characters or hyphens. First character must be a letter. Can't contain two consecutive hyphens. Can't end with a hyphen.

Master username   Info

Type a login ID for the master user of your DB instance.

```
admin
```

1 to 16 alphanumeric characters. The first character must be a letter.

☑ Auto generate a password

Amazon RDS can generate a password for you, or you can specify your own password.

▼ **Set up EC2 connection - *optional***

You can also set up a connection to an EC2 instance after creating the database. Go to the database list page or the database details page, choose **Actions**, and then choose **Set up to EC2 connection**.

Compute resource

Choose whether to set up a connection to a compute resource for this database. Setting up a connection will automatically change connectivity settings so that the compute resource can connect to this database.

● Don't connect to an EC2 compute resource	○ Connect to an EC2 compute resource
Don't set up a connection to a compute resource for this database. You can manually set up a connection to a compute resource later.	Set up a connection to an EC2 compute resource for this database.

▶ **View default settings for Easy create**

Easy create sets the following configurations to their default values, some of which can be changed later. If you want to change any of these settings now, use Standard create.

ⓘ You are responsible for ensuring that you have all of the necessary rights for any third-party products or services that you use with AWS services.

Cancel   **Create database**

Figure 7.12: Creating RDS database - part 2

Figure 7.13 shows the details of the RDS database instance.

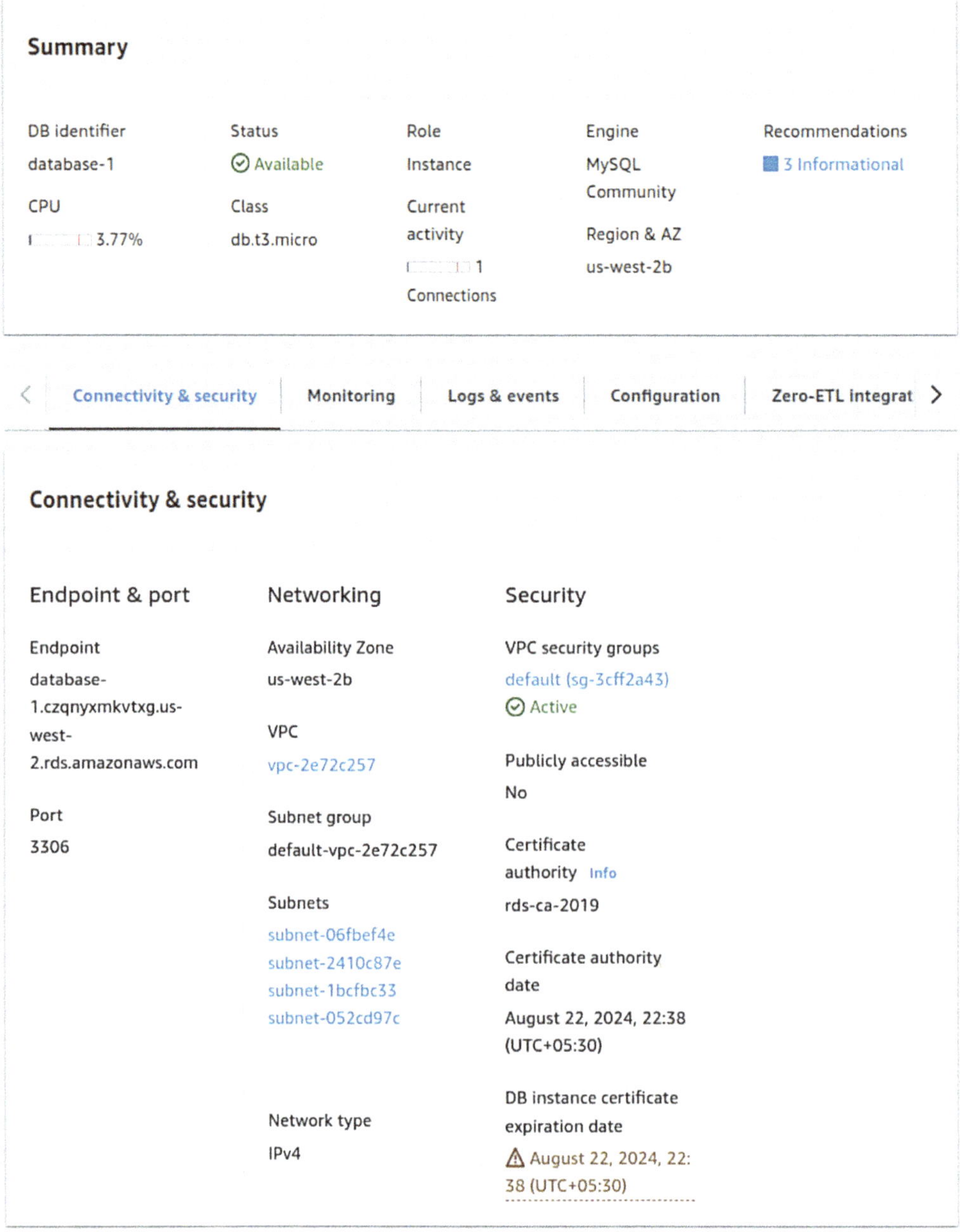

Summary

DB identifier	Status	Role	Engine	Recommendations
database-1	⊘ Available	Instance	MySQL Community	◼ 3 Informational
CPU	Class	Current activity	Region & AZ	
⌐ ⌐ 3.77%	db.t3.micro	⌐ ⌐ 1 Connections	us-west-2b	

< **Connectivity & security**   Monitoring   Logs & events   Configuration   Zero-ETL integrat >

Connectivity & security

Endpoint & port

Endpoint
database-1.czqnyxmkvtxg.us-west-2.rds.amazonaws.com

Port
3306

Networking

Availability Zone
us-west-2b

VPC
vpc-2e72c257

Subnet group
default-vpc-2e72c257

Subnets
subnet-06fbef4e
subnet-2410c87e
subnet-1bcfbc33
subnet-052cd97c

Network type
IPv4

Security

VPC security groups
default (sg-3cff2a43)
⊘ Active

Publicly accessible
No

Certificate authority Info
rds-ca-2019

Certificate authority date
August 22, 2024, 22:38 (UTC+05:30)

DB instance certificate expiration date
⚠ August 22, 2024, 22:38 (UTC+05:30)

Figure 7.13: RDS database details

Figure 7.14 shows the security group configuration used for the RDS instance. The RDS instance is not public-facing and access is provided only to traffic coming from the microservices instances. To allow traffic from the microservices instances, the custom source option is selected, and the security group used for the microservices is provided.

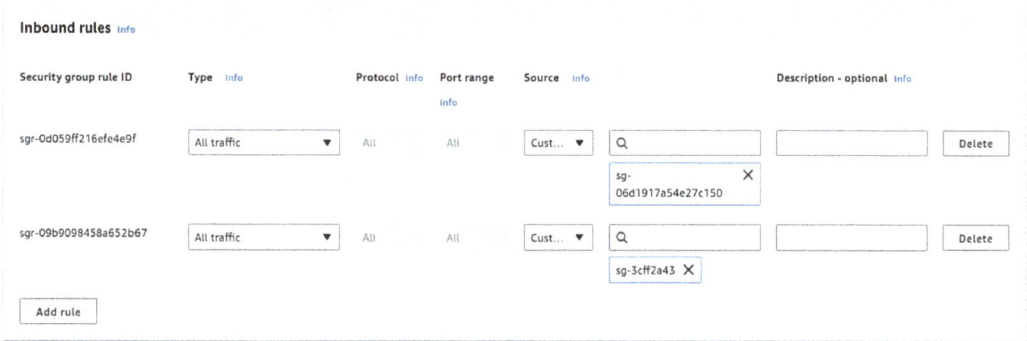

Figure 7.14: Security group for RDS database

The Flask application uses SQLAlchemy to interface with MySQL for object-relational mapping. The SQLAlchemy engine is configured to connect to the RDS endpoint URL with database credentials. Figure 7.15 shows how to connect to the RDS database instance and query the MySQL database.

```
ubuntu@ip-172-31-25-162:~/ecommerce/user$ mysql --host=database-1.czqnyxmkvtxg.us-west-2.rds.amazonaws.com
--port=3306 --user=admin --password=S9c1Zl6tC93AuTfKCLLV
mysql: [Warning] Using a password on the command line interface can be insecure.
Welcome to the MySQL monitor.  Commands end with ; or \g.
Your MySQL connection id is 52
Server version: 8.0.35 Source distribution

Copyright (c) 2000, 2023, Oracle and/or its affiliates.

Oracle is a registered trademark of Oracle Corporation and/or its
affiliates. Other names may be trademarks of their respective
owners.

Type 'help;' or '\h' for help. Type '\c' to clear the current input statement.

mysql> SHOW DATABASES;
+--------------------+
| Database           |
+--------------------+
| information_schema |
| mysql              |
| orderdb            |
| performance_schema |
| product            |
| review             |
| sys                |
| user               |
+--------------------+
8 rows in set (0.00 sec)

mysql> SELECT * FROM orderdb.order;
+----+---------+---------+---------------------+---------------------+
| id | user_id | is_open | date_added          | date_updated        |
+----+---------+---------+---------------------+---------------------+
|  1 |       1 |       0 | 2024-01-20 02:30:35 | 2024-01-20 02:30:39 |
|  2 |       1 |       0 | 2024-01-20 02:31:39 | 2024-01-20 02:31:46 |
+----+---------+---------+---------------------+---------------------+
2 rows in set (0.00 sec)
```

Figure 7.15: Querying MySQL database on RDS instance

7.5   Microservices App Using EC2, S3, CloudFront & RDS

In this section, we provide the source code of the E-Commerce microservices application that is deployed on EC2 and uses S3 for storing files, CloudFront as CDN, and RDS for persisting data.

The source code of the frontend service and Flask templates is the same as the microservices application described in the previous chapter. The implementations of the routes for the User, Product, Order, and Review services are also similar to the ones provided in the previous chapter. For the sake of brevity, we are providing only the code differences in the microservices to support S3, CloudFront, and RDS.

Box 7.1 shows the code of the user microservice. When a new user registers, their password is hashed using *sha256_crypt*, and a random avatar image is generated locally using the *avinit* library. This image file is then uploaded to an Amazon S3 bucket using the *boto3* SDK. The S3 URL for this image file is returned by the *s3uploading* function.

The user data (including hashed passwords, usernames, and photo URL) is saved in a MySQL database hosted on Amazon RDS. Flask-SQLAlchemy is used to interface the Flask app with this RDS database for object-relational mapping and sessions.

Once uploaded to S3, the user avatar images are served via CloudFront, which acts as a content delivery network (CDN) to provide fast access to these image assets. The CloudFront URL is configured in the Flask app settings. When user data is retrieved, the S3/CloudFront URL is used to display the user's photo.

This separation of user data in RDS and user images in S3, while utilizing CloudFront for fast image delivery, allows the microservice to scale. The app can handle large volumes of user registrations and image serving without slowing down the main database.

■ **Box 7.1: Flask user microservice**

```
#Only the differences from the User service
#explained in previous chapter are shown,
#where SQLite is replaced with RDS and images are stored on S3.

app = Flask(__name__)
app.config['SECRET_KEY'] = "DoWgTDq87Kmne3TsCjNFabP"
app.config['BUCKET_NAME'] = 'microservices-ecommerce-app'
app.config['CLOUDFRONT_URL'] = 'https://dn2avtdn1xu.cloudfront.net'
app.config['AWS_ACCESS_KEY'] = 'EXAMPLEKEY'
app.config['AWS_SECRET_KEY'] = 'EXAMPLESECRET'
app.config['MYSQL_RDS_ENDPOINT'] = 'db.czkv.us-west-2.rds.amazonaws.com'
app.config['MYSQL_RDS_USER'] = 'admin'
app.config['MYSQL_RDS_PASSWORD'] = 'S9c1Zl6tC93AuTfKCLLV'
app.config['SQLALCHEMY_TRACK_MODIFICATIONS'] = False
app.config['ENV'] = "development"
app.config['DEBUG'] = True
app.config['SQLALCHEMY_DATABASE_URI']  = 'mysql+pymysql://'+
                    app.config['MYSQL_RDS_USER']+':'+
                    app.config['MYSQL_RDS_PASSWORD']+'@'+
                    app.config['MYSQL_RDS_ENDPOINT']+':3306/user'
app.config['SQLALCHEMY_ECHO'] = True
app.config['UPLOAD_FOLDER'] = 'uploads'
```

```python
db.init_app(app)
login_manager.init_app(app)

migrate = Migrate(app, db)
app.session_interface = CustomSessionInterface()

class User(UserMixin, db.Model):
    id = db.Column(db.Integer, primary_key=True)
    username = db.Column(db.String(255), unique=True, nullable=False)
    email = db.Column(db.String(255), unique=True, nullable=False)
    first_name = db.Column(db.String(255), unique=False, nullable=True)
    last_name = db.Column(db.String(255), unique=False, nullable=True)
    password = db.Column(db.String(255), unique=False, nullable=False)
    photo = db.Column(db.String(255), unique=False, nullable=True)
    is_admin = db.Column(db.Boolean, default=False)
    authenticated = db.Column(db.Boolean, default=False)
    api_key = db.Column(db.String(255), unique=True, nullable=True)
    date_added = db.Column(db.DateTime, default=datetime.utcnow)
    date_updated = db.Column(db.DateTime, onupdate=datetime.utcnow)

    def encode_api_key(self):
        self.api_key = sha256_crypt.hash(self.username +
                        str(datetime.utcnow))

    def encode_password(self):
        self.password = sha256_crypt.hash(self.password)

    def __repr__(self):
        return '<User %r>' % (self.username)

    def to_json(self):
        return {
            'first_name': self.first_name,
            'last_name': self.last_name,
            'username': self.username,
            'email': self.email,
            'photo': self.photo,
            'id': self.id,
            'api_key': self.api_key,
            'is_active': True,
            'is_admin': self.is_admin
        }

def s3uploading(filename):
    s3 = boto3.client('s3',
        aws_access_key_id=app.config['AWS_ACCESS_KEY'],
        aws_secret_access_key=app.config['AWS_SECRET_KEY'])
    bucket = app.config['BUCKET_NAME']
    path_filename_disk = os.path.join(app.config['UPLOAD_FOLDER'],
                            filename)
    path_filename_s3 = "photos/" + filename
    print(path_filename_s3)
    s3.upload_file(path_filename_disk, bucket, path_filename_s3)
```

```python
    url = app.config['CLOUDFRONT_URL']+'/'+path_filename_s3
    return url

@app.route('/api/user/create', methods=['POST'])
def post_register():
    first_name = request.form['first_name']
    last_name = request.form['last_name']
    email = request.form['email']
    username = request.form['username']
    password = sha256_crypt.hash((str(request.form['password'])))
    user = User()
    user.email = email
    user.first_name = first_name
    user.last_name = last_name
    user.password = password
    user.username = username
    user.authenticated = True
    name=first_name+' '+ last_name
    filename = "user"+str(int(time.time()*1000))+".png"
    imgpath=os.path.join(app.config['UPLOAD_FOLDER'],
                    filename)
    r = lambda: random.randint(0,255)
    colors=[]
    colors.append('#%02X%02X%02X' % (r(),r(),r()))
    avinit.get_png_avatar(name, output_file=imgpath,
                    colors=colors)
    uploadedFileURL = s3uploading(filename)
    user.photo = uploadedFileURL
    db.session.add(user)
    db.session.commit()
    response = jsonify({'message': 'User added',
            'result': user.to_json()})
    return response
```

Box 7.2 shows the code of the product microservice. When a new product is created, the product image file is first saved locally, then uploaded to an Amazon S3 bucket using the *boto3* SDK. The S3 URL for this image file is returned by the *s3uploading* function. The product data (including name, description, price, and image URL) is inserted into a MySQL database hosted on Amazon RDS. Flask-SQLAlchemy provides the interface to RDS for object-relational mapping and database sessions.

Once uploaded to S3, the product images are served via CloudFront content delivery network. This provides fast, reliable access to the images stored in S3. The CloudFront URL is configured in the Flask application settings. When retrieving product data, this URL is used to display the associated product image.

This architecture separates the product images from the core product data. Images are stored in Amazon S3 for scalable, redundant storage, while critical product data lives in RDS. The use of CloudFront accelerates image loading times. The Flask application coordinates with S3, CloudFront, and RDS using *boto3* and *SQLAlchemy* libraries.

■ Box 7.2: Flask product microservice

```
#Only the differences from the Product service
#explained in previous chapter are shown,
#where SQLite is replaced with RDS and images are stored on S3.

app = Flask(__name__)
app.config['SECRET_KEY'] = "DoWgTDq87Kmne3TsCjNFabP"
app.config['BUCKET_NAME'] = 'microservices-ecommerce-app'
app.config['CLOUDFRONT_URL'] = 'https://dn2avtdn1xu.cloudfront.net'
app.config['AWS_ACCESS_KEY'] = 'EXAMPLEKEY'
app.config['AWS_SECRET_KEY'] = 'EXAMPLESECRET'
app.config['MYSQL_RDS_ENDPOINT'] = 'db.czkv.us-west-2.rds.amazonaws.com'
app.config['MYSQL_RDS_USER'] = 'admin'
app.config['MYSQL_RDS_PASSWORD'] = 'S9c1Zl6tC93AuTfKCLLV'
app.config['SQLALCHEMY_TRACK_MODIFICATIONS'] = False
app.config['ENV'] = "development"
app.config['DEBUG'] = True
app.config['SQLALCHEMY_DATABASE_URI']  = 'mysql+pymysql://'+
                       app.config['MYSQL_RDS_USER']+':'+
                       app.config['MYSQL_RDS_PASSWORD']+'@'+
                       app.config['MYSQL_RDS_ENDPOINT']+':3306/product'
app.config['SQLALCHEMY_ECHO'] = True
app.config['UPLOAD_FOLDER'] = 'uploads'

db.init_app(app)
migrate = Migrate(app, db)

class Product(db.Model):
    id = db.Column(db.Integer, primary_key=True)
    name = db.Column(db.String(255), unique=True, nullable=False)
    slug = db.Column(db.String(255), unique=True, nullable=False)
    price = db.Column(db.Float, default=0)
    image = db.Column(db.String(255), unique=False, nullable=True)
    description = db.Column(db.Text)
    date_added = db.Column(db.DateTime, default=datetime.utcnow)
    date_updated = db.Column(db.DateTime, onupdate=datetime.utcnow)

    def to_json(self):
        return {
            'id': self.id,
            'name': self.name,
            'description': self.description,
            'slug': self.slug,
            'price': self.price,
            'image': self.image
        }

def s3uploading(filename):
    s3 = boto3.client('s3',
        aws_access_key_id=app.config['AWS_ACCESS_KEY'],
        aws_secret_access_key=app.config['AWS_SECRET_KEY'])
    bucket = app.config['BUCKET_NAME']
    path_filename_disk = os.path.join(app.config['UPLOAD_FOLDER'],
```

```
                                        filename)
    path_filename_s3 = "photos/" + filename
    print(path_filename_s3)
    s3.upload_file(path_filename_disk, bucket, path_filename_s3)
    url = app.config['CLOUDFRONT_URL']+'/'+path_filename_s3
    return url

@app.route('/api/product/create', methods=['POST'])
def post_create():
    name = request.form.get('name')
    slug = request.form.get('slug')
    description = request.form.get('description')
    price = request.form.get('price')
    image = request.files.get('image')
    filename = secure_filename(image.filename)
    image.save(os.path.join(app.config['UPLOAD_FOLDER'],
                            filename))
    uploadedFileURL = s3uploading(filename)
    item = Product()
    item.name = name
    item.slug = slug
    item.image = uploadedFileURL
    item.price = price
    item.description=description
    db.session.add(item)
    db.session.commit()
    response = jsonify({'message': 'Product added',
                'product': item.to_json()})
    return response
```

Box 7.3 shows the code of the order microservice.

■ Box 7.3: Flask order microservice

```
#Only the differences from the Order service explained in
#previous chapter are shown, where SQLite is replaced with RDS.

app = Flask(__name__)
app.config['SECRET_KEY'] = "DoWgTDq87Kmne3TsCjNFabP"
app.config['BUCKET_NAME'] = 'microservices-ecommerce-app'
app.config['CLOUDFRONT_URL'] = 'https://dn2avtdn1xu.cloudfront.net'
app.config['AWS_ACCESS_KEY'] = 'EXAMPLEKEY'
app.config['AWS_SECRET_KEY'] = 'EXAMPLESECRET'
app.config['MYSQL_RDS_ENDPOINT'] = 'db.czkv.us-west-2.rds.amazonaws.com'
app.config['MYSQL_RDS_USER'] = 'admin'
app.config['MYSQL_RDS_PASSWORD'] = 'S9c1Zl6tC93AuTfKCLLV'
app.config['SQLALCHEMY_TRACK_MODIFICATIONS'] = False
app.config['ENV'] = "development"
app.config['DEBUG'] = True
app.config['SQLALCHEMY_DATABASE_URI']  = 'mysql+pymysql://'+
                        app.config['MYSQL_RDS_USER']+':'+
                        app.config['MYSQL_RDS_PASSWORD']+'@'+
                        app.config['MYSQL_RDS_ENDPOINT']+':3306/orderdb'
app.config['SQLALCHEMY_ECHO'] = True
```

Box 7.4 shows the code of the review microservice.

■ Box 7.4: Flask review microservice

```
#Only the differences from the Review service
#explained in previous chapter are shown,
#where SQLite is replaced with RDS.

app = Flask(__name__)
app.config['SECRET_KEY'] = "DoWgTDq87Kmne3TsCjNFabP"
app.config['BUCKET_NAME'] = 'microservices-ecommerce-app'
app.config['CLOUDFRONT_URL'] = 'https://dn2avtdn1xu.cloudfront.net'
app.config['AWS_ACCESS_KEY'] = 'EXAMPLEKEY'
app.config['AWS_SECRET_KEY'] = 'EXAMPLESECRET'
app.config['MYSQL_RDS_ENDPOINT'] = 'db.czkv.us-west-2.rds.amazonaws.com'
app.config['MYSQL_RDS_USER'] = 'admin'
app.config['MYSQL_RDS_PASSWORD'] = 'S9c1Zl6tC93AuTfKCLLV'
app.config['SQLALCHEMY_TRACK_MODIFICATIONS'] = False
app.config['ENV'] = "development"
app.config['DEBUG'] = True
app.config['SQLALCHEMY_DATABASE_URI']  = 'mysql+pymysql://'+
                    app.config['MYSQL_RDS_USER']+':'+
                    app.config['MYSQL_RDS_PASSWORD']+'@'+
                    app.config['MYSQL_RDS_ENDPOINT']+':3306/review'
app.config['SQLALCHEMY_ECHO'] = True
app.config['UPLOAD_FOLDER'] = 'uploads'
```

Box 7.5 shows the instructions for setting up databases for microservices.

■ Box 7.5: Instructions for setting up databases for microservices

```
#Connect to RDS MySQL database instance and create databases
mysql --host=db.czkv.us-west-2.rds.amazonaws.com
    --port=3306 --user=admin
    --password=S9c1Zl6tC93AuTfKCLLV
#Run within mysql shell
    #Create Database
    CREATE DATABASE user;
    CREATE DATABASE product;
    CREATE DATABASE orderdb;
    CREATE DATABASE review;
    #Show Databases
    SHOW DATABASES;
    #Exit mysql shell
    exit

#For User, Product, Order and Review services
#initialize DB, create migrations and upgrade
flask db init
flask db migrate
flask db upgrade
```

7.6   Persisting Data with DynamoDB

DynamoDB is a fully managed NoSQL database provided by AWS. Using a non-relational database like DynamoDB provides several advantages compared to traditional RDBMS for modern applications:

- **Flexibility**: DynamoDB is schema-less so each item can have different attributes. This provides flexibility to evolve the data model easily as requirements change without modifying entire tables. RDS schema changes often require complex migrations. With DynamoDB, new attributes can be directly added to items without impacting existing code. Nested hierarchies allow complex relationships to be modeled within an item.
- **High Scalability**: DynamoDB is designed for massive scale and throughput unlike RDBMS constrained by compute power. DynamoDB automatically partitions data over sufficient servers to meet provisioned capacity. Sharding RDS data is complex to implement. DynamoDB scales seamlessly without sharding complexity.
- **Low Latency**: DynamoDB provides low latency for reads and writes, enabling real-time experiences. RDS performance degrades significantly under load, affecting latency.
- **High Availability**: DynamoDB replicates data across multiple availability zones (AZs) providing built-in high availability (HA). RDS Multi-AZ helps with failover but increases latency due to synchronous replication.
- **Fully Managed**: DynamoDB is serverless and fully managed by AWS. It does not require capacity provisioning, software patching, or cluster management. RDS still requires management of underlying EC2 instances, scaling capacity, patching, backups, and HA configurations.
- **Pay-Per-Use Pricing**: DynamoDB has simple pay-per-request pricing with generous free tier. RDS has a minimum instance fee even for small workloads.

Figure 7.16 shows the list of DynamoDB tables for the E-Commerce application including Orders, Products, Reviews and Users. For the Orders table, we use username as the partition key and order ID as the sort key. For the Products table, we use slug as the partition key. For the Reviews table, we use product slug as the partition key. For the Users table, we use username as the partition key.

DynamoDB > Tables

Name ▲	Status	Partition key	Sort key	Indexes	Deletion protection	Read capacity mode	Write capacity mode	Total size	Table class
orders	⊘ Active	username (S)	order_id (S)	0	⊖ Off	Provisioned (1)	Provisioned (1)	147 bytes	Standard
products	⊘ Active	slug (S)	-	0	⊖ Off	Provisioned (1)	Provisioned (1)	201 bytes	Standard
reviews	⊘ Active	product_slug (S)	-	0	⊖ Off	Provisioned (1)	Provisioned (1)	135 bytes	Standard
users	⊘ Active	username (S)	-	0	⊖ Off	Provisioned (1)	Provisioned (1)	1.1 kilobytes	Standard

Figure 7.16: DynamoDB tables for the E-Commerce application

Figure 7.17 shows an item in the users DynamoDB table.

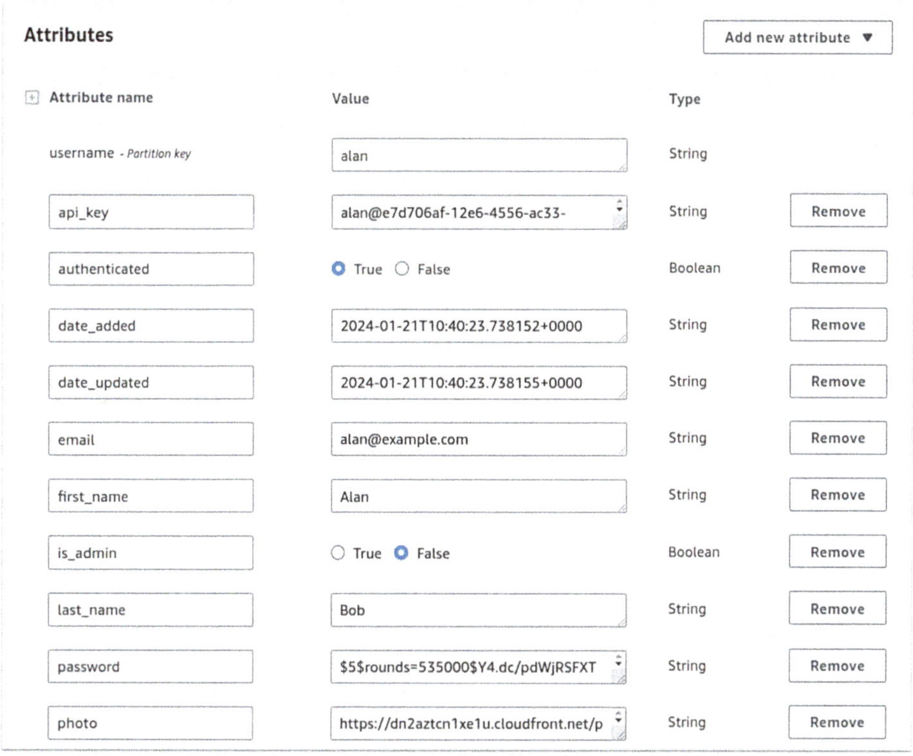

Figure 7.17: Users table in DynamoDB

Figure 7.18 shows an item in the products DynamoDB table.

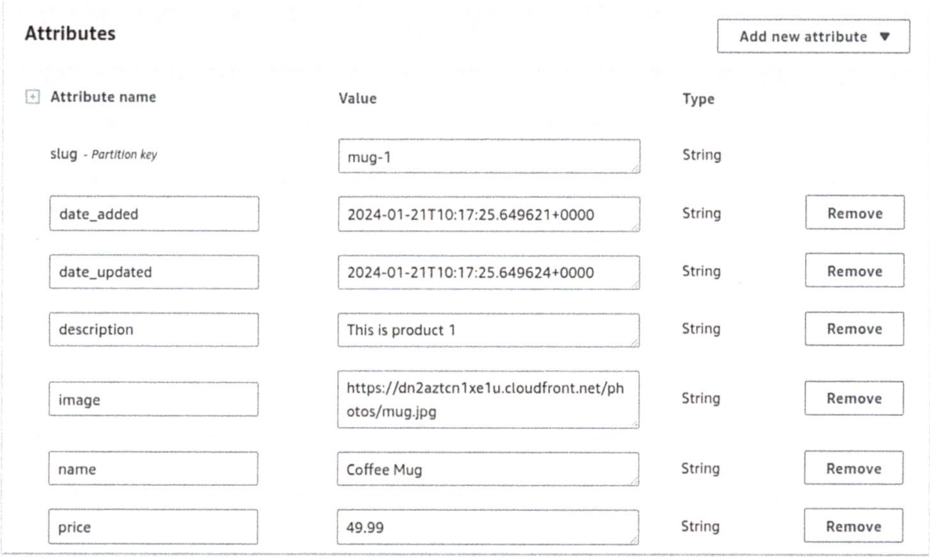

Figure 7.18: Products table in DynamoDB

Figure 7.19 shows an item in the orders DynamoDB table.

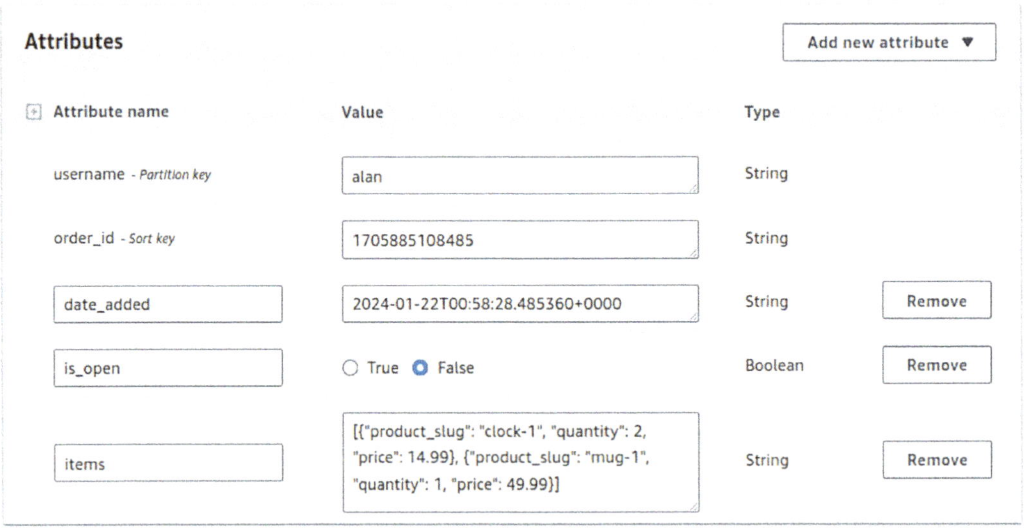

Figure 7.19: Orders table in DynamoDB

Figure 7.20 shows an item in the reviews DynamoDB table.

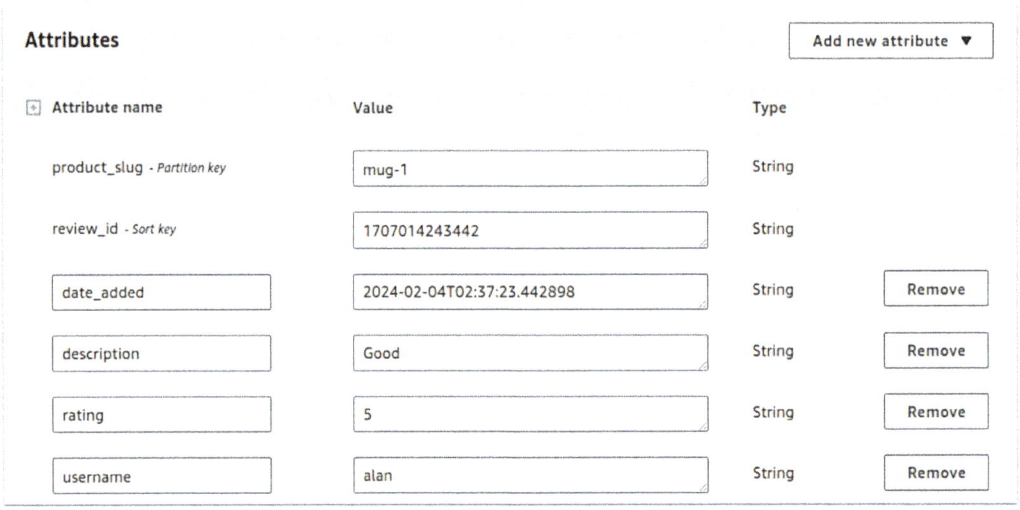

Figure 7.20: Reviews table in DynamoDB

7.7 Microservices App Using EC2, S3, CloudFront & DynamoDB

Box 7.6 shows the code of the frontend microservice configuration and API clients. It defines config variables like service URLs for user, product, order, and review microservices. Flask-Login is initialized for handling user sessions. It has classes like *UserClient*, *ProductClient*, *OrderClient*, and *ReviewClient* that call respective microservices APIs. For example, *UserClient* calls the user service to register and log in the user. When a user logs in, an API key is stored in a session to authenticate subsequent requests. Product service API is called to get all the products that are displayed on the home page. Order service API is called to get the user's order.

■ **Box 7.6: Frontend microservice configuration and API clients**

```
import os
import requests
from flask import Flask
from flask_migrate import Migrate
from flask import render_template, session
from flask redirect, url_for, flash, request, jsonify
from flask_login import current_user
from flask_wtf import FlaskForm
from wtforms import StringField, PasswordField
from wtforms import SubmitField, HiddenField, IntegerField
from wtforms.validators import DataRequired, Email
from flask_bootstrap import Bootstrap
from flask_login import LoginManager
from flask import session, request
import json


login_manager = LoginManager()
bootstrap = Bootstrap()

app = Flask(__name__, static_folder='static')
app.config['UPLOAD_FOLDER'] = 'static/images'
app.config['SECRET_KEY'] = "DoWgTDq87Kmne3TsCjNFabP"
app.config['WTF_CSRF_SECRET_KEY'] = "sEWQkE9oYBiF5fVJnm278i7"
app.config['ENV'] = "development"
app.config['DEBUG'] = True

USER_SERVICE_URL='http://localhost:5001'
PRODUCT_SERVICE_URL='http://localhost:5002'
ORDER_SERVICE_URL='http://localhost:5003'
REVIEW_SERVICE_URL='http://localhost:5004'

login_manager.init_app(app)
login_manager.login_message = "Please login"
login_manager.login_view = "login"

class UserClient:
    @staticmethod
    def post_login(form):
        api_key = False
        payload = {
```

```
                    'username': form.username.data,
                    'password': form.password.data
                }
            url = USER_SERVICE_URL+'/api/user/login'
            response = requests.request("POST", url=url, data=payload)
            if response:
                d = response.json()
                if d['user'] is not None:
                    user = d['user']
            return user

    @staticmethod
    def get_user():
        headers = {
            'Authorization': 'Basic ' + session['user_api_key']
        }
        url = USER_SERVICE_URL+'/api/user'
        response = requests.request(method="GET",
                        url=url, headers=headers)
        user = response.json()
        return user

    @staticmethod
    def get_user_with_username(username):
        response = requests.request(method="GET",
                url=USER_SERVICE_URL+'/api/user/' + str(username))
        user = response.json()
        return user

    @staticmethod
    def post_user_create(form):
        user = False
        payload = {
            'email': form.email.data,
            'password': form.password.data,
            'first_name': form.first_name.data,
            'last_name': form.last_name.data,
            'username': form.username.data
        }
        url = USER_SERVICE_URL+'/api/user/create'
        response = requests.request("POST", url=url, data=payload)
        if response:
            user = response.json()
        return user

    @staticmethod
    def does_exist(username):
        url = USER_SERVICE_URL+'/api/user/' + username + '/exists'
        response = requests.request("GET", url=url)
        return response.status_code == 200

class ProductClient:
    @staticmethod
    def get_products():
```

```
            r = requests.get(PRODUCT_SERVICE_URL+'/api/products')
            products = r.json()
            return products

    @staticmethod
    def get_product(slug):
        response = requests.request(method="GET",
                url=PRODUCT_SERVICE_URL+'/api/product/' + slug)
        product = response.json()
        return product

class OrderClient:
    @staticmethod
    def get_order():
        headers = {
            'Authorization': 'Basic ' + session['user_api_key']
        }
        url = ORDER_SERVICE_URL+'/api/order'
        response = requests.request(method="GET",
                            url=url, headers=headers)
        order = response.json()
        return order

    @staticmethod
    def post_add_to_cart(username, product_slug, price, qty=1):
        payload = {
            'username': username,
            'product_slug': product_slug,
            'qty': qty,
            'price': price
        }
        url = ORDER_SERVICE_URL+'/api/order/add-item'

        headers = {
            'Authorization': 'Basic ' + session['user_api_key']
        }
        response = requests.request("POST", url=url,
                        data=payload, headers=headers)
        if response:
            order = response.json()
            return order

    @staticmethod
    def post_checkout():
        url = ORDER_SERVICE_URL+'/api/order/checkout'

        headers = {
            'Authorization': 'Basic ' + session['user_api_key']
        }
        response = requests.request("POST", url=url,
                                headers=headers)
        order = response.json()
        return order
```

```python
    @staticmethod
    def get_order_from_session():
        default_order = {
            'items': {},
            'total': 0,
        }
        return session.get('order', default_order)

    @staticmethod
    def get_cart():
        headers = {
            'Authorization': 'Basic ' + session['user_api_key']
        }
        r = requests.get(ORDER_SERVICE_URL+'/api/cart',
                        headers=headers)
        products = r.json()
        return products

    @staticmethod
    def get_orders():
        headers = {
            'Authorization': 'Basic ' + session['user_api_key']
        }
        r = requests.get(ORDER_SERVICE_URL+'/api/orders',
                        headers=headers)
        orders = r.json()
        return orders

class ReviewClient:
    @staticmethod
    def post_review(username, product_slug, rating, review):
        payload = {
            'username': username,
            'product_slug': product_slug,
            'rating': rating,
            'review': review
        }
        url = REVIEW_SERVICE_URL+'/api/review/add'

        headers = {
            'Authorization': 'Basic ' + session['user_api_key']
        }
        response = requests.request("POST", url=url,
                    data=payload, headers=headers)
        if response:
            order = response.json()
            return order

    @staticmethod
    def get_reviews(product_slug):
        headers = {
            'Authorization': 'Basic ' + session['user_api_key']
        }
        r = requests.get(REVIEW_SERVICE_URL+'/api/reviews/'+
```

```
                                    str(product_slug), headers=headers)
        orders = r.json()
        return orders

@login_manager.user_loader
def load_user(user_id):
    return None

def get_user_name_photo():
    try:
        response = UserClient.get_user()
        user = response['result']
        user_name = user['first_name']+" "+user['last_name']
        user_photo = user['photo']
    except:
        user_name=''
        user_photo=''
    return user_name, user_photo
```

Box 7.7 shows the code of the Flask routes in the frontend service. The routes render templates to display pages like register, login, home, product, cart, and orders. Within the routes, the respective microservice APIs are called via client classes to fetch data.

■ Box 7.7: Frontend microservice routes

```
@app.route('/', methods=['GET'])
def home():
    if current_user.is_authenticated:
        session['order'] = OrderClient.get_order_from_session()
    try:
        products = ProductClient.get_products()
    except requests.exceptions.ConnectionError:
        products = {
            'results': []
        }
    user_name, user_photo = get_user_name_photo()
    return render_template('home.html', products=products,
        user_name = user_name, user_photo=user_photo)

@app.route('/register', methods=['GET', 'POST'])
def register():
    form = RegistrationForm(request.form)
    if request.method == "POST":
        if form.validate_on_submit():
            username = form.username.data
            user = UserClient.does_exist(username)
            if user:
                flash('Please try another username', 'error')
                return render_template('register/index.html', form=form)
            else:
                user = UserClient.post_user_create(form)
                if user:
                    flash('Please login', 'success')
```

```python
                            return redirect(url_for('login'))
            else:
                flash('Errors found', 'error')
        return render_template('register.html', form=form)

@app.route('/login', methods=['GET', 'POST'])
def login():
    if current_user.is_authenticated:
        return redirect(url_for('home'))
    form = LoginForm()
    if request.method == "POST":
        if form.validate_on_submit():
            user = UserClient.post_login(form)
            if user:
                session['user_api_key'] = user['api_key']
                session['user'] = user
                order = OrderClient.get_order()
                if order.get('result', False):
                    session['order'] = order['result']
                flash('Welcome back, ' + user['first_name'], 'success')
                return redirect(url_for('home'))
            else:
                flash('Cannot login', 'error')
        else:
            flash('Errors found', 'error')
    return render_template('login.html', form=form)

@app.route('/logout', methods=['GET'])
def logout():
    session.clear()
    return redirect(url_for('home'))

@app.route('/product/<slug>', methods=['GET', 'POST'])
def product(slug):
    response = ProductClient.get_product(slug)
    item = response['result']
    form = ItemForm(product_id=item['slug'])
    reviewslist=[]
    reviews=ReviewClient.get_reviews(item['slug'])
    for review in reviews['results']:
        try:
            reviewdict={}
            reviewdict['rating']=review['rating']
            reviewdict['description']=review['description']
            reviewdict['date_added']=review['date_added']
            reviewer=UserClient.get_user_with_username(review['username'])
            reviewdict['photo']=reviewer['result']['photo']
            reviewdict['user_name']=reviewer['result']['first_name']+' '+
                                    reviewer['result']['last_name']
            reviewslist.append(reviewdict)
        except:
            pass
    if request.method == "POST":
        if 'user' not in session:
```

```
                    flash('Please login', 'error')
                    return redirect(url_for('login'))
            order = OrderClient.post_add_to_cart(
                username=session['user']['username'],
                product_slug=item['slug'],
                price=item['price'], qty=1)
            session['order'] = order['result']
            flash('Item has been added to cart', 'success')

    user_name, user_photo = get_user_name_photo()
    return render_template('product.html', product=item,
        form=form, reviews=reviewslist,
        user_name = user_name, user_photo=user_photo)

@app.route('/checkout', methods=['GET'])
def summary():
    if 'user' not in session:
        flash('Please login', 'error')
        return redirect(url_for('login'))
    if 'order' not in session:
        flash('No order found', 'error')
        return redirect(url_for('home'))
    order = OrderClient.get_order()
    if len(order['result']['items']) == 0:
        flash('No order found', 'error')
        return redirect(url_for('home'))
    OrderClient.post_checkout()
    return redirect(url_for('thank_you'))

@app.route('/order/thank-you', methods=['GET'])
def thank_you():
    if 'user' not in session:
        flash('Please login', 'error')
        return redirect(url_for('login'))
    if 'order' not in session:
        flash('No order found', 'error')
        return redirect(url_for('home'))
    session.pop('order', None)
    flash('Thank you for your order', 'success')
    user_name, user_photo = get_user_name_photo()
    return render_template('thanks.html',
        user_name = user_name, user_photo=user_photo)

@app.route('/cart', methods=['GET'])
def cart():
    if 'user' not in session:
        flash('Please login', 'error')
        return redirect(url_for('login'))
    try:
        result = OrderClient.get_cart()
        products=result['result']
        productsInCart=[]
        totalamount=0
        for p in products:
```

```python
                resp = ProductClient.get_product(str(p['product_slug']))
                itemdict={}
                itemdict['quantity']=p['quantity']
                itemdict['name']=resp['result']['name']
                itemdict['description']=resp['result']['description']
                itemdict['slug']=resp['result']['slug']
                itemdict['price']=resp['result']['price']
                itemdict['image']=resp['result']['image']
                itemdict['total']=int(p['quantity'])*
                              float(resp['result']['price'])
                totalamount=totalamount+float(itemdict['total'])
                totalamount=round(totalamount,2)
                productsInCart.append(itemdict)
    except requests.exceptions.ConnectionError:
            productsInCart=[]
    user_name, user_photo = get_user_name_photo()
    return render_template('cart.html', products=productsInCart,
        totalamount=totalamount, user_name = user_name,
        user_photo=user_photo)

@app.route('/orders', methods=['GET'])
def orders():
    if 'user' not in session:
        flash('Please login', 'error')
        return redirect(url_for('login'))
    try:
        result = OrderClient.get_orders()
        orders=result['result']
        ordersPlaced=[]
        for p in orders:
            itemdict={}
            itemdict['itemscount']=len(p['items'])
            itemdict['date_added']=p['date_added']
            itemdict['id']=p['order_id']
            itemdict['amount']=p['amount']
            itemdict['productimages']=[]
            for q in p['items']:
                resp=ProductClient.get_product(q['product_slug'])
                itemdict['productimages'].append(resp['result']['image'])
            ordersPlaced.append(itemdict)
    except:
        ordersPlaced=[]
    user_name, user_photo = get_user_name_photo()
    return render_template('orders.html', orders=ordersPlaced,
        user_name = user_name, user_photo=user_photo)

@app.route('/postreview', methods=['POST'])
def postreview():
    ratinginput = request.form.get('ratinginput')
    reviewinput = request.form.get('reviewinput')
    productslug = request.form.get('productslug')
    response = UserClient.get_user()
    user = response['result']
    username = user['username']
```

```
    ReviewClient.post_review(username, productslug,
                ratinginput, reviewinput)
    flash('Thank you for your review', 'success')
    return redirect('/product/'+productslug)

if __name__ == '__main__':
    app.run(host='0.0.0.0', port=5000)
```

Box 7.8 shows the code of the user service. It uses Amazon S3, CloudFront, and DynamoDB to store and serve user data and profile images. The app configures S3, CloudFront, and DynamoDB credentials and settings. It defines a User model that maps to a DynamoDB table using the PynamoDB library. PynamoDB handles the DynamoDB functionality like creating tables, constructing query parameters, serializing objects, etc. When a new user registers, their password is hashed using *sha256_crypt* and a random avatar image is generated locally using the *avinit* library. This image file is then uploaded to an Amazon S3 bucket using the *boto3* SDK. The S3 URL for this image file is returned by the *s3uploading* function. The user data (including hashed passwords, usernames, and photo URL) is saved in a DynamoDB table using PynamoDB.

▪ Box 7.8: User microservice

```
import os
from flask import Flask, send_from_directory, send_file
from flask_login import LoginManager
from datetime import datetime
from flask_login import UserMixin
from passlib.hash import sha256_crypt
from flask import make_response, request, jsonify
from flask_login import current_user
from flask_login import login_user, logout_user, login_required
from passlib.hash import sha256_crypt
from flask import g
from flask.sessions import SecureCookieSessionInterface
from flask_login import user_loaded_from_header
import time, random
import avinit
import base64
import boto3
from boto3.session import Session
from pynamodb.models import Model
from pynamodb.attributes import UnicodeAttribute, NumberAttribute
from pynamodb.attributes import BooleanAttribute, UTCDateTimeAttribute
from pynamodb.connection import Connection
import uuid

login_manager = LoginManager()
basedir = os.path.abspath(os.path.dirname(__file__))

app = Flask(__name__)
app.config['AWS_ACCESS_KEY'] = 'EXAMPLEKEY'
app.config['AWS_SECRET_KEY'] = 'EXAMPLESECRET'
```

```python
app.config['REGION'] = 'us-west-2'
app.config['SECRET_KEY'] = "DoWgTDq87Kmne3TsCjNFabP"
app.config['BUCKET_NAME'] = 'microservices-ecommerce-app'
app.config['CLOUDFRONT_URL'] = 'https://dn2avtdn1xu.cloudfront.net'
app.config['ENV'] = "development"
app.config['DEBUG'] = True
app.config['SQLALCHEMY_ECHO'] = True
app.config['UPLOAD_FOLDER'] = 'uploads'

login_manager.init_app(app)

class User(Model):
    class Meta:
        table_name = "users1"
        region = "us-west-2"
        aws_access_key_id = app.config['AWS_ACCESS_KEY']
        aws_secret_access_key = app.config['AWS_SECRET_KEY']

    username = UnicodeAttribute(hash_key=True)
    email = UnicodeAttribute()
    first_name = UnicodeAttribute()
    last_name = UnicodeAttribute()
    password = UnicodeAttribute()
    photo = UnicodeAttribute()
    is_admin = BooleanAttribute()
    authenticated = BooleanAttribute()
    api_key = UnicodeAttribute()
    date_added = UTCDateTimeAttribute(default=datetime.utcnow)
    date_updated = UTCDateTimeAttribute()

    def encode_api_key(self):
        self.api_key = self.username+'@'+str(uuid.uuid4())

    def encode_password(self):
        self.password = sha256_crypt.hash(self.password)

    def __repr__(self):
        return '<User %r>' % (self.username)

    def is_active(self):
        return True

    def is_authenticated(self):
        return True

    def is_anonymous(self):
        return False

    def get_id(self):
        return str(self.username)

    def to_json(self):
        return {
            'first_name': self.first_name,
```

```
            'last_name': self.last_name,
            'username': self.username,
            'email': self.email,
            'photo': self.photo,
            'api_key': self.api_key,
            'is_active': True,
            'is_admin': self.is_admin
        }

# Create the DynamoDB table if needed
if not User.exists():
    User.create_table(read_capacity_units=1,
                write_capacity_units=1, wait=True)

@login_manager.user_loader
def load_user(user_id):
    return User.get(user_id)

@login_manager.unauthorized_handler
def unauthorized():
    return "Unauthorized", 401


@login_manager.request_loader
def load_user_from_request(request):
    api_key = request.headers.get('Authorization')
    if api_key:
        api_key = api_key.replace('Basic ', '', 1)
        splitkey = api_key.split('@')
        try:
            user = User.get(splitkey[0])
            if user.api_key==api_key:
                return user
        except:
            return None
    return None

def s3uploading(filename):
    s3 = boto3.client('s3',
        aws_access_key_id=app.config['AWS_ACCESS_KEY'],
        aws_secret_access_key=app.config['AWS_SECRET_KEY'])
    bucket = app.config['BUCKET_NAME']
    path_filename_disk = os.path.join(app.config['UPLOAD_FOLDER'],
                                    filename)
    path_filename_s3 = "photos/" + filename
    s3.upload_file(path_filename_disk, bucket, path_filename_s3)
    url = app.config['CLOUDFRONT_URL']+'/'+path_filename_s3
    return url

@app.route('/api/user/create', methods=['POST'])
def post_register():
    first_name = request.form['first_name']
    last_name = request.form['last_name']
    email = request.form['email']
```

```
    username = request.form['username']
    password = sha256_crypt.hash((str(request.form['password'])))
    name=first_name+' '+ last_name
    filename = "user"+str(int(time.time()*1000))+".png"
    imgpath=os.path.join(app.config['UPLOAD_FOLDER'], filename)
    r = lambda: random.randint(0,255)
    colors=[]
    colors.append('#%02X%02X%02X' % (r(),r(),r()))
    avinit.get_png_avatar(name, output_file=imgpath, colors=colors)
    uploadedFileURL = s3uploading(filename)
    # Create new user
    user = User(
        username = username,
        email = email,
        first_name = first_name,
        last_name = last_name,
        password = password,
        photo = uploadedFileURL,
        is_admin = False,
        authenticated = True,
        api_key = '',
        date_added = datetime.utcnow(),
        date_updated = datetime.utcnow()
    )
    # Save to DynamoDB
    user.save()
    response = jsonify({'message': 'User added',
                'result': user.to_json()})
    return response

@app.route('/api/user/login', methods=['POST'])
def post_login():
    username = request.form['username']
    try:
        user = User.get(username)
    except:
        return make_response(jsonify({'message': 'Not found'}), 401)
    if user:
        if sha256_crypt.verify(str(request.form['password']),
                            user.password):
            user.encode_api_key()
            user.save()
            login_user(user)
            return make_response(jsonify({'message': 'Logged in',
                            'user': user.to_json()}))
    return make_response(jsonify({'message': 'Not logged in'}), 401)

@app.route('/api/user/logout', methods=['POST'])
def post_logout():
    if current_user.is_authenticated:
        logout_user()
        return make_response(jsonify({'message': 'You are logged out'}))
    return make_response(jsonify({'message': 'You are not logged in'}))
```

```
@app.route('/api/user/<username>/exists', methods=['GET'])
def get_username(username):
    try:
        item = User.get(username)
    except:
        return make_response(jsonify({'message': 'Not found'}), 401)
    if item is not None:
        response = jsonify({'result': True})
    else:
        response = jsonify({'message': 'Cannot find username'}), 404
    return response

@login_required
@app.route('/api/user', methods=['GET'])
def get_user():
    if current_user.is_authenticated:
        return make_response(jsonify({'result': current_user.to_json()}))

    return make_response(jsonify({'message': 'Not logged in'})), 401

@app.route('/api/user/<username>', methods=['GET'])
def userid(username):
    try:
        item = User.get(username)
    except DoesNotExist:
        return make_response(jsonify({'message': 'Not found'}), 401)

    if item is not None:
        response = jsonify({'result': item.to_json()})
    else:
        response = jsonify({'message': 'Cannot find user'}), 404
    return response

@app.route('/uploads/<filename>')
def uploaded_file(filename):
    return send_from_directory(app.config['UPLOAD_FOLDER'], filename)

@user_loaded_from_header.connect
def user_loaded_from_header(self, user=None):
    g.login_via_header = True

if __name__ == '__main__':
    app.run(host='0.0.0.0', port=5001)
```

Box 7.9 shows the code of the product service. It uses Amazon S3, CloudFront, and DynamoDB to store and serve product images and data. The Product model has attributes like name, description, price, and product image. When a new product is created via the *api/product/create* endpoint, it accepts the product data and saves an image file uploaded to the server. It uploads the image to an S3 bucket using *boto3* and generates a public URL via CloudFront. The image URL is saved in the Product model along with other data. The model is saved to DynamoDB using PynamoDB. When retrieving a product via *api/product/<slug>*, it queries DynamoDB to get the product data including the CloudFront image URL. This allows serving dynamic product data from a managed NoSQL database while storing images in S3 and serving them via CloudFront for fast access. The code implements best practices like using secure filenames, separating configuration, validating user input, and handling errors. The core domain logic is separated from the persistence and file storage mechanisms for maintainability.

■ **Box 7.9: Product microservice**

```python
import os
from flask import Flask, send_from_directory
from flask_migrate import Migrate
from flask import jsonify, request
from datetime import datetime
from werkzeug.utils import secure_filename
import base64
import boto3
from pynamodb.models import Model
from pynamodb.attributes import UnicodeAttribute, NumberAttribute
from pynamodb.attributes import BooleanAttribute, UTCDateTimeAttribute
from pynamodb.connection import Connection
import uuid

basedir = os.path.abspath(os.path.dirname(__file__))


app = Flask(__name__)
app.config['SECRET_KEY'] = "DoWgTDq87Kmne3TsCjNFabP"
app.config['BUCKET_NAME'] = 'microservices-ecommerce-app'
app.config['CLOUDFRONT_URL'] = 'https://dn2avtdn1xu.cloudfront.net'
app.config['AWS_ACCESS_KEY'] = 'EXAMPLEKEY'
app.config['AWS_SECRET_KEY'] = 'EXAMPLESECRET'
app.config['ENV'] = "development"
app.config['DEBUG'] = True
app.config['UPLOAD_FOLDER'] = 'uploads'

class Product(Model):
    class Meta:
        table_name = "products"
        region = "us-west-2"
        aws_access_key_id = app.config['AWS_ACCESS_KEY']
        aws_secret_access_key = app.config['AWS_SECRET_KEY']
    slug = UnicodeAttribute(hash_key=True)
    name = UnicodeAttribute()
    description = UnicodeAttribute()
    image = UnicodeAttribute()
    price = UnicodeAttribute()
    date_added = UTCDateTimeAttribute(default=datetime.utcnow)
    date_updated = UTCDateTimeAttribute()

    def to_json(self):
        return {
            'slug': self.slug,
            'name': self.name,
            'description': self.description,
            'price': self.price,
```

```
                   'image': self.image
         }

# Create the DynamoDB table if needed
if not Product.exists():
    Product.create_table(read_capacity_units=1,
             write_capacity_units=1, wait=True)

def s3uploading(filename):
    s3 = boto3.client('s3',
        aws_access_key_id=app.config['AWS_ACCESS_KEY'],
        aws_secret_access_key=app.config['AWS_SECRET_KEY'])
    bucket = app.config['BUCKET_NAME']
    path_filename_disk = os.path.join(app.config['UPLOAD_FOLDER'],
                              filename)
    path_filename_s3 = "photos/" + filename
    s3.upload_file(path_filename_disk, bucket, path_filename_s3)
    url = app.config['CLOUDFRONT_URL']+'/'/'+path_filename_s3
    return url

@app.route('/api/products', methods=['GET'])
def products():
    # Scan with limit of max 50 items
    products = Product.scan()
    items = []
    for item in products:
        items.append(item.to_json())
    return jsonify({
        "results": items
    })

@app.route('/api/product/create', methods=['POST'])
def post_create():
    name = request.form.get('name')
    slug = request.form.get('slug')
    description = request.form.get('description')
    price = request.form.get('price')
    image = request.files.get('image')
    filename = secure_filename(image.filename)
    image.save(os.path.join(app.config['UPLOAD_FOLDER'], filename))
    uploadedFileURL = s3uploading(filename)
    # Create new user
    item = Product(
        slug = slug,
        name = name,
        image = uploadedFileURL,
        price = price,
        description = description,
        date_added = datetime.utcnow(),
        date_updated = datetime.utcnow()
    )
    # Save to DynamoDB
    item.save()
    response = jsonify({'message': 'Product added',
```

```
                         'product': item.to_json()})
    return response

@app.route('/api/product/<slug>', methods=['GET'])
def product(slug):
    try:
        item = Product.get(slug)
    except:
        response = jsonify({'message': 'Product not found'}), 404
    if item is not None:
        response = jsonify({'result': item.to_json()})
    else:
        response = jsonify({'message': 'Product not found'}), 404
    return response

@app.route('/uploads/<filename>')
def uploaded_file(filename):
    return send_from_directory(app.config['UPLOAD_FOLDER'],
                               filename)

if __name__ == '__main__':
    app.run(host='0.0.0.0', port=5002)
```

Box 7.10 shows the code for the order service. It uses Flask to create APIs for adding items to an order, getting open orders, checking out orders, getting the cart, and getting all orders. Orders are stored in a DynamoDB table. The Order model defines the schema with *username* as the hash key and *order_id* as the range key. Additional attributes track whether the order is open, the JSON encoded list of items, and the order date. When adding items, it first checks if there is an existing open order for that user. If not, it creates a new order. It then adds the item to the list or increments the quantity if it already exists. To get the open order, it scans for orders with that username and checks if the order status is open (*is_open=True*). On checkout, it finds the open order and sets *is_open* to False to close it. The cart returns the open order's items. The */api/orders* endpoint returns all non-open orders.

■ Box 7.10: Order microservice

```
import os
from flask import Flask
from flask_migrate import Migrate
from flask import jsonify, request, make_response
from flask import Flask
from flask_sqlalchemy import SQLAlchemy
from datetime import datetime
import requests
import boto3
from pynamodb.models import Model
from pynamodb.attributes import UnicodeAttribute, NumberAttribute
from pynamodb.attributes import BooleanAttribute, UTCDateTimeAttribute
from pynamodb.connection import Connection
import uuid
import json
```

```
import time

basedir = os.path.abspath(os.path.dirname(__file__))

app = Flask(__name__)
app.config['SECRET_KEY'] = "DoWgTDq87Kmne3TsCjNFabP"
app.config['BUCKET_NAME'] = 'microservices-ecommerce-app'
app.config['CLOUDFRONT_URL'] = 'https://dn2avtdn1xu.cloudfront.net'
app.config['AWS_ACCESS_KEY'] = 'EXAMPLEKEY'
app.config['AWS_SECRET_KEY'] = 'EXAMPLESECRET'
app.config['ENV'] = "development"
app.config['DEBUG'] = True
USER_SERVICE_URL='http://localhost:5001'

class Order(Model):
    class Meta:
        table_name = "ordersn"
        region = "us-west-2"
        aws_access_key_id = app.config['AWS_ACCESS_KEY']
        aws_secret_access_key = app.config['AWS_SECRET_KEY']
    username = UnicodeAttribute(hash_key=True)
    order_id = UnicodeAttribute(range_key=True)
    is_open = BooleanAttribute()
    items = UnicodeAttribute()
    date_added = UTCDateTimeAttribute(default=datetime.utcnow)

    def to_json(self):
        items = []
        amount=0
        for i in json.loads(self.items):
            items.append(i)
            amount=amount+float(i['price'])*float(i['quantity'])
            amount=round(amount,2)

        return {
            'items': items,
            'order_id': self.order_id,
            'is_open': self.is_open,
            'username': self.username,
            'date_added': self.date_added.strftime("%b %d, %Y"),
            'amount': amount
        }

# Create the DynamoDB table if needed
if not Order.exists():
    Order.create_table(read_capacity_units=1,
            write_capacity_units=1, wait=True)

class UserClient:
    @staticmethod
    def get_user(api_key):
        headers = {
            'Authorization': api_key
        }
```

```
        response = requests.request(method="GET",
                    url=USER_SERVICE_URL+'/api/user', headers=headers)
        if response.status_code == 401:
            return False
        user = response.json()
        return user

@app.route('/api/order/add-item', methods=['POST'])
def order_add_item():
    api_key = request.headers.get('Authorization')
    response = UserClient.get_user(api_key)
    if not response:
        return make_response(jsonify({'message': 'Not logged in'}), 401)
    user = response['result']
    product_slug = request.form['product_slug']
    qty = int(request.form['qty'])
    price = float(request.form['price'])
    username = user['username']
    orders = Order.scan(Order.username.startswith(username))
    known_order=None
    if orders is None:
        response = jsonify({'message': 'No order found',
                            'result': []})
    else:
        items=[]
        for order in orders:
            if order.is_open==True:
                known_order=order
    if known_order is None:
        itemslist=[]
        order_id=str(int(time.time()*1000))
        known_order = Order(
            username = username,
            order_id=order_id,
            is_open = True,
            date_added = datetime.utcnow()
        )
        itemslist.append({'product_slug': product_slug,
                        'quantity': qty, 'price': price})
        known_order.items=json.dumps(itemslist)
    else:
        found = False
        itemslist=json.loads(known_order.items)
        newitemslist=[]
        for item in itemslist:
            if item['product_slug'] == product_slug:
                found = True
                item['quantity'] = int(item['quantity'])+qty
            newitemslist.append(item)
        if found is False:
            newitemslist.append({'product_slug': product_slug,
                            'quantity': qty, 'price': price})
        known_order.items=json.dumps(newitemslist)
    known_order.save()
```

```
        response = jsonify({'result': known_order.to_json()})
        return response


@app.route('/api/order', methods=['GET'])
def order():
    api_key = request.headers.get('Authorization')
    response = UserClient.get_user(api_key)
    if not response:
        return make_response(jsonify({'message': 'Not logged in'}), 401)
    user = response['result']
    orders = Order.scan(Order.username.startswith(user['username']))
    open_order=None
    for order in orders:
        if order.is_open==True:
            open_order=order
    if open_order is None:
        response = jsonify({'message': 'No order found'})
    else:
        response = jsonify({'result': open_order.to_json()})
    return response


@app.route('/api/order/checkout', methods=['POST'])
def checkout():
    api_key = request.headers.get('Authorization')
    response = UserClient.get_user(api_key)
    if not response:
        return make_response(jsonify({'message': 'Not logged in'}), 401)
    user = response['result']
    orders = Order.scan(Order.username.startswith(user['username']))
    open_order=None
    for order in orders:
        if order.is_open==True:
            open_order=order
            open_order.is_open=False
            open_order.save()
    response = jsonify({'result': open_order.to_json()})
    return response

@app.route('/api/cart', methods=['GET'])
def cart():
    api_key = request.headers.get('Authorization')
    response = UserClient.get_user(api_key)
    if not response:
        return make_response(jsonify({'message': 'Not logged in'}), 401)
    user = response['result']
    orders = Order.scan(Order.username.startswith(user['username']))
    if orders is None:
        response = jsonify({'message': 'No order found', 'result': []})
    else:
        items=[]
        orderitems=[]
        for order in orders:
```

```
            if order.is_open==True:
                orderitems=order.to_json()['items']
        response = jsonify({'result': orderitems})
    return response


@app.route('/api/orders', methods=['GET'])
def orders():
    api_key = request.headers.get('Authorization')
    response = UserClient.get_user(api_key)
    if not response:
        return make_response(jsonify({'message': 'Not logged in'}), 401)
    user = response['result']
    orders = Order.scan(Order.username.startswith(user['username']))
    if orders is None:
        response = jsonify({'message': 'No order found', 'result': []})
    else:
        items=[]
        for order in orders:
            if order.is_open==False:
                items.append(order.to_json())
        response = jsonify({'result': items})
    return response


if __name__ == '__main__':
    app.run(host='0.0.0.0', port=5003)
```

Box 7.11 shows the code of the review service. It implements APIs for adding and retrieving product reviews. A Review data model is defined using the PynamoDB ORM. It maps Review objects to a DynamoDB table. The attributes like *product_slug*, *username*, *rating*, and *description* are mapped to DynamoDB attributes. The */api/review/add* endpoint allows adding a new review by taking in parameters like *username*, *product_slug*, *rating*, and *description* from the request and creating a new Review object to save to DynamoDB. The */api/reviews/<product_slug>* endpoint retrieves reviews for a product by querying the Review table on the *product_slug* hash key. The matching review items are returned as JSON.

■ **Box 7.11: Review microservice**

```
import os
from flask import Flask, send_from_directory
from flask_migrate import Migrate
from flask import jsonify, request
from datetime import datetime
from flask_migrate import Migrate
from werkzeug.utils import secure_filename
import boto3
from pynamodb.models import Model
from pynamodb.attributes import UnicodeAttribute, NumberAttribute
from pynamodb.attributes import BooleanAttribute, UTCDateTimeAttribute
from pynamodb.connection import Connection
import uuid

basedir = os.path.abspath(os.path.dirname(__file__))
```

```
app = Flask(__name__)
app.config['SECRET_KEY'] = "DoWgTDq87Kmne3TsCjNFabP"
app.config['BUCKET_NAME'] = 'microservices-ecommerce-app'
app.config['CLOUDFRONT_URL'] = 'https://dn2avtdn1xu.cloudfront.net'
app.config['AWS_ACCESS_KEY'] = 'EXAMPLEKEY'
app.config['AWS_SECRET_KEY'] = 'EXAMPLESECRET'
app.config['ENV'] = "development"
app.config['DEBUG'] = True
app.config['UPLOAD_FOLDER'] = 'uploads'

class Review(Model):
    class Meta:
        table_name = "reviews"
        region = "us-west-2"
        aws_access_key_id = app.config['AWS_ACCESS_KEY']
        aws_secret_access_key = app.config['AWS_SECRET_KEY']

    product_slug = UnicodeAttribute(hash_key=True)
    review_id = UnicodeAttribute(range_key=True)
    username = UnicodeAttribute()
    description = UnicodeAttribute()
    rating = UnicodeAttribute()
    date_added = UTCDateTimeAttribute(default=datetime.utcnow)
    date_updated = UTCDateTimeAttribute()

    def to_json(self):
        return {
            'username': self.username,
            'product_slug': self.product_slug,
            'review_id': self.review_id,
            'rating': self.rating,
            'description': self.description,
            'date_added': self.date_added.strftime("%b %d, %Y")
        }

# Create the DynamoDB table if needed
if not Review.exists():
    Review.create_table(read_capacity_units=1,
        write_capacity_units=1, wait=True)

@app.route('/api/review/add', methods=['POST'])
def post_create():
    username = request.form.get('username')
    product_slug = request.form.get('product_slug')
    rating = request.form.get('rating')
    description = request.form.get('review')
    review_id=str(int(time.time()*1000))
    # Create new review
    item = Review(
        product_slug = product_slug,
        review_id = review_id,
        username = username,
        rating = rating,
```

```
            description = description,
            date_added = datetime.utcnow(),
            date_updated = datetime.utcnow()
        )
    item.save()

    response = jsonify({'message': 'Review added',
                    'review': item.to_json()})
    return response

@app.route('/api/reviews/<product_slug>', methods=['GET'])
def reviews(product_slug):
    reviews = Review.scan(Review.product_slug.startswith(product_slug))
    items = []
    for item in reviews:
        items.append(item.to_json())
    return jsonify({
        "results": items
    })

if __name__ == '__main__':
    app.run(host='0.0.0.0', port=5004)
```

Summary

In this chapter, we covered improvements for the initial E-commerce microservices application to leverage AWS services like S3, CloudFront, RDS, and DynamoDB. We first presented an architecture using S3 for file storage, CloudFront CDN for fast file delivery, and RDS MySQL for the database backend. We explained how S3 provides highly durable and scalable object storage for files like user photos and product images. We described how CloudFront accelerates delivery of these static assets using edge caching worldwide. We discussed how RDS automates database administration tasks allowing developers to focus on the application logic instead. We then walked through the steps for creating an S3 bucket, setting its access policy to public, and enabling static website hosting. We explained how to create a CloudFront distribution using the S3 bucket as the origin source. We described how to launch an RDS MySQL instance, configure its security group for private access, and connect to it programmatically using Flask-SQLAlchemy. Next, we covered an alternative architecture using S3, CloudFront, and DynamoDB instead of RDS. We explained the benefits of DynamoDB like flexible schemas, high scalability, low latency, and serverless nature compared to limitations of relational databases. We presented the steps for creating tables, defining models, and performing CRUD operations using the PynamoDB library to map the domain objects to DynamoDB. We provided source code snippets demonstrating integration with S3, CloudFront, RDS, and DynamoDB in the microservices.

8

CONTAINERIZING MICROSERVICES WITH DOCKER, ECR AND ECS

THIS CHAPTER COVERS

- Virtualization vs Containerization
- Docker Overview
- Containerizing Microservices Application with Docker
- Deploying Containerized Microservices Application on AWS

8.1   Introduction

Containerization has revolutionized the way modern applications are developed and deployed. Unlike virtual machines, which virtualize the hardware layer, containers virtualize the operating system, allowing multiple isolated user-space instances to run on a single host. This provides a lightweight and portable encapsulation of an application and its dependencies into a single unit.

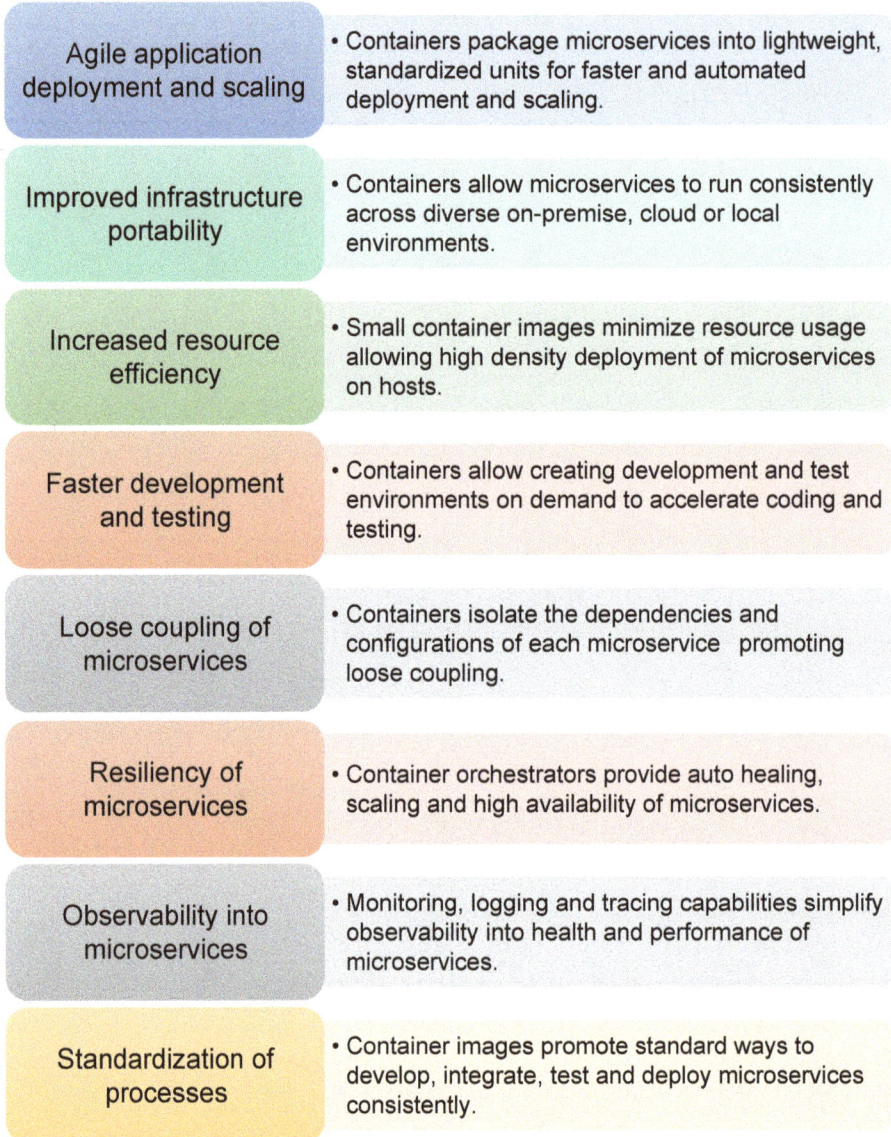

Agile application deployment and scaling	• Containers package microservices into lightweight, standardized units for faster and automated deployment and scaling.
Improved infrastructure portability	• Containers allow microservices to run consistently across diverse on-premise, cloud or local environments.
Increased resource efficiency	• Small container images minimize resource usage allowing high density deployment of microservices on hosts.
Faster development and testing	• Containers allow creating development and test environments on demand to accelerate coding and testing.
Loose coupling of microservices	• Containers isolate the dependencies and configurations of each microservice promoting loose coupling.
Resiliency of microservices	• Container orchestrators provide auto healing, scaling and high availability of microservices.
Observability into microservices	• Monitoring, logging and tracing capabilities simplify observability into health and performance of microservices.
Standardization of processes	• Container images promote standard ways to develop, integrate, test and deploy microservices consistently.

Figure 8.1: Benefits of containerization for microservices

Containers have become an essential technology for deploying microservices. Microservices architecture structures an application as a collection of loosely coupled services. Each service implements specific business capabilities and can be independently developed, tested, deployed, and scaled. Containers enable packing each microservice into a standardized unit along with its dependencies and configuration. In a microservices architecture, each microservice is packaged into a container image along with configuration files and dependencies.

Figure 8.1 shows the key benefits of containerization for microservices. Containerization enables packing microservices into lightweight, standardized, and portable images that simplify deployment and orchestration. Containers provide isolated environments for securely running microservices and give flexibility to deploy across diverse infrastructures. By leveraging containers, organizations can accelerate development of reliable and scalable microservices applications.

8.2 Virtualization vs Containerization

Virtualization and containerization are two different approaches to running applications in isolated environments. Figure 8.2 shows a comparison of a virtual machine and container.

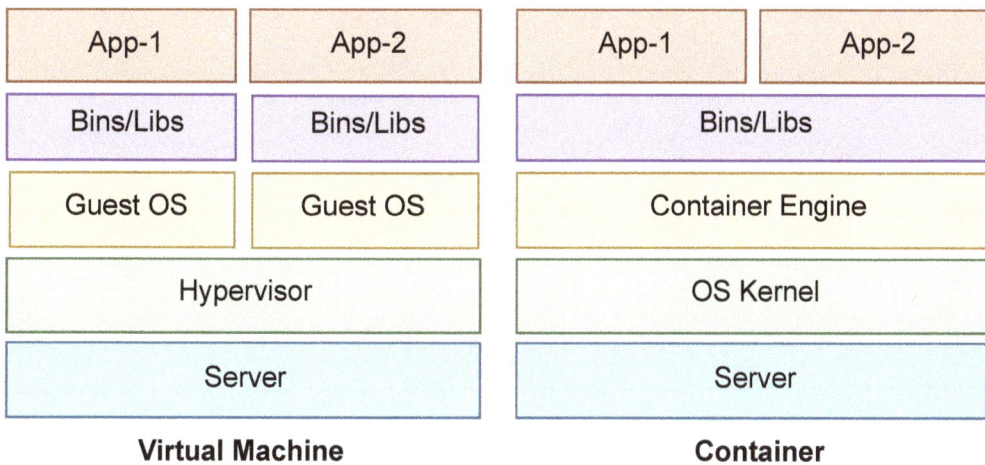

Figure 8.2: Virtual Machine versus Container

A virtual machine runs on a physical server hardware that hosts the virtual machine. This provides the CPU, memory, and storage. A hypervisor layer is used to emulate hardware and allow multiple guest operating systems to run. Virtual machines include a full guest operating system with kernels, binaries, and libraries that run inside the guest OS to support applications. A container runs on a physical or virtual server that hosts the containers. Containers do not emulate hardware or need a hypervisor. Containers share the host OS kernel and only package the necessary libraries and binaries. Container engine is a software that creates and manages containers, e.g. Docker. The binaries and libraries are packaged inside the container image. Only libraries needed by the apps are included. The key difference is containers leverage the host OS kernel instead of virtualizing hardware like VMs. This makes containers more lightweight and portable.

Figure 8.3 shows a comparison of virtualization and containerization. Virtualization provides abstraction of physical hardware into virtual machines. A hypervisor allows multiple VMs to run on a single server. Each VM includes a full operating system, libraries, binaries,

	Virtualization	Containerization
Virtualizes	Hardware resources like CPU, memory, storage, networking	Operating system kernel to isolate user space instances
Isolation Level	Strong isolation boundary provided by hypervisor. VMs are completely isolated.	Weak isolation as containers share same kernel. Use namespaces, cgroups for isolation.
Overhead	High - VMs require full guest operating system to be installed increasing storage and memory needs.	Low - Containers directly use host OS kernel, share binaries and libraries.
Boot Time	Slow boot time due to booting up complete guest OS.	Fast boot time as no OS boot required.
Portability	Limited portability between environments due to dependency on hypervisor and hardware.	Highly portable as can run on any system with container runtime.
Scalability	Slow and manual process to scale up/down VMs. Boot time limits rapid scaling.	Fast and automated scaling of containers using orchestration platforms.
Microservices Suitability	Low due to high overhead, resource needs. Limits density Slow scaling.	High density deployment. Fast deployment and scaling aligns to microservices.
Security	Strong isolation provides high security.	Weak isolation through namespaces and cgroups provides lower security.
Use Cases	Long running apps, apps with strong security needs.	Agile and portable applications like microservices.

Figure 8.3: Virtualization versus Containerization

and application code. VMs provide complete isolation and strong security boundaries between workloads. However, they tend to be heavyweight, requiring substantial resources.

In contrast, containerization provides operating system-level virtualization by isolating user space instances. Containers package up just the application code, configurations, and dependencies. The container runtime engine runs on the host OS and shares the OS kernel with other containers. This makes containers extremely lightweight and portable. However, containers provide weaker isolation than VMs.

The following characteristics of containerization make containers better suited than VMs for deploying microservices architectures:

- **Speed and density**: Containers have very fast startup times and low resource footprint allowing high-density deployment of microservices. Many containers can run on a host.
- **Agility**: Containerized microservices can be quickly orchestrated and reconfigured for agile development and deployment.
- **Portability**: Containers can run consistently across on-premises and cloud environments due to standardized runtimes.

- **Scalability**: Microservices in containers can be rapidly scaled up/down to handle bursty traffic patterns, improving resource utilization.
- **Availability**: Orchestrators like Kubernetes can be used to restart failed containers and reschedule workloads for high availability.
- **Observability**: Container orchestrators provide health checks, logging, and monitoring for microservices visibility.
- **Loose coupling**: Containers isolate dependencies of each microservice, enabling loose coupling between services.
- **Developer productivity**: Containers provide local development environments that closely match production for faster coding.

In contrast, VMs would add overhead, slow down deployment cycles, and reduce portability of microservices across environments. The lightweight nature of containers makes them ideal for componentizing microservices applications.

However, containers may not provide adequate isolation for untrusted workloads or highly sensitive data. VMs would be better suited in those cases though at the cost of reduced agility and scalability. For most microservices use cases, containers provide the right blend of agility and isolation.

8.3 Docker Overview

Docker is an open-source platform for developing, shipping, and running applications inside containers. Containers allow developers to package an application with all its dependencies into a standardized unit that can run consistently on any infrastructure. Docker provides capabilities to build and manage containers, enabling portability across environments and easier scaling.

Docker has revolutionized software development and IT operations by bringing concepts from Linux container technology to create lightweight, portable application environments. It has become a hugely popular platform for automating the deployment, scaling, and management of containerized applications. Figure 8.4 shows the key benefits of using Docker for microservices.

8.3.1 Docker Architecture

Docker utilizes a client-server architecture to build, run, and manage containers. Figure 8.5 shows the Docker architecture and how the various components of Docker interact. The Docker Client is a command-line tool that allows users to interact with the Docker daemon or engine. The Docker daemon runs as a background service on Docker hosts and is responsible for building container images, running containers, and distributing workloads across a cluster.

Docker hosts are the physical or virtual machines that run the Docker daemon and containers. Containers are isolated runtime environments where applications run with their dependencies packaged inside. Images are read-only templates that containers are launched from. Images are made up of layered filesystems that share common files to optimize storage and image transfers.

Benefit	Description
Portability	Docker containers can run consistently across different operating systems and cloud platforms. Avoid vendor and technology lock-in.
Agile Deployment	Containers are lightweight and fast to deploy compared to VMs. Launch new instances quickly.
Developer Productivity	Reuse images to get started faster. Standard components improve efficiency.
Isolation	Containers provide isolated environments for applications. Ideal for multi-tenant environments.
Resource Optimization	Containers are lightweight and minimize resource usage compared to VMs. Higher density.
Scalability	Easy to scale horizontally by spinning up new containers quickly.
Microservices	Well suited for building applications using microservices architecture.
Security	Isolation and namespaces reduce attack surface. Image verification improves security.
Faster Time to Market	Streamlines development, testing and deployment. Enables CI/CD.
Consistent Environment	Containers provide the same environment across the pipeline.
Cloud and OS Portability	Applications are portable across different operating systems and cloud platforms.

Figure 8.4: Benefits of Docker for microservices

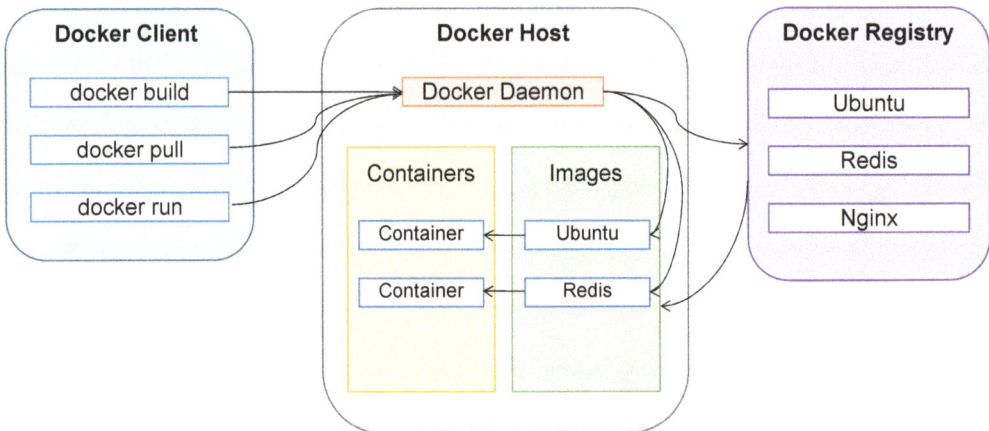

Figure 8.5: Docker architecture

Docker registries are repositories for storing and distributing images. Docker Hub is the default public registry, but private registries can also be deployed for internal use. Images are pushed to and pulled from registries by the Docker daemon when instructed by Docker clients.

Component	Description
Docker Client	CLI tool to interact with Docker daemon to build, run and manage Docker objects like containers, images, networks.
Docker Daemon	Background service that runs on Docker hosts to build, run and distribute containers.
Docker Host	Physical or virtual machine that runs the Docker daemon.
Docker Container	Isolated runtime environments for running applications packaged with dependencies.
Docker Image	Read-only templates used to create container environments. Images are made of layered filesystems.
Docker Registry	Repositories for storing and distributing Docker images like Docker Hub or private registries.
Docker Network	Enables communication between containers across hosts using drivers like bridge, overlay, macvlan etc.
Docker Storage	Manages filesystem layers for container images and persistent storage volumes for containers.
Docker Compose	Tool for defining and running multi-container Docker apps in an isolated env.
Docker Swarm	Container orchestration built into Docker for clustering multiple Docker hosts and scheduling containers.

Figure 8.6: Docker components

Figure 8.6 shows the components of Docker. Let us review each component in detail.

Docker Client

The Docker client is a command-line interface (CLI) that allows users to interact with the Docker daemon. It is the primary interface for running Docker commands to build, run, and manage Docker objects like containers, images, volumes, and networks. The client can run on the host machine and connect to the local Docker daemon, or it can connect remotely to a daemon hosted on another machine. The client and daemon communicate via sockets or a RESTful API.

Figure 8.7 shows the commands available on the Docker client. The client takes user inputs and communicates them to the Docker daemon which carries them out. The daemon then responds back with a result or status to the client.

Command	Description
docker container	Manage containers (run, start, stop, list)
docker image	Manage images (build, list, remove)
docker build	Build images from Dockerfiles
docker push/pull	Push/pull images to registries
docker run	Run a command in a container
docker ps	List running containers
docker network	Manage networks
docker volume	Manage data volumes
docker compose	Define apps with multi container workflows

Figure 8.7: Docker client commands

Docker Daemon

The Docker daemon (dockerd) is a persistent background service that manages the entire Docker environment. It runs on the host machines that make up the Docker environment. As a daemon service, it runs in the background and does not need user interaction.

The daemon receives and executes commands sent from the Docker client. The key functions performed by the Docker daemon are as follows:

- **Image management**: Pulling, building, and storing images
- **Container lifecycle management**: Running, stopping, and restarting containers
- **Network management**: Creating networks for communication between containers
- **Storage and volumes**: Managing storage volumes mounted inside containers
- **Communications**: Managing communication between the client and daemon
- **Security**: Applying security policies and authorizing requests

The Docker daemon listens for requests from the Docker client and manages Docker objects like images, containers, networks, and volumes. It also communicates with other daemons to manage Docker services across a distributed system.

Docker Host

A Docker host is a system running the Docker daemon and containers. This can be a physical server, on-premises, or cloud-based server, or it can be a virtual machine. The Docker daemon runs natively on Linux-based systems. For Windows and Mac, a Linux VM runs transparently with the daemon to provide full Docker functionality.

The Docker host provides the environment in which containers actually run. When a user runs a Docker container, it is the Docker daemon on the host that instantiates and runs the container. The key functions performed by the Docker host are as follows:

- **Container execution**: Launching container processes
- **Image management**: Storing Docker images ready for container deployment
- **Networking**: Managing virtual networks for inter-container and external communication
- **Storage**: Providing data volumes that can be mounted inside containers

- **Security**: Applying Linux security features (such as namespaces, control groups, and SELinux, for instance).
- **Resource allocation**: Assigning memory limits and CPU shares to containers

A physical or virtual system running the Docker daemon can host many containers. Multiple Docker hosts can also be clustered together using swarm mode to create a distributed Docker environment.

Docker Containers

Docker containers are runtime instances of Docker images. They provide isolated, standardized, and portable environments for applications to run without interference between each other or with the underlying host system.

Containers include the application code, system tools, libraries, and dependencies required to run the application, bundled into a single package. This allows the containerized application to run quickly and reliably from one computing environment to another.

The key properties of Docker containers are as follows:

- **Isolation**: Containers are isolated from each other and the host environment via namespaces and control groups. This allows containers to run side-by-side without impacting each other. Namespaces provide isolation for resources like process trees, networks, user IDs, and mounted file systems. Control groups limit the amount of resources like CPU and memory available to containers. Together, they prevent processes in one container from affecting processes in another container.
- **Portability**: Containers are portable across environments because they conform to standardized formats like OCI (Open Container Initiative) standards. The format defines how things like container images, runtimes, and config are implemented. Adhering to common standards allows containers to run consistently regardless of whether the target environment is a desktop, on-premises data center, cloud provider, etc. The container runtime environment and host OS are abstracted away from the application code.
- **Lightweight**: Containers have a small footprint and minimum overhead because they share the host kernel instead of needing their own complete OS. This makes them more efficient than virtual machines which require their own guest OS. Sharing the host OS allows containers to be more lightweight, using fewer resources than VMs in some cases. The host provides the kernel while containers package up just the user space components like libraries and settings. This efficient approach powers more applications per host.
- **Secure**: Containers limit the attack surface and adopt a principle of least privilege to enhance security. They contain only the minimal components needed to run an application, reducing the points of entry for attackers. Access to the container's processes, filesystem, and resources is locked down tightly via namespaces, control groups and capabilities like read-only volumes. Images are signed, and container content is hashed for tamper-proofing.
- **Scalable**: Containerized applications can be dynamically orchestrated and replicated across multiple hosts on demand to scale horizontally. The lightweight nature of containers allows more processes to run on the same hardware resources. Container orchestrators (like Docker Swarm and Kubernetes) automate container deployments

and scaling. More container instances can be spun up to handle increased loads and then spun down when traffic reduces. This facilitates elastic scaling.

• **Developer Friendly**: Container formats and standards make the developer experience more consistent. Containers encourage practices like immutable infrastructure, easing version changes. Building images with Dockerfiles enables repeatable builds across environments. Images can be rebuilt frequently without friction to bake in changes. Common base images provide standardized starting points.

When running a containerized application, the Docker client sends a request to the Docker daemon to launch a container based on a specific Docker image. The Docker daemon pulls the image from a registry if not already cached locally. The daemon creates a set of namespaces and control groups to create an isolated container environment. A thin writable container layer is added over the image base to store any state as the container runs. Signals are handled to track container status so it can be managed by the daemon.

At runtime, the container has private access to its own filesystem, processes, network interfaces, hostname, memory, and other resources, isolated from the host and other containers. It runs natively on the host kernel but confined within the resources allocated to it. The containerized process cannot see resources or processes in other containers. It can access storage volumes mounted from the host if configured. Network traffic can be managed via the default bridge network or custom network configurations. Multiple containers can run side by side with minimal overhead. The host operating system and hardware are abstracted away from the application code running inside the containers.

A container lifecycle moves through the following phases:

• **Creation**: A container is created in the stopped state when 'docker run' is executed. The image layers are extracted, and a container is created with a read-write layer over the image.
• **Start**: The 'docker start' command starts a created container by launching its primary process. The container state changes to running once process starts.
• **Stop**: Issuing a 'docker stop' command stops a running container by sending a SIGTERM to the primary process. After timeout, SIGKILL kills the process.
• **Restart**: Stopped containers can be restarted using 'docker start'. The container retains changes made in previous running state.
• **Removal**: The 'docker rm' command removes a stopped container from the Docker host, freeing up disk space used by its writable layer.

Containers are designed to be ephemeral in nature. Running containers can be gracefully stopped and restarted. When no longer needed, they can be definitively removed.

Docker Images

Docker images are read-only templates used to launch Docker containers. They provide the filesystem and configuration required for a specific type of container. For example, an image may contain an Ubuntu OS, Node.js runtime, and application files needed to run a Node.js app.

Images are made up of a series of layers representing the instructions needed to assemble the image. Each layer tracks changes compared to the layer below it. The layers contain things like the OS files, applications, configuration, dependencies, and environment variables.

When launched, a container is created from the image with a thin writable layer over it where state can be persisted. Any changes are stored in this writable layer only, leaving the underlying image itself intact.

The key properties of Docker images are as follows:
- **Read-only**: Images are read-only templates from which containers are launched.
- **Layered**: Made up of filesystem layers, each representing container instructions.
- **Lightweight**: Image layers are cached and copied on write, making images efficient.
- **Modular**: Layers can be reused across images, leading to smaller image sizes.
- **Versioned**: Image tags identify the image version, allowing version control.
- **Distributed**: Can be pushed and pulled from public or private registries.
- **Buildable**: Can be built from base images or Dockerfiles to customize.
- **Secure**: Digitally signed for integrity and provenance assurance.

Images provide the starting point for defining, sharing, and reusing portable application environments.

Docker Registries

Docker registries are repositories for storing and distributing Docker images. They can be public like Docker Hub or private within an organization. Images are pushed to registries from development environments and pulled from registries into runtime environments. This enables the distribution of images to wherever they need to run.

The key tasks performed by a Docker registry are as follows:
- **Store**: Maintain a catalog of image repositories containing images and metadata.
- **Retrieve**: Allow users to search for, pull, and download images via CLI or UI.
- **Share**: Manage permissions around image access and updates.
- **Secure**: Authenticate clients and control access to image repositories.
- **Replicate**: Mirror images across distributed registry instances.
- **Scale**: Support demands of growing repositories, bandwidth, and traffic.

Public registries like Docker Hub provide open repositories for sharing public images. Private registries allow companies to maintain proprietary images internally. Images can also be exported and imported as tar files for offline distribution. Registries enable the sharing, discovery, and distribution of Docker images to power container deployments.

Docker Networking

By default, containers are attached to a virtual bridge network on the Docker host. This bridge network allows communication between containers on the same host. Docker has several built-in network drivers that provide different networking capabilities for containers. The key network drivers are as follows:
- **Bridge**: The default network driver. It provides container isolation by creating a private network internal to the host. Containers on this network can communicate via IP addresses.
- **Host**: Removes network isolation between the container and host machine. Containers share the host's networking namespace.
- **Overlay**: Allows containers connected to different Docker daemons to communicate. It creates a distributed network between multiple Docker daemon hosts.
- **MACVLAN**: Assigns a MAC address to each container allowing them to appear as physical devices on the network. Communication with external devices and networks is enabled directly.

- **None**: Removes all networking capabilities from a container. Useful for containers that do not require external access.

In addition to default networks, developers can define custom Docker networks to configure connectivity between containers and external systems according to the needs of their applications. There are many third-party network drivers (like Weave, Calico, Flannel, Cilium, etc.) that provide advanced networking and policy options. Networking capabilities are integral to connecting and managing communications for Docker environments.

8.3.2   Docker Storage and Volumes

Containers are ephemeral with any data written inside the container deleted on container deletion. For persisting data beyond container lifecycles, external volumes need to be mounted into containers.

Docker utilizes storage drivers to manage the contents of images and containers. The default storage driver is overlay2, which uses a layered union filesystem to efficiently store and share containers. Other drivers like devicemapper, btrfs, and zfs offer different performance trade-offs.

When a container is created from an image, a thin writable container layer is added on top of the underlying image layers. All changes made to the running container are written to this thin writable layer. The container layer is deleted when the container is removed, preserving the immutable image layers below it. This allows sharing of common read-only parts across multiple containers created from the same image.

Docker Volumes provide the ability to connect file systems from the host machine into containers. This allows sharing and persisting data between containers and the host. Even when containers are destroyed, volumes allow retaining important data outside the containers. Volumes enable stateful applications using containers. Volumes provide persistent data storage independent of container lifecycle.

Docker Bind mounts provide a way to map a host file or directory to a location within the container. Bind mounts can be configured per container. Bind mounts are similar to volumes; however, unlike volumes, they always exist on the host, do not need creation/deletion, and are dependent on the host directory structure. A tmpfs mount is a temporary file storage created in memory that allows containers to write files that are not persisted across container restarts.

Docker's storage and volumes architecture ensures immutable infrastructure through images, overlay-writable layers for containers, and stateful data persistence via mounted volumes. Storage volumes and mounts allow containers to persist data, share data between containers, and share data with non-Docker workloads.

8.3.3   Dockerfile

A Dockerfile is a text file that contains instructions for how a Docker image is built. It configures the environment and contains commands to assemble the image. A Dockerfile starts with specifying a base image, which forms the foundation for the rest of the instructions. Typically, an OS image like Ubuntu or Alpine Linux is used. The base image gets pulled from a registry like Docker Hub. Next, various commands can be executed to install dependencies, add files, and set environment variables.

Instruction	Description
FROM	Sets the base image to build upon
RUN	Executes a command during the image build process
COPY	Copies files from the host into the image filesystem
ADD	Similar to COPY but with extra features like URL handling
ENV	Sets an environment variable in the image
CMD	Provides the default command to run when starting a container
ENTRYPOINT	Configures a container to run as an executable program
EXPOSE	Informs Docker that a container listens on the specified network ports
WORKDIR	Sets the working directory for other Dockerfile commands and the running container
USER	Sets the user or UID to use when running image commands and the container
VOLUME	Creates a mount point for externally mounted volumes or other containers
LABEL	Adds metadata to the image in key-value pairs
ARG	Defines a build-time variable that can be passed at build-time with docker build
HEALTHCHECK	Tests a container runs correctly using commands like curl
ONBUILD	Adds triggers that get executed when the image is used as a base for another build

Figure 8.8: Dockerfile instructions

Figure 8.8 shows the instructions used within a Dockerfile. Box 8.1 shows a sample Dockerfile. This demonstrates several common Dockerfile instructions like FROM, RUN, WORKDIR, COPY, EXPOSE, ENV, and CMD to build an image that runs a Python Flask app. Each instruction creates a new layer in the image. This layered architecture allows Docker images to be lightweight, fast, and cacheable. When building the image, Docker uses cached layers if possible, only rebuilding layers that change. Once all instructions are executed, the Dockerfile produces a ready-to-run image.

■ **Box 8.1: Dockerfile sample**

```
# Start from the latest ubuntu image
FROM ubuntu:latest

# Update packages and install python
RUN apt-get update && apt-get install -y python3
```

```
# Set the working directory
WORKDIR /app

# Copy source code to container
COPY . /app/

# Install dependencies
RUN pip install -r requirements.txt

# Expose port for flask app
EXPOSE 5000

# Set environment variables
ENV FLASK_ENV=development

# Run flask app
CMD [ "python", "./app.py" ]
```

To build an image from a Dockerfile, the *'docker build'* command is used. This executes each step and caches the results. Build arguments can also be passed to parameterize the build process. Images get tagged with a name and version that identify them.

Once an image is built, Docker containers can be spun up from it. Containers allow shipping an application with its runtime environment all packaged together. This facilitates portability across different environments. Containers also isolate apps from each other through separate file systems, processes and networks.

Running a container uses the *'docker run'* command. Parameters like network ports, volumes, and environment variables can be specified when starting a container. Docker offers great flexibility in how containers get networked together and integrate with the host system resources.

8.3.4   Docker Compose

Docker Compose is a tool for defining and running multi-container Docker applications. With Docker Compose, you define the various services and their parameters in a YAML file. This covers everything needed to run the whole application stack. With a single command, Docker Compose can create all images, spin up containers, connect them, and start the application. This simplifies orchestrating the many services of a complex application.

Figure 8.9 shows the components of a Docker Compose file. The Docker Compose file starts by listing the different services or containers that make up the app. Under each service, details like the Dockerfile path, ports, volumes, dependencies, and other configs can be added. Networks can also be configured to allow inter-container communication within the app. Service discovery makes it easy to access containers by name. Deployment parameters like the number of replicas and resource limits can be specified as needed. With a single *'docker-compose up'* command, everything gets built as per the compose file. Images are created, containers spun up, linked together, and apps started automatically. No need to manually build, create networks, or manage containers.

Compose can also integrate with various production-grade tools. Docker Swarm enables scaling the app across multiple hosts. Kubernetes provides complete orchestration and

Component	Description
version	Specifies Compose file format version
services	Defines the different services/containers that make up the app
build	Specifies Dockerfile and options to build the service image
ports	Exposes ports to host machine for external access
volumes	Mounts external folders/files into the service containers
networks	Configures networks connecting the app services
depends_on	Specifies dependencies between services for start order
environment	Sets environment variables required by the services
deploy	Configures deployment parameters like replicas and resources
command	Overrides default command when starting service containers
image	Specifies custom image to use instead of building an image
restart	Defines restart policy if containers exit or crash
links	Alias for inter-service communication and discovery

Figure 8.9: Docker Compose components

management of containerized apps. CI/CD pipelines can build, test, and deploy the application on every code change.

The compose file serves as a single source of truth for the app's environment. As requirements evolve, the file can be edited to add services, update config, or re-architect the stack. The same file works seamlessly from development to production.

Box 8.2 shows a sample Docker Compose YAML file. This defines a *web* service built from a Dockerfile, a *db* service using a PostgreSQL image, a *redis* service with 2 replicas, a *worker* service depending on *db* and *redis*, a network, and volumes for persisting data. The *web* service exposes port 5000, sets an environment variable, and mounts code. The *db* and *redis* services set required environment variables.

■ **Box 8.2: Sample Docker Compose file**

```
version: "3.8"
services:
  web:
    build: ./web
    ports:
      - "5000:5000"
    volumes:
      - ./web/code:/code
    environment:
      - DEBUG=1
  db:
    image: postgres:13
    environment:
      - POSTGRES_DB=appdb
      - POSTGRES_USER=appuser
      - POSTGRES_PASSWORD=password
  redis:
    image: redis:alpine
    deploy:
      replicas: 2
  worker:
    build: ./worker
    depends_on:
      - db
      - redis
    restart: on-failure

networks:
  - app-network
volumes:
  - db-data:/var/lib/db
  - cache-data:/var/cache
```

8.4 Containerizing Microservices Application with Docker

In this section, we will describe the steps for containerizing the microservices E-Commerce application using Docker. Figure 8.10 shows the architecture of the containerized application comprising containers for frontend, user, order, product, and review microservices.

The records of users, products, orders, and reviews are stored in a MySQL database. A separate container for MySQL is used. The user, order, product, and review microservices connect to the MySQL container to store and retrieve data.

For storing user profile photos and product images, we use a MinIO container. MinIO is an open-source object storage server with Amazon S3 compatible API. MinIO supports standard S3 API operations like PUT, GET, DELETE, LIST, HEAD, and supports features like bucket policies, encryption, lifecycle management, and versioning. MinIO is a good choice for building a private or hybrid cloud object storage for backups, archives, data lakes, media repositories, and more. Its S3 compatibility makes it easy to migrate applications from AWS S3 to MinIO for greater control, security, and cost savings.

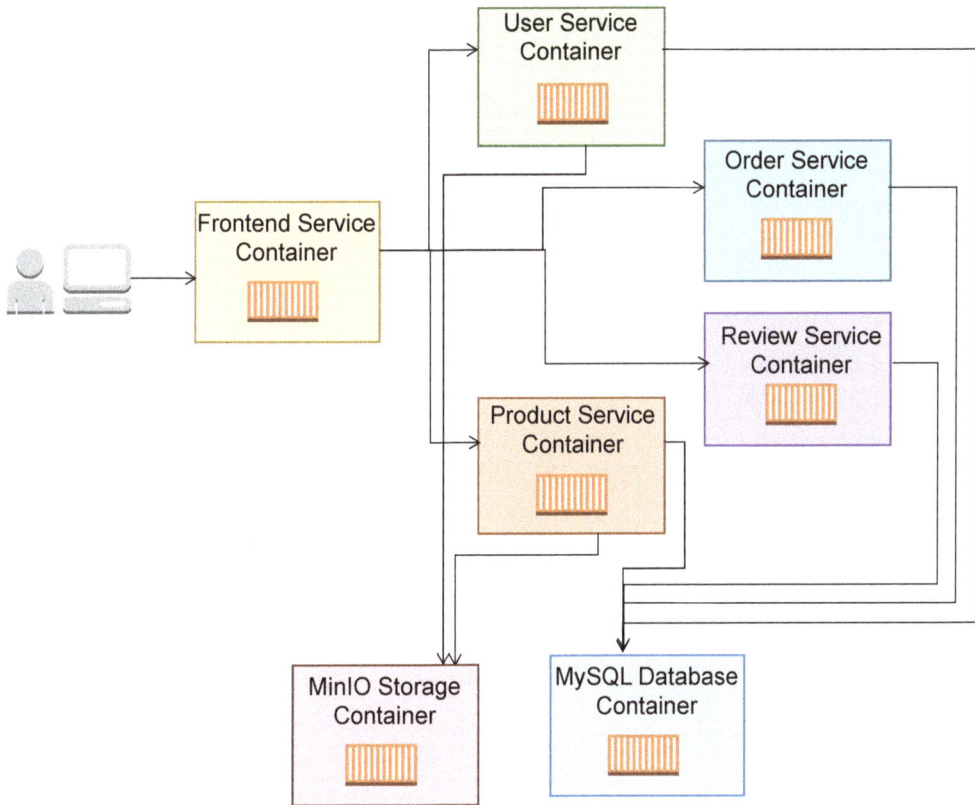

Figure 8.10: Containerized Microservices E-Commerce application

The source code of the Flask templates is the same as the microservices application described in Chapter 6. The implementations of the routes for the frontend, user, product, order, and review microservices are also similar to the ones provided in the Chapter 6. For the sake of brevity, we are providing only the code differences in the microservices to support MySQL database and MinIO storage.

Box 8.6 shows the code of the frontend microservice. It loads configuration from environment variables like the URLs for the backend services (user, product, order, and review). This allows the frontend to call those services. A *healthcheck* endpoint is implemented that returns an HTTP 200 status to indicate the frontend service is up and running.

■ Box 8.3: Frontend microservice

```
#Only the differences from the Frontend service explained in
#previous chapter are shown.

app = Flask(__name__, static_folder='static')
app.config['UPLOAD_FOLDER'] = 'static/images'
app.config['SECRET_KEY'] = os.getenv("SECRET_KEY")
app.config['WTF_CSRF_SECRET_KEY'] = os.getenv("WTF_CSRF_SECRET_KEY")
```

```
app.config['ENV'] = "development"
app.config['DEBUG'] = True

USER_SERVICE_URL=os.getenv("USER_SERVICE_URL")
PRODUCT_SERVICE_URL= os.getenv("PRODUCT_SERVICE_URL")
ORDER_SERVICE_URL= os.getenv("ORDER_SERVICE_URL")
REVIEW_SERVICE_URL= os.getenv("REVIEW_SERVICE_URL")

@app.route('/healthcheck', methods=['GET'])
def health_check():
    return make_response(jsonify({'message': 'Healthy'}), 200)
```

Box 8.4 shows the code of the user microservice. When a new user registers, their password is hashed using *sha256_crypt* and a random avatar image is generated locally using the *avinit* library. This image file is then uploaded to a MinIO bucket using the *boto3* SDK. The MinIO URL for this image file is returned by the *s3uploading* function. The user data (including hashed passwords, usernames, and photo URL) is saved in a MySQL database.

■ Box 8.4: User microservice

```
#Only the differences from the User service explained in
#previous chapter are shown.

app = Flask(__name__)
app.config['SECRET_KEY'] = os.getenv("SECRET_KEY")
app.config['BUCKET_NAME'] = os.getenv("BUCKET_NAME")
app.config['CLOUDFRONT_URL'] = os.getenv("CLOUDFRONT_URL")
app.config['STORAGE_PROVIDER']=os.getenv("STORAGE_PROVIDER")
app.config['AWS_ACCESS_KEY'] = os.getenv("AWS_ACCESS_KEY")
app.config['AWS_SECRET_KEY'] = os.getenv("AWS_SECRET_KEY")
app.config['STORAGE_HOST'] = os.getenv("STORAGE_HOST")
app.config['STORAGE_PORT'] = os.getenv("STORAGE_PORT")
app.config['STORAGE_HOST_EXT'] = os.getenv("STORAGE_HOST_EXT")
app.config['STORAGE_PORT_EXT'] = os.getenv("STORAGE_PORT_EXT")
app.config['SQLALCHEMY_DATABASE_URI'] =
                    os.getenv("SQLALCHEMY_DATABASE_URI")
app.config['SQLALCHEMY_TRACK_MODIFICATIONS'] = False
app.config['ENV'] = "development"
app.config['DEBUG'] = True
app.config['SQLALCHEMY_ECHO'] = True
app.config['UPLOAD_FOLDER'] = 'uploads'

class User(UserMixin, db.Model):
    id = db.Column(db.Integer, primary_key=True)
    username = db.Column(db.String(255), unique=True, nullable=False)
    email = db.Column(db.String(255), unique=True, nullable=False)
    first_name = db.Column(db.String(255), unique=False, nullable=True)
    last_name = db.Column(db.String(255), unique=False, nullable=True)
    password = db.Column(db.String(255), unique=False, nullable=False)
    photo = db.Column(db.String(255), unique=False, nullable=True)
    is_admin = db.Column(db.Boolean, default=False)
    authenticated = db.Column(db.Boolean, default=False)
    api_key = db.Column(db.String(255), unique=True, nullable=True)
```

```
        date_added = db.Column(db.DateTime, default=datetime.utcnow)
        date_updated = db.Column(db.DateTime, onupdate=datetime.utcnow)

        def encode_api_key(self):
            self.api_key = sha256_crypt.hash(self.username +
                                             str(datetime.utcnow))

        def encode_password(self):
            self.password = sha256_crypt.hash(self.password)

        def __repr__(self):
            return '<User %r>' % (self.username)

        def to_json(self):
            return {
                'first_name': self.first_name,
                'last_name': self.last_name,
                'username': self.username,
                'email': self.email,
                'photo': self.photo,
                'id': self.id,
                'api_key': self.api_key,
                'is_active': True,
                'is_admin': self.is_admin
            }

def s3uploading(filename):
    if app.config['STORAGE_PROVIDER']=='minio':
        storage_endpoint='http://'+app.config['STORAGE_HOST']+':'+
                         app.config['STORAGE_PORT']
        s3 = boto3.client('s3', endpoint_url=storage_endpoint,
                aws_access_key_id=app.config['AWS_ACCESS_KEY'],
                aws_secret_access_key=app.config['AWS_SECRET_KEY'])
    else:
        s3 = boto3.client('s3',
                aws_access_key_id=app.config['AWS_ACCESS_KEY'],
                aws_secret_access_key=app.config['AWS_SECRET_KEY'])

    bucket = app.config['BUCKET_NAME']
    path_filename_disk = os.path.join(app.config['UPLOAD_FOLDER'],
                                      filename)
    path_filename_s3 = "photos/" + filename
    print(path_filename_s3)
    s3.upload_file(path_filename_disk, bucket, path_filename_s3)
    if app.config['STORAGE_PROVIDER']=='minio':
        url= 'http://'+app.config['STORAGE_HOST_EXT']+':'+
                app.config['STORAGE_PORT_EXT']+"/"+
                app.config['BUCKET_NAME']+"/"+path_filename_s3
    else:
        url = app.config['CLOUDFRONT_URL']+'/'+path_filename_s3
    return url

@app.route('/api/user/create', methods=['POST'])
def post_register():
```

```
    first_name = request.form['first_name']
    last_name = request.form['last_name']
    email = request.form['email']
    username = request.form['username']
    password = sha256_crypt.hash((str(request.form['password'])))
    user = User()
    user.email = email
    user.first_name = first_name
    user.last_name = last_name
    user.password = password
    user.username = username
    user.authenticated = True
    name=first_name+' '+ last_name
    filename = "user"+str(int(time.time()*1000))+".png"
    imgpath=os.path.join(app.config['UPLOAD_FOLDER'], filename)
    r = lambda: random.randint(0,255)
    colors=[]
    colors.append('#%02X%02X%02X' % (r(),r(),r()))
    avinit.get_png_avatar(name, output_file=imgpath, colors=colors)
    uploadedFileURL = s3uploading(filename)
    user.photo = uploadedFileURL
    db.session.add(user)
    db.session.commit()
    response = jsonify({'message': 'User added',
                'result': user.to_json()})
    return response

@app.route('/healthcheck', methods=['GET'])
def health_check():
    return make_response(jsonify({'message': 'Healthy'}), 200)
```

Box 8.5 shows the code of the product microservice. When a new product is created, the product image file is first saved locally, then uploaded to a MinIO bucket using the *boto3* SDK. The MinIO URL for this image file is returned by the *s3uploading* function. The product data (including name, description, price, and image URL) is inserted into a MySQL database.

■ Box 8.5: Product microservice

```
#Only the differences from the Product service explained in
#previous chapter are shown.

app = Flask(__name__)
app.config['SECRET_KEY'] = os.getenv("SECRET_KEY")
app.config['BUCKET_NAME'] = os.getenv("BUCKET_NAME")
app.config['CLOUDFRONT_URL'] = os.getenv("CLOUDFRONT_URL")
app.config['STORAGE_PROVIDER']=os.getenv("STORAGE_PROVIDER")
app.config['AWS_ACCESS_KEY'] = os.getenv("AWS_ACCESS_KEY")
app.config['AWS_SECRET_KEY'] = os.getenv("AWS_SECRET_KEY")
app.config['STORAGE_HOST'] = os.getenv("STORAGE_HOST")
app.config['STORAGE_PORT'] = os.getenv("STORAGE_PORT")
app.config['STORAGE_HOST'] = os.getenv("STORAGE_HOST")
app.config['STORAGE_PORT'] = os.getenv("STORAGE_PORT")
```

```
app.config['STORAGE_HOST_EXT'] = os.getenv("STORAGE_HOST_EXT")
app.config['STORAGE_PORT_EXT'] = os.getenv("STORAGE_PORT_EXT")
app.config['SQLALCHEMY_DATABASE_URI'] =
                    os.getenv("SQLALCHEMY_DATABASE_URI")
app.config['SQLALCHEMY_TRACK_MODIFICATIONS'] = False
app.config['ENV'] = "development"
app.config['DEBUG'] = True
app.config['SQLALCHEMY_ECHO'] = True
app.config['UPLOAD_FOLDER'] = 'uploads'

class Product(db.Model):
    id = db.Column(db.Integer, primary_key=True)
    name = db.Column(db.String(255), unique=True, nullable=False)
    slug = db.Column(db.String(255), unique=True, nullable=False)
    price = db.Column(db.Float, default=0)
    image = db.Column(db.String(255), unique=False, nullable=True)
    description = db.Column(db.Text)
    date_added = db.Column(db.DateTime, default=datetime.utcnow)
    date_updated = db.Column(db.DateTime, onupdate=datetime.utcnow)

    def to_json(self):
        return {
            'id': self.id,
            'name': self.name,
            'description': self.description,
            'slug': self.slug,
            'price': self.price,
            'image': self.image
        }

def s3uploading(filename):
    if app.config['STORAGE_PROVIDER']=='minio':
        storage_endpoint='http://'+app.config['STORAGE_HOST']+':'+
                        app.config['STORAGE_PORT']
        s3 = boto3.client('s3', endpoint_url=storage_endpoint,
                aws_access_key_id=app.config['AWS_ACCESS_KEY'],
                aws_secret_access_key=app.config['AWS_SECRET_KEY'])
    else:
        s3 = boto3.client('s3',
            aws_access_key_id=app.config['AWS_ACCESS_KEY'],
            aws_secret_access_key=app.config['AWS_SECRET_KEY'])

    bucket = app.config['BUCKET_NAME']
    path_filename_disk = os.path.join(app.config['UPLOAD_FOLDER'],
                            filename)
    path_filename_s3 = "photos/" + filename
    print(path_filename_s3)
    s3.upload_file(path_filename_disk, bucket, path_filename_s3)
    if app.config['STORAGE_PROVIDER']=='minio':
        url= 'http://'+app.config['STORAGE_HOST_EXT']+':'+
                app.config['STORAGE_PORT_EXT']+"/"+
                app.config['BUCKET_NAME']+"/"+path_filename_s3
    else:
        url = app.config['CLOUDFRONT_URL']+'/'+path_filename_s3
```

```
        return url

@app.route('/api/product/create', methods=['POST'])
def post_create():
    name = request.form.get('name')
    slug = request.form.get('slug')
    description = request.form.get('description')
    price = request.form.get('price')
    image = request.files.get('image')

    filename = secure_filename(image.filename)
    image.save(os.path.join(app.config['UPLOAD_FOLDER'], filename))
    uploadedFileURL = s3uploading(filename)

    item = Product()
    item.name = name
    item.slug = slug
    item.image = uploadedFileURL
    item.price = price
    item.description=description

    db.session.add(item)
    db.session.commit()

    response = jsonify({'message': 'Product added',
                'product': item.to_json()})
    return response
```

Box 8.6 shows the code of the order microservice.

■ Box 8.6: Order microservice

```
#Only the differences from the Order service explained in
#previous chapter are shown.

app = Flask(__name__)
app.config['SECRET_KEY'] = os.getenv("SECRET_KEY")
app.config['SQLALCHEMY_DATABASE_URI'] =
            os.getenv("SQLALCHEMY_DATABASE_URI")
app.config['SQLALCHEMY_TRACK_MODIFICATIONS'] = False
app.config['ENV'] = "development"
app.config['DEBUG'] = True
app.config['SQLALCHEMY_ECHO'] = True
app.config['UPLOAD_FOLDER'] = 'uploads'
USER_SERVICE_URL=os.getenv("USER_SERVICE_URL")

@app.route('/healthcheck', methods=['GET'])
def health_check():
    return make_response(jsonify({'message': 'Healthy'}), 200)
```

Box 8.7 shows the code of the review microservice.

■ Box 8.7: Review microservice

```
#Only the differences from the Review service explained in
#previous chapter are shown.

app = Flask(__name__)
app.config['SECRET_KEY'] = os.getenv("SECRET_KEY")
app.config['SQLALCHEMY_DATABASE_URI']  =
                    os.getenv("SQLALCHEMY_DATABASE_URI")
app.config['SQLALCHEMY_TRACK_MODIFICATIONS'] = False
app.config['ENV'] = "development"
app.config['DEBUG'] = True
app.config['SQLALCHEMY_ECHO'] = True

@app.route('/healthcheck', methods=['GET'])
def health_check():
    return make_response(jsonify({'message': 'Healthy'}), 200)
```

Box 8.8 shows the code of the Dockerfile which is used for building the container images for all the microservices. The Dockerfile uses the Python 3.11.6 slim image as the base image to keep the eventual container image small and optimized. It creates a */app* directory inside the container to hold the application code and sets this as the working directory. The application code is copied from the host machine into the */app* directory to add it to the image. The Dockerfile installs required dependencies like the *libcairo* library and *MariaDB* client libraries using *apt-get*. It also installs the Python dependencies defined in requirements.txt using *pip*. The container exposes port 5000 for the application traffic and starts the Gunicorn WSGI server when launched, serving the application based on the configuration in */app/gunicorn.py*.

■ Box 8.8: Dockerfile for building Docker images

```
FROM python:3.11.6-slim
RUN mkdir /app
WORKDIR /app
ADD . /app/
RUN apt-get update
RUN apt install -y libcairo-5c-dev
RUN apt install -y mariadb-client-core
RUN pip3 install -r requirements.txt
EXPOSE 5000
CMD ["gunicorn", "wsgi:app", "-c", "/app/gunicorn.py"]
```

Box 8.9 shows the Docker Compose file for the E-Commerce application. It provides a full environment for the microservices, their persistent storage, and the frontend service, enabling local development and testing of the entire E-Commerce application stack. The Docker Compose file defines services for a MySQL database container, a MinIO object storage container, and microservice containers for user, product, order, review, and frontend. The MySQL container stores user, product, order, and review data accessed by the respective microservices. MinIO provides S3-compatible object storage for storing images and files, used by the user and product services. The microservices are configured with environment variables for their database and object storage connections. The frontend service depends on the other microservices and is configured with their internal docker host URLs for API access. Each microservice exposes a port mapping to publish its container port externally. They depend on the database and object storage containers to ensure those are running before starting.

■ **Box 8.9: Docker Compose file**

```
version: "3"

services:
  db:
    restart: always
    image: mysql
    container_name: database
    ports:
      - "3306:3306"
    volumes:
      - ~/mysql/database/mysql-data:/var/lib/mysql
    environment:
      - MYSQL_ROOT_PASSWORD=c1Zl6tC93AuTfKC

  storage:
    restart: always
    image: quay.io/minio/minio
    container_name: minio1
    ports:
      - "9000:9000"
      - "9001:9001"
    volumes:
      - ~/minio/data:/data
    environment:
      - MINIO_ROOT_USER=AKIAIOSFODNN7EXAMPLE
      - MINIO_ROOT_PASSWORD=wJalrXUtnFEMI/K7MDENG/bPxRfiCYEXAMPLEKEY
    command: server /data --console-address ":9001"

  user-service:
    restart: always
    image: asbind/ecomuser:v6
    container_name: user-container
    ports:
      - "5001:5000"
    depends_on:
      - "db"
      - "storage"
    environment:
      - SECRET_KEY=DoWgTDq87Kmne3TsCjNFabP
      - BUCKET_NAME=ecommerce
      - AWS_ACCESS_KEY=AKIAIOSFODNN7EXAMPLE
      - AWS_SECRET_KEY=wJalrXUtnFEMI/K7MDENG/bPxRfiCYEXAMPLEKEY
      - STORAGE_PROVIDER=minio
```

```
    - STORAGE_HOST=storage
    - STORAGE_PORT=9000
    - STORAGE_HOST_EXT=localhost
    - STORAGE_PORT_EXT=9000
    - SQLALCHEMY_DATABASE_URI=mysql+pymysql://
                        root:c1Z16tC93AuTfKC@db:3306/userdb

product-service:
  restart: always
  image: asbind/ecomproduct:v6
  container_name: product-container
  ports:
    - "5002:5000"
  depends_on:
    - "db"
    - "storage"
  environment:
    - SECRET_KEY=DoWgTDq87Kmne3TsCjNFabP
    - BUCKET_NAME=ecommerce
    - AWS_ACCESS_KEY=AKIAIOSFODNN7EXAMPLE
    - AWS_SECRET_KEY=wJalrXUtnFEMI/K7MDENG/bPxRfiCYEXAMPLEKEY
    - STORAGE_PROVIDER=minio
    - STORAGE_HOST=storage
    - STORAGE_PORT=9000
    - STORAGE_HOST_EXT=localhost
    - STORAGE_PORT_EXT=9000
    - SQLALCHEMY_DATABASE_URI=mysql+pymysql://
                        root:c1Z16tC93AuTfKC@db:3306/productdb

order-service:
  restart: always
  image: asbind/ecomorder:v6
  container_name: order-container
  ports:
    - "5003:5000"
  depends_on:
    - "db"
    - "user-service"
  environment:
    - SECRET_KEY=DoWgTDq87Kmne3TsCjNFabP
    - SQLALCHEMY_DATABASE_URI=mysql+pymysql://
                        root:c1Z16tC93AuTfKC@db:3306/orderdb
    - USER_SERVICE_URL=http://user-service:5000

review-service:
  restart: always
  image: asbind/ecomreview:v6
  container_name: review-container
  ports:
    - "5004:5000"
  depends_on:
    - "db"
  environment:
    - SECRET_KEY=DoWgTDq87Kmne3TsCjNFabP
```

```
      - SQLALCHEMY_DATABASE_URI=mysql+pymysql://
                            root:c1Z16tC93AuTfKC@db:3306/reviewdb

  frontend-service:
    restart: always
    image: asbind/ecomfrontend:v6
    container_name: frontend-container
    ports:
      - "5000:5000"
    depends_on:
      - "user-service"
      - "product-service"
      - "order-service"
      - "review-service"
    environment:
      - SECRET_KEY=DoWgTDq87Kmne3TsCjNFabP
      - WTF_CSRF_SECRET_KEY=sEWQkE9oYBiF5fVJnm278i7
      - USER_SERVICE_URL=http://user-service:5000
      - PRODUCT_SERVICE_URL=http://product-service:5000
      - ORDER_SERVICE_URL=http://order-service:5000
      - REVIEW_SERVICE_URL=http://review-service:5000
```

Box 8.10 shows the instructions for building Docker images and setting up the application. These instructions take you through the full process of building images, configuring volumes, starting the application stack, creating databases, running migrations, seeding data, and calling service APIs to test the application flow. The instructions show how to build Docker images for each of the microservices (frontend, user, product, order, and review). Each service has its own Dockerfile, which is used to build an image. The image is tagged with the service name and a version. The images are then pushed to a Docker registry for distribution. Next, local directories are created on the host for persistent storage volumes that will be mounted into the MySQL and MinIO containers. The Docker Compose file is then used to start the full multi-container application stack, including the database, object storage, and all microservices. The Docker Compose file handles networking and depends on the pre-built images from the registry. With the stack running, the instructions show how to exec into the MySQL container and create databases for each microservice. Migrations are then performed within each service's container to initialize the database schema. A cURL example for creating a product by calling the product service API is shown.

■ **Box 8.10: Instructions for building Docker images and setting up the application**

```
#Login to your docker hub account
docker login --username mydockerusername
------


#Build docker images
docker build -f Dockerfile -t ecomfrontend:v1 .
docker tag ecomfrontend:v1 mydockerusername/ecomfrontend:v1
docker push mydockerusername/ecomfrontend:v1

docker build -f Dockerfile -t ecomuser:v1 .
```

```
docker tag ecomuser:v1 mydockerusername/ecomuser:v1
docker push mydockerusername/ecomuser:v1

docker build -f Dockerfile -t ecomproduct:v1 .
docker tag ecomproduct:v1 mydockerusername/ecomproduct:v1
docker push mydockerusername/ecomproduct:v1

docker build -f Dockerfile -t ecomorder:v1 .
docker tag ecomorder:v1 mydockerusername/ecomorder:v1
docker push mydockerusername/ecomorder:v1

docker build -f Dockerfile -t ecomreview:v1 .
docker tag ecomreview:v1 mydockerusername/ecomreview:v1
docker push mydockerusername/ecomreview:v1
------

#Create local directories for MinIO and MySQL volumes
mkdir -p ~/mysql/database
mkdir -p ~/minio/data

#Run docker-compose
docker-compose -f docker-compose-mysql-minio up

---
#Create databases for microservices

docker exec -it database mysql -u root -p

#Within mysql shell run following
SHOW DATABASES;
CREATE DATABASE userdb;
CREATE DATABASE orderdb;
CREATE DATABASE productdb;
CREATE DATABASE reviewdb;

-----
#Run DB migrations within containers

docker exec -it user-container /bin/bash
rm -rf migrations/
flask db init
flask db migrate
flask db upgrade

docker exec -it order-container /bin/bash
rm -rf migrations/
flask db init
flask db migrate
flask db upgrade

docker exec -it product-container /bin/bash
rm -rf migrations/
flask db init
flask db migrate
```

```
flask db upgrade

docker exec -it review-container /bin/bash
rm -rf migrations/
flask db init
flask db migrate
flask db upgrade


-----


#Create product
curl -X POST -F "name=Mug" -F "slug=mug-1"
              -F "description=This is a mug"
              -F "price=49.99" -F "image=@mug.jpg"
        http://localhost:5002/api/product/create

#Cleanup by removing all containers:
docker rm -f $(docker ps -aq)
```

Figure 8.11 shows the output of the *docker-compose up* command. It shows the containers for MinIO, MySQL, and all the microservices being created.

```
[arshdeep@arshdeep microservices-ecommerce-docker]$ docker-compose -f docker-compose-mysql-minio.yaml up
[+] Running 7/0
 ✓ Container minio1              Created                                              0.0s
 ✓ Container database           Created                                              0.0s
 ✓ Container review-container    Created                                              0.0s
 ✓ Container product-container   Created                                              0.0s
 ✓ Container user-container      Created                                              0.0s
 ✓ Container order-container     Created                                              0.0s
 ✓ Container frontend-container  Created                                              0.0s
Attaching to database, frontend-container, minio1, order-container, product-container, review-container,
user-container
database          | 2024-01-30 11:05:10+00:00 [Note] [Entrypoint]: Entrypoint script for MySQL Server 8
.3.0-1.el8 started.
database          | 2024-01-30 11:05:10+00:00 [Note] [Entrypoint]: Switching to dedicated user 'mysql'
database          | 2024-01-30 11:05:10+00:00 [Note] [Entrypoint]: Entrypoint script for MySQL Server 8
.3.0-1.el8 started.
minio1            | MinIO Object Storage Server
minio1            | Copyright: 2015-2024 MinIO, Inc.
minio1            | License: GNU AGPLv3 <https://www.gnu.org/licenses/agpl-3.0.html>
minio1            | Version: RELEASE.2024-01-29T03-56-32Z (go1.21.6 linux/amd64)
minio1            |
minio1            | Status:         1 Online, 0 Offline.
minio1            | S3-API: http://172.20.0.2:9000  http://127.0.0.1:9000
minio1            | Console: http://172.20.0.2:9001 http://127.0.0.1:9001
minio1            |
minio1            | Documentation: https://min.io/docs/minio/linux/index.html
minio1            | Warning: The standard parity is set to 0. This can lead to data loss.
database          | '/var/lib/mysql/mysql.sock' -> '/var/run/mysqld/mysqld.sock'
user-container    | [2024-01-30 11:05:11 +0000] [1] [INFO] Starting gunicorn 20.0.4
user-container    | [2024-01-30 11:05:11 +0000] [1] [INFO] Listening at: http://0.0.0.0:5000 (1)
user-container    | [2024-01-30 11:05:11 +0000] [1] [INFO] Using worker: sync
user-container    | [2024-01-30 11:05:11 +0000] [7] [INFO] Booting worker with pid: 7
review-container  | [2024-01-30 11:05:11 +0000] [1] [INFO] Starting gunicorn 20.0.4
review-container  | [2024-01-30 11:05:11 +0000] [1] [INFO] Listening at: http://0.0.0.0:5000 (1)
review-container  | [2024-01-30 11:05:11 +0000] [1] [INFO] Using worker: sync
review-container  | [2024-01-30 11:05:11 +0000] [7] [INFO] Booting worker with pid: 7
product-container | [2024-01-30 11:05:11 +0000] [1] [INFO] Starting gunicorn 20.0.4
product-container | [2024-01-30 11:05:11 +0000] [1] [INFO] Listening at: http://0.0.0.0:5000 (1)
```

Figure 8.11: Docker-Compose command output

Figure 8.12 shows the output of the *docker ps* command with details of all the running containers.

```
[arshdeep@arshdeep ]$ docker ps
CONTAINER ID   IMAGE               COMMAND               CREATED       STATUS          PORTS
                                                         NAMES
cfd43d60c41b   asbind/ecomfrontend:v6  "gunicorn wsgi:app -…"  5 minutes ago  Up 51 seconds   0.0.0.0:
5000->5000/tcp, :::5000->5000/tcp                        frontend-container
c5ee0b5802ed   asbind/ecomorder:v6     "gunicorn wsgi:app -…"  5 minutes ago  Up 51 seconds   0.0.0.0:
5003->5000/tcp, :::5003->5000/tcp                        order-container
f491972c48d9   asbind/ecomuser:v6      "gunicorn wsgi:app -…"  5 minutes ago  Up 52 seconds   0.0.0.0:
5001->5000/tcp, :::5001->5000/tcp                        user-container
07d10d070f76   asbind/ecomreview:v6    "gunicorn wsgi:app -…"  5 minutes ago  Up 52 seconds   0.0.0.0:
5004->5000/tcp, :::5004->5000/tcp                        review-container
a54a45eedf4c   asbind/ecomproduct:v6   "gunicorn wsgi:app -…"  5 minutes ago  Up 52 seconds   0.0.0.0:
5002->5000/tcp, :::5002->5000/tcp                        product-container
520c2069b23d   quay.io/minio/minio     "/usr/bin/docker-ent…"  4 hours ago   Up 52 seconds   0.0.0.0:
9000-9001->9000-9001/tcp, :::9000-9001->9000-9001/tcp   minio1
e2187a98fe64   mysql                   "docker-entrypoint.s…"  4 hours ago   Up 52 seconds   0.0.0.0:
3306->3306/tcp, :::3306->3306/tcp, 33060/tcp            database
```

Figure 8.12: Viewing running Docker containers

Figure 8.13 shows how to create a MinIO bucket. To create a bucket, browse to URL: *http://localhost:9001* to access the MinIO console and login with MinIO credentials as provided in the Docker Compose file.

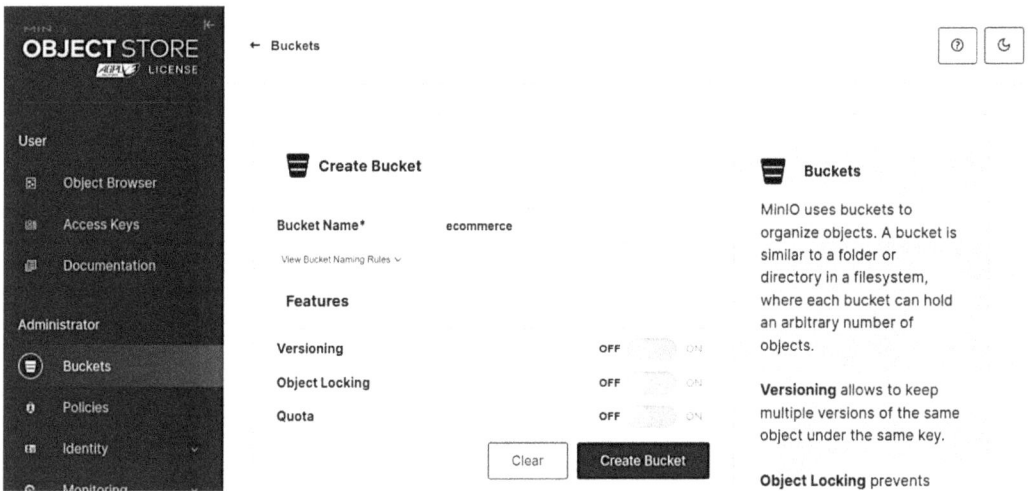

Figure 8.13: Creating a bucket within MinIO

Figure 8.14 shows how to change the access policy of the MinIO bucket to public.

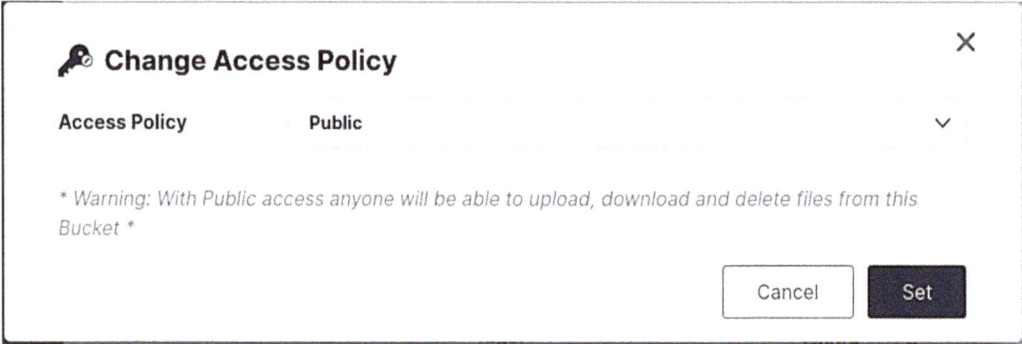

Figure 8.14: Changing access policy of MinIO bucket to public

Figure 8.15 shows the details of the MinIO bucket.

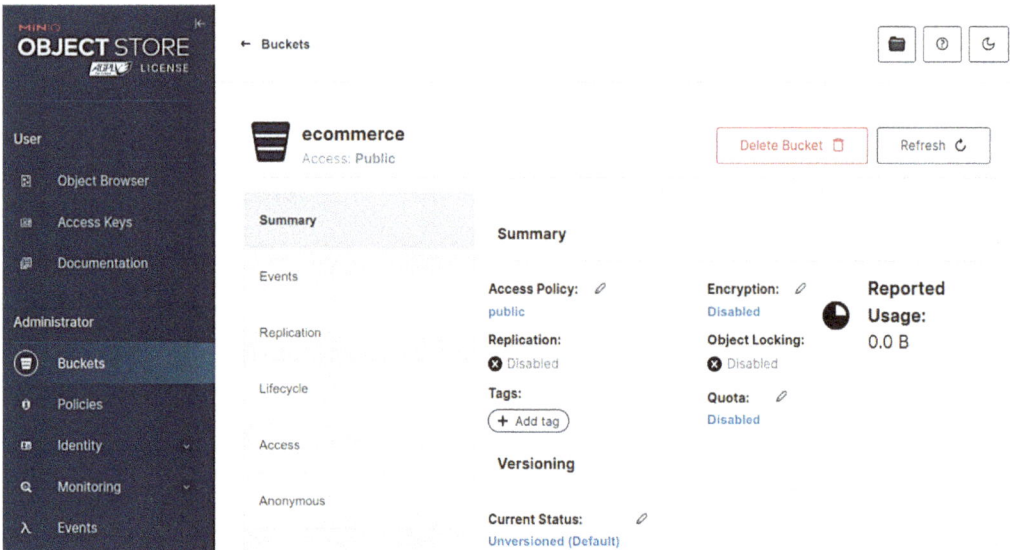

Figure 8.15: Viewing MinIO bucket details

8.5 Deploying Containerized Microservices Application on AWS

In this section, we describe how to deploy the containerized application on AWS using services like ECR, ECS, ALB, S3, CloudFront, and RDS. Figure 8.16 shows the deployment architecture of the E-Commerce microservices application on AWS.

To deploy the application on AWS, we will leverage several managed services to run the containers and provide storage, databases, load balancing, and content delivery. The Docker images will be stored in Elastic Container Registry (ECR), AWS's managed Docker registry. Images can be pushed to ECR repositories from the local development environment.

The containers will run on Elastic Container Service (ECS), AWS's container orchestration service. Within ECS we will use Fargate, which is a serverless option. Fargate removes the need to provision and manage EC2 instances. We just define the task configuration and Fargate handles the underlying infrastructure. Task definitions will define the containers to run for each microservice.

The frontend service will sit behind an Internet-facing (public) Application Load Balancer, providing external access to the application. The ALB will route to the frontend containers. The user, product, order, and review services will sit behind internal ALBs to receive traffic from the frontend. The internal ALBs will provide access between services.

Amazon S3 will store user profile photos and product images. Cloudfront CDN will cache and optimize delivery of the S3 content to the frontend. The MySQL database will run on Amazon RDS, taking advantage of its management, backups, and high availability. The microservices will connect to the RDS instance for data storage and retrieval.

With this AWS architecture utilizing ECS, ALBs, S3, RDS, and more, we can reliably deploy the containerized microservices application and frontend. Managed AWS services will provide scalability, security, and high availability.

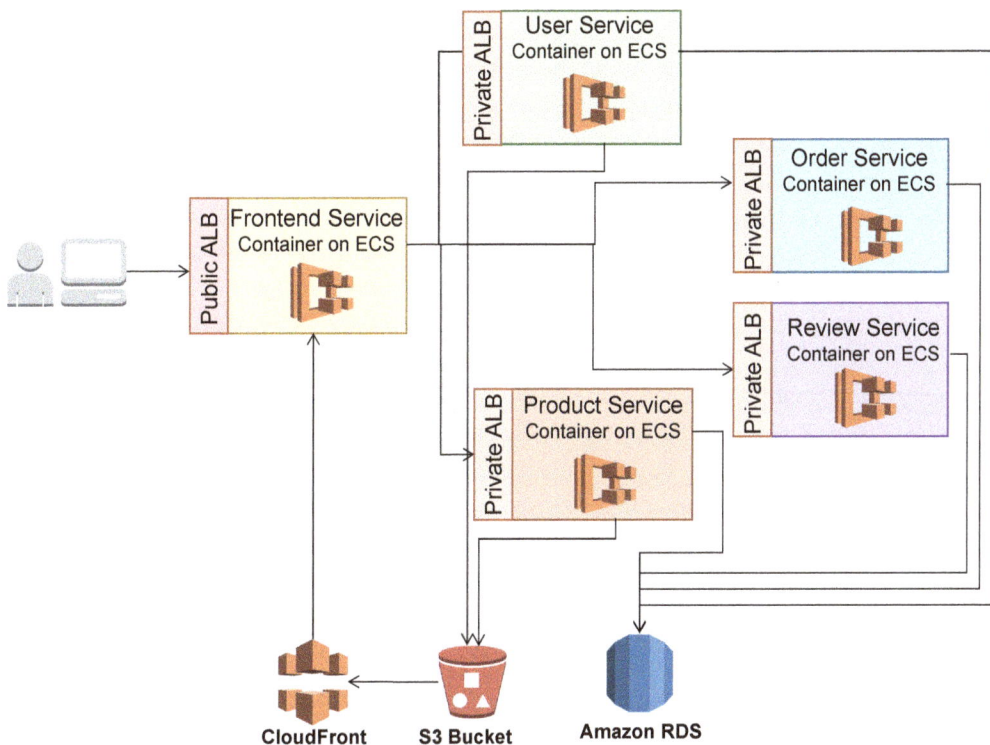

Figure 8.16: Architecture of E-Commerce microservices application on AWS

8.5.1 Amazon Elastic Container Registry (ECR)

Amazon Elastic Container Registry (ECR) is a fully managed container image registry by AWS that enables storing, managing, and deploying Docker container images. ECR provides secure, reliable, and scalable storage for container images used by Amazon ECS, Amazon EKS, AWS Fargate, and other container workloads on AWS.

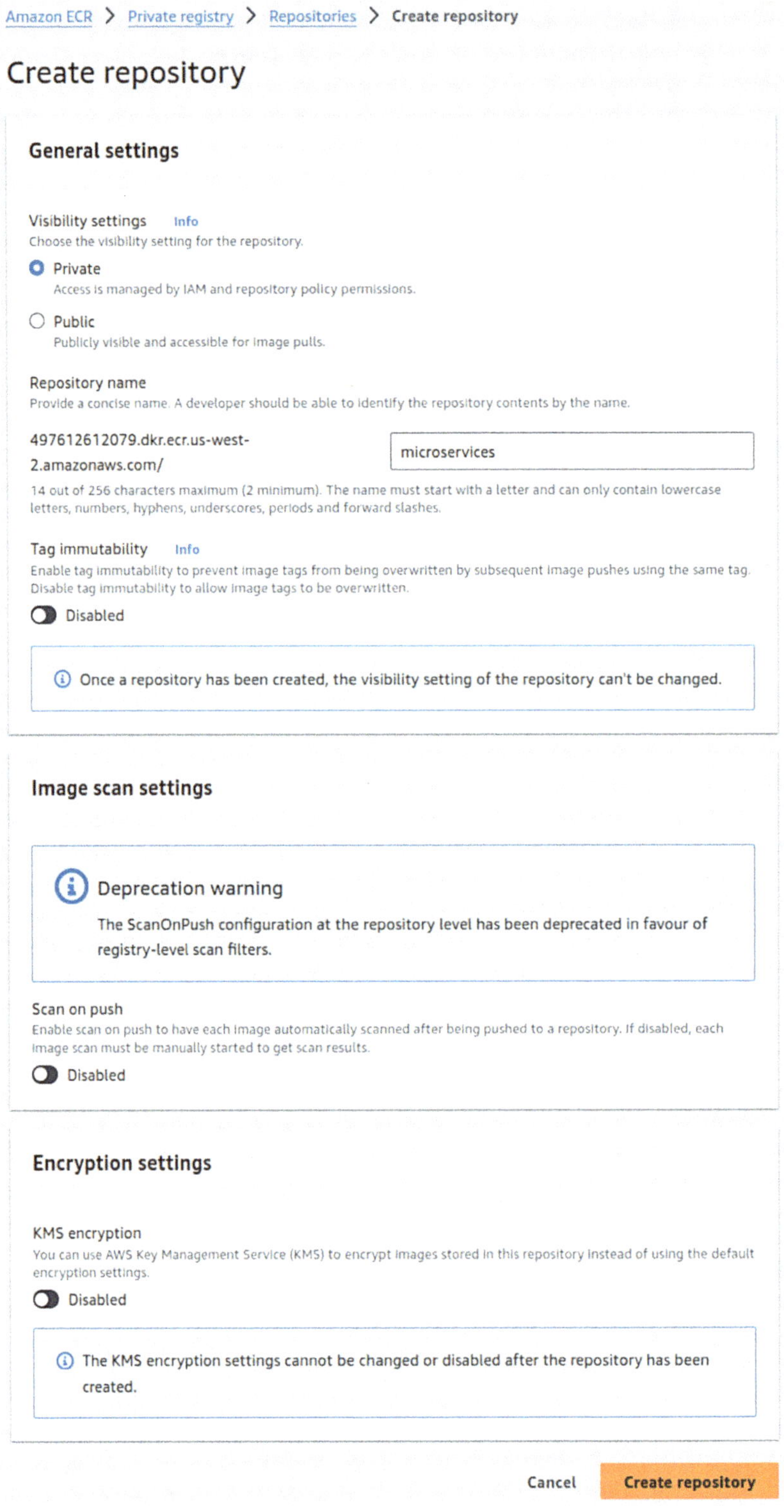

Amazon ECR > Private registry > Repositories > Create repository

Create repository

General settings

Visibility settings   Info
Choose the visibility setting for the repository.

○ **Private**
   Access is managed by IAM and repository policy permissions.

○ **Public**
   Publicly visible and accessible for image pulls.

Repository name
Provide a concise name. A developer should be able to identify the repository contents by the name.

497612612079.dkr.ecr.us-west-
2.amazonaws.com/ | microservices |

14 out of 256 characters maximum (2 minimum). The name must start with a letter and can only contain lowercase
letters, numbers, hyphens, underscores, periods and forward slashes.

Tag immutability   Info
Enable tag immutability to prevent image tags from being overwritten by subsequent image pushes using the same tag.
Disable tag immutability to allow image tags to be overwritten.

🔵 Disabled

> ⓘ Once a repository has been created, the visibility setting of the repository can't be changed.

Image scan settings

> ⓘ **Deprecation warning**
>
> The ScanOnPush configuration at the repository level has been deprecated in favour of
> registry-level scan filters.

Scan on push
Enable scan on push to have each image automatically scanned after being pushed to a repository. If disabled, each
image scan must be manually started to get scan results.

🔵 Disabled

Encryption settings

KMS encryption
You can use AWS Key Management Service (KMS) to encrypt images stored in this repository instead of using the default
encryption settings.

🔵 Disabled

> ⓘ The KMS encryption settings cannot be changed or disabled after the repository has been
> created.

Cancel   **Create repository**

Figure 8.17: Creating Amazon ECR repository

The key benefits of ECR include private image storage within AWS accounts, access control through IAM policies, encryption of images at rest, high availability by replicating across availability zones, auto-scaling infrastructure, integration with AWS container services, and configurable lifecycle policies to automatically clean up old images.

To use ECR, Docker images are built locally or using CI/CD pipelines, tagged appropriately, and pushed to ECR repositories using Docker or AWS CLI. Container services like ECS and EKS can then pull the images from ECR to deploy containers without managing registry connectivity or authentication.

ECR provides fine-grained access control using IAM policies and repository policies to control who can access repositories. Temporary authorization tokens provide secure access for tools like Docker CLI. ECR also enables identity federation and access scopes to implement secure, multi-tenant registries.

For production workloads, ECR replicates images across availability zones for high durability and uptime. It provides DDoS protection, compliance certifications, and backup/restore capabilities. ECR autoscales infrastructure to handle peak loads of millions of requests per minute with low latency. It also minimizes data transfer using image layering.

The tight integration between ECR and AWS container services like ECS and EKS streamlines the workflow of building, storing, and deploying container images. With its enterprise-grade scalability, security, availability, and performance, ECR enables organizations to build robust and production-ready container infrastructure on AWS.

Figure 8.17 shows how to create a private ECR repository. Box 8.11 provides instructions for building Docker images and pushing to the ECR repository. The source code of the application is the same as used in the previous section with Docker. We use *awscli* to retrieve an authentication token and authenticate our Docker client to ECR. Next, we build Docker images using the 'docker build' command. After a build is completed, we tag the image and then push it to ECR. Note the naming convention for the Docker images of frontend, user, product, order, and review is selected such that all these images can be pushed to the same ECR repository. Figure 8.18 shows the images pushed to the ECR repository.

■ **Box 8.11: Instructions for building Docker images and pushing to Amazon ECR**

```
#Login into ECR account
aws ecr get-login-password --region us-west-2 | docker login
        --username AWS --password-stdin
        4936001209.dkr.ecr.us-west-2.amazonaws.com


------


#Build docker images and push to ECR

docker build -f Dockerfile -t ecomfrontend:v1 .
docker tag ecomfrontend:v1 4936001209.dkr.ecr.us-west-2.amazonaws.com/
                                    microservices:ecomfrontend_v1
docker push 4936001209.dkr.ecr.us-west-2.amazonaws.com/
                                    microservices:ecomfrontend_v1

docker build -f Dockerfile -t ecomuser:v1 .
docker tag ecomuser:v1 4936001209.dkr.ecr.us-west-2.amazonaws.com/
```

```
                                                microservices:ecomuser_v1
docker push 4936001209.dkr.ecr.us-west-2.amazonaws.com/
                                                microservices:ecomuser_v1

docker build -f Dockerfile -t ecomproduct:v1 .
docker tag ecomproduct:v1 4936001209.dkr.ecr.us-west-2.amazonaws.com/
                                                microservices:ecomproduct_v1
docker push 4936001209.dkr.ecr.us-west-2.amazonaws.com/
                                                microservices:ecomproduct_v1

docker build -f Dockerfile -t ecomorder:v1 .
docker tag ecomorder:v1 4936001209.dkr.ecr.us-west-2.amazonaws.com/
                                                microservices:ecomorder_v1
docker push 4936001209.dkr.ecr.us-west-2.amazonaws.com/
                                                microservices:ecomorder_v1

docker build -f Dockerfile -t ecomreview:v1 .
docker tag ecomreview:v1 4936001209.dkr.ecr.us-west-2.amazonaws.com/
                                                microservices:ecomreview_v1
docker push 4936001209.dkr.ecr.us-west-2.amazonaws.com/
                                                microservices:ecomreview_v1
```

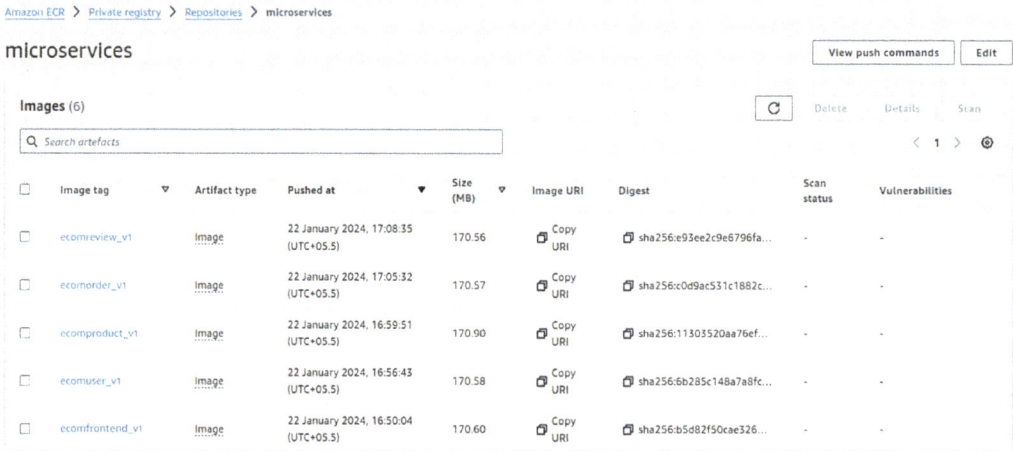

Amazon ECR > Private registry > Repositories > **microservices**

microservices

Images (6)

	Image tag	Artifact type	Pushed at	Size (MB)	Image URI	Digest	Scan status	Vulnerabilities
	ecomreview_v1	Image	22 January 2024, 17:08:35 (UTC+05.5)	170.56	Copy URI	sha256:e93ee2c9e6796fa...	-	-
	ecomorder_v1	Image	22 January 2024, 17:05:32 (UTC+05.5)	170.57	Copy URI	sha256:c0d9ac531c1882c...	-	-
	ecomproduct_v1	Image	22 January 2024, 16:59:51 (UTC+05.5)	170.90	Copy URI	sha256:11303520aa76ef...	-	-
	ecomuser_v1	Image	22 January 2024, 16:56:43 (UTC+05.5)	170.58	Copy URI	sha256:6b285c148a7a8fc...	-	-
	ecomfrontend_v1	Image	22 January 2024, 16:50:04 (UTC+05.5)	170.60	Copy URI	sha256:b5d82f50cae326...	-	-

Figure 8.18: Docker images for E-Commerce application pushed to ECR

8.5.2   Amazon Elastic Container Service (ECS)

Amazon Elastic Container Service (ECS) is a fully managed container orchestration service that enables running and scaling Docker containers on AWS infrastructure. ECS eliminates the need to install, operate, and scale your own container orchestration software by providing a simple API and user interface to launch and stop containers.

Amazon ECS supports launching containers onto Fargate or EC2 infrastructure. With Fargate, containers run on a serverless infrastructure managed by AWS. You don't need to provision any EC2 instances. Instead, Fargate launches containers onto its serverless compute engine. This simplifies infrastructure management as Fargate handles all the underlying servers.

With EC2 launch type, you provision your own EC2 instances as the infrastructure for ECS. ECS manages installing the agent and scheduling containers across your EC2 fleet. EC2 allows more control over the underlying instances including choice of instance type, VPCs, and configuring servers directly. However, you also take on more operational overhead of managing, scaling, securing, and paying for the EC2 instances even when not running containers.

ECS handles starting/stopping tasks and scheduling containers across the cluster based on resource needs and optimization. This removes the manual work of scaling EC2 fleets up and down. ECS abstracts away servers, networking, load balancing, and OS management overhead allowing you to just focus on building and running container images rather than instance management.

ECS integrates with other AWS services like Elastic Load Balancing, Elastic Block Store, IAM, and CloudWatch for monitoring and high availability across availability zones. ECS supports Docker containers natively, and you can further manage clusters using AWS CloudFormation, Terraform, or Kubernetes YAML files. It is cost-efficient leveraging auto-scaling groups, spot instances, and no upfront cluster management fees. The key benefits of ECS include fully managed infrastructure, easy scaling, integration with AWS, Docker image support, and infrastructure flexibility.

To use ECS, you first create a cluster, which is a logical grouping of resources like EC2 instances to run containers on. ECS can automatically provision and manage EC2 instances, or you can run it on your own on-premise servers. For our E-Commerce application, we create an ECS cluster using the Fargate option as shown in Figure 8.19. Fargate is simpler and more hands-off, while EC2 provides more customization of the infrastructure.

After creating a cluster, you define task definitions which act as a blueprint for the tasks you want to run on ECS. Amazon ECS task definitions specify the details of containers that make up your application, including the Docker image to use from a repository, CPU and memory resource allocations, networking and port configurations, environment variables, secrets, mount points, IAM roles, and permissions. To create a new task definition, go to the ECS console and select Task Definitions > Create New Task Definition. Give the task definition a name and select compatibility for EC2 or Fargate. Define the container details like image, memory, ports, etc. Specify the host and container networking modes. Add any additional configuration such as environment variables. Set IAM roles and permissions for the containers. Once created, the task definition can be used to run containers across the ECS cluster based on the parameters configured. Figures 8.20, 8.21, and 8.22 show the steps for creating a task definition for the frontend service of the E-Commerce application. Similarly create the task definitions for other services (user, product, order, and review).

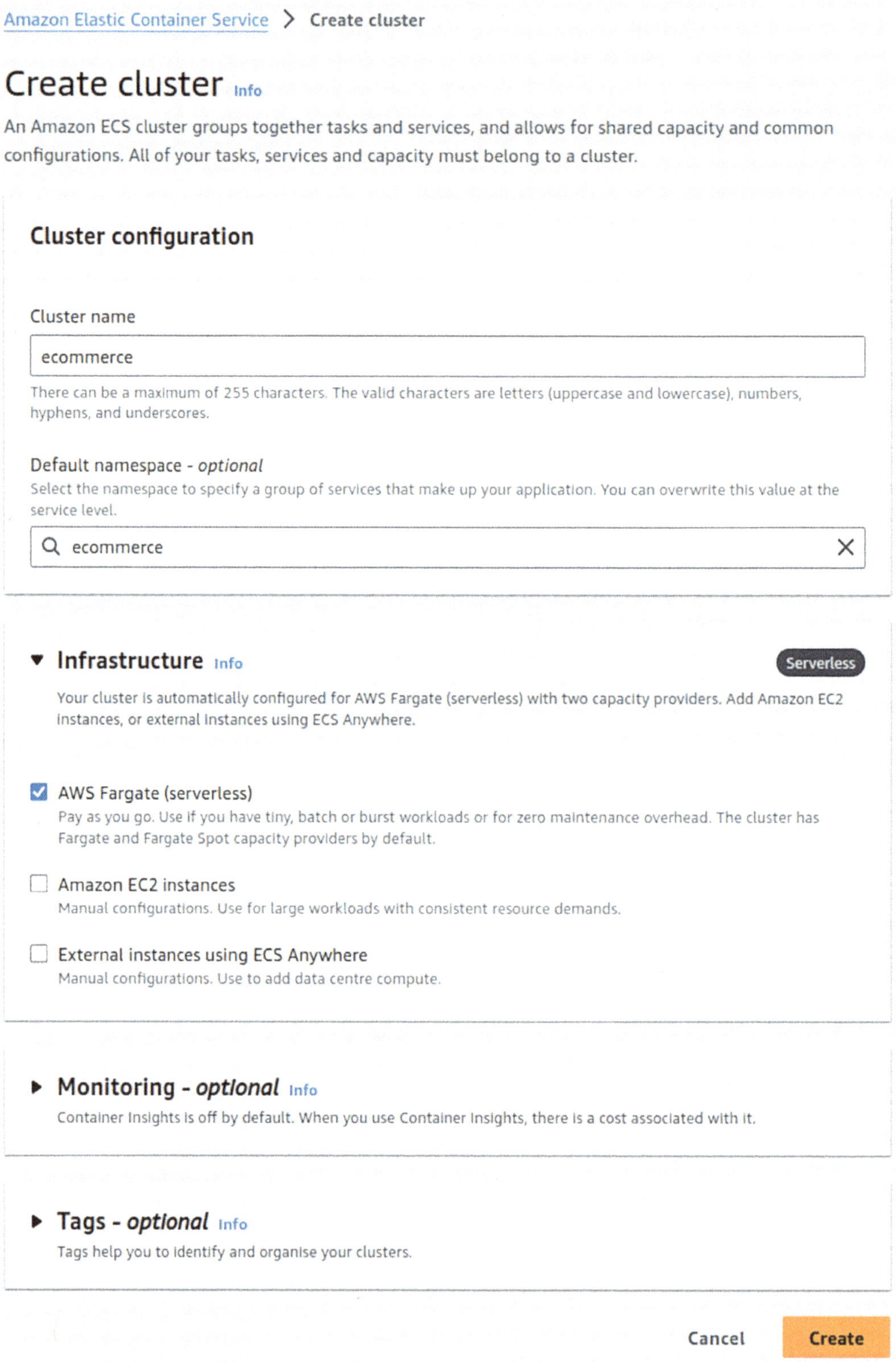

Amazon Elastic Container Service > Create cluster

Create cluster Info

An Amazon ECS cluster groups together tasks and services, and allows for shared capacity and common configurations. All of your tasks, services and capacity must belong to a cluster.

Cluster configuration

Cluster name

    ecommerce

There can be a maximum of 255 characters. The valid characters are letters (uppercase and lowercase), numbers, hyphens, and underscores.

Default namespace - *optional*
Select the namespace to specify a group of services that make up your application. You can overwrite this value at the service level.

    Q ecommerce   ✕

▼ **Infrastructure** Info   [Serverless]

    Your cluster is automatically configured for AWS Fargate (serverless) with two capacity providers. Add Amazon EC2 instances, or external instances using ECS Anywhere.

☑ AWS Fargate (serverless)
    Pay as you go. Use if you have tiny, batch or burst workloads or for zero maintenance overhead. The cluster has Fargate and Fargate Spot capacity providers by default.

☐ Amazon EC2 instances
    Manual configurations. Use for large workloads with consistent resource demands.

☐ External instances using ECS Anywhere
    Manual configurations. Use to add data centre compute.

▶ **Monitoring - *optional*** Info
    Container Insights is off by default. When you use Container Insights, there is a cost associated with it.

▶ **Tags - *optional*** Info
    Tags help you to identify and organise your clusters.

                                                    Cancel   [Create]

Figure 8.19: Creating an ECS cluster

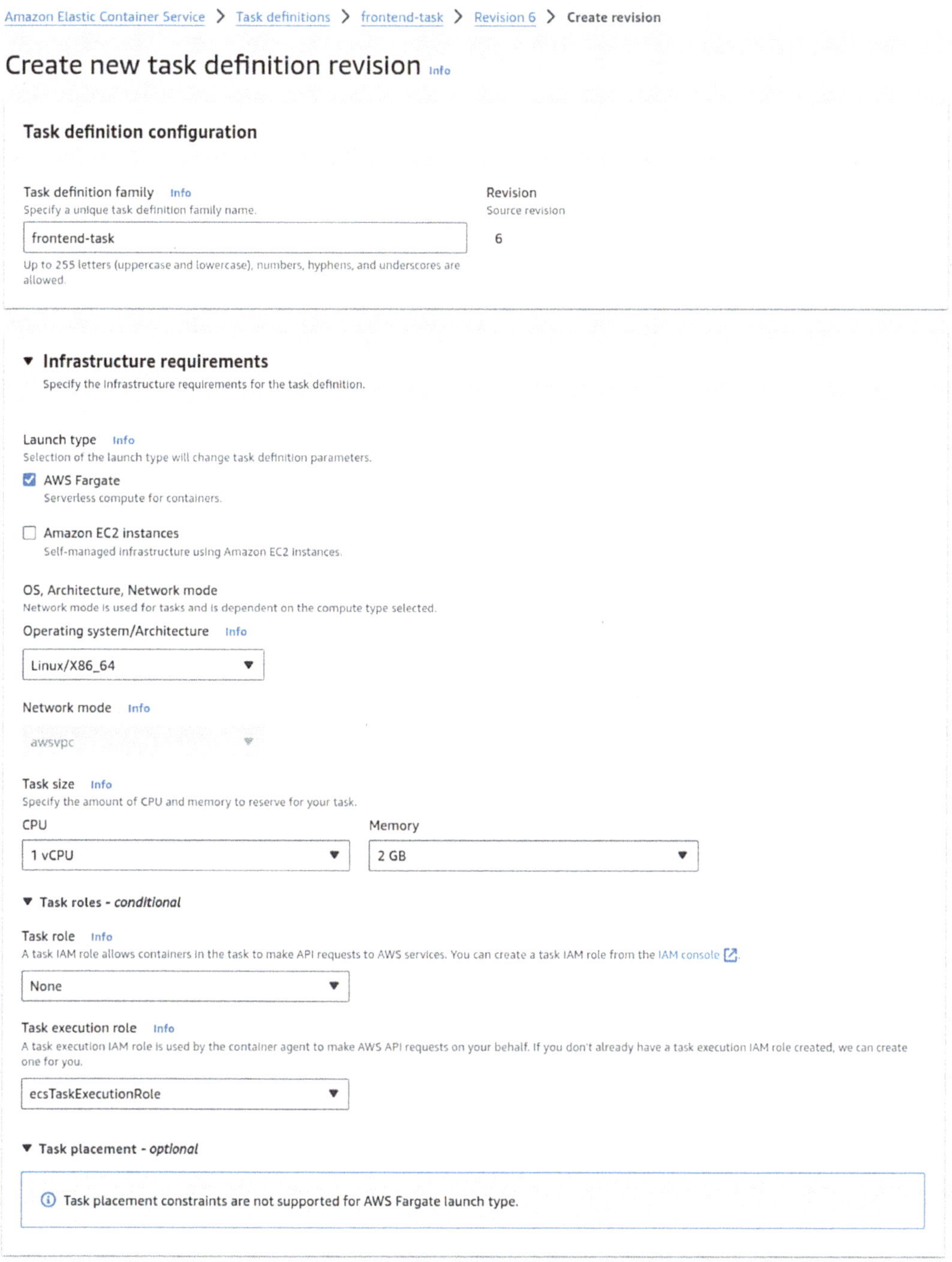

Amazon Elastic Container Service > Task definitions > frontend-task > Revision 6 > **Create revision**

Create new task definition revision Info

Task definition configuration

Task definition family   Info
Specify a unique task definition family name.

| frontend-task |

Up to 255 letters (uppercase and lowercase), numbers, hyphens, and underscores are allowed.

Revision
Source revision

6

▼ **Infrastructure requirements**
Specify the infrastructure requirements for the task definition.

Launch type   Info
Selection of the launch type will change task definition parameters.

☑ **AWS Fargate**
Serverless compute for containers.

☐ **Amazon EC2 instances**
Self-managed infrastructure using Amazon EC2 instances.

OS, Architecture, Network mode
Network mode is used for tasks and is dependent on the compute type selected.

Operating system/Architecture   Info

| Linux/X86_64 ▼ |

Network mode   Info

| awsvpc ▼ |

Task size   Info
Specify the amount of CPU and memory to reserve for your task.

CPU	Memory
1 vCPU ▼	2 GB ▼

▼ Task roles - *conditional*

Task role   Info
A task IAM role allows containers in the task to make API requests to AWS services. You can create a task IAM role from the IAM console ↗.

| None ▼ |

Task execution role   Info
A task execution IAM role is used by the container agent to make AWS API requests on your behalf. If you don't already have a task execution IAM role created, we can create one for you.

| ecsTaskExecutionRole ▼ |

▼ Task placement - *optional*

ⓘ Task placement constraints are not supported for AWS Fargate launch type.

Figure 8.20: Creating an ECS task definition - part 1

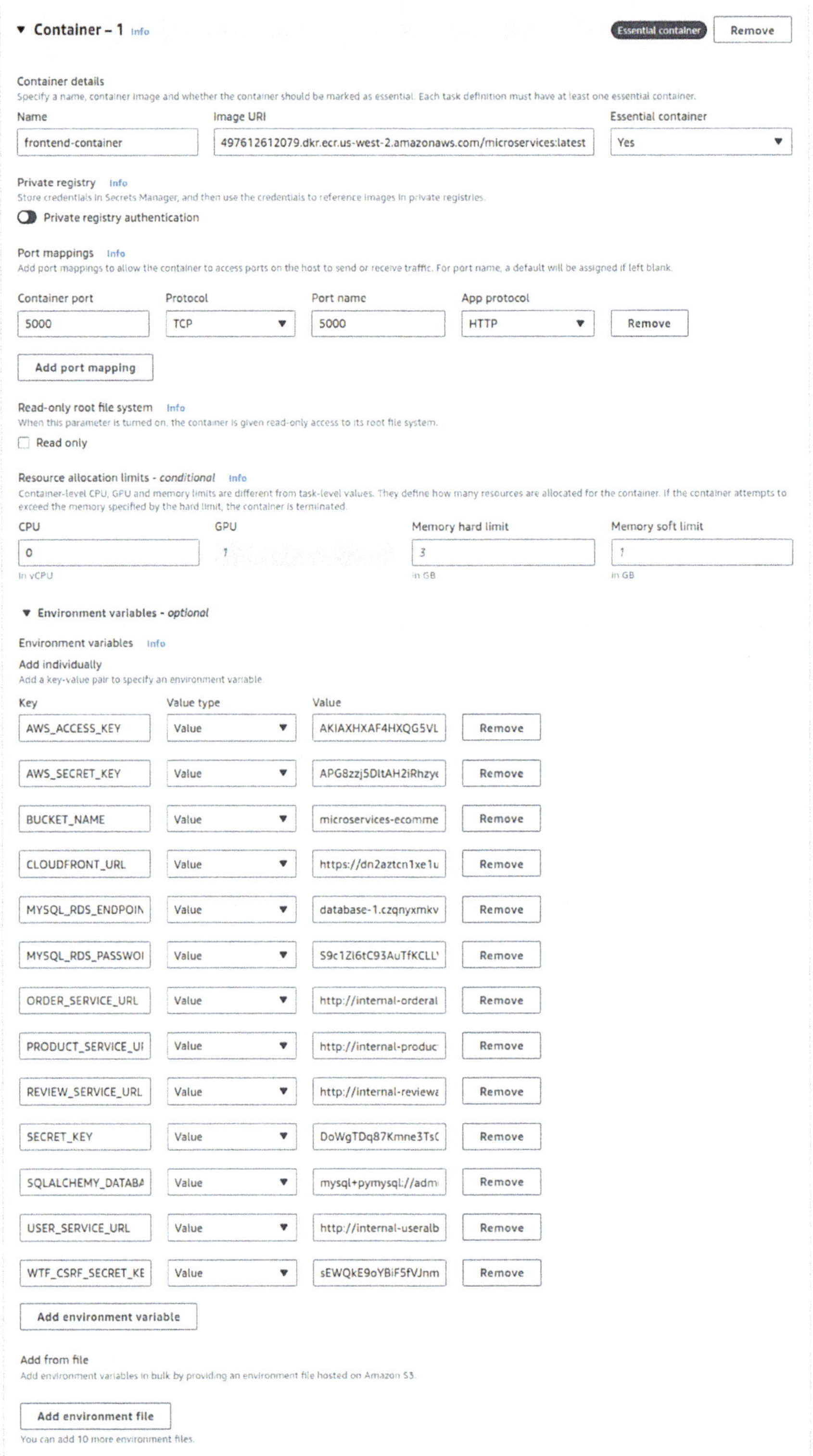

Figure 8.21: Creating an ECS task definition - part 2

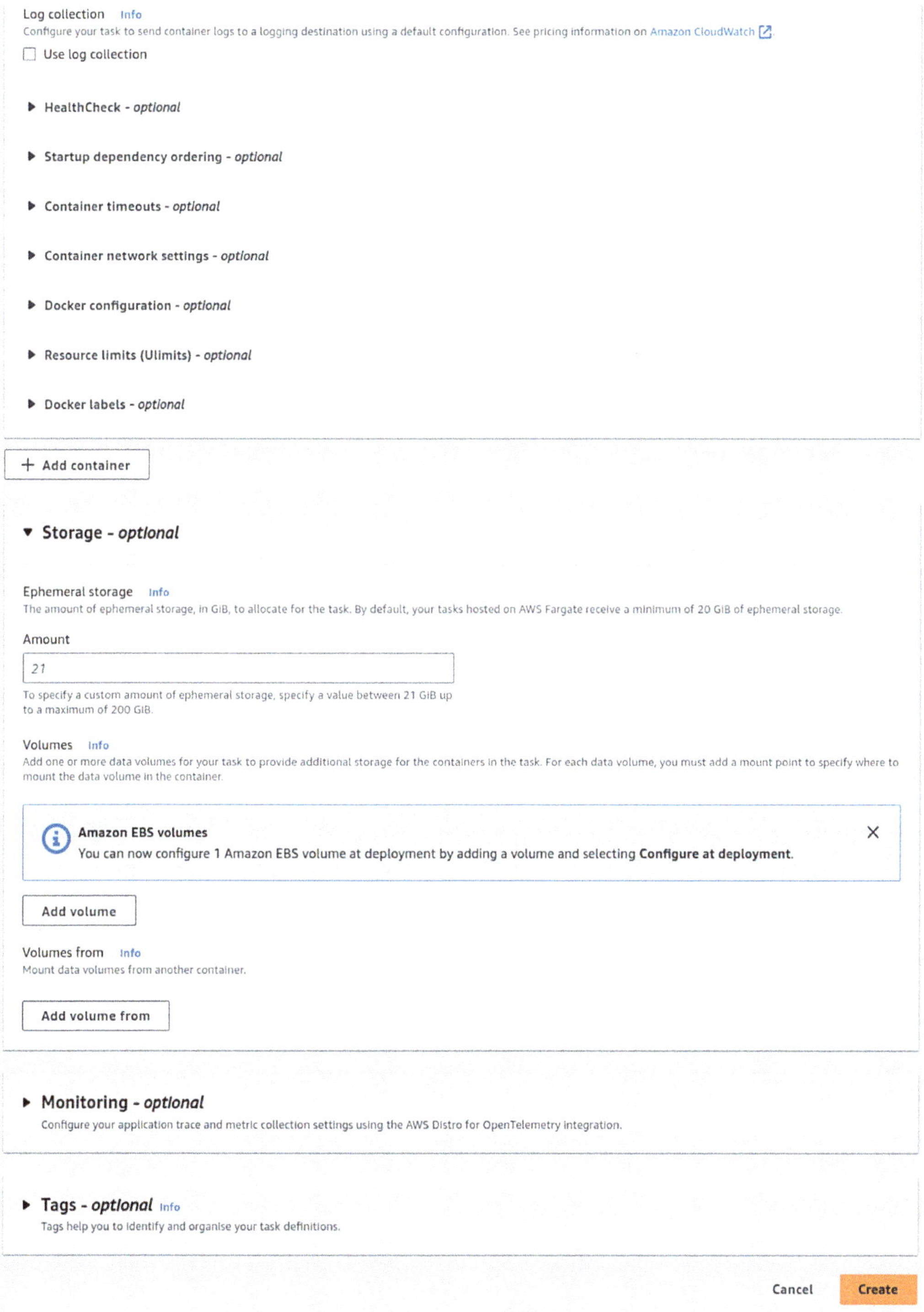

Log collection   Info
Configure your task to send container logs to a logging destination using a default configuration. See pricing information on Amazon CloudWatch [↗].

☐ Use log collection

▶ HealthCheck - *optional*

▶ Startup dependency ordering - *optional*

▶ Container timeouts - *optional*

▶ Container network settings - *optional*

▶ Docker configuration - *optional*

▶ Resource limits (Ulimits) - *optional*

▶ Docker labels - *optional*

[+ Add container]

▼ Storage - *optional*

Ephemeral storage   Info
The amount of ephemeral storage, in GiB, to allocate for the task. By default, your tasks hosted on AWS Fargate receive a minimum of 20 GiB of ephemeral storage.

Amount

```
21
```

To specify a custom amount of ephemeral storage, specify a value between 21 GiB up to a maximum of 200 GiB.

Volumes   Info
Add one or more data volumes for your task to provide additional storage for the containers in the task. For each data volume, you must add a mount point to specify where to mount the data volume in the container.

> ⓘ **Amazon EBS volumes**   ✕
> You can now configure 1 Amazon EBS volume at deployment by adding a volume and selecting **Configure at deployment**.

[Add volume]

Volumes from   Info
Mount data volumes from another container.

[Add volume from]

▶ Monitoring - *optional*
Configure your application trace and metric collection settings using the AWS Distro for OpenTelemetry integration.

▶ Tags - *optional* Info
Tags help you to identify and organise your task definitions.

Cancel   [Create]

Figure 8.22: Creating an ECS task definition - part 3

Figure 8.23 shows the ECS task definitions created for frontend, user, product, order, and review microservices of the E-Commerce application.

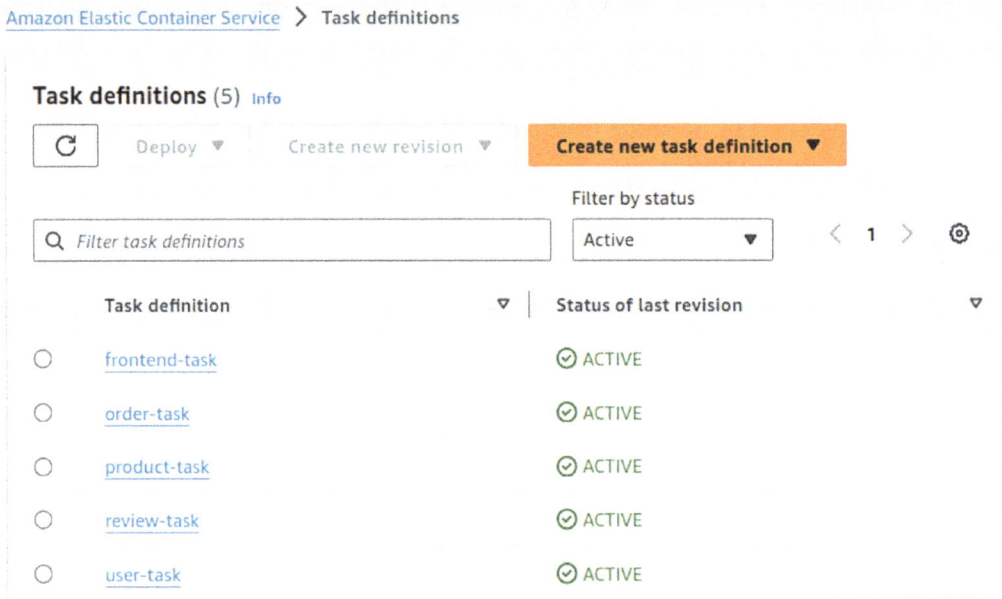

Figure 8.23: ECS task definitions for microservices of E-Commerce app

8.5.3   Amazon Application Load Balancer (ALB)

Amazon Application Load Balancer (ALB) provides managed load balancing for containerized applications running on Amazon ECS. ALB makes it easy to distribute incoming traffic across multiple containers and route requests based on the content of the request.

ALB supports path-based and host-based request routing to different target groups. This enables directing traffic to different containers based on the URL path or hostname. You can implement advanced request routing logic like A/B testing and blue-green deployments.

When creating an ECS service, you can specify an ALB to distribute traffic across the tasks in your service. The ALB will target the containers running on your ECS cluster using dynamic host-port mapping. This avoids having to specify fixed host-ports in the task definitions.

When used with ECS, the ALB acts as the single point of ingress for all traffic to your containers. This simplifies tasks like TLS termination as the encryption offload happens at the load balancer. ALB provides built-in health checks and monitors the status of your ECS tasks. If a task fails its health checks, ALB will stop sending requests to that container and reroute traffic to the healthy tasks. ALB will also drain and reroute connections when ECS needs to scale down or replace tasks to deploy new versions.

Since ALB manages the complexities of request routing, service discovery, health checks, and application availability, it streamlines running containerized workloads at scale. The ECS integration provides automatic container discovery and dynamic mapping, eliminating the need to directly manage changing IP addresses or ports.

Figures 8.24 and 8.25 show the steps to create a target group for ALB. Figures 8.26, 8.27, and 8.28 show the steps for creating an ALB.

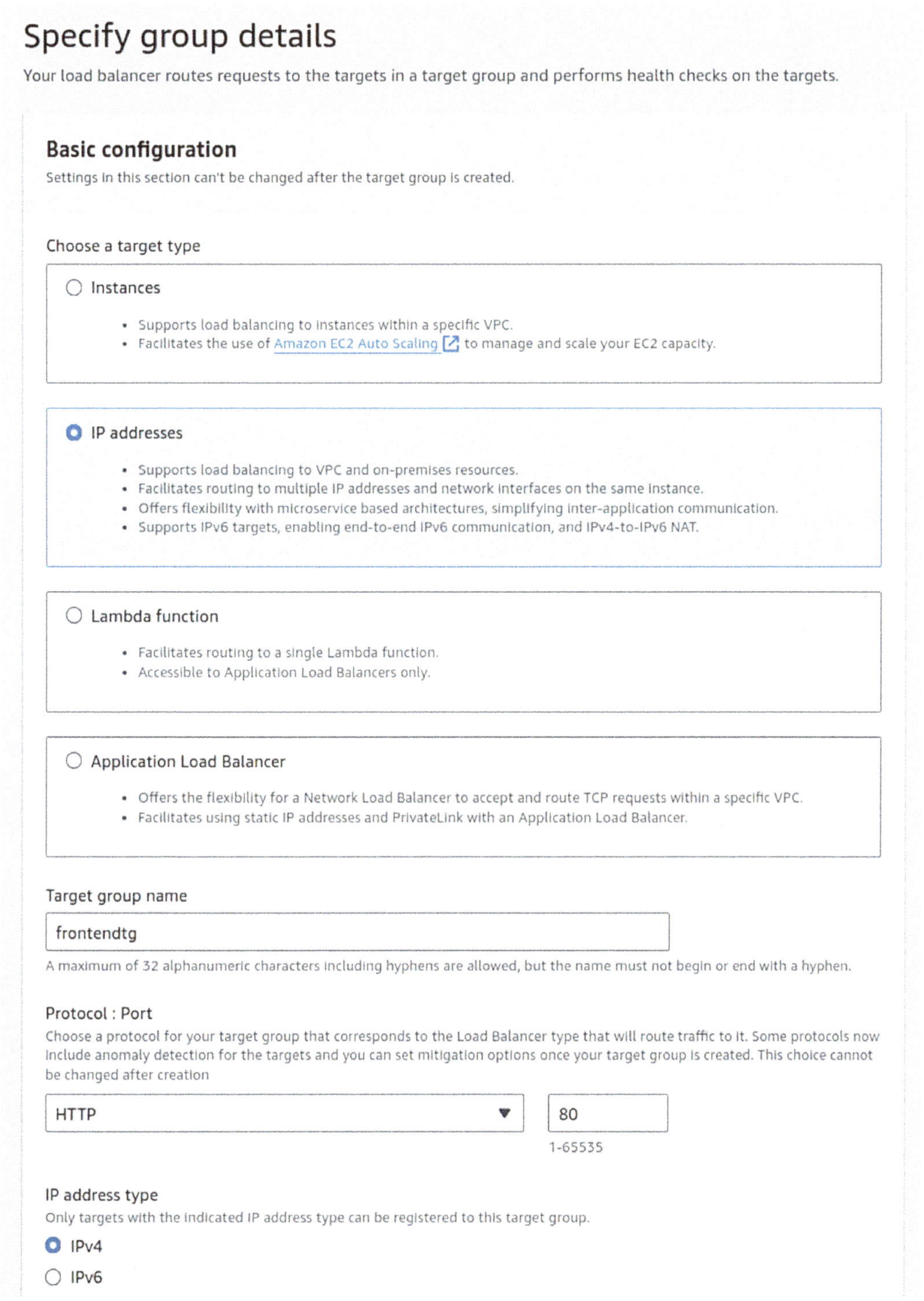

Specify group details

Your load balancer routes requests to the targets in a target group and performs health checks on the targets.

Basic configuration
Settings in this section can't be changed after the target group is created.

Choose a target type

○ Instances
- Supports load balancing to instances within a specific VPC.
- Facilitates the use of Amazon EC2 Auto Scaling ☑ to manage and scale your EC2 capacity.

◉ IP addresses
- Supports load balancing to VPC and on-premises resources.
- Facilitates routing to multiple IP addresses and network interfaces on the same instance.
- Offers flexibility with microservice based architectures, simplifying inter-application communication.
- Supports IPv6 targets, enabling end-to-end IPv6 communication, and IPv4-to-IPv6 NAT.

○ Lambda function
- Facilitates routing to a single Lambda function.
- Accessible to Application Load Balancers only.

○ Application Load Balancer
- Offers the flexibility for a Network Load Balancer to accept and route TCP requests within a specific VPC.
- Facilitates using static IP addresses and PrivateLink with an Application Load Balancer.

Target group name

| frontendtg |

A maximum of 32 alphanumeric characters including hyphens are allowed, but the name must not begin or end with a hyphen.

Protocol : Port

Choose a protocol for your target group that corresponds to the Load Balancer type that will route traffic to it. Some protocols now include anomaly detection for the targets and you can set mitigation options once your target group is created. This choice cannot be changed after creation

| HTTP ▼ | 80 |

1-65535

IP address type
Only targets with the indicated IP address type can be registered to this target group.

◉ IPv4
○ IPv6

Figure 8.24: Creating a target group for ALB - part 1

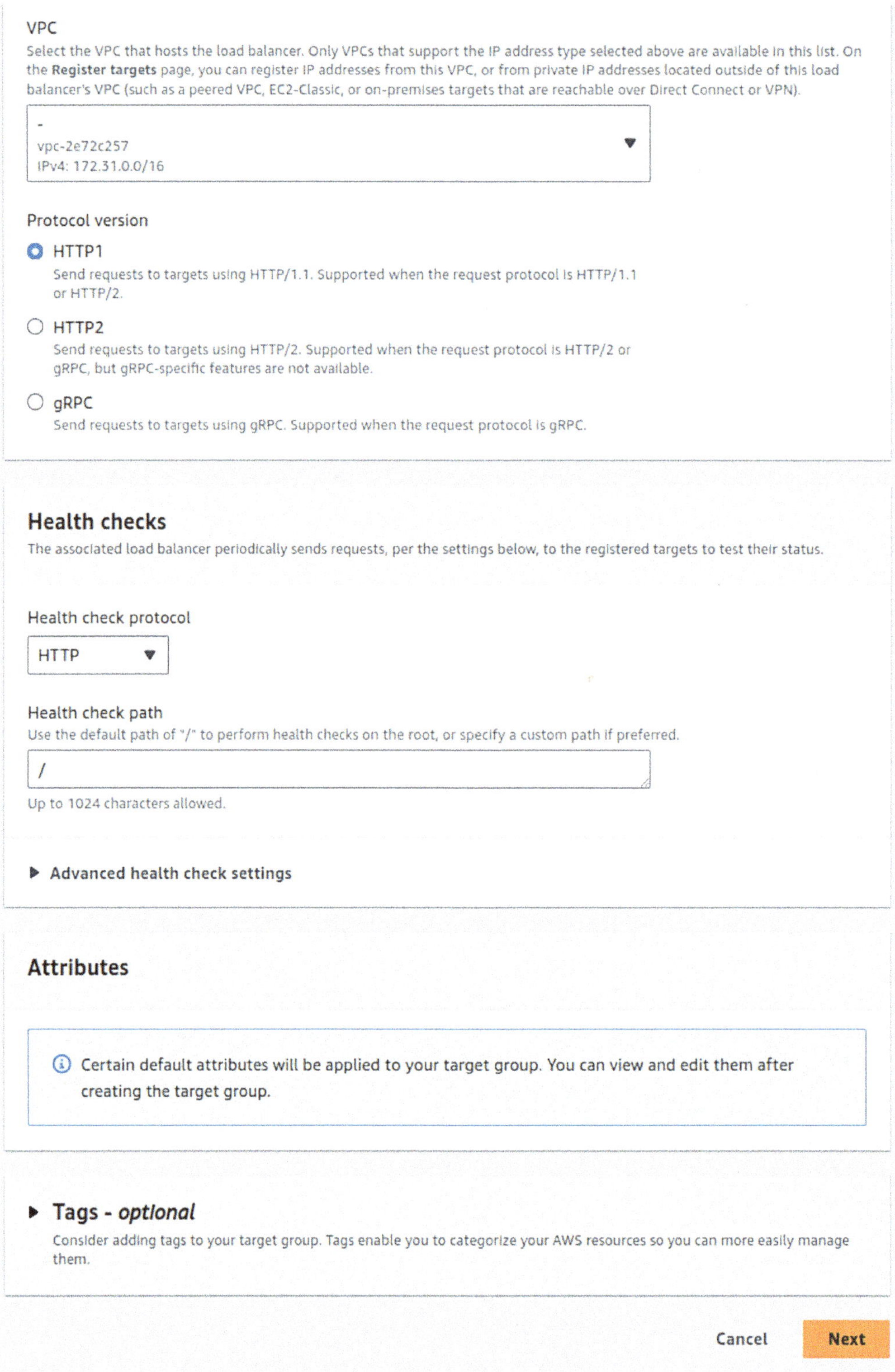

VPC

Select the VPC that hosts the load balancer. Only VPCs that support the IP address type selected above are available in this list. On the **Register targets** page, you can register IP addresses from this VPC, or from private IP addresses located outside of this load balancer's VPC (such as a peered VPC, EC2-Classic, or on-premises targets that are reachable over Direct Connect or VPN).

```
-
vpc-2e72c257                                                                    ▼
IPv4: 172.31.0.0/16
```

Protocol version

🔘 **HTTP1**
   Send requests to targets using HTTP/1.1. Supported when the request protocol is HTTP/1.1 or HTTP/2.

⭕ **HTTP2**
   Send requests to targets using HTTP/2. Supported when the request protocol is HTTP/2 or gRPC, but gRPC-specific features are not available.

⭕ **gRPC**
   Send requests to targets using gRPC. Supported when the request protocol is gRPC.

Health checks

The associated load balancer periodically sends requests, per the settings below, to the registered targets to test their status.

Health check protocol

```
HTTP        ▼
```

Health check path
Use the default path of "/" to perform health checks on the root, or specify a custom path if preferred.

```
/
```

Up to 1024 characters allowed.

▶ **Advanced health check settings**

Attributes

ⓘ Certain default attributes will be applied to your target group. You can view and edit them after creating the target group.

▶ **Tags - *optional***
Consider adding tags to your target group. Tags enable you to categorize your AWS resources so you can more easily manage them.

Cancel   **Next**

Figure 8.25: Creating a target group for ALB - part 2

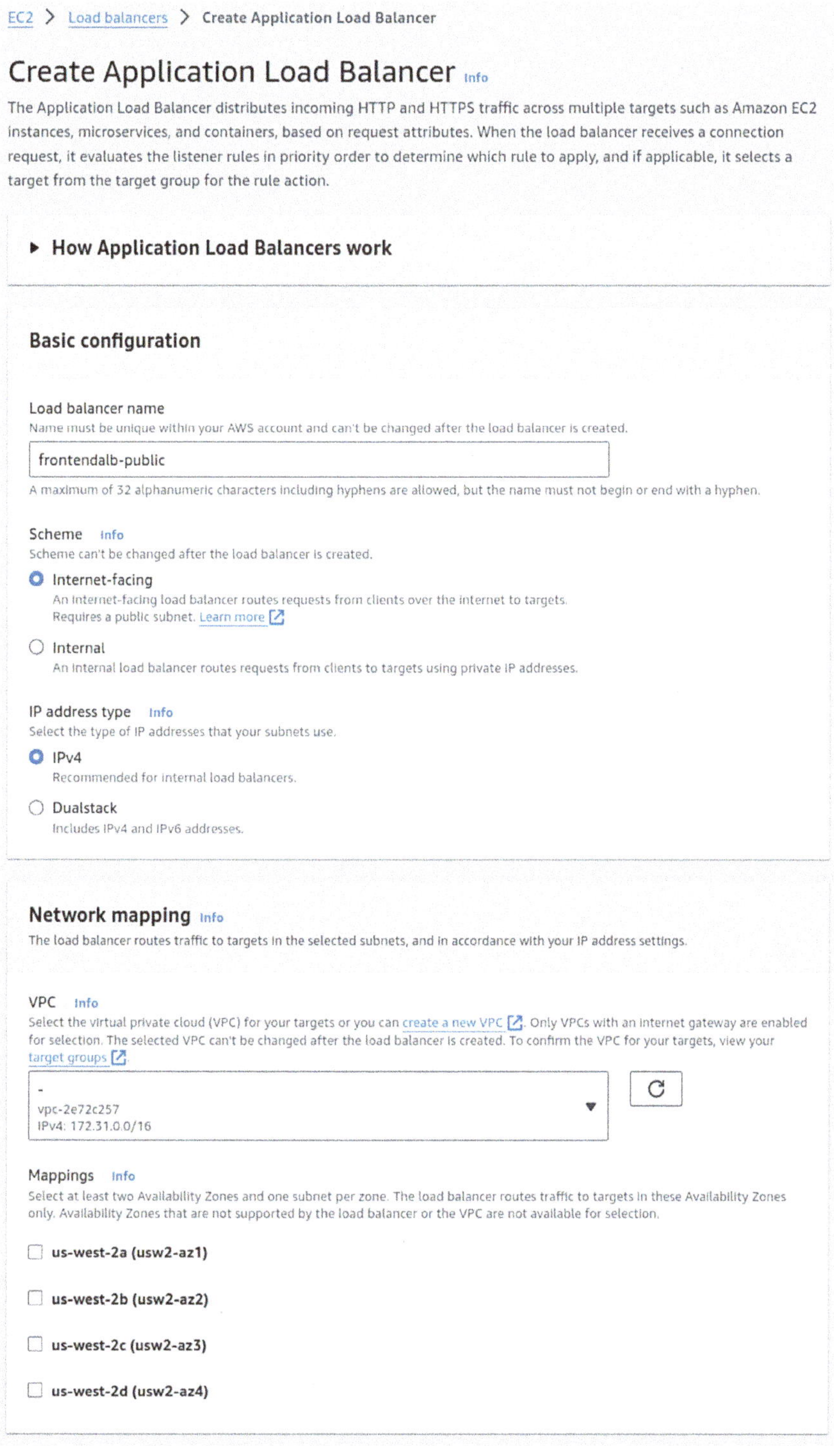

EC2 > Load balancers > Create Application Load Balancer

Create Application Load Balancer Info

The Application Load Balancer distributes incoming HTTP and HTTPS traffic across multiple targets such as Amazon EC2 instances, microservices, and containers, based on request attributes. When the load balancer receives a connection request, it evaluates the listener rules in priority order to determine which rule to apply, and if applicable, it selects a target from the target group for the rule action.

▶ **How Application Load Balancers work**

Basic configuration

Load balancer name
Name must be unique within your AWS account and can't be changed after the load balancer is created.

```
frontendalb-public
```

A maximum of 32 alphanumeric characters including hyphens are allowed, but the name must not begin or end with a hyphen.

Scheme Info
Scheme can't be changed after the load balancer is created.

🔘 Internet-facing
An internet-facing load balancer routes requests from clients over the internet to targets.
Requires a public subnet. Learn more ↗

⭕ Internal
An internal load balancer routes requests from clients to targets using private IP addresses.

IP address type Info
Select the type of IP addresses that your subnets use.

🔘 IPv4
Recommended for internal load balancers.

⭕ Dualstack
Includes IPv4 and IPv6 addresses.

Network mapping Info

The load balancer routes traffic to targets in the selected subnets, and in accordance with your IP address settings.

VPC Info
Select the virtual private cloud (VPC) for your targets or you can create a new VPC ↗. Only VPCs with an internet gateway are enabled for selection. The selected VPC can't be changed after the load balancer is created. To confirm the VPC for your targets, view your target groups ↗

```
-
vpc-2e72c257                                              ▼        ⟳
IPv4: 172.31.0.0/16
```

Mappings Info
Select at least two Availability Zones and one subnet per zone. The load balancer routes traffic to targets in these Availability Zones only. Availability Zones that are not supported by the load balancer or the VPC are not available for selection.

☐ **us-west-2a (usw2-az1)**

☐ **us-west-2b (usw2-az2)**

☐ **us-west-2c (usw2-az3)**

☐ **us-west-2d (usw2-az4)**

Figure 8.26: Creating an ALB - part 1

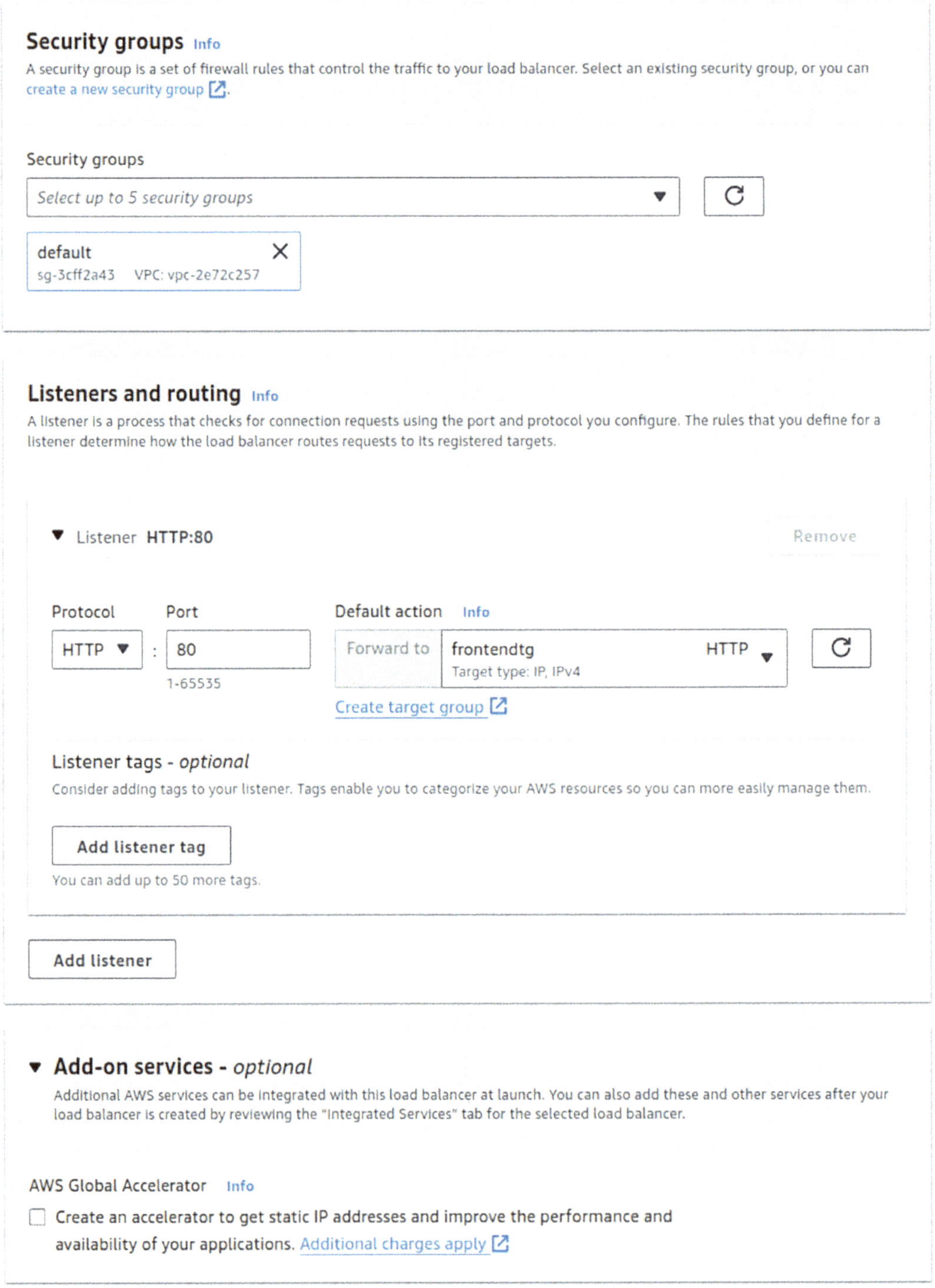

Security groups Info

A security group is a set of firewall rules that control the traffic to your load balancer. Select an existing security group, or you can create a new security group.

Security groups

Select up to 5 security groups

default   ✕
sg-3cff2a43   VPC: vpc-2e72c257

Listeners and routing Info

A listener is a process that checks for connection requests using the port and protocol you configure. The rules that you define for a listener determine how the load balancer routes requests to its registered targets.

▼ Listener **HTTP:80**   Remove

Protocol   Port   Default action Info

HTTP ▼   :   80   Forward to   frontendtg   HTTP ▼
             1-65535   Target type: IP, IPv4

                         Create target group

Listener tags - *optional*

Consider adding tags to your listener. Tags enable you to categorize your AWS resources so you can more easily manage them.

Add listener tag

You can add up to 50 more tags.

Add listener

▼ Add-on services - *optional*

Additional AWS services can be integrated with this load balancer at launch. You can also add these and other services after your load balancer is created by reviewing the "Integrated Services" tab for the selected load balancer.

AWS Global Accelerator   Info

☐ Create an accelerator to get static IP addresses and improve the performance and availability of your applications. Additional charges apply

Figure 8.27: Creating an ALB - part 2

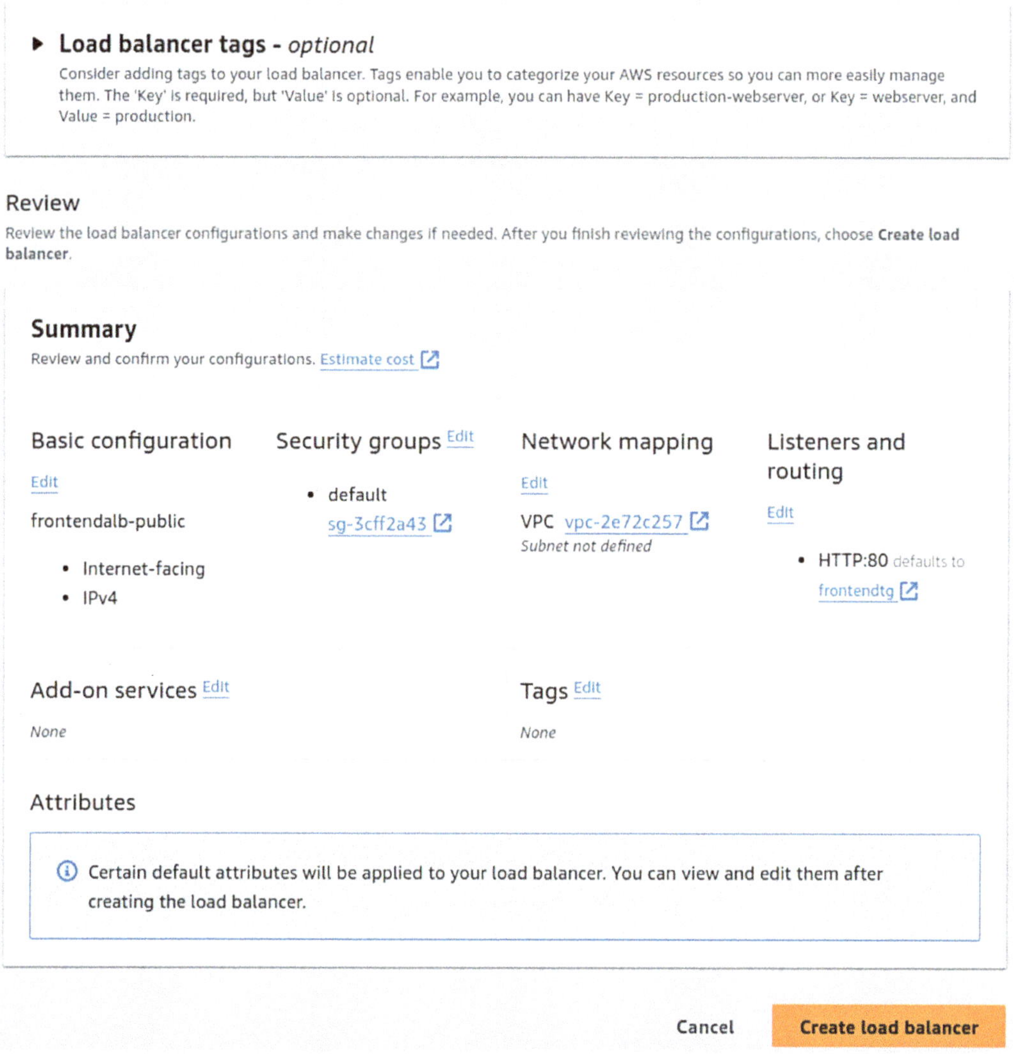

▶ **Load balancer tags -** *optional*

Consider adding tags to your load balancer. Tags enable you to categorize your AWS resources so you can more easily manage them. The 'Key' is required, but 'Value' is optional. For example, you can have Key = production-webserver, or Key = webserver, and Value = production.

Review

Review the load balancer configurations and make changes if needed. After you finish reviewing the configurations, choose **Create load balancer**.

Summary

Review and confirm your configurations. Estimate cost ☑

Basic configuration	Security groups Edit	Network mapping	Listeners and routing
Edit	• default	Edit	Edit
frontendalb-public	sg-3cff2a43 ☑	VPC vpc-2e72c257 ☑	
• Internet-facing		*Subnet not defined*	• HTTP:80 defaults to
• IPv4			frontendtg ☑

Add-on services Edit		Tags Edit
None		*None*

Attributes

ⓘ Certain default attributes will be applied to your load balancer. You can view and edit them after creating the load balancer.

Cancel   **Create load balancer**

Figure 8.28: Creating an ALB - part 3

8.5.4 Creating ECS Services

While the ECS task definitions specify how to build containers, ECS services define how to run them. A service controls the number of tasks running and how they are distributed across the ECS cluster. To create a new ECS service, go to the ECS console and select the ECS cluster created previously. Then choose the option to create a service and select a task definition. Give the service a name and set the desired number of tasks to run. Select the minimum healthy percent, which is the threshold for how many tasks can be down before replacement. Choose the subnets and security groups for the containers to run in.

When creating an ECS service, you can specify an existing Application Load Balancer to route traffic to your containers. Under the Load Balancing section, select your existing load balancer. Then specify the listener and target group that are configured for your load balancer. The listener defines which port to route requests to, while the target group points to the list of containers that will receive traffic. The health check path is used to monitor container health. The load balancer will route traffic only to healthy containers that pass the configured health check.

Amazon Elastic Container Service ❯ Clusters ❯ ecommerce ❯ **Create service**

Create Info

Environment   `AWS Fargate`

Existing cluster

ecommerce

▼ **Compute configuration** *(advanced)*

Compute options   Info
To ensure task distribution across your compute types, use appropriate compute options.

⊙ **Capacity provider strategy**
Specify a launch strategy to distribute your tasks across one or more capacity providers.

◉ **Launch type**
Launch tasks directly without the use of a capacity provider strategy.

Launch type   Info
Select either managed capacity (Fargate), or custom capacity (EC2 or user-managed, External instances). External instances are registered to your cluster using the ECS Anywhere capability.

| FARGATE ▼ |

Platform version   Info
Specify the platform version on which to run your service.

| LATEST ▼ |

Figure 8.29: Creating an ECS service - part 1

Figures 8.29, 8.30, and 8.31 show the steps for creating an ECS service for the frontend microservice of the E-Commerce application. The service will start running containerized tasks based on the selected task definition and configured parameters.

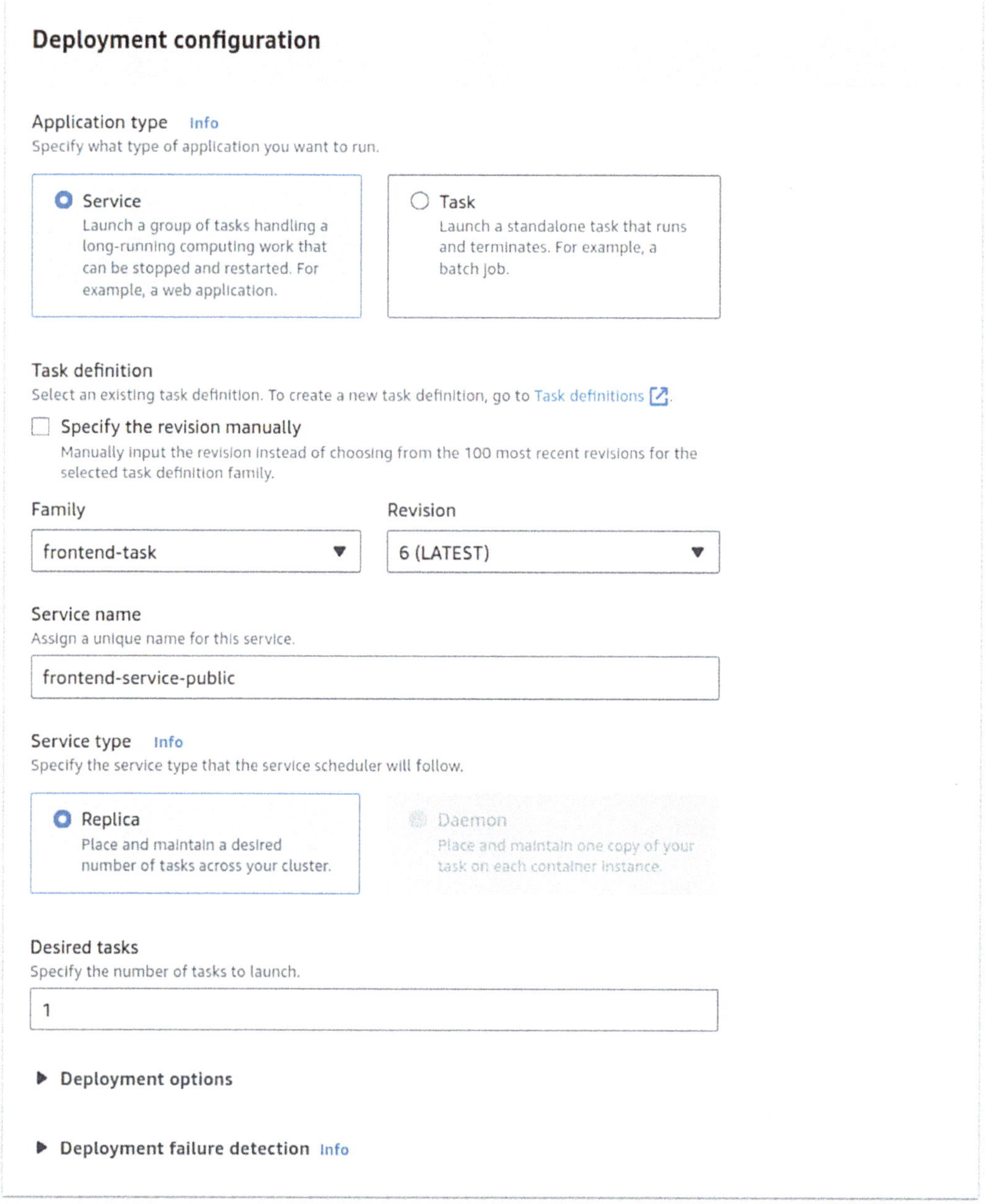

Deployment configuration

Application type   Info
Specify what type of application you want to run.

● Service	○ Task
Launch a group of tasks handling a long-running computing work that can be stopped and restarted. For example, a web application.	Launch a standalone task that runs and terminates. For example, a batch job.

Task definition
Select an existing task definition. To create a new task definition, go to Task definitions ↗.

☐ Specify the revision manually
  Manually input the revision instead of choosing from the 100 most recent revisions for the selected task definition family.

Family	Revision
frontend-task ▼	6 (LATEST) ▼

Service name
Assign a unique name for this service.

frontend-service-public

Service type   Info
Specify the service type that the service scheduler will follow.

● Replica	⚙ Daemon
Place and maintain a desired number of tasks across your cluster.	Place and maintain one copy of your task on each container instance.

Desired tasks
Specify the number of tasks to launch.

1

▶ Deployment options

▶ Deployment failure detection Info

Figure 8.30: Creating an ECS service - part 2

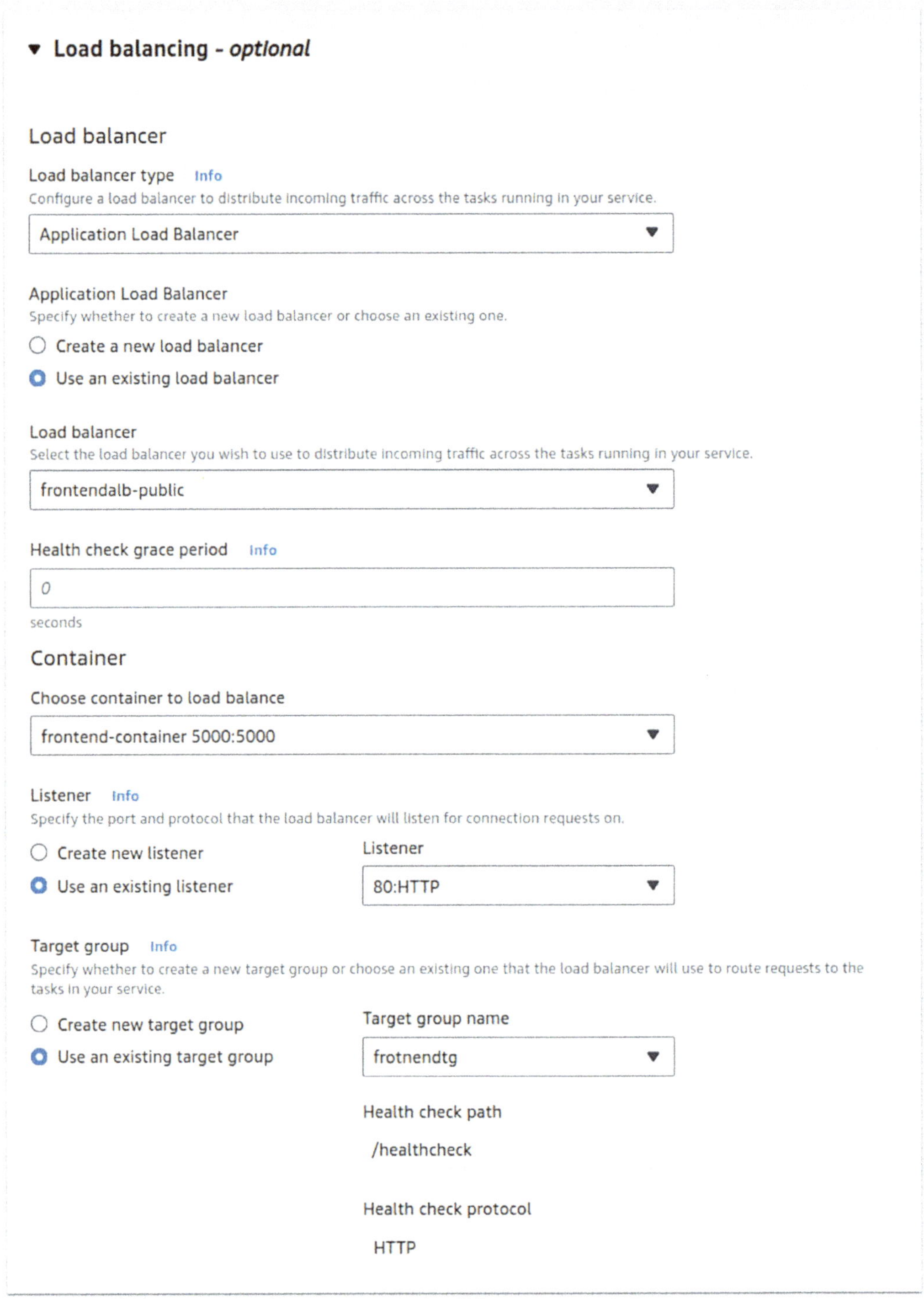

▼ **Load balancing** - *optional*

Load balancer

Load balancer type   Info
Configure a load balancer to distribute incoming traffic across the tasks running in your service.

```
Application Load Balancer                                    ▼
```

Application Load Balancer
Specify whether to create a new load balancer or choose an existing one.

○ Create a new load balancer

● Use an existing load balancer

Load balancer
Select the load balancer you wish to use to distribute incoming traffic across the tasks running in your service.

```
frontendalb-public                                          ▼
```

Health check grace period   Info

```
0
```

seconds

Container

Choose container to load balance

```
frontend-container 5000:5000                                ▼
```

Listener   Info
Specify the port and protocol that the load balancer will listen for connection requests on.

○ Create new listener   Listener

● Use an existing listener
```
                               80:HTTP                      ▼
```

Target group   Info
Specify whether to create a new target group or choose an existing one that the load balancer will use to route requests to the tasks in your service.

○ Create new target group   **Target group name**

● Use an existing target group
```
                               frotnendtg                   ▼
```

                               Health check path

                                /healthcheck

                               Health check protocol

                                HTTP

Figure 8.31: Creating an ECS service - part 3

Similarly, create ECS services for the user, product, order, and review microservices. Figure 8.32 shows all the ECS services for the E-Commerce application.

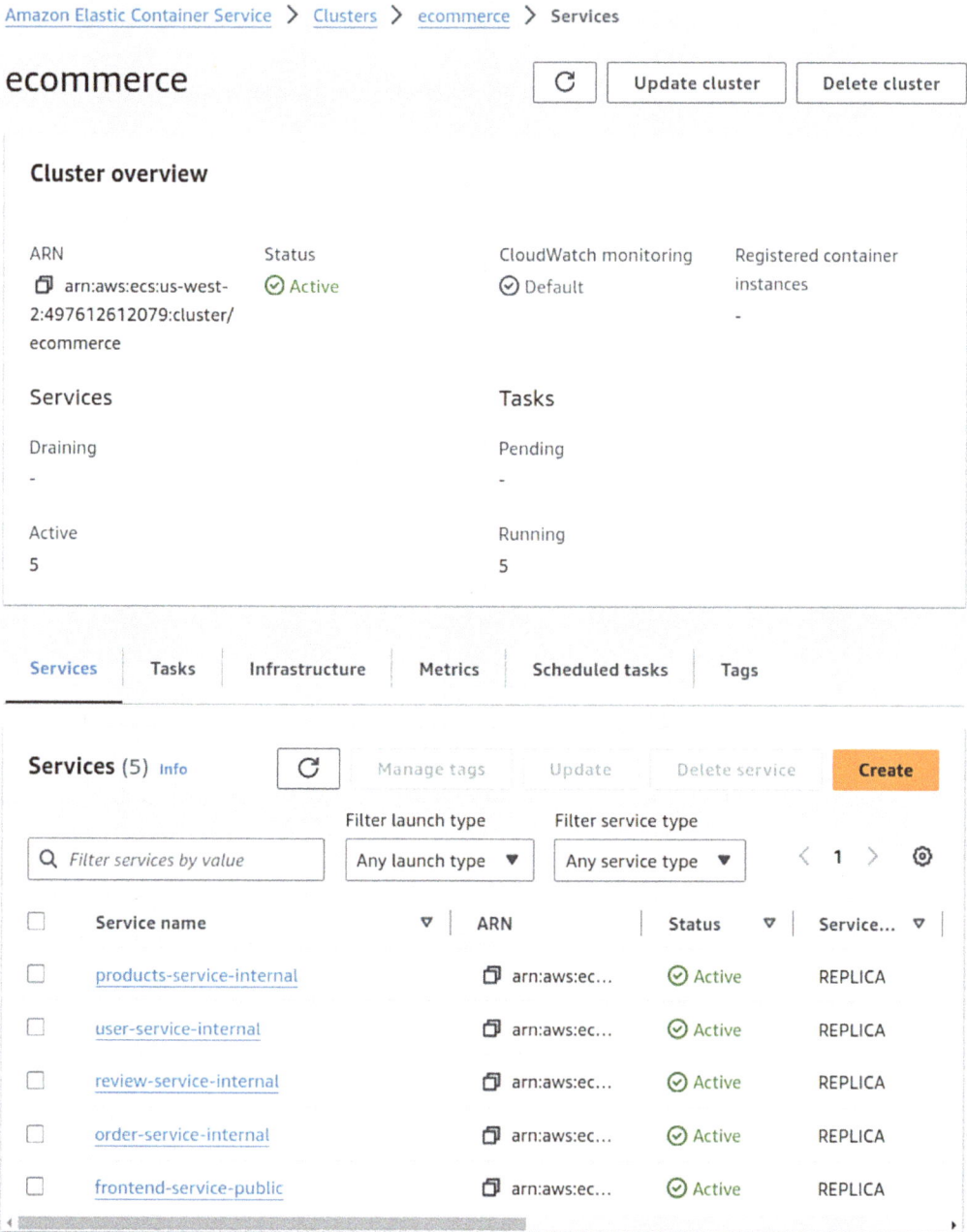

Figure 8.32: ECS services for E-Commerce application

With all the services running, you can browse to the public DNS of the Internet facing ALB attached to the frontend service to access the E-Commerce application.

Summary

In this chapter, we covered containerizing microservices applications using Docker and deploying them on AWS. We described how containerization provides several benefits for building and running microservices compared to virtual machines. Containers are lightweight, portable, and fast, making them a good fit for the microservices architecture. We presented an overview of Docker, which has emerged as the leading container platform. Docker provides capabilities to build, share, and run containerized applications using images, containers, and registries. We explained the Docker architecture comprising the Docker client, daemon, images, containers, and registries. We described key components like Dockerfiles for image builds, Docker Compose for multi-container apps, and networking/volumes for data persistence. We explained containerizing a microservices E-Commerce application with Docker. The application comprised microservices for frontend, user management, product catalog, orders, and reviews. We showed sample code for each microservice modified to integrate a MySQL database and MinIO object storage. A Dockerfile was presented to build images for the services. We demonstrated using Docker Compose to start the full application stack including the database, object storage, and all microservices containers. Next, we described deploying the containerized application to AWS using ECS, ECR, ALB, and other services. We explained pushing built images to Elastic Container Registry (ECR) for private Docker image storage on AWS. We then showed creating an ECS cluster and task definitions to describe how to run the containers. Application Load Balancers were configured to route traffic to the microservices. We presented steps to create ECS services that specify how many tasks to run for each microservice. The services integrate with the ALBs for load balancing across containers. Together, ECR, ECS, ALB, and other AWS services provide a complete environment to deploy the containerized microservices application on the cloud.

CHAPTER 9

IMPLEMENTING HIGH-PERFORMANCE MICROSERVICES WITH GRPC

THIS CHAPTER COVERS

- gRPC Overview
- Microservices Application using gRPC

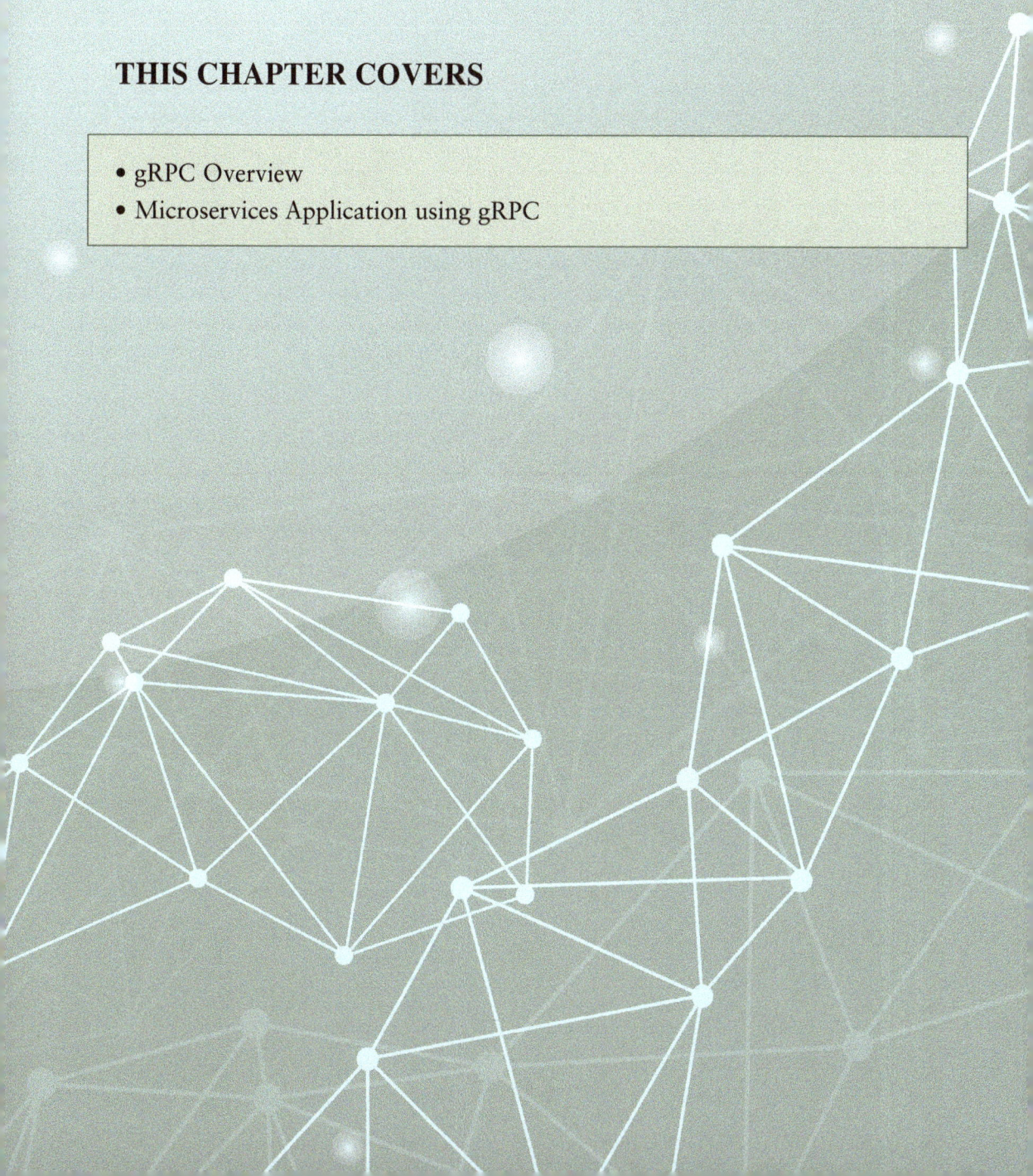

9.1   Introduction

gRPC is a modern, high-performance remote procedure call (RPC) framework that can be used for communication between microservices. gRPC has emerged as a popular alternative to REST for building microservices applications. gRPC uses protocol buffers as the mechanism for serializing structured data between the client and server. gRPC encodes data in binary format using protocol buffers, which are faster, smaller, and less ambiguous than JSON format which is used by REST.

There are several key benefits of gRPC over REST:
- gRPC is a high-performance framework that uses HTTP/2 as a transport mechanism which supports multiplexing, bidirectional streaming, and header compression. This removes much of the overhead associated with REST over HTTP/1.x resulting in reduced latency. Protocol buffers are also more compact and efficient than JSON providing faster serialization. This makes gRPC services up to 10x faster than REST according to benchmarks.
- gRPC provides better API contracts by using protocol buffers. The required structure of requests and responses is explicitly defined in *.proto* definition files which serve as documentation. The strict contracts enable stronger type safety and reduce bugs. Code can be automatically generated from the *.proto* definitions for multiple languages.
- gRPC supports bidirectional streaming, allowing a client to act as a server and vice versa. This is useful for high throughput, low-latency scenarios like real-time chat. REST APIs are unidirectional by nature. Additionally, gRPC allows clients to query or alter just parts of a large message through its support of partial responses. This provides performance benefits.
- gRPC fits better conceptually for connecting microservices since it treats each service interaction as a function call. The *.proto* file defines the function signatures and structured data schema. gRPC calls also simplify client-server interactions to a single network hop compared to REST which requires multiple round trips between calls.

gRPC makes it easier to develop, maintain, and scale mission-critical microservices by providing an efficient, strongly-typed interface definition framework over HTTP/2. Its performance and scalability gains compared to REST make gRPC a compelling choice for microservices architectures going forward.

Figure 9.1 shows a comparison of gRPC and REST. gRPC powers efficient service-to-service communication for microservices. The RPC paradigm, protobuf serialization, and focus on streaming provide significant advantages over REST. However, REST still suits public APIs due to wider language and browser support. For internal communication between microservices, gRPC is emerging as the clear choice.

In the previous chapters, we described the implementation of different versions of a microservices E-Commerce application using REST. In this chapter, we will cover the migration of the REST version of the E-Commerce application to gRPC and dive deeper into the technical details of gRPC. We will demonstrate the advantages of gRPC through the E-Commerce application example.

Feature	gRPC	REST
Contract Definition	Strongly typed .proto schema	Open API Specification (JSON Schema)
	Precise method signatures and request/response types	Flexible documentation of endpoints and payload
Serialization	Protocol Buffers (Protobuf)	JSON, XML
	Smaller payloads due to binary encoding	Readable payloads
	Faster serialization/deserialization	Slower serialization, human readable
	Breaking changes can be handled via proto versioning	Breaking changes harder to detect
API Paradigm	RPC-style call/response	Resources and CRUD actions as endpoints
	Unary, server streaming, client streaming, bidirectional streaming	Request-response only, continuations for streaming
	Strong coupling between client and server	Loosely coupled
Traffic	HTTP/2 multiplexing reduces chattiness	Typically multiple request-response needed per operation
	Uni-directional streams	Significantly more round trips
Streaming	Built-in support for streaming requests and responses	Need continuations, long polling, websockets
	Low-latency streaming	Streaming added on top of HTTP
Browser Support	No native browser support	Broad support with JavaScript HTTP clients
Code Generation	Server and client stubs generated from .proto	Handwritten servers and clients
	Faster and easier client implementations	More flexible but requires manual effort
Tooling	Growing ecosystem but still maturing	Mature tools like Postman, Swagger UI, proxies

Figure 9.1: gRPC vs. REST

9.2 gRPC Overview

gRPC provides high-performance RPC-based communication for microservices along with strong service contracts. The key capabilities and features of gRPC are as follows:

- **Efficient Serialization with Protocol Buffers**: gRPC uses Protocol Buffers (Protobuf), an efficient binary serialization format, to serialize structured data between clients and servers. Protobuf is smaller, faster, and less ambiguous than formats like JSON/XML. Protobuf messages are strongly typed and language agnostic, enabling code generation in multiple languages. This facilitates polyglot microservices. The binary protobuf format also results in smaller payload sizes compared to JSON leading to reduced network bandwidth utilization.

- **Bi-directional Streaming**: gRPC supports streaming semantics where a client and server can stream unlimited sequences of requests and responses to each other. This is useful for high throughput, low latency scenarios. Server-side streaming allows sending multiple responses for a single client request. Client-side streaming allows sending a stream of requests from the client. Bidirectional streaming allows asynchronous full-duplex communication which is critical for services like chat, real-time analytics, etc.

- **Contract-first Development with .proto files**: gRPC uses *.proto* files to define service contracts and message schemas. This facilitates contract-first development. The *.proto* files serve as documentation and generate strongly typed code stubs in target languages for both clients and servers. Updating a *.proto* file automatically updates all client/server implementations providing consistency across polyglot systems.
- **Pluggable Authentication and Encryption**: gRPC supports TLS encryption for securing communication between clients and servers. It also supports a variety of authentication mechanisms like OAuth2. Sensitive headers and payload can be encrypted, while metadata like routing data can remain unencrypted.
- **Easy Code Generation and Integration**: gRPC provides plugins for popular IDEs like Visual Studio and tooling like protoc for easy code generation from *.proto* files. gRPC tools generate client libraries in many languages, making it easy to build polyglot microservices. gRPC integrates well with existing systems through grpc-gateway, which provides reverse proxying to REST/JSON APIs.

There are four types of service methods supported in gRPC:

- **Unary RPCs**: This is similar to a normal function call where the client sends a single request and gets back a single response. The client blocks until the server responds.
- **Server Streaming RPCs**: The client sends a request, and the server responds with a stream of responses. The client blocks until the server closes the stream.
- **Client Streaming RPCs**: The client sends a stream of requests to the server. The server blocks until the client closes the request stream and returns a single response.
- **Bidirectional Streaming**: Both sides send a stream of requests and responses. The order of messages is maintained across the streams.

9.3 Microservices Application using gRPC

Figure 9.2 shows the architecture of the E-Commerce microservices application using gRPC. To migrate the REST version of the E-Commerce application as described in the previous chapters, the following steps have to be followed:

- **Define .proto files**: The first step is to define *.proto* files for each microservice (user, product, order, and review). These files will contain the service and message definitions including RPC methods, request/response structures, enums, constants, and comments. Protocol buffers data types should be used to define message fields.
- **Generate stubs**: Next, the protoc compiler is used to generate client and server stubs from the *.proto* files. For Python, grpcio-tools stubs should be generated, including the client stubs for the UI and server stubs for each backend service. The generated stubs can be placed within the respective microservice codebases.
- **Update frontend microservice**: The frontend microservice needs to be updated to use the gRPC client stubs by importing them and modifying the service calls to directly invoke gRPC methods instead of REST APIs. Any streaming requests/responses need to be handled appropriately.
- **Modify backend microservices**: The backend microservices (user, product, order, and

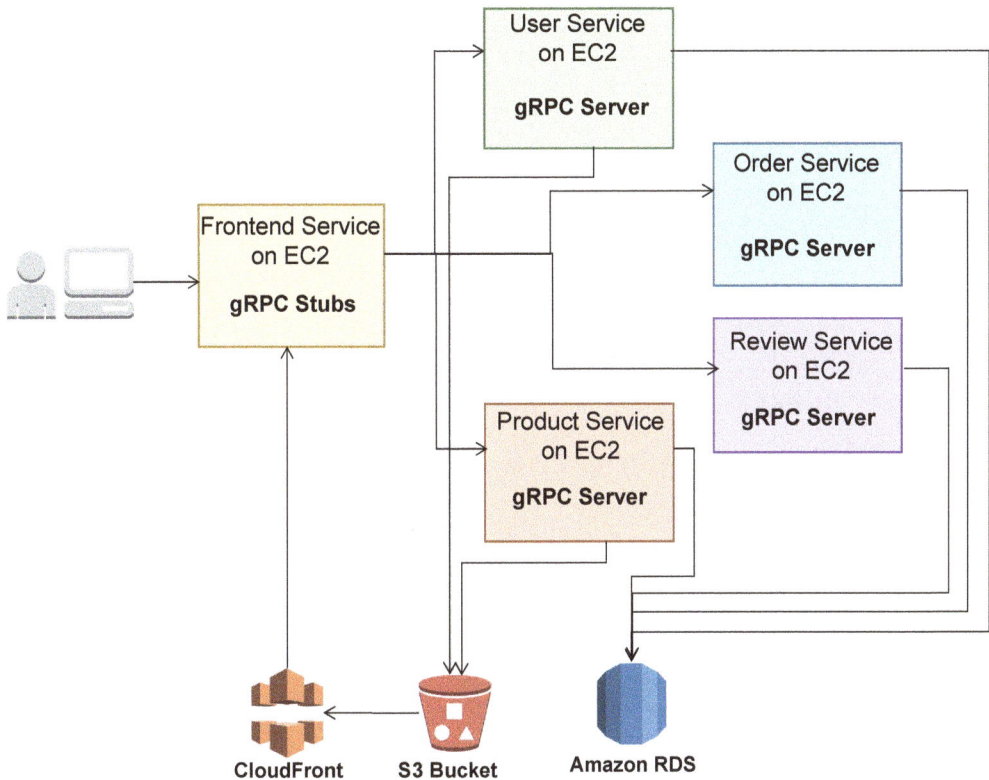

Figure 9.2: E-Commerce microservices application using gRPC

review) have to be modified by importing and extending the generated gRPC server stubs, implementing the service handler methods defined in the *.proto* files, and using protocol buffers data types.

9.3.1 Define Proto Files

The *.proto* files define clean service interfaces and message schemas for the core functionalities of each microservice using Protocol Buffers. The structure and namespaces help in generating appropriate client/server code later.

Box 9.1 shows the *user.proto* file which defines the gRPC service and message schemas for the User microservice. It starts by declaring the *UserService* with four RPC methods - *GetUserById* for retrieving a User object, *CreateUser* for creating a new User, *LoginUser* to handle user login, and *CheckUsername* to verify username availability. The key requests and responses for each of these RPC methods are then defined as message types. The *GetUserRequest* contains the id field to fetch a user, while *CreateUserRequest* includes fields like first name, last name, and username, which are required to create a new user record. The *LoginRequest* has username and password fields for handling login, and *UsernameRequest* just needs the username to check its availability. The *UsernameResponse* returns a boolean result field for the username check. The *User* message defines the actual structure of a *User* object with important fields like id, name, email, photo, admin status, and API key. Primitive protocol buffers data types like string and int32 are used to define these message fields.

■ Box 9.1: User proto file

```
syntax = "proto3";

service UserService {
  rpc GetUserById(GetUserRequest) returns (User);
  rpc CreateUser(CreateUserRequest) returns (User);
  rpc LoginUser(LoginRequest) returns (User);
  rpc CheckUsername(UsernameRequest) returns (UsernameResponse);
}

message EmptyUser {}

message GetUserRequest {
  int32 id = 1;
}

message CreateUserRequest {
  string first_name = 1;
  string last_name = 2;
  string username = 3;
  string email = 4;
  string password = 5;
  string photo = 6;
}

message LoginRequest {
  string username = 1;
  string password = 2;
}

message UsernameRequest {
  string username = 1;
}

message UsernameResponse {
  bool result = 1;
}

message User {
  int32 id = 1;
  string first_name = 2;
  string last_name = 3;
  string username = 4;
  string email = 5;
  string photo = 6;
  bool is_admin = 7;
  string api_key = 8;
}
```

Box 9.2 shows the *product.proto* file which defines the *ProductService* with RPC methods to get products, get a product by ID or slug, and create a new product. The requests and responses are defined as messages - *Empty*, *ProductList*, *ProductRequest*, *ProductCreateRequest*, and *Product*. The *ProductList* message contains repeated *Product* fields to return a list. The *Product* message has fields like id, name, description, slug, image, and price to define the structure of a product.

■ Box 9.2: Product proto file

```
syntax = "proto3";

service ProductService {
    rpc GetProducts(Empty) returns (ProductList);
    rpc GetProduct(ProductRequest) returns (Product) {}
    rpc GetProductWithID(ProductRequestID) returns (Product) {}
    rpc CreateProduct(ProductCreateRequest) returns (Product) {}
}

message Empty {}

message ProductList {
    repeated Product products = 1;
}

message ProductRequest {
    string slug = 1;
}

message ProductRequestID {
    int32 id = 1;
}

message ProductCreateRequest {
    string name = 2;
    string description = 3;
    string slug = 4;
    float price = 5;
    string image = 6;
}

message Product {
    int32 id = 1;
    string name = 2;
    string description = 3;
    string slug = 4;
    float price = 5;
    string image = 6;
    string date_added=7;
}
```

Box 9.3 shows the *order.proto* file which defines the *OrderService* with RPC methods to add items, get order/cart, checkout, and get orders. The requests and responses have message types like *AddItemRequest*, *GetOrderRequest*, *OrderResponse*, and *GetCartResponse*. The

OrderResponse defines the overall order structure. The *OrderItem* is used to define order line items.

■ Box 9.3: Order proto file

```
syntax = "proto3";

package order;

service OrderService {
  rpc AddItem (AddItemRequest) returns (OrderResponse) {}
  rpc GetOrder (GetOrderRequest) returns (OrderResponse) {}
  rpc Checkout (CheckoutRequest) returns (OrderResponse) {}
  rpc GetCart (GetCartRequest) returns (GetCartResponse) {}
  rpc GetOrders (GetOrdersRequest) returns (GetOrdersResponse) {}
}

message AddItemRequest {
  int32 user_id = 1;
  int32 product_id = 2;
  int32 qty = 3;
  float price = 4;
}

message GetOrderRequest {
  int32 user_id = 1;
}

message CheckoutRequest {
  int32 user_id = 1;
}

message GetCartRequest {
  int32 user_id = 1;
}

message GetOrdersRequest {
  int32 user_id = 1;
}

message OrderResponse {
  int32 id = 1;
  string items = 2;
  bool is_open = 3;
  int32 user_id = 4;
  string date_added = 5;
  float amount = 6;
}

message GetCartResponse {
    string items = 1;
}

message GetOrdersResponse {
```

```
    repeated OrderResponse orders = 1;
}

message OrderItem {
  float price = 1;
  int32 product = 2;
  int32 quantity = 3;
}
```

Box 9.4 shows the *review.proto* file which defines the *ReviewService* with RPC methods to add a review and get reviews for a product. The *ReviewRequest* contains the user id, product id, rating, and description to add a review. The *GetReviewsRequest* has the product id to fetch the reviews. The *ReviewsList* returns repeated *Review* objects in response. The *Review* message defines the review structure including id, user id, product id, rating, description, and date fields.

■ Box 9.4: Review proto file

```
syntax = "proto3";

service ReviewService {
  rpc AddReview (ReviewRequest) returns (Review) {}
  rpc GetReviews (GetReviewsRequest) returns (ReviewsList) {}
}

message ReviewRequest {
  int32 user_id = 1;
  int32 product_id = 2;
  float rating = 3;
  string description = 4;
}

message GetReviewsRequest {
  int32 product_id = 1;
}

message ReviewsList {
  repeated Review reviews = 1;
}

message Review {
  int32 id = 1;
  int32 user_id = 2;
  int32 product_id = 3;
  float rating = 4;
  string description = 5;
  string date_added = 6;
}
```

9.3.2 Generate stubs

The gRPC Python stubs for the user service can be generated using the protoc compiler. For Python, we use the following command:

python -m grpc_tools.protoc -I. –python_out=. –grpc_python_out=. user.proto

This command runs the protoc compiler to generate gRPC Python stub code from the *user.proto* file. The *-I.* parameter specifies the current directory as the source include path to resolve any imports. The *–python_out=.* indicates that regular Python code should be generated for the protocol buffer messages into the current directory. Similarly, *–grpc_python_out=.* generates the Python gRPC stub classes in the current directory itself.

This command will output two Python files - *user_pb2.py* and *user_pb2_grpc.py*. The *user_pb2.py* file contains the protocol buffer message descriptors and lookup infrastructure generated from the original *.proto* file. It defines a descriptor pool called DESCRIPTOR that holds descriptors for all the message types defined in the *.proto*. It also contains a symbol database *_sym_db* that maps message names to their descriptors for lookup. The file has methods like *BuildMessageAndEnumDescriptors* and *BuildTopDescriptorsAndMessages* that register all the message descriptors into the descriptor pool and symbol database. It also defines *_serialized_start* and *_serialized_end* constants that specify byte ranges for serializing the message types.

The *user_pb2_grpc.py* file defines the client and server classes for the gRPC service specified in the *.proto* file. The *UserServiceStub* acts as the client, providing methods to serialize requests, make gRPC calls, and deserialize responses for the service RPC methods like *GetUserById* and *CreateUser*. The *UserServiceServicer* is the server class that needs implementation for the RPC method handlers. The *add_UserServiceServicer_to_server* function registers these RPC method handlers with a gRPC server. The *UserService* base class defines the service and enables making direct RPC calls.

Similarly, generate the server stubs for the product, order, and review services. For each service, two files will be generated - *service_pb2.py* contains the descriptor definitions and lookup infrastructure for the messages, and *service_pb2_grpc.py* defines the gRPC client and server classes. The protoc compiler autogenerates these classes from the proto definitions, relieving the user from writing repetitive boilerplate serialization and RPC glue code. This bridges the high-level service definition from the *.proto* file to the underlying gRPC transport and serialization mechanisms. The generated stub code handles serialization and RPC invocation while the user implements the service by providing RPC method handlers.

9.3.3 Update frontend microservice

The next step is to update the frontend microservice to use the gRPC client stubs by importing them and modifying the service calls to directly invoke gRPC methods instead of REST APIs. Box 9.5 shows the frontend microservice configuration code and some utility functions.

■ Box 9.5: Frontend microservice configuration

```
import os, time, json, random
from flask import Flask
from flask_migrate import Migrate
from flask import render_template, session
from flask import redirect, url_for, flash, request, jsonify
from flask_login import current_user
from flask_wtf import FlaskForm
from wtforms import StringField, PasswordField
from flask import SubmitField, HiddenField, IntegerField
from wtforms.validators import DataRequired, Email
from flask_bootstrap import Bootstrap
from flask_login import LoginManager, UserMixin
from flask_login import current_user, login_user
from flask import logout_user, login_required
from flask import session, request
from werkzeug.utils import secure_filename
import grpc
import product_pb2, product_pb2_grpc
import review_pb2, review_pb2_grpc
import order_pb2, order_pb2_grpc
import user_pb2, user_pb2_grpc
import boto3
import requests
import avinit

login_manager = LoginManager()
bootstrap = Bootstrap()

app = Flask(__name__, static_folder='static')
app.config['UPLOAD_FOLDER'] = 'static/images'
app.config['SECRET_KEY'] = "DoWgTDq87Kmne3TsCjNFabP"
app.config['WTF_CSRF_SECRET_KEY'] = "sEWQkE9oYBiF5fVJnm278i7"
app.config['ENV'] = "development"
app.config['DEBUG'] = True
app.config['BUCKET_NAME'] = 'microservices-ecommerce-app'
app.config['CLOUDFRONT_URL'] = 'https://dn2aztcn1xe1u.cloudfront.net'
app.config['UPLOAD_FOLDER'] = 'uploads'
app.config['AWS_ACCESS_KEY'] = 'EXAMPLEKEY'
app.config['AWS_SECRET_KEY'] = 'EXAMPLESECRET'

USER_SERVICE_URL='localhost:50054'
PRODUCT_SERVICE_URL='localhost:50051'
ORDER_SERVICE_URL='localhost:50053'
REVIEW_SERVICE_URL='localhost:50052'

login_manager.init_app(app)
```

```python
login_manager.login_message = "Please login"
login_manager.login_view = "login"

@login_manager.user_loader
def load_user(user_id):
    userclient=UserClient()
    user=userclient.get_user(user_id)
    return User(user)


def get_user_name_photo():
    try:
        user_name = session['user']['first_name']+" "+
                                session['user']['last_name']
        user_photo = session['user']['photo']
    except:
        user_name=''
        user_photo=''
    return user_name, user_photo


def s3uploading(filename):
    s3 = boto3.client('s3',
        aws_access_key_id=app.config['AWS_ACCESS_KEY'],
        aws_secret_access_key=app.config['AWS_SECRET_KEY'])
    bucket = app.config['BUCKET_NAME']
    path_filename_disk = os.path.join(app.config['UPLOAD_FOLDER'],
                                filename)
    path_filename_s3 = "photos/" + filename
    s3.upload_file(path_filename_disk, bucket, path_filename_s3)
    url = app.config['CLOUDFRONT_URL']+'/'+path_filename_s3
    return url
```

Box 9.6 shows the implementation of the frontend service including the gRPC clients to communicate with backend services (user, product, order, and review). These gRPC clients encapsulate communication with all the backend services, allowing the frontend to get/post data from them easily. The frontend just calls these clients without worrying about the gRPC complexities. The *User* class is used to represent a User object for Flask-Login. The *UserClient* is a gRPC client to talk to the user microservice. It has methods to login, register, and get a user. The *ProductClient* is a gRPC client to talk to the product microservice. It has methods to get products, get a product by id/slug, and create a product. The *OrderClient* is a gRPC client to talk to the order microservice. It has methods to get orders, add to cart, and checkout. The *ReviewClient* is a gRPC client to talk to the review microservice. It has methods to get reviews for a product, and add a review. The clients initialize a gRPC channel and stub to talk to the backend services. The methods make gRPC requests and return the response in a dictionary format. This allows the Flask frontend to call these clients to retrieve data from the services and pass it to the templates for rendering.

■ Box 9.6: Frontend microservice clients and gRPC stubs

```python
class User(UserMixin):
    def __init__(self, user_data):
        self.id = user_data.get('id')

    def get_id(self):
        return self.id

class UserClient:
    def __init__(self):
        self.channel = grpc.insecure_channel(USER_SERVICE_URL)
        self.stub = user_pb2_grpc.UserServiceStub(self.channel)

    def post_login(self, username, password):
        request = user_pb2.LoginRequest(username=username,
                                        password=password)
        response = self.stub.LoginUser(request)
        try:
            userdic = {
            'id': response.id,
            'first_name': response.first_name,
            'last_name': response.last_name,
            'username': response.username,
            'email': response.email,
            'photo': response.photo,
            'is_admin': response.is_admin,
            'api_key': response.api_key
            }
        except:
            userdic={}
            userdic['api_key']=False
        return userdic

    def get_user(self, user_id):
        request = user_pb2.GetUserRequest(id=user_id)
        response = self.stub.GetUserById(request)
        userdic = {
            'id': response.id,
            'first_name': response.first_name,
            'last_name': response.last_name,
            'username': response.username,
            'email': response.email,
            'photo': response.photo,
            'is_admin': response.is_admin,
            'api_key': response.api_key
            }
        return userdic

    def post_user_create(self, first_name, last_name,
                    username, email, password, photo):
        request = user_pb2.CreateUserRequest(first_name=first_name,
            last_name=last_name, username=username,
            email=email, password=password, photo=photo)
```

```python
        response = self.stub.CreateUser(request)

        userdic = {
            'id': response.id,
            'first_name': response.first_name,
            'last_name': response.last_name,
            'username': response.username,
            'email': response.email,
            'photo': response.photo,
            'is_admin': response.is_admin,
            'api_key': response.api_key
            }
        return userdic

    def does_exist(self, username):
        request = user_pb2.UsernameRequest(username=username)
        response = self.stub.CheckUsername(request)
        return response.result

class ProductClient:
    def __init__(self):
        self.channel = grpc.insecure_channel(PRODUCT_SERVICE_URL)
        self.stub = product_pb2_grpc.ProductServiceStub(self.channel)

    def get_products(self):
        request = product_pb2.Empty()
        response = self.stub.GetProducts(request)
        # Convert response to list
        products = []
        for p in response.products:
            product = {
            'id': p.id,
            'name': p.name,
            'price': round(p.price,2),
            'description': p.description,
            'slug': p.slug,
            'image': p.image
            }
            products.append(product)

        productsdic={}
        productsdic['results']=products
        return productsdic

    def get_product(self, slug):
        request = product_pb2.ProductRequest(slug=slug)
        response = self.stub.GetProduct(request)
        product = {
            'id': response.id,
            'name': response.name,
            'price': round(response.price,2),
            'description': response.description,
            'slug': response.slug,
            'image': response.image
```

```
            }
        productsdic={}
        productsdic['result']=product
        return productsdic

    def get_product_with_id(self, pid):
        request = product_pb2.ProductRequestID(id=pid)
        response = self.stub.GetProductWithID(request)
        product = {
            'id': response.id,
            'name': response.name,
            'description': response.description,
            'slug': response.slug,
            'price': round(response.price,2),
            'image': response.image
            }
        productsdic={}
        productsdic['result']=product
        return productsdic

    def create_product(self, name, description,
                    slug, price, uploadedFileURL):
        request = product_pb2.ProductCreateRequest(name=name,
                    description=description, slug=slug,
                    price=price, image=uploadedFileURL)
        response = self.stub.CreateProduct(request)
        product = {
            'id': response.id,
            'name': response.name,
            'price': round(response.price,2),
            'description': response.description,
            'slug': response.slug,
            'image': response.image
            }
        productsdic={}
        productsdic['result']=product
        return productsdic

class OrderClient:
    def __init__(self):
        self.channel = grpc.insecure_channel(ORDER_SERVICE_URL)
        self.stub = order_pb2_grpc.OrderServiceStub(self.channel)

    def get_order(self, user_id):
        request = order_pb2.GetOrderRequest(user_id=user_id)
        response = self.stub.GetOrder(request)
        orderdic={}
        try:
            order = {
                'id': response.id,
                'items': json.loads(response.items),
                'is_open': response.is_open,
                'user_id': response.user_id,
                'date_added': response.date_added,
```

```
                        'amount': round(response.amount,2)
            }
        except:
            order={}
        orderdic['result']=order
        return orderdic

    def get_orders(self, user_id):
        request = order_pb2.GetOrdersRequest(user_id=user_id)
        response = self.stub.GetOrders(request)
        orders = []
        for p in response.orders:
            product = {
                'id': p.id,
                'items': json.loads(p.items),
                'is_open': p.is_open,
                'user_id': p.user_id,
                'date_added': p.date_added,
                'amount': round(p.amount,2)
            }
            orders.append(product)

        ordersdic={}
        ordersdic['result']=orders
        return ordersdic

    def get_cart(self, user_id):
        request = order_pb2.GetCartRequest(user_id=user_id)
        response = self.stub.GetCart(request)
        items=json.loads(response.items)
        ordersdic={}
        ordersdic['result']=items
        return ordersdic

    def post_add_to_cart(self, user_id, product_id, price, qty=1):
        request = order_pb2.AddItemRequest(user_id=user_id,
                        product_id=product_id, qty=qty, price=qty)
        response = self.stub.AddItem(request)

        order = {
            'id': response.id,
            'items': json.loads(response.items),
            'is_open': response.is_open,
            'user_id': response.user_id,
            'date_added': response.date_added,
            'amount': round(response.amount,2)
        }
        orderdic={}
        orderdic['result']=order
        return orderdic

    def post_checkout(self, user_id):
        request = order_pb2.CheckoutRequest(user_id=user_id)
        response = self.stub.Checkout(request)
```

```
        order = {
            'id': response.id,
            'items': json.loads(response.items),
            'is_open': response.is_open,
            'user_id': response.user_id,
            'date_added': response.date_added,
            'amount': round(response.amount,2)
        }
        orderdic={}
        orderdic['result']=order
        return orderdic

class ReviewClient:
    def __init__(self):
        self.channel = grpc.insecure_channel(REVIEW_SERVICE_URL)
        self.stub = review_pb2_grpc.ReviewServiceStub(self.channel)

    def get_reviews(self, product_id):
        request = review_pb2.GetReviewsRequest(product_id=product_id)
        response = self.stub.GetReviews(request)
        reviews = []
        for p in response.reviews:
            review = {
                'id': p.id,
                'user_id': p.user_id,
                'product_id':p.product_id,
                'rating': p.rating,
                'date_added': p.date_added,
                'description': p.description
            }
            reviews.append(review)
        reviewsdic={}
        reviewsdic['result']=reviews
        return reviewsdic

    def post_review(self, user_id, product_id, rating, description):
        request = review_pb2.ReviewRequest(user_id=int(user_id),
                        product_id=int(product_id),
                        rating=float(rating), description=description)
        response = self.stub.AddReview(request)
        review = {
            'id': response.id,
            'user_id': response.user_id,
            'product_id': response.product_id,
            'rating': response.rating,
            'description': response.description,
            'date_added': response.date_added
        }
        reviewdic={}
        reviewdic['result']=review
        return reviewdic
```

Box 9.7 shows the implementation of the frontend service routes. It uses the gRPC clients as shown earlier. Also, it manages the user session and renders templates.

■ **Box 9.7: Frontend microservice routes**

```python
@app.route('/', methods=['GET'])
def home():
    if current_user.is_authenticated:
        user_id=session['user']['id']
        orderclient=OrderClient()
        order = orderclient.get_order(user_id)
        session['order'] = order['result']
    try:
        productclient = ProductClient()
        products = productclient.get_products()
    except requests.exceptions.ConnectionError:
        products = {
            'results': []
        }
    user_name, user_photo = get_user_name_photo()
    return render_template('home.html',
        products=products, user_name = user_name,
        user_photo=user_photo)


@app.route('/register', methods=['GET', 'POST'])
def register():
    form = RegistrationForm(request.form)
    if request.method == "POST":
        if form.validate_on_submit():
            username = form.username.data
            userclient=UserClient()
            exist = userclient.does_exist(username)
            if exist:
                flash('Please try another username', 'error')
                return render_template('register/index.html',
                                        form=form)
            else:
                name=form.first_name.data+' '+ form.last_name.data
                filename = "user"+str(int(time.time()*1000))+".png"
                imgpath=os.path.join(app.config['UPLOAD_FOLDER'],
                                filename)
                r = lambda: random.randint(0,255)
                colors=[]
                colors.append('#%02X%02X%02X' % (r(),r(),r()))
                avinit.get_png_avatar(name,
                        output_file=imgpath, colors=colors)
                uploadedFileURL = s3uploading(filename)
                user = userclient.post_user_create(form.first_name.data,
                        form.last_name.data, form.username.data,
                        form.email.data, form.password.data,
                        uploadedFileURL)
                if user:
                    flash('Please login', 'success')
                    return redirect(url_for('login'))
        else:
            flash('Errors found', 'error')
    return render_template('register.html', form=form)
```

```python
@app.route('/login', methods=['GET', 'POST'])
def login():
    if current_user.is_authenticated:
        return redirect(url_for('home'))
    form = LoginForm()
    if request.method == "POST":
        if form.validate_on_submit():
            userclient=UserClient()
            user = userclient.post_login(form.username.data,
                                    form.password.data)
            if user['api_key']:
                loginuser = User(user)
                login_user(loginuser)
                session['user_api_key'] = user['api_key']
                sessiondict={}
                sessiondict['first_name'] = user['first_name']
                sessiondict['last_name'] = user['last_name']
                sessiondict['id'] = user['id']
                sessiondict['username'] = user['username']
                sessiondict['email'] = user['email']
                sessiondict['api_key'] = user['api_key']
                sessiondict['photo'] = user['photo']
                session['user'] = sessiondict
                user_id=session['user']['id']

                flash('Welcome, ' + user['first_name'], 'success')
                return redirect(url_for('home'))
            else:
                flash('Cannot login', 'error')
        else:
            flash('Errors found', 'error')
    return render_template('login.html', form=form)

@app.route('/logout', methods=['GET'])
def logout():
    if current_user.is_authenticated:
        session.clear()
        logout_user()
    return redirect(url_for('home'))

@app.route('/product/<slug>', methods=['GET', 'POST'])
def product(slug):
    productclient = ProductClient()
    response = productclient.get_product(slug)
    item = response['result']
    form = ItemForm(product_id=item['id'])
    reviewslist=[]
    reviewclient=ReviewClient()
    result=reviewclient.get_reviews(item['id'])
    reviews=result['result']
    user_id=session['user']['id']
    for review in reviews:
        try:
```

```
                reviewdict={}
                reviewdict['rating']=review['rating']
                reviewdict['description']=review['description']
                reviewdict['date_added']=review['date_added']
                userclient = UserClient()
                reviewer = userclient.get_user(review['user_id'])
                reviewdict['photo']=reviewer['photo']
                reviewdict['user_name']=reviewer['first_name']+' '+
                                         reviewer['last_name']
                reviewslist.append(reviewdict)
        except:
            pass

    if request.method == "POST":
        if 'user' not in session:
            flash('Please login', 'error')
            return redirect(url_for('login'))
        orderclient=OrderClient()
        order = orderclient.post_add_to_cart(user_id,
                        product_id=item['id'],
                        price=item['price'], qty=1)
        session['order'] = order['result']
        flash('Item has been added to cart', 'success')
    user_name, user_photo = get_user_name_photo()
    return render_template('product.html', product=item,
        form=form, reviews=reviewslist,
        user_name = user_name, user_photo=user_photo)

@app.route('/checkout', methods=['GET'])
def summary():
    if 'user' not in session:
        flash('Please login', 'error')
        return redirect(url_for('login'))
    if 'order' not in session:
        flash('No order found', 'error')
        return redirect(url_for('home'))
    user_id=session['user']['id']
    orderclient=OrderClient()
    order = orderclient.get_order(user_id)
    if len(order['result']['items']) == 0:
        flash('No order found', 'error')
        return redirect(url_for('home'))
    orderclient=OrderClient()
    orderclient.post_checkout(user_id)
    return redirect(url_for('thank_you'))

@app.route('/order/thank-you', methods=['GET'])
def thank_you():
    if 'user' not in session:
        flash('Please login', 'error')
        return redirect(url_for('login'))

    if 'order' not in session:
        flash('No order found', 'error')
```

```
                return redirect(url_for('home'))

        session.pop('order', None)
        flash('Thank you for your order', 'success')
        user_id=session['user']['id']
        user_name, user_photo = get_user_name_photo()
        return render_template('thanks.html', user_name = user_name,
                               user_photo=user_photo)

@app.route('/cart', methods=['GET'])
def cart():
    if 'user' not in session:
        flash('Please login', 'error')
        return redirect(url_for('login'))
    try:
        user_id=session['user']['id']
        orderclient=OrderClient()
        result = orderclient.get_cart(user_id)
        products=result['result']
        productsInCart=[]
        totalamount=0
        for p in products:
            productclient = ProductClient()
            resp = productclient.get_product_with_id(p['product'])
            itemdict={}
            itemdict['quantity']=p['quantity']
            itemdict['name']=resp['result']['name']
            itemdict['description']=resp['result']['description']
            itemdict['id']=resp['result']['id']
            itemdict['slug']=resp['result']['slug']
            itemdict['price']=resp['result']['price']
            itemdict['image']=resp['result']['image']
            itemdict['total']=p['quantity']*resp['result']['price']
            totalamount=totalamount+itemdict['total']
            totalamount=round(totalamount,2)
            productsInCart.append(itemdict)
    except requests.exceptions.ConnectionError:
        productsInCart=[]
    user_name, user_photo = get_user_name_photo()
    return render_template('cart.html', products=productsInCart,
        totalamount=totalamount,
        user_name = user_name, user_photo=user_photo)

@app.route('/orders', methods=['GET'])
def orders():
    if 'user' not in session:
        flash('Please login', 'error')
        return redirect(url_for('login'))
    try:
        user_id=session['user']['id']
        orderclient=OrderClient()
        result = orderclient.get_orders(user_id)
        orders=result['result']
        ordersPlaced=[]
```

```python
        for p in orders:
            itemdict={}
            itemdict['itemscount']=len(p['items'])
            itemdict['id']=p['id']
            itemdict['date_added']=p['date_added']
            itemdict['amount']=p['amount']
            itemdict['productimages']=[]
            for q in p['items']:
                productclient = ProductClient()
                resp=productclient.get_product_with_id(q['product'])
                itemdict['productimages'].append(resp['result']['image'])

            ordersPlaced.append(itemdict)
    except requests.exceptions.ConnectionError:
        ordersPlaced=[]
    user_name, user_photo = get_user_name_photo()
    return render_template('orders.html', orders=ordersPlaced,
            user_name = user_name, user_photo=user_photo)


@app.route('/postreview', methods=['POST'])
def postreview():
    ratinginput = request.form.get('ratinginput')
    reviewinput = request.form.get('reviewinput')
    productslug = request.form.get('productslug')
    user_id = session['user']['id']
    product_id = request.form.get('productid')
    reviewclient = ReviewClient()
    response = reviewclient.post_review(user_id,
            product_id, ratinginput, reviewinput)
    flash('Thank you for your review', 'success')
    return redirect('/product/'+productslug)


@app.route('/api/product/create', methods=['POST'])
def post_create():
    name = request.form.get('name')
    slug = request.form.get('slug')
    description = request.form.get('description')
    price = request.form.get('price')
    price = round(float(price), 2)
    image = request.files.get('image')
    filename = secure_filename(image.filename)
    image.save(os.path.join(app.config['UPLOAD_FOLDER'], filename))
    uploadedFileURL = s3uploading(filename)
    productclient = ProductClient()
    product = productclient.create_product(name, description,
                        slug, price, uploadedFileURL)
    response = jsonify({'message': 'Product added', 'product': product})
    return response


if __name__ == '__main__':
    app.run(host='0.0.0.0', port=5000)
```

9.3.4 Modify backend microservices

Next, we modify the backend microservices (user, product, order, and review) by importing and extending the generated gRPC server stubs, implementing the service handler methods defined in the *.proto* files, and using protocol buffers data types.

Box 9.8 shows the user microservice. It defines the SQLAlchemy User model and configures the Flask app and SQLAlchemy for connecting to a MySQL database.

■ **Box 9.8: User microservice**

```
import os
from flask import Flask, send_from_directory, send_file
from flask_migrate import Migrate
from flask_sqlalchemy import SQLAlchemy
from datetime import datetime
from flask_login import UserMixin
from passlib.hash import sha256_crypt
from flask import make_response, request, jsonify
import time, random

db = SQLAlchemy()
basedir = os.path.abspath(os.path.dirname(__file__))

app = Flask(__name__)
app.config['SECRET_KEY'] = "DoWgTDq87Kmne3TsCjNFabP"
app.config['BUCKET_NAME'] = 'microservices-ecommerce-app'
app.config['CLOUDFRONT_URL'] = 'https://dn2aztu.cloudfront.net'
app.config['AWS_ACCESS_KEY'] = 'EXAMPLEKEY'
app.config['AWS_SECRET_KEY'] = 'EXAMPLESECRET'
app.config['MYSQL_RDS_ENDPOINT'] = 'db.czqy.us-west-2.rds.amazonaws.com'
app.config['MYSQL_RDS_USER'] = 'admin'
app.config['MYSQL_RDS_PASSWORD'] = 'S9c1Z16tC93AuTfKCLLV'
app.config['SQLALCHEMY_TRACK_MODIFICATIONS'] = False
app.config['ENV'] = "development"
app.config['DEBUG'] = True
app.config['SQLALCHEMY_DATABASE_URI'] = 'mysql+pymysql://'+
                app.config['MYSQL_RDS_USER']+':'+
                app.config['MYSQL_RDS_PASSWORD']+'@'+
                app.config['MYSQL_RDS_ENDPOINT']+':3306/user'
app.config['SQLALCHEMY_ECHO'] = True
app.config['UPLOAD_FOLDER'] = 'uploads'


db.init_app(app)
migrate = Migrate(app, db)

class User(UserMixin, db.Model):
    id = db.Column(db.Integer, primary_key=True)
    username = db.Column(db.String(255), unique=True, nullable=False)
    email = db.Column(db.String(255), unique=True, nullable=False)
    first_name = db.Column(db.String(255), unique=False, nullable=True)
    last_name = db.Column(db.String(255), unique=False, nullable=True)
    password = db.Column(db.String(255), unique=False, nullable=False)
    photo = db.Column(db.String(255), unique=False, nullable=True)
```

```
    is_admin = db.Column(db.Boolean, default=False)
    authenticated = db.Column(db.Boolean, default=False)
    api_key = db.Column(db.String(255), unique=True, nullable=True)
    date_added = db.Column(db.DateTime, default=datetime.utcnow)
    date_updated = db.Column(db.DateTime, onupdate=datetime.utcnow)

    def encode_api_key(self):
        self.api_key = sha256_crypt.hash(self.username +
                        str(datetime.utcnow))

    def encode_password(self):
        self.password = sha256_crypt.hash(self.password)

    def __repr__(self):
        return '<User %r>' % (self.username)

    def to_json(self):
        return {
            'first_name': self.first_name,
            'last_name': self.last_name,
            'username': self.username,
            'email': self.email,
            'photo': self.photo,
            'id': self.id,
            'api_key': self.api_key,
            'is_active': True,
            'is_admin': self.is_admin
        }
```

Box 9.9 shows the implementation of the gRPC server for the user service. It defines the gRPC methods for getting a user by ID, creating a new user, logging in a user, and checking if a username is taken. User data is serialized/deserialized between protobuf messages and SQLAlchemy User model.

The user gRPC server shown in Box 9.9 and the user microservice in Box 9.8 work together to provide a gRPC service with common user management functionality by integrating with a persistence layer using Flask, SQLAlchemy, and MySQL. The protobuf messages define the interface contract and data structures.

■ **Box 9.9: User gRPC server**

```
import grpc
from concurrent import futures
import io
import os
from passlib.hash import sha256_crypt
import user_pb2
import user_pb2_grpc
from app import app, db, User

class UserService(user_pb2_grpc.UserServiceServicer):
  def GetUserById(self, request, context):
    with app.app_context():
```

```
      user = User.query.filter_by(id=request.id).first()
      if user:
        p=user_pb2.User()
        p.id = user.id
        p.first_name = user.first_name
        p.last_name = user.last_name
        p.username = user.username
        p.email = user.email
        p.photo = user.photo
        p.is_admin = user.is_admin
        p.api_key = user.api_key
        return p
      return user_pb2.EmptyUser()

  def CreateUser(self, request, context):
    with app.app_context():
      # Create user logic
      first_name = request.first_name
      last_name = request.last_name
      email = request.email
      username = request.username
      password = sha256_crypt.hash(request.password)
      user = User()
      user.email = email
      user.first_name = first_name
      user.last_name = last_name
      user.password = password
      user.username = username
      user.authenticated = True
      user.photo = request.photo
      db.session.add(user)
      db.session.commit()
      p=user_pb2.User()
      p.id = user.id
      p.first_name = user.first_name
      p.last_name = user.last_name
      p.username = user.username
      p.email = user.email
      p.photo = user.photo
      p.is_admin = user.is_admin
      return p

  def LoginUser(self, request, context):
    with app.app_context():
      user = User.query.filter_by(username=request.username).first()
      if user:
        if sha256_crypt.verify(request.password, user.password):
          user.encode_api_key()
          db.session.commit()
          #login_user(user)
          p=user_pb2.User()
          p.id = user.id
          p.first_name = user.first_name
          p.last_name = user.last_name
```

```
              p.username = user.username
              p.email = user.email
              p.photo = user.photo
              p.is_admin = user.is_admin
              p.api_key = user.api_key
              return p
        return user_pb2.EmptyUser()

   def CheckUsername(self, request, context):
     with app.app_context():
       item = User.query.filter_by(username=request.username).first()
       u= user_pb2.UsernameResponse()
       if item is not None:
         u.result=True
       else:
         u.result=False
       return u

def serve():
  server = grpc.server(futures.ThreadPoolExecutor(max_workers=10))
  user_pb2_grpc.add_UserServiceServicer_to_server(UserService(),
                         server)
  server.add_insecure_port('[::]:50054')
  server.start()
  print("gRPC server started on port 50054")
  server.wait_for_termination()

if __name__ == '__main__':
  serve()
```

Box 9.10 shows the implementation of the product microservice. It defines the Flask application and SQLAlchemy model for Product. It configures the Flask app with database and other settings and sets up SQLAlchemy with a MySQL database for products.

■ **Box 9.10: Product microservice**

```
import os
from flask import Flask, send_from_directory
from flask_migrate import Migrate
from flask import jsonify, request
from flask_sqlalchemy import SQLAlchemy
from datetime import datetime
from flask_migrate import Migrate
from werkzeug.utils import secure_filename
import boto3

db = SQLAlchemy()
basedir = os.path.abspath(os.path.dirname(__file__))

app = Flask(__name__)
app.config['SECRET_KEY'] = "DoWgTDq87Kmne3TsCjNFabP"
app.config['BUCKET_NAME'] = 'microservices-ecommerce-app'
app.config['CLOUDFRONT_URL'] = 'https://dn2aztcn1xe1u.cloudfront.net'
```

```
app.config['AWS_ACCESS_KEY'] = 'EXAMPLEKEY'
app.config['AWS_SECRET_KEY'] = 'EXAMPLESECRET'
app.config['MYSQL_RDS_ENDPOINT'] = 'db.czqy.us-west-2.rds.amazonaws.com'
app.config['MYSQL_RDS_USER'] = 'admin'
app.config['MYSQL_RDS_PASSWORD'] = 'S9c1Zl6tC93AuTfKCLLV'
app.config['SQLALCHEMY_TRACK_MODIFICATIONS'] = False
app.config['ENV'] = "development"
app.config['DEBUG'] = True
app.config['SQLALCHEMY_DATABASE_URI']  = 'mysql+pymysql://'+
                    app.config['MYSQL_RDS_USER']+':'+
                    app.config['MYSQL_RDS_PASSWORD']+'@'+
                    app.config['MYSQL_RDS_ENDPOINT']+':3306/product'
app.config['SQLALCHEMY_ECHO'] = True
app.config['UPLOAD_FOLDER'] = 'uploads'
db.init_app(app)
migrate = Migrate(app, db)

class Product(db.Model):
    id = db.Column(db.Integer, primary_key=True)
    name = db.Column(db.String(255), unique=True, nullable=False)
    slug = db.Column(db.String(255), unique=True, nullable=False)
    price = db.Column(db.Float, default=0)
    image = db.Column(db.String(255), unique=False, nullable=True)
    description = db.Column(db.Text)
    date_added = db.Column(db.DateTime, default=datetime.utcnow)
    date_updated = db.Column(db.DateTime, onupdate=datetime.utcnow)

    def to_json(self):
        return {
            'id': self.id,
            'name': self.name,
            'description': self.description,
            'slug': self.slug,
            'price': self.price,
            'image': self.image
        }
```

Box 9.11 shows the implementation of the gRPC server for the product service. It implements the gRPC service with methods for CRUD operations on products. It uses Flask app and SQLAlchemy models to interact with the database. It defines a *ProductService* servicer class that implements the RPC methods like *GetProducts*, *GetProduct*, and *CreateProduct*.

■ Box 9.11: Product gRPC server

```
import grpc
from concurrent import futures
import io
import os
import product_pb2
import product_pb2_grpc
from app import app, db, Product
```

```python
class ProductService(product_pb2_grpc.ProductServiceServicer):
  def GetProducts(self, request, context):
    with app.app_context():
      products = Product.query.all()

      product_list = product_pb2.ProductList()
      for product in products:
        p = product_pb2.Product()
        p.id = product.id
        p.name = product.name
        p.description = product.description
        p.slug = product.slug
        p.price = product.price
        p.image = product.image
        product_list.products.append(p)

      return product_list

  def GetProduct(self, request, context):
    with app.app_context():
      product = Product.query.filter_by(slug=request.slug).first()
      if not product:
        context.set_code(grpc.StatusCode.NOT_FOUND)
        context.set_details('Product not found')
        return product_pb2.Product()
      p = product_pb2.Product()
      p.id = product.id
      p.name = product.name
      p.description = product.description
      p.slug = product.slug
      p.price = product.price
      p.image = product.image
      return p

  def GetProductWithID(self, request, context):
    with app.app_context():
      product = Product.query.filter_by(id=request.id).first()
      if not product:
        context.set_code(grpc.StatusCode.NOT_FOUND)
        context.set_details('Product not found')
        return product_pb2.Product()
      p = product_pb2.Product()
      p.id = product.id
      p.name = product.name
      p.description = product.description
      p.slug = product.slug
      p.price = product.price
      p.image = product.image
      return p

  def CreateProduct(self, request, context):
    with app.app_context():
      product = Product()
      product.name = request.name
```

```
            product.description = request.description
            product.slug = request.slug
            product.price = request.price
            product.image = request.image
            db.session.add(product)
            db.session.commit()
            p = product_pb2.Product()
            p.id = product.id
            p.name = product.name
            p.description = product.description
            p.slug = product.slug
            p.price = product.price
            p.image = product.image
            p.date_added = product.date_added.strftime("%b %d, %Y")
            return p

def serve():
  server = grpc.server(futures.ThreadPoolExecutor(max_workers=10))
  product_pb2_grpc.add_ProductServiceServicer_to_server(
                              ProductService(), server)
  server.add_insecure_port('[::]:50051')
  server.start()
  print("gRPC server started on port 50051")
  server.wait_for_termination()

if __name__ == '__main__':
    serve()
```

Box 9.12 shows the implementation of the order microservice. It defines the Flask application and SQLAlchemy models used by the order service. It defines *Order* and *OrderItem* models to represent orders and items. It configures the Flask app with database and other settings and sets up SQLAlchemy with a MySQL database for orders and items.

■ Box 9.12: Order microservice

```
import os
from flask import Flask
from flask_migrate import Migrate
from flask import jsonify, request, make_response
from flask import Flask
from flask_sqlalchemy import SQLAlchemy
from datetime import datetime
import requests
import boto3

db = SQLAlchemy()
basedir = os.path.abspath(os.path.dirname(__file__))

app = Flask(__name__)
app.config['SECRET_KEY'] = "DoWgTDq87Kmne3TsCjNFabP"
app.config['MYSQL_RDS_ENDPOINT'] = 'db.czqy.us-west-2.rds.amazonaws.com'
app.config['MYSQL_RDS_USER'] = 'admin'
app.config['MYSQL_RDS_PASSWORD'] = 'S9c1Z16tC93AuTfKCLLV'
```

```python
app.config['SQLALCHEMY_TRACK_MODIFICATIONS'] = False
app.config['ENV'] = "development"
app.config['DEBUG'] = True
app.config['SQLALCHEMY_DATABASE_URI']  = 'mysql+pymysql://'+
                app.config['MYSQL_RDS_USER']+':'+
                app.config['MYSQL_RDS_PASSWORD']+'@'+
                app.config['MYSQL_RDS_ENDPOINT']+':3306/orderdb'
app.config['SQLALCHEMY_ECHO'] = True

USER_SERVICE_URL='http://127.0.0.1:5001'

db.init_app(app)
migrate = Migrate(app, db)

class Order(db.Model):
    id = db.Column(db.Integer, primary_key=True)
    user_id = db.Column(db.Integer)
    items = db.relationship('OrderItem', backref='orderItem')
    is_open = db.Column(db.Boolean, default=True)
    date_added = db.Column(db.DateTime, default=datetime.utcnow)
    date_updated = db.Column(db.DateTime, onupdate=datetime.utcnow)

    def create(self, user_id):
        self.user_id = user_id
        self.is_open = True
        return self

    def to_json(self):
        items = []
        amount=0
        for i in self.items:
            items.append(i.to_json())
            amount=amount+i.price*i.quantity
            amount=round(amount,2)

        return {
            'id': self.id,
            'items': items,
            'is_open': self.is_open,
            'user_id': self.user_id,
            'date_added': self.date_added.strftime("%b %d, %Y"),
            'amount': amount
        }

class OrderItem(db.Model):
    id = db.Column(db.Integer, primary_key=True)
    order_id = db.Column(db.Integer, db.ForeignKey('order.id'))
    product_id = db.Column(db.Integer)
    price = db.Column(db.Float, default=0)
    quantity = db.Column(db.Integer, default=1)
    date_added = db.Column(db.DateTime, default=datetime.utcnow)
    date_updated = db.Column(db.DateTime, onupdate=datetime.utcnow)

    def __init__(self, product_id, quantity, price):
```

```
            self.product_id = product_id
            self.quantity = quantity
            self.price = price

    def to_json(self):
        return {
            'price': self.price,
            'product': self.product_id,
            'quantity': self.quantity
        }
```

Box 9.13 shows the implementation of the gRPC server for the order service. It defines an *OrderService* class that implements the gRPC methods like *AddItem*, *GetOrder*, *Checkout*, *GetCart*, and *GetOrders*. These methods access the *Order* and *OrderItem* models to retrieve and store order data.

▪ Box 9.13: Order gRPC server

```
import os
import json
import grpc
from concurrent import futures
import order_pb2
import order_pb2_grpc
from app import app, db, Order, OrderItem

class OrderService(order_pb2_grpc.OrderServiceServicer):
  def AddItem(self, request, context):
  with app.app_context():
    user_id = request.user_id
    product_id = request.product_id
    qty = request.qty
    price = request.price
    known_order = Order.query.filter_by(user_id=user_id,
                                         is_open=1).first()
    if known_order is None:
      known_order = Order()
      known_order.is_open = True
      known_order.user_id = user_id
      order_item = OrderItem(product_id, qty, price)
      known_order.items.append(order_item)
    else:
      found = False
      for item in known_order.items:
        if item.product_id == product_id:
          found = True
          item.quantity += qty
      if found is False:
        order_item = OrderItem(product_id, qty, price)
        known_order.items.append(order_item)
    db.session.add(known_order)
    db.session.commit()
    orderjson=known_order.to_json()
```

```
    p = order_pb2.OrderResponse()
    p.id = orderjson['id']
    p.items = json.dumps(orderjson['items'])
    p.is_open = orderjson['is_open']
    p.user_id = orderjson['user_id']
    p.date_added = orderjson['date_added']
    p.amount = orderjson['amount']
    return p

def GetOrder(self, request, context):
with app.app_context():
  open_order = Order.query.filter_by(user_id=request.user_id,
                                      is_open=1).first()

  if open_order is not None:
    orderjson=open_order.to_json()
    p = order_pb2.OrderResponse()
    p.id = orderjson['id']
    p.items = json.dumps(orderjson['items'])
    p.is_open = orderjson['is_open']
    p.user_id = orderjson['user_id']
    p.date_added = orderjson['date_added']
    p.amount = orderjson['amount']
    return p
  else:
    return order_pb2.OrderResponse()

def Checkout(self, request, context):
with app.app_context():
  order_model = Order.query.filter_by(user_id=request.user_id,
                                      is_open=1).first()
  order_model.is_open = 0

  db.session.add(order_model)
  db.session.commit()
  orderjson=order_model.to_json()
  p = order_pb2.OrderResponse()
  p.id = orderjson['id']
  p.items = json.dumps(orderjson['items'])
  p.is_open = orderjson['is_open']
  p.user_id = orderjson['user_id']
  p.date_added = orderjson['date_added']
  p.amount = orderjson['amount']
  return p

def GetCart(self, request, context):
with app.app_context():
  open_order = Order.query.filter_by(user_id=request.user_id,
                                      is_open=1).first()
  items=[]
  if open_order is not None:
    for item in open_order.items:
      items.append(item.to_json())
  p=order_pb2.GetCartResponse()
  p.items=json.dumps(items)
```

```
      return p

  def GetOrders(self, request, context):
  with app.app_context():
    orders = Order.query.filter_by(user_id=request.user_id,
                                   is_open=0)
    orders_list = order_pb2.GetOrdersResponse()
    for order in orders:
      p = order_pb2.OrderResponse()
      orderjson=order.to_json()
      print(orderjson)
      p.id = orderjson['id']
      p.items = json.dumps(orderjson['items'])
      p.is_open = orderjson['is_open']
      p.user_id = orderjson['user_id']
      p.date_added = orderjson['date_added']
      p.amount = orderjson['amount']
      orders_list.orders.append(p)
    return orders_list

def serve():
  server = grpc.server(futures.ThreadPoolExecutor(max_workers=10))
  order_pb2_grpc.add_OrderServiceServicer_to_server(OrderService(),
                                                    server)
  server.add_insecure_port('[::]:50053')
  server.start()
  print("gRPC server started on port 50053")
  server.wait_for_termination()

if __name__ == '__main__':
    serve()
```

Box 9.14 shows the implementation of the review microservice. It defines the Flask application and SQLAlchemy model for Review. It configures the Flask app with database and other settings and sets up SQLAlchemy with a MySQL database for reviews.

■ Box 9.14: Review microservice

```
import os
from flask import Flask, send_from_directory
from flask_migrate import Migrate
from flask import jsonify, request
from flask_sqlalchemy import SQLAlchemy
from datetime import datetime
from flask_migrate import Migrate
from werkzeug.utils import secure_filename
import boto3

db = SQLAlchemy()
basedir = os.path.abspath(os.path.dirname(__file__))

app = Flask(__name__)
app.config['SECRET_KEY'] = "DoWgTDq87Kmne3TsCjNFabP"
```

```
app.config['MYSQL_RDS_ENDPOINT'] = 'db.czqy.us-west-2.rds.amazonaws.com'
app.config['MYSQL_RDS_USER'] = 'admin'
app.config['MYSQL_RDS_PASSWORD'] = 'S9c1Z16tC93AuTfKCLLV'
app.config['SQLALCHEMY_TRACK_MODIFICATIONS'] = False
app.config['ENV'] = "development"
app.config['DEBUG'] = True
app.config['SQLALCHEMY_DATABASE_URI']  = 'mysql+pymysql://'+
                    app.config['MYSQL_RDS_USER']+':'+
                    app.config['MYSQL_RDS_PASSWORD']+'@'+
                    app.config['MYSQL_RDS_ENDPOINT']+':3306/review'
app.config['SQLALCHEMY_ECHO'] = True
app.config['UPLOAD_FOLDER'] = 'uploads'

db.init_app(app)
migrate = Migrate(app, db)

class Review(db.Model):
    id = db.Column(db.Integer, primary_key=True)
    user_id = db.Column(db.Integer)
    product_id = db.Column(db.Integer)
    rating = db.Column(db.Float, default=0)
    description = db.Column(db.Text)
    date_added = db.Column(db.DateTime, default=datetime.utcnow)
    date_updated = db.Column(db.DateTime, onupdate=datetime.utcnow)

    def to_json(self):
        return {
            'id': self.id,
            'user_id': self.user_id,
            'product_id': self.product_id,
            'rating': self.rating,
            'description': self.description,
            'date_added': self.date_added.strftime("%b %d, %Y")
        }
```

Box 9.15 shows the implementation of the gRPC server for the review service. It implements the *ReviewService* class with methods - *GetReviews* and *AddReview*.

■ Box 9.15: Review gRPC server

```
import grpc
from concurrent import futures
import io
import os
import review_pb2
import review_pb2_grpc
from app import app, db, Review

class ReviewService(review_pb2_grpc.ReviewServiceServicer):
  def GetReviews(self, request, context):
    with app.app_context():
      reviews = Review.query.filter_by(product_id=request.product_id)
      reviews_list = review_pb2.ReviewsList()
```

```
        for review in reviews:
          p = review_pb2.Review()
          p.id = review.id
          p.user_id = review.user_id
          p.product_id = review.product_id
          p.rating = review.rating
          p.description = review.description
          p.date_added = review.date_added.strftime("%b %d, %Y")
          reviews_list.reviews.append(p)
        return reviews_list

    def AddReview(self, request, context):
      with app.app_context():
        review = Review()
        review.user_id = request.user_id
        review.product_id = request.product_id
        review.rating = request.rating
        review.description = request.description
        db.session.add(review)
        db.session.commit()
        p = review_pb2.Review()
        p.id = review.id
        p.user_id = review.user_id
        p.product_id = review.product_id
        p.rating = review.rating
        p.description = review.description
        p.date_added = review.date_added.strftime("%b %d, %Y")
        return p

def serve():
  server = grpc.server(futures.ThreadPoolExecutor(max_workers=10))
  review_pb2_grpc.add_ReviewServiceServicer_to_server(ReviewService(),
                                                       server)
  server.add_insecure_port('[::]:50052')
  server.start()
  print("gRPC server started on port 50052")
  server.wait_for_termination()

if __name__ == '__main__':
    serve()
```

Summary

In this chapter, we covered migrating a REST-based microservices application to gRPC. gRPC is an efficient remote procedure call (RPC) framework that uses protocol buffers for serializing structured data between clients and servers. gRPC provides several benefits compared to REST, such as higher performance, bidirectional streaming, better service contracts, and ease of code generation. We first presented an overview of gRPC and its key capabilities. gRPC enables efficient serialization using Protocol Buffers, which are faster, smaller, and less ambiguous than JSON or XML. It supports bidirectional streaming RPCs, which are useful for high throughput, low latency applications. gRPC promotes a contract-first development approach using *.proto* files to define services and message schemas. These files serve as documentation and generate strongly typed client/server code stubs. gRPC also provides built-in support for authentication, encryption, load balancing, and monitoring. gRPC enables easy code generation from *.proto* files and integration with existing systems. We then described the process of migrating a REST-based microservices E-Commerce application to gRPC. This involved defining *.proto* files for each microservice (user, product, order, and review). These files contain service and message definitions including RPC methods, requests, responses, and comments. The next step was using the protoc compiler to generate client and server stubs from the *.proto* files. After this, the frontend microservice was updated to use the gRPC client stubs instead of making REST calls. This required modifying service invocations to call gRPC methods directly. Finally, the backend microservices (user, product, order, and review) were modified to implement the gRPC services by extending the generated server stubs and implementing the RPC handlers. This chapter presented a systematic approach to migrate a microservices application from REST to gRPC by leveraging *.proto* files for service contracts, utilizing protoc for stub generation, modifying the frontend to use gRPC clients, and implementing the gRPC services in the backends.

10 SERVERLESS MICROSERVICES WITH LAMBDA AND API GATEWAY

THIS CHAPTER COVERS

- Serverless Microservices Application
- Cognito User Pool
- DynamoDB Tables
- IAM Role
- Lambda Functions
- API Gateway
- Static Website Frontend

10.1 Introduction

The serverless architectural pattern has emerged as a popular approach for building cloud-native applications. The granularity of the serverless model aligns costs directly with usage and brings significant operational benefits. The cloud provider handles provisioning, scaling, patching, and maintenance of the underlying servers. This enables development teams to focus on writing business logic. Services can be developed independently and deployed rapidly. Automated scaling and fault tolerance reduce manual intervention. Pay-per-use pricing and shutting down unused capacity provide cost savings. For event-driven and bursty workloads, serverless is often the most efficient and agile approach compared to traditional application servers.

Category	Serverless	Server-based
Infrastructure	No servers to manage. AWS handles infrastructure.	Servers must be provisioned and managed.
Scaling	Auto-scaling. Services scale independently.	Manual scaling by adding servers.
Availability	Built-in redundancy and fault tolerance.	High availability and fault tolerance must be custom built.
Performance	Fast scaling to meet demand.	Scaling limited by server capacity.
Costs	Pay per use and execution duration.	Pay for allocated capacity even if unused.
Deployments	Faster deployments with no servers to provision.	Slower due to server provisioning.
Language support	Several languages like Python, Node, Java, C# .NET supported.	Any language can be used on servers.
Monitoring	CloudWatch, X-Ray provide metrics and tracing.	Custom instrumentation required.
Flexibility	Loosely coupled services, easier to modify.	Tighter coupling makes changes harder.
Complexity	Simpler architecture and dev workflow.	Complexity in managing many servers.
Latency	Added latency of cold starts for functions.	Low latency when servers already running.
Dependencies	Limitations on packages that can be included.	Any dependencies can be installed.

Figure 10.1: Comparison of serverless and server-based approaches

The traditional monolithic architecture runs the entire application stack on one or more servers or virtual machines. Scaling requires launching additional identical instances. The entire application may scale unnecessarily when only certain services require additional capacity. There is also increased risk from a change or failure affecting the entire monolith.

Scaling, fault tolerance, and high availability must be built into every layer.

Figure 10.1 shows a comparison of serverless and server-based approaches for microservices applications. Serverless provides automation, rapid scaling, reduced operational overhead, and finer billing granularity. Server-based architecture gives more control over languages, dependencies, and performance tuning. The choice depends on the application architecture, workload patterns, and team skills.

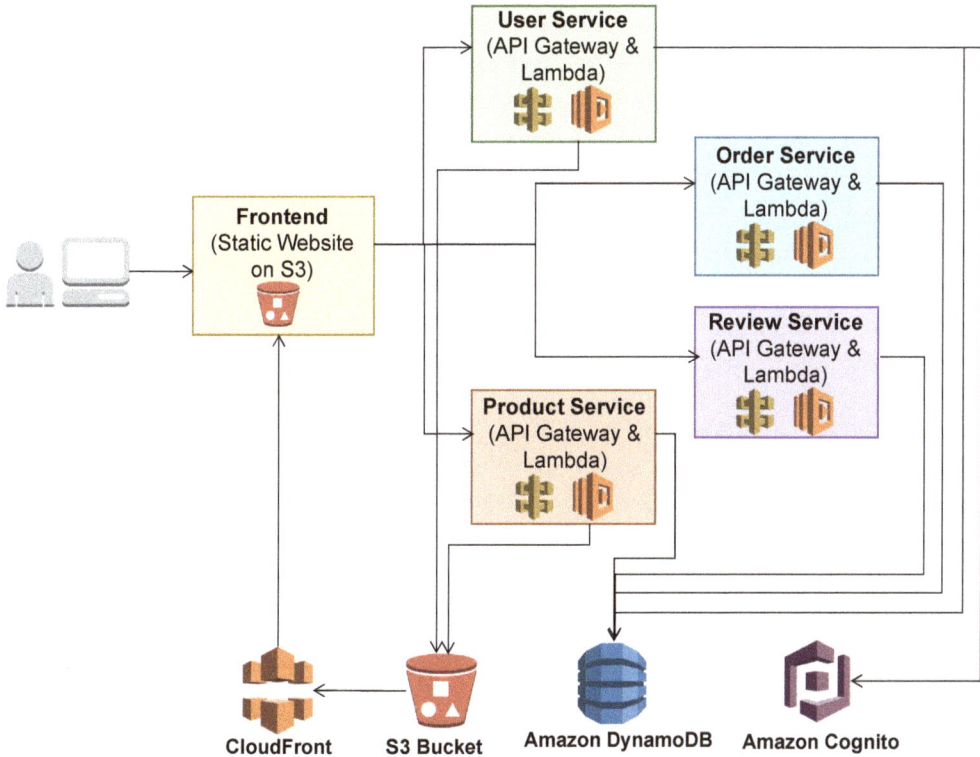

Figure 10.2: Architecture of serverless E-Commerce application

In the previous chapters, we described the implementation of different versions of a microservices E-Commerce application using server-based or container-based approaches. In this chapter, we will cover the migration of the server version of the E-Commerce application to serverless and dive deeper into the technical details of serverless architectures. We will demonstrate the advantages of serverless approach through the E-Commerce application example.

We will go through the steps to build and deploy the E-Commerce application using API Gateway, Lambda, DynamoDB, Cognito, S3, CloudFront, and IAM. By the end of the chapter, you will have a clear understanding of developing robust and scalable cloud-native applications using a serverless architecture on AWS. The techniques can be applied to build APIs and microservices for a variety of domains beyond E-Commerce as well.

Figure 10.2 shows the architecture of the serverless E-Commerce application. The serverless E-Commerce application will leverage the following AWS services:

- **API Gateway**: This fully managed service provides a RESTful API frontend to the various microservices in our architecture. API Gateway handles all the tasks involved in accepting and processing a large number of concurrent API calls, including traffic management, CORS support, authorization, access control, throttling, monitoring, and API version management. API Gateway has native support for deploying RESTful APIs that can be accessed over HTTP. It handles mapping incoming requests to various backend services.

- **Lambda**: The core backend services (user, product, order, and review) will be implemented as independent, serverless Lambda functions. Lambda provides a runtime environment to execute code in response to trigger events. In our E-Commerce application, Lambda functions will be triggered by API calls from API Gateway and will perform operations like user management, product catalog management, order processing, and review management. Lambda auto-scales to support any volume of traffic and runs code on a high availability compute infrastructure. It is inherently fault-tolerant.

- **DynamoDB**: A fully managed NoSQL database service will provide persistence for the product catalog, order data, and review data. DynamoDB provides fast and predictable performance at any scale, making it a great fit for serverless applications. It has built-in fault tolerance and replication across availability zones. DynamoDB allows creating databases that scale up or down automatically. For serverless workloads, DynamoDB provides on-demand capacity which scales instantly to accommodate traffic spikes and drops down during idle periods without any manual intervention.

- **Cognito**: We will leverage Amazon Cognito to handle user management, authentication, and authorization for our E-Commerce application. Cognito provides user directories that can scale to millions of users. It supports sign-up, sign-in, and access control for web and mobile apps. Cognito will integrate with API Gateway and Lambda to handle user authentication and authorization for our REST APIs.

- **S3**: User-uploaded images, such as profile pictures, and product images will be stored on Amazon S3, which provides highly durable object storage. The Lambda functions will securely upload the images to S3 buckets.

- **CloudFront**: To optimize performance and availability for serving user profile pictures and product images, we will use CloudFront as a content delivery network (CDN). Using CloudFront CDN will provide users across the globe fast access to images stored in S3.

- **IAM**: Each Lambda function will be assigned an IAM role that defines its permissions. We will create an execution role that grants basic Lambda execution permissions and permission to write logs to CloudWatch Logs. Additionally, we will attach policies for access to S3, DynamoDB, and Cognito to this role.

The above combination of services allows building a secure, scalable, and operationally simple E-Commerce application. The loose coupling between the frontend, backend, and data storage services enables independent scaling. New features can be added easily by launching new functions. The backend code only needs to focus on business logic without managing infrastructure.

10.2   Serverless Microservices Application

10.2.1   Cognito User Pool

To enable user management and authentication, a user pool will be created in Amazon Cognito. Figures 10.3, 10.4, 10.5, and 10.6 show the steps for creating a Cognito user pool.

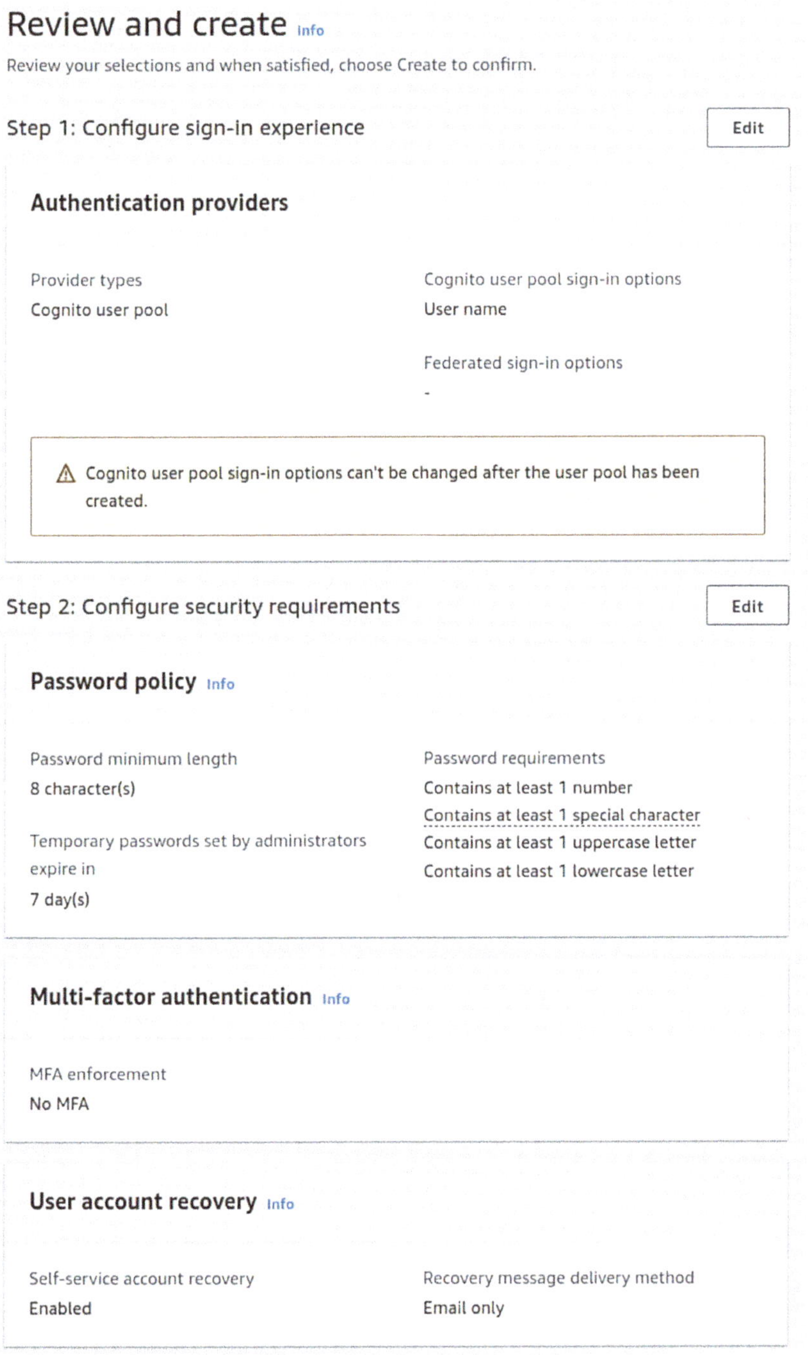

Review and create Info

Review your selections and when satisfied, choose Create to confirm.

Step 1: Configure sign-in experience   [Edit]

Authentication providers

Provider types   Cognito user pool sign-in options
Cognito user pool   User name

                                        Federated sign-in options
                                        -

> ⚠ Cognito user pool sign-in options can't be changed after the user pool has been created.

Step 2: Configure security requirements   [Edit]

Password policy Info

Password minimum length   Password requirements
8 character(s)   Contains at least 1 number
                                        Contains at least 1 special character
Temporary passwords set by administrators   Contains at least 1 uppercase letter
expire in   Contains at least 1 lowercase letter
7 day(s)

Multi-factor authentication Info

MFA enforcement
No MFA

User account recovery Info

Self-service account recovery   Recovery message delivery method
Enabled   Email only

Figure 10.3: Creating Cognito user pool - part 1

The user pool will allow users to sign in with a username and password. Additional user attributes like *family_name*, *given_name*, and *picture* are specified.

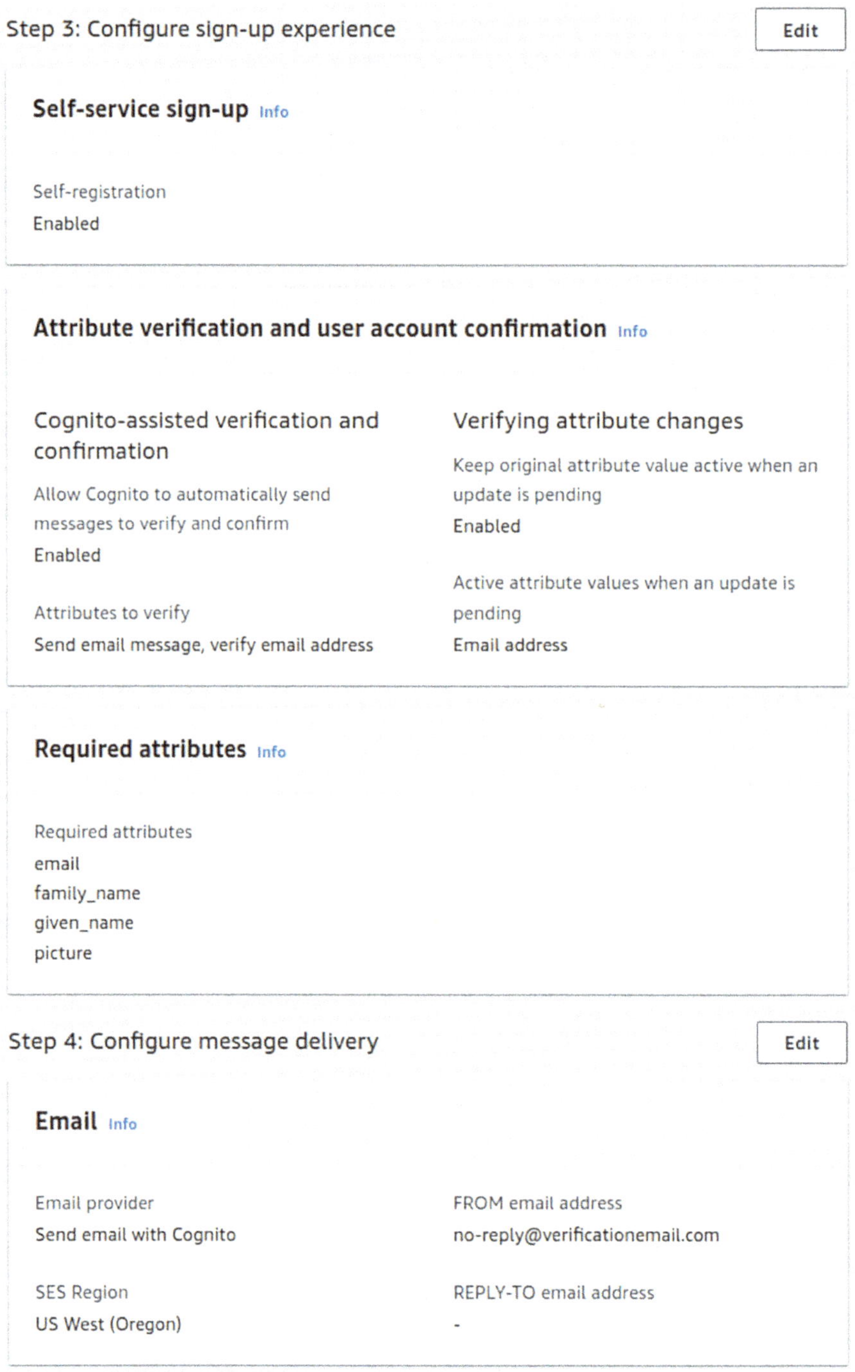

Step 3: Configure sign-up experience   [Edit]

Self-service sign-up Info

Self-registration
Enabled

Attribute verification and user account confirmation Info

Cognito-assisted verification and confirmation

Allow Cognito to automatically send messages to verify and confirm
Enabled

Attributes to verify
Send email message, verify email address

Verifying attribute changes

Keep original attribute value active when an update is pending
Enabled

Active attribute values when an update is pending
Email address

Required attributes Info

Required attributes
email
family_name
given_name
picture

Step 4: Configure message delivery   [Edit]

Email Info

Email provider
Send email with Cognito

SES Region
US West (Oregon)

FROM email address
no-reply@verificationemail.com

REPLY-TO email address
-

Figure 10.4: Creating Cognito user pool - part 2

A client app is set up in Cognito, which is given access to read the user data. The client app ID will be used within the user login and signup lambda functions to authenticate users. Cognito handles secure storage of user credentials, authentication, and authorization to access the user data.

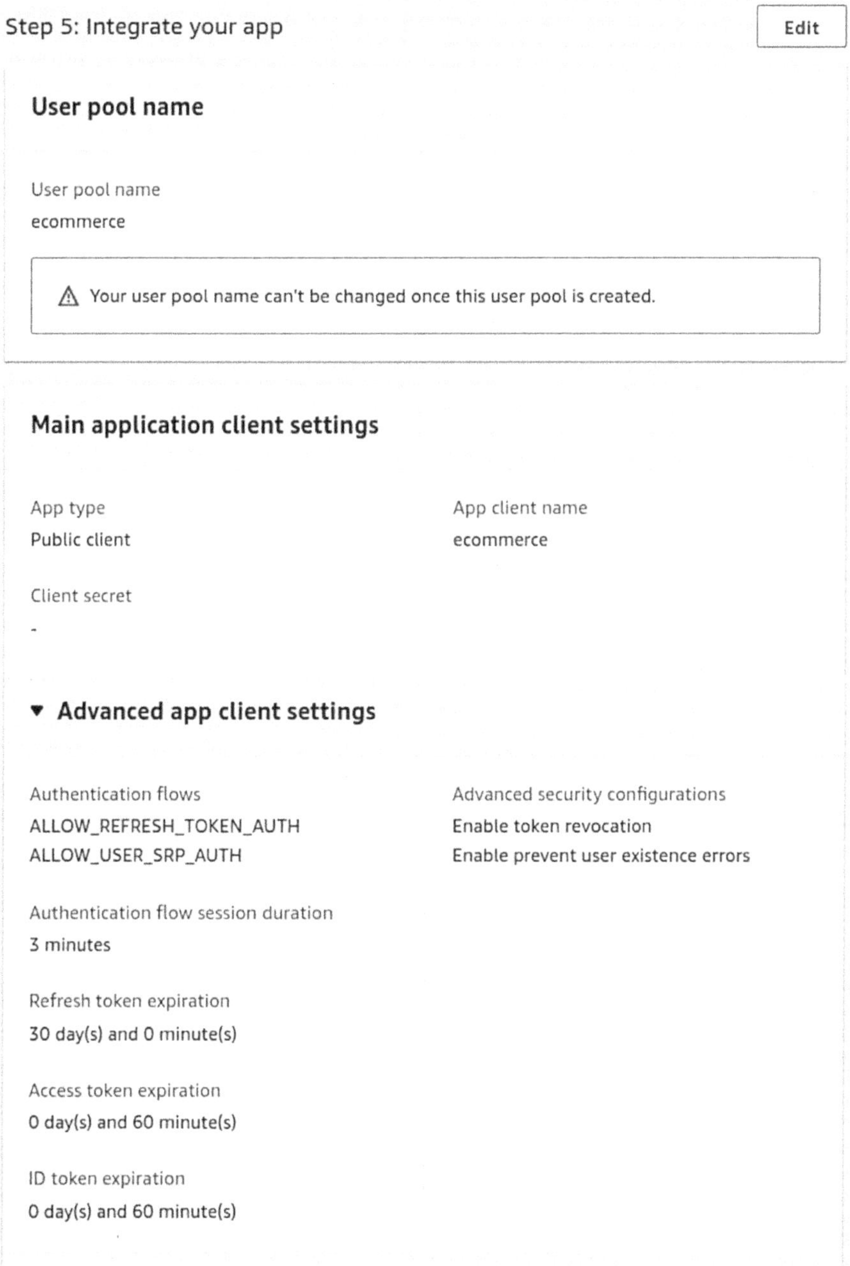

Step 5: Integrate your app   [Edit]

User pool name

User pool name
ecommerce

> ⚠ Your user pool name can't be changed once this user pool is created.

Main application client settings

App type   App client name
Public client   ecommerce

Client secret
-

▼ Advanced app client settings

Authentication flows   Advanced security configurations
ALLOW_REFRESH_TOKEN_AUTH   Enable token revocation
ALLOW_USER_SRP_AUTH   Enable prevent user existence errors

Authentication flow session duration
3 minutes

Refresh token expiration
30 day(s) and 0 minute(s)

Access token expiration
0 day(s) and 60 minute(s)

ID token expiration
0 day(s) and 60 minute(s)

Figure 10.5: Creating Cognito user pool - part 3

▼ **Attribute read and write permissions for this app**

Choose the standard and custom attributes that this app can read and write. Required attributes are locked as writable. We recommend that you set immutable custom attributes as writable to allow the app client to set initial values during sign-up.

Attribute ▲	Read	Write
address	⊘ Read	⊘ Write
birthdate	⊘ Read	⊘ Write
email	⊘ Read	⊘ Write
email_verified	⊘ Read	⊖ Not writable
family_name	⊘ Read	⊘ Write
gender	⊘ Read	⊘ Write
given_name	⊘ Read	⊘ Write
locale	⊘ Read	⊘ Write
middle_name	⊘ Read	⊘ Write
name	⊘ Read	⊘ Write
nickname	⊘ Read	⊘ Write
phone_number	⊘ Read	⊘ Write
phone_number_verified	⊘ Read	⊖ Not writable
picture	⊘ Read	⊘ Write
preferred_username	⊘ Read	⊘ Write
profile	⊘ Read	⊘ Write
updated_at	⊘ Read	⊘ Write
website	⊘ Read	⊘ Write
zoneinfo	⊘ Read	⊘ Write

Figure 10.6: Creating Cognito user pool - part 4

Figure 10.7 shows the details of the Cognito user pool.

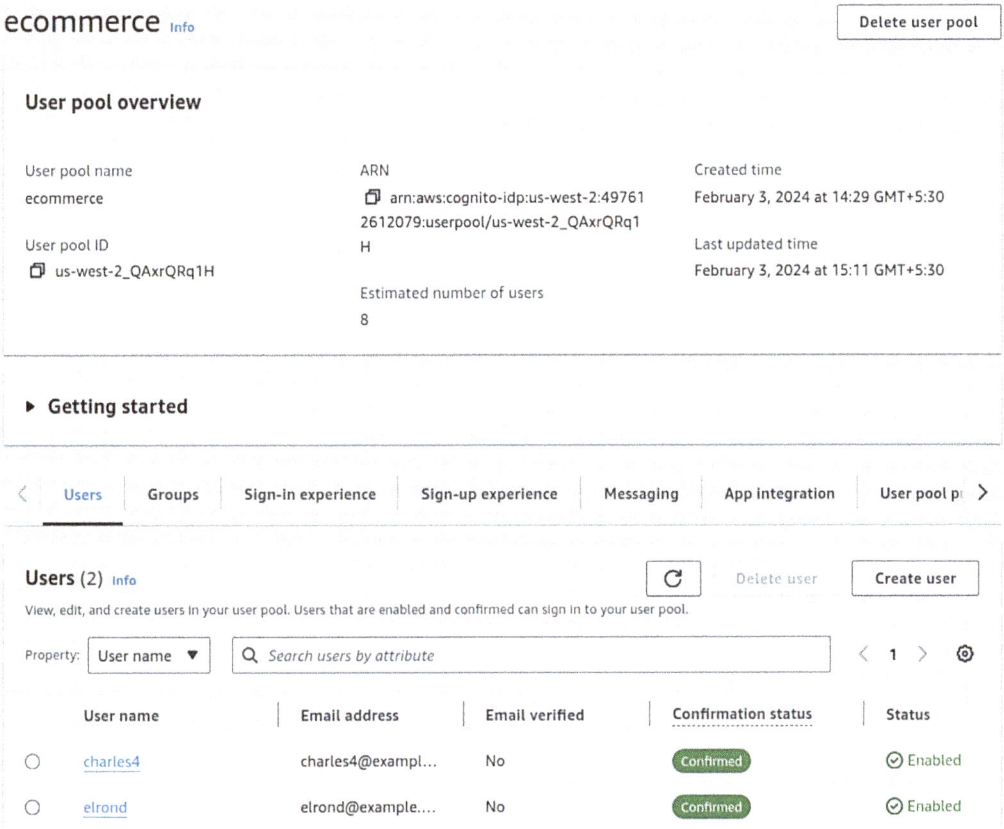

Figure 10.7: Cognito user pool

10.2.2   DynamoDB Tables

Next, we will create the DynamoDB tables for orders, products, and reviews. Figure 10.8 shows how to create a DynamoDB table for orders. Use the *username* field as the partition key and *order_id* as the sort key. Figure 10.9 shows an item and its attributes within the order table.

Similarly, create tables for products and reviews. For the product table, use the *slug* field as the partition key. For the review table, use the *slug* field as the partition key and *review_id* as the sort key. Figures 10.10, and 10.11 show the items and their attributes in the product and review tables.

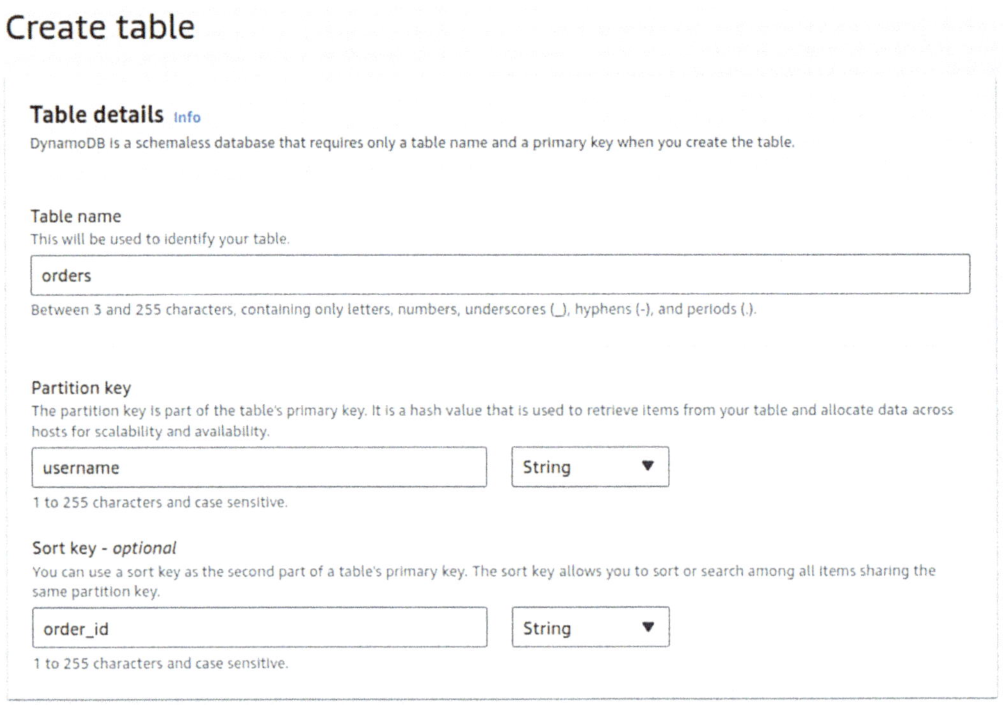

Create table

Table details Info
DynamoDB is a schemaless database that requires only a table name and a primary key when you create the table.

Table name
This will be used to identify your table.

> orders

Between 3 and 255 characters, containing only letters, numbers, underscores (_), hyphens (-), and periods (.).

Partition key
The partition key is part of the table's primary key. It is a hash value that is used to retrieve items from your table and allocate data across hosts for scalability and availability.

> username | String ▼

1 to 255 characters and case sensitive.

Sort key - *optional*
You can use a sort key as the second part of a table's primary key. The sort key allows you to sort or search among all items sharing the same partition key.

> order_id | String ▼

1 to 255 characters and case sensitive.

Figure 10.8: Creating DynamoDB table for orders

Attributes   Add new attribute ▼

⊞ Attribute name	Value	Type	
username *- Partition key*	charles4	String	
order_id *- Sort key*	1707040464730	String	
date_added	2024-02-04T09:54:24.730407	String	Remove
is_open	○ True ◉ False	Boolean	Remove
items	[{"product_slug": "mug-1", "quantity": 1, "price": 29.0, "image": "https://dn2aztcn1xe1u.cloudfront.net/photos/mug.jpg", "name": "Mug"}]	String	Remove

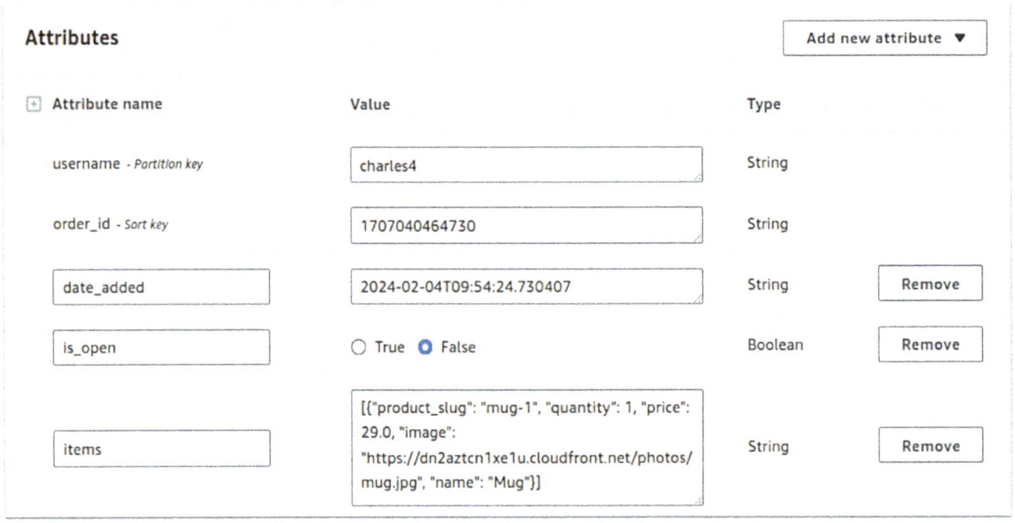

Figure 10.9: DynamoDB table for orders

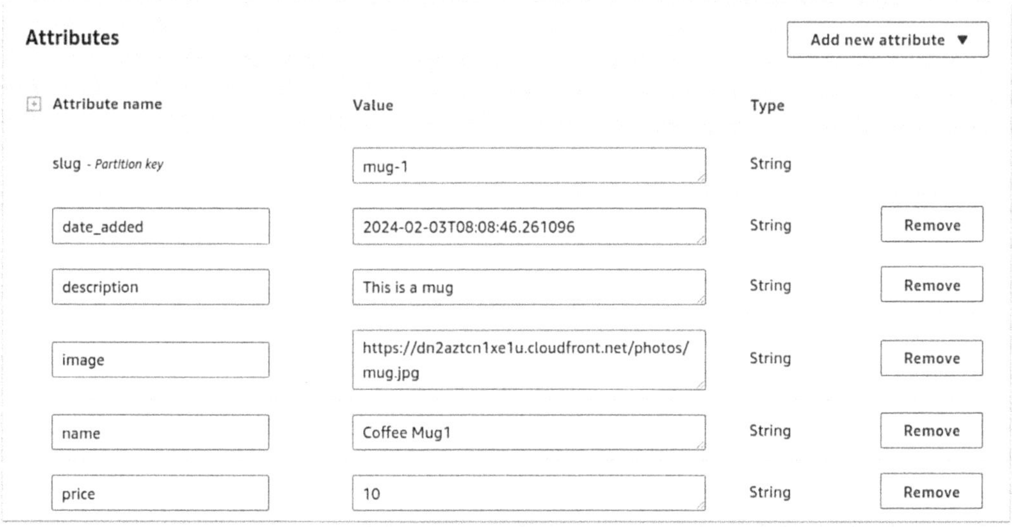

Figure 10.10: DynamoDB table for products

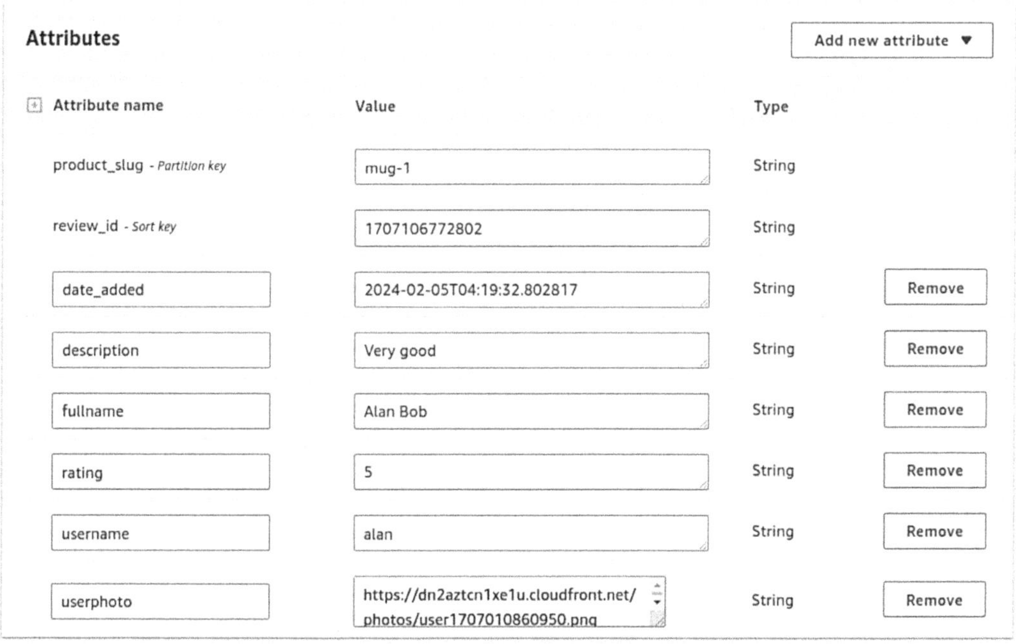

Figure 10.11: DynamoDB table for reviews

10.2.3　IAM Role

Next, we will create an IAM role that will be attached to all the lambda functions as shown in Figure 10.12. This role grants basic Lambda execution permissions and permission to write logs to CloudWatch Logs. To this role, we attach policies for access to S3, DynamoDB, and Cognito. The lambda functions will programmatically assume this role at runtime to gain access to the required resources.

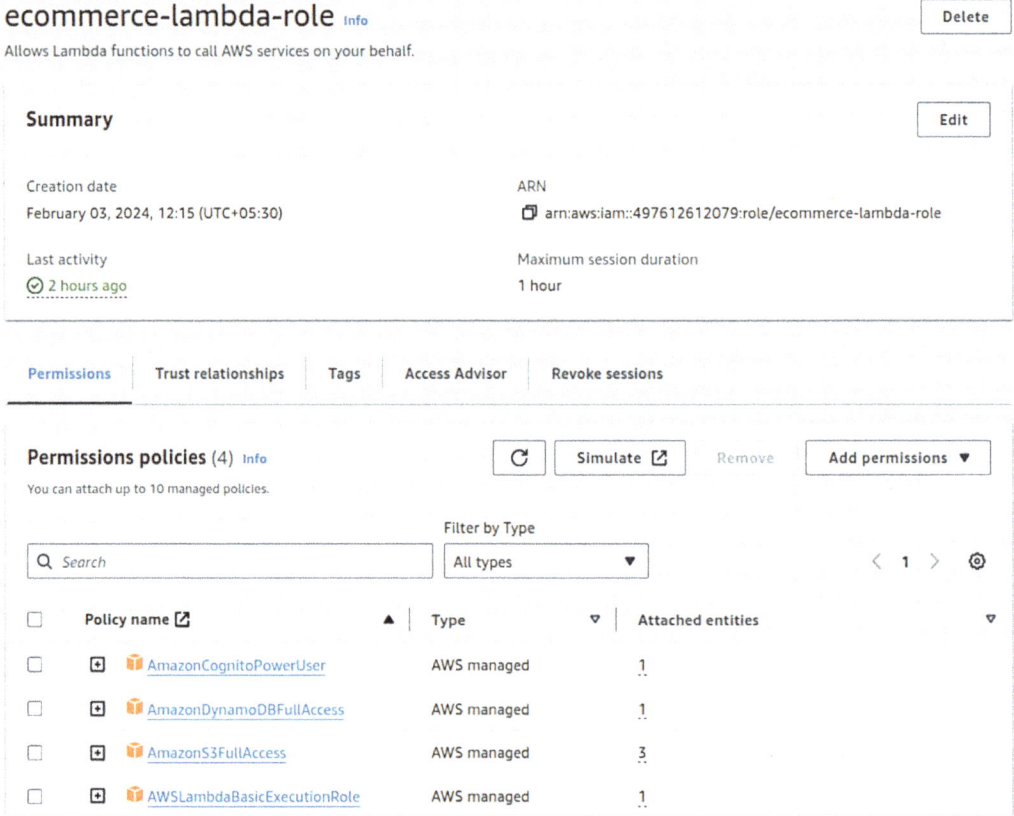

Policy name	Type	Attached entities
AmazonCognitoPowerUser	AWS managed	1
AmazonDynamoDBFullAccess	AWS managed	1
AmazonS3FullAccess	AWS managed	3
AWSLambdaBasicExecutionRole	AWS managed	1

Figure 10.12: Creating IAM role

10.2.4　Lambda Functions

Next, we will create lambda functions for the user, product, order, and review services. Figure 10.13 shows how to create a lambda function from the AWS console. We will use Python 3.9 as the runtime and attach the IAM role created previously to the lambda function.

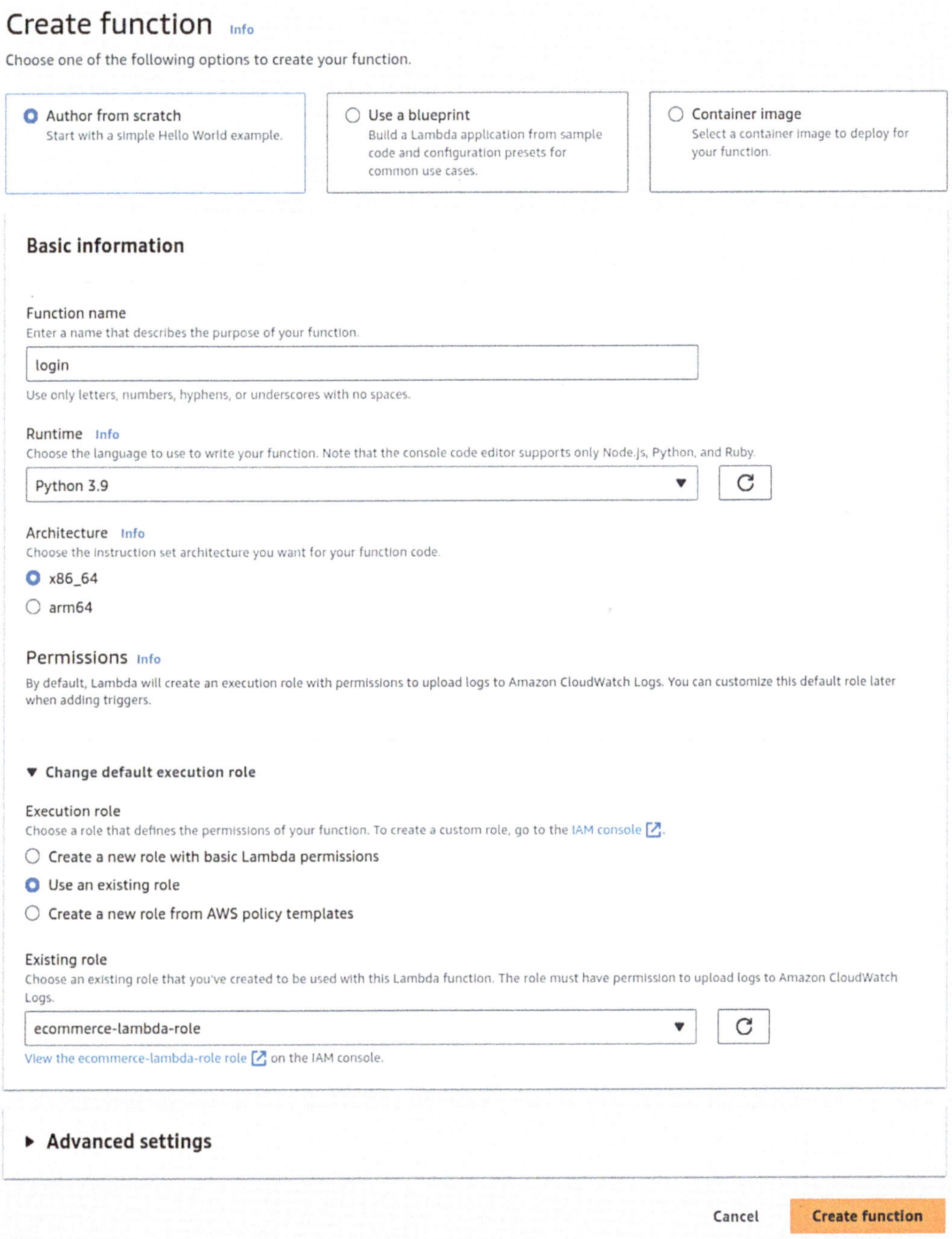

Create function Info

Choose one of the following options to create your function.

● Author from scratch	○ Use a blueprint	○ Container image
Start with a simple Hello World example.	Build a Lambda application from sample code and configuration presets for common use cases.	Select a container image to deploy for your function.

Basic information

Function name
Enter a name that describes the purpose of your function.

> login

Use only letters, numbers, hyphens, or underscores with no spaces.

Runtime Info
Choose the language to use to write your function. Note that the console code editor supports only Node.js, Python, and Ruby.

> Python 3.9   ▼   ⟳

Architecture Info
Choose the instruction set architecture you want for your function code.

● x86_64
○ arm64

Permissions Info

By default, Lambda will create an execution role with permissions to upload logs to Amazon CloudWatch Logs. You can customize this default role later when adding triggers.

▼ **Change default execution role**

Execution role
Choose a role that defines the permissions of your function. To create a custom role, go to the IAM console ↗.

○ Create a new role with basic Lambda permissions
● Use an existing role
○ Create a new role from AWS policy templates

Existing role
Choose an existing role that you've created to be used with this Lambda function. The role must have permission to upload logs to Amazon CloudWatch Logs.

> ecommerce-lambda-role   ▼   ⟳

View the ecommerce-lambda-role role ↗ on the IAM console.

▶ **Advanced settings**

Cancel   **Create function**

Figure 10.13: Creating lambda function - part 1

After creating the lambda function, we copy the Python code into the code editor of the lambda function as shown in Figure 10.14.

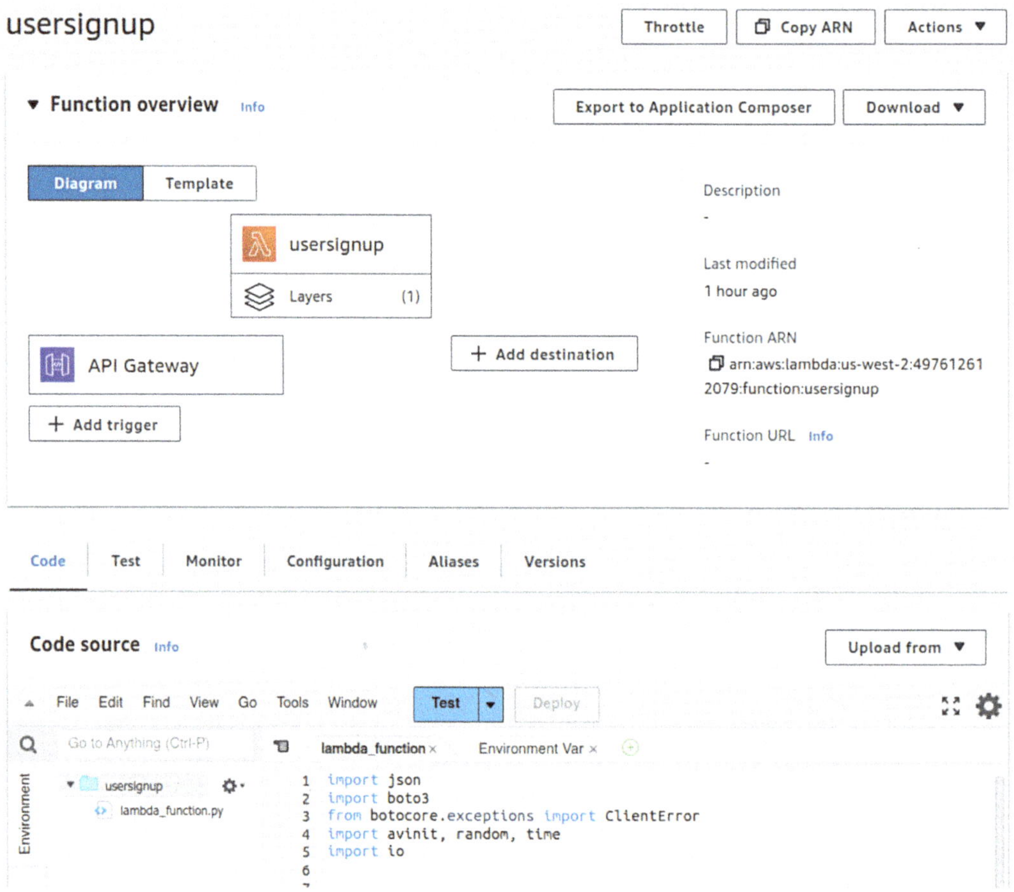

Figure 10.14: Creating lambda function - part 2

Box 10.1 shows the instructions for creating a layer for use in the lambda functions. We first launch an EC2 instance using Amazon Linux 2. Within the instance, we install Python 3.9 from source, since it needs to match the Lambda runtime. This requires installing dependencies like gcc and openssl-devel using yum, downloading the Python source code, unpacking it, configuring and compiling it, then installing it. Next, the folder structure to hold the Python packages is created following AWS recommendations for organizing Lambda layers. The needed Python packages are pip-installed into this folder structure individually using the *–target* parameter to place them in the site-packages area. Any required system libraries are installed using yum. These libraries, along with their dependencies, are copied over into the layer folder. This makes all necessary libs available alongside the Python packages. The entire layer folder is zipped up into a single compressed file for deployment. The AWS CLI is configured with API credentials to enable publishing the layer. The layer zip file is uploaded using the lambda *publish-layer-version* CLI command, specifying parameters like layer name, description, compatible Python runtime, and pointing to the local zip file.

■ Box 10.1: Instructions for creating a layer for use in a lambda function

```
#Install Python 3.9 on Amazon Linux 2 instance
sudo yum update -y
sudo yum install -y gcc openssl-devel bzip2-devel libffi-devel
cd /opt
sudo wget https://www.python.org/ftp/python/3.9.0/Python-3.9.0.tgz
sudo tar xzf Python-3.9.0.tgz
cd Python-3.9.0
sudo ./configure --enable-optimizations
sudo make altinstall


#Create folder structure for python packages
cd ~/
mkdir -p mylayer/aws-layer/aws-layer/python/lib/python3.9/site-packages


#Install python packages at the created path
cd ~/mylayer

pip3.9 install cairosvg --target
      aws-layer/python/lib/python3.9/site-packages

pip3.9 install cffi --target
      aws-layer/python/lib/python3.9/site-packages

pip3.9 install avinit[png] --target
      aws-layer/python/lib/python3.9/site-packages

pip3.9 install PyJWT --target
      aws-layer/python/lib/python3.9/site-packages

#Install required libraries
sudo yum install cairo cairo-dev

#Copy required libraries along with the dependencies
cd ~/mylayer/aws-layer/aws-layer/python/lib/
sudo cp -r /usr/lib64/libcairo* .
sudo cp -r /usr/lib64/libX* .
sudo cp -r /usr/lib64/libglvnd* .
sudo cp -r /usr/lib64/libgl* .
sudo cp -r /usr/lib64/libx* .
sudo cp -r /usr/lib64/libpng* .
sudo cp -r /usr/lib64/libpixman* .
sudo cp -r /usr/lib64/libway* .
sudo cp -r /usr/lib64/libEGL* .
sudo cp -r /usr/lib64/libGL* .
sudo cp -r /usr/lib64/libgbm* .
sudo cp -r /usr/lib64/libgl* .
sudo cp -r /usr/lib64/libxshmfence* .

#Create zip of layer
cd ~/mylayer/aws-layer/
```

```
zip -r9 lambda-layer.zip .

#Configure AWS CLI
aws configure

#Upload layer zip to AWS
aws lambda publish-layer-version --layer-name Avinit14
        --description "My Python layer"
        --zip-file fileb://lambda-layer.zip
        --compatible-runtimes python3.9
```

Figure 10.15 shows how to add the published layer to a lambda function through the Lambda console UI layers section.

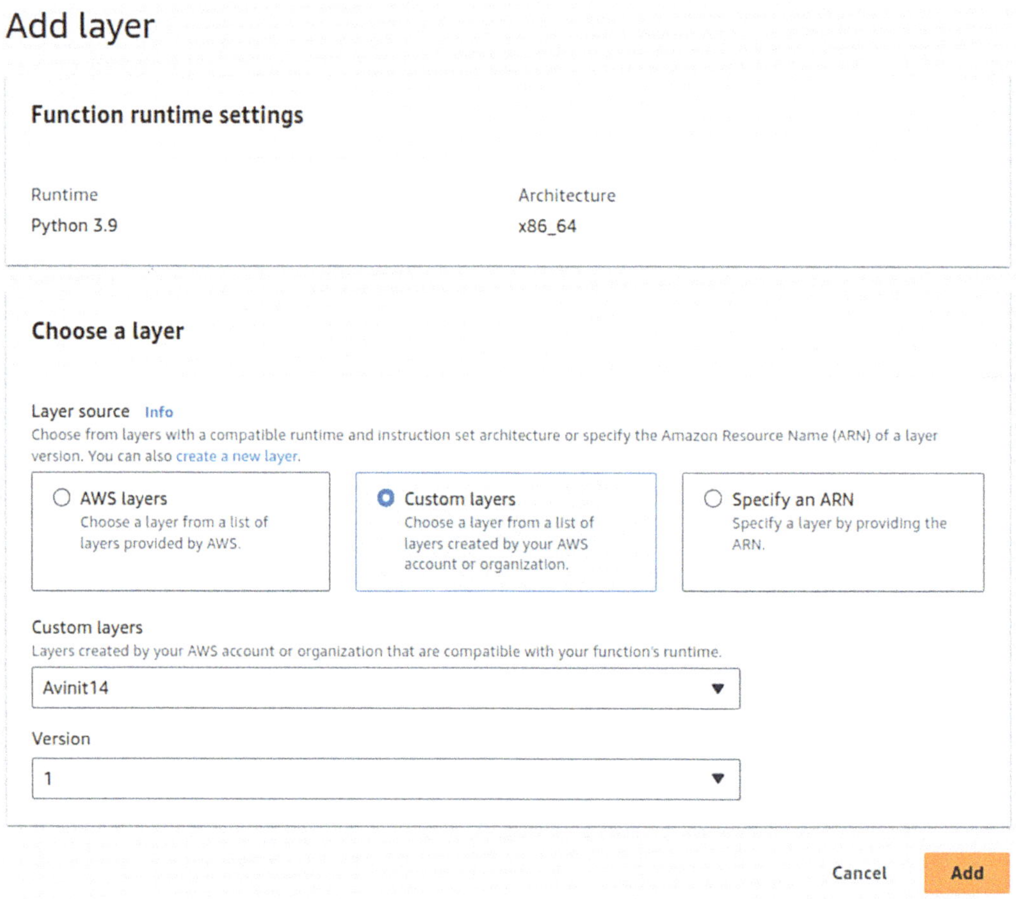

Add layer

Function runtime settings

Runtime   Architecture
Python 3.9   x86_64

Choose a layer

Layer source   Info
Choose from layers with a compatible runtime and instruction set architecture or specify the Amazon Resource Name (ARN) of a layer version. You can also create a new layer.

○ AWS layers   ● Custom layers   ○ Specify an ARN
  Choose a layer from a list of   Choose a layer from a list of   Specify a layer by providing the
  layers provided by AWS.   layers created by your AWS   ARN.
                                   account or organization.

Custom layers
Layers created by your AWS account or organization that are compatible with your function's runtime.

Avinit14   ▼

Version

1   ▼

                                                     Cancel   **Add**

Figure 10.15: Adding a layer to a lambda function

Next, we configure an environment variable *LD_LIBRARY_PATH* to point to the layer's lib folder so the function can locate the libraries packaged in the layer, as shown in Figure 10.16.

Similarly, create the other lambda functions. Attach the lambda layer to all the functions that use the dependencies packaged in the layer. Figure 10.17 shows the list of all the lambda functions for the E-Commerce application.

Edit environment variables

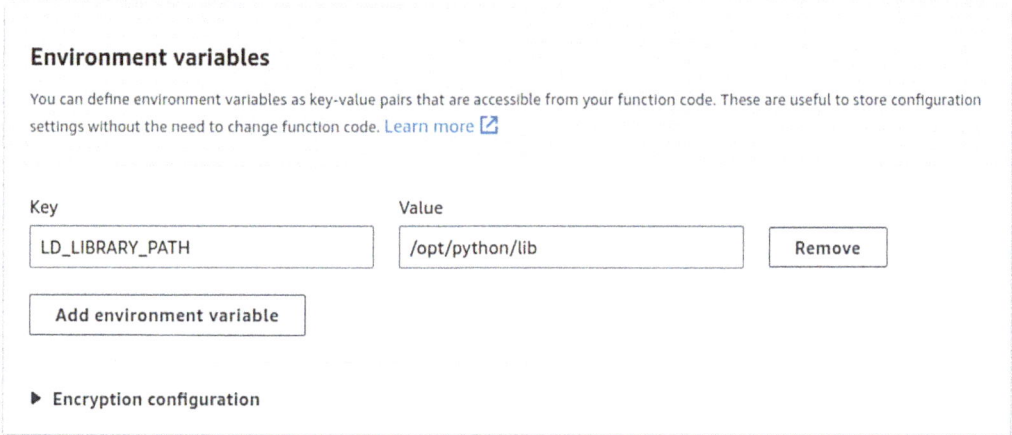

Environment variables

You can define environment variables as key-value pairs that are accessible from your function code. These are useful to store configuration settings without the need to change function code. Learn more ⧉

Key	Value	
LD_LIBRARY_PATH	/opt/python/lib	Remove

Add environment variable

▶ **Encryption configuration**

Figure 10.16: Configuring environment variables in lambda function

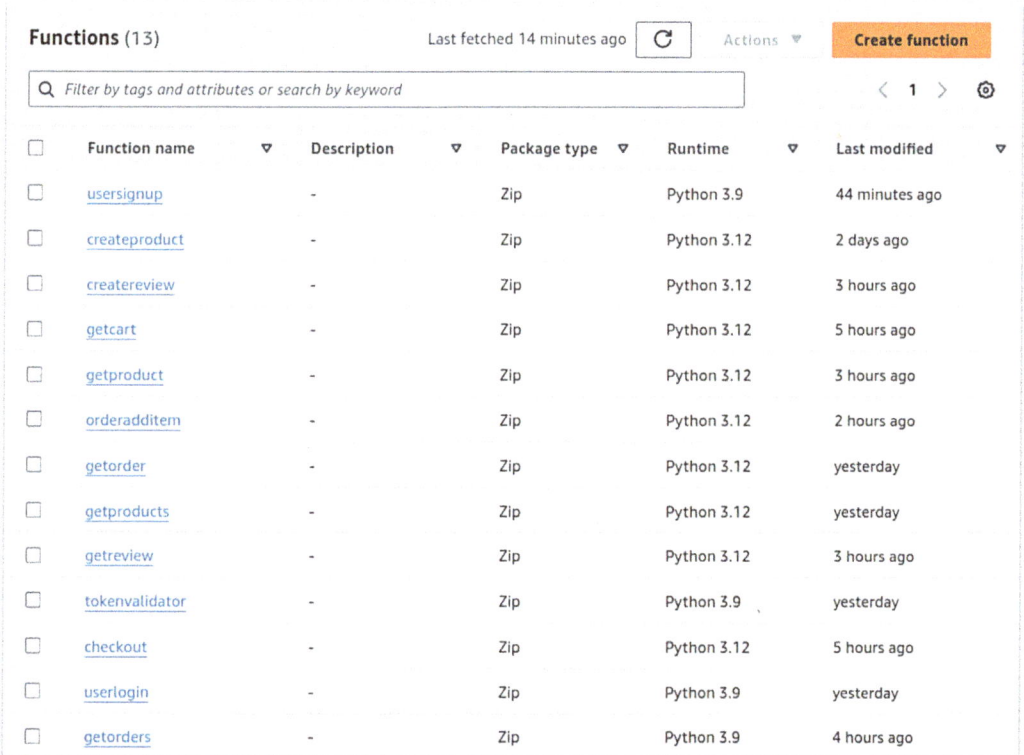

Functions (13)   Last fetched 14 minutes ago ↻   Actions ▾   **Create function**

🔍 *Filter by tags and attributes or search by keyword*   ⟨ 1 ⟩   ⚙

	Function name	▽	Description	▽	Package type	▽	Runtime	▽	Last modified	▽
☐	usersignup		-		Zip		Python 3.9		44 minutes ago	
☐	createproduct		-		Zip		Python 3.12		2 days ago	
☐	createreview		-		Zip		Python 3.12		3 hours ago	
☐	getcart		-		Zip		Python 3.12		5 hours ago	
☐	getproduct		-		Zip		Python 3.12		3 hours ago	
☐	orderadditem		-		Zip		Python 3.12		2 hours ago	
☐	getorder		-		Zip		Python 3.12		yesterday	
☐	getproducts		-		Zip		Python 3.12		yesterday	
☐	getreview		-		Zip		Python 3.12		3 hours ago	
☐	tokenvalidator		-		Zip		Python 3.9		yesterday	
☐	checkout		-		Zip		Python 3.12		5 hours ago	
☐	userlogin		-		Zip		Python 3.9		yesterday	
☐	getorders		-		Zip		Python 3.9		4 hours ago	

Figure 10.17: Lambda functions for E-Commerce application

Box 10.2 shows the code of the lambda function for user signup. This function enables user registration using Amazon Cognito for user management. The Cognito user pool ID, client ID, S3 bucket name, and CloudFront URL are specified. In the handler, the signup data like username, password, name, email, and picture are extracted from the request body. A unique filename is generated for the user photo, which is uploaded to S3. The CloudFront URL of the photo is assigned to the picture variable. The *sign_up* API of Cognito SDK is called to create the user by passing username, password, and attributes like name, email, and picture. If successful, the *admin_confirm_sign_up* API is called to confirm the user. The user data like username, name, picture, and email is returned in the response.

■ Box 10.2: User signup lambda function

```
import json
import boto3
from botocore.exceptions import ClientError
import avinit, random, time
import io


REGION="us-west-2"
USER_POOL_ID="us-west-2_QAxrQRq"
CLIENT_ID="6egeuf4gpmv878phrcf8pv"
cognitoclient = boto3.client('cognito-idp', region_name=REGION)
s3 = boto3.client('s3')
BUCKET_NAME='microservices-ecommerce-app'
CLOUDFRONT_URL = 'https://dn2aztcn.cloudfront.net'

def lambda_handler(event, context):
    body = event['body'].strip()
    body=body.replace('\n','')
    body=json.loads(body)
    username=body['username']
    password=body['password']
    given_name=body['given_name']
    family_name=body['family_name']
    email=body['email']

    name=given_name+' '+ family_name
    filename = "user"+str(int(time.time()*1000))+".png"
    imgpath='/tmp/'+filename
    r = lambda: random.randint(0,255)
    colors=[]
    colors.append('#%02X%02X%02X' % (r(),r(),r()))
    avinit.get_png_avatar(name, output_file=imgpath, colors=colors)
    path_filename_s3 = "photos/" + filename
    with open(imgpath, 'rb') as f:
        s3.upload_fileobj(f, BUCKET_NAME, path_filename_s3)

    url = CLOUDFRONT_URL+'/'+path_filename_s3
    picture=url
    result=False
    message=""
    response={}
```

```
returndata={}
userdata={}
response = cognitoclient.sign_up(
    ClientId=CLIENT_ID,
    Username=username,
    Password=password,
    UserAttributes=[
        {
            'Name': 'given_name',
            'Value': given_name
        },
        {
            'Name': 'family_name',
            'Value': family_name
        },
        {
            'Name': 'email',
            'Value': email
        },
        {
            'Name': 'picture',
            'Value': picture
        },
    ]
)
result=True
message="Signup successful"
response = cognitoclient.admin_confirm_sign_up(
    UserPoolId=USER_POOL_ID,
    Username=username
)
userdata['username']=username
userdata['given_name']=given_name
userdata['family_name']=family_name
userdata['picture']=picture
userdata['email']=email
returndata['result']=result
returndata['message']=message
returndata['userdata']=userdata
return {
    "statusCode": 200,
    "headers": {
            "Content-Type": "application/json",
            "Access-Control-Allow-Origin" : "*",
            "Access-Control-Allow-Methods" : "*"
        },
    "body": json.dumps(returndata)
}
```

Box 10.3 shows the code of the lambda function for user login. It takes the username and password from the request body, calls the Amazon Cognito *admin_initiate_auth* API to authenticate the user, and if successful, generates a JSON Web Token (JWT) containing user info like username, first name, last name, and email. It retrieves this additional user info by calling the Cognito *admin_get_user* API. The token is returned in the response to the caller. The lambda function demonstrates using Cognito for user authentication and generating signed JWTs for the authenticated user with relevant claims, which can be used for authorization by other microservices.

■ Box 10.3: User login lambda function

```
import json
import boto3
from botocore.exceptions import ClientError
import jwt
import datetime

REGION="us-west-2"
USER_POOL_ID="us-west-2_QAxrQRq"
CLIENT_ID="6egeuf4gpmv878phrcf8pv"
JWT_SECRET = 'mysecretkey'
cognitoclient = boto3.client('cognito-idp', region_name=REGION)

def lambda_handler(event, context):
    body = event['body'].strip()
    body=body.replace('\n','')
    body=json.loads(body)

    username=body['username']
    password=body['password']
    result=False
    message=""
    response={}
    returndata={}
    userdata={}

    response = cognitoclient.admin_initiate_auth(
        UserPoolId=USER_POOL_ID,
        ClientId=CLIENT_ID,
        AuthFlow='ADMIN_NO_SRP_AUTH',
        AuthParameters={
            'USERNAME': username,
            'PASSWORD': password
        }
    )

    if 'ResponseMetadata' in response:
        if response['ResponseMetadata']['HTTPStatusCode']==200:
            result=True
            message="Login successful"
            response = cognitoclient.admin_get_user(
                UserPoolId=USER_POOL_ID,
                Username=username
            )
            # Generate JWT with user info and expiry
            token = jwt.encode({
                'username': username,
                'exp': datetime.datetime.utcnow() +
                        datetime.timedelta(days=1)
```

```
                    }, JWT_SECRET, algorithm='HS256')

                userdata['token'] = token
                for item in response['UserAttributes']:
                    if item['Name']=='given_name':
                        userdata['given_name']=item['Value']
                    elif item['Name']=='family_name':
                        userdata['family_name']=item['Value']
                    elif item['Name']=='email':
                        userdata['email']=item['Value']
                    elif item['Name']=='picture':
                        userdata['picture']=item['Value']
            else:
                return False
                message="Something went wrong"

        userdata['username']=username
        returndata['result']=result
        returndata['message']=message
        returndata['userdata']=userdata
        return {
            "statusCode": 200,
            "headers": {
                "Access-Control-Allow-Origin" : "*",
                "Access-Control-Allow-Methods" : "*"
            },
            "body": json.dumps(returndata)
        }
```

Box 10.4 shows the code of the lambda function for token validation, which is used as a custom authorizer in API Gateway. It validates the JWT passed in the authorization header of the API request. The code imports the PyJWT library to decode the JWT and specifies a secret key *JWT_SECRET* to validate the signature. In the lambda handler, it extracts the token from the event headers. It uses the *jwt.decode* method to validate the token signature with the secret and HS256 algorithm. If valid, it returns an IAM policy granting access to the API. If invalid due to expired or invalid signature, it returns a response indicating an invalid token. This allows secure access to the backend APIs only for requests with a valid JWT. Using a custom authorizer with JWT validation ensures only authenticated users can access the REST APIs.

■ **Box 10.4: Token validation lambda function**

```
import jwt
import os

JWT_SECRET = 'mysecretkey'

def lambda_handler(event, context):
    token = event['headers']['authorization']
    validate_token = lambda token: jwt.decode(token,
                JWT_SECRET, algorithms=['HS256'])
    try:
```

```
        payload = validate_token(token)
        print('Token valid')
        # Return a policy
        return {
          "principalId": "user",
          "policyDocument": {
            "Version": "2012-10-17",
            "Statement": [
                {
                    "Action": "execute-api:Invoke",
                    "Effect": "Allow",
                    "Resource": event["methodArn"]
                }
            ]
          }
        }
    except jwt.ExpiredSignatureError:
        print('Token expired')
        return {"response":"Invalid token"}
    except jwt.InvalidTokenError:
        print('Invalid token')
        return {"response":"Invalid token"}
```

Box 10.5 shows the code of the lambda function for creating a product. It receives the product details like name, slug, description, price, and image in the request body. It extracts the base64 encoded image data, decodes it, and uploads the image to an S3 bucket. It constructs the product item with required attributes like slug, name, description, price, image URL, and date added. The product item is inserted into the DynamoDB products table using the *put_item* method. The response body contains a success message and the details of the new product item.

■ Box 10.5: Create product lambda function

```python
import json
import boto3
from botocore.exceptions import ClientError
import base64
import time
import io
from datetime import datetime

dynamodb = boto3.resource('dynamodb')
table = dynamodb.Table('products')
s3 = boto3.client('s3')
BUCKET_NAME='microservices-ecommerce-app'
CLOUDFRONT_URL = 'https://dn2aztcn1xe1u.cloudfront.net'

def lambda_handler(event, context):
    body = event['body'].strip()
    body=body.replace('\n','')
    body=json.loads(body)
    name = body['name']
```

```
    slug = body['slug']
    description = body['description']
    price = body['price']
    image = body['image']
    filename=body['filename']
    image_data = base64.b64decode(image)
    image_object = io.BytesIO(image_data)

    # Upload image to S3
    path_filename_s3 = "photos/" + filename
    s3.upload_fileobj(image_object, BUCKET_NAME, path_filename_s3)
    url = CLOUDFRONT_URL+'/'+path_filename_s3

    # Create product in DynamoDB
    item = {
            'slug': slug,
            'name': name,
            'description': description,
            'price': price,
            'image': url,
            'date_added': datetime.now().isoformat()
        }
    table.put_item(
       Item=item
    )
    response = {
        "statusCode": 200,
        "body": json.dumps({"message": "Product created",
                            "product": item})
    }
    return response
```

Box 10.6 shows the code of the lambda function to retrieve a single product from DynamoDB based on the product slug provided in the path parameter. It first gets the slug from the path parameter of the event. It then queries the products table in DynamoDB using the slug as the partition key. If a matching item is found, it returns a 200 response with the product details in the body. If no matching item is found, it returns a 404 response indicating the product was not found.

■ Box 10.6: Get product lambda function

```
import json
import boto3
from botocore.exceptions import ClientError
import base64
import time
import io
from datetime import datetime
from boto3.dynamodb.conditions import Key

dynamodb = boto3.resource('dynamodb')
table = dynamodb.Table('products')
```

```
s3 = boto3.client('s3')

def lambda_handler(event, context):
    slug = event['pathParameters']['slug']
    response = table.query(KeyConditionExpression=Key('slug').eq(slug))
    item = response['Items'][0] if response['Items'] else None
    if item:
        return {
            "statusCode": 200,
            "headers": {
                "Content-Type": "application/json",
                "Access-Control-Allow-Origin" : "*",
                "Access-Control-Allow-Methods" : "*"
            },
            "body": json.dumps({"result": item})
        }
    else:
        return {
            "statusCode": 404,
            "headers": {
                "Content-Type": "application/json",
                "Access-Control-Allow-Origin" : "*",
                "Access-Control-Allow-Methods" : "*"
            },
            "body": json.dumps({"message": "Product not found"})
        }
```

Box 10.7 shows the code of the lambda function to retrieve all products from the DynamoDB products table and return them in a JSON response. In the handler, it scans the products table to get all items. It then returns a JSON response with a status code of 200, appropriate headers for CORS, and the products array in the body.

■ Box 10.7: Get all products lambda function

```
import json
import boto3
from botocore.exceptions import ClientError
import base64
import time
import io
from datetime import datetime

dynamodb = boto3.resource('dynamodb')
table = dynamodb.Table('products')
s3 = boto3.client('s3')

def lambda_handler(event, context):
    response = table.scan()
    items = response['Items']
    return {
        "statusCode": 200,
        "headers": {
            "Content-Type": "application/json",
```

```
            "Access-Control-Allow-Origin" : "*",
            "Access-Control-Allow-Methods" : "*"
        },
        "body": json.dumps({"results": items})
    }
```

Box 10.8 shows the code of the lambda function for adding items to an order in a shopping cart. It receives the order details like username, product information, and quantity in the request body. It queries the DynamoDB orders table to check if an open order already exists for that user. If not, it creates a new order. If an open order exists, it checks if the item being added already exists in the order. If so, it increments the quantity, otherwise, it adds the new item to the order's items list. Finally, it updates the order in DynamoDB and returns a success response.

■ **Box 10.8: Order add item lambda function**

```
import json
import boto3
from botocore.exceptions import ClientError
import time
from datetime import datetime
from boto3.dynamodb.conditions import Key, Attr

dynamodb = boto3.resource('dynamodb')
table = dynamodb.Table('orders')

def lambda_handler(event, context):
    body = event['body'].strip()
    body=body.replace('\n','')
    body=json.loads(body)
    username = body['username']
    product_slug = body['product_slug']
    qty = int(body['qty'])
    price = float(body['price'])
    image = body['image']
    name = body['name']
    response = table.query(
        KeyConditionExpression=Key('username').eq(username))
    orders = response['Items']
    known_order=None
    if orders is None:
        response = {
            "statusCode": 200,
            "headers": {
                "Content-Type": "application/json",
                "Access-Control-Allow-Origin" : "*",
                "Access-Control-Allow-Methods" : "*"
            },
            "body": json.dumps({"message": "No order found",
                        "result": []})
        }
        return response
```

```
        else:
            items=[]
            for order in orders:
                if order['is_open']==True:
                    known_order=order

        if known_order is None:
            itemslist=[]
            itemslist.append({'product_slug': product_slug,
                              'quantity': qty, 'price': price,
                              'image': image, 'name': name})
            order_id=str(int(time.time()*1000))
            known_order = {
                'username': username,
                'order_id': order_id,
                'is_open': True,
                'items': json.dumps(itemslist),
                'date_added': datetime.now().isoformat()
            }
            table.put_item(
                Item=known_order
            )
        else:
            found = False
            itemslist=json.loads(known_order['items'])
            newitemslist=[]
            for item in itemslist:
                if item['product_slug'] == product_slug:
                    found = True
                    item['quantity'] = int(item['quantity'])+qty
                newitemslist.append(item)
            if found is False:
                newitemslist.append({'product_slug': product_slug,
                                     'quantity': qty, 'price': price,
                                     'image': image, 'name': name})
            known_order['items']=json.dumps(newitemslist)
            table.put_item(
                Item=known_order
            )
        response = {
                "statusCode": 200,
                "headers": {
                    "Content-Type": "application/json",
                    "Access-Control-Allow-Origin" : "*",
                    "Access-Control-Allow-Methods" : "*"
                },
                "body": json.dumps({"message": "Order found",
                            "result": known_order})
            }
        return response
```

Box 10.9 shows the code of the lambda function for order checkout. It takes the username from the input event and queries the DynamoDB orders table to get all the orders for that user. It checks if any open order exists for that user and closes it by setting *is_open* to false and saving the order back to DynamoDB. The function returns a response with the open order details if found.

> ■ **Box 10.9: Checkout lambda function**

```python
import json, boto3, time
from botocore.exceptions import ClientError
from datetime import datetime
from boto3.dynamodb.conditions import Key, Attr

dynamodb = boto3.resource('dynamodb')
table = dynamodb.Table('orders')

def lambda_handler(event, context):
    print(event)
    body = event['body'].strip()
    body=body.replace('\n','')
    body=json.loads(body)
    username = body['username']
    response = table.query(
        KeyConditionExpression=Key('username').eq(username))
    orders = response['Items']
    open_order=None
    if orders is None:
        response = {
            "statusCode": 200,
            "headers": {
                    "Access-Control-Allow-Origin" : "*",
                    "Access-Control-Allow-Methods" : "*"
            },
            "body": json.dumps({"message": "No order found",
                            "result": []})
        }
        return response
    else:
        orderitems=[]
        for order in orders:
            if order['is_open']==True:
                open_order=order
                open_order['is_open']=False
                table.put_item(
                    Item=open_order
                )
    response = {
            "statusCode": 200,
            "headers": {
                    "Access-Control-Allow-Origin" : "*",
                    "Access-Control-Allow-Methods" : "*"
            },
            "body": json.dumps({"message": "Order found",
                            "result": open_order})
        }
    return response
```

Box 10.10 shows the code of the lambda function to retrieve an open order for a user. It takes the username from the input event body and queries the orders DynamoDB table with the username as the hash key to get all orders for that user. The orders list is iterated to check if any order has *is_open=True*. If found, that open order is returned in the response JSON. If no open order exists, a response with an empty result is returned.

■ **Box 10.10: Get order lambda function**

```python
import json
import boto3
from botocore.exceptions import ClientError
import time
from datetime import datetime
from boto3.dynamodb.conditions import Key, Attr

dynamodb = boto3.resource('dynamodb')
table = dynamodb.Table('orders')


def lambda_handler(event, context):
    body = event['body'].strip()
    body=body.replace('\n','')
    body=json.loads(body)
    username = body['username']
    response = table.query(
        KeyConditionExpression=Key('username').eq(username))
    orders = response['Items']
    open_order=None
    if orders is None:
        response = {
            "statusCode": 200,
            "body": json.dumps({"message": "No order found",
                                "result": []})
        }
        return response
    else:
        for order in orders:
            if order['is_open']==True:
                open_order=order

    if open_order is None:
        response = {
            "statusCode": 200,
            "body": json.dumps({"message": "No order found",
                                "result": []})
        }
        return response
    else:
        response = {
                "statusCode": 200,
                "body": json.dumps({"message": "Open order found",
                                    "result": open_order})
            }
        return response
```

Box 10.11 shows the code of the lambda function to retrieve closed orders for a user from the orders DynamoDB table. It takes the username as input and queries the orders table to get all orders for that user. It then filters these orders to only keep those where *is_open=False*, indicating closed orders. The filtered orders are returned in the response body as a JSON object containing a message and the order details in a result array.

■ Box 10.11: Get all orders lambda function

```python
import json, boto3, time
from botocore.exceptions import ClientError
from datetime import datetime
from boto3.dynamodb.conditions import Key, Attr

dynamodb = boto3.resource('dynamodb')
table = dynamodb.Table('orders')

def lambda_handler(event, context):
    print(event)
    body = event['body'].strip()
    body=body.replace('\n','')
    body=json.loads(body)
    username = body['username']
    response = table.query(
        KeyConditionExpression=Key('username').eq(username))
    orders = response['Items']
    orderslist=[]

    if orders is None:
        response = {
            "statusCode": 200,
            "headers": {
                    "Access-Control-Allow-Origin" : "*",
                    "Access-Control-Allow-Methods" : "*"
            },
            "body": json.dumps({"message": "No order found",
                            "result": []})
        }
        return response
    else:
        for order in orders:
            if order['is_open']==False:
                orderslist.append(order)

    response = {
            "statusCode": 200,
            "headers": {
                    "Access-Control-Allow-Origin" : "*",
                    "Access-Control-Allow-Methods" : "*"
            },
            "body": json.dumps({"message": "Order found",
                            "result": orderslist})
        }
    return response
```

Box 10.12 shows the code of the lambda function to retrieve the current open order for a user from the orders DynamoDB table. It takes the username from the input event body. It then queries the orders table to get all orders for that user. It loops through the orders to find the one where *is_open=True*. It extracts the items from that open order. It calculates the total order amount by looping through the order items, multiplying the quantity by the price, and summing it up. Finally, it returns a 200 response with the order items array and total order amount in the response body. This allows the frontend to show the current open cart and total for a user.

■ **Box 10.12: Get cart lambda function**

```python
import json
import boto3
from botocore.exceptions import ClientError
import time
from datetime import datetime
from boto3.dynamodb.conditions import Key, Attr

dynamodb = boto3.resource('dynamodb')
table = dynamodb.Table('orders')

def lambda_handler(event, context):
    body = event['body'].strip()
    body=body.replace('\n','')
    body=json.loads(body)
    username = body['username']
    response = table.query(
        KeyConditionExpression=Key('username').eq(username))
    orders = response['Items']
    known_order=None
    orderitems=[]
    totalamount=0
    if orders is None:
        response = {
            "statusCode": 200,
            "headers": {
            "Access-Control-Allow-Origin" : "*",
            "Access-Control-Allow-Methods" : "*"
          },
            "body": json.dumps({"message": "No order found",
                                "result": []})
        }
        return response
    else:
        for order in orders:
            if order['is_open']==True:
                orderitems=order['items']

    try:
        for item in json.loads(orderitems):
            totalamount=totalamount+
                int(item['quantity'])*float(item['price'])
    except:
```

```
        pass
    response = {
            "statusCode": 200,
            "headers": {
            "Access-Control-Allow-Origin" : "*",
            "Access-Control-Allow-Methods" : "*"
        },
            "body": json.dumps({"message": "Order found",
                "result": orderitems, "totalamount": totalamount})
        }
    return response
```

Box 10.13 shows the code of the lambda function to create a product review in DynamoDB. It first gets the review data like username, product identifier, rating, and description from the request body. It generates a unique review ID and constructs a review item object with all the data. The item is then inserted into the reviews DynamoDB table. It returns a 200 success response with the inserted review item in the body.

■ Box 10.13: Post review lambda function

```
import json
import boto3
from botocore.exceptions import ClientError
import time
from datetime import datetime

dynamodb = boto3.resource('dynamodb')
table = dynamodb.Table('reviews')

def lambda_handler(event, context):
    print(event)
    body = event['body'].strip()
    body=body.replace('\n','')
    body=json.loads(body)
    username = body['username']
    product_slug = body['product_slug']
    description = body['description']
    rating = body['rating']
    fullname = body['fullname']
    userphoto = body['userphoto']
    review_id=str(int(time.time()*1000))
    item = {
            'product_slug': product_slug,
            'review_id': review_id,
            'username': username,
            'rating': rating,
            'description': description,
            'fullname': fullname,
            'userphoto': userphoto,
            'date_added': datetime.now().isoformat()
        }
    table.put_item(
       Item=item
```

```
    )
    response = {
        "statusCode": 200,
        "headers": {
                "Content-Type": "application/json",
                "Access-Control-Allow-Origin" : "*",
                "Access-Control-Allow-Methods" : "*"
            },
        "body": json.dumps({"message": "Review posted", "review": item})
    }
    return response
```

Box 10.14 shows the code of the lambda function to retrieve product reviews from DynamoDB. It takes the product slug from the request path parameters. It queries the reviews table on the *product_slug* to get all reviews for that product. It returns a JSON response containing the list of review items.

■ **Box 10.14: Get review lambda function**

```
import json
import boto3
from botocore.exceptions import ClientError
import base64
import time
import io
from datetime import datetime
from boto3.dynamodb.conditions import Key, Attr

dynamodb = boto3.resource('dynamodb')
table = dynamodb.Table('reviews')

def lambda_handler(event, context):
    slug = event['pathParameters']['slug']
    response = table.query(
        KeyConditionExpression=Key('product_slug').eq(slug))

    items = response['Items']

    return {
        "statusCode": 200,
        "headers": {
                "Content-Type": "application/json",
                "Access-Control-Allow-Origin" : "*",
                "Access-Control-Allow-Methods" : "*"
            },
        "body": json.dumps({"results": items})
    }
```

10.2.5 API Gateway

Amazon API Gateway is used to create RESTful APIs that connect to backend services like Lambda functions and DynamoDB. API Gateway handles all the tasks involved in accepting and processing API calls, such as traffic management, authorization, access control, monitoring, and API version management.

Figure 10.18 shows the list of APIs for the E-Commerce application. To implement the API, we first define the top-level API resources - *user*, *product*, *order*, and *review*. For each of these resources, we define the second-level resources, for example, *create* and *login* for the *user* resource. Next, we configure the HTTP methods (like GET and POST) for these resources.

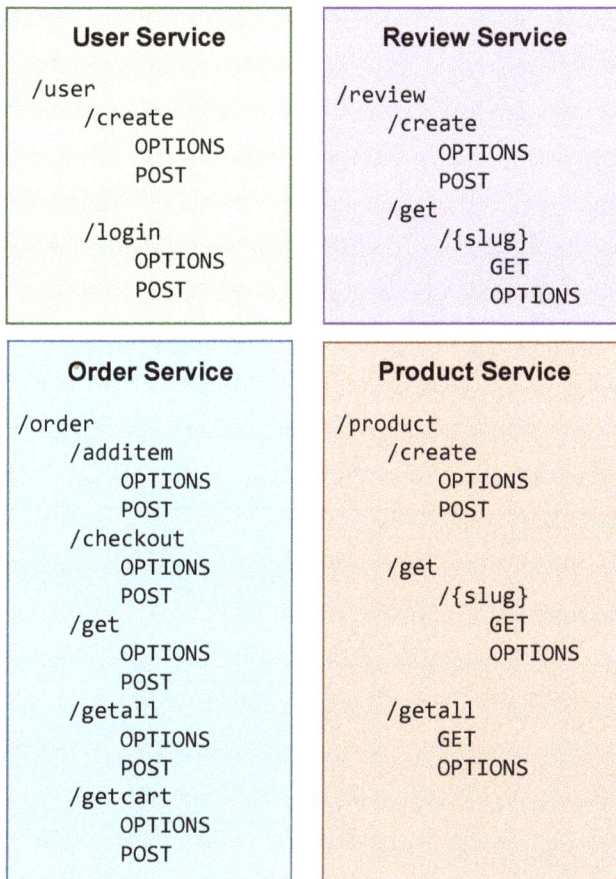

```
        User Service

/user
    /create
            OPTIONS
            POST

    /login
            OPTIONS
            POST
```

```
        Review Service

/review
    /create
            OPTIONS
            POST
    /get
            /{slug}
                GET
                OPTIONS
```

```
        Order Service

/order
    /additem
            OPTIONS
            POST
    /checkout
            OPTIONS
            POST
    /get
            OPTIONS
            POST
    /getall
            OPTIONS
            POST
    /getcart
            OPTIONS
            POST
```

```
        Product Service

/product
    /create
            OPTIONS
            POST

    /get
            /{slug}
                GET
                OPTIONS

    /getall
            GET
            OPTIONS
```

Figure 10.18: APIs for the E-Commerce application

The integration type then needs to be set up for each method. We use the lambda function as the integration type for each method and select the specific function to be invoked. Figure 10.19 shows the API Gateway resources for the E-Commerce application on the left and the API method for getting cart items on the right.

Once integrations are set up, methods need to be tested to verify that they are working as expected. The API Gateway provides a test console to send test requests and view responses.

The next step is deploying the API to make it accessible via an endpoint URL. Deployment generates a live API URL that can be shared and accessed by client applications. Multiple stages like dev, test, and prod can be used to manage different deployment environments. For security, authorization, and access controls need to be implemented. API Keys can be used for simple authorization.

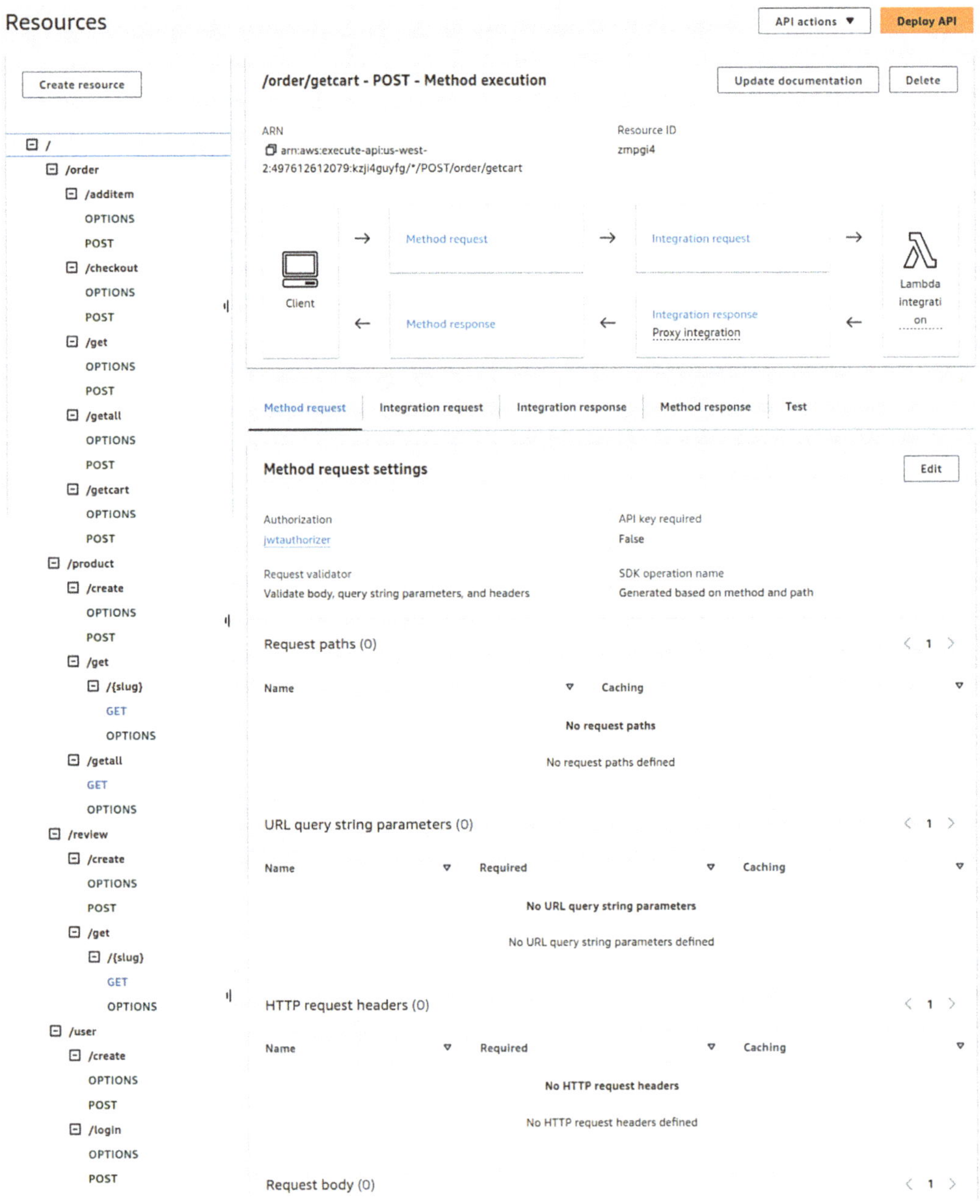

Figure 10.19: API Gateway resources for the E-Commerce application

API Gateway allows implementing custom authorizers to perform authentication and authorization for API calls. A custom authorizer is a lambda function that verifies the caller's identity and returns an IAM policy for access control. We set up a custom authorizer as shown in Figure 10.20. To set up the custom authorizer, we use the authorizer lambda function (token authorizer described previously) to validate the token and generate IAM policies. In API Gateway, we create an authorizer resource and select the lambda function. Finally, we attach the authorizer to API methods or resources to require authorization. When a request hits the API, the API Gateway checks if a valid token is present, calls the authorizer lambda to verify it, and allows or denies access based on the returned IAM policy.

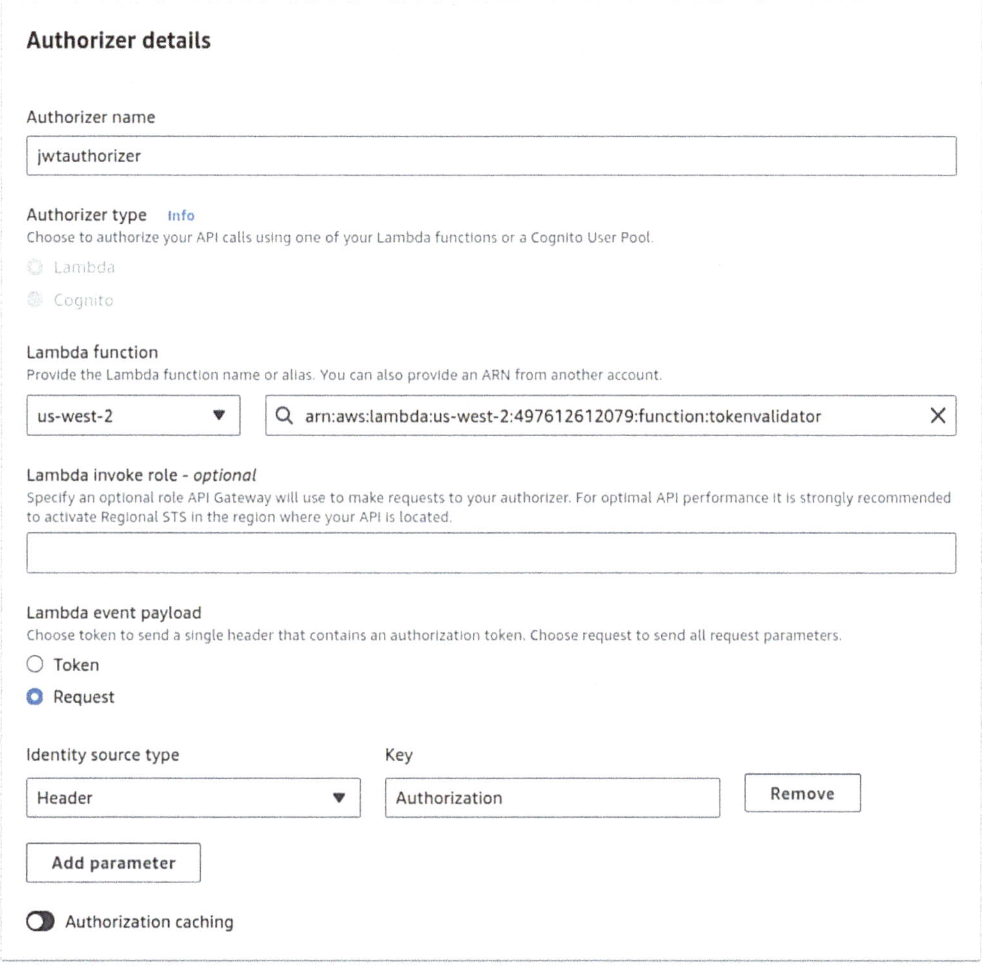

Authorizer details

Authorizer name

jwtauthorizer

Authorizer type   Info
Choose to authorize your API calls using one of your Lambda functions or a Cognito User Pool.

○ Lambda

○ Cognito

Lambda function
Provide the Lambda function name or alias. You can also provide an ARN from another account.

us-west-2 ▼   🔍 arn:aws:lambda:us-west-2:497612612079:function:tokenvalidator   ✕

Lambda invoke role - *optional*
Specify an optional role API Gateway will use to make requests to your authorizer. For optimal API performance it is strongly recommended to activate Regional STS in the region where your API is located.

Lambda event payload
Choose token to send a single header that contains an authorization token. Choose request to send all request parameters.

○ Token

● Request

Identity source type   Key

Header   ▼   Authorization   Remove

Add parameter

◖ Authorization caching

Figure 10.20: Creating a custom authorizer in API Gateway

CORS (Cross-Origin Resource Sharing) allows requests to be made from one domain to another domain in the browser. By default, browsers block CORS requests for security. To enable CORS, the server needs to include certain headers like *Access-Control-Allow-Origin* in the response. In API Gateway, CORS can be enabled as shown in Figure 10.21. In Lambda functions, CORS headers need to be manually added to the response. The *Access-Control-Allow-Origin* header specifies which domains can request the API. The *Access-Control-Allow-Methods* specifies the allowed HTTP methods. Enabling CORS in API Gateway and Lambda removes cross-origin errors and allows frontends to access the APIs from a different domain.

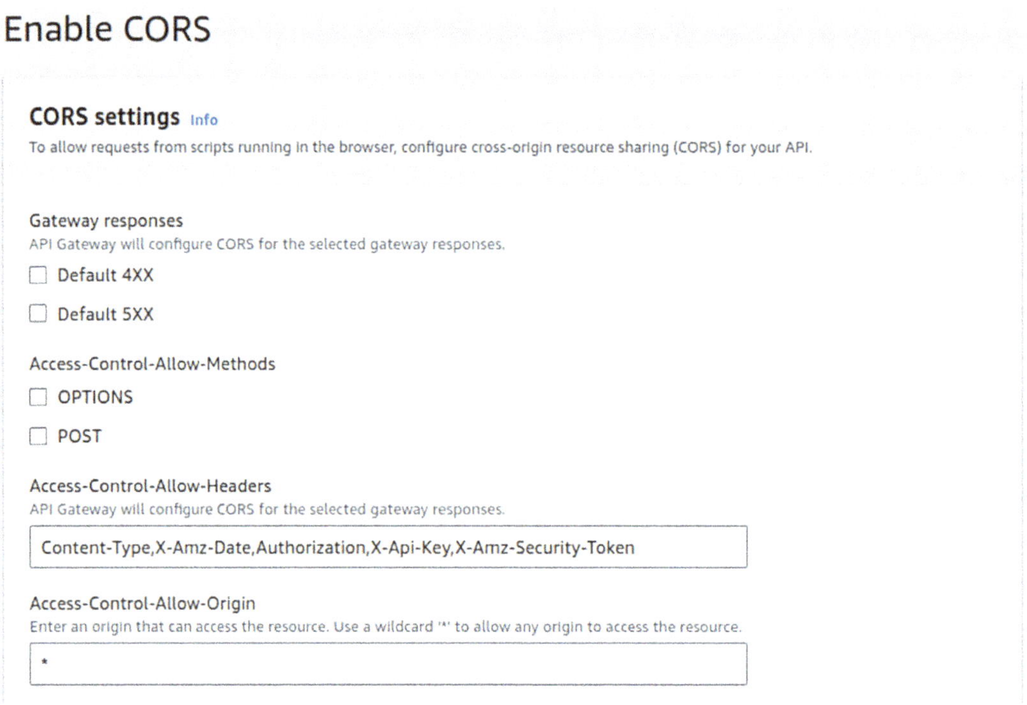

Enable CORS

CORS settings Info

To allow requests from scripts running in the browser, configure cross-origin resource sharing (CORS) for your API.

Gateway responses

API Gateway will configure CORS for the selected gateway responses.

☐ Default 4XX

☐ Default 5XX

Access-Control-Allow-Methods

☐ OPTIONS

☐ POST

Access-Control-Allow-Headers

API Gateway will configure CORS for the selected gateway responses.

```
Content-Type,X-Amz-Date,Authorization,X-Api-Key,X-Amz-Security-Token
```

Access-Control-Allow-Origin

Enter an origin that can access the resource. Use a wildcard '*' to allow any origin to access the resource.

```
*
```

Figure 10.21: Enabling CORS for a resource in API Gateway

10.2.6   Static Website Frontend

The frontend for the serverless E-Commerce application comprises static HTML pages for login, register, home, product, cart, and orders. A common JavaScript file (process.js) is used in all HTML pages to dynamically populate data in these pages.

Box 10.15 shows the HTML code of the login page. It has a form to enter username and password to log in.

■ **Box 10.15: Login page**

```
<!DOCTYPE html>
<html lang="en">
<head>
    <meta charset="UTF-8">
    <meta name="viewport" content="width=device-width,
        initial-scale=1.0">
    <title>Login</title>
    <link rel="stylesheet" href="assets/css/bootstrap.min.css">
    <link rel="stylesheet" href="assets/css/all.css">
    <link rel="stylesheet" href="assets/css/star-rating.css">
    <link rel="stylesheet" href="assets/css/theme.css">
    <link rel="stylesheet" href="static/css/style.css">
</head>
<body>
    <nav class="navbar navbar-expand-lg navbar-dark bg-dark">
```

```
            <a class="navbar-brand" href="/">Home</a>
            <button class="navbar-toggler" type="button"
                data-toggle="collapse" data-target="#navbarNav"
                aria-controls="navbarNav" aria-expanded="false"
                aria-label="Toggle navigation">
                <span class="navbar-toggler-icon"></span>
            </button>
            <div class="collapse navbar-collapse" id="navbarNav">
                <ul class="navbar-nav ml-auto" id="navbar-container">
                    <li class="nav-item"><a class="nav-link text-white mr-3"
                        href="/login.html">Login</a></li>
                    <li class="nav-item"><a class="nav-link text-white mr-3"
                        href="/register.html">Register</a></li>
                </ul>
            </div>
        </nav>
        <div class="container mt-5">
            <h2>Login</h2>
            <form id="loginform" method='post' action="/login">
                <input type="text" name="username" id="username"
                 class="form-control" placeholder="Enter username"><br>
                <input type="password" name="password" id="password"
                class="form-control" placeholder="Enter password"><br>
                <button type="submit" class="btn btn-primary">Login</button>
            </form>
        </div>
        <script src="assets/js/jquery-3.5.1.min.js"></script>
        <script src="assets/js/popper.min.js"></script>
        <script src="assets/js/bootstrap.min.js"></script>
        <script src="assets/js/star-rating.js"></script>
        <script src="assets/js/theme.js"></script>
        <script src="assets/js/process.js"></script>
</body>
</html>
```

Box 10.16 shows the HTML code of the register page. It has a form to enter username, password, first name, last name, and email to register a new user.

■ Box 10.16: Register page

```
<!DOCTYPE html>
<html lang="en">
<head>
    <meta charset="UTF-8">
    <meta name="viewport" content="width=device-width,
                        initial-scale=1.0">
    <title>Register</title>
    <link rel="stylesheet" href="assets/css/bootstrap.min.css">
    <link rel="stylesheet" href="assets/css/all.css">
    <link rel="stylesheet" href="assets/css/star-rating.css">
    <link rel="stylesheet" href="assets/css/theme.css">
    <link rel="stylesheet" href="static/css/style.css">
</head>
```

```
<body>
    <nav class="navbar navbar-expand-lg navbar-dark bg-dark">
        <a class="navbar-brand" href="/">Home</a>
        <button class="navbar-toggler" type="button"
            data-toggle="collapse" data-target="#navbarNav"
            aria-controls="navbarNav" aria-expanded="false"
            aria-label="Toggle navigation">
            <span class="navbar-toggler-icon"></span>
        </button>
        <div class="collapse navbar-collapse" id="navbarNav">
            <ul class="navbar-nav ml-auto" id="navbar-container">
                <li class="nav-item"><a class="nav-link text-white mr-3"
                    href="/login.html">Login</a></li>
                <li class="nav-item"><a class="nav-link text-white mr-3"
                    href="/register.html">Register</a></li>
            </ul>
        </div>
    </nav>
    <div class="container mt-5">
        <h2>Register</h2>
        <h4 id="message"></h4>
        <form id="signupform" method='post' action="#">
        <input type="text" name="username" id="username"
            class="form-control" placeholder="Enter username"><br>
        <input type="password" name="password" id="password"
            class="form-control" placeholder="Enter password"><br>
        <input type="text" name="given_name" id="given_name"
            class="form-control" placeholder="Enter first name"><br>
        <input type="text" name="family_name" id="family_name"
            class="form-control" placeholder="Enter last name"><br>
        <input type="text" name="email" id="email" class="form-control"
                placeholder="Enter email"><br>
        <button type="submit" class="btn btn-primary">Register</button>
        </form>
    </div>
    <script src="assets/js/jquery-3.5.1.min.js"></script>
    <script src="assets/js/popper.min.js"></script>
    <script src="assets/js/bootstrap.min.js"></script>
    <script src="assets/js/star-rating.js"></script>
    <script src="assets/js/theme.js"></script>
    <script src="assets/js/process.js"></script>
</body>
</html>
```

Box 10.17 shows the HTML code of the home page, which displays the products in a grid format. The products are dynamically populated via JavaScript.

■ Box 10.17: Home page

```
<!DOCTYPE html>
<html lang="en">
<head>
    <meta charset="UTF-8">
```

```
    <meta name="viewport" content="width=device-width,
                                    initial-scale=1.0">
    <title>Home</title>
    <link rel="stylesheet" href="assets/css/bootstrap.min.css">
    <link rel="stylesheet" href="assets/css/all.css">
    <link rel="stylesheet" href="assets/css/star-rating.css">
    <link rel="stylesheet" href="assets/css/theme.css">
    <link rel="stylesheet" href="static/css/style.css">
</head>
<body>
    <nav class="navbar navbar-expand-lg navbar-dark bg-dark">
        <a class="navbar-brand" href="index.html">Home</a>
        <button class="navbar-toggler" type="button"
            data-toggle="collapse" data-target="#navbarNav"
            aria-controls="navbarNav" aria-expanded="false"
            aria-label="Toggle navigation">
            <span class="navbar-toggler-icon"></span>
        </button>
        <div class="collapse navbar-collapse" id="navbarNav">
            <ul class="navbar-nav ml-auto" id="navbar-container"></ul>
        </div>
    </nav>
  <div class="container mt-5">
    <div class="row" id="products-container"></div>
  </div>
    <script src="assets/js/jquery-3.5.1.min.js"></script>
    <script src="assets/js/popper.min.js"></script>
    <script src="assets/js/bootstrap.min.js"></script>
    <script src="assets/js/star-rating.js"></script>
    <script src="assets/js/theme.js"></script>
    <script src="assets/js/process.js"></script>
</body>
</html>
```

Box 10.18 shows the HTML code of the product page. This page displays the details of a single product. It has sections to show product info, reviews, and a form to add a new review. The product and review data are dynamically populated via JavaScript.

■ Box 10.18: Product page

```
<!DOCTYPE html>
<html lang="en">
<head>
    <meta charset="UTF-8">
    <meta name="viewport" content="width=device-width,
                       initial-scale=1.0">
    <title>Product</title>
    <link rel="stylesheet" href="assets/css/bootstrap.min.css">
    <link rel="stylesheet" href="assets/css/all.css">
    <link rel="stylesheet" href="assets/css/star-rating.css">
    <link rel="stylesheet" href="assets/css/theme.css">
    <link rel="stylesheet" href="static/css/style.css">
</head>
```

```
<body>
    <nav class="navbar navbar-expand-lg navbar-dark bg-dark">
        <a class="navbar-brand" href="index.html">Home</a>
        <button class="navbar-toggler" type="button"
            data-toggle="collapse" data-target="#navbarNav"
            aria-controls="navbarNav" aria-expanded="false"
            aria-label="Toggle navigation">
            <span class="navbar-toggler-icon"></span>
        </button>
        <div class="collapse navbar-collapse" id="navbarNav">
            <ul class="navbar-nav ml-auto" id="navbar-container"></ul>
        </div>
    </nav>
  <div class="container mt-5" id="product-container"></div>
  <div class="container mt-5" id="review-container"></div>
  <div class="container mt-5" id="postreview-container">
  <form action="#" method="post" id="reviewform">
    <input type="hidden" name="productslug"
        id="reviewformproductslug" value="">
    <div class="form-group">
      <h4>Add Review</h4>
      <input required class="rating" id="ratinginput"
        name="ratinginput" type="number" value="0" title=""
        data-theme="krajee-fas" data-min=0 data-max=5 data-step=1
        data-size="sm" data-show-caption="false" data-show-clear="false"
        data-display-only="false">
      <textarea class="form-control" rows="5"
        id="reviewinput" name="reviewinput"></textarea>
    </div>
    <button type="submit" class="btn btn-primary">Post Review</button>
  </form>
  <br><br>
  </div>
    <script src="assets/js/jquery-3.5.1.min.js"></script>
    <script src="assets/js/popper.min.js"></script>
    <script src="assets/js/bootstrap.min.js"></script>
    <script src="assets/js/star-rating.js"></script>
    <script src="assets/js/theme.js"></script>
    <script src="assets/js/process.js"></script>
</body>
</html>
```

Box 10.19 shows the HTML code of the cart page. The cart page shows the items added to the cart by the user. It has a cart container to display the cart items. The cart data is dynamically populated via JavaScript.

■ Box 10.19: Cart page

```
<!DOCTYPE html>
<html lang="en">
<head>
    <meta charset="UTF-8">
    <meta name="viewport" content="width=device-width,
```

```
                                initial-scale=1.0">
    <title>Cart</title>
    <link rel="stylesheet" href="assets/css/bootstrap.min.css">
    <link rel="stylesheet" href="assets/css/all.css">
    <link rel="stylesheet" href="assets/css/star-rating.css">
    <link rel="stylesheet" href="assets/css/theme.css">
    <link rel="stylesheet" href="static/css/style.css">
</head>
<body>
    <nav class="navbar navbar-expand-lg navbar-dark bg-dark">
        <a class="navbar-brand" href="index.html">Home</a>
        <button class="navbar-toggler" type="button"
            data-toggle="collapse" data-target="#navbarNav"
            aria-controls="navbarNav" aria-expanded="false"
            aria-label="Toggle navigation">
            <span class="navbar-toggler-icon"></span>
        </button>
        <div class="collapse navbar-collapse" id="navbarNav">
            <ul class="navbar-nav ml-auto" id="navbar-container"></ul>
        </div>
    </nav>
  <div class="container mt-5" id="cart-container"></div>
    <script src="assets/js/jquery-3.5.1.min.js"></script>
    <script src="assets/js/popper.min.js"></script>
    <script src="assets/js/bootstrap.min.js"></script>
    <script src="assets/js/star-rating.js"></script>
    <script src="assets/js/theme.js"></script>
    <script src="assets/js/process.js"></script>
</body>
</html>
```

Box 10.20 shows the HTML code of the orders page. This page lists the orders placed by the logged-in user. It has an orders container to display the order info. The orders data is dynamically populated via JavaScript.

■ Box 10.20: Orders page

```
<!DOCTYPE html>
<html lang="en">
<head>
    <meta charset="UTF-8">
    <meta name="viewport" content="width=device-width,
                            initial-scale=1.0">
    <title>Orders</title>
    <link rel="stylesheet" href="assets/css/bootstrap.min.css">
    <link rel="stylesheet" href="assets/css/all.css">
    <link rel="stylesheet" href="assets/css/star-rating.css">
    <link rel="stylesheet" href="assets/css/theme.css">
    <link rel="stylesheet" href="static/css/style.css">
</head>
<body>
    <nav class="navbar navbar-expand-lg navbar-dark bg-dark">
        <a class="navbar-brand" href="index.html">Home</a>
```

```
            <button class="navbar-toggler" type="button"
                data-toggle="collapse" data-target="#navbarNav"
                aria-controls="navbarNav" aria-expanded="false"
                aria-label="Toggle navigation">
                <span class="navbar-toggler-icon"></span>
            </button>
            <div class="collapse navbar-collapse" id="navbarNav">
                <ul class="navbar-nav ml-auto" id="navbar-container"></ul>
            </div>
        </nav>
    <div class="container mt-5" id="orders-container"></div>
        <script src="assets/js/jquery-3.5.1.min.js"></script>
        <script src="assets/js/popper.min.js"></script>
        <script src="assets/js/bootstrap.min.js"></script>
        <script src="assets/js/star-rating.js"></script>
        <script src="assets/js/theme.js"></script>
        <script src="assets/js/process.js"></script>
</body>
</html>
```

Boxes 10.21, 10.22, 10.23 show the JavaScript code of the process.js file, which is a common JavaScript file used in all the HTML pages to dynamically populate data on these pages. This acts as the front-end logic to display pages, while calling backend services via APIs. It handles user sessions, navigation, communication with APIs, and dynamic rendering using AJAX. It handles routing based on the URL pathname, calling the right page loading logic. Events like form submission or button click are handled by calling the corresponding logic.

When the login form is submitted, it calls the *login* API with the username and password. If successful, it stores the auth token, username, name, and user photo URL in sessionStorage. Then it redirects to the home page. Similarly, for user registration, it calls the *create user* API and handles the response. To check if the user is logged in, it checks sessionStorage for the auth token. If present, the navbar with cart and logout links is loaded, otherwise, links to login/register are shown. The cart count badge is updated by calling the *get cart* API.

The home page loads all products by calling the *get all products* API. The cart page calls the *get cart* API and displays the items, quantity, and total amount. Checkout calls the *checkout* API to complete the order. The orders page calls the *get all orders* API to display past orders. It formats the date and calculates totals for each order. The product page loads details by calling the *get product* API with the slug. It also loads reviews by calling the *get reviews* API. To post a review, it calls the *create review* API with data like rating, text, and product slug. Adding to cart calls the *add item to cart* API.

Box 10.21 shows part 1 of the process.js file with implementations of the following functions:
- clearSession() - Clears sessionStorage to log the user out
- urlParam() - Retrieves the value of a query parameter from a URL
- formattedDate() - Formats a date object to a string
- checkIfLoggedIn() - Checks if token and username are present in sessionStorage
- loadNavbar() - Loads the navbar HTML dynamically using session data
- updateCartCount() - Calls API to get cart data and updates cart count

■ Box 10.21: Common JavaScript for all web pages (process.js) - part 1

```javascript
$(document).ready(function () {
    var pathname = window.location.pathname;
    if (pathname == '/index.html') {
        loadHomePage();
    } else if (pathname == '/cart.html') {
        loadCartPage();
    } else if (pathname == "/orders.html") {
        loadOrdersPage();
    } else if (pathname == "/product.html") {
        loadProductPage();
    } else if (pathname == "/thanks.html") {
        loadThanksPage();
    }

    $("#loginform").submit(function (event) {
        processLogin();
        event.preventDefault();
    });

    $("#signupform").submit(function (event) {
        processSignup();
        event.preventDefault();
    });

    $("#reviewform").submit(function (event) {
        processPostReview();
        event.preventDefault();
    });

    $('body').on('click', '#addtocartbtn', function (event) {
        processAddToCart();
        event.preventDefault();
    });

    $('body').on('click', '#checkoutlink', function (event) {
        processCheckout();
        event.preventDefault();
    });

    $("#logoutlink").click(function (event) {
        clearSession();
        event.preventDefault();
    });
});

function clearSession() {
    sessionStorage.clear();
    location.href = 'login.html';
};

$.urlParam = function (name) {
    var results = new RegExp('[\?&]' + \
```

```
                name +\ '=([^&#]*)').exec(window.location.href);
    return results[1] || 0;
}

function formattedDate(datetime) {
    var date = new Date(datetime);
    var formatted = date.toLocaleDateString('en-US', {
        month: 'short',
        day: 'numeric',
        year: 'numeric'
    });
    return formatted;
}

function checkIfLoggedIn() {
    var token = sessionStorage.getItem('token');
    var username = sessionStorage.getItem('username');
    if (token == null || username == null) {
        return false;
    } else {
        return true;
    }
}

function loadNavbar() {
    $("#navbar-container").html('<li class="nav-item">\
    <a class="nav-link text-white mr-3" href="cart.html">Cart\
     <span class="badge" id="cartcount"></span></a></li>\
     <li class="nav-item"><a class="nav-link text-white mr-3"\
      href="orders.html">Orders</a></li><li class="nav-item">\
      <a class="nav-link text-white mr-3" href="#" id="logoutlink">\
      Logout</a></li><span style="margin-top:8px;\
      margin-left: 20px;color:#fff">' +\
        sessionStorage.getItem('name') +\
        '</span><img src="' + sessionStorage.getItem('userphoto') +\
        '" class="mr-3 rounded-circle" style="width:30px;height:30px;\
        margin-top:5px;margin-left: 20px;">');
}
```

Box 10.22 shows part 2 of the process.js file with implementations of the following functions:

- loadHomePage() - Retrieves a list of products by calling the API and displays them
- loadCartPage() - Checks if the user is logged in, gets cart data by calling the API, and displays cart items
- loadOrdersPage() - Checks if the user is logged in, gets order history by calling the API, and displays the orders
- loadProductPage() - Retrieves product data and reviews by slug from the API and displays product details and reviews
- loadThanksPage() - Loads the thank-you page which is displayed after an order is completed

■ Box 10.22: Common JavaScript for all web pages (process.js) - part 2

```javascript
function loadHomePage() {
    loggedin = checkIfLoggedIn();
    if (loggedin) {
        loadNavbar();
        updateCartCount();
    } else {
        $("#navbar-container").html('<li class="nav-item">\
            <a class="nav-link text-white mr-3" href="/login.html">\
            Login</a></li><li class="nav-item"><a class="nav-link \
            text-white mr-3" href="/register.html">Register</a></li>');
    }
    var htmlstr = "";
    $.ajax({
        url: 'https://azji3ghygf.execute-api.us-west-2.amazonaws.com\
            /dev/product/getall',
        type: 'GET',
        crossDomain: true,
        contentType: "application/json",
        success: function (data) {
            $.each(data.results, function (index, value) {
                htmlstr = htmlstr + '<div class="col-md-4">\
                <div class="card mb-4"><a href="product.html?slug=' +\
                 value.slug + '"><img src="' + value.image +\
                 '" class="card-img-top"></a><div class="card-body">\
                 <a href="product.html?slug=' + value.slug +\
                  '"><h5 class="card-title">' + value.name +\
                  '</h5></a><p class="card-text">Price: $' +\
                   value.price +'</p></div></div></div>';
            });
            $('#products-container').html(htmlstr);
        },
        error: function () {
            console.log("Failed");
        }
    });
}

function loadCartPage() {
    loggedin = checkIfLoggedIn();
    if (loggedin) {
        loadNavbar();
        updateCartCount();
    } else {
        location.href = "login.html"
    }
    var htmlstr = "";
    var datadir = {
        username: sessionStorage.getItem('username')
    };
    var htmlstr = '<div class="container mt-5"><h2>Shopping Cart</h2>\
                <table class="table"><thead><tr><th>Product</th>\
```

```
                    <th>Price</th><th>Quantity</th><th>Amount</th></tr>\
                    </thead><tbody>';
    $.ajax({
        url: 'https://azji3ghygf.execute-api.us-west-2.amazonaws.com/\
                  dev/order/getcart',
        type: 'POST',
        crossDomain: true,
        dataType: 'json',
        contentType: "application/json",
        headers: {
            'authorization': sessionStorage.getItem('token')
        },
        success: function (data) {
            if (data.totalamount > 0) {
            var resultsjson = JSON.parse(data.result);
            $.each(resultsjson, function (index, value) {
            htmlstr = htmlstr + '<tr><td><img src="' + value.image +\
             '" style="max-width: 80px;">' + value.name + '</td><td>' +\
               value.price + '</td><td>' + value.quantity +\
                 '</td><td>' + value.price + '</td></tr>';
            });
            htmlstr = htmlstr + '</tbody></table><strong>\
            Total Amount: $' +data.totalamount + \
            '</strong><br><br><button class="btn btn-primary" \
            id="checkoutlink">Checkout</button></div>';
            } else {
                htmlstr = htmlstr + '<tr><td colspan="4">\
                Your cart is empty</td></tr></tbody></table>';
            }
            $('#cart-container').html(htmlstr);
        },
        error: function () {
            console.log("Failed");
        },
        data: JSON.stringify(datadir)
    });
}

function loadOrdersPage() {
    loggedin = checkIfLoggedIn();
    if (loggedin) {
        loadNavbar();
        updateCartCount();
    } else {
        location.href = "login.html"
    }
    var htmlstr = "";
    var datadir = {
        username: sessionStorage.getItem('username')
    };
    var htmlstr = '<div class="container mt-5"><h2>Orders</h2>\
                   <table class="table"><thead><tr><th>Order ID</th>\
                   <th>Date</th><th>Items</th><th>Total Amount</th>\
                   </tr></thead><tbody>';
```

```
    $.ajax({
        url: 'https://azji3ghygf.execute-api.us-west-2.amazonaws.com/\
                    dev/order/getall',
        type: 'POST',
        crossDomain: true,
        dataType: 'json',
        contentType: "application/json",
        headers: {
            'authorization': sessionStorage.getItem('token')
        },
        success: function (data) {
            if (data.message == "Order found") {
                var totalamount = 0
                $.each(data.result, function (index, value) {
                htmlstr = htmlstr + '<tr><td>' + value.order_id +\
                 '</td><td>' + formattedDate(value.date_added) +\
                  '</td><td>';
                $.each(JSON.parse(value.items),
                    function (index1, value1) {
                    htmlstr = htmlstr + '<img src="' + value1.image +\
                     '" style="max-width: 50px;">';
                    totalamount = totalamount + value1.price;
                });
                htmlstr = htmlstr + '</td><td>$' + totalamount +\
                 '</td></tr>';
                });
            } else {
                htmlstr = htmlstr + '<tr><td colspan="4">\
                        No orders found</td></tr></tbody></table>';
            }
            $('#orders-container').html(htmlstr);
        },
        error: function () {
            console.log("Failed");
        },
        data: JSON.stringify(datadir)
    });
}

function loadProductPage() {
    loggedin = checkIfLoggedIn();
    if (loggedin) {
        loadNavbar();
        updateCartCount();
    } else {
        location.href = "login.html"
    }
    var htmlstr = "";
    const queryString = window.location.search;
    const urlParams = new URLSearchParams(queryString);
    const slug = urlParams.get('slug')
    $("#reviewformproductslug").val(slug);
    var htmlstr = '';
    $.ajax({
```

```
    url: 'https://azji3ghygf.execute-api.us-west-2.amazonaws.com/\
                    dev/product/get/' + slug,
    type: 'GET',
    crossDomain: true,
    dataType: 'json',
    contentType: "application/json",
    headers: {
        'authorization': sessionStorage.getItem('token')
    },
    success: function (data) {
    htmlstr = htmlstr + '<div class="row"><div class="col-md-6">\
    <img src="' + data.result.image + '" width="100%">\
        </div><div class="col-md-6"><h2>' + data.result.name +\
        '</h2><p>' + data.result.description + '</p>\
        <h4>Price: $' + data.result.price + '</h4><br>\
        <input type="hidden" name="cartproductslug" \
        id="cartproductslug" value="' + data.result.slug +\
         '"><input type="hidden" name="cartproductqty" \
         id="cartproductqty" value="1"><input type="hidden"\
          name="cartproductprice" id="cartproductprice" \
          value="' + data.result.price + '"><input type="hidden" \
          name="cartproductname" id="cartproductname" \
          value="' + data.result.name + '"><input type="hidden"\
           name="cartproductimage" id="cartproductimage" \
           value="' + data.result.image + '">\
           <button type="submit" class="btn btn-primary"\
            id="addtocartbtn">Add To Cart</button></div></div>';
        $('#product-container').html(htmlstr);
    },
    error: function () {
        console.log("Failed");
    }
});

var htmlstr1 = '';
$.ajax({
    url: 'https://azji3ghygf.execute-api.us-west-2.amazonaws.com/\
                       dev/review/get/' + slug,
    type: 'GET',
    crossDomain: true,
    dataType: 'json',
    contentType: "application/json",
    headers: {
        'authorization': sessionStorage.getItem('token')
    },
    success: function (data) {
        htmlstr1 = htmlstr1 + '<h3>Reviews</h3>';
        $.each(data.results, function (index, value) {
        htmlstr1 = htmlstr1 + '<div class="media mb-3">\
        <img src="' + value.userphoto + '" class="mr-3"\
        width="50"><div class="media-body"><h5 class="mt-0">'\
        + value.fullname + ' - <small><i> ' + \
        formattedDate(value.date_added) +'</i></small></h5>\
        <input required class="rating" type="number" value="'\
```

```
               + value.rating + '" title=""  > ' + \
                value.description + '</div>    </div>';
               });
               $('#review-container').html(htmlstr1);
               $(".rating").rating({min:0, max:5, step:0.5, size:'xs',
                   theme: 'krajee-fas', displayOnly: true,
                   'showClear': false, 'showCaption': false});
           },
           error: function () {
               console.log("Failed");
           }
       });
}

function loadThanksPage() {
    loggedin = checkIfLoggedIn();
    if (loggedin) {
        loadNavbar();
        updateCartCount();
    } else {
        location.href = "login.html"
    }
}
```

Box 10.23 shows part 3 of the process.js file with implementations of the following functions:

- processLogin() - Calls the *login* API and saves user data in sessionStorage upon successful login
- processSignup() - Calls the *create user* API to register a new user
- processPostReview() - Calls the *create review* API to post a review
- processAddToCart() - Calls the *add item to cart* API
- processCheckout() - Calls the *checkout* API to complete the order
- updateCartCount() - Helper to update cart count in navbar

■ **Box 10.23: Common JavaScript for all web pages (process.js) - part 3**

```
function processLogin() {
    var username = $("#username").val();
    var password = $("#password").val();
    var datadir = {
        username: username,
        password: password
    };
    $.ajax({
        url: 'https://azji3ghygf.execute-api.us-west-2.amazonaws.com/\
                        dev/user/login',
        type: 'POST',
        crossDomain: true,
        dataType: 'json',
        contentType: "application/json",
        success: function (data) {
        if (data.result) {
```

```
            sessionStorage.setItem('username', data.userdata.username);
            sessionStorage.setItem('name', data.userdata.given_name +\
                         ' ' + data.userdata.family_name);
            sessionStorage.setItem('token', data.userdata.token);
            sessionStorage.setItem('userphoto', data.userdata.picture);
            location.href = 'index.html';
        } else {
            $("#message").html(data.message);
        }
        },
        error: function () {
            console.log("Failed");
        },
        data: JSON.stringify(datadir)
    });
}

function processSignup() {
    var username = $("#username").val();
    var password = $("#password").val();
    var given_name = $("#given_name").val();
    var family_name = $("#family_name").val();
    var email = $("#email").val();
    var datadir = {
        username: username,
        password: password,
        given_name: given_name,
        family_name: family_name,
        email: email
    };
    $.ajax({
        url: 'https://azji3ghygf.execute-api.us-west-2.amazonaws.com/\
                         dev/user/create',
        type: 'POST',
        crossDomain: true,
        dataType: 'json',
        contentType: "application/json",
        success: function (data) {
            $("#message").html("Thanks for signing up. Please login.");
            $("#signupform").hide();
        },
        error: function () {
            console.log("Failed");
        },
        data: JSON.stringify(datadir)
    });
}

function processPostReview() {
    var datadir = {
        username: sessionStorage.getItem('username'),
        userphoto: sessionStorage.getItem('userphoto'),
        fullname: sessionStorage.getItem('name'),
        product_slug: $("#reviewformproductslug").val(),
```

```
                    rating: $("#ratinginput").val(),
                    description: $("#reviewinput").val()
            };
        $.ajax({
                url: 'https://azji3ghygf.execute-api.us-west-2.amazonaws.com/\
                                    dev/review/create',
                type: 'POST',
                crossDomain: true,
                dataType: 'json',
                contentType: "application/json",
                headers: {
                    'authorization': sessionStorage.getItem('token')
                },
                success: function (data) {
                    location.reload();
                },
                error: function () {
                    console.log("Failed");
                },
                data: JSON.stringify(datadir)
        });
}

function processAddToCart() {
    var datadir = {
            username: sessionStorage.getItem('username'),
            fullname: sessionStorage.getItem('name'),
            product_slug: $("#cartproductslug").val(),
            name: $("#cartproductname").val(),
            qty: $("#cartproductqty").val(),
            price: $("#cartproductprice").val(),
            image: $("#cartproductimage").val()
    };
    $.ajax({
            url: 'https://azji3ghygf.execute-api.us-west-2.amazonaws.com/\
                                dev/order/additem',
            type: 'POST',
            crossDomain: true,
            dataType: 'json',
            contentType: "application/json",
            headers: {
                'authorization': sessionStorage.getItem('token')
            },
            success: function (data) {
                updateCartCount();
            },
            error: function () {
                console.log("Failed");
            },
            data: JSON.stringify(datadir)
    });
}

function processCheckout() {
```

```
    loggedin = checkIfLoggedIn();
    if (loggedin) {

    } else {
        location.href = "login.html"
    }
    var datadir = {
        username: sessionStorage.getItem('username')
    };

    $.ajax({
        url: 'https://azji3ghygf.execute-api.us-west-2.amazonaws.com/\
                              dev/order/checkout',
        type: 'POST',
        crossDomain: true,
        dataType: 'json',
        contentType: "application/json",
        headers: {
            'authorization': sessionStorage.getItem('token')
        },
        success: function (data) {
            location.href = "thanks.html"
        },
        error: function () {
            console.log("Failed");
        },
        data: JSON.stringify(datadir)
    });
}

function updateCartCount() {
    var datadir = {
        username: sessionStorage.getItem('username')
    };
    $.ajax({
        url: 'https://azji3ghygf.execute-api.us-west-2.amazonaws.com/\
                            dev/order/getcart',
        type: 'POST',
        crossDomain: true,
        dataType: 'json',
        contentType: "application/json",
        headers: {
            'authorization': sessionStorage.getItem('token')
        },
        success: function (data) {
            var cartcount = 0;
            if (data.totalamount > 0) {
                var resultsjson = JSON.parse(data.result);
                $.each(resultsjson, function (index, value) {
                    cartcount = cartcount + 1;
                });
            }
            $('#cartcount').html(cartcount);
        },
```

```
            error: function () {
                console.log("Failed");
            },
            data: JSON.stringify(datadir)
    });
}
```

Summary

In this chapter, we covered the implementation of serverless microservices applications. We started by describing the benefits of the serverless approach over traditional server-based architectures for building cloud-native applications. We presented a comparison of serverless versus server-based systems across various dimensions like infrastructure management, scaling, availability, performance, costs, deployment speed, language support, monitoring, flexibility, complexity, latency, and dependency management. Serverless simplifies the architecture and DevOps workflow by eliminating infrastructure management. It provides automatic scaling, built-in high availability, and faster deployments. The granular billing model of serverless aligns costs closely with usage. The independent scaling of services, event-driven nature, and lack of idle capacity provide cost savings. However, serverless functions have additional latency for cold starts and limitations on packages that can be included. Next, we described the architecture of a serverless E-Commerce application comprising API Gateway, Lambda functions implementing the backend services, DynamoDB for data storage, S3 for storing images, CloudFront CDN, Cognito for user management and authentication, and frontend with static web pages. We then presented a step-by-step implementation, first setting up the backend, creating a Cognito user pool, creating tables in DynamoDB, IAM roles, and lambda functions for each service. The lambda functions were assigned the IAM role and given permissions to access other AWS resources like S3, DynamoDB, and Cognito. We also showed how to create and deploy a layer to package dependencies used by Lambda. The API Gateway configuration was discussed next. We described how to create resources, methods, and integration with Lambda. We described implementing authorization using API keys and JWT tokens validated through a custom authorizer Lambda. Enabling CORS was also covered. For the front-end, we showed HTML, CSS, and JavaScript code for the static web pages like login, register, home, product, cart, and orders. Common logic was placed in a process.js file that made AJAX calls to APIs and handled routing, authentication, and session management. In this chapter, we presented a pattern for developing microservices applications using a serverless architecture on AWS. We provided details on leveraging API Gateway, Lambda, DynamoDB, S3, CloudFront, Cognito, and IAM to build a complete end-to-end system. The chapter serves as a practical guide and reference for implementing cloud-native, serverless microservices on AWS.

CHAPTER

11

MICROSERVICES OBSERVABILITY AND MONITORING

THIS CHAPTER COVERS

- Observability and Monitoring
- Logging
- Metrics
- Distributed Tracing with OpenTelemetry
- OpenTelemetry and Jaeger
- Prometheus and Grafana
- AWS X-Ray and CloudWatch
- Best Practices for Observability and Monitoring

11.1 Introduction

Microservices have become a popular architectural approach for building scalable, resilient, and maintainable applications. However, the distributed nature of microservices also introduces complexity. Each service is developed, deployed, and scaled independently, leading to a system with many moving parts. When something goes wrong, the complexity makes it difficult to pinpoint the root cause. This is where observability and monitoring become critical.

	Observability	Monitoring
Goal	Understand internal system behavior to gain insights	Track key metrics to assess system health
Pillars	Logs, metrics, traces	Metrics
Scope	Whole system	Specific metrics
Data	Rich, contextual data	Targeted metrics
Analysis	Ad hoc, interactive	Predefined alerts and dashboards
Use Cases	Troubleshooting, debugging	Alerting, SRE
Key Metrics	Any relevant metrics	Golden signals - latency, traffic, errors, saturation
Implementation	Instrumentation, platforms	Monitoring tools, loggers

Figure 11.1: Observability versus Monitoring

Observability provides deep visibility into the runtime behavior and internals of the system. Monitoring tracks key metrics to detect anomalies and triggers alerts to draw attention to issues. Together, they enable developers to understand what is happening and respond quickly. Figure 11.1 shows a comparison of observability and monitoring.

In monolithic applications, developers have full access to and control over the codebase. Issues can be identified by debugging locally. In contrast, microservices are owned by independent teams. The services run as black boxes to each other. Developers cannot simply debug through the entire system.

As a result, microservices must provide observability into their runtime behavior and expose monitoring data. The core pillars of observability are:

- **Logs**: Logs record discrete events that happened, such as errors, debug messages, and state changes. They provide rich contextual details useful for debugging specific issues.
- **Metrics**: Metrics are numerical measurements that represent the health and performance of a system. Metrics are aggregated over time to reveal trends.
- **Traces**: Traces record the end-to-end journey of a request through the system. This shows how services interact and helps pinpoint latency issues.

Figure 11.2 shows an overview of the three pillars of observability.

Observability and monitoring provide the deep insights required to operate resilient microservices in production. In this chapter, we will cover observability and monitoring techniques for microservices applications. With the help of an E-Commerce microservices application, we will demonstrate how to instrument each service for logs, metrics, and traces, and aggregate the data to gain system-wide visibility. As we instrument the E-Commerce application, we will explore various techniques and tools for logging, metrics, and tracing.

Pillar	Logs	Metrics	Traces
Definition	Text records of discrete events	Numeric measurements aggregated over time	Distributed request flow data
Key attributes	Timestamp, text, log levels	Name, labels, numeric values	Trace ID, spans, relationships
Generation	Log statements in code	Counters, gauges, histograms in code	Automatic instrumentation
Data types	Unstructured text	Time series data	Graph data model
Key capabilities	Searchable records, filtering	Aggregation, trends, baselines, alerts	End-to-end visualization, latency analysis
Analysis approach	Ad hoc, interactive	Reports, dashboards, alerts	Trace inspection and drilling down
Common uses	Debugging, auditing, tracking	Anomaly detection, SLO tracking, capacity planning	Troubleshooting bottlenecks and errors
Challenges	Data overload, parsing text	Metric explosion, dashboard overload, alert fatigue	Complex asynchronous flows, cross-service tracing
Tools	ELK, Splunk, Datadog	Prometheus, Grafana	Jaeger, Zipkin

Figure 11.2: Three pillars of observability

11.2 Logging

Logs provide detailed records of events that occur within an application. They are indispensable for understanding runtime behavior and troubleshooting issues. A log message typically contains fields such as:

- Timestamp: When the event occurred
- Log Level: Severity like INFO, WARN, ERROR
- Message: Description of the event
- Context: Relevant variables and traces

Some common use cases for logs include:

- Errors and exception debugging
- Auditing security events and user actions
- Tracking workflow and business process execution
- Analyzing usage patterns

In monolithic applications, the standard practice is to write logs to a single file or database table. However, this approach does not scale for microservices. Each service instance generates its own separate log stream. With multiple services and instances, logs become dispersed across the environment. To aggregate logs in a microservices architecture, a centralized logging pipeline is required. There are two primary approaches:

- **Push Model**: In the push model, each service instance is responsible for actively sending its logs to a centralized logging backend. This requires configuring the logging library to push logs to the backend. The benefit of push model is that services own and control the log transmission. However, there is increased complexity to configure push transport and a risk of overflow if the backend cannot keep up.
- **Pull Model**: In the pull model, a dedicated agent on each host collects logs from all service instances and ships them to the centralized backend. The agent pulls logs from where the services write them (usually stdout/stderr or log files). Popular log collection agents include Fluentd, Logstash, Filebeat, and Vector. Agents are configured with sources to pull from and sinks to push to. The benefit of the pull model is that the services don't need additional configuration. Pulling spreads the load of transmission. However, an agent is required on each host, and the log files may be lost if the agent is down.

Traditionally, application logs have been free-form plain text intended for humans. However, machine readability unlocks more value from logs. Structured logging outputs logs in a structured format like JSON. This allows logs to be parsed, indexed, and queried more easily. Popular structured logging libraries like Serilog and Zap provide out-of-the-box support for outputting logs in JSON.

With the logging architecture decided, we need to instrument each microservice to generate meaningful logs. At a minimum, every service should log the following:

- **Start-up**: Logs when the service starts successfully.
- **Shut-down**: Logs when the service is terminating.
- **Incoming requests**: Logs all incoming requests with key metadata like method and parameters.
- **Outgoing requests**: Any requests made to downstream services.
- **Errors**: Detailed logs for any errors encountered.

Once logs are aggregated in the backend store, they can be analyzed in various ways as follows:

- **Searching**: Log data can be searched for specific terms, timestamps, log levels, etc. This allows finding relevant logs for debugging issues.
- **Statistical Analysis**: Logs contain numerical counts, durations, sizes, and other details that can be statistically analyzed for trends.
- **Alerting**: Alert rules can trigger notifications for specific log events like error spikes. This enables proactive identification of problems.
- **Visualization**: Logs with numeric fields can be visualized in charts to spot trends.
- **Machine Learning**: Logs are great training data for machine learning models. The models can learn to parse, classify, and react to logs automatically.

Effective logging is foundational to microservices observability. With proper logs, developers gain deep insights into application execution and behavior. Logs help uncover precise reasons when things fail.

11.3 Metrics

While logs and traces provide deep insights into discrete events and transactions, metrics give a broad view of overall system behavior and health. Metrics are numerical measurements that are aggregated over time into time series data. Monitoring metrics allows teams to track trends, set alerts, and react to anomalies. In conjunction with traces and logs, metrics provide a comprehensive observability solution.

Metric Type	Metric	Description
Infrastructure Metrics	Infrastructure metrics indicate the performance and capacity of the underlying hosts and network.	
Host Metrics	CPU	Overall CPU utilization percentage. High CPU may usage indicate insufficient resources.
	Memory	Memory usage vs. total memory. Consistently high memory points to a need to scale up hosts.
	Disk I/O	Read/writes to disk, important for disk-bound applications.
	Network I/O	Network bytes in/out to watch for bottlenecks.
Container Metrics	Container CPU/memory	Usage metrics for running containers to watch for resource contention.
	Container restarts	Frequency of unexpected restarts due to failures.
	Container status	Signals for stopped or crashed containers.
Application Metrics	Application metrics provide insights into the runtime behavior of services and application code.	
Throughput	Request rate	Number of requests served per second by an endpoint. Measures service load.
	Response rate	Requests per second successfully completed. In conjunction with error rates, identifies saturated endpoints.
Latency	Request duration	End-to-end latency experienced by users. Highlights slow endpoints.
	Database latency	Time taken for database queries. Indicates slow DB operations.
Traffic	Requests by endpoint	Volume of requests by endpoint path to understand usage patterns.
	Requests by region	Geographical breakdown of traffic.
	Requests by user	Volume of requests generated per user to watch for spikes.
Errors	5xx errors	Rate of server-side failures.
	4xx errors	Rate of client-side errors.
	Exceptions	Application-specific exception rates.
Business Metrics	Business metrics represent key business events and KPIs. These vary based on the application. For an E-Commerce app, the following metrics can be tracked: orders placed per minute, revenue generated per minute, new users per minute, cart additions per minute, checkouts per minute, purchase conversion rate, etc.	

Figure 11.3: Types of metrics

Some common use cases for metrics include:
- **Detect problems**: Metrics act as canaries to detect emerging issues via thresholds.
- **Establish baselines**: Understand typical behavior as a baseline for anomalies.
- **Inform capacity**: Metric trends help plan resource capacity.
- **Optimize performance**: Identify optimization opportunities through metrics.
- **Drive actions**: Metrics can trigger alerts and auto-scaling actions.

- **Root-cause analysis**: Metrics explain the sequence of events after an incident and help in root-cause analysis.

Figure 11.3 shows the kinds of metrics that provide valuable signals into the health of microservices. To start collecting metrics, each service must be instrumented. Libraries like Prometheus Client for Python simplify instrumentation. The next step is aggregating metrics from all sources into a unified store. Prometheus is a popular choice that handles scraping, storing, querying, and alerting time series metrics. Prometheus operates on a pull model where the services expose metrics on an HTTP endpoint that Prometheus scrapes. A single Prometheus server can scrape thousands of instances.

While Prometheus excels at storing and analyzing metric data, it does not provide much visualization. Grafana is commonly paired with Prometheus to build dashboards and graphs from time series data. This provides an intuitive view of latency trends and spikes.

Metrics provide invaluable signals for assessing the health of microservices and reacting to emerging issues. By instrumenting services and infrastructure for metrics, we gain visibility into traffic patterns, performance trends, and business health. When used alongside traces and logs, metrics enable a proactive monitoring strategy. The ability to establish baselines and alert on anomalies transforms monitoring from reactive to proactive.

11.4 Distributed Tracing with OpenTelemetry

In microservices architectures, requests often traverse multiple services. Each service is a black box to external callers. When problems occur, identifying the root cause can be challenging due to the complexity of interactions between the services.

Distributed tracing provides deep insights into request flows across service boundaries. It records cross-service communication to construct end-to-end transaction traces. Teams can analyze these traces to visualize flows, isolate performance issues, and pinpoint where failures occur.

The key concepts in distributed tracing are as follows:
- **Trace**: A trace encompasses a full transaction, representing the lifecycle of a single end-user request through the distributed system.
- **Span**: A span represents an individual unit of work within a trace. It may be thought of as a logical thread. Each service will generate one or more spans per request.
- **Context Propagation**: The context contains tracing metadata that is propagated across service boundaries to connect spans originating from the same request.
- **Instrumentation**: Code that generates tracing data and context propagation automatically without manual intervention.

Figure 11.4 shows a trace topology and a trace with multiple spans. When a user request enters the system, a trace ID is generated. This trace ID is injected into outbound requests and logged against all activity for that request. The result is a complete transaction trace across services. OpenTelemetry provides libraries for instrumenting applications to emit telemetry data including traces, metrics, and logs.

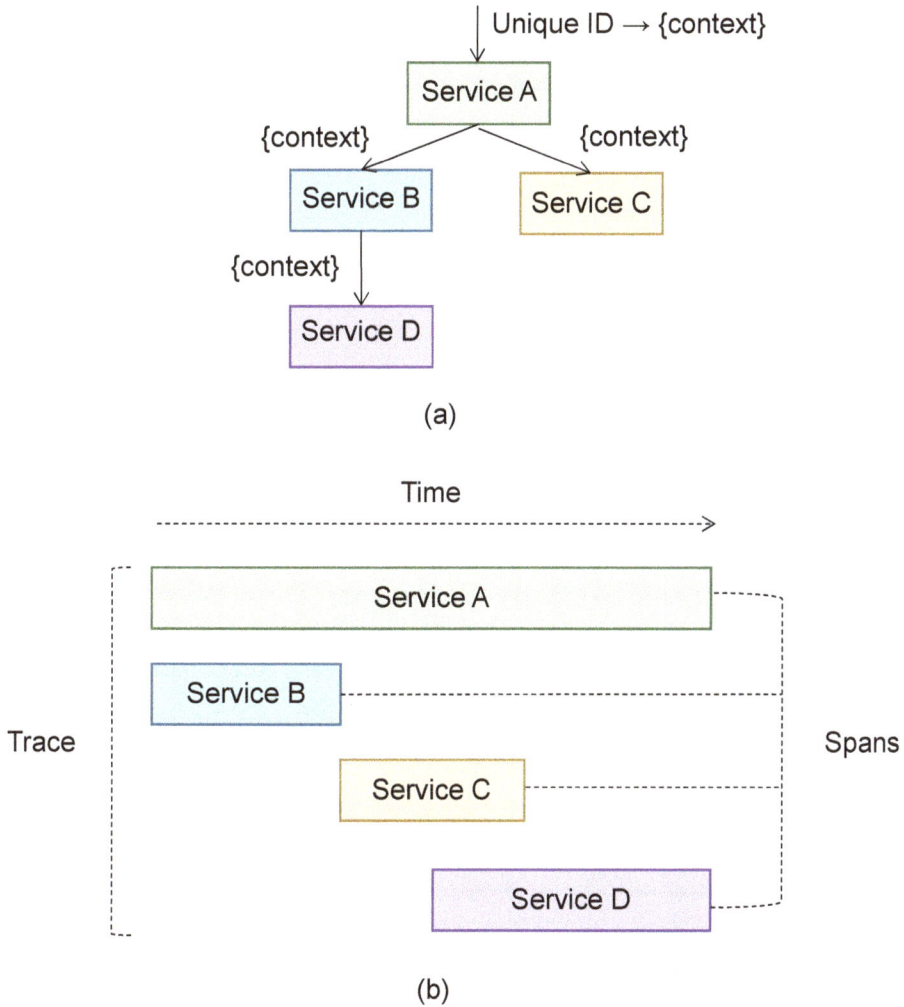

Figure 11.4: (a) Trace topology, (b) Trace and span

OpenTelemetry consists of three components:
- **SDK**: The libraries used by applications to generate telemetry.
- **Collector**: Receives, processes, and exports telemetry data.
- **Backend**: Stores, analyzes, and visualizes the telemetry.

The OpenTelemetry SDK automatically instruments code to create spans and propagate context. The collector aggregates data across services and sends it to the backend. To enable distributed tracing in a microservices application, we need to add the OpenTelemetry SDK dependency to each service. With the SDK initialized, any application code is automatically instrumented to produce spans and propagate context. The SDK will:
- Generate root span for incoming requests
- Create child spans for outbound calls
- Inject context into outbound HTTP requests
- Export spans in batch to a backend like Jaeger

A key aspect of distributed tracing is propagating the trace context across services so that spans from the same request get connected. The context is transmitted using different mechanisms depending on the communication protocol:

- **HTTP**: For HTTP requests between services, the OpenTelemetry SDK injects context into request headers using the *W3C TraceContext* format.
- **Messaging**: For asynchronous messaging, context can be attached to messages via formats like *B3* propagation.
- **RPC**: Some RPC protocols like gRPC have built-in context propagation.

Once services are instrumented, we can observe traces in a tool like Jaeger UI. A trace view provides valuable insights such as:

- **Visualize flow**: Quickly see which services interacted and where time is spent.
- **Isolate failures**: Identify the exact service where errors originate.
- **Find bottlenecks**: Spot services with high latency impacting performance.
- **Understand volumes**: See traffic volumes and how they flow through the system.

We can drill down into a trace to inspect timings, logs, tags, and other metadata on each span. In addition, Jaeger provides aggregation and filtering to analyze trends. For example, we can view error rates, filter by endpoints, and aggregate by duration. These capabilities help developers diagnose the root cause of issues from production traffic.

Distributed tracing is invaluable for shedding light into the black box of microservices interactions. By instrumenting services with OpenTelemetry, we can generate traces mapping the end-to-end flow of requests across services. The trace data acts as a blueprint for diagnosing issues and optimizing flows. Traces become part of the narrative describing how the system behaves. Just as logs tell us what happened, and metrics tell us how fast something happened, the traces show us where it happened.

11.5   OpenTelemetry and Jaeger

Distributed tracing is critical for understanding how requests flow through complex microservices architectures. By instrumenting services with distributed tracing, we can track requests end-to-end, monitor performance, pinpoint errors, and gain deep visibility into inter-service communication.

OpenTelemetry provides a vendor-neutral open-source framework for instrumenting microservices and exporting traces to different backends like Jaeger. In this section, we will do a deep dive into how OpenTelemetry is implemented in Python for the E-Commerce microservices application.

Boxes 11.1 and 11.2 show the code excerpts from the frontend and user services of the E-Commerce application with OpenTelemetry instrumentation. The first step is configuring the OpenTelemetry *TracerProvider*, which manages spans and span processors. This is done in both the frontend and user services. Next, we set up the Jaeger exporter, which will send spans to a Jaeger agent. The *JaegerExporter* sends spans in batches to a Jaeger agent. We add it to the *TracerProvider* as a *BatchSpanProcessor*, which will export spans asynchronously.

OpenTelemetry provides auto-instrumentation for many popular frameworks like Flask and Requests. This makes it easy to add tracing without having to manually instrument every bit of code. The *FlaskInstrumentor* and *RequestsInstrumentor* enable the auto-instrumentation for Flask and Requests. Now any requests handled by the Flask application will automatically generate spans. Outgoing requests made with the Requests library will also be instrumented. This handles a lot of the tracing boilerplate for us. Our code is now transparently instrumented to create spans any time a request is handled.

For more advanced tracing, we may want to create root spans to capture specific operations that aren't covered by the auto-instrumentation. In our services, we create a tracer instance using the *trace.get_tracer()* function. This tracer is then used to start root spans using the *tracer.start_as_current_span()* function. Any code executed within this context will become part of the span. This is used in the frontend and user services to create spans for custom operations. We can also set attributes on spans to capture metadata using the *span.set_attribute()* function.

A key part of distributed tracing is propagating the trace context across service boundaries. This connects all the spans into a single end-to-end trace. OpenTelemetry provides propagation APIs to inject trace context into requests and extract it on the server side. In the frontend, we inject the context into request headers before making a call using the *W3CBaggagePropagator().inject()* function. The W3CPropagator adds the tracing headers into the carrier (headers). On the receiving end in the user service, we extract the context from the incoming headers using *TraceContextTextMapPropagator().extract()* function. Now the user service can access the same tracing context as the frontend. Any spans it starts will become part of the same distributed trace. This allows seamless distributed tracing across all services based on the propagated context.

> ■ **Box 11.1: Frontend service excerpt with OpenTelemetry instrumentation**
>
> ```
> import os
> import requests
> from flask import Flask
> from flask_migrate import Migrate
> from flask import render_template, session
> from flask import redirect, url_for, flash, request, jsonify
> from flask_login import current_user
> from flask_bootstrap import Bootstrap
> from flask_login import LoginManager
> from flask import session, request
> import json, time
> from datetime import datetime, timedelta
> from opentelemetry import trace, baggage
> from opentelemetry.exporter.jaeger.thrift import JaegerExporter
> from opentelemetry.context import attach, detach
> from opentelemetry.context.context import Context
> from opentelemetry.propagate import extract
> from opentelemetry.trace.status import Status, StatusCode
> from opentelemetry.trace import SpanKind, TraceFlags
> from opentelemetry.sdk.resources import SERVICE_NAME, Resource
> from opentelemetry.semconv.trace import SpanAttributes
> from opentelemetry.sdk.trace import TracerProvider
> from opentelemetry.sdk.trace.export import (
>     ConsoleSpanExporter,
>     SimpleSpanProcessor,
>     BatchSpanProcessor,
> ```

```
)
from opentelemetry.instrumentation.flask import FlaskInstrumentor
from opentelemetry.instrumentation.requests import RequestsInstrumentor
from opentelemetry.baggage.propagation import W3CBaggagePropagator
from opentelemetry.context import get_current
from opentelemetry import propagators
from opentelemetry.trace.propagation.tracecontext import
                              TraceContextTextMapPropagator

login_manager = LoginManager()
bootstrap = Bootstrap()

app = Flask(__name__, static_folder='static')
app.config['UPLOAD_FOLDER'] = 'static/images'
app.config['SECRET_KEY'] = "DoWgTDq87Kmne3TsCjNFabP"
app.config['WTF_CSRF_SECRET_KEY'] = "sEWQkE9oYBiF5fVJnm278i7"
app.config['ENV'] = "development"
app.config['DEBUG'] = True

USER_SERVICE_URL='http://localhost:5001'
PRODUCT_SERVICE_URL='http://localhost:5002'
ORDER_SERVICE_URL='http://localhost:5003'
REVIEW_SERVICE_URL='http://localhost:5004'

login_manager.init_app(app)
login_manager.login_message = "Please login"
login_manager.login_view = "login"

service_name = 'ecommerce-frontend'
agent_host = os.environ.get('AGENT_HOST', 'localhost')
agent_port = os.environ.get('AGENT_PORT', '6831')

trace.set_tracer_provider(
    TracerProvider(
        resource=Resource.create({SERVICE_NAME: service_name})
    )
)

jaeger_exporter = JaegerExporter(
    agent_host_name = agent_host,
    agent_port = int(agent_port),
)

trace.get_tracer_provider().add_span_processor(
    BatchSpanProcessor(jaeger_exporter)
)

FlaskInstrumentor().instrument_app(app)
RequestsInstrumentor().instrument()
tracer = trace.get_tracer('ecommerce-frontend')

class UserClient:
    @staticmethod
    def post_login(form):
```

```
            api_key = False
            payload = {
                'username': form.username.data,
                'password': form.password.data
            }
            url = USER_SERVICE_URL+'/api/user/login'
            response = requests.post( url=url, data=payload)
            if response:
                d = response.json()
                #print("This is response from user api: " + str(d))
                if d['user'] is not None:
                    user = d['user']
            return user

    @staticmethod
    def get_user():
        with tracer.start_as_current_span("api1_span") as span:
            ctx = baggage.set_baggage("user",
                        json.dumps(session['user']))
            headers = {}
            W3CBaggagePropagator().inject(headers, ctx)
            TraceContextTextMapPropagator().inject(headers, ctx)
            print(headers)
            headers['Authorization']='Basic '+session['user_api_key']
            url = USER_SERVICE_URL+'/api/user'
            response = requests.get(url=url, headers=headers)
            user = response.json()
            print(user)
            return user

    @staticmethod
    def get_user_with_username(username):
        response = requests.get(url=USER_SERVICE_URL+'/api/user/' +
                            str(username))
        user = response.json()
        return user

    @staticmethod
    def post_user_create(form):
        user = False
        payload = {
            'email': form.email.data,
            'password': form.password.data,
            'first_name': form.first_name.data,
            'last_name': form.last_name.data,
            'username': form.username.data
        }
        url = USER_SERVICE_URL+'/api/user/create'
        response = requests.post(url=url, data=payload)
        if response:
            user = response.json()
        return user

    @staticmethod
```

```python
    def does_exist(username):
        url = USER_SERVICE_URL+'/api/user/' + username + '/exists'
        response = requests.get(url=url)
        return response.status_code == 200

def get_user_name_photo():
    with tracer.start_as_current_span('get_user_name_photo') as span:
        try:
            response = UserClient.get_user()
            user = response['result']
            user_name = user['first_name']+" "+user['last_name']
            user_photo = user['photo']
            ctx = baggage.set_baggage("username", user_name)
        except:
            user_name=''
            user_photo=''
        return user_name, user_photo

@app.route('/', methods=['GET'])
def home():
    with tracer.start_as_current_span('home_page') as span:
        if current_user.is_authenticated:
            session['order'] = OrderClient.get_order_from_session()

        try:
            products = ProductClient.get_products()
        except:
            products = {
                'results': []
            }

        span = trace.get_current_span()

        if 'user' in session:
            print(session['user'])
            span.add_event(json.dumps({'event': 'home_page',
                                    'value': session['user']}))
            span.set_attribute('user', session['user']['username'])
            span.set_status(Status(status_code=StatusCode.OK))
            ctx = get_current()
            propagator = W3CBaggagePropagator()
            ctx = baggage.set_baggage("test2", "value2", context=ctx)
            output = {}
            propagator.inject(output, context=ctx)
            print(output.get("baggage"))

        user_name, user_photo = get_user_name_photo()
        return render_template('home.html', products=products,
            user_name = user_name, user_photo=user_photo)
```

■ Box 11.2: User service excerpt with OpenTelemetry instrumentation

```python
import os
from flask import Flask, send_from_directory, send_file
from flask_login import LoginManager
from datetime import datetime
from flask_login import UserMixin
from passlib.hash import sha256_crypt
from flask import make_response, request, jsonify
from flask_login import current_user, login_user, login_required
from passlib.hash import sha256_crypt
from flask import g
from flask.sessions import SecureCookieSessionInterface
from flask_login import user_loaded_from_header
import time, random, json
import base64
from opentelemetry import trace, baggage
from opentelemetry.exporter.jaeger.thrift import JaegerExporter
from opentelemetry.context import attach, detach
from opentelemetry.context.context import Context
from opentelemetry.propagate import extract
from opentelemetry.trace.status import Status, StatusCode
from opentelemetry.trace import SpanKind, TraceFlags
from opentelemetry.sdk.resources import SERVICE_NAME, Resource
from opentelemetry.semconv.trace import SpanAttributes
from opentelemetry.sdk.trace import TracerProvider
from opentelemetry.sdk.trace.export import (
    ConsoleSpanExporter,
    SimpleSpanProcessor,
    BatchSpanProcessor,
)
from opentelemetry.instrumentation.flask import FlaskInstrumentor
from opentelemetry.instrumentation.requests import RequestsInstrumentor
from opentelemetry.baggage.propagation import W3CBaggagePropagator
from opentelemetry.context import get_current
from opentelemetry import propagators
from opentelemetry.trace.propagation.tracecontext import
                            TraceContextTextMapPropagator


login_manager = LoginManager()
basedir = os.path.abspath(os.path.dirname(__file__))

app = Flask(__name__)
app.config['SECRET_KEY'] = "DoWgTDq87Kmne3TsCjNFabP"
app.config['BUCKET_NAME'] = 'microservices-ecommerce-app'
app.config['CLOUDFRONT_URL'] = 'https://dn2aztcn1xe1u.cloudfront.net'
app.config['ENV'] = "development"
app.config['DEBUG'] = True
app.config['SQLALCHEMY_ECHO'] = True
app.config['UPLOAD_FOLDER'] = 'uploads'
login_manager.init_app(app)

service_name = 'ecommerce-user'
agent_host = os.environ.get('AGENT_HOST', 'localhost')
```

```
agent_port = os.environ.get('AGENT_PORT', '6831')

trace.set_tracer_provider(
    TracerProvider(
        resource=Resource.create({SERVICE_NAME: service_name})
    )
)

jaeger_exporter = JaegerExporter(
    agent_host_name = agent_host,
    agent_port = int(agent_port),
)

trace.get_tracer_provider().add_span_processor(
    BatchSpanProcessor(jaeger_exporter)
)

FlaskInstrumentor().instrument_app(app)
RequestsInstrumentor().instrument()
tracer = trace.get_tracer('ecommerce-user')


@login_required
@app.route('/api/user', methods=['GET'])
def get_user():
    headers = dict(request.headers)
    print(f"Received headers: {headers}")
    carrier ={'traceparent': headers['Traceparent']}
    ctx = TraceContextTextMapPropagator().extract(carrier=carrier)
    print(f"Received context: {ctx}")

    if 'Baggage' in headers:
        b2 ={'baggage': headers['Baggage']}
        ctx2 = W3CBaggagePropagator().extract(b2, context=ctx)
        print(f"Received context2: {ctx2}")
    else:
        ctx2=get_current()

    # Start a new span
    with tracer.start_span("get_user", context=ctx2):
        span = trace.get_current_span()
      # Use propagated context
        print(baggage.get_baggage('user', ctx2))
        if current_user.is_authenticated:
            span.add_event(json.dumps({'event': 'user_api',
                        'value': current_user.to_json()}))
            return make_response(jsonify({'result':
                            current_user.to_json()}))
        return make_response(jsonify({'message': 'Not logged in'})), 401
```

With OpenTelemetry, distributed tracing can be easily added to Python microservices. It provides comprehensive instrumentation while avoiding vendor lock-in.

Next, we will look at Jaeger, which provides a powerful UI for querying, visualizing, and analyzing distributed traces. Once our services are configured to export traces, we can use

Jaeger to understand the system architecture and request flow.

When a new trace is exported, it will appear in the Jaeger Search screen. We can search and filter traces by fields like service, operation, duration, tags, etc. Figure 11.5 shows how to search and view traces for the frontend service.

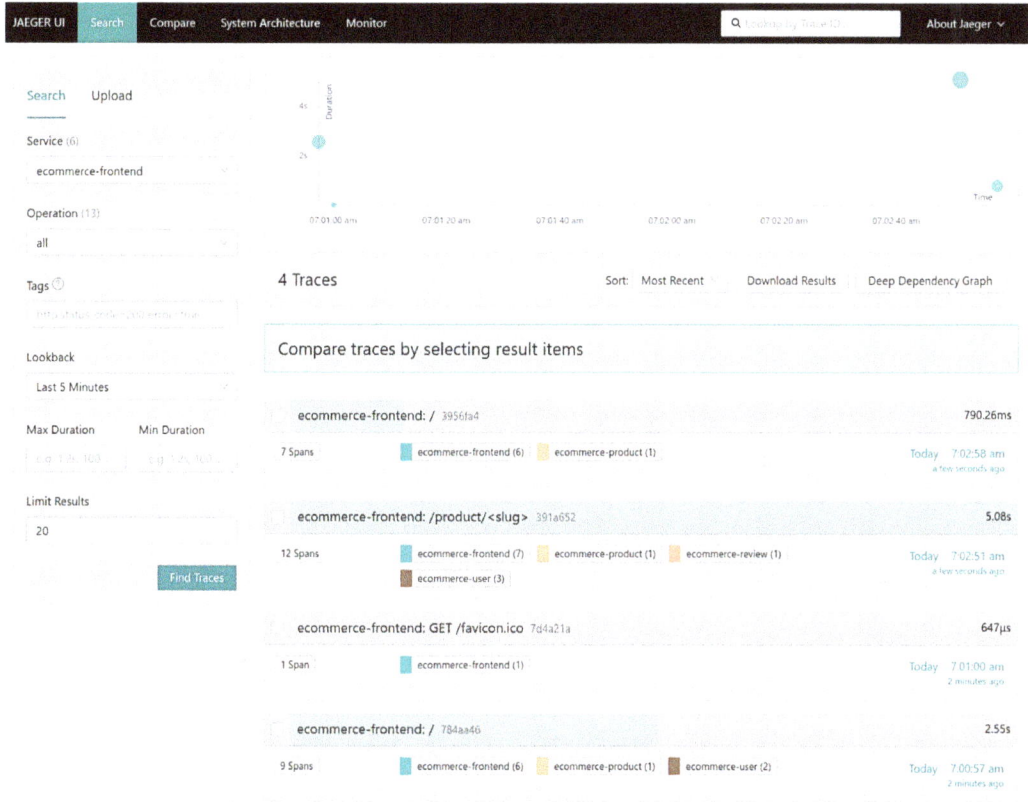

Figure 11.5: Viewing traces in Jaeger

Clicking on a trace opens up the Trace Detail view. This visualizes the entire trace showing the root span and all child spans. Each span represents an operation or function call. Figure 11.6 shows the trace detail view. The span graph is interactive and hovering over a span reveals key information like start time, duration, tags, and logs. Clicking a span opens the span detail panel with additional data. We can examine the trace to understand the exact path a request took through the system. Long durations, errors, or gaps indicate issues to debug.

Inside the span detail panel, we can inspect everything about that particular span:

- Operation name: the function or code block being traced
- Start time and duration
- Tags: key-value metadata like user ID or request name
- Logs: debug statements or trace events
- Context: trace ID, span ID, flags
- Process: service name and IDs
- Warnings: errors or problems

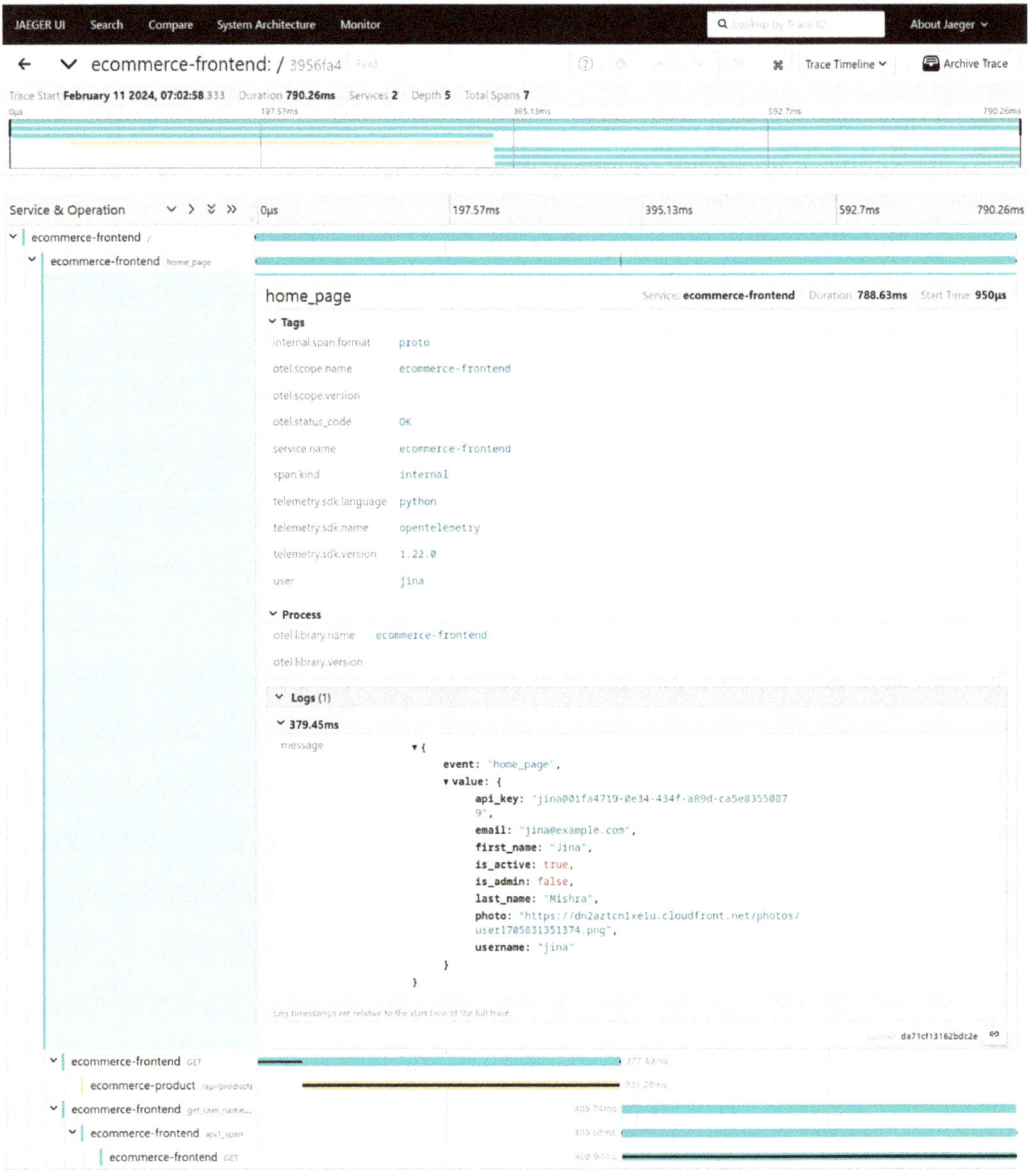

Figure 11.6: Viewing details of a trace in Jaeger

This helps narrow down latency or errors to a specific span segment. We can pinpoint where time is being spent or issues occurring.

Analyzing traces over time reveals the system architecture. Looking at span start times and durations illustrates the request flow through different services. For example, a trace starting in the frontend, calling the user service, and then the order service. Over time, the most common trace shapes indicate the core request paths. Long durations or errors in a span highlight problem areas to optimize. Jaeger provides a map view of services and their connections derived from trace data as shown in Figure 11.7. This can uncover hidden dependencies and bottlenecks.

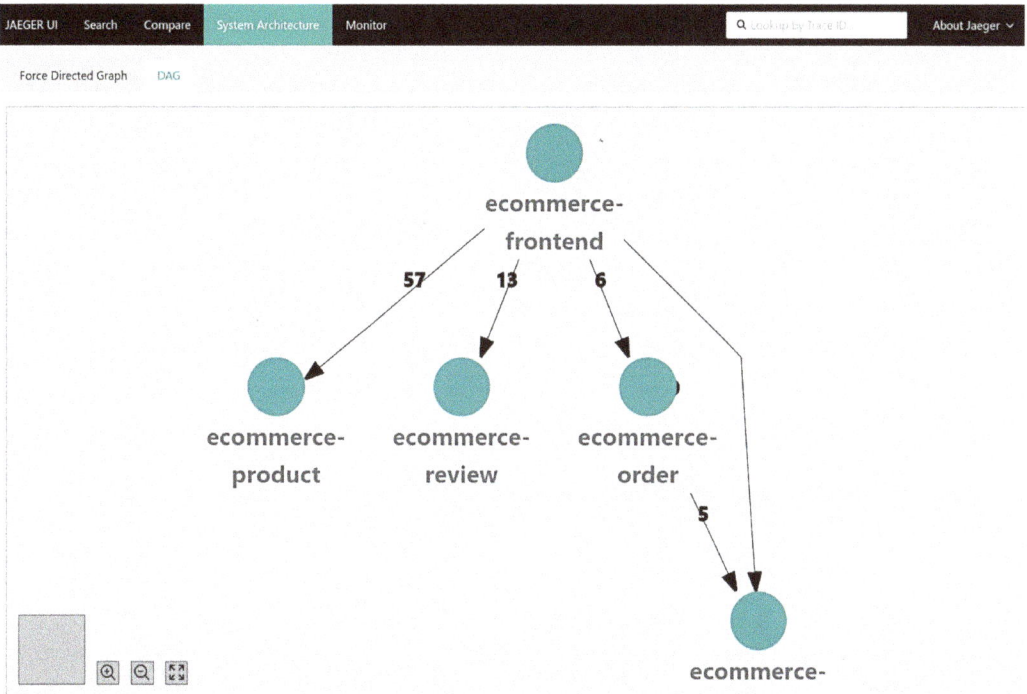

Figure 11.7: Viewing system architecture in Jaeger

Some key insights provided by Jaeger into system architecture include:
- Request flow: sequence of services called
- Critical paths: most common traces
- Latency hotspots: long durations indicate slow services
- Traffic volume: number of traces between services
- Errors: spans with problems or warnings

Jaeger provides many tools for troubleshooting microservices architectures via distributed tracing data. Instrumenting services with OpenTelemetry gives powerful observability into the entire system.

11.6 Prometheus and Grafana

Microservices architectures composed of multiple independent services provide benefits like easier scalability and flexibility. However, the distributed nature also brings challenges in monitoring and troubleshooting. Using a monitoring system like Prometheus and visualization tool like Grafana can help tackle these challenges.

Prometheus is an open-source monitoring and alerting toolkit. It scrapes and stores time series data like metrics and allows querying them through its own powerful query language called PromQL. Some key aspects of Prometheus are as follows:
- A pull-based monitoring system where Prometheus server scrapes metrics exposed by services over HTTP periodically.
- A multi-dimensional time series database to store the metric data with annotations.
- A built-in query language and API to filter and aggregate metric data.

- A rich set of client libraries for instrumenting application code to expose metrics easily.
- Good integration with Grafana for building dashboards. Alerting support to trigger alerts based on metric thresholds.

In a microservices setup, each service exposes metrics related to service health, performance, errors, etc. The Prometheus server scrapes these metrics periodically and stores them. This data can then be visualized or alerted on.

Box 11.3 shows the code excerpt of the frontend service with instrumentation for Prometheus metrics. To expose metrics, the Prometheus client library is added in the service code. We instrument the frontend service to increment the request count and observe request latency on each request. We use Prometheus counters to track login counts, add-to-cart counts, and order checkout counts. The frontend service exposes a metrics HTTP endpoint that Prometheus scrapes from.

■ **Box 11.3: Frontend service excerpt with Prometheus metrics**

```
import os
import requests
from flask import Flask
from flask_migrate import Migrate
from flask import render_template, session
from flask import redirect, url_for, flash, request, jsonify
from flask_login import current_user
from flask_bootstrap import Bootstrap
from flask_login import LoginManager
from flask import session, request
import json, time
from datetime import datetime, timedelta
import logging
import boto3
from prometheus_client import Counter, Histogram
from prometheus_client import make_wsgi_app
from werkzeug.middleware.dispatcher import DispatcherMiddleware
from werkzeug.serving import run_simple
from flask_prometheus_metrics import register_metrics

login_manager = LoginManager()
bootstrap = Bootstrap()

app = Flask(__name__, static_folder='static')
app.config['UPLOAD_FOLDER'] = 'static/images'
app.config['SECRET_KEY'] = "DoWgTDq87Kmne3TsCjNFabP"
app.config['WTF_CSRF_SECRET_KEY'] = "sEWQkE9oYBiF5fVJnm278i7"
app.config['ENV'] = "development"
app.config['DEBUG'] = True

USER_SERVICE_URL='http://localhost:5001'
PRODUCT_SERVICE_URL='http://localhost:5002'
ORDER_SERVICE_URL='http://localhost:5003'
REVIEW_SERVICE_URL='http://localhost:5004'

login_manager.init_app(app)
```

```
login_manager.login_message = "Please login"
login_manager.login_view = "login"

# Counters
REQUEST_COUNT = Counter('request_count',
                'Total Request Count', ['method', 'endpoint'])
LOGIN_COUNT = Counter('login_count', 'Total Login Count')
ADD_TO_CART_COUNT = Counter('add_to_cart', 'Add to Cart Count')
CHECKOUT_COUNT = Counter('checkout_count', 'Checkout Count')

# Histograms
REQUEST_LATENCY=Histogram('request_latency_seconds','Request latency')

@app.before_request
def before_request():
  request.start_time = time.time()

@app.after_request
def after_request(response):
  request_latency = time.time() - request.start_time
  REQUEST_LATENCY.observe(request_latency)
  REQUEST_COUNT.labels(request.method, request.path).inc()
  return response

@app.route('/', methods=['GET'])
def home():
    REQUEST_COUNT.labels(request.method, request.url_rule.rule).inc()
    if current_user.is_authenticated:
        session['order'] = OrderClient.get_order_from_session()
    try:
        products = ProductClient.get_products()
    except:
        products = {
            'results': []
        }
    user_name, user_photo = get_user_name_photo()
    return render_template('home.html', products=products,
                user_name = user_name, user_photo=user_photo)

@app.route('/login', methods=['GET', 'POST'])
def login():

    if current_user.is_authenticated:
        return redirect(url_for('home'))
    form = LoginForm()
    if request.method == "POST":
        if form.validate_on_submit():
            user = UserClient.post_login(form)
            if user:
                session['user_api_key'] = user['api_key']
                session['user'] = user
                order = OrderClient.get_order()
                if order.get('result', False):
                    session['order'] = order['result']
```

```
                        flash('Welcome back, ' + user['first_name'], 'success')
                        LOGIN_COUNT.inc()
                        return redirect(url_for('home'))
                else:
                        flash('Cannot login', 'error')
            else:
                    flash('Errors found', 'error')
        return render_template('login.html', form=form)

@app.route('/product/<slug>', methods=['GET', 'POST'])
def product(slug):
        response = ProductClient.get_product(slug)
        item = response['result']
        form = ItemForm(product_id=item['slug'])
        reviewslist=[]
        try:
                reviews=ReviewClient.get_reviews(item['slug'])
                for review in reviews['results']:
                        reviewdict={}
                        reviewdict['rating']=review['rating']
                        reviewdict['description']=review['description']
                        reviewdict['date_added']=review['date_added']
                        reviewer=UserClient.get_user_with_username(review['username'])
                        reviewdict['photo']=reviewer['result']['photo']
                        reviewdict['user_name']=reviewer['result']['first_name']+
                                            ' '+reviewer['result']['last_name']
                        reviewslist.append(reviewdict)
        except:
                pass
        if request.method == "POST":
                start_time = time.time()
                if 'user' not in session:
                        flash('Please login', 'error')
                        return redirect(url_for('login'))
                order = OrderClient.post_add_to_cart(
                        username=session['user']['username'],
                        product_slug=item['slug'], price=item['price'], qty=1)
                session['order'] = order['result']
                flash('Item has been added to cart', 'success')
                ADD_TO_CART_COUNT.inc()
        user_name, user_photo = get_user_name_photo()
        return render_template('product.html',
                        product=item, form=form, reviews=reviewslist,
                user_name = user_name, user_photo=user_photo)

@app.route('/checkout', methods=['GET'])
def summary():
        start_time = time.time()
        if 'user' not in session:
                flash('Please login', 'error')
                return redirect(url_for('login'))
        if 'order' not in session:
                flash('No order found', 'error')
```

```
            return redirect(url_for('home'))
    order = OrderClient.get_order()
    if len(order['result']['items']) == 0:
        flash('No order found', 'error')
        return redirect(url_for('home'))
    OrderClient.post_checkout()
    return redirect(url_for('thank_you'))

@app.route('/order/thank-you', methods=['GET'])
def thank_you():
    if 'user' not in session:
        flash('Please login', 'error')
        return redirect(url_for('login'))
    if 'order' not in session:
        flash('No order found', 'error')
        return redirect(url_for('home'))
    session.pop('order', None)
    flash('Thank you for your order', 'success')
    CHECKOUT_COUNT.inc()
    user_name, user_photo = get_user_name_photo()
    return render_template('thanks.html',
            user_name = user_name, user_photo=user_photo)

if __name__ == '__main__':
    # provide app's version and deploy environment/config name
    register_metrics(app, app_version="v0.1.2", app_config="staging")
    # Plug metrics WSGI app to your main app with dispatcher
    dispatcher = DispatcherMiddleware(app.wsgi_app,
                {"/metrics": make_wsgi_app()})
    run_simple(hostname="0.0.0.0", port=5000, application=dispatcher)
```

Box 11.4 shows the commands are for setting up Prometheus and Grafana monitoring using Docker containers. The first command runs a Prometheus container, mapping port 9090 on the host to 9090 in the container, using host network mode, and mounting a prometheus.yml config file into the container. This will start up a Prometheus instance to collect metrics. The second command creates a named volume called "grafana-storage" to store Grafana data. The third command runs a Grafana container, mapping port 3000 on the host to 3000 in the container, using the host network, and mounting the "grafana-storage" volume to the Grafana data directory. This will start up a Grafana instance to visualize the metrics collected by Prometheus.

▪ Box 11.4: Running Prometheus and Grafana containers

```
#Create prometheus container
docker run -p 9090:9090 --network=host -v
    prometheus.yml:/etc/prometheus/prometheus.yml
    prom/prometheus

#Create volume for grafana container
docker volume create grafana-storage

#Create grafana container
```

```
docker run -p 3000:3000 -d --network=host
    --name=grafana
    --volume grafana-storage:/var/lib/grafana
    grafana/grafana
```

Prometheus server needs to be configured to scrape the instrumented microservices. The configuration is done in prometheus.yml file as shown in Box 11.5. This configures scraping of metrics from the frontend service. Similarly, we can add other services to the configuration file. Prometheus will periodically scrape the */metrics* endpoint on these services to collect metrics. Multiple services can be targeted by Prometheus using such scrape configuration. Figure 11.8 shows the output of the */metrics* endpoint exposed by the frontend service.

■ **Box 11.5: Prometheus configuration file**

```
scrape_configs:
  - job_name: 'frontend'
    scrape_interval: 5s
    static_configs:
      - targets: ['localhost:5000']
```

```
# TYPE python_gc_objects_collected_total counter
python_gc_objects_collected_total{generation="0"} 37400.0
python_gc_objects_collected_total{generation="1"} 4995.0
python_gc_objects_collected_total{generation="2"} 6.0
# HELP python_gc_objects_uncollectable_total Uncollectable objects found during GC
# TYPE python_gc_objects_uncollectable_total counter
python_gc_objects_uncollectable_total{generation="0"} 0.0
python_gc_objects_uncollectable_total{generation="1"} 0.0
python_gc_objects_uncollectable_total{generation="2"} 0.0
# HELP python_gc_collections_total Number of times this generation was collected
# TYPE python_gc_collections_total counter
python_gc_collections_total{generation="0"} 239.0
python_gc_collections_total{generation="1"} 21.0
python_gc_collections_total{generation="2"} 1.0
# HELP python_info Python platform information
# TYPE python_info gauge
python_info{implementation="CPython",major="3",minor="11",patchlevel="7",version="3.11.7"} 1.0
# HELP process_virtual_memory_bytes Virtual memory size in bytes.
# TYPE process_virtual_memory_bytes gauge
process_virtual_memory_bytes 6.7162112e+08
# HELP process_resident_memory_bytes Resident memory size in bytes.
# TYPE process_resident_memory_bytes gauge
process_resident_memory_bytes 2.3064576e+07
# HELP process_start_time_seconds Start time of the process since unix epoch in seconds.
# TYPE process_start_time_seconds gauge
process_start_time_seconds 1.70769960732e+09
# HELP process_cpu_seconds_total Total user and system CPU time spent in seconds.
# TYPE process_cpu_seconds_total counter
process_cpu_seconds_total 5.359999999999999
# HELP process_open_fds Number of open file descriptors.
# TYPE process_open_fds gauge
process_open_fds 6.0
# HELP process_max_fds Maximum number of open file descriptors.
# TYPE process_max_fds gauge
process_max_fds 1024.0
# HELP app_request_latency_seconds Application Request Latency
# TYPE app_request_latency_seconds histogram
app_request_latency_seconds_bucket{endpoint="/",le="0.005",method="GET"} 0.0
app_request_latency_seconds_bucket{endpoint="/",le="0.01",method="GET"} 0.0
app_request_latency_seconds_bucket{endpoint="/",le="0.025",method="GET"} 0.0
```

Figure 11.8: Prometheus metrics exported by the frontend service

Figure 11.9 shows the details of the Prometheus target for scraping metrics.

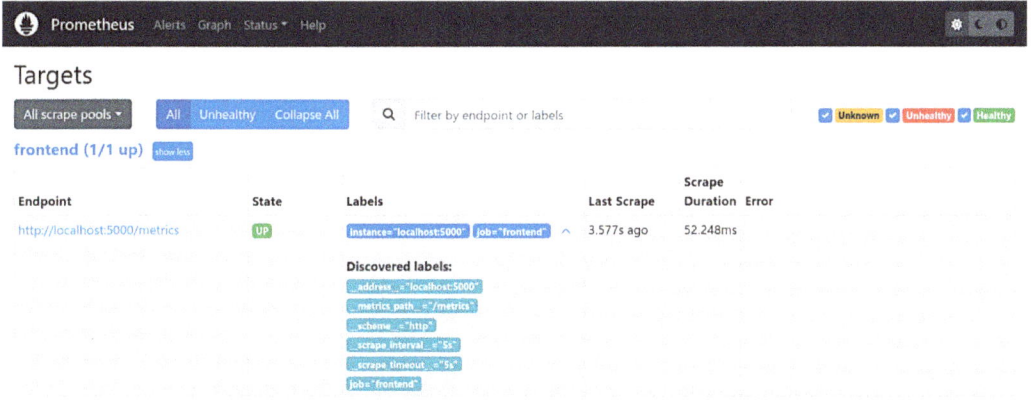

Figure 11.9: Viewing the Prometheus target for scraping metrics

Figures 11.10 and 11.11 show examples of plotting the Prometheus metrics for request counts and add-to-cart counts.

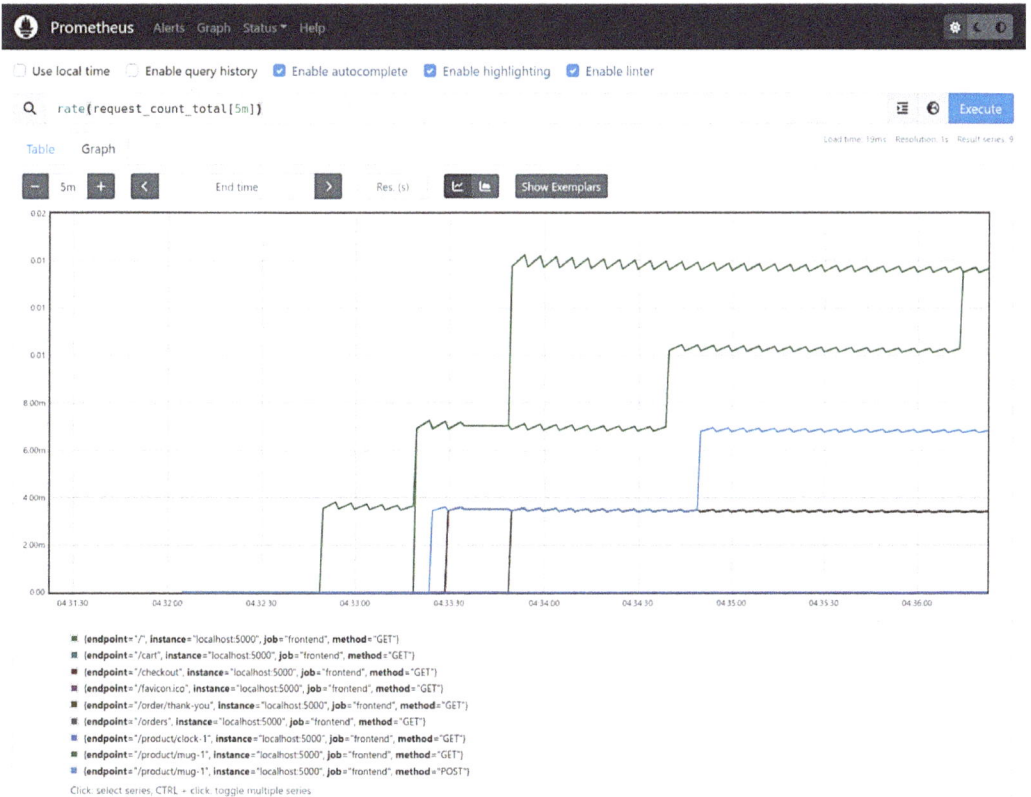

Figure 11.10: Prometheus metric for request count

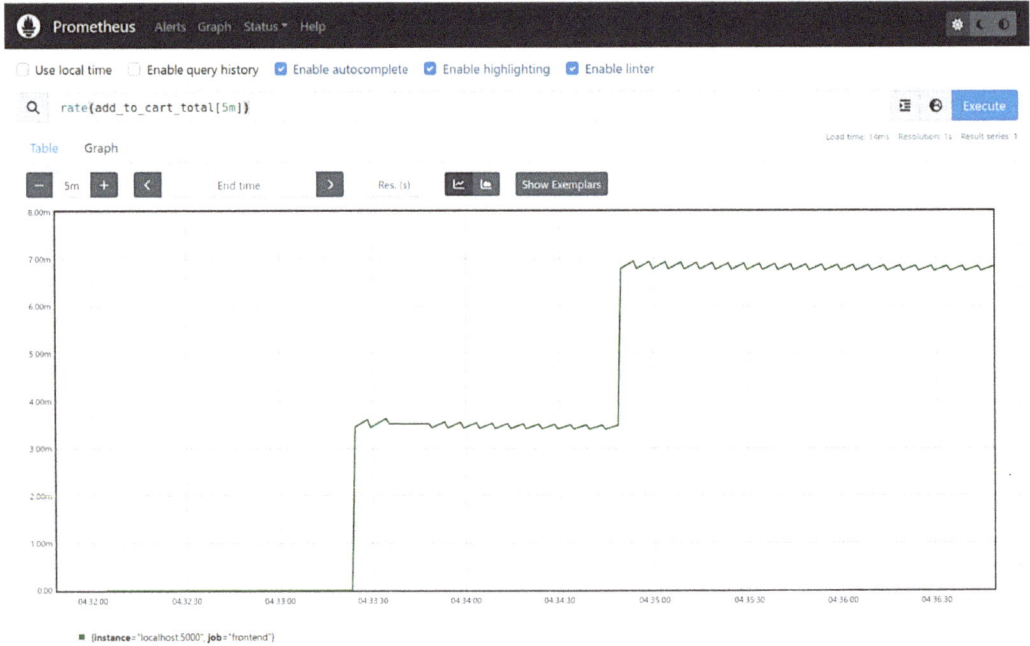

Figure 11.11: Prometheus metric for add-to-cart count

While Prometheus provides a querying interface to filter and analyze metric data, however, visualizing the metrics over time is better done using Grafana. Grafana is a visualization tool that can query multiple data sources, including Prometheus. It provides an intuitive UI to create dashboards composed of various graphs, tables, and visuals.

Grafana can visualize Prometheus metrics for microservices applications such as:

- Time series graph of request latency to spot spikes
- Uptime graphs for services using counters
- Tables showing top erroring services based on error counters
- Gauges indicating current request throughput
- Alert notification panels to show critical alerts

Grafana dashboards give a single pane of glass view into the entire system's metrics. This helps spot problems like degraded performance in specific services. Alerting can be configured for critical issues.

Once the Grafana container is running, you can access the Grafana UI at http://localhost:3000. You will be prompted to create a new account and log in. Figure 11.12 shows how to add Prometheus as a data source in Grafana.

Next, we create a simple dashboard with Prometheus metrics. Figure 11.13 shows how to create a chart for add-to-cart count. Similarly, we create other charts and add them to the dashboard as shown in Figure 11.14.

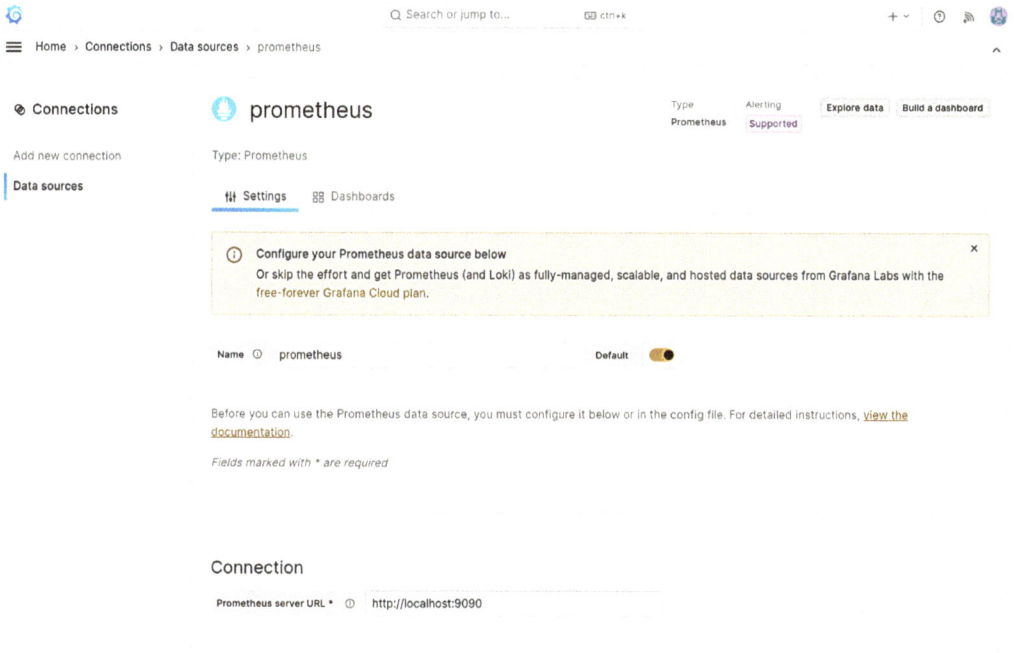

Figure 11.12: Configuring Prometheus data source in Grafana

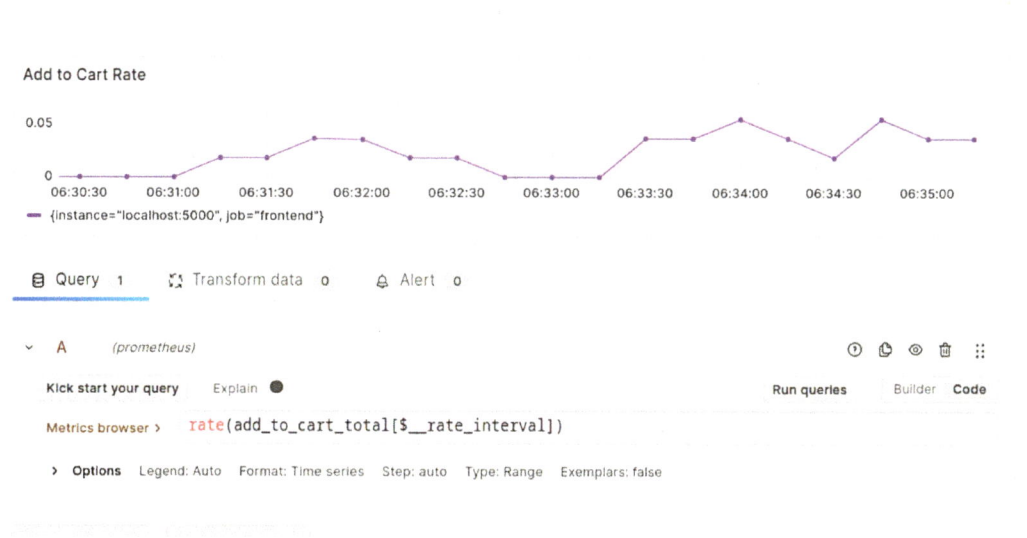

Figure 11.13: Creating a chart in Grafana

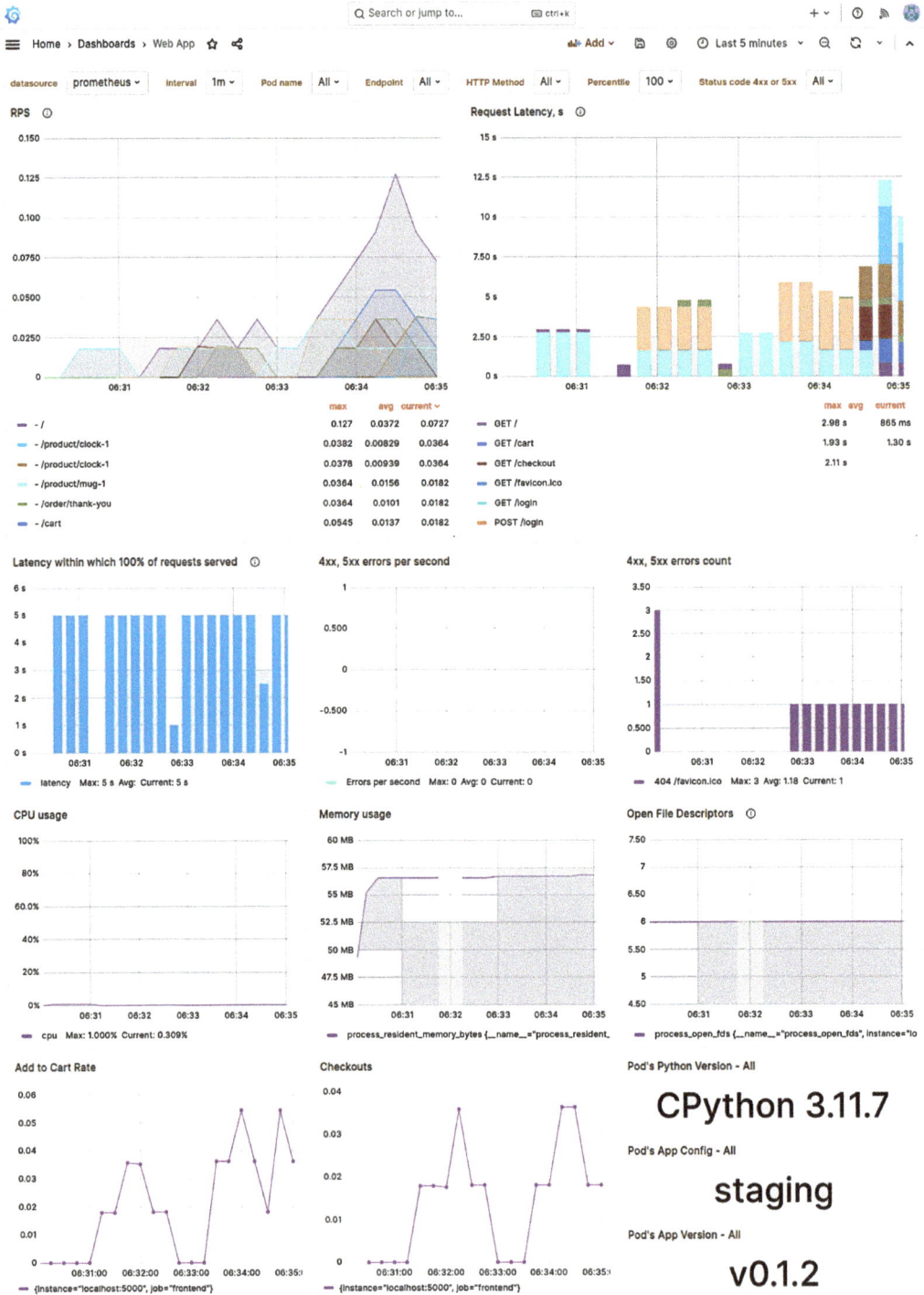

Figure 11.14: Grafana dashboard for the E-Commerce application

11.7 AWS X-Ray and CloudWatch

The decentralized nature of microservices brings challenges related to distributed tracing and logging. AWS provides services like X-Ray and CloudWatch Logs that help address these challenges and enable effective monitoring in microservices environments.

X-Ray is an AWS service that provides application tracing and performance insights for microservices applications. It traces requests as they flow through the various microservices and records a detailed service map of a distributed system.

The key capabilities of X-Ray are as follows:

- **Distributed tracing**: X-Ray traces requests across microservices, enabling you to visualize request flows and identify performance bottlenecks.
- **Service map**: The service map provides a bird's eye view of the microservices app, showing all components and how they connect.
- **Trace analytics**: Detailed latency, error, and other metrics are provided for tracing data. This allows performance optimization.
- **Annotations and metadata**: Additional data such as debug info and environment data can be added to traces using annotations and metadata.
- **Integration with AWS services**: Many AWS services like API Gateway, Lambda, ECS, and more are integrated with X-Ray for automatic tracing.

To use X-Ray, the X-Ray SDK needs to be installed in each microservice. The SDK instruments the application code and handles transmission of trace data to the X-Ray daemon process. The X-Ray daemon runs on EC2 or on-premises servers. The X-Ray daemon aggregates and samples trace data before sending it to the X-Ray service. X-Ray provides granular tracing data and visibility into request flows in complex microservices architectures. Developers can use the insights to improve application performance and availability.

CloudWatch Logs is a service that allows collection, storage, and analysis of log data from distributed applications and infrastructure. With microservices, the log data is generated across many services hosted on different servers. CloudWatch Logs can aggregate all this disparate log data into centralized log streams for each application.

The key capabilities of CloudWatch Logs are as follows:

- **Centralized log storage**: Log data from all microservices is collected in one place for easier access and analysis.
- **Search and filter logs**: CloudWatch allows searching and filtering the log data to isolate specific requests, errors, etc.
- **Real-time monitoring**: Logs can be monitored in real-time for issues or metrics crossing thresholds.
- **Log retention**: Logs can be stored securely for any retention period, from days to years.
- **Analysis and insights**: CloudWatch integrations with services like Lambda and Elasticsearch allow sophisticated log analytics.
- **Alerting**: CloudWatch alarms can trigger SNS notifications or Lambda functions based on log metrics.

To start collecting logs in CloudWatch, the CloudWatch Logs agent needs to be installed on each EC2 instance or server running the microservices. The agent will detect print and log statements in the application code and transmit log data to CloudWatch. With a centralized logging solution, DevOps teams get application visibility, and can use logs for monitoring, auditing, and debugging microservices environments.

Box 11.6 shows the code excerpt of the frontend service with instrumentation for AWS X-Ray for tracing and CloudWatch for logs. For X-Ray, the X-Ray SDK is imported and configured to enable tracing for the Flask app. The XRayMiddleware is used to instrument the Flask app to generate trace data. The *patch_all()* method instruments all supported libraries like requests to generate traces. The *@xray_recorder.capture()* decorator is used to create a segment around routes. This captures tracing data for requests to these endpoints. Within the routes, subsegments are created using *xray_recorder.begin_subsegment()* to trace specific functions or blocks. Metadata and annotations are added to segments using methods like *put_metadata()* and *put_annotation()* to add additional context. The generated trace data is sent to the X-Ray service, where it can be viewed in the console. The trace data provides insights into request latency, flows through the app, and errors.

For CloudWatch Logs, the CloudWatch client is initialized, and a log group and stream are created to store the log data. A *CloudWatchLogHandler* is created to send log data to CloudWatch using the client. This handler is added to the main application logger. Within routes, the logger is used to log messages at different severity levels like *logger.info()* and *logger.error()* which are sent to CloudWatch. Structured log messages with contextual data can be logged, which makes searching and parsing easier. The CloudWatch console can be used to search and filter log data, set up alerts, and analyze trends.

■ **Box 11.6: Frontend service excerpt with X-Ray tracing and CloudWatch logging**

```
import os
import requests
from flask import Flask
from flask_migrate import Migrate
from flask import render_template, session
from flask import redirect, url_for, flash, request, jsonify
from flask_login import current_user
from flask_bootstrap import Bootstrap
from flask_login import LoginManager
from flask import session, request
import json, time
from datetime import datetime, timedelta
from aws_xray_sdk.core import xray_recorder, patch_all
from aws_xray_sdk.ext.flask.middleware import XRayMiddleware
import logging
import boto3
from watchtower import CloudWatchLogHandler

login_manager = LoginManager()
bootstrap = Bootstrap()

app = Flask(__name__, static_folder='static')
app.config['UPLOAD_FOLDER'] = 'static/images'
app.config['SECRET_KEY'] = "DoWgTDq87Kmne3TsCjNFabP"
app.config['WTF_CSRF_SECRET_KEY'] = "sEWQkE9oYBiF5fVJnm278i7"
```

```python
app.config['ENV'] = "development"
app.config['DEBUG'] = True


plugins = ('EC2Plugin',)
xray_recorder.configure(service='Ecommerce Frontend',
                plugins=plugins, sampling=False)
XRayMiddleware(app, xray_recorder)
patch_all()


cw_logs_client = boto3.client('logs',
    aws_access_key_id='enter-key',
    aws_secret_access_key='enter-secret',
    region_name='us-west-2')

USER_SERVICE_URL='http://172.31.22.221:5000'
PRODUCT_SERVICE_URL='http://172.31.23.59:5000'
ORDER_SERVICE_URL='http://172.31.24.13:5000'
REVIEW_SERVICE_URL='http://172.31.16.29:5000'

login_manager.init_app(app)
login_manager.login_message = "Please login"
login_manager.login_view = "login"

# Log group and stream names
log_group_name = 'my-log-group'
log_stream_name = 'my-log-stream'

# Check if log group exists, if not then create it
log_groups = cw_logs_client.describe_log_groups()
log_group_exists = False
for group in log_groups['logGroups']:
    if group['logGroupName'] == log_group_name:
        log_group_exists = True
        break
if not log_group_exists:
    cw_logs_client.create_log_group(logGroupName=log_group_name)

# Check if log stream exists, if not then create it
log_streams = cw_logs_client.describe_log_streams(
                    logGroupName=log_group_name)
log_stream_exists = False
for stream in log_streams['logStreams']:
    if stream['logStreamName'] == log_stream_name:
        log_stream_exists = True
        break
if not log_stream_exists:
    cw_logs_client.create_log_stream(logGroupName=log_group_name,
                            logStreamName=log_stream_name)

# Create CloudWatch Logs handler
cw_handler = CloudWatchLogHandler(log_group=log_group_name,
                stream_name=log_stream_name,
                boto3_client=cw_logs_client)
```

```python
# Configure logger and add handler
logger = logging.getLogger()
logger.setLevel(logging.INFO)
logger.addHandler(cw_handler)

@app.route('/', methods=['GET'])
@xray_recorder.capture('home')
def home():
    logger.info('Handling home page')
    if current_user.is_authenticated:
        session['order'] = OrderClient.get_order_from_session()

    try:
        products = ProductClient.get_products()
    except:
        products = {
            'results': []
        }
    document = xray_recorder.current_segment()
    if 'user' in session:
        document.put_annotation('user', session['user'])
        document.put_metadata('page', 'home page')
        document.put_metadata('user', session['user'])

    user_name, user_photo = get_user_name_photo()
    return render_template('home.html', products=products,
        user_name = user_name, user_photo=user_photo)

@app.route('/login', methods=['GET', 'POST'])
@xray_recorder.capture('login')
def login():
    logger.info('Handling login')
    if current_user.is_authenticated:
        return redirect(url_for('home'))
    form = LoginForm()
    if request.method == "POST":
        if form.validate_on_submit():
            user = UserClient.post_login(form)
            if user:
                session['user_api_key'] = user['api_key']
                session['user'] = user
                order = OrderClient.get_order()
                if order.get('result', False):
                    session['order'] = order['result']
                return redirect(url_for('home'))
            else:
                flash('Cannot login', 'error')
        else:
            flash('Errors found', 'error')
    return render_template('login.html', form=form)
```

Figure 11.15 shows a trace map of the E-Commerce application in AWS X-Ray. Figure 11.16 shows a list view with details of the nodes of the E-Commerce application.

Trace Map   5m   15m   30m   1h   3h

Q *Filter by X-Ray group*   +   Q *Select a node*

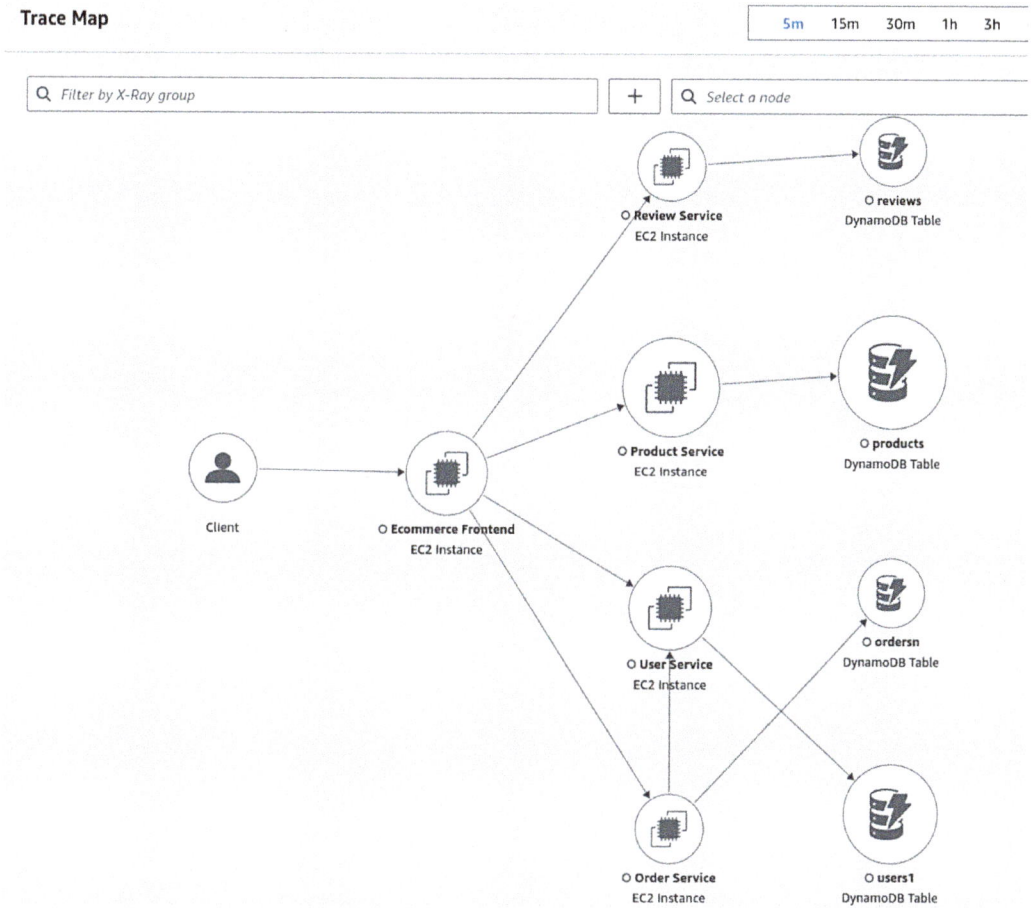

Figure 11.15: Trace map of E-Commerce application in AWS X-Ray

Nodes (8)   View on map   View logs ☑   View traces   View dashboard

Q *Enter the node name or look for a property*   ⟨ 1 ⟩ ⊚

	Name ▲	Type ▽	Alarms ▽	Latency (avg) ▽	Faults (5xx) ▽	Requests ▽
○	Order Service	EC2 Instance	-	26ms	0.00/min	2.20/min
○	orders	DynamoDB Table	-	10ms	0.00/min	6.00/min
○	Product Service	EC2 Instance	-	5ms	0.00/min	23.60/min
○	products	DynamoDB Table	-	4ms	0.00/min	47.20/min
○	Review Service	EC2 Instance	-	24ms	0.00/min	0.80/min
○	reviews	DynamoDB Table	-	22ms	0.00/min	1.60/min
○	User Service	EC2 Instance	-	20ms	0.00/min	6.20/min
○	users	DynamoDB Table	-	6ms	0.00/min	12.80/min

Figure 11.16: List view showing nodes of E-Commerce application in AWS X-Ray

Figure 11.17 shows the traces for the E-Commerce application in AWS X-Ray. The user can filter by service/node, time range, error, etc.

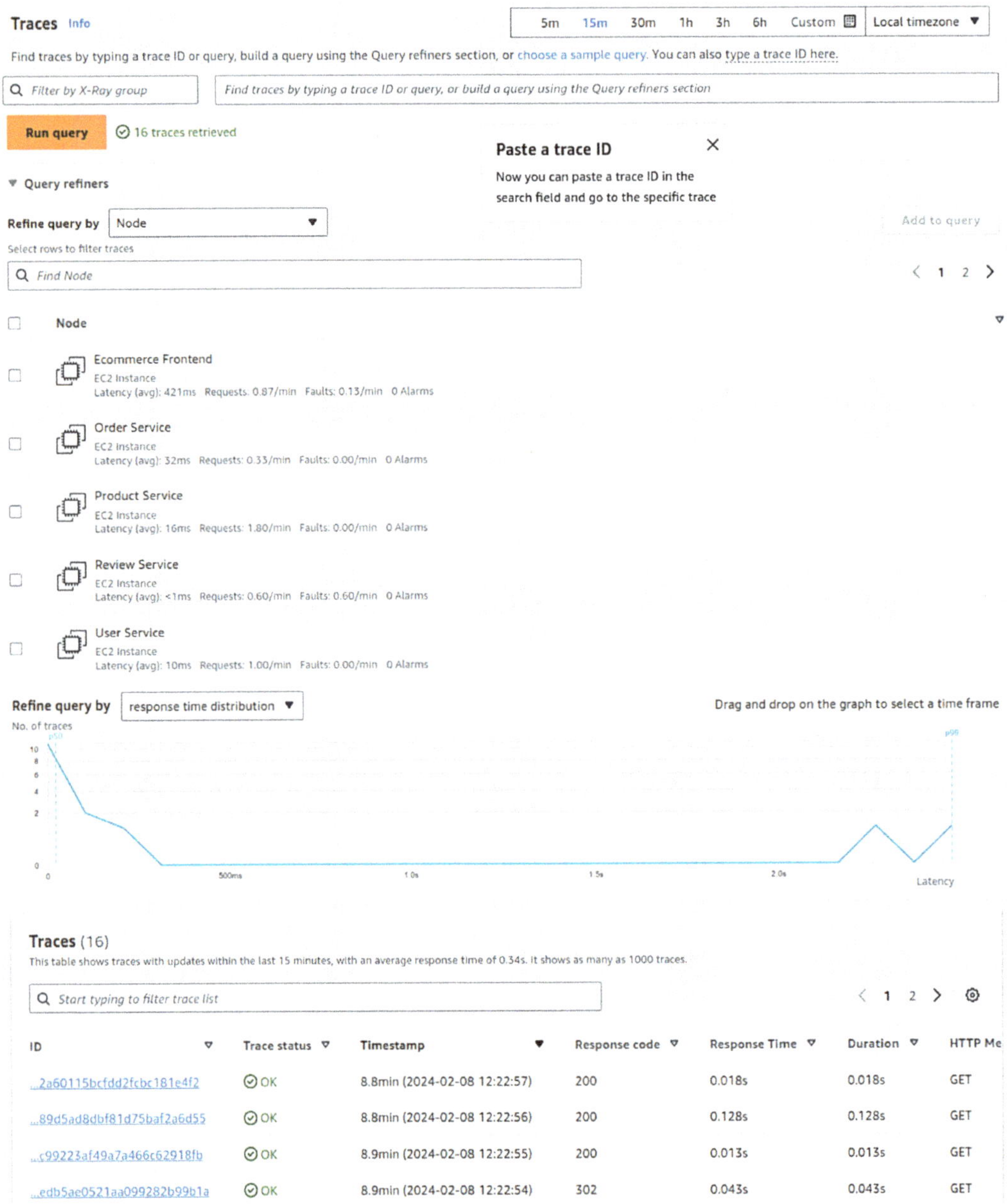

Figure 11.17: Viewing traces for E-Commerce application in AWS X-Ray

Figure 11.18 shows a detailed view of a single trace. The segments timeline provides a timeline view in trace detail with all segments in that trace shown sequentially. The segment detail pane on the right shows the segment metadata and other details.

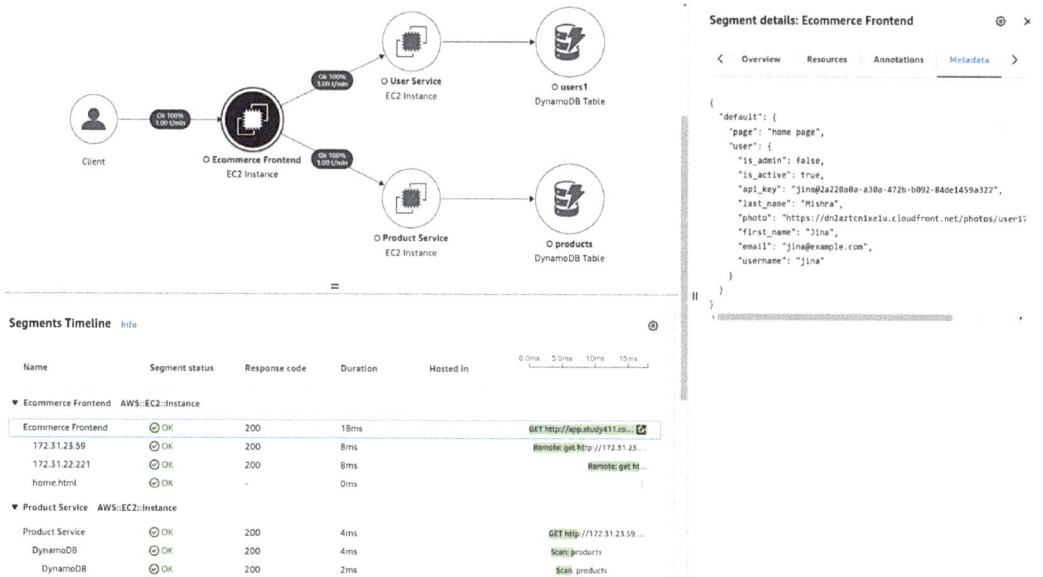

Figure 11.18: View trace details and metadata in AWS X-Ray

Figure 11.19 shows the metrics tab for the frontend service with metrics like requests, errors, and latency distributions.

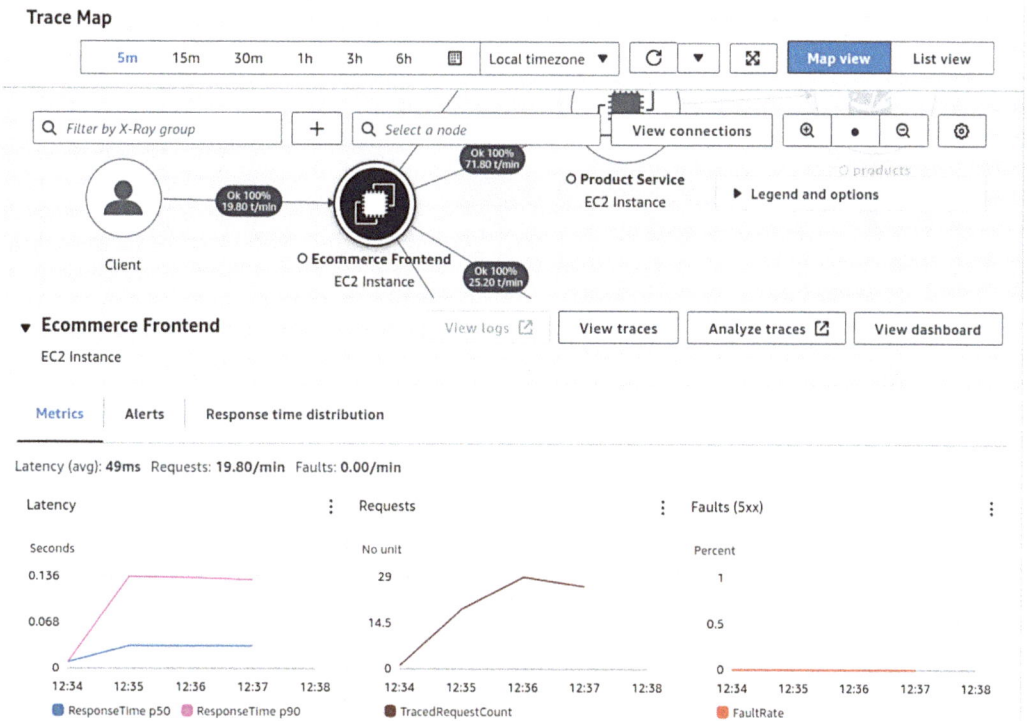

Figure 11.19: Viewing service metrics in AWS X-Ray

Figure 11.20 shows an example of detecting and analyzing a fault in the review service of the E-Commerce application with X-Ray.

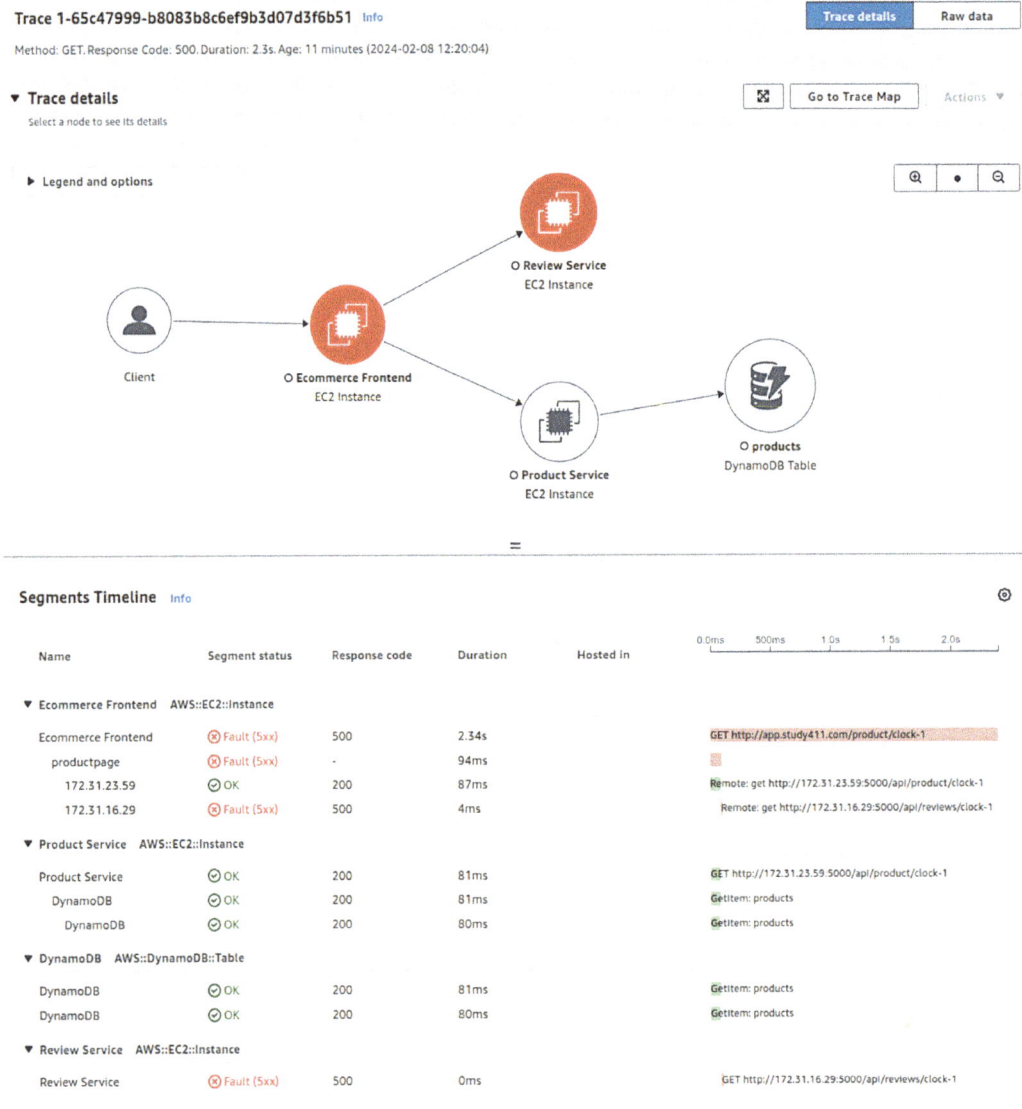

Trace 1-65c47999-b8083b8c6ef9b3d07d3f6b51 Info   Trace details   Raw data

Method: GET. Response Code: 500. Duration: 2.3s. Age: 11 minutes (2024-02-08 12:20:04)

▼ **Trace details**   Go to Trace Map   Actions ▾

Select a node to see its details

▶ Legend and options

Client — O Ecommerce Frontend (EC2 Instance) — O Review Service (EC2 Instance), O Product Service (EC2 Instance) — O products (DynamoDB Table)

Segments Timeline Info

Name	Segment status	Response code	Duration	Hosted in	
▼ Ecommerce Frontend	AWS::EC2::Instance				
Ecommerce Frontend	⊗ Fault (5xx)	500	2.34s		GET http://app.study411.com/product/clock-1
productpage	⊗ Fault (5xx)	-	94ms		
172.31.23.59	⊘ OK	200	87ms		Remote: get http://172.31.23.59:5000/api/product/clock-1
172.31.16.29	⊗ Fault (5xx)	500	4ms		Remote: get http://172.31.16.29:5000/api/reviews/clock-1
▼ Product Service	AWS::EC2::Instance				
Product Service	⊘ OK	200	81ms		GET http://172.31.23.59:5000/api/product/clock-1
DynamoDB	⊘ OK	200	81ms		Getitem: products
DynamoDB	⊘ OK	200	80ms		Getitem: products
▼ DynamoDB	AWS::DynamoDB::Table				
DynamoDB	⊘ OK	200	81ms		Getitem: products
DynamoDB	⊘ OK	200	80ms		Getitem: products
▼ Review Service	AWS::EC2::Instance				
Review Service	⊗ Fault (5xx)	500	0ms		GET http://172.31.16.29:5000/api/reviews/clock-1

Figure 11.20: Detecting and analyzing faults with AWS X-Ray

Figure 11.21 shows a CloudWatch log group and stream with the logs generated by the frontend service.

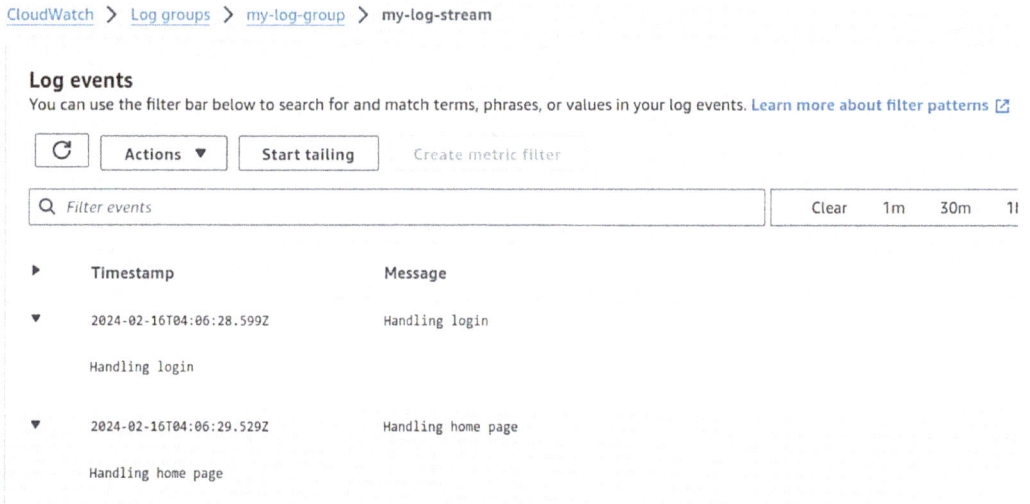

Figure 11.21: Viewing application logs in CloudWatch

Distributed tracing with X-Ray and centralized logging with CloudWatch Logs provide invaluable observability and monitoring capabilities for microservices applications on AWS. Using these services, teams can gain insights into request flows, system health, errors, and operational patterns to optimize the complex microservices architecture. The automated collection and retention of tracing and log data gives DevOps teams visibility into both real-time performance and historical trends. This enables faster troubleshooting, streamlined debugging, and data-driven refinement of microservices environments.

11.8   Best Practices for Observability and Monitoring

In this section, we describe some best practices for Microservices Observability and Monitoring as recommended by AWS in its Well-Architected Framework.

- **Implement Centralized Logging**: Capture logs from all microservices components, including application code, frameworks, application servers, and infrastructure. Send the logs to a centralized logging solution like Amazon CloudWatch Logs. This allows for easy aggregation and analysis of logs across all services.
- **Instrument Code for Custom Metrics**: Instrument the microservices code to capture custom application metrics like request rates, response times, and error rates. Publish these metrics to a monitoring system like Amazon CloudWatch, and set alarms on critical metrics to receive notifications of issues.
- **Implement Distributed Tracing**: Use a distributed tracing solution like AWS X-Ray to track requests across microservices and identify performance bottlenecks or errors. Correlate traces with logs and metrics for deeper insights into the behavior of the microservices.
- **Visualize Metrics on Dashboards**: Create dashboards to visualize key metrics like request rates, error rates, latencies, and saturation levels for each microservice. This

will provide quick insights into the health and performance of the services.

- **Monitor Infrastructure Metrics**: Monitor infrastructure metrics from underlying hosts or containers, such as CPU, memory, and disk usage, to identify resource bottlenecks. Automatically scale resources based on utilization to avoid performance issues.
- **Perform Synthetic Transactions**: Implement synthetic transactions that simulate user interactions with the microservices at regular intervals. Alert if these transactions fail or if their performance degrades, allowing you to proactively monitor services from a customer's perspective.
- **Implement Service Discovery and Load Balancing**: Set up service discovery and load balancing across microservice instances to distribute traffic and remove unhealthy hosts from the load balancing rotation. Monitor the health of service instances to ensure optimal performance.
- **Monitor End-to-End Transactions**: In addition to monitoring individual microservices, monitor end-to-end business transactions that span multiple services. Gain insights into inter-service communications and identify performance issues across the entire system.
- **Align Monitoring with SLIs/SLOs**: Define Service Level Indicators (SLIs) and Service Level Objectives (SLOs) for your microservices, and align your monitoring metrics and alerts to track whether these objectives are being met. Monitor service-level indicators like uptime, latency, and error rates to ensure you are meeting your SLOs.
- **Ensure High Availability for Monitoring Systems**: Replicate metrics, logs, and traces to multiple availability zones to ensure that your monitoring system remains highly available. Send notifications via multiple channels, such as email, SMS, and chat apps, to ensure reliable alerting.
- **Automate Failover and Rollback**: Automate the failover of unhealthy microservices instances and the rollback of bad releases to accelerate recovery and minimize human intervention. Use service health metrics to trigger automated actions like auto-scaling, rerouting traffic, and self-healing instances.
- **Continuously Analyze Telemetry Data**: Regularly analyze the telemetry data (metrics, logs, and traces) collected from your microservices to identify new metrics or dimensions worth monitoring, improve the context and quality of logs, expand tracing to newer services and test cases, and increase the depth of synthetic monitoring scenarios. Treat observability and monitoring as a continuous process that evolves alongside your application.
- **Implement Chaos Engineering**: Regularly conduct chaos engineering experiments to simulate various failure scenarios, such as service disruptions, network latency, or resource constraints. This helps you understand how your microservices behave under duress and identify potential weaknesses in your monitoring and observability practices.
- **Monitor Dependency Services**: Monitor the performance and availability of external services and third-party APIs that your microservices depend on. Identify issues with these dependencies that could be impacting the performance or reliability of your microservices, and set up alerts to notify you when these dependencies are experiencing problems.

- **Track Usage and Cost**: Monitor the usage and costs associated with your microservices, including resources consumed (such as compute, storage, and network), API calls, and third-party service usage. This will help you optimize resource utilization, identify cost-saving opportunities, and ensure that you are staying within your budget.
- **Implement Canary Deployments**: Use canary deployments to gradually roll out new versions of your microservices to a small subset of users or traffic. Monitor the performance and behavior of the canary instances closely before promoting the new version to your entire production environment. This approach helps you catch issues early and minimizes the impact of bad releases.
- **Establish Observability Ownership**: Assign clear ownership and responsibility for observability and monitoring within your organization. Establish a dedicated team or assign individuals to champion observability best practices, continuously improve monitoring capabilities, and drive the adoption of new observability tools and techniques across your microservices ecosystem.
- **Ensure Data Retention and Archival**: Establish data retention policies for your logs, metrics, and traces based on your organization's compliance and auditing requirements. Implement archival solutions, such as Amazon S3 or Amazon Glacier, to store this data cost-effectively for long-term analysis and historical insights.
- **Integrate with Collaboration Tools**: Integrate your monitoring and alerting systems with collaboration tools like Slack to facilitate real-time communication and collaboration during incidents or performance issues. Share dashboard links, alert notifications, and troubleshooting information within these channels to enable faster response times and more effective incident management.
- **Educate and Train Teams**: Provide regular training and education to your development, operations, and support teams on microservices observability and monitoring best practices, tools, and techniques. Ensure that everyone involved in building, deploying, and maintaining microservices has a solid understanding of the observability principles and practices that enable successful operations.

Summary

In this chapter, we covered the importance of observability and monitoring techniques for microservices architectures. We explained how the decentralized nature of microservices brings complexity in debugging and troubleshooting. To address this, microservices must provide observability into their runtime behavior and expose monitoring data. We described the three core pillars of observability - logs, metrics, and traces. Logs record discrete events and provide rich contextual details useful for debugging. Metrics are numerical measurements that reveal trends and enable alerting on anomalies. Traces follow the journey of a request across services to pinpoint latency issues. We explained logging techniques for microservices. A centralized logging pipeline is required to aggregate logs across services. We compared push and pull logging models. For metrics, we described how to instrument services to expose Prometheus metrics. These metrics can be visualized in Grafana dashboards. Next, we covered distributed tracing concepts like traces, spans, and context propagation. OpenTelemetry provides open-source libraries for instrumenting microservices and exporting traces to backends like Jaeger. We demonstrated how Jaeger enables analyzing request flows, volumes, and errors. Next, we described using Prometheus for metrics collection and Grafana for visualization. We showed how to configure Prometheus scrape jobs and create Grafana dashboards that provide insights into service health and performance. Next, we explained how AWS X-Ray is used for distributed tracing of microservices on AWS. X-Ray traces requests across services and records a detailed service map. We demonstrated how CloudWatch Logs enables centralized logging by aggregating logs across services. Observability and monitoring are critical for operating resilient microservices in production. By instrumenting services for logs, metrics, and traces, teams gain deep visibility into the runtime behavior and internal workings of microservices systems. This enables rapid debugging, informed optimization, and proactive incident response.

12 MICROSERVICES SECURITY

THIS CHAPTER COVERS

- Authentication and Authorization
- API Gateway and Perimeter Security
- Secure Communication
- Data Security
- Monitoring and Logging
- Secure Development Practices
- Secure Deployment and Automation
- Incident Response and Disaster Recovery
- Containerization and Isolation
- Least Privilege and Separation of Concerns
- Network Security
- Vulnerability Management
- Chaos Engineering for Microservices Security
- Security Automation
- DevSecOps for Microservices Security

12.1   Introduction

Microservices architecture has emerged as a popular approach for building modern, cloud-native applications. While microservices offer numerous benefits, they also introduce new security challenges that must be addressed to ensure the overall integrity and security of the system.

In a microservices architecture, the attack surface expands as multiple services communicate across boundaries. The distributed nature and increased number of service interactions make it more challenging to implement centralized security controls, monitoring, and logging. Authentication, authorization, and secure communication become more complex to manage across different services.

This chapter will cover the best practices and strategies for securing microservices architectures. Figure 12.1 provides an overview of the security best practices for microservices. By implementing these best practices, organizations can build resilient and secure microservices architectures that can withstand potential threats and attacks.

Best Practice	Description
Authentication and Authorization	Implement centralized identity and access management with JWT/OAuth2, RBAC, service-to-service authentication (mTLS and API keys)
API Gateway and Perimeter Security	Enforce security at API gateway level with rate limiting, IP whitelisting, throttling, authentication, and authorization
Secure Communication	Encrypt communication between services (TLS, gRPC); use service meshes and messaging queues.
Data Security	Classify data sensitivity, encrypt data, secure storage, and access controls
Monitoring and Logging	Collect centralized logs, metrics, and traces; analyze for security events/anomalies
Secure Development Practices	Secure coding, security code reviews, security testing (SAST, DAST, and penetration testing)
Secure Deployment and Automation	Infrastructure as Code (CloudFormation, Terraform), security testing in pipelines
Incident Response and Disaster Recovery	Develop and test incident response and disaster recovery plans
Containerization and Isolation	Deploy microservices as containers for isolation and resource controls
Least Privilege and Separation of Concerns	Grant minimum permissions, separate by access levels
Network Security	Segment networks, isolate environments (VPCs, NACLs), encrypt in-network traffic
Vulnerability Management	Regular scanning, patching, updates for vulnerabilities
Chaos Engineering	Introduce failures to test resilience, identify weaknesses
Security Automation	Automate security tasks - scanning, compliance, configurations

Figure 12.1: Microservices security best practices

12.2 Authentication and Authorization

In a microservices architecture, where multiple services communicate with each other to perform complex tasks, secure authentication and authorization mechanisms are crucial for protecting the system from unauthorized access and maintaining data integrity. Implementing a centralized identity and access management (IAM) system is the foundation for managing user identities, authentication, and authorization across all microservices.

12.2.1 Centralized Identity and Access Management (IAM)

A centralized IAM system is responsible for creating, managing, and revoking user identities, as well as controlling access to resources based on user roles and permissions. This centralized approach ensures consistency in identity and access management across the entire microservices architecture.

An IAM system provides the following core functionalities:

- **User Registration and Identity Management**: The IAM system handles the creation, modification, and deletion of user identities. This includes processes for onboarding new users, updating user information, and revoking user access when necessary.
- **Authentication**: The IAM system provides mechanisms for authenticating users, verifying their identities, and issuing credentials (e.g., access tokens) that can be used for subsequent requests to microservices.
- **Authorization**: The IAM system manages user roles, permissions, and access control policies. It determines which users or groups are authorized to access specific resources or perform specific actions within the microservices architecture.
- **Auditing and Logging**: The IAM system maintains a comprehensive audit trail of user activities, including successful and failed authentication attempts, changes to user identities and permissions, and resource access logs. This information is essential for security monitoring, incident response, and compliance purposes.
- **Integration with Microservices**: The IAM system provides APIs or integration points that allow microservices to authenticate users, validate access tokens, and retrieve user information and permissions for authorization purposes.

By centralizing identity and access management, organizations can ensure consistent and secure user authentication and authorization across all microservices, reducing the complexity and potential vulnerabilities associated with managing identities and permissions in a distributed manner.

12.2.2 Token-based Authentication

Token-based authentication is a widely adopted approach for securing microservices architectures. It involves issuing a security token, such as a JSON Web Token (JWT) or an OAuth2 access token, to a user or client upon successful authentication. This token can then be included in subsequent requests to microservices as proof of identity and authorization.

JSON Web Tokens (JWTs) are compact, self-contained tokens that carry information about the user's identity, permissions, and other relevant data in a digitally signed format. JWTs consist of three parts as follows:

- **Header**: Contains metadata about the token, such as the algorithm used for signing the token.

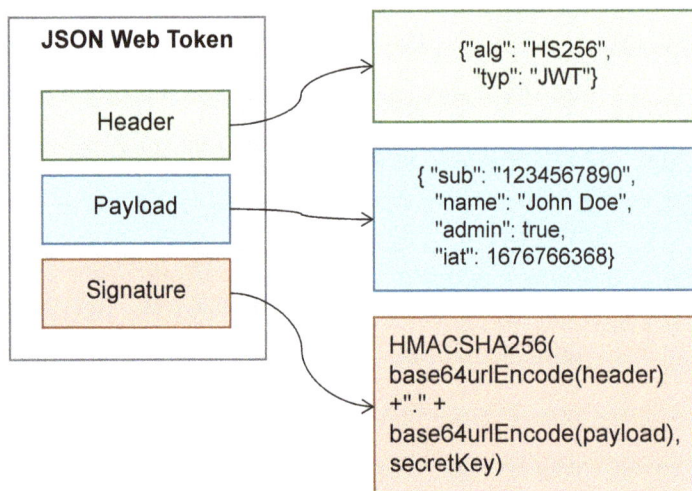

Figure 12.2: JSON Web Token (JWT)

- **Payload**: Contains claims or statements about the user, such as their identity, roles, permissions, and expiration time.
- **Signature**: A digital signature that ensures the integrity and authenticity of the token.

Figure 12.2 shows the parts of a JWT. When a user or client authenticates with the IAM system, the IAM system generates a JWT containing the user's identity, roles, and other relevant information. This JWT is then returned to the user or client and should be included in the *Authorization* header of subsequent requests to microservices.

Each microservice can validate the JWT using a shared secret or public key to verify its integrity and authenticity. The microservice can then extract the user's identity and permissions from the JWT and use this information to make authorization decisions.

OAuth2 is another widely adopted protocol for token-based authentication and authorization. OAuth2 is particularly useful in scenarios where users or clients need to access resources owned by third-party services or applications. It allows users to grant limited access to their resources without sharing their credentials with the third-party service.

Figure 12.3 shows the OAuth flow. The user tries to access a feature in the client app that requires authorization to the cloud app resources. The client app redirects the user to the cloud app's authorization server with a request to access specific resources. The user logs in to the cloud app and is prompted to grant permission to the client. If approved, the authorization server issues an access token to the client app. This token serves as proof of delegated authorization. The client app presents the access token to the cloud app when making API calls to access the user's protected resources. The cloud app verifies the token is valid and the requested scopes are permitted. If authorization checks pass, the cloud app responds with the requested resource. The user retains control over the authorization, with the ability to revoke access. The client app does not handle the user's credentials directly. This allows secure access delegation in the OAuth flow.

Both JWTs and OAuth2 offer advantages in terms of scalability, flexibility, and security compared to traditional session-based authentication methods.

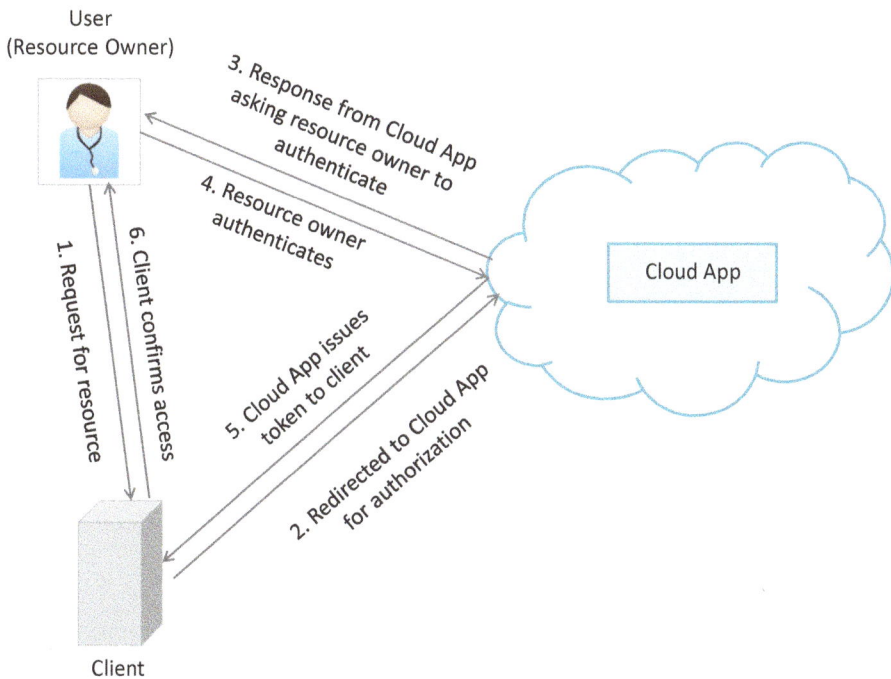

Figure 12.3: OAuth flow

12.2.3 Role-based Access Control (RBAC)

Role-based access control (RBAC) is a widely adopted model for managing user permissions and access to resources within a microservices architecture. RBAC assigns permissions to roles rather than directly to individual users, simplifying the management of user access and reducing the risk of granting excessive privileges.

In an RBAC model, the following components are defined:

- **Roles**: Roles represent a set of permissions or privileges within the system. Examples of roles could include Administrator, User, Manager, or Guest.
- **Permissions**: Permissions define the actions or operations that a user can perform on specific resources. These can include read, write, update, delete, or other specific actions relevant to the microservices architecture.
- **Resources**: Resources are the objects or entities within the system that require access control, such as microservices, data, files, or specific API endpoints.
- **Users**: Users represent individual identities within the system, such as employees, customers, or external partners.

Figure 12.4 shows the components of RBAC. The user management, user role assignments, and access policy management can be part of a centralized IAM system. The IAM system maps users to one or more roles based on their responsibilities and access requirements. Each role is then assigned a set of permissions that determine the actions that role can perform on specific resources.

When a user authenticates and obtains an access token (such as JWT or OAuth2 token), the token contains information about the user's identity and their assigned roles. As the

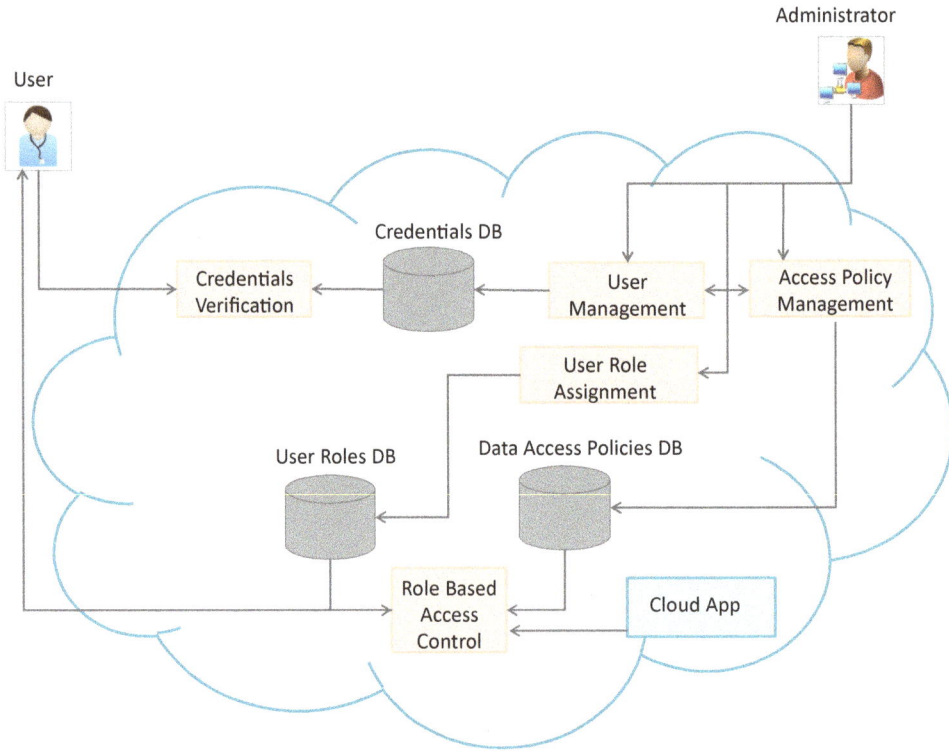

Figure 12.4: Role-based access control (RBAC) system

user interacts with different microservices, the microservices can inspect the access token to determine the user's roles and the associated permissions. This allows the microservices to make authorization decisions based on the user's assigned roles and the specific permissions required to perform an action on a resource.

For example, consider a scenario where a user with the Administrator role attempts to access a microservice that manages user accounts. The microservice would validate the user's access token, extract the user's role information, and check if the Administrator role has the necessary permissions to perform user management operations (e.g., create, update, or delete user accounts). If the permissions match, the microservice would allow the user to perform the requested action; otherwise, it would deny access.

RBAC simplifies the management of user permissions by decoupling them from individual user identities. Instead of assigning permissions directly to each user, administrators can define roles and assign permissions to those roles. As new users are added to the system, they can be assigned to appropriate roles, inheriting the associated permissions without the need for manual configuration for each user.

12.2.4   Service-to-Service Authentication

In a microservices architecture, services often need to communicate with each other to perform complex tasks or retrieve data. Securing these inter-service communications is essential to prevent unauthorized access, data tampering, and other security risks. Mutual TLS (mTLS) and API keys are two common approaches for implementing secure service-to-service authentication in a microservices architecture.

Mutual TLS, also known as two-way TLS or client-certificate authentication, is an extension of the standard TLS protocol that provides mutual authentication between the client and server. In the context of microservices, mTLS ensures that both the client (microservice) and the server (microservice) authenticate each other before establishing a secure communication channel.

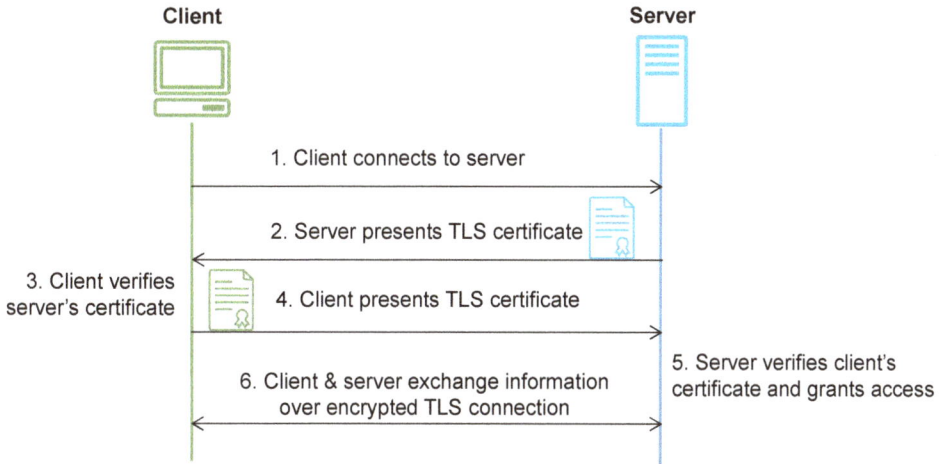

Figure 12.5: mTLS flow

Figure 12.5 shows the mTLS flow. The steps in this flow are as follows:

1. The client (microservice) initiates a TLS handshake with the server (microservice) and presents its client certificate, which contains its identity and public key.
2. The server validates the client's certificate against a trusted certificate authority (CA) and verifies the client's identity.
3. If the client's certificate is valid, the server responds with its own server certificate, which contains its identity and public key.
4. The client validates the server's certificate against a trusted CA and verifies the server's identity.
5. If both certificates are valid, a secure TLS connection is established, and the client and server can exchange data securely.

mTLS provides strong mutual authentication and encryption for communication between microservices. Each microservice has a unique identity (certificate) that is verified by the other party, preventing unauthorized services from accessing sensitive data or functionality.

API keys is another approach for service-to-service authentication where a unique key or token is assigned to each microservice or client. The API key acts as a shared secret between the client and the server, allowing the server to verify the client's identity and authorize access to resources or APIs. When a client (microservice) wants to access a server (microservice), it includes the API key in the request headers or as a query parameter. The server validates the API key against a list of authorized keys and grants or denies access based on the validity of the key. API keys can be generated, rotated, and revoked by a centralized system.

12.3 API Gateway and Perimeter Security

In a microservices architecture, the API gateway serves as the single entry point for all
external requests, acting as a reverse proxy and enforcing security policies. It provides a
consistent and secure interface for clients to access microservices, hiding the complexity of
the underlying architecture. The API gateway plays a crucial role in securing the perimeter of
the microservices system, protecting against various threats and ensuring the overall security
of the architecture. Figure 12.6 shows the API Gateway functionality.

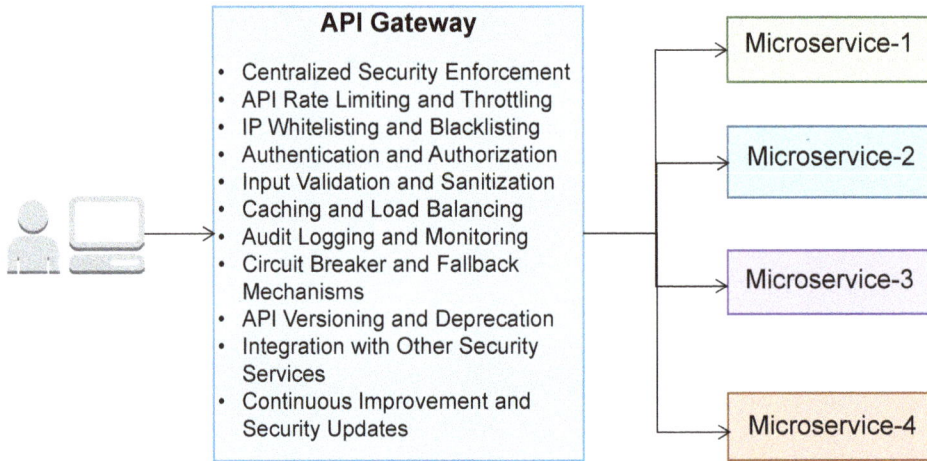

Figure 12.6: API Gateway

API Gateway provides the following functionality:

- **Centralized Security Enforcement**: The API gateway centralizes the enforcement
  of security policies, reducing the need for individual microservices to implement
  security controls independently. By consolidating security functions, the API gateway
  simplifies the overall security management and reduces the risk of inconsistent or
  misconfigured security controls across different microservices.
- **API Rate Limiting and Throttling**: The API gateway implements API rate limiting
  and throttling to protect microservices from abuse and Distributed Denial of Service
  (DDoS) attacks. Rate limiting controls the number of requests a client can make
  within a specific time frame, preventing clients from overwhelming the system with
  excessive requests. Throttling limits the number of concurrent requests a client can
  make, ensuring fair distribution of resources and preventing resource exhaustion. By
  implementing rate limiting and throttling, the API gateway effectively manages the
  flow of incoming requests and prevents malicious actors from monopolizing system
  resources.
- **IP Whitelisting and Blacklisting**: The API gateway implements security controls
  such as IP whitelisting and blacklisting to restrict access to microservices based on
  the client's IP address. Whitelisting involves creating a list of trusted IP addresses or
  address ranges that are allowed to access the microservices, while blacklisting involves
  maintaining a list of known malicious or untrusted IP addresses that are denied access.

By implementing IP whitelisting and blacklisting, the API gateway can effectively control access to microservices and mitigate the risk of unauthorized access from untrusted sources.

- **Authentication and Authorization**: The API gateway is responsible for enforcing authentication and authorization policies for all incoming requests. It should validate the authenticity of the client and determine whether the client has the necessary permissions to access the requested resources or microservices. The API gateway can implement various authentication mechanisms, such as API keys, JSON Web Tokens (JWT), or OAuth2, to validate client identities. Once authenticated, the API gateway applies role-based access control (RBAC) or attribute-based access control (ABAC) policies to authorize access to specific microservices or resources based on the client's roles, permissions, or attributes.

- **Input Validation and Sanitization**: The API gateway implements input validation and sanitization mechanisms to protect microservices from malicious inputs, such as cross-site scripting (XSS), SQL injection, or other types of code injection attacks. By validating and sanitizing incoming requests, the API gateway can prevent malicious payloads from reaching the microservices and potentially compromising the system.

- **Caching and Load Balancing**: In addition to security enforcement, the API gateway provides caching and load balancing capabilities to improve the overall performance and scalability of the microservices architecture. Caching frequently accessed responses can reduce the load on microservices and improve response times for clients. Load balancing distributes incoming requests across multiple instances of a microservice, ensuring high availability and fault tolerance.

- **Audit Logging and Monitoring**: The API gateway implements comprehensive audit logging and monitoring mechanisms to track all incoming requests, responses, and security-related events. Audit logs provide valuable insights into system behavior and can be used for security analysis, incident response, and compliance purposes. Monitoring tools can be integrated with the API gateway to collect metrics, track performance, and generate alerts for anomalous behaviors or security incidents.

- **Circuit Breaker and Fallback Mechanisms**: The API gateway implements circuit breakers and fallback mechanisms to enhance the resilience and reliability of the microservices architecture. Circuit breakers prevent cascading failures by isolating failing microservices, while fallback mechanisms provide alternative responses or graceful degradation when microservices are unavailable. These mechanisms help maintain the overall availability and stability of the system, even in the face of partial failures.

- **API Versioning and Deprecation**: As microservices evolve over time, the API gateway supports versioning and deprecation of APIs. Versioning allows clients to continue using older versions of an API while new versions are introduced, enabling smooth transitions and backward compatibility. Deprecation allows for the controlled retirement of outdated APIs, providing clients with ample notice and time to migrate to newer versions.

- **Integration with Other Security Services**: The API gateway integrates with other security services and tools to enhance the overall security posture of the microservices architecture. This may include integrating with Web Application Firewalls (WAFs) for additional security controls, Security Information and Event Management (SIEM) systems for centralized logging and threat detection, or external authentication and authorization services for enhanced identity management.

- **Continuous Improvement and Security Updates**: The API gateway and its security controls are continuously evaluated and updated to address emerging threats, vulnerabilities, and best practices. Regular security updates, patches, and configuration changes are applied to ensure the API gateway remains secure and effective in protecting the microservices architecture.

By implementing these security controls and best practices at the API gateway level, organizations can establish a robust perimeter security layer for their microservices architecture, effectively protecting against a wide range of threats and ensuring the overall security and resilience of the system.

12.4   Secure Communication

Ensuring secure communication between microservices is crucial to maintain the confidentiality, integrity, and availability of data and services. Microservices often communicate with each other over insecure networks, making them susceptible to various threats, such as eavesdropping, tampering, and man-in-the-middle attacks. To mitigate these risks, several best practices and techniques can be employed to secure communication between microservices.

12.4.1   Encryption in Transit

Encrypting communication between microservices is essential to prevent unauthorized access and eavesdropping. Transport Layer Security (TLS) is the most widely used protocol for securing communication over the internet. TLS provides confidentiality through encryption, ensuring that data transmitted between microservices cannot be read by unauthorized parties. It also ensures integrity by verifying that the data has not been tampered with during transmission.

To implement TLS, both the client and server microservices must support the protocol and have valid TLS certificates. These certificates are used to establish a secure connection and verify the identity of the communicating parties. It is crucial to use trusted Certificate Authorities (CAs) to issue these certificates and follow industry best practices for managing and rotating them.

In addition to TLS, other secure protocols like gRPC can be used for communication between microservices. gRPC is a modern, high-performance remote procedure call (RPC) framework that supports several features, including transport security using TLS. It provides a secure and efficient way to define service contracts and communicate between microservices, making it a popular choice for building microservices architectures.

12.4.2   Secure Communication Channels

Secure communication channels, such as service meshes or secure messaging systems, can be used to facilitate secure communication between microservices. These channels provide a reliable and secure way to transmit data between microservices, even in complex and distributed architectures.

Service Meshes

A service mesh is an infrastructure layer that provides a dedicated communication network for microservices. It acts as a transparent, application-aware proxy that secures communication between services through features like mTLS, traffic encryption, and policy enforcement. Popular service mesh solutions include Istio, Linkerd, and Consul Connect. Service meshes simplify the implementation of secure communication by providing a centralized control plane for managing security policies and certificates across all microservices.

Messaging Systems

Secure messaging systems like Apache Kafka, RabbitMQ, or Amazon Simple Queue Service (SQS) can be used to facilitate communication between microservices through asynchronous messaging. These systems provide secure channels for transmitting messages, enabling microservices to communicate without direct connections. Transport-level security mechanisms like TLS can be used to encrypt communication between microservices and the messaging system, ensuring confidentiality and integrity.

12.4.3 Auditing and Monitoring

Auditing and monitoring secure communication between microservices are essential for detecting potential security breaches and ensuring compliance with security policies. Logging and monitoring tools like AWS CloudTrail, Amazon CloudWatch, or third-party solutions like Datadog or Splunk can be used to collect and analyze logs and metrics related to communication between microservices.

Auditing logs should capture information about successful and failed connections, encryption status, authentication and authorization events, and any security-related errors or anomalies. Regular analysis of these logs can help identify potential security issues, such as unauthorized access attempts, insecure configurations, or protocol downgrade attacks.

Monitoring tools can track metrics related to secure communication, such as the number of TLS connections, encryption algorithms used, certificate expiration dates, and performance of secure communication channels. Alerting mechanisms should be implemented to notify security teams of potential security incidents or breaches related to communication between microservices.

12.5 Data Security

In a microservices architecture, data is often distributed across multiple services, databases, and storage systems. Ensuring the security of this distributed data is crucial to protect sensitive information and maintain compliance with data privacy regulations. Several best practices and techniques can be employed for data security in microservices architectures, including data classification, encryption, secure storage, and access controls.

12.5.1 Data Classification and Sensitivity

The first step in securing data is to classify it based on its sensitivity and criticality. Data classification helps organizations understand the value and potential impact of data breaches, allowing them to prioritize security controls and resources.

Common data classification levels include:
- **Public data**: Information that is generally available and does not require any confidentiality measures.
- **Internal data**: Information that is intended for internal use only and should not be shared outside the organization.
- **Confidential data**: Sensitive information that could cause significant harm if disclosed, such as personal data, financial records, or intellectual property.
- **Restricted data**: Highly sensitive data that requires strict access controls and protection measures, such as trade secrets, classified government information, or personal health records.

By classifying data into these categories, organizations can determine the appropriate security measures and access controls required for each data type.

12.5.2 Encryption at Rest and in Transit

Encryption is a fundamental security control that protects data from unauthorized access by converting it into an unreadable format using cryptographic algorithms and keys.

Encryption at Rest

Encryption should be applied to data at rest (stored data). For data at rest, industry-standard algorithms like AES-256 should be used to encrypt sensitive data before storing it. Full disk encryption or encryption at the file/object level should be applied to databases, storage volumes, and backups. Secure practices for key generation, storage, and rotation are critical for robust encryption of stored data. Cloud services like AWS Key Management Service facilitate secure key management and encryption for data at rest.

Encryption in Transit

Encryption should be applied to data in transit (data being transmitted between systems or services). For data in transit, Transport Layer Security (TLS) or protocols like gRPC enable encryption for all communication between microservices and external clients. End-to-end encryption should be implemented for sensitive data moving through messaging systems and event streams. Secure communication channels like service meshes or secure WebSockets allow for encrypted communication between microservices.

12.5.3 Secure Storage Solutions

Cloud providers offer secure storage solutions that can be integrated into microservices architectures. For example:
- **AWS S3 (Simple Storage Service)**: AWS S3 provides object storage with built-in encryption, access controls, and audit logging. S3 supports server-side encryption using AWS-managed keys or customer-managed keys for added control and security.
- **AWS Secrets Manager**: AWS Secrets Manager is a secure storage solution for secrets, such as API keys, database credentials, and other confidential information. It provides automatic rotation, encryption at rest, and auditing capabilities.
- **HashiCorp Vault**: Vault is an open-source secrets management tool that can be used to securely store and access sensitive data, such as API keys, passwords, and certificates. Vault supports various storage backends, cloud providers, and on-premises systems.

When using these secure storage solutions, follow best practices for access controls, credential rotation, and auditing to maintain the security of stored data.

12.5.4 Data Access Controls and Restricted Access

Implementing access controls and restricting access to sensitive data is crucial to prevent unauthorized access and data breaches. Role-Based Access Control (RBAC) and attribute-based access control (ABAC) are two common approaches for managing data access in microservices architectures.

Role-Based Access Control (RBAC)

For RBAC, define roles with specific permissions and access levels based on job functions or responsibilities. RBAC assigns users to appropriate roles based on their job requirements and the principle of least privilege. It implements access policies that grant or deny access to specific data resources based on user roles and permissions.

Attribute-Based Access Control (ABAC)

For ABAC, define access policies based on user attributes (e.g., job title, department, location) and resource attributes (e.g., data classification, resource owner). Grant or deny access to resources based on the evaluation of these attributes against defined access policies. ABAC provides fine-grained control over data access and enables dynamic access decisions based on context.

In addition to access controls, organizations should implement the principle of least privilege, granting users and microservices only the minimum necessary access to perform their intended functions. Regularly reviewing and auditing access to sensitive data can help identify and mitigate potential security risks.

12.5.5 Data Lifecycle Management and Disposal

Implementing secure data lifecycle management practices ensures that sensitive data is protected throughout its lifecycle, from creation to disposal. This includes:

- **Data Creation**: Ensure that sensitive data is created and handled securely from the start, following best practices for encryption, secure storage, and access controls.
- **Data Use and Processing**: Implement controls to monitor and log access to sensitive data, ensuring that it is used only for authorized purposes and by authorized entities.
- **Data Sharing and Transfer**: If sensitive data needs to be shared or transferred, ensure that it is encrypted, and secure communication channels are used to prevent unauthorized access or interception.
- **Data Archiving and Backup**: Sensitive data that needs to be archived or backed up should be encrypted, and backups should be stored securely with access controls and audit logging.
- **Data Disposal and Deletion**: When sensitive data is no longer needed, it should be securely deleted or disposed of to prevent unauthorized access.

By following best practices for data classification, encryption, secure storage, access controls, and data lifecycle management, organizations can effectively protect sensitive data and maintain compliance with data privacy regulations.

12.6   Monitoring and Logging

In a microservices architecture, where applications are composed of multiple, independent services communicating with each other, monitoring, logging, and incident response play a crucial role in maintaining a secure and resilient system. By implementing robust monitoring and logging practices, organizations can gain valuable insights into the behavior of their microservices, detect security incidents promptly, and respond effectively to mitigate potential threats.

12.6.1   Centralized Logging and Monitoring

To effectively monitor and log microservices, organizations should adopt a centralized approach. By collecting logs, metrics, and traces from all microservices into a centralized platform, teams can gain a comprehensive view of the entire system's behavior. Centralized logging and monitoring solutions, such as AWS CloudWatch, Elasticsearch, Logstash, and Kibana (ELK Stack), or third-party solutions like Datadog or Splunk, can be used to collect and analyze logs from multiple sources.

Centralized logging solutions should be designed to handle the high volume of logs generated by microservices. Logs can be filtered, aggregated, and analyzed to identify patterns, trends, and anomalies. Effective log management practices, such as log rotation and compression, should be implemented to optimize storage and performance.

12.6.2   Collecting Logs, Metrics, and Traces

Microservices generate various types of logs, including application logs, infrastructure logs, and security logs. Application logs provide insights into the behavior of individual microservices, including errors, warnings, and debugging information. Infrastructure logs, such as container logs or Kubernetes logs, provide information about the underlying infrastructure supporting the microservices. Security logs, including authentication and authorization logs, access logs, and firewall logs, provide valuable data for detecting security incidents and breaches.

In addition to logs, collecting metrics and traces is essential for understanding the performance and behavior of microservices. Metrics, such as CPU utilization, memory usage, and request latency, provide insights into the health and performance of microservices. Traces, which capture the end-to-end flow of requests through multiple microservices, help identify bottlenecks and performance issues.

By collecting logs, metrics, and traces, organizations can gain a comprehensive understanding of their microservices architecture, which is essential for identifying and addressing security issues.

12.6.3   Log Analysis and Security Event Detection

Once logs, metrics, and traces are collected, organizations should implement log analysis practices to identify security events and anomalies. Log analysis can be performed using various techniques, including:
  • **Pattern and anomaly detection**: By analyzing log patterns and identifying deviations from normal behavior, organizations can detect potential security incidents or breaches. Machine learning algorithms and statistical methods can be used to identify anomalous

behavior, such as sudden spikes in traffic, unusual access patterns, or unexpected error rates.

- **Security information and event management (SIEM)**: SIEM solutions, like AWS Security Hub, Splunk, or QRadar, correlate security events from multiple sources, including logs, network traffic, and endpoint data. SIEM solutions can detect known attack patterns, identify potential threats, and provide insights into the overall security posture of the organization.
- **Security log analysis**: Analyzing security logs, such as authentication and authorization logs, network firewall logs, and intrusion detection system (IDS) logs, can help identify unauthorized access attempts, policy violations, and potential security breaches.
- **User behavior analytics (UBA)**: UBA solutions analyze user behavior patterns and detect anomalies that may indicate compromised accounts, insider threats, or malicious activity. By establishing baselines for normal user behavior, UBA can identify deviations that may require further investigation.

By implementing log analysis practices, organizations can identify security incidents promptly, reducing the potential impact of threats and enabling a more effective incident response.

12.6.4 Alerting and Notifications

Implementing effective alert mechanisms is crucial for timely incident response. Organizations should define alert policies based on security events, performance thresholds, and other relevant criteria. Alert policies should consider the severity and potential impact of incidents, ensuring that high-priority alerts are promptly addressed.

Alert mechanisms can include email notifications, messaging services, or integration with incident response platforms. Alerts should be sent to designated security teams or incident response personnel, ensuring that the right people are notified and can take appropriate action.

Upon receiving an alert, organizations should follow a well-defined incident response plan. An incident response plan outlines the steps to be taken to contain, investigate, and mitigate security incidents.

12.7 Secure Development Practices

Secure development practices are crucial in ensuring the overall security of a microservices architecture. Adopting a comprehensive approach to security throughout the software development lifecycle (SDLC) helps identify and mitigate potential vulnerabilities early, reducing the risk of introducing security flaws into production environments.

12.7.1 Secure Coding Practices and Code Reviews

Adhering to secure coding practices is fundamental to developing secure microservices. Developers should be trained in secure coding principles and best practices, including input validation, output encoding, proper error handling, and secure use of cryptographic libraries. Adopting coding guidelines and standards, such as the OWASP Secure Coding Practices, can help developers write secure code and avoid common vulnerabilities.

Conducting regular code reviews is essential for identifying and addressing security issues early in the development process. Code reviews should focus on identifying potential security vulnerabilities, adherence to secure coding practices, and compliance with security requirements. Automated tools like static code analysis (SCA) can assist in detecting security vulnerabilities, such as SQL injection, cross-site scripting (XSS), and buffer overflows, in the source code.

12.7.2   Security Testing

Security testing is a critical practice that should be integrated into the development lifecycle to identify and address security vulnerabilities before they are introduced into production environments. There are several types of security testing that should be employed:

- **Static Application Security Testing (SAST)**: SAST tools analyze the source code and byte code of applications to identify potential security vulnerabilities. These tools can detect issues like SQL injection, cross-site scripting (XSS), and insecure cryptographic practices.
- **Dynamic Application Security Testing (DAST)**: DAST tools simulate real-world attacks against running applications, testing for vulnerabilities like SQL injection, XSS, and broken authentication. These tools can help identify vulnerabilities that may not be detected during static analysis.
- **Penetration Testing**: Penetration testing, also known as ethical hacking, involves manually simulating real-world attacks to identify and exploit vulnerabilities in the system. Penetration testing can help uncover vulnerabilities that may be missed by automated tools and provide a more comprehensive assessment of the overall security posture.
- **API Security Testing**: As microservices communicate primarily through APIs, testing the security of these APIs is crucial. API security testing involves validating the authentication and authorization mechanisms, input validation, error handling, and adherence to security best practices for API design and implementation.

12.7.3   Secure Libraries, Frameworks, and Tools

Choosing secure libraries, frameworks, and tools is essential to reduce the risk of introducing known vulnerabilities into microservices. Developers should stay informed about the latest security advisories and vulnerabilities related to the third-party libraries and frameworks they use. When selecting libraries, frameworks, and tools, developers should consider factors like the maturity of the project, the frequency of security updates, and the size of the user community. Using popular and widely-adopted libraries and frameworks can increase the likelihood of timely security updates and community support.

12.7.4   Dependency Management and Patching

Effective dependency management is crucial in microservices architectures, where each microservice may have its own set of dependencies. Maintaining an up-to-date inventory of all dependencies, including direct and transitive dependencies, is essential for managing security risks. Developers should regularly check for updates to dependencies and promptly apply security patches to address known vulnerabilities. Automating dependency management and patching can help streamline this process and ensure consistent and timely updates across all microservices.

12.7.5 Secure Software Development Lifecycle (SSDLC)

Adopting a Secure Software Development Lifecycle (SSDLC) ensures that security is integrated into every phase of the software development process, from requirements gathering and design to testing, deployment, and maintenance. Different phases in SSDLC are as follows:

- **Design**: In the design phase, security requirements should be defined, ánd threat modeling should be conducted to identify potential security risks and appropriate countermeasures. Security controls and mitigation strategies should be incorporated into the design to address identified risks.
- **Development**: During the development phase, secure coding practices, code reviews, and security testing should be implemented to identify and address security vulnerabilities proactively.
- **Testing**: In the testing phase, a comprehensive security testing strategy should be employed, including static analysis, dynamic analysis, penetration testing, and other techniques to identify and remediate security issues.
- **Deployment**: The deployment phase should include secure deployment practices, such as applying the principle of least privilege, implementing secure configuration management, and automating security tasks like vulnerability scanning and compliance checks.
- **Maintenance**: In the maintenance phase, regular patching and updates should be applied to address newly discovered vulnerabilities. Security monitoring and incident response procedures should be established to detect and respond to security incidents.

By adopting an SSDLC and integrating security practices throughout the software development lifecycle, organizations can significantly reduce the risk of introducing security vulnerabilities into their microservices and maintain a strong security posture.

12.7.6 Security Champions and Training

Establishing security champions within development teams can promote a culture of security and facilitate the adoption of secure development practices. Security champions can serve as subject matter experts, providing guidance and support to their teams on security-related issues, and acting as liaisons between development and security teams. Regular security training for developers is essential to raise awareness and keep them informed about the latest security threats, vulnerabilities, and best practices. Training should cover topics such as secure coding practices, security testing techniques, secure design principles, and incident response procedures.

12.8 Secure Deployment and Automation

In a microservices architecture, the deployment and automation processes play a critical role in ensuring the secure and reliable delivery of software. With multiple microservices interacting with each other, a single vulnerability or misconfiguration can compromise the entire system. Therefore, it's essential to implement secure deployment practices and automation to mitigate security risks, maintain consistency, and enhance the overall security posture.

12.8.1 Secure Deployment Pipelines

Deployment pipelines define the stages and workflows for building, testing, and deploying microservices. A secure deployment pipeline should incorporate the following:

- **Continuous Integration (CI) and Continuous Deployment (CD)**: Implement CI/CD practices to automate the build, test, and deployment processes. This ensures that changes to microservices are consistently built, tested, and deployed in a controlled and repeatable manner.

- **Version Control**: Use a secure version control system (e.g., Git) to manage code changes and track the history of microservices. Implement strict access controls, audit logging, and branch protection policies to enhance security and prevent unauthorized modifications.

- **Code Reviews**: Implement mandatory code reviews to identify potential security vulnerabilities, coding errors, and deviations from secure coding practices. Automated code analysis tools (e.g., SonarQube, Checkmarx) can be integrated into the pipeline to identify common security issues and code quality problems.

- **Security Testing**: Integrate various security testing practices into the deployment pipeline, such as static application security testing (SAST), dynamic application security testing (DAST), and penetration testing. These tests should be performed at different stages of the pipeline to identify and remediate security vulnerabilities before deployment.

- **Automated Vulnerability Scanning**: Implement automated vulnerability scanning for microservices and their dependencies using tools like AWS Inspector or OWASP Dependency-Check. These tools should be integrated into the deployment pipeline to identify known vulnerabilities in application code, third-party libraries, and container images.

- **Compliance Checks**: Automate compliance checks against industry standards (e.g., PCI-DSS, HIPAA, GDPR) and organizational security policies to ensure that microservices meet the required security and regulatory requirements.

- **Approval Gates**: Implement manual or automated approval gates at critical stages of the deployment pipeline to enforce review and approval processes. This ensures that microservices meet predefined security criteria and pass necessary checks before being promoted to the next stage or production deployment.

- **Audit Logging**: Enable detailed audit logging throughout the deployment pipeline to capture all activities, changes, approvals, and security events. These logs can be used for forensics, incident response, and compliance auditing purposes.

12.8.2 Infrastructure as Code (IaC)

Infrastructure as Code (IaC) enables the management and provisioning of infrastructure resources using declarative configuration files. IaC tools like AWS CloudFormation or Terraform provide a consistent, repeatable, and automated approach to infrastructure deployment. IaC tools provide the following functionalities:

- **Secure Configuration Management**: IaC tools are used to define infrastructure configurations, security controls, and policies as code. This ensures that infrastructure resources are consistently provisioned with the desired security configurations, reducing the risk of misconfigurations and drift.

- **Immutable Infrastructure**: IaC tools help in adopting an immutable infrastructure approach, where infrastructure components are treated as disposable and replaced entirely during updates or changes. This reduces the risk of accidental modifications or drift, as infrastructure components are always deployed from a known, secure baseline.
- **Automated Deployment**: IaC tools help in automating the deployment of infrastructure resources, ensuring consistent and repeatable infrastructure provisioning across multiple environments (e.g., development, staging, and production).
- **Validate Configurations**: Validation checks and testing should be done to ensure that infrastructure configurations adhere to security best practices and organizational policies. Tools like AWS Config Rules, AWS Control Tower, or third-party solutions like Bridgecrew can be used to validate and enforce secure configurations.
- **Separation of Environments**: Maintain separate infrastructure configurations and deployments for different environments (e.g., development, staging, and production). This separation ensures that changes in one environment do not inadvertently impact other environments and reduces the risk of accidental exposure or data leakage.

12.8.3 Secure Automation and Orchestration

Automation and orchestration tools like AWS Lambda, AWS Step Functions, or Apache Airflow enable the automation of various tasks, including deployment, scaling, and monitoring of microservices. These tools should be configured and used securely to maintain a robust and secure microservices architecture. The following best practices should be adopted for secure automation and orchestration:

- **Secure Execution Environment**: Ensure that automation and orchestration tools run in a secure execution environment, such as AWS Lambda or AWS Fargate, which provides isolation, resource constraints, and secure runtime environments.
- **Least Privilege Access**: Apply the principle of least privilege when granting permissions and access to automation and orchestration tools. These tools should only have the minimum necessary permissions and access to resources required to perform their intended functions.
- **Secure Event Sources**: When using event-driven architectures, validate and secure the event sources that trigger automation and orchestration workflows. Implement input validation, filtering, and whitelisting to prevent unauthorized or malicious events from triggering workflows.
- **Audit Logging and Monitoring**: Enable detailed audit logging and monitoring for automation and orchestration tools to capture all activities, events, and security-related information. These logs can be used for forensics, incident response, and compliance auditing purposes.
- **Secure Communication**: Ensure that communication between automation and orchestration tools and other microservices is secure, using encrypted channels (e.g., TLS or gRPC) and authentication mechanisms (e.g., API keys or JWT).
- **Secure Configuration Management**: Store and manage configuration files, scripts, and other artifacts used by automation and orchestration tools in a secure version control system.
- **Regularly Update and Patch**: Regularly update and patch automation and orchestration tools, runtime environments, and dependencies to address known vulnerabilities.

12.9   Incident Response and Disaster Recovery

Having robust incident response and disaster recovery capabilities is crucial for securing microservices architectures. The distributed nature of microservices introduces complexity in responding to security incidents and recovering from failures. Organizations need to implement comprehensive incident response and disaster recovery plans tailored to microservices environments.

Incident Response

An effective incident response plan is essential for quickly detecting, containing, and remediating security incidents in a microservices architecture. Key aspects of incident response for microservices include:

- Monitor and analyze logs from all microservices using centralized logging and monitoring tools. Configure alerts to notify response teams of potential incidents.
- Implement automated response procedures to isolate and shutdown compromised microservices. For example, integrate incident response tools with orchestrators like Kubernetes to automatically quarantine affected containers.
- Develop an incident classification and severity matrix focused on microservices. Classify incidents based on impact to specific microservices and data assets.
- Maintain a regularly updated inventory of all microservices and their functions. This helps identify the blast radius of incidents and prioritize response efforts.
- Implement Chaos Engineering techniques like fault injection to proactively test and improve incident response capabilities for microservices failures.
- Ensure incidents can be quickly contained within microservice boundaries to avoid lateral movement across the ecosystem. Microservice isolation and segmentation model limits damage.
- Re-deploy compromised microservices from secure templates and configurations to quickly restore services after cleanup. Automated deployment pipelines facilitate rapid rebuilding.
- Perform forensic analysis of compromised microservices in an isolated environment to determine the root cause and identify security gaps.
- Establish clear responsibilities and train incident response teams on microservices-specific response procedures.
- Update response plans periodically based on learnings from real incidents and response tests. Continuously improve the plan.

Disaster Recovery

Microservices architectures need flexible and scalable disaster recovery capabilities to handle different types of failures. Key aspects of disaster recovery for microservices include:

- Implement disaster recovery solutions for each microservice rather than a single monolithic system. Recovery time objectives (RTO) and recovery point objectives (RPO) should be defined per service.
- Leverage Infrastructure-as-Code tools like Terraform to provision replaceable and automated disaster recovery environments.
- Utilize microservices versioning and blue-green deployments for easy rollback to

stable versions in case of disasters.

- Set up redundant microservices across multiple availability zones to provide high availability during outages.
- For stateful microservices, implement asynchronous data replication and automatic failover across availability zones.
- Build capabilities to independently scale up instances of critical microservices during disasters to meet increased demand.
- Test disaster recovery plans through structured DR drills. Simulate different disasters like availability zone (AZ) outages, data corruption, service unavailability, and execute failover procedures.
- Integrate Chaos Engineering experiments into disaster recovery testing by inducing controlled failures and observing system behavior.
- Evaluate gaps in the ability to meet RTO/RPOs for microservices. Address issues and continue improving recovery processes.
- Analyze disaster scenarios that can cross microservice boundaries. Develop organization-wide DR strategies for widespread disasters.
- Validate backup systems and integrity of replicated microservices data through test restores. Ensure no data loss from backups.

With comprehensive incident response and disaster recovery plans tailored to microservices, organizations can rapidly respond to security events and recover from failures while minimizing disruption to services. Conducting regular response testing and drills is key to keeping plans effective.

12.10   Containerization and Isolation

Containers play a crucial role in modern microservices architectures, providing a consistent runtime environment and isolation between different components of the system. By leveraging container technologies like Docker and Kubernetes, organizations can achieve better security, scalability, and portability for their microservices.

12.10.1   Consistent Runtime Environments

Containers facilitate the creation of immutable runtime environments, ensuring that each microservice runs in a consistent and predictable state. Unlike traditional monolithic applications, where components often share resources and dependencies, each microservice runs in its own isolated container, encapsulating all the necessary libraries, tools, and configuration files required for its operation. This approach leads to several security benefits:

- **Reduced Attack Surface**: By encapsulating each microservice in a separate container, the potential attack surface is significantly reduced. If one microservice is compromised, the impact is limited to that specific container, minimizing the risk of spreading to other parts of the system.
- **Reproducible Environments**: Containers provide a consistent and reproducible runtime environment across different stages of the development lifecycle, from local development to production deployment. This consistency helps identify and address security issues early in the development process, reducing the risk of introducing vulnerabilities during deployment or runtime.

- **Simplified Dependency Management**: Each container contains only the required dependencies and libraries for the specific microservice, minimizing the risk of conflicting or outdated dependencies. This approach simplifies dependency management and reduces the potential for vulnerabilities introduced by third-party libraries or frameworks.
- **Controlled Resource Utilization**: Containers enable fine-grained control over resource allocation and utilization, allowing organizations to limit the resources (CPU, memory, network, etc.) available to each microservice. This isolation prevents one microservice from monopolizing shared resources, which could lead to denial of service or performance degradation for other components.

12.10.2 Container Isolation and Security

Container technologies like Docker and Kubernetes provide several security features to ensure isolation between containers and protect against unauthorized access or resource sharing.

- **Kernel Namespaces**: Kernel namespaces provide isolation between different aspects of the container's runtime, such as process trees, network interfaces, and mount points. This isolation prevents containers from accessing or modifying resources outside their designated namespace, enhancing security and preventing unintended interactions between containers.
- **Control Groups (cgroups)**: Control groups, or cgroups, enable resource allocation and limitation for containers, ensuring that each container receives only the resources it requires. This feature prevents resource exhaustion attacks, where a malicious container attempts to consume an excessive amount of system resources, impacting the performance of other containers or the host system.
- **Secure Computing Mode (seccomp)**: Seccomp is a kernel feature that enables filtering and restricting system calls available to containers. By applying seccomp profiles, organizations can limit the system calls that containers can execute, reducing the attack surface and potential for privilege escalation or system compromise.
- **AppArmor and SELinux**: AppArmor and SELinux are Linux kernel security modules that provide mandatory access control (MAC) functionality. These modules can be used to define fine-grained security policies that restrict the access and permissions granted to containers, providing an additional layer of security beyond traditional discretionary access control (DAC).
- **User Namespaces**: User namespaces provide a way to map user and group IDs within a container to different IDs on the host system. This feature enables running containers with non-root user privileges, reducing the impact of potential privilege escalation attacks and limiting the consequences of a compromised container.

12.10.3 Patching and Updating Container Images

Regular patching and updating of container images are essential to address known vulnerabilities and security issues in the underlying operating system, libraries, and dependencies. Adopting a continuous integration and continuous deployment (CI/CD) pipeline with automated vulnerability scanning and patching helps ensure that microservices are running on up-to-date and secure container images.

Organizations should establish processes and tools for:

- **Vulnerability Scanning**: Regularly scan container images for known vulnerabilities in the underlying operating system, libraries, and application dependencies. Tools like Trivy, Anchore, or Clair can be integrated into the CI/CD pipeline to scan images and identify vulnerabilities.
- **Patch Management**: Implement a patch management process to address identified vulnerabilities by updating container images with the latest security patches and updates. This process should include rebuilding container images with updated base images, libraries, or application code, and pushing the updated images to a secure container registry.
- **Automated Deployment**: Automate the deployment of updated container images to production environments, ensuring that microservices are running on the latest patched and secure images. Kubernetes and other container orchestration platforms provide mechanisms for rolling updates and deployments, allowing organizations to update microservices with minimal downtime.
- **Vulnerability Monitoring**: Monitor security advisories and vulnerability databases to stay informed about newly discovered vulnerabilities in the software components and dependencies used within container images. Implement processes to quickly assess the impact of these vulnerabilities on your microservices and prioritize patching efforts accordingly.
- **Immutable Infrastructure**: Adopt an immutable infrastructure approach, where container images are treated as immutable artifacts. When a vulnerability is discovered, a new container image is built, incorporating the necessary security patches, and deployed to replace the existing vulnerable container instances. This approach ensures that microservices always run on consistent and secure container images.

By leveraging containerization and isolation technologies, organizations can enhance the security of their microservices architectures. Immutable containers, consistent runtime environments, container isolation features, and regular patching and updating of container images contribute to a more secure and resilient microservices ecosystem.

12.11 Least Privilege and Separation of Concerns

Applying the principle of least privilege is one of the most important security best practices for microservices architectures. It involves granting each microservice only the minimum set of permissions, access, and capabilities needed to perform its intended function. This limits the blast radius in case a service is compromised, preventing the attacker from pivoting to other parts of the system. Some key ways to implement least privilege for microservices include:

12.11.1 Identity and Access Management

Have a central identity provider that manages authentication and issues security tokens to validate each microservice's identity. Services should use these tokens to communicate with each other and access resources like databases, rather than sharing long-lived credentials. Use role-based access control (RBAC) to assign permissions to microservices based on their roles and implement authorization checks before allowing access. For example, an

Order microservice may have read and write access to the orders database, while the User microservice only gets read access.

12.11.2   OS-Level Security and Containerization

Run microservices inside containers with locked-down capabilities using technologies like Docker and Kubernetes. This creates isolation between containers and applies the principle of least privilege to processes and resources like storage, memory, and network. Use Kubernetes pod security policies, AppArmor, Seccomp, or tools like OPA Gatekeeper to restrict container capabilities and prevent privilege escalation attacks. For example, the User microservice containers do not need access to the Docker daemon or host file system. Removing such unneeded privileges shrinks the attack surface.

12.11.3   Secure Service-to-Service Communication

Microservices should only expose the minimal set of APIs required for other authorized services to integrate with them. Avoid overly permissive APIs. Implement service authentication using mTLS, API keys, or OAuth integrations so that only trusted first-party services in the architecture can directly access other microservices. Do not expose services directly to third-party apps or public internet traffic without additional security controls. Encrypt service-to-service communication using TLS or mutual TLS (mTLS) to prevent eavesdropping or man-in-the-middle attacks during transit between microservices.

12.11.4   Access Controls on Shared Resources

Use attribute-based access control (ABAC) or centralized authorization services to implement fine-grained access controls when multiple microservices share common resources like databases, message queues, object storage, or caching layers. Grant each microservice least privilege access only to the specific data objects it requires. For example, the User table may grant read access to Order and Product services, but not allow modifying user data from those services. The User service manages updates to that table.

12.11.5   Separation of Concerns and Domain Decomposition

The separation of concerns principle recommends decomposing large, complex systems into discrete, specialized components that focus on a single business capability or domain entity. In microservices, this takes the form of breaking monoliths into autonomous services aligned to domains like Customers, Orders, Payments, etc. Services become experts in their domain and only have access to resources required for their domain. For example, an E-Commerce application may have separate microservices for managing inventory, orders, customer profiles, recommendations, and payment processing. Instead of a single process touching multiple areas, requests flow across services focused on their own domain. This decomposition limits the impact of bugs or security issues. A flaw in the recommendation algorithm only affects that service, not order processing or payment data.

12.11.6   Microservice Domains as Trust Boundaries

Aligning services to business domains also creates trust boundaries from a security perspective. Instead of one large application with access to everything, you have secure domains with clear interfaces interacting via APIs. Domains authorize and integrate with other domains safely via APIs and contracts. Changes or issues are localized to domains due to loose coupling. This enables implementing least privilege controls at a domain level in addition to the individual microservice level. Fine-grained scoping of access and trust zones mapped to business capabilities reduces risk and exposure. Security teams gain visibility into protection considerations and attack surface for each domain.

Applying least privilege and separation of concerns is critical for limiting the attack surface and improving the security posture of microservices architectures. Taken together, these best practices reduce the likelihood of widespread lateral compromise, enforce tiered access controls, and facilitate accountability across decentralized services.

12.12   Network Security

In a microservices architecture, network security is crucial for ensuring secure communication between services and preventing unauthorized access to resources. By implementing various network security controls, you can create secure boundaries between microservices, isolate traffic, and protect against potential attacks.

12.12.1   Network Segmentation and Isolation

Network segmentation is the process of dividing a network into multiple smaller networks, known as segments or subnets. Each segment is isolated from the others, preventing direct communication between them. This isolation helps contain the impact of a potential security breach within a single segment, reducing the overall risk to the system.

In a microservices architecture, network segmentation can be achieved using Virtual Private Clouds (VPCs) and Network Access Control Lists (NACLs). VPCs are logically isolated virtual networks within a cloud provider's infrastructure, allowing you to define your own network topology and control traffic flow. NACLs are stateless firewalls that act as a virtual firewall for your VPCs, controlling inbound and outbound traffic at the subnet level.

By segmenting your microservices into different VPCs or subnets based on their function, sensitivity, or access levels, you can effectively isolate them from each other and limit the potential spread of security incidents. For example, you might have separate VPCs for public-facing services, internal services, and sensitive data processing services, each with its own set of security controls and access rules.

12.12.2   Secure Communication Protocols

Within the same network, microservices should communicate using secure protocols to protect data in transit. HTTPS and WebSocket Secure (WSS) are two commonly used protocols for secure communication within a microservices architecture.

12.12.3   Firewalls and Network Access Controls

Firewalls and network access controls are essential for controlling inbound and outbound traffic to and from microservices. These controls can be implemented at various levels, such as network firewalls, host-based firewalls, and cloud-based security groups.

Network firewalls are typically deployed at the perimeter of a network, controlling traffic flow between the internal network and external networks. They can be configured to allow or block specific types of traffic based on predefined rules, such as source and destination IP addresses, ports, and protocols. Host-based firewalls are software-based firewalls that run on individual servers or containers, controlling traffic to and from the specific host or container. These firewalls can provide granular control over network traffic, allowing or blocking specific ports and protocols for individual microservices.

Cloud providers, such as AWS, offer security groups, which act as virtual firewalls for instances within a VPC. Security groups control inbound and outbound traffic at the instance level, allowing you to define rules based on IP addresses, ports, and protocols. These rules can be tailored to the specific needs of each microservice, providing an additional layer of network security.

By carefully configuring firewalls and network access controls, you can restrict access to microservices from unauthorized sources, limit the exposure of sensitive ports and services, and enforce consistent network security policies across your microservices architecture.

12.12.4 Network Monitoring and Logging

Monitoring and logging network traffic are essential for identifying potential security incidents and analyzing network behavior. Network monitoring tools, such as Wireshark or tcpdump, can capture and analyze network traffic, providing visibility into communication patterns and potential security threats. Centralized logging solutions, like AWS CloudWatch Logs or third-party tools like Splunk or Graylog, can collect and analyze logs from various network devices, including firewalls, routers, and load balancers. These logs can provide valuable insights into network traffic, security events, and potential vulnerabilities.

By monitoring network traffic and analyzing logs, you can detect anomalies, identify unauthorized access attempts, and investigate security incidents. Regular reviews of network logs and monitoring data can help you identify patterns, trends, and potential security risks, allowing you to proactively address them and strengthen your network security posture.

12.12.5 Network Access Controls for External Connections

In addition to securing communication within the internal network, it's crucial to implement appropriate network access controls for external connections to a microservices architecture. This includes controlling access from external clients, third-party services, and even public internet access.

For external clients accessing your microservices, you should implement network access controls to restrict access based on source IP addresses, geographic regions, or specific client applications. IP whitelisting, which allows only a predefined set of IP addresses or IP address ranges to access your services, can be an effective way to control external access.

When integrating with third-party services or APIs, it's essential to ensure secure communication by using secure protocols like HTTPS and implementing network access controls. You can restrict access to specific IP addresses or ranges for these third-party services and enforce secure communication channels.

If your microservices require public internet access, such as for communicating with external APIs or services, you should implement appropriate network security controls. This may include using NAT gateways or internet gateways within your VPC to control and monitor outbound internet traffic. Additionally, you can implement egress filtering, which allows you to control outbound traffic based on predefined rules, such as destination IP addresses, ports, and protocols.

12.12.6 Network Security Automation

As the complexity of your microservices architecture grows, managing network security configurations manually can become increasingly challenging. To streamline network security management and reduce the risk of human error, it's essential to adopt automation and Infrastructure-as-Code practices.

Infrastructure-as-Code (IaC) tools, such as AWS CloudFormation or Terraform, allow you to define your entire network infrastructure, including VPCs, subnets, security groups, and network access controls, as code. By treating your infrastructure as code, you can version control your network configurations, apply consistent security settings across multiple environments, and automate the deployment and management of your network infrastructure. Security as code principles can be applied to network security configurations, where security policies, access controls, and network settings are defined as code and version controlled alongside your infrastructure code. This approach ensures that security configurations are consistently applied across all environments and can be easily reviewed, audited, and updated as needed.

Automation tools, such as Ansible, Chef, or Puppet, can be used to automate the deployment and management of network security configurations. These tools can enforce security policies, apply software updates and patches, and manage network access controls across multiple microservices and environments.

By adopting Infrastructure-as-Code and security automation practices, you can streamline the management of your network security configurations, reduce the risk of human error, and ensure consistent and repeatable deployment of security controls across your microservices architecture.

12.13 Vulnerability Management

Vulnerabilities in software systems are an inevitable reality that organizations must address proactively. Microservices architectures, with their distributed and componentized nature, introduce additional complexities in vulnerability management. A comprehensive vulnerability management program is essential to identify, assess, and mitigate potential vulnerabilities in a timely manner, ensuring the security and resilience of microservices.

12.13.1 Understanding Vulnerabilities

A vulnerability is a weakness or flaw in a software system that can be exploited by an attacker to gain unauthorized access, compromise data, or disrupt operations. Vulnerabilities can exist in various components of a microservices architecture, including:

- **Microservices code**: Vulnerabilities can arise from coding errors, misconfigurations, or insecure coding practices, such as using vulnerable libraries or frameworks, improper input validation, or insufficient authentication and authorization mechanisms.
- **Third-party libraries and frameworks**: Microservices often rely on third-party libraries and frameworks, which can introduce vulnerabilities if not patched or updated

regularly. These dependencies need to be monitored and managed to address potential security issues.

- **Infrastructure and runtime environments**: Vulnerabilities can exist in the underlying infrastructure, such as operating systems, containers, orchestration platforms (such as Kubernetes), and cloud services. These components need to be kept up-to-date with the latest security patches and updates.
- **Communication channels and protocols**: Vulnerabilities can arise in the communication channels and protocols used by microservices for service-to-service communication, APIs, and messaging systems. Insecure configurations or outdated protocols can expose sensitive data or enable unauthorized access.

12.13.2 Vulnerability Management Process

A comprehensive vulnerability management process involves several key steps to identify, assess, and mitigate vulnerabilities effectively:

- **Vulnerability Discovery**: A critical first step in vulnerability management is discovering where vulnerabilities exist within the microservices environment. This involves subscribing to security advisories to stay informed on new vulnerabilities, using automated scanning tools regularly to check for vulnerabilities in code and dependencies, and performing thorough manual testing like code reviews, static analysis, dynamic testing, and penetration testing to uncover vulnerabilities that automated tools may miss.
- **Vulnerability Assessment**: Once vulnerabilities have been discovered, they must be evaluated to understand their severity, potential exploitability, and possible impact on the system. Factors like attack vectors, complexity of exploitation, and consequences like data theft or service disruption should be analyzed to determine the risk level of each vulnerability. An assessment allows prioritization based on the affected microservice's criticality, the likelihood of a successful attack, and the potential damage to the overall system.
- **Vulnerability Remediation**: With vulnerabilities prioritized based on risk, steps can be taken to remediate them through patching, upgrading dependencies, implementing compensating controls if immediate fixes aren't feasible, and controlled update deployments. Patch management strategies tailored for microservices environments are necessary to address vulnerabilities efficiently while avoiding service disruptions. Techniques like immutable infrastructure and canary releases facilitate safe, incremental updates and rollbacks if issues arise.
- **Continuous Monitoring and Improvement**: Ongoing vigilance through continuous monitoring, reviews to improve processes, and learning from incidents enables proactive adaptation of vulnerability management programs. Implementing continuous alerting helps promptly detect new threats or incidents requiring a response. Regularly reviewing and updating vulnerability management tools, policies, and processes based on evolving threats and industry best practices maximizes their effectiveness. Conducting post-incident analysis identifies areas for improvement to incorporate into future vulnerability management activities.

12.13.3 Automation and Integration

Automating vulnerability management tasks and integrating vulnerability management practices into the software development lifecycle (SDLC) can significantly improve efficiency and reduce the risk of human errors.

- **Automation**: Automating repetitive vulnerability management tasks can improve efficiency and reduce errors. Automated tools should be leveraged to regularly perform vulnerability scanning, assessment, and reporting. Integrating scanning into continuous integration and continuous deployment (CI/CD) pipelines enables early detection of vulnerabilities during development. Infrastructure-as-Code (IaC) tools like Terraform, CloudFormation, and Ansible allow infrastructure configurations and patching strategies to be defined and managed in code. With automated vulnerability management workflows in place, issues can be identified and addressed rapidly with minimal human effort.

- **Integration with SDLC**: Incorporating vulnerability management practices throughout the software development lifecycle (SDLC) embeds security into each phase of microservices delivery. Threat modeling and risk assessments during design help identify potential vulnerabilities and mitigations early on. Implementing secure development practices and requirements reduces the likelihood of introducing vulnerabilities while coding. Security testing as part of QA uncovers vulnerabilities to remediate before deployment. Vulnerability scanning during release management minimizes security risks at deployment. With vulnerability management tightly integrated across the entire SDLC, microservices can be developed, tested, and deployed more securely.

By implementing a comprehensive vulnerability management program, organizations can effectively identify, assess, and mitigate vulnerabilities in their microservices architectures. Regular scanning, assessment, patching, and monitoring, combined with automation, integration with the SDLC, and collaboration across teams and stakeholders, can significantly enhance the security posture and resilience of microservices.

12.14 Chaos Engineering for Microservices Security

Chaos engineering is a disciplined approach to testing the resilience and reliability of systems by introducing controlled failures and disruptions into the production environment. In a microservices architecture, chaos engineering plays a crucial role in identifying potential security weaknesses, assessing the resilience of individual microservices, and improving the overall security posture of the system.

Microservices architectures are inherently complex, with numerous interconnected components and dependencies. As the number of microservices grows, the complexity of the system increases, making it more challenging to predict how the system will behave under various failure scenarios. Chaos engineering helps organizations proactively identify and address these potential failure points by intentionally injecting controlled failures and disruptions into the production environment.

The concept of chaos engineering originated from the practices of Netflix, which pioneered the use of chaos experiments to test the resilience of its distributed systems. Netflix recognized that traditional testing methods, such as unit tests and integration tests, were not sufficient to capture the complexities of their highly distributed architecture. By introducing controlled failures, they could observe how their systems responded and identify potential weaknesses before they became critical issues.

The primary goals of chaos engineering in a microservices architecture are:

- **Identifying Failure Modes**: Chaos engineering experiments help uncover potential failure modes that may not be evident during normal operations. By injecting controlled failures, such as network disruptions, service crashes, or resource constraints, organizations can observe how their microservices respond to these scenarios and identify weaknesses or vulnerabilities in their design or implementation.
- **Assessing Resilience**: Chaos engineering provides an opportunity to assess the resilience of individual microservices and the overall system. By observing how the system responds to failures, organizations can determine whether their resilience strategies, such as retries, circuit breakers, and fallback mechanisms, are effective in mitigating the impact of failures and maintaining system availability.
- **Improving Security**: Chaos engineering experiments can reveal security vulnerabilities and weaknesses that may not be evident during normal operations. By introducing controlled failures and disruptions, organizations can observe how their security controls and mechanisms respond and identify potential areas for improvement.
- **Testing Incident Response**: Chaos engineering experiments simulate real-world failure scenarios, allowing organizations to test their incident response processes and procedures. This enables teams to identify areas for improvement in their incident response practices, such as communication, collaboration, and decision-making.

12.14.1   Implementing Chaos Engineering in Microservices

Chaos engineering involves several key steps to ensure a systematic and controlled approach to testing the resilience of microservices:

- **Setting Objectives**: Before conducting chaos experiments, teams should clearly define the objectives they aim to achieve. These objectives may include testing specific failure scenarios, assessing the resilience of individual microservices, or validating incident response procedures.
- **Baseline Measurement**: Establishing a baseline measurement of the system's performance and behavior under normal conditions is essential. This baseline provides a reference point for comparing the system's behavior during and after chaos experiments.
- **Experiment Design**: Designing chaos experiments involves determining the type of failure or disruption to introduce, the scope of the experiment, and the metrics to measure during the experiment. Teams should carefully plan experiments to ensure they are safe, controlled, and aligned with the defined objectives.
- **Execution and Monitoring**: When executing chaos experiments, teams should closely monitor the system's behavior, performance, and metrics to observe the impact of the introduced failures or disruptions. Monitoring tools, such as Amazon CloudWatch or third-party solutions like Datadog, can help collect and analyze relevant metrics.
- **Analysis and Remediation**: After conducting chaos experiments, teams should analyze the collected data and observations to identify any weaknesses, vulnerabilities, or areas for improvement in their microservices architecture. Based on the insights gained, teams can implement remediation measures to address identified issues and

improve the overall security and resilience of the system.

- **Continuous Improvement**: Chaos engineering is an ongoing process that should be integrated into the development and operations lifecycle. As the microservices architecture evolves, teams should continue to design and execute chaos experiments to validate the resilience and security of the system and identify new areas for improvement.

12.14.2 Tools and Frameworks for Chaos Engineering

Several tools and frameworks are available to facilitate the implementation of chaos engineering in microservices architectures:

- **Chaos Monkey**: Developed by Netflix, Chaos Monkey is a tool that randomly terminates instances and services within a microservices architecture. It helps identify single points of failure and tests the resilience of the system to handle unexpected instance terminations.
- **Chaos Toolkit**: The Chaos Toolkit is an open-source framework that enables the design and execution of chaos experiments across various domains, including microservices, cloud infrastructure, and distributed systems. It provides a simple and extensible mechanism for defining and running chaos experiments.
- **Gremlin**: Gremlin is a commercial chaos engineering platform that offers a comprehensive suite of tools for designing, executing, and analyzing chaos experiments. It supports a wide range of failure scenarios across different infrastructure and application components.
- **Chaos Mesh**: Chaos Mesh is an open-source chaos engineering platform designed specifically for Kubernetes environments. It provides a comprehensive set of fault injection methods and supports a range of fault types, such as network failures, pod terminations, and resource constraints.
- **Chaos Engineering for AWS**: AWS provides several services and tools that can be used for chaos engineering in microservices architectures deployed on AWS. These include AWS Fault Injection Simulator, AWS Systems Manager, and AWS CloudFormation for infrastructure provisioning and fault injection.

12.15 Security Automation

In a microservices architecture, where multiple services and components interact with each other, manual security management can be challenging and prone to errors. Security automation is a crucial practice that helps organizations streamline and automate various security tasks, reducing the risk of human error and improving efficiency.

Security automation involves the use of tools, scripts, and workflows to automate security-related processes, such as vulnerability scanning, configuration management, compliance checks, and incident response. By automating these tasks, organizations can achieve consistent, repeatable, and scalable security practices, ensuring that their microservices architecture remains secure and compliant with industry standards and best practices.

12.15.1 Automating Security Checks and Scans

Automated security checks and scans are essential for identifying and mitigating vulnerabilities in microservices. By integrating security scanning tools into the continuous integration and continuous deployment (CI/CD) pipeline, organizations can automatically scan their code, infrastructure, and running services for vulncrabilities.

- **Static Code Analysis**: Automated static code analysis tools, such as SonarQube or GitLab Code Quality, can be integrated into the CI/CD pipeline to scan the source code for security vulnerabilities, coding errors, and best practice violations. These tools analyze the code without executing it, providing early detection of potential security issues.
- **Dynamic Application Security Testing (DAST)**: DAST tools, like OWASP ZAP or Burp Suite, simulate real-world attacks by sending malicious payloads to running applications. Integrating these tools into the deployment pipeline enables automated security testing of microservices in their runtime environment, helping to identify vulnerabilities that may have been missed during static analysis.
- **Infrastructure Scanning**: Tools like AWS Inspector, Aqua Security, or Prisma Cloud can be used to scan the infrastructure provisioned for microservices. These tools identify misconfigurations, vulnerable packages, and security issues in the underlying infrastructure, such as virtual machines, containers, or serverless functions.
- **Dependency Scanning**: Tools like Snyk, OWASP Dependency-Check, or Dependency-Track can be integrated into the CI/CD pipeline to scan project dependencies for known vulnerabilities. These tools check the libraries and frameworks used by microservices against vulnerability databases and provide reports on known issues and available updates.

12.15.2 Automated Configuration Management

Maintaining consistent and secure configurations across multiple microservices and environments is a significant challenge. Automation tools like Ansible, Puppet, or Terraform can be used to define and manage infrastructure and configurations as code. This approach ensures that microservices and their underlying infrastructure are consistently deployed and configured according to predefined security standards.

- **Infrastructure-as-Code (IaC)**: IaC tools like AWS CloudFormation or Terraform allow you to define and manage the infrastructure required for microservices as code. This includes creating virtual networks, security groups, access controls, and other infrastructure components. By treating infrastructure as code, you can ensure consistent and repeatable deployment of secure infrastructure across multiple environments.
- **Configuration as Code**: Tools like Ansible or Puppet can be used to define and manage the configuration of microservices and their runtime environments as code. This includes configuring security settings, installing software packages, applying patches, and enforcing security policies. Configuration as code ensures that microservices are consistently deployed and configured across multiple environments, reducing the risk of misconfigurations and vulnerabilities.

12.15.3 Compliance and Governance Automation

Automating compliance and governance checks helps organizations ensure that their microservices architecture adheres to industry standards, regulatory requirements, and internal security policies. Tools like AWS Config or third-party solutions like CloudSploit can be used to continuously monitor and assess the compliance of microservices and their infrastructure.

- **Compliance Checks**: Automated compliance checks can be performed to ensure that microservices and their underlying infrastructure meet specific security standards, such as PCI-DSS, HIPAA, or NIST. These checks can verify that appropriate security controls are in place, such as encryption, access controls, and logging.
- **Governance Checks**: Automated governance checks can be used to enforce internal security policies and best practices across microservices. These checks can validate that microservices are configured according to predefined security guidelines, such as network segmentation, resource tagging, or secure communication protocols.
- **Remediation and Reporting**: In addition to compliance and governance checks, automation tools can also assist with remediation and reporting. When non-compliant resources or configurations are identified, automated workflows can be triggered to remediate issues or generate reports for further analysis and action.

12.15.4 Incident Response Automation

Automating incident response processes can help organizations quickly detect, analyze, and respond to security incidents, minimizing the potential impact and reducing the time required for manual intervention. Automation tools and workflows can be used to orchestrate various incident response tasks, such as alert triage, incident investigation, and mitigation actions.

- **Security Monitoring and Alerting**: Security monitoring tools like AWS CloudTrail, Amazon GuardDuty, or third-party solutions like Splunk or Datadog can be used to collect and analyze security-related logs, metrics, and events from microservices. These tools can generate alerts when suspicious activities or potential security incidents are detected, triggering automated incident response workflows.
- **Automated Incident Triage**: Automated incident triage workflows can prioritize and categorize incoming security alerts based on predefined rules and severity levels. This helps security teams focus on the most critical incidents and reduces the time required for manual triage.
- **Incident Investigation and Analysis**: Automated workflows can assist in incident investigation and analysis by collecting and correlating relevant data from various sources, such as logs, network traffic, and infrastructure configurations. This data can be used to identify the root cause of the incident and guide the appropriate mitigation actions.
- **Automated Mitigation and Remediation**: Based on the incident analysis, automated workflows can be triggered to mitigate or remediate the identified security issues. This could include actions such as isolating or terminating compromised resources, revoking access credentials, applying security patches, or deploying new versions of microservices with resolved vulnerabilities.
- **Incident Reporting and Documentation**: Automated incident response workflows can generate detailed reports and documentation for security incidents. These reports

can include information about the incident timeline, root cause analysis, mitigation actions taken, and recommendations for preventing similar incidents in the future.

By adopting security automation practices, organizations can streamline and improve the security of their microservices architecture. Automated security checks and scans help identify vulnerabilities and misconfigurations early in the development lifecycle. Automated configuration management ensures consistent and secure deployment of microservices and their infrastructure. Compliance and governance automation help organizations adhere to industry standards and internal security policies. Incident response automation enables quick detection and mitigation of security incidents, minimizing potential impact.

12.16   DevSecOps for Microservices Security

Integrating security practices into the DevOps processes and culture is crucial for building and operating secure microservices architectures. DevSecOps, which stands for Development, Security, and Operations, is an approach that emphasizes collaboration and automation to embed security throughout the entire software development lifecycle (SDLC).

One of the core principles of DevSecOps is 'shifting security left', which means integrating security considerations early in the development process. By incorporating security practices from the initial stages of software development, organizations can identify and mitigate potential vulnerabilities before they are introduced into production environments. In the context of microservices, shifting security left involves practices such as secure by design, where security should be a fundamental consideration during the design phase of microservices and threat modeling and risk assessments should be conducted to identify potential security risks and determine appropriate mitigation strategies. It also involves secure coding practices, where developers should be trained in secure coding practices and follow guidelines like the OWASP Secure Coding Practices, with code reviews, static code analysis, and security testing integrated into the development process. Additionally, security should be incorporated into the CI/CD pipeline through practices like static code analysis, dependency scanning, dynamic application security testing (DAST), infrastructure scanning, and compliance checks.

Automation is a key enabler of DevSecOps, as it helps streamline security processes, reduce the risk of human error, and ensure consistent and repeatable security practices across the entire microservices architecture. In the context of microservices, automation can be applied to processes such as automated security scans by integrating automated security scanning tools into the CI/CD pipeline to scan code, dependencies, infrastructure, and running applications for vulnerabilities. It can also involve automated configuration management through the use of Infrastructure-as-Code (IaC) and Configuration-as-Code (CaC) tools to define and manage infrastructure and configurations for microservices in a secure and consistent manner. Automated compliance checks can be implemented to ensure that microservices and their infrastructure adhere to security standards, regulatory requirements, and internal security policies. Automated incident response processes, including security monitoring, alerting, triage, investigation, and mitigation actions, can be employed to quickly detect and respond to security incidents.

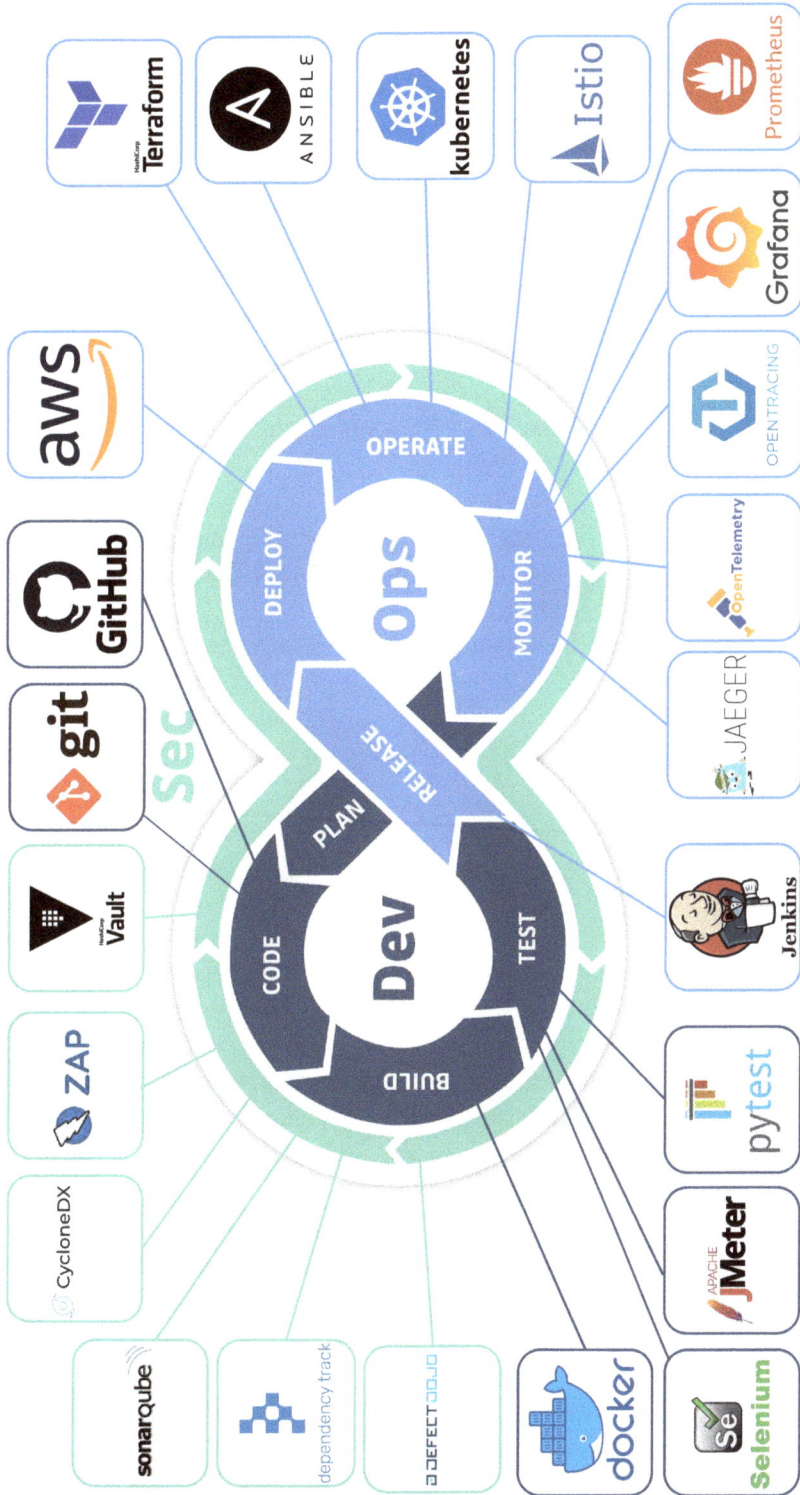

Figure 12.7: DevSecOps tools/platforms

DevSecOps is not just about tools and processes; it is also about fostering a culture of security within the organization. This involves practices such as cross-functional collaboration, where collaboration between development, security, and operations teams is encouraged, and knowledge sharing, joint decision-making, and collective ownership of security practices are facilitated. Continuous learning and improvement should be promoted by conducting regular security training, sharing best practices, and incorporating lessons learned from security incidents or exercises.

Figure 12.7 shows some popular DevSecOps tools/platforms categorized into the different phases of the software development lifecycle. These include:

- **Code**:
  - **Git & GitHub**: Distributed version control system and platform for collaborative code development and code reviews.
- **Build**:
  - **Docker**: Platform for building, packaging, and distributing applications as lightweight and portable containers.
- **Test**:
  - **pytest**: Python-based testing framework for writing and executing unit tests.
  - **Apache JMeter**: Open-source load testing tool for analyzing and measuring the performance of web applications.
  - **Selenium**: Suite of tools for automating web browsers and testing web applications.
- **Release**:
  - **Jenkins**: Open-source automation server for building, testing, and deploying software projects.
- **Deploy**:
  - **AWS**: Cloud computing platform providing a wide range of cloud services for deploying, operating, and securing cloud-based microservices applications.
- **Operate**:
  - **Terraform**: Infrastructure as Code (IaC) tool for provisioning and managing cloud infrastructure resources across multiple providers.
  - **Ansible**: Configuration management and automation tool for deploying and managing applications and infrastructure.
  - **Kubernetes**: Open-source container orchestration system for automating deployment, scaling, and management of containerized applications.
  - **Istio**: Open-source service mesh for connecting, securing, and monitoring microservices.
- **Monitor**:
  - **Prometheus**: Open-source monitoring and alerting system for collecting and analyzing metrics from different sources.
  - **Grafana**: Open-source data visualization and analytics platform for monitoring and observability.
  - **OpenTelemetry & Jaeger**: Open-source observability framework and tracing system for distributed applications and microservices.
- **Security**:
  - **HashiCorp Vault**: Secrets management solution for securely storing and accessing sensitive data, such as API keys, passwords, and certificates.

- **SonarQube**: Static code analysis tool for identifying code quality issues, security vulnerabilities, and code coverage.
- **CycloneDX**: Software Bill of Materials (SBOM) standard for tracking software components and dependencies.
- **Defect Dojo**: Security automation and vulnerability management platform for tracking and managing application security issues.
- **Dependency Track**: Software Composition Analysis (SCA) tool for identifying and managing vulnerabilities in third-party dependencies.

The adoption of microservices architectures and cloud platforms further augments the DevSecOps methodology, enabling organizations to develop and deliver features incrementally through sprints. The specifics of the tools and processes that underpin DevSecOps practices for developing, operating, and securing microservices will be explored in-depth in a follow-on book dedicated to this topic.

Summary

In this chapter, we covered various best practices and strategies for securing microservices architectures. We covered authentication and authorization and presented the importance of a centralized identity and access management (IAM) system for managing user identities and access. We described token-based authentication using JSON Web Tokens and OAuth2 for stateless user authentication. We also covered role-based access control and attribute-based access control for authorization. Next, we discussed API gateways and perimeter security. We described how API gateways act as reverse proxies, enforcing security policies like rate limiting, IP whitelisting, authentication, authorization, and input validation. API gateways also facilitate capabilities like monitoring, logging, circuit breaking, and graceful degradation. We then covered best practices for securing communication between microservices, including encryption in transit using TLS, mutual TLS for service-to-service authentication, and secure communication channels like service meshes. We also highlighted the importance of monitoring and logging secure communication. For data security, we outlined various techniques like data classification, encryption at rest and in transit, secure storage solutions, and access controls like RBAC and ABAC. Proper data lifecycle management from creation to disposal was also emphasized. Next, we described monitoring, logging, and incident response strategies tailored for microservices. We highlighted centralized logging, log analysis for security, alerting mechanisms, and the importance of a well-defined incident response plan. We covered leveraging containerization and isolation technologies like Docker and Kubernetes to enhance security through immutable infrastructure and microservice isolation. Regular scanning and patching of container images was also emphasized. For operational security, we presented the principles of least privilege access and separation of concerns, limiting the impact of potential attacks or issues. We also discussed network security, microservices domains as trust boundaries, and network segmentation for isolation. Vulnerability management, chaos engineering, security automation, and secure development practices were also covered as essential elements of the security posture. This chapter provided a comprehensive overview of the critical security considerations and best practices for building, deploying, and operating secure microservices architectures.

BIBLIOGRAPHY

[1] Mell, Peter, and Timothy Grance. The NIST Definition of Cloud Computing, NIST, Sept. 2011.

[2] Bahga, Arshdeep and Vijay Krishna Madisetti. "Analyzing Massive Machine Maintenance Data in a Computing Cloud." IEEE Transactions on Parallel and Distributed Systems 23 (2012): 1831-1843.

[3] Bahga, Arshdeep and Vijay Krishna Madisetti. "Cloud-Based Information Technology Framework for Data Driven Intelligent Transportation Systems." Journal of Transportation Technologies 3 (2013): 131-141.

[4] "Network Functions Virtualization." ETSI, etsi.org/technologies-clusters/technologies/nfv. Accessed 2024.

[5] "OpenFlow Switch Specification." Open Networking Foundation, www.opennetworking.org. Accessed 2024.

[6] "CloudStack." The Apache Software Foundation, cloudstack.apache.org. Accessed 2024.

[7] "Eucalyptus." Eucalyptus Systems Inc., www.eucalyptus.com. Accessed 2024.

[8] "OpenStack." OpenStack Foundation, www.openstack.org. Accessed 2024.

[9] IBM SOA Foundation, www.ibm.com/software/solutions/soa/offerings.html. IBM, 2012.

[10] Windows Communication Foundation, msdn.microsoft.com/en-us/library/vstudio/ms735119. Microsoft. Accessed 2024.

[11] Oracle SOA Suite, www.oracle.com/us/products/middleware/soa/suite/overview/index.html. Oracle. Accessed 2024.

[12] Salesforce SOA, wiki.developerforce.com/page/SalesforceSOADemo. salesforce.com. Accessed 2024.

[13] Bahga, Arshdeep and Vijay Krishna Madisetti. "A Cloud-based Approach for Interoperable Electronic Health Records (EHRs)." IEEE Journal of Biomedical and Health Informatics 17 (2013): 894-906.

[14] "The Python Standard Library." Python Software Foundation, docs.python.org/2/library/. Accessed 2024.

[15] Fielding, Roy T. and Richard N. Taylor. "Principled design of the modern Web architecture." Proceedings of the 2000 International Conference on Software Engineering. ICSE 2000 the New Millennium (2000): 407-416.

[16] Codd, E. F.. "A relational model of data for large shared data banks." Commun. ACM 13 (1970): 377-387.

[17] Bahga, Arshdeep and Vijay Krishna Madisetti. "Rapid Prototyping of Multitier Cloud-Based Services and Systems." Computer 46 (2013): 76-83.

[18] Amazon Web Services, aws.amazon.com. Accessed 2024.

[19] "boto." Amazon Web Services, boto.readthedocs.io/en/latest. Accessed 2024.

[20] Bahga, Arshdeep and Vijay Krishna Madisetti. "Performance Evaluation Approach for Multi-Tier Cloud Applications." Journal of Software Engineering and Applications 06 (2013): 74-83.

[21] Cloud Security Alliance. Trusted Cloud Initiative, cloudsecurityalliance.org/research/tci/. Accessed 2024.

[22] "Kerberos." MIT, web.mit.edu/kerberos. Accessed 2024.

[23] "The OAuth 2.0 Authorization Framework." IETF Tools, tools.ietf.org/html/rfc6749. Accessed 2024.

[24] "Well-Architected Framework." Amazon Web Services, aws.amazon.com/architecture/well-architected/. Accessed 2024.

[25] Microsoft. Azure Architecture - Microservices, 2022, docs.microsoft.com/en-us/azure/architecture/guide/architecture-styles/microservices. Accessed 1 Feb. 2024.

[26] Merkel, Dirk. "Docker: lightweight Linux containers for consistent development and deployment." Linux Journal 2014 (2014): 2.

[27] Jamshidi, Pooyan et al. "Cloud Migration Patterns: A Multi-cloud Service Architecture Perspective." ICSOC Workshops (2015).

[28] Pahl, Claus et al. "Architectural Principles for Cloud Software." ACM Transactions on Internet Technology (TOIT) 18 (2018): 1 - 23.

[29] Pahl, Claus. "Containerization and the PaaS Cloud." IEEE Cloud Computing 2 (2015): 24-31.

[30] Villegas, David et al. "Cloud federation in a layered service model." J. Comput. Syst. Sci. 78 (2012): 1330-1344.

[31] Zimmermann, Olaf. "Microservices tenets." Computer Science - Research and Development 32 (2017): 301-310.

[32] Ebert, Christof et al. "DevOps." IEEE Software 33 (2022): 94-100.

[33] El-Gazzar, Rania Fahim. "A Literature Review on Cloud Computing Adoption Issues in Enterprises." TDIT (2014).

[34] Pérez, Alfonso et al. "Serverless computing for container-based architectures." Future Gener. Comput. Syst. 83 (2018): 50-59.

[35] Yu, Eric S. K. and Stephanie Deng. "Understanding Software Ecosystems: A Strategic Modeling Approach." IWSECO@ICSOB (2011).

[36] Villamizar, Mario et al. "Infrastructure Cost Comparison of Running Web Applications in the Cloud Using AWS Lambda and Monolithic and Microservice Architectures." 2016 16th IEEE/ACM International Symposium on Cluster, Cloud and Grid Computing (CCGrid) (2016): 179-182.

[37] Villamizar, Mario et al. "Evaluating the monolithic and the microservice architecture pattern to deploy web applications in the cloud." 2015 10th Computing Colombian Conference (10CCC) (2015): 583-590.

[38] Alshuqayran, Nuha et al. "A Systematic Mapping Study in Microservice Architecture." 2016 IEEE 9th International Conference on Service-Oriented Computing and Applications (SOCA) (2016): 44-51.

[39] Gopal, Hemanth et al. "Security, Privacy and Challenges in Microservices Architecture and Cloud Computing- Survey." ArXiv abs/2212.14422 (2022): n. pag.

[40] Bhardwaj, Aditya and C. Rama Krishna. "Virtualization in Cloud Computing: Moving from Hypervisor to Containerization—A Survey." Arabian Journal for Science and Engineering 46 (2021): 8585 - 8601.

[41] Velepucha, Victor and Pamela Flores. "A Survey on Microservices Architecture: Principles, Patterns and Migration Challenges." IEEE Access 11 (2023): 88339-88358.

[42] Soni, Madhavi and Varshapriya Jyotinagar. "SQL vs NoSQL Databases for the Microservices: A Comparative Survey." 2023 2nd International Conference on Edge Computing and Applications (ICECAA) (2023): 17-22.

[43] Usman, Muhammad et al. "A Survey on Observability of Distributed Edge & Container-Based Microservices." IEEE Access 10 (2022): 86904-86919.

[44] Carvalho, Luiz et al. "Re-engineering Legacy Systems as Microservices: An Industrial Survey of Criteria to Deal with Modularity and Variability of Features." Handbook of Re-Engineering Software Intensive Systems into Software Product Lines (2023).

[45] Koyya, Krishna Mohan and B. Muthukumar. "A Survey of Saga Frameworks for Distributed Transactions in Event-driven Microservices." 2022 Third International Conference on Smart Technologies in Computing, Electrical and Electronics (ICSTCEE) (2022): 1-6.

[46] Jain, Garvit et al. "A Survey on Trending Topics of Microservices." International Journal of Emerging Trends in Engineering Research (2021): n. pag.

[47] Sekhar, Repana Reddy and Veena Gadad. "Microservices, Saga Pattern and Event Sourcing: A Survey." (2020).

[48] Ghofrani, Javad and Daniel Lübke. "Challenges of Microservices Architecture: A Survey on the State of the Practice." Central-European Workshop on Services and their Composition (2018).

[49] Saleh Sedghpour, Mohammad Reza and Paul Townend. "Service Mesh and eBPF-Powered Microservices: A Survey and Future Directions." 2022 IEEE International Conference on Service-Oriented System Engineering (SOSE) (2022): 176-184.

[50] Waseem, Muhammad et al. "Understanding the Issues, Their Causes and Solutions in Microservices Systems: An Empirical Study." ArXiv abs/2302.01894 (2023): n. pag.

[51] Abdelfattah, Amr S. and Tomás Cerný. "Microservices Security Challenges and Approaches." Integrated Spatial Databases (2022).

[52] Kalubowila, D. C. A. et al. "Optimization of Microservices Security." 2021 3rd International Conference on Advancements in Computing (ICAC) (2021): 49-54.

[53] Rangaiyengar, Rupashree et al. "Multi-Layer Observability for Fault Localization in Microservices Based Systems." 2023 IEEE International Conference on Software Analysis, Evolution and Reengineering (SANER) (2023): 733-737.

[54] Li, Yongkang et al. "Serverless Computing: State-of-the-Art, Challenges and Opportunities." IEEE Transactions on Services Computing 16 (2023): 1522-1539.

[55] Jonas, Eric et al. "Cloud Programming Simplified: A Berkeley View on Serverless Computing." ArXiv abs/1902.03383 (2019): n. pag.

[56] Butt, Umer Ahmed et al. "Cloud Security Threats and Solutions: A Survey." Wireless Personal Communications 128 (2022): 387-413.

INDEX

www.ingramcontent.com/pod-product-compliance
Lightning Source LLC
Chambersburg PA
CBHW040138200326
41458CB00025B/6302